THE REBEL EMPRESSES

Elisabeth of Austria and Eugénie of France, Power and
Glamour in the Struggle for Europe

NANCY GOLDSTONE

Little, Brown and Company

New York • Boston • London

Little, Brown and Company
Hachette Book Group
1290 Avenue of the Americas, New York, NY 10104
littlebrown.com

First Edition: February 2025

Little, Brown and Company is a division of Hachette Book Group, Inc. The Little, Brown name and logo are trademarks of Hachette Book Group, Inc.

The publisher is not responsible for websites (or their content) that are not owned by the publisher.

The Hachette Speakers Bureau provides a wide range of authors for speaking events. To find out more, go to hachettespeakersbureau.com or email hachettespeakers@hbgusa.com.

Little, Brown and Company books may be purchased in bulk for business, educational, or promotional use. For information, please contact your local bookseller or the Hachette Book Group Special Markets Department at special.markets@hbgusa.com.

Illustration credits begin on page 597.

ISBN 9780316419420
LCCN 2024943219

Printing 2, 2025

LSC-C

Printed in the United States of America

For Larry and Lee, always

Contents

Map of Europe 1815   x-xi

Introduction   3

1. A Scandal in Bavaria   11
2. The Empire Strikes Back   31
3. An Imperial Bait and Switch   42
4. The Reign in Spain   63
5. Mademoiselle de Montijo   75
6. The Wild Countess of Teba   92
7. An Imperial Coup   111
8. The Rose of Bavaria   127
9. Making France Great Again   145
10. Love in the Time of Cholera   163
11. An Empress on the Rise   181
12. An Imperial Education   203
13. The Disciples of the Dagger   227
14. Three Weddings and a War   247
15. Regent of the Empire   263
16. His Cheatin' Imperial Heart   285
17. Imperial Expeditions   309
18. An Imperial Time Out   329
19. The Empress Rolls the Dice   345
20. The Metamorphosis   365

Contents

21. Government by the Heroine   381
22. The Empress Takes a Stand   395
23. An Unfortunate Fall-Off in Imperial Greatness   413
24. The Empress to the Rescue   425
25. An Exhibition of Imperial Honor   441
26. The Empress Breaks Free   457
27. The Reign in Spain — Again   471
28. By the Skin of the Empress's Teeth   485
29. The Search for Solace   503
30. The Ex-Empress Steps In   517
31. The Imperial Cabin in the Woods   531
32. The New Disciples of the Dagger   547

Acknowledgments   557
Notes   559
Bibliography   589
Illustration Credits   597
Index   599

Time's book is before me lying,
All things that have happened here,
Good with Evil ever vying—
All before my gaze stands clear.

—The great German poet Heinrich Heine

EUROPE
1815

Scale of Miles
0 100 200 300 400 500

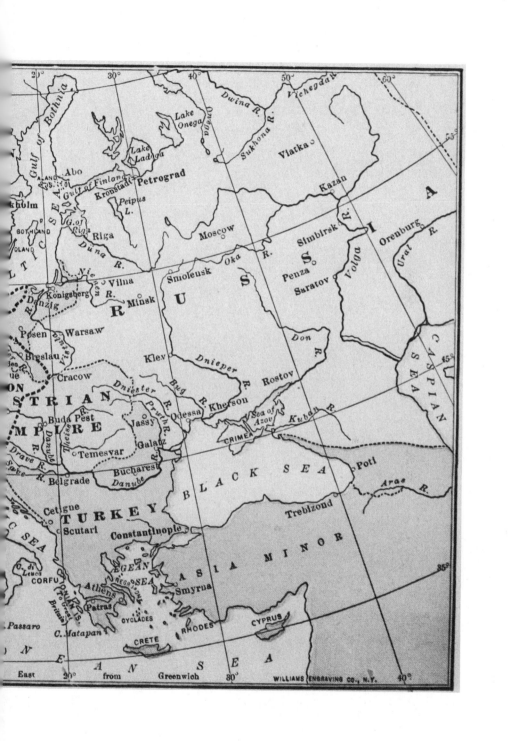

Dwina R. Vichegda R.

Gulf of Bothnia

Lake Onega

Onega R.

Sukhona R.

Vlatka

Lake Ladoga

Abo

ALAND IS.

Gulf of Finland

Kronstadt Petrograd

Kazan

Peipus L.

BALTIC SEA

G. of Riga

GOTHLAND

OLAND

Riga

Duna R.

Moscow

Oka R.

Volga R.

Simbirsk R.

Orenburg

Ural R.

Penza

Saratov

R U S S I A

Niemen R.

Vilna

Smoleusk

Konigsberg

Danzig

Minsk

R R.

Posen Warsaw

Vistula R.

Breslau

Kiev

Dnieper R.

Don R.

CASPIAN SEA

Cracow

Dniester R.

Bug R.

Rostov

AUSTRIAN EMPIRE

Buda Pest

Theiss R.

Pruth R.

Jassy

Odessa

Kherson

Sea of Azov

Kuban R.

Drave R.

Danube R.

Temesvar

Galaz

CRIMEA

Save R.

Belgrade

Bucharest

Danube

Poti

B L A C K   S E A

Aras R.

Cetigne

TURKEY

Treblzond

ADRIATIC SEA

Scutari

Constantinople

ASIA MINOR

C. di Leuca

CORFU

EGEAN SEA

NEGROPONT

Athens

Smyrna

IONIAN IS.

Patras

CYCLADES

CYPRUS

C. Passaro

C. Matapan

RHODES

CRETE

IONIAN   SEA

East   from   Greenwich

WILLIAMS ENGRAVING CO., N.Y.

THE

*R*EBEL

EMPRESSES

Introduction

The railway station at Salzburg, Austria, late in the afternoon of August 18, 1867—

THE STREETS OF THE PICTURESQUE ALPINE TOWN, ordinarily drowsy in the summer heat, were crowded with expectant spectators. Visiting aristocrats in expensive silks, the women shaded by delicate, lace-edged bonnets and elaborate parasols, jostled for position along the main route from the imperial palace to the railway depot with native villagers equally colorful in their dirndls and traditional Bavarian lederhosen. The atmosphere breathed official pageantry. The buildings were dressed up with tapestries and garlands of flowers; a long, plush carpet had been rolled out from the street through the main vestibule of the train station all the way to the platform; and idling on the pavement by the entranceway was a grand carriage pulled by six horses. It was evident that an important meeting was about to take place. Franz Joseph, the distinguished emperor of Austria, and his wife, Elisabeth, affectionately known as Sisi, were for the first time hosting their counterparts, Napoleon III of France and his wife, the Empress Eugénie, to a state visit.

Following protocol, the main body of the Austrian court—the principal ministers and ambassadors, supported by their secretaries and staffs; senior household functionaries and ladies-in-waiting; even members of the imperial orchestra—had obediently uprooted themselves and made the nearly 200-mile journey from Vienna to Salzburg. The arrival of the Emperor of the French, as Napoleon III showily styled himself, happened to coincide with Franz Joseph's thirty-seventh birthday, and a special mass had been celebrated at the Salzburg cathedral that morning. The highlight of the service was a soaring performance of Mozart by the court musicians, "somewhat to the astonishment and altogether to the delight of the Salzburgers, who are, I mourn to say, accustomed to a very indifferent execution of their own divine maestro's church music," the foreign correspondent for the London *Daily Telegraph,* sent to report on the historic imperial encounter, noted in his widely syndicated account of these proceedings.

But the deliberate conjuring of a holiday atmosphere belied the underlying gravity of the rendezvous. Austria and France, openly hostile for the majority of the past four centuries, had both recently suffered searing diplomatic and military defeats. Their treasuries were depleted and their armies strained. The upstart kingdom of Prussia, under the direction of its wily chief minister, Otto von Bismarck, had taken advantage of the perceived weakness of these two formerly dominant powers to pursue a policy of ruthless territorial expansion. If Franz Joseph and Napoleon III could not find a way to overcome their differences and meet the crisis, all of Europe would waver once again on the cusp of war.

And yet, even with so much at stake, the world's attention was focused not on the two monarchs who held the fate of millions in their hands, but rather on their wives. This was the first time that Elisabeth and Eugénie, both renowned for their stunning good looks and high-fashion wardrobes, and consequently objects of intense fascination at home and abroad, were scheduled to meet. Which of these imperial goddesses would outshine the other in a face-to-face beauty contest was debated openly in the press. Bowing to this reality, also imported from Vienna to Salzburg (and currently dominating the station waiting room), was a life-sized statue of Sisi surrounded by a heady profusion of tropical flowers, a blatant exercise of hometown advantage.

By four in the afternoon, the 200 or so most prominent members of the court and military who had been invited to greet the Emperor and Empress of the French on their arrival had taken their coveted positions on the train platform. Half an hour later, Franz Joseph and

Elisabeth appeared and made their way graciously through the crowd to the front line, so that the expected guests would have no trouble locating them among the sea of unfamiliar faces. Finally, at 5 p.m. exactly, the omnipresent court musicians began to play, the imperial guard formally presented arms, and the incoming engine, which had evidently been awaiting this signal, rolled deliberately into the station. Napoleon III, lifting his top hat and bowing courteously in a gesture of appreciation at the splendid welcome arranged by his hosts, could be seen clearly through the main cabin window.

The train stopped. Eugénie and her husband disembarked just as Elisabeth and Franz Joseph moved forward to meet them. The foreign correspondents took up their pens and craned their heads. The competition was on.

Each woman had her partisans. On Sisi's side was the *Daily Telegraph* man. "The Empress Elisabeth, who looked, if possible, lovelier than ever, was dressed in blue and white (Bavarian colors), and wore a plain black straw hat with a plume of black feathers," he reported dutifully, in acknowledgment of his readership's seemingly insatiable demand for details of the latest in style trends and accessories. "Elisabeth of Austria is more than a head taller than Eugénie of France; the former is as lithe and slender as a young poplar; the latter has grown stout of late, which makes her look shorter than she really is," he continued critically. The *Daily Telegraph* was momentarily disconcerted to discover that the visiting French empress, mindful of the potential ravages to the complexion of a day's hard traveling, had taken precautions against the elements that hindered the pursuit of journalistic excellence. "A thick black veil hid the Empress Eugénie's face from view," the correspondent confessed. "But the spirited, refined countenance of Elisabeth no envious covering concealed," he recovered loyally.

The London *Standard* columnist, on the other hand, was definitely in the French camp. "The Empress Eugénie was very simply attired in a pretty travelling dress, which was very short, showing to advantage her admirably formed small feet," he declared. "The short dress formed quite a strange contrast to the long sweeping trains of all the other ladies present. Her Majesty looked just ready for a mountain excursion, nimble, agile in her movements, elastic." Faced like his competitor with the debacle of the veil, the *Standard* man was compelled to fall back on the expedient of imagination. "In the whole demeanor of the Empress Eugénie is a freshness, a vivacity," he enthused, omitting altogether the small detail that he could not actually see her face. "She is delightfully natural, and the grace of her manner is something rarely seen... It is not at all unlikely that those who read this may think it is an exaggeration, and call it fulsome flattery. No one, however, who was present and saw the charming woman will think so. On the contrary,... you feel—you cannot but feel—her exquisite grace just as you cannot but feel in your whole heart and your whole body the freshness of the morning," he gushed poetically.

It wasn't until a few hours later that the press finally got what it wanted: a sight of Elisabeth and Eugénie side by side in all their glory at the celebratory concert held at the Salzburg opera house as part of the evening's entertainment. There, even the most jaded among the correspondents were dazzled in spite of themselves, and conceded the contest a draw. "The Empresses, who looked remarkably well, and made an admirable contrast of blonde with brunet [*sic*], were in white silk, the dress of the Empress Elisabeth relieved with zig zag bands of black," judged the reporter for the New York *World*. "Both Empresses wore tiaras of diamonds, and Eugénie... under the brilliant light, looked nearly as young as her sister sovereign."

THUS DID THE NINETEENTH CENTURY reduce Elisabeth and Eugénie, two of the most layered women of their time, to attractive footnotes on the pages of history. This age belongs instead to Victoria, its most enduring female monarch, who remained at her post for an astonishing sixty-three years, beating the former record, held by the equally redoubtable Elizabeth I, by nearly two decades. The passage of time, and with it the hunger for nostalgia, has only increased Victoria's renown. She is perhaps more respected and beloved today than she was in her own era.

But it is a mistake to overlook her sister sovereigns in France and Austria. Fearless, adventurous, and athletic; defiantly, even fiercely independent, Sisi and Eugénie represented, each in her own way, a new kind of empress, one who rebelled against traditional expectations and restrictions. Their beauty was undeniable but so too was their influence on a world that was fast becoming recognizably modern. As railroads for the first time crisscrossed kingdoms, and telegraphs linked continents, their lives would become so entwined that it is impossible to understand one without the other, or indeed the whole glorious whirlwind of a century in which they lived, without the beguiling power of their stories.

ELISABETH

Sisi's father, Duke Max, with his zither

1

A Scandal in Bavaria

The spirit of the Revolution is immortal.

—Heinrich Heine

ELISABETH WAS BORN IN MUNICH, the capital city of the kingdom of Bavaria, on December 24—Christmas Eve—1837. At the time of her birth, she had a six-year-old brother, Ludwig, and a three-year-old sister, Helene, whom everyone called "Nene." Elisabeth herself was soon dubbed "Sisi." Her mother, Duchess Ludovika, was the youngest surviving daughter of Maximilian Joseph, the first king of Bavaria, and so had royal blood in her veins. The same could not be said of Sisi's father, Duke Max. Duke Max was only a second cousin.

But what her father lacked in pedigree he more than made up for in personality. Duke Max could have stepped right off the stage of a Bavarian comic opera. Handsome, exuberant, an expert sportsman and self-proclaimed man of letters as well as an amateur composer of folk songs, Sisi's father aimed to enjoy life. Just weeks after her birth, Duke Max, accompanied by three friends, two servants, his doctor, and his zither instructor, set off on an eight-month jaunt to Egypt and the Holy Land, with stopovers in Greece and Rome. "I was driven by an irresistible feeling, by an unconquerable urge away from the eternal uniformity of an everyday life that is comfortable to the point of discomfort, in which one no longer lives but vegetates," he rhapsodized in the travelogue of his experiences that he published upon his return. "Unfortunately," he added pointedly, "there are people who can hardly comprehend why one might decide to undertake a journey of this sort. I feel sorry for those creatures so fond of peace and quiet, those slaves to habit"—an allusion that undoubtedly included his wife, who, with two young children and now a new baby to look after, strangely did not share her husband's carefree wanderlust.

Not that Duchess Ludovika didn't have her own marital complaints. Growing up as the youngest daughter of the second wife of the king of Bavaria, she had watched as, one by one, each of her older siblings secured a brilliant future as the spouse of a successor to a prestigious throne. Her two eldest (twin) sisters married into the royal families of Saxony and Prussia; then, her next two sisters, also twins, wedded the heir to the Austrian empire and the Crown Prince of Saxony, respectively. Ludovika naturally expected that she, too, would make a splendid match and in so doing come into possession of the numerous servants, jewels, gowns, carriages, castles, and other assorted windfalls associated with sovereign rule.

But then, in 1825, just as she turned seventeen and was finally poised to make her own graceful entrance into the royal marriage market, her father suddenly died and her thirty-nine-year-old half brother, Ludwig (son of King Maximilian Joseph's first wife), acceded to the Bavarian throne. King Ludwig I had no intention of sharing the royal palace with his father's second family, so he promptly evicted his stepmother and half sister from their Munich home. This snub did not improve Ludovika's marital prospects.

Still, all was not lost. Ludovika and her mother cast themselves on the hospitality of her older sister Sophia, who had married into the imperial family of Austria. At Archduchess Sophia's court in Vienna, Ludovika met and favorably impressed the Crown Prince of Portugal; the two fell in love. But Lisbon was deemed too far away by Ludovika's mother, who wanted this last daughter to remain close to her. Besides, the crown prince had rebelled against his father and consequently was judged to be unsuitable. So, instead of becoming queen of Portugal,

Ludovika was required to stay in Germany and wed her cousin Duke Max, a suitor who was as indifferent to her charms as she was to his. To add insult to injury, because of this marriage, Ludovika was stripped of the sovereign title "Princess *of* Bavaria," to which she had been born, and was instead forced to adopt her husband's trumped-up, déclassé insignia of "Duke and Duchess *in* Bavaria," a perpetual reminder of her reduced station. Even so, the couple managed to maintain enough of a position on the outskirts of the social register that Elisabeth's birth made the London papers. "The Duchess LOUISA, consort of Duke MAXIMILIAN of Bavaria, gave birth to a Princess on the 25th ult [last]," the London *Times* reported on January 4, 1838, in a mention notable for getting both the date of the newborn's arrival and her family's title wrong.

THAT BAVARIA EVEN HAD a king was a relatively new phenomenon. For over 200 years, right up until the beginning of the nineteenth century, Bavaria was an electorate, and for a thousand years before that, merely a duchy, indistinguishable from the dozens of other duchies that made up what is today called Germany.

But all of that changed with the advent of Napoleon Bonaparte, the greatest warrior of his age — of perhaps any age. It had not taken a crystal ball to see that the Corsican general turned emperor of France, having already swept through and plundered Italy and Egypt, would eventually turn his sights eastward, a policy that would put him in direct conflict with powerful Austria. Since the most direct route a French army could take to get to Austria, or an Austrian army could take to get to France, was for one or the other to fight their way through Bavaria first, living in this unfortunately situated state was a little like being in the collision path of two enormous, speeding locomotives bearing down on each other from opposite directions. There was no getting out of the way by declaring neutrality; the only hope for survival was to wait until the last moment and then jump aboard the train most likely to prevail in the inevitable crash.

And so that was what Duchess Ludovika's father, Maximilian Joseph, had done. In August of 1805, just weeks away from invasion by one side or the other, he weighed the quality and quantity of the two forces and came down firmly on the side of France, signing a treaty of alliance that provided Napoleon with Bavarian money, supplies, and soldiers. The wisdom of his decision was immediately confirmed when the French army walloped a combined Austrian-Russian offensive on December 2, 1805, at Austerlitz. For this perspicuity, Napoleon awarded Maximilian Joseph the conquered territories of the Tyrol, the Vorarlberg, and Trent to the south; Passau to the east; and Augsberg and Eichstatt to the west—a considerable addition to Bavarian lands and subjects. He also raised the electorate of Bavaria to a monarchy. "If you had not been on my side in this war, Prince Murat would now be King of Bavaria instead of you," Napoleon observed coolly to the newly made sovereign.

With French friendship came more victories and spoils. When Napoleon followed up his initial triumph against Austria by defeating Prussia, he reorganized Germany, allotting the Lutheran city of Bayreuth to King Maximilian Joseph as further compensation for his participation. Suddenly, by the annexation of all these new provinces, Bavaria, whose citizenry had for centuries been overwhelmingly rigidly Catholic, found itself contending with 1.2 million new Protestant subjects.

Napoleon had a remedy for that, too. "Religion is an affair of conscience, not of State," he noted, and so on May 1, 1808, under the influence of his new overlord, Maximilian Joseph granted Bavaria its first written constitution, which was based on the principles of the French Revolution (as interpreted by Napoleon). This highly progressive document guaranteed tolerance of religion and equal rights under the law to Catholics, Lutherans, and Calvinists (Jews had to wait until 1813 to be included in these reforms); abolished both serfdom and special privileges for aristocrats (although the nobles were allowed to retain their titles and property); pledged to uphold freedom of the press; and established an elected national assembly with the power to help draft laws and exercise control over state expenditures and tax revenues.

This was the genius of Napoleon—he won over large groups of even those he defeated in battle by portraying himself as the champion of the downtrodden. "Have confidence in the great Sovereign [i.e., himself] upon whom your lot depends!" he boomed to the crowds who greeted him throughout Germany. "You can experience nothing but improvements." But in fact the burden of the endless supplies and soldiers he demanded, and the exorbitant taxes he levied, fell predominantly on the lower classes.

There is perhaps such a thing as too much success. Napoleon's speedy subjugation of Germany only served to fuel his ambitions. He went after Spain next, where he got bogged down in a costly invasion that depleted his resources, and then, in 1812, disastrously targeted Russia. "The extravagance of these gigantic schemes brought about the fall of Napoleon," the Austrian foreign minister reported simply.

Bavaria, which was forced to contribute some 30,000 soldiers to Napoleon's Moscow offensive, reeled when just over 200 of these martyred servicemen managed to survive and straggle home. In the wake of the cataclysm, Maximilian Joseph reevaluated. Demonstrating once again a formidable talent for political pragmatism, he waited until Austria was just about to launch a counteroffensive, and then suddenly leapt off the French train and onto the (soon-to-be-victorious) Austrian one. "It produced an excellent impression that you declared your country to be on our side before the Battle of Leipzig," Francis II, the winning emperor, asserted after Napoleon surrendered. "It is on that account that I am in favor of Bavaria's remaining great," he added, by which he meant that, as a reward for his excellent timing, Maximilian Joseph would be allowed to hold on to both his monarchy *and* all the territory he'd accumulated under French rule.

And that was how Bavaria came out of the Napoleonic Wars a regional power, and the reason Duchess Ludovika's older sisters had all succeeded in marrying royalty. But despite his defeat and death, some six years later on the Island of Saint Helena, Napoleon's influence over southern Germany was not completely eradicated. Bavaria retained its elected assembly and religious and civil rights even after the war had ended. It was a kingdom, true — but a kingdom with a constitution. As a child growing up in Munich, Sisi had the benefit of this.

THE YEARS OF WAR were long past by the time she was born. Maximilian Joseph had died and been succeeded by his eldest son, Ludwig I, Duchess Ludovika's older half brother. Ludwig, who prided himself on his artistic sensibilities, was busy remaking his capital into an idealized, Bavarian-sized version of the ancient Greek and Roman cities whose treasures he marveled at on his frequent trips abroad. Elisabeth's earliest years thus unfolded against a noisy background of marble-cutting and masonry, as one soaring, ornately columned and frescoed edifice after another took shape along the main avenues leading to the royal palace. She even lived in one of these new, faux-classical mansions, which the king, aware that his favorite brother-in-law, Duke Max, could not afford to purchase on his own, had generously built for him at the treasury's expense. This was the home Sisi and her family occupied during the winters when they were in town.

That King Ludwig I enjoyed Duke Max's company enough to give him a house was not surprising — the two men had much in common. Like Ludwig, Sisi's father appreciated good-looking women and cheated publicly and energetically on his wife. The king and the duke also shared a keen interest in the literary arts. In addition to the memoir of his wanderings, Duke Max penned ironic verses and stories, and composed songs for the guitar; Ludwig published love sonnets. It must be confessed that despite their obvious passion for their subjects, neither man displayed a talent above the ordinary. Heinrich Heine, the most celebrated lyricist of the era, observed:

> *King Ludwig was a noble poet*
> *He sang — but Apollo lamented*
> *As on his knees he besought the king:*
> *"Stop! Stop! I become demented."*

It wasn't just the monarch who appreciated Duke Max's outsized personality and eccentric, amusing behavior. The townspeople were on his side, too. Elisabeth's father was beloved for having an aesthetic that mirrored that of his fellow citizens. The duke despised stuffy aristocratic ceremony. Thumbing his nose at convention, he installed a practice show ring in the backyard of his fancy marble residence, where he trained horses to perform circus tricks. He much preferred Bavarian folk songs and zither tunes to symphonies, and succeeded, much to the pride of his countrymen, in having one of his pieces played at Buckingham Palace on the same program with the overture to a new opera by Carl Maria von Weber, a celebrated German composer. Duke Max was also known for having organized a group of his friends, mostly fellow amateur musicians and scribblers (and, of course, his zither instructor), into a Knights of the Round Table society where, costumed as King Arthur, he presided once a month over dinners at which copious amounts of beer were consumed, and boisterous singing continued long into the night.

To have such a man for a father was glorious; to have him as a husband was something else. Duchess Ludovika, forced to put up with Duke Max's numerous mistresses and illegitimate children, as well as his other foibles, was often not on speaking terms with her waggish marriage partner. But at least she could console herself that Duke Max was not as ungenerous to his wife and children as King Ludwig was to his. Sensitive to the charge that his numerous building projects were an extravagance the treasury could ill afford, the king of Bavaria compensated for his public munificence by keeping his private household on a budget so tight that the queen could not afford a new gown, and the royal family dined regularly on black bread and onions. With this example in front of her, Duchess Ludovika knew enough to accept her situation.

To their considerable credit, neither of Elisabeth's parents took their dissatisfaction with one another out on their offspring, and the result was that Sisi had a very happy, almost idyllic childhood. She was part of a large, lively family and loved it. The one marital responsibility that Duke Max apparently took seriously was procreation, and a new baby appeared every two years with a punctuality a field marshal would have envied. By the time Elisabeth was seven, in addition to her older siblings Ludwig and Nene, she had a younger brother, Karl Theodore, called "Gackel" (German for Cock), born August 9, 1839, and two younger sisters, Marie, whose birthday was October 4, 1841, and Mathilde, "Spatz" (Sparrow), who came along on September 30, 1843.

As this meant that Duchess Ludovika was nearly always either pregnant or just recovering from birth, and with Duke Max not much more than a large child himself, parental oversight was not taxing. Sisi and her brothers and sisters grew up in a fond, unfussy atmosphere where levity was valued over lessons; riding, romping, and zither-playing were educational requirements; and everyone had his or her own tree at Christmas.

Almost as soon as she learned to scamper about under her own momentum, Elisabeth's most joyous times were spent at the family's summer estate, Possenhofen Castle. Situated about twenty miles southwest of Munich, amidst one of the most beautiful landscapes Bavaria had to offer, Possi, as this sprawling, romantic château was known, might have been conjured up as a child's vision of a magical residence in a fairy tale. There were green parks and shaded woods filled with forest animals, the whole ringed by snow-capped mountain peaks, and a large, crystal-blue lake perfect for fishing, swimming, or boating. (The family maintained a replica of a Venetian gondola as an added amusement.) At Possi, Elisabeth, who loved animals, kept rabbits and ponies, and looked after a flock of guinea hens. She had two lambs of her own, and even a fawn; and this was in addition to the family's many dogs.

Although she was under the charge of a governess, Sisi's real instruction came from her father, whom she idolized. Duke Max wasn't around his children all that often, but when he was, he made it count. His focus was overwhelmingly on outdoor physical exercise. "I don't want you to strut like princes, or drag your feet like common mortals," he lectured his progeny. "You must learn to move like angels with wings upon your feet." Whereupon he took them for hours-long hikes through the forests and up into the mountains. "I am never tired of walking, and I thank my father for it," Elisabeth would later report. Duke Max was equally insistent that his children be as agile on horseback as they were scrambling up the rocks beside him on their own two legs. Those who showed promise were introduced to more advanced skills, like riding bareback.

And no one in the family demonstrated more innate talent or sheer, comprehensive, stunning athletic ability than Sisi. The attention she could not pay to her studies—"there were times when she had literally to be tied to her chair," the governess complained—found its home instead in the saddle and in the wild, free terrain of the wooded hills and mountains adjoining Possi. Elisabeth could no more do without swimming, or fishing, or running through the forest, or especially galloping through the countryside, than she could do without air. She was so good, such a natural, that her father even admitted her to his backyard show ring while she was still a child, and initiated her into the seductive art of trick riding. "If you and I, Sisi, had not been born princes, we would have been performers in a circus," Duke Max observed solemnly.

But her father's influence extended far beyond athletics. Among his children, he seems to have recognized Elisabeth's as the spirit closest to his own, and by his attentions fostered the quixotic in her. He taught her to play the zither and together they stood in the squares of the villages surrounding Possi and performed impromptu open-air duets that drew applause and sometimes coins from the passersby. "This is the only money I have earned in my life," Sisi would later reveal. He fed her imagination by telling her stories of knights and classical Greek heroes. He introduced her to the poetry of Heinrich Heine, a German Jew forced to convert to Lutheranism in order to obtain a university degree, with whose liberal democratic political views Duke Max agreed. Duke Max revered Heine, whose work reflected a love of nature and restless romanticism. In emulation of her father and Heine, Sisi, too, was scribbling verses at a young age.

And then, while she was still a child, Sisi's family and indeed all of Bavaria were suddenly jolted by the appearance of a force so powerful, so inflammatory, that it rivaled Napoleon himself in its ability to upend society and bring back the dark days of conflict and chaos. On October 5, 1846, just a few months before Elisabeth's ninth birthday, a carriage bearing the notorious adventuress Lola Montez rolled into Munich.

IT IS DIFFICULT TO CONCEIVE of a historical figure more exuberantly, irrepressibly, irreverently entertaining than Lola Montez. Born in Ireland sometime in February 1820 (the exact date is unknown), the product of an illegitimate, fourteen-year-old Irish mother and one Ensign Edward Gilbert, a recently deployed British soldier, Lola began life as plain old Eliza Gilbert. When she was three years old, her father was transferred to India; however, she and her parents had no sooner arrived at the new posting than Ensign Gilbert succumbed to cholera. Rather than return home, Eliza's mother, not yet twenty and very pretty, decided to stay in India with her young daughter and within a year was married again, this time to a Scottish lieutenant. As was customary among the British living in India, Eliza was cared for by ayahs who coddled and indulged her.

Then, at the age of six, just like Mary Lennox in Frances Hodgson Burnett's famous children's book *The Secret Garden*, Eliza was suddenly uprooted from her hot, crowded, colorful surroundings and sent to live with her stepfather's upright, chilly family in the small town of Montrose, on the northeast coast of Scotland, to begin her education. The unhappy child understandably felt out of place — certainly no one in Montrose had ever seen anyone like this strange, willful creature before — and to compensate, she played pranks, told whoppers, and in general did her best to shock the neighborhood.

At twelve, to everyone's relief, she was sent to an English girls' boarding school in the fashionable town of Bath. By the time she was ready to graduate, and her mother had returned to England to fetch her back to India, Eliza had grown into her looks, which were famously striking—a dark-haired beauty with arresting eyes.

And this was when the trouble began. To relieve the tedium of the long voyage from Calcutta, Eliza's mother had struck up a flirtation with a good-looking thirty-year-old British officer, Lieutenant Thomas James. Lieutenant James continued to hover even after the ship docked, and so had a chance to meet his mistress's adorable seventeen-year-old daughter. Lola would later claim that she ran off with James because her mother intended to marry her to a sixty-year-old widower in India, but it's difficult to believe anything Lola said, because she was such a charmingly inventive hustler. What is known is that Eliza Gilbert became Eliza James at a church just outside Dublin on July 23, 1837.

Lieutenant James would be the first of multiple husbands and lovers. Eliza accompanied her spouse to India but left him a few years later, citing abusive behavior. On the long voyage back to England, she took up with another handsome British officer, Lieutenant Lennox. For about a year after her return, Lennox paid her expenses and introduced her to popular haunts and London society. But then they, too, split up and Eliza was left without a visible means of financial support.

It was while she was at this crossroads that twenty-three-year-old Eliza demonstrated her resilience. She booked passage for Cádiz (where living was cheap), received two months' worth of instruction in Andalusian choreography, and returned to England on April 14, 1843, not as Eliza James, but rather as the professional *danseuse* Doña Lola Montez, having reinvented herself as the widow of a fictitious Spanish aristocrat.

It was a bluff of monumental proportions. She had only the Spanish she had managed to pick up locally; she had never danced profession-ally; she knew no one of importance in either Seville or Madrid. It should never have worked—but it did. From that moment on, Eliza James became Lola Montez, a persona she inhabited for the rest of her life. So much so that when she made her debut on the London stage six weeks later, and several of Lieutenant Lennox's friends who happened to be in the audience recognized her and pointed out to the newspapers that she was in fact neither Spanish nor a widow, but rather the adulterous ex-wife of a British soldier in India who was still very much alive, Lola merely doubled down and published a letter to the editor, explaining with great dignity that she was "a native of Seville ... [and] until the 14th of April last, when I landed in England, I *never set my foot* in this country, and *I never saw London before in my life.*"

This was the beginning of a historic, not to say epic, career. When the startled London stage manager declined to engage her further, Lola took her act on the road. Everywhere she went, scandal and sensation followed. She smoked in public—and cigars, at that—at a time when it was considered outrageous for a woman to do so. She carried a dagger and a small pistol and brandished them during the many arguments she provoked. In Berlin, she was famously arrested for striking a Prussian policeman in the face with her riding crop, and then, after the officer filed charges against her, was deported for tearing up and stamping on the court order summoning her for questioning by the authorities. She intercepted Franz Liszt, perhaps the most popular musician of the period, while he was on tour, ingratiated herself, and then used him as a reference to secure dancing engagements. She had a love affair with a newspaper editor in Paris who was unfortunately killed in a duel, and caused a frenzy in the press by sweeping into the courthouse dressed all in black—Lola looked exceptionally well in black—and giving dramatic testimony against his murderer at the subsequent trial.* Afterwards, she left France and wandered aimlessly through Germany, scrounging around for theaters at which to perform. She was temporarily between engagements and lovers, and consequently low on funds, when on a whim she trundled into eight-year-old Sisi's hometown and met her uncle, Ludwig I, king of Bavaria.

He never had a chance. Ludwig was by this time sixty years old. He had a long-suffering wife, for whom he had never felt any real desire,

---

* Lola may truly be said to be a woman ahead of her time. She anticipated reality television by nearly 200 years.

and eight adult children. He was going deaf. His skin was pockmarked. It had been years since his last dalliance, and he missed the thrill that, in his opinion, only a ravishing young creature could provide. Ludwig worshipped feminine loveliness. Unique among his fellow monarchs, he commissioned his court painter, Joseph Karl Stieler, to produce a series of portraits of the most striking women of his acquaintance. The king was a true democrat when it came to love: his Gallery of Beauties was open to the public and contained over thirty paintings, not simply likenesses of highborn ladies, but also those of lowly merchants' and cobblers' daughters, and even one of a Jewess. (Although cruelly none of his wife.)

But for all his pretensions of being a sophisticated philanderer and man of the world, nothing in Ludwig's experience prepared him for an operator on the scale of Lola Montez. Informed that she needed the king's approval to dance at the Royal Court Theater, Lola obtained a private audience with Ludwig on October 8, 1846, three days after her arrival in Munich. She showed up wearing a close-fitting gown of ebony velvet and her most appealing expression. It was later rumored that she had undressed and danced (or worse) while closeted alone with the king but this was just malicious gossip. The aging Ludwig, who had never heard of this bewitchingly exotic young Spanish dancer before the interview, needed no such encouragement. He was a lost man the moment he set eyes on her.

It did not take Lola long to figure out that, consequently, Bavaria offered a path to advancement superior to any that had been available at her previous addresses. Within weeks, she admitted to Ludwig that she loved him, and allowed him to convince her to stay on in Munich as his sweetheart.

Lola stayed, and Ludwig paid. The king, conspicuous for parsimony when it came to himself and his family, not only footed the bill for his new favorite's lodging at the best hotel in Munich, but he also bought her a mansion in town, which he then gave her a free hand to remodel and redecorate in lavish style. Soon thereafter, Ludwig commanded the royal treasury to bestow an annual allowance of 10,000 florins on

Lola—more than the highest official in the kingdom earned, and certainly more than the queen had access to in all their years of marriage. Lola was given the best horses and a grand carriage in which to ride around the city; she bought anything she wanted and sent the bill to the king; and of course she had her portrait painted by Stieler, who added it with great fanfare to the Gallery of Beauties, where it drew crowds of spectators.

Throughout, Lola, who was nothing if not consistent, continued to behave as immoderately as she had prior to arriving in Munich. Having no need to earn a living, she put her dancing career on hold and instead insisted on being treated as a grand lady, much to the dismay and resistance of the Bavarian upper class. She again got into altercations with the police and tore up official summonses, and she regularly humiliated the queen by appearing at the same public functions attended by the royal family, during which, in front of the pitying eyes of all Munich society, Ludwig would leave his wife alone to watch as he slavishly paid court to the brazen younger woman. In one memorable incident, Lola started a riot after Turk, the large dog she kept, attacked a workman on the street. Rather than restrain her pet, she slapped the underling five times in the face for trying to defend himself. The onlookers took the side of the laborer and chased Lola and Turk into a shop; word got around and hundreds gathered outside the establishment, demanding her arrest. Lola only managed to escape by waiting until dark and then climbing out a second-story window and down a ladder in the back.*

But nothing Lola did weakened Ludwig's infatuation. In vain his advisers showed him a thick dossier of newspaper and diplomatic reports detailing her true identity, age, and history; she explained it all away as lies concocted by jealous competitors and Jesuits. The Prussian ambassador warned, "Every conception of the dignity of the throne is trampled underfoot," and even one of the king's most loyal supporters

---

* Turk, not as adept at aerial descents, had to wait until the following morning to be liberated.

despaired that Lola "has insulted all classes of society, offended everyone, and the city and the nation are so up in arms that with the best will it is too late to improve her position." Worse, Ludwig promised to raise his "Lolita," as he called her, to the highest levels of nobility by bestowing upon her the title and privileges of a countess. In preparation for this, on February 3, 1847, a mere four months after the dancer's arrival, he ordered his ministers to draw up and sign the appropriate legal papers granting her Bavarian citizenship.

And it was at this point that that pesky constitution came into play. By law, the king could not unilaterally bestow citizenship on a foreigner. He needed one of his councilors to countersign the order. This, Ludwig's chief minister, an ultraconservative Catholic who had been in power for twenty years, refused to do. When the king insisted, the minister, as well as all the rest of the Council of State, also ultraconservative Catholics, threatened to resign. Ludwig, who had never been crossed this way before, bristled and accepted the mass resignation. He then replaced the council with a new, more progressive ministry that was led for the first time in Bavarian history by a Protestant. It was understood that the new chief minister would sign Lola's citizenship papers. The liberal councilor had no more liking for the Spanish dancer than had his conservative predecessor, but acquiescing was worth it to him to gain power. He signed.

Ironically, the change in government was popular in Munich. While it was true that nobody cared for Lola, the ultraconservative ministers had been chipping away at civil liberties for years. They had restricted access to foreign publications deemed subversive, imposed censorship, and curtailed the religious and constitutional rights of those of differing beliefs. Many Catholics in Munich, like Elisabeth's parents, were more liberal. Duke Max openly advocated freedom of the press, and Duchess Ludovika, along with other women of rank, had once cornered Ludwig in his castle to berate him for indulging the ultraconservative party's intolerance of Protestants. The king's appointment of a more progressive councilor raised expectations of pending democratic reforms.

But, of course, that hadn't been Ludwig's intention at all. Ludwig had chosen the Protestant minister not for his views, but because he was the only experienced official Ludwig could find who was willing to sign Lola's citizenship papers. The king believed, as he always had, that his commands should be obeyed instantly and without question. He did not want freedom of the press, nor a liberal agenda, and he certainly did not want his subjects to have the right to tell him what to do.

He just wanted Lola. And Lola wanted to be a countess.

And so a countess she became six months later, on August 25, 1847. "I feel constrained to point out once again to Your Majesty the consequences of Your Majesty's action," Ludwig's new minister, who had countersigned this second document only after vigorous resistance, warned. "They will be very serious."

He was right. When the Bavarian population discovered Lola's elevation, there was outrage. It was reported with amusement in the foreign papers (but not in the Munich press, which was prohibited from running negative stories about Lola) that an aristocratic counteroffensive was waged during performances at the opera house, with one of the doyennes of society flagrantly wielding "an enormous fan, held up between her face and the box of the new countess." The queen, who had to find out about her rival's triumph by reading about it in the *State Gazette,* stood up to her husband for the first time in their thirty-seven years of marriage and point-blank refused to receive the interloper.★ On October 16, 1847, the Chamber of Representatives, meeting for only the eleventh time in Bavarian history, entered the fray by voting unanimously for freedom of the press, and even threatened to withhold the money required to fund the all-important new railroads running through Bavaria if this and other "grievances" were not addressed, "the fact being that the most serious cases of interference with the press have been on account of attacks on Lola Montez," as a London paper was quick to point out. When Ludwig refused to comply with their

---

★ According to Bavarian law, Lola could not legally be considered a countess, despite the countersigned order, unless notice of her elevation was published in an official state publication, so she made Ludwig do this.

demands, the representative assembly, citing the constitution, threatened to depose him. The mood in the city, ordinarily placid, turned so ugly that Duke Max and Duchess Ludovika, worried about street violence, packed up the children and, to Elisabeth's intense joy, moved to out-of-the-way Possi to celebrate the Christmas holidays and her tenth birthday.

This turned out to be a prudent decision. The family was still at their country house when Lola, now countess of Landsfeld, got into an argument with the University of Munich.

Undeterred by the increasingly vocal campaign against her, the new countess continued to flout propriety, just as she always had. Having secured wealth and title beyond anything she could have hoped for elsewhere, Lola was determined to have a good time with them. Problem was, Munich was so provincial and staid. Its amusements could not compare with those of Paris or London. And then, she was being ostracized by the people she considered to be her social peers, and Ludwig was clearly a bore. ("I come after everyone else, in all situations," the king grumbled of his beloved. "If there is no one else to talk with or nothing else to do, then I may remain, otherwise I am driven away...If Turk the dog could talk, he would be heard with greater attentiveness," he observed dolefully.)

And so, Lola had to make her own fun. This she did by befriending a group of students (all of them male, of course; no women were allowed to attend the university) and inviting them over to her splendid new house for late-night parties. The one on New Year's Eve got so out of hand that she was knocked out cold when her admirers, dancing drunkenly around the main salon, hoisted their benefactress high into the air and whacked her head on the crystal chandelier. She even secretly took the handsomest among them as her lover.

The professors and the rest of the predominantly conservative student body were appalled. Nothing daunted, the countess's young partisans formed themselves into a club. To distinguish their fraternity, they wore matching red caps provided by Lola. On February 9, 1848, some of the members, given away by their crimson headgear, were jeered by a mob of their schoolmates and chased off campus into a nearby pub. Trapped by a rapidly growing crowd, one of them dashed off a note to Lola, begging for assistance.

Upon receipt of this SOS, Lola immediately sallied forth to deliver her entourage from captivity. But no sooner had she neared her destination than the enraged scholars, recognizing the countess, turned and began to chase her. Lola banged on the gates of the surrounding houses, but no one would let her in. She eventually found refuge in a church, but then, angered by the insults of the throng outside, left this sanctuary, pistol in hand, to confront her pursuers. The gun was torn from her and she was fighting for her life when the police arrived and rescued her.

Indignant at the riot and the shocking treatment of his favorite, Ludwig retaliated by closing the university for a year and ordering those students who were not citizens of Munich to leave the city within twenty-four hours. But this punishment, rather than intimidating the academic community and Lola's numerous other detractors within the capital, only encouraged them to adopt even more aggressive tactics against her. The next day, an assembly of some 2,000 of Ludwig's subjects marched to the square adjoining the palace and demanded that the university be reopened and the countess of Landsfeld deported. The king imperiously denied their petition but privately begged Lola to leave the city, just for a day, as he had been informed by his general that neither the Munich police nor the Bavarian army was willing to fire on the local population to protect her. This, Lola, who had never run away from a fight in her life, declined to do.

By the following morning, February 11, 1848, the opposing lines were drawn and the combatants were ready. Battle was joined at 7 a.m., when hundreds of townspeople descended on Lola's expensive new house and began to wreck it. They dug up paving stones from the street and threw them at the windows, shattering the glass. They surged through her garden and tried to batter down her doors. Lola, ever the warrior, burst out of her mansion, waving her pistol, but her servants ran out and overpowered her, shouting for her carriage. The driver pulled up quickly, the still-struggling countess was pitched unceremoniously into the compartment, and the coach took off at breakneck speed. Later that day, Ludwig was forced to bow to reality and rescind his order to close the university. There was great rejoicing in the streets; the brave patriots of Munich had risen up as one and heroically saved the kingdom from the evil clutches of a phony Spanish dancer.

But sometimes even an episode as fundamentally trivial as running a twenty-eight-year-old adventuress out of town has deeper ramifications. History has a way of choosing its own turning points, and the expulsion of Lola Montez from Bavaria ended up being one of them. It was as if a lever had been applied to the weight of absolute monarchy, lifting it ever so slightly and exposing its vulnerability. As the Austrian ambassador pointed out worriedly in his account of these events home to Vienna, "The people have triumphed over the royal power and are conscious of their undeniable victory; they have learned the power of their will and the manner of using it with success." And as if to underscore this truth, not two weeks later, the citizens of Paris took to the streets and this time evicted not a mistress from her mansion, but *the King of France himself* from the realm.

News of the forced abdication and flight of the French monarch resounded over Europe, stunning the established authorities and raising the hopes of liberal reformers everywhere. On March 6, a mob of over 10,000 of Ludwig's subjects broke into the royal armory in Munich and distributed the weapons stockpiled inside to the public. Within days, the fever of revolution had spread to Berlin, where students and citizens clashed with armed and mounted hussars, forcing the king of Prussia to agree to the writing of a national constitution similar to the document already in place in Bavaria. By March 14, the people of Vienna had also taken to the streets, wresting the promise of a more democratic system from the Austrian emperor and compelling the resignation of his principal minister, whose autocratic vision of order and status quo had been embraced by the crowned heads of Europe for decades. "It was public opinion, the example set by Prussia and Bavaria,...which prompted the united movement in all classes of society," the foreign correspondent for the London *Observer* asserted of the Viennese revolt.

Elisabeth and her family remained safely at Possi throughout the turmoil, so she would not have seen the barricades being raised in the streets, nor the soldiers guarding the palace, nor heard the drums beating to call for additional troops to quell the rioters. She would find out only later that the countess of Landsfeld, in addition to fleeing, had been stripped of her citizenship, and had an outstanding warrant for her arrest, should she ever try to slip back into the country.

But even as a ten-year-old, Sisi could not have helped but be aware of the dénouement of the violent outbursts against Lola, for on March 20, 1848, her Uncle Ludwig, for twenty-three years the sole ruler in Munich, signed a royal patent of abdication. "We have been graciously pleased to resign our crown in favour of our beloved son his Royal Highness the Crown Prince Maximilian...While I descend from the throne my heart yet glows with affection for Bavaria and for Germany," Ludwig concluded graciously in the royal address that accompanied this bombshell.

Perhaps. But a little later, privately, the king penned a poem, "To Lola," that likely depicted his sentiments more accurately.

> 'Twere better far that I had never known thee
> For whom my heart's blood I would gladly give;
> With grief beyond expression thou has filled me,
> Most burning love of all the years I live . . .
>
> The dream of years evermore has vanished
> And I awaken in a wilderness.
> What I have felt of joy and pleasure banished;
> My crown is forfeit, and my happiness.

2

The Empire Strikes Back

In the world's history every event is not the direct consequence
of another, but all events mutually act and react on one another.

—Heinrich Heine

FORTUNATELY FOR BAVARIA, Sisi's thirty-seven-year-old cousin Maximilian II, the new king, proved to be far less dogmatic (and certainly
less susceptible to the charms of itinerant *femmes fatales*) than his
father. On March 22, 1848, just two days after Ludwig's abdication,
Maximilian issued a proclamation granting a general amnesty to all
who had been swept up in the political turmoil precipitated by Lola.
He then went even further and promised to put in place "without
delay" a series of reforms such as freedom of the press and religious
toleration, with specific legislation aimed at "improving the situation
of the Jews." He also called for more representative elections as well
as tax relief. "We have entered a new era of our political life," Maximilian II declared in a speech he made to the Chamber of Representatives. "Not only Bavaria but Germany looks on, contemplating the
deliberations which are about to take place...Let us set a good example to all its people. Let our devise be freedom and legality," he finished firmly.

And with that, the anger and resentment faded and the atmosphere
in Munich assumed its former placidity. "A very striking contrast with

the fermentation prevailing in the other German States, is presented by Bavaria," a London paper pointed out a few weeks later. "The whole country is not only perfectly tranquil, but continues to increase in enthusiasm and affection for their new king." With the crisis behind them, it was once again safe for Elisabeth's parents to think about returning to the capital with the children.

But other members of Duchess Ludovika's family did not have it so easy. Prussia, ruled by her older sister Elise's husband, Frederick William IV, had seen an escalation of protests despite the king's bending to the popular will and accepting the necessity of a national constitution. But the real worry was Austria, where Ludovika's closest sister, Sophia, only three years her senior, was married to the emperor's younger brother, Archduke Francis Charles. As in Prussia, the Austrian ruler had been forced by mass uprisings in Vienna to agree to a constitution and a more representative government, but these concessions only increased the desire for reform. On May 15, 1848, a mob of some 10,000 students, laborers, and guardsmen, many of them armed, had again taken to the streets, forcing the entire imperial family, including Sophia and Archduke Francis Charles and their three youngest children, Maximilian, age fifteen; Karl, age fourteen; and Ludwig, age six, to flee the unruly capital for the more placid town of Innsbruck. "Their Majesties quitted Vienna in so much haste that they took neither change of linen nor clothes," it was later reported.

As Possi was only about 88 miles north of Innsbruck, Duchess Ludovika hastened in June to her sister's side, bringing fourteen-year-old Nene, ten-year-old Sisi, and eight-year-old Gackel with her to help amuse their cousins. Duke Max, who detested the stuffy atmosphere of the Austrian court, declined to accompany his wife on this expedition. Knowing how difficult it was for her restless younger daughter to leave the joys of Possi in the summer, even for so scenic a destination as the mountains of Innsbruck, Duchess Ludovika, as much as she wished to project a decorous image, wisely threw protocol and dignity aside and allowed Elisabeth to take her dogs and caged songbirds along with her on the long carriage ride.

★   ★   ★

FOR SISI, THIS VISIT was unmemorable. The novelty of the enormous imperial palace—with its grand rooms, ornate ceilings, and golden chandeliers, where she and her family were given apartments—soon wore off. The surrounding mountains were as lovely as promised, but she could not just wander off on her own as she could at Possi. Days were more structured at the imperial court than they were in Bavaria. Sisi was happiest when she and Gackel found opportunities to slip away from the adults to play.

This was not the case, however, with her sister Nene. Nene was at the age when she no longer wished to be considered a child. She willingly stayed in the gilded drawing rooms with her mother and Aunt Sophia. Unlike the experience of many adolescents, puberty had not been unkind to Nene. She was tall for her age, attractive, and graceful. Her manners were respectful, and she was clearly serious and intelligent. Much to her mother's pride and relief, Nene made an excellent impression on Sophia.

Elisabeth, on the other hand, received almost no notice from the imperial family, with one great exception: her cousin Karl. Karl was smitten. For a fourteen-year-old to take an interest in a ten-year-old is unusual. This is perhaps explained by Karl's being used to drawing rooms and etiquette and obedience—all of Sophia's sons were, most especially her eldest, Franz Joseph, whose earnest compliancy set the tone for the rest of his siblings. Nene's deportment was no mystery to Karl; in his experience, this was the way people were supposed to behave. But Sisi! Sisi didn't give a thought to the rules. She was creative, mercurial, and had a boundless energy that gave off its own fascinating light. Karl did everything he could think of to make her like him. He gave her flowers. He sent her trinkets. Long after the visit was over, he continued to write to her, often tucking some article of jewelry inside the letters. Sisi responded dutifully, if sporadically, to these tokens. If only he had thought to send a rabbit instead of a ring.

Elisabeth was too young to know it, of course, but this cozy family visit coincided with yet another of those slippery turning points in history. For while Sisi was blithely (if unconsciously) charming Karl, and Duchess Ludovika was casually (if deliberately) promoting Nene, pious, devoted Aunt Sophia was plotting a coup.

ARCHDUCHESS SOPHIA WAS FORTY-THREE years old the summer that Sisi and Gackel frisked in and out of the grand salon of the royal palace at Innsbruck. She had first come to the Habsburg court in Vienna nearly a quarter century earlier, a hopeful nineteen-year-old bride, only to discover that the family she had married into, while still unquestionably the most prestigious dynasty in Europe, had some significant shortcomings. Not even the most robust genetic blueprint can withstand generations of inbreeding, and both Emperor Ferdinand I and his younger brother, Archduke Francis Charles (Sophia's husband), were testament to this unfortunate scientific truth. Ferdinand was prone to epileptic seizures, among other ailments, and had such a low IQ that the London papers openly referred to him as "a cretin," "an idiot of the worst class," and a "mental nullity." Although married, he could not sire children. Archduke Francis Charles was not quite as intellectually and physically challenged as his brother—Sophia had four sons by him—but he was not that much more competent either. The archduke spent most of his time hunting.

Sophia was neither a deep thinker nor a brilliant political strategist, but, faced with liege lords like her husband and his brother, she did not have to be. It was enough that she was intelligent and determined, with strong views as to which actions the monarchy should take, to place her in a position to influence events.

The archduchess's reaction to the popular uprisings in Vienna, and especially to Ferdinand's capitulation to the demands for a constitution and a more liberal, representative government (which in her opinion had resulted in the imperial family's having to flee), was anger and humiliation. She referred dismissively to the revolutionaries as "a mess of students." When, early in June 1848, just before Duchess Ludovika and her children's visit, a deputation of Viennese ladies arrived at Innsbruck to respectfully petition the imperial family to return to the city, it was reported that both Sophia and her sister-in-law the empress "declared that they would not re-enter Vienna till all the students had been expelled from it, and the former order of things restored."

The question was how to do this. The situation was made infinitely more complicated by the fact that Vienna wasn't the only trouble spot. In addition to Austria, the Habsburg empire included Hungary, Bohemia, Transylvania, and much of northern Italy. By the summer of 1848, *every one* of these locales had caught the revolutionary fever sparked by France and Bavaria. The Hungarian capital of Pesth was demanding democratic representation and an independent government. There were armed demonstrations in the streets of Prague in favor of liberalization. Even the imperial dominions of Lombardy and Venetia were under threat, as the king of Sardinia (whose domain included the northern Italian principality of Piedmont, and thus bordered imperial lands), taking advantage of the public outcry for a free, united Italy, was at war with Austria.

And then fate lent a hand and the solution revealed itself. On June 6, 1848, just as Sophia and her sister-in-law were scoldingly turning away the disappointed emissaries from the Viennese ladies' society, a new wave of violence hit Prague. Soldiers under the command of the general in charge of the Austrian forces in Bohemia, Prince Alfred of Windischgraetz, clashed with demonstrators in several locations, including one of the main squares. During this latter encounter, an errant bullet was shot into a nearby building. It happened to be Windischgraetz's own quarters. His wife of thirty-one years, who had been standing at the window anxiously observing the conflict in the street, was struck— and died.

In the wake of this personal tragedy, Windischgraetz did not wait to receive orders from Innsbruck. He did not care that he exceeded his authority. He brought out the heavy artillery and began bombarding the city. Eight days later, with at least 46 confirmed dead and 130 wounded, the revolutionaries, mostly students and workers, surrendered. A state of siege was declared; private homes were searched; hundreds of civilians were arrested. Twenty thousand people fled the city.

When Windischgraetz finally relinquished Prague from martial law a month later, he did so only after publicly warning the citizenry that "even the slightest attempt at a new rebellion will result in an immediate imposition of the most severe military power."

In Innsbruck, Archduchess Sophia rejoiced at hearing this news. To her, Prince Windischgraetz was a hero, and his subjugation of Prague was an unqualified victory for the throne. His repressive methods and swift results were a vindication of everything she believed. This was what should be done with unruly Vienna and Hungary as well.

So, she reached out to the prince, and also to two other generals who she knew could be counted on to be sympathetic to a hard-line response to the unrest: Field Marshal Joseph Radetzky, who was in command of the Austrian forces in Italy, and Colonel Josip Jellačić, stationed in Hungary. All three agreed that Ferdinand ought never to have given in to the radicals' demands in the first place, and that what was needed was a fresh start to the monarchy, backed by force. To help ensure the success of what was shaping up nicely to be a military coup, Windischgraetz also suggested getting political advice from his brother-in-law, Prince Felix Schwarzenberg. It was so well known that these four men were in league with Sophia that they were openly referred to as "the Camarilla [cabal]."

The process of "setting things in order," as Sophia euphemistically called it, began that summer. On July 25, 1848, Field Marshal Radetzky beat the king of Sardinia's forces at Custoza in northern Italy and secured military control of Lombardy and Venetia. On September 11, Jellačić's divisions went on the offensive in Hungary. Soon thereafter, Windischgraetz left Prague and marched the majority of his army, complete with artillery, southeast to Olmütz, only about 200 miles north of Vienna, under the pretext of engaging in practice maneuvers.

Matters came to a head on October 6, 1848. The Viennese citizenry, enraged at imperial attempts to suppress the revolt in Hungary (which they rightly took as auguring poorly for their own prospects for democratic reform), once again took violently to the streets. Focusing their anger on the minister of war, a mob surrounded his offices, forced its way into the building, and brutally murdered him, stabbing him multiple times and eventually hanging his mutilated, naked body from a nearby lamppost.

The horror over this butchery provided Sophia's cohorts with the desired pretext for declaring martial law. By October 23, Windischgraetz and his regiments had marched down from Olmütz and surrounded Vienna. The field marshal gave the capital forty-eight hours to surrender, and when it did not, he unleashed the full force of his arsenal against the civilian population, as he had in Prague. This time, 2,000 people died, and thousands more were injured or had their homes or businesses destroyed in the shelling. Two thousand more were arrested after the revolutionaries finally capitulated, with twenty-five summarily executed for treason. It was all over, with Windischgraetz's soldiers in complete control, by the first week in November.

While Sophia's co-conspirator was busy raining death and destruction on the imperial capital, the archduchess took it upon herself to reinvigorate the monarchy. Her half brother Ludwig's abdication in favor of his son had succeeded so well in Bavaria that Sophia had the happy thought to emulate this strategy by deposing Ferdinand. This turned out to be a relatively simple undertaking. Ferdinand's wife had had quite enough of her irate subjects. The empress added her voice to her clever sister-in-law's, reminding her husband that he was older and sickly, and that it would be better to let someone else take up the burden of all these troubles. Ferdinand accepted these arguments meekly and prepared to abdicate.

By the established order of succession, the throne should then have gone to Sophia's husband, Archduke Francis Charles. But the fourth member of the archduchess's inner circle, Prince Schwarzenberg (Windischgraetz's brother-in-law, responsible for political advice), counseled against this. The success of the coup would rise and fall on the military, he noted. Consequently, the monarchy needed "an Emperor we can show to the soldiers."

And that's how Sophia's eldest son got the job. Eighteen-year-old Franz Joseph, who had embraced discipline and routine at an early age, and who had never opposed his mother's wishes in his entire life, admired soldiers and felt at home in their company. He had technically been in the army since he was thirteen, when he was named honorary colonel-in-chief of a regiment. He started participating in field exercises when he was seventeen and so was used to taking orders. He had even already seen action in battle in Italy (although naturally from a rearguard, heavily defended position). Moreover, Franz Joseph was well acquainted with both Field Marshals Windischgraetz and Radetzky, having served under each of them, and respected their authority and experience enormously. He was young, slim, attractive, athletic, and an excellent horseman. He looked particularly handsome in uniform. He was perfect.

And so, on the morning of December 2, 1848, in the great hall of the archbishop's palace at Olmütz (Vienna being considered still too risky to chance), before an assembly that included the imperial family and the main conspirators—Windischgraetz, Colonel Jellaçić (who returned from Hungary for the occasion), and Schwarzenberg—among other assorted officers and diplomats, Franz Joseph formally ascended the throne. "God bless you Franzl," the deposed Ferdinand murmured affably afterward, patting his nephew's head. "Be good. I don't mind."

The manifest cynicism of pretending to hand so vast and complex a responsibility as the rule of the Austrian empire over to a teenager did not go unnoticed. "What a boy of eighteen, governed by his mother, the most thoroughly hated woman in Germany, can do to arrest the march of destruction, is not easy to be imagined," wondered an editorial in London's *Daily News*. The Hungarian *Zeitung* of Pesth informed its readership of the new emperor's ascension with this scathing exchange: "Sophie says to her son, who is still a minor, 'You are King!' He answers: 'I am King, and my first care will be to fight against the revolt in Hungary.' What a scandal!"

But in Olmütz, these criticisms were brushed aside by the undeniable success of the intrigue. To underscore the importance of the military to the imperial throne, the inaugural ceremony had ended with a review of Windischgraetz's troops. The cheers from the assembled divisions when Franz Joseph made his appearance were gratifyingly hearty. But clearly even the soldiers were aware of who was now really in control of the monarchy, as it wasn't until Archduchess Sophia arrived that the ovation reached its crescendo.

THE ASCENSION OF FRANZ JOSEPH marked the end of any hope for democratic reform in the Austrian empire. Three months later, on March 6, 1849, the new emperor abruptly and unilaterally dissolved the representative Diet, which had been charged with writing a national constitution, and instead substituted a significantly watered-down version written by one of his imperial ministers. It didn't matter anyway, as it never went into effect—none of the rights promised by Ferdinand did—and even this more monarchically friendly constitution was revoked a short time later, when Sophia and her son finally dropped all pretense of ruling as anything but a repressive autocracy.

But what was really heartbreaking was what happened to Hungary, long the bulwark of the Austrian empire. Although the Hungarian Diet had initially asked merely for representation at the imperial court, certain basic human rights, and more control over local affairs, both Windischgraetz and Jellačić nonetheless sent in armies, and on March 4, 1849, Franz Joseph, acting again on the advice of his mother and her circle, publicly revoked Ferdinand's earlier pledge to recognize the kingdom's right to an independent constitution. The stunned Hungarians, who up until this point had been negotiating in good faith with Vienna, fought back. Many of their officers were seasoned professionals who had served in the Austrian military, so they were familiar with the tactics used by their former colleagues. Moreover, even the foot soldiers, although hastily recruited and untried, were utterly committed to defending their country. This combination proved irresistible. By May 1849, the Hungarian army had succeeded in driving both Windischgraetz's and Jellačić's troops out of the kingdom and back across the border into their own territory.

Faced with this unexpected setback, Windischgraetz, casting around for alternatives, came up with the novel plan of petitioning Tsar

Nicholas I to send in an army of Russian soldiers to help Franz Joseph subdue the Hungarians. This was a highly unusual move. World-class powers like Austria do not as a rule ask other world-class powers to invade their property. For one thing, it's a public admission of weakness, which carries with it the danger that other, unsolicited, less well-meaning powers will be encouraged to invade as well. Then there is also the risk that even a friendly ally like the tsar of Russia would expect some recompense for helping out, not to mention that once Russian soldiers have fought their way onto your lands, it can be quite difficult getting them out again.

But Sophia, in her zeal to crush all those whom she viewed as threats to imperial authority, threw her support behind this contingency. She even had Franz Joseph write what amounted to a thank-you note to Nicholas as an added impetus. "From my childhood, I have been accustomed to see in Your Majesty...the sincerest, most faithful friend of my family," the eighteen-year-old Austrian emperor penned dutifully to the fifty-three-year-old tsar. "It is enough for me to be convinced that Your Majesty, with the great wisdom that distinguishes him, ... [will lend] the help of his powerful arm."

It worked. Nicholas, believing Austria to be indebted to him by this appeal, agreed to provide troops and artillery. The Hungarians continued to fight bravely, but with the addition of 100,000 Russian soldiers and their 12,000 cannons in June, the defenders were heavily outnumbered. Within two months it was clear that they could not hold out. On August 11, 1849, the general in charge of the Hungarian forces surrendered to his Russian counterpart. At the same time, Hungary's leading statesman, Lajos Kossuth, fled the kingdom with about 4,000 of his supporters.

This turned out to be a prudent expedient. Those who stayed behind were subjected to shocking brutality. One hundred fourteen Hungarians, thirteen generals, and the former prime minister were summarily executed, and over 2,000 were imprisoned. (When petitioned for mercy, Prince Schwarzenberg was said to have responded complacently, "That's all right, but we must hang a few first.") Even Nicholas was repulsed by the wanton revenge. "The punishment...upon those who surrendered to our army is infamous, and an insult to us," the tsar wrote to his general. "I am deeply wounded by it."★ Frustrated that so many of the rebels had gotten away, the Austrians, with the warm approval of the new emperor and his mother, hanged seventy-five people in effigy, a meaningless gesture that merely deepened the hatred the conquered felt for the imperial government.

By such gratuitous acts of violence and humiliation was the reign of Franz Joseph cemented. From this point on, the heavy mantle of totalitarianism shrouded the Austrian empire. Sophia could congratulate herself on the success of her strategy, but although she did not realize it, the victory had come at a price. For as the brilliant orator and former president of the Hungarian Diet, Lajos Kossuth, now a refugee forced into exile, observed: "A Dynasty which is founded upon the freedom of the people will always excite enthusiasm, for a faithful heart can only belong to a free man...But not a sparrow will fall to support the policy of an oppressive Government."

★ You know you've reached a new low when the tsar of Russia thinks you're barbaric.

3

An Imperial Bait and Switch

One does not send the Emperor of Austria packing.

—Duchess Ludovika

BACK IN BAVARIA, SISI, who had not even reached puberty when her Aunt Sophia was busy rearranging the imperial succession and imposing martial law on her far-flung subjects, was aware of none of this. Her life, after her return from the Innsbruck visit, had continued along its peaceful, customary path. She spent her summers riding and tromping through the glorious countryside around Possi and her winters in now-quieted Munich. The big event of 1849 in her family was not the vengeful suppression of Hungary but rather the birth of a new baby brother, Maximilian (nicknamed Mapperl), on December 7, 1849, just a few weeks before her own twelfth birthday. As before, Sisi sat down to a sociable, if necessarily somewhat chaotic, breakfast every morning at eight with her mother and her numerous siblings (her father was rarely around and certainly not for breakfast) and afterwards squirmed through lessons with her governess until two. She took up drawing, and made sketches of her pets, as well as of the mountains surrounding Possi. But poetry remained her secret passion.

There was something that had changed since the return from Innsbruck, though, and that was her mother's attitude toward Nene. Sophia had evidently given her sister enough encouragement that Duchess

Ludovika believed her eldest daughter had a chance of one day marrying into the imperial family, and she was determined that Helene be prepared should this golden opportunity arise.

And so, for the next three years, Nene was the focus of Duchess Ludovika's attention (such as there was of it, what with a new baby, a household full of rambunctious children, and a husband who, although he occupied the same domicile, basically lived an entirely separate existence).* In return, Nene, as a dutiful eldest daughter, did all she could to fulfill her mother's expectations, although clearly the burden of responsibility weighed heavily on her. She grew shy and reserved, so as not to make a mistake. As this made her seem off-puttingly wooden and remote, Duchess Ludovika had then to remind her daughter to smile, and to make an effort to master the art of charming those around her through conversation, as was expected of those seeking royal husbands. Additionally, French, dancing, and music were added to the curriculum. Although Sisi was given instruction in these as well, she did not excel at the lessons and Duchess Ludovika did not push her as she did Helene. Beauty, as the duchess well knew, was a significant factor in the calculus of imperial marriages, and her second daughter, while certainly a sweet-natured, modest youngster, was also, alas, "as round-faced as any peasant girl," her mother sighed.

This concentration on Helene was of benefit to Elisabeth during those first formative years of adolescence. Because Nene was being thrust into the adult world prematurely, Sisi, coasting along almost unnoticed in her wake, was allowed the freedom to grow up at her own pace. Moreover, as there was no cause for competition between them—Sisi had neither the ability nor the desire to conform to drawing-room manners, and would have driven the entire family mad if she were not allowed to spend the preponderance of her free time running around outside or perfecting her riding—the two sisters shared a special relationship. Elisabeth looked up to Helene and admired her greatly for being so accomplished,

---

* So removed was Duke Max generally from family life that he had two of his favorite illegitimate daughters over to a private luncheon with him nearly every day in his quarters on the first floor.

attractive, and mature, while for Nene, Sisi was the closest member of the family with whom she could just be herself.

Adolescence came, and with it a growth spurt and hormones. Sisi remained a fearless outdoorswoman—there was nothing she would not dare while on horseback—and a devoted animal lover, but to these avocations was now added the usual interest in boys. She developed such a crush on a young count in her father's service that she would crouch behind a strategically placed bush and wait there for hours hoping to catch a glimpse of him. Unable to hide her infatuation, she was soon discovered, and the object of her affection was sent away. When, tragically, the young man died soon thereafter from a sudden illness, she cried for days and composed a long poem mourning the loss of her dead sweetheart, although she was forced to acknowledge in these lovelorn verses the "hard truth" that he had not reciprocated her feelings.

Which is all to say that by the summer of 1853, fifteen-year-old Elisabeth, for all her tiptoeing into the adult world, was still very much a naïve and sheltered schoolgirl. And this was where matters stood in June, when Duchess Ludovika's fondest hopes materialized. A letter from Archduchess Sophia arrived at Possi by special messenger, inviting nineteen-year-old Helene, accompanied by her parents, to help celebrate Franz Joseph's twenty-third birthday at the imperial family's country home in Bad Ischl that August. Duchess Ludovika grasped the import of this summons immediately. Given his choice of all the most eligible princesses in Europe, the emperor of Austria had decided to marry Nene.

ACTUALLY, THIS WAS NOT COMPLETELY ACCURATE. Franz Joseph did indeed wish to marry, but it was his mother who had chosen the bride. By the beginning of 1853, with Austrian military rule firmly in place—"Soldiers administer the government in every one of the provinces of the empire," the London *Daily News* noted—Archduchess Sophia at last felt that she could turn her attention to happier projects. At the top of this list was finding an appropriate match for her eldest son. There was some sense of urgency about this. Franz Joseph was a normal young man with a healthy sex drive. Although the archduchess had placed him in the care of one of her closest advisers, Count Karl Grünne (Schwarzenberg had died), a former soldier who understood these matters, and who discreetly arranged for his charge to satisfy himself with lower-class women, this system obviously could not go on forever. There was evidence that the emperor himself was getting tired of it and wanted a more fulfilling relationship. He had fallen in love twice already—once with a princess whom Sophia suspected of harboring Hungarian sympathies, and, when that had been discouraged, with the niece of the king of Prussia. His mother would have been quite happy with this latter match, but unfortunately the young woman in question was a Protestant who refused to convert (the Austrian imperial family was exclusively, rigidly Catholic), and who was in any event already engaged to another man. But the speed and intensity with which Franz Joseph transferred his affections were a little disconcerting, and the archduchess understood that if she didn't act quickly, there was a danger that the young emperor would be dazzled by some thoroughly unsuitable female. Although Sophia knew he would never marry without her approval, it would just be easier all around if she found him the right person before that happened.

All thoughts of marriage had to be put on hold in February, however, when the Austrian court received a decisive scare. One of the more distressing side effects of a repressive autocracy is that those citizens who feel strongly about registering a complaint often resort to irregular methods to make their case, there being no legitimate avenue by which to express an opposing opinion. This uncomfortable truth was brought home to Franz Joseph on Sunday, February 18, 1853, when, while he was out for an afternoon stroll in Vienna, a young man of about his own age suddenly accosted him from behind. Drawing a knife from his pocket, the interloper lunged at his target and succeeded in stabbing the unsuspecting emperor through the collar of his coat. Luckily for Franz Joseph, he was wearing his dress uniform, which was stiff with gold brocade. Although the gash was serious and bled profusely, the embroidery saved his life by preventing the knife from going deeper. "Long live Kossuth!" his assailant shouted in Hungarian as he was led away by the police, later to be hanged.

It took almost two months for Franz Joseph to recover, and his mother never really got over it. She noted the anniversary of this date, and gave thanksgiving for his survival, for the rest of her life. But it also renewed her determination to get his marriage settled as quickly as possible. Sadly, this assassination attempt was not the only sign of the monarchy's unpopularity. An insurrection had again broken out in Milan, requiring yet more soldiers and repression; and Tsar Nicholas, having helped Austria secure Hungary, was now expecting Franz Joseph to return the favor and send troops to aid him annex Crimea, an act of aggression that was sure to provoke even more resistance. A royal wedding, always an event of consuming interest, would make for a nice distraction from these troubles, and would showcase the emperor's softer, more sympathetic side.

Ordinarily in these cases, a bride was chosen because she brought in a prestigious alliance or shored up a deteriorating one. Sophia's focus was on Germany, where Austria's formerly dominant influence was being contested by Berlin. A Prussian marriage would have been her first choice—Prussia had by far the strongest military in the region and Sophia would have much preferred to ally with Berlin rather than compete with it—but of course that match had already fallen through and even her older sister, Elise, the queen of Prussia, could not revive it. The archduchess next tried to get her son interested in a princess of Saxony (whose mother, Amalie, was another of Sophia's sisters), but Franz Joseph did not find the young woman attractive.

That left Bavaria. It wasn't an optimal match—Franz Joseph couldn't marry an actual high-ranking royal princess, because the current king, Maximilian II, had thoughtlessly sired only sons—but as Bavaria was the largest and most strategically placed realm in southern Germany, the alliance made enough sense that Sophia was willing to lower her standards and consider a candidate from Duchess Ludovika's humbler line of the family. Aware that she had not seen her sister's eldest daughter for some time, the archduchess took the precaution of asking the Austrian ambassador in Munich to report on Helene's appearance, manners, and general social graces. The diplomat made haste to write back praising Nene in such glowing terms that Sophia was inspired to relate his findings to her son, who, prior to this, seems to have had only the vaguest recollection of his cousin, if he remembered her at all. But now, as his mother had intended, his interest was piqued, and he agreed with her plan to meet Helene at Ischl in preparation for announcing their engagement.

As Franz Joseph's birthday was August 18, it was agreed that the bride-to-be and her parents would be invited to arrive on the 16th. This way, the emperor would have two full days to approve his mother's choice, which both considered more than sufficient. Helene and her family would then spend the next two weeks, until August 31, in Ischl, to permit time for the numerous social functions associated with the celebration of an imperial engagement. This round of brilliant fêtes and quality family time would have the added advantage of giving Franz Joseph and Helene a chance to get to know each other a little before officially embarking on their life's journey together.

MEANWHILE, BACK AT POSSI, all was in motion. It does not take a clairvoyant to deduce the effect the invitation to Ischl had on Duchess Ludovika. She had only two months to get Nene ready. Ball gowns, tea dresses, and riding outfits in the latest fashions had to be ordered, fitted, and finished. The dancing master and French tutor worked overtime. Helene needed to be instructed in court etiquette, and to work on her conversational skills.

And Nene wasn't the duchess's only problem. Duke Max flatly refused to attend. It was summer and he wasn't about to go sit around indoors at a lot of parties with his wife's relatives, whom he knew to be a boring, stuffy lot. Duchess Ludovika was aware that although it looked odd for the prospective bride's father to absent himself, it was better than having him there embarrassing Helene by making his contempt obvious. Realizing that Franz Joseph's brothers would also be at

Ischl to celebrate the emperor's birthday, Ludovika decided to take Elisabeth along instead. It would help Nene to have her sister to distract and soothe her, and there was always the chance that the nice young Karl would renew his attentions. Although Sisi's face was still too round for her mother's taste, Duchess Ludovika noted with approval that this flaw was somewhat disguised by the masses of glorious auburn hair that hung down in luxurious tresses to her daughter's waist. Also, Elisabeth's figure, shaped by hours of exercise, was exceptionally slim and willowy. Of course, she chattered like the child she was and could barely sit still from one minute to the next, but her mother doubted that anyone besides Karl would pay much attention to her.

And so at last the great day came, and Duchess Ludovika ushered Nene and Sisi into the carriage. (There was so much baggage that it had to travel by a second coach with the servants.) This time, Elisabeth's dogs and parakeets were left behind with the younger children—not even Gackel, Sisi's usual partner in crime, was allowed to accompany his older sisters on the visit. The trip to Ischl was Elisabeth's first grown-up adventure, and she was excited to be included and careful to be on her best behavior. But everyone in the family knew that the star of the upcoming performance was Helene.

ISCHL WAS A CHARMING RESORT TOWN about halfway between Munich and Vienna. Built on the banks of an impossibly blue river, surrounded by the inevitable majestic mountains, it was, like Innsbruck, as picturesque and romantic a setting as could be found in Austria. The imperial family had had a villa in Ischl for decades, and Sophia had brought her boys for their summer holidays all their young lives, so over the years it had become quite fashionable. Franz Joseph loved the vacation spot for its restful beauty and happy childhood memories, so much so that he made sure to celebrate all of his birthdays there. The local population was proud of this distinction and each year looked forward to the gala events planned to commemorate the occasion.

Ischl was over 100 miles from Munich, and as so often happens on long journeys, complications arose that added to the travel time.

Duchess Ludovika could not pass by so close to Salzburg without stopping to call upon a recently bereaved relative who lived there, and while she and her daughters were visiting, she came down with a headache, which forced her to rest. Although she pushed herself and still managed to arrive on the evening of the 16th as planned, she, Helene, and Elisabeth were over an hour and a half late getting to their hotel. To the duchess's anxiety over their tardiness was then added the aggravation of learning that the coach carrying their servants and luggage had fallen behind and was nowhere to be seen. This meant that they had only the mourning dresses they had donned for the Salzburg visit with which to greet the imperial family.

The calamity of having to introduce herself to her future husband in the wrinkled, high-necked, long-sleeved black gown she had traveled in was not calculated to ease Helene's nerves. This consciousness of not looking her best, and perhaps not measuring up, was then heightened considerably when Archduchess Sophia, inspecting her guests prior to ushering them over to her apartments to join the rest of the family for tea, took one look at Nene and immediately sent for her own lady-in-waiting to come help arrange her niece's hair. During this preliminary period, the only person in the room who seems to have remained undismayed was Elisabeth, who had the advantage of being ignored. Sophia, in a long letter to her sister Amalie, the queen of Saxony, recorded that "with profound delight I looked on as Sissy [*sic*] did her own hair, with elegance and grace in all her movements." But this observation is most likely an example of artful backpedaling, as the missive was written days later, when events had already upended the archduchess's careful planning. The fact that the lady-in-waiting was not instructed to give Elisabeth's braids even a once-over is a far more telling sign that neither her aunt nor her mother was paying the slightest attention to her.

This interlude of beautification must have been hurried, as the rest of the imperial family were already gathered in Sophia's rooms by the time Duchess Ludovika and her daughters made their entrance. It was a small group—just Franz Joseph, his younger brothers Maximilian and Karl, and a sprinkling of other relatives, including Sophia's and Ludovika's sister Elise, the queen of Prussia. (Amalie remained behind in Dresden.) The atmosphere was apparently awkward from the very beginning. The emperor, who had been waiting around all day to get a glimpse of his future bride, registered a marked lack of enthusiasm upon meeting her. (Note to future ambassadors: Perhaps be a bit more circumspect about raising the expectations of potential suitors.) Helene, already insecure about her appearance — who knows what those middle-aged women had done to her hair — noted his reaction and retreated into reticence. The absence of a spark between the couple was obvious, and this naturally put a damper on the rest of the party.

Except for Sisi. Sisi, who saw Helene through the eyes of an adoring younger sister, had no inkling that the evening was not going as expected. "Nene is fortunate, since she has seen so many people already, but I haven't," she confessed to Sophia's lady-in-waiting. "I am so anxious that I cannot eat." But Elisabeth, while shy, was also pleased to be considered adult enough to be included among the guests, and it showed. Her eyes were bright and her face was animated. Moreover, she was so young that her timidity was to be expected, and consequently only added to her unguarded authenticity.

Karl certainly thought so. Still Elisabeth's devoted admirer, twenty-year-old Karl had been awaiting her arrival every bit as impatiently as Franz Joseph had been looking forward to seeing Helene. And so it was that Karl, with a gaze as penetrating as any suspicious husband's, was the first to detect what was happening. As soon as the party was over, he went up to his mother and complained that "the moment the Emperor beheld Sissy, an expression of such satisfaction appeared in his face that one could no longer doubt whom he would choose."

Sophia, a practical woman, put this assertion down to nonsense. It defied reason that a grown man could take a romantic interest in someone who was so obviously still a juvenile. "As if he would look at that little brat!" she scoffed in reply.

It must therefore have come as something of a shock to learn, early the next morning, that Karl had been right. Sophia barely had time to get out of bed before Franz Joseph, who had evidently spent a warm and restless night contemplating the joys of married life, burst in on her to announce that Elisabeth was the one. "Oh, but how sweet Sisi is, she's as fresh as a budding almond, and what a magnificent crown of hair frames her face! What lovely, soft eyes she has, and lips like strawberries," he enthused. But, his mother protested, what about Helene? "Don't you think that Helene is clever, that she has a beautiful, slender figure?" the archduchess urged. "Well, yes, a little grave and quiet, certainly pleasant and nice," her son responded dismissively. "But Sisi—Sisi—such loveliness, such exuberance, like a little girl's and yet so sweet!"*

Although caught by surprise by his ardor, Sophia recovered quickly. After all, her son had only seen Elisabeth once. A more prolonged exposure was sure to reveal Sisi's adolescent gaucheness, and her older sister's poise. Cautioning Franz Joseph "not to rush the matter, to consider it well" (to which he unpromisingly muttered that "neither should one protract it"), Sophia alerted her sister Elise, who in turn informed Duchess Ludovika of the problem.

There is no record of Ludovika's reaction to the news that the emperor of Austria was on the verge of rejecting graceful, age-appropriate Helene in favor of a fifteen-year-old who kept a pen full of pet rabbits, but it is not difficult to guess her thoughts. It seems that she kept Sisi in the dark but dropped a word to Helene to make a particular effort to shine at the ball scheduled for that evening.

And Nene did. This time, she got to put on the dress that had been designed expressly for this occasion—a gorgeous, rustling, white silk gown that accentuated her height and slim waist. Her hair, into which a garland of ivy was delicately woven (there was thankfully no mention of the archduchess's lady-in-waiting being in attendance), was also styled as planned. She knew herself to look every inch a future empress. Consequently, when Helene made her entrance into the ballroom that

---

* Lucky they left eleven-year-old Marie at home! Think how fresh and sweet she'd have looked.

evening, she carried her head high. "Many gentlemen," Sophia noted afterwards in her letter to Amalie in Dresden, were "absolutely enchanted by her."

Sisi, by contrast, was attired in a simple, pink-and-white cotton tarlatan frock. To give a sense of the disparity between the two sisters' costumes, cotton tarlatan was what Meg from *Little Women* was intending to wear to the neighborhood dance until kind friends took pity on her and lent her a nicer gown.

There is no question that Franz Joseph was well aware of his mother's preference. But the emperor was also in the grip of romantic infatuation. Ironically, it was at Sophia's behest that he had come to Ischl primed to fall in love. That it happened not to be with the cousin his mother had chosen for him seemed, in the heat of the moment, to be of small import. Here was one decision at least that he could make for himself. And so this most deferential of sons, who had never previously opposed his parent in word or deed, chose this occasion to stubbornly assert himself.

The first dance passed without anyone escorting either Helene or Elisabeth to the floor. The emperor, too, sat this first movement out, although this was unusual for him. For the second dance, Sophia solicited a member of the imperial staff to pair with Sisi (thus leaving Nene free to partner with her son) on the grounds that, having never attended a ball before, the young girl needed the practice. The aide rose chivalrously to the challenge and gamely led Elisabeth through the polka (although she admitted nervously to him that she didn't think she could do it without her instructor on hand to call out the steps in advance). But instead of Franz Joseph's taking the hint and asking Helene to dance, the emperor merely sat again on the sidelines and watched Sisi.

At last came the third dance, a cotillion. This time, Franz Joseph rose and crossed the room. In front of dozens of eyes, all pretending not to notice, he made his way to his Bavarian cousins. Begging the pleasure of a whirl around the room, he offered his arm—to Sisi. Nor did he leave her afterwards as was customary, but instead asked her to sit by him so that he could present her with a bouquet of flowers. And it was at this point that everyone in the room except Elisabeth understood that Franz Joseph had made his choice. "Since she had never before made an appearance in high society," Sophia explained later to Amalie, "she was unable to fathom the import of the attention (which informed the whole world about the Emperor's intentions towards her)."

Sisi might not have known what it meant, but Helene did. The humiliation of that moment must have been profound. To be so publicly and crassly passed over for her younger sister in front of all those unfamiliar, haughty faces — the barons, duchesses, queens, princes, and other state officials who made up the exclusive inner circle of the imperial court! That Nene did not break down but stayed through the rest of that evening, making small talk, dancing, and smiling, revealed more about her character, courage, and overall fitness to be an empress than all the silk ball gowns, dancing lessons, and French instruction in Europe could ever have provided.

And this was just the beginning of Helene's mortification. The next day, the 18th, was Franz Joseph's birthday, which was celebrated with yet another formal family meal, followed by an afternoon drive to a nearby village. This time, at the emperor's insistence, Elisabeth took what previously had been her sister's place beside him, while Nene was demoted to Sisi's spot farther down the table. Archduchess Sophia then invited both of her nieces to ride in her carriage along with Franz Joseph for the afternoon's excursion, to give her son a few hours of uninterrupted time to get to know both young women better. She was clearly hoping that he would recognize the obvious superiority of the elder's conversation and overall deportment. Nene knew that this was her last chance, and she did her best. Helene "talked a lot and in a most entertaining fashion," Sophia reported approvingly. "I am greatly charmed by the girl, my eye follows her, which is always the case when I take a liking to a young person."

But even the archduchess was forced to concede by the end of that outing that the battle was lost. No sooner had the imperial carriage returned to Ischl than Franz Joseph solicited yet another private interview with his parent. Without further preliminaries, he charged Sophia with the task of communicating to Duchess Ludovika his desire to marry Sisi. But he warned that Ludovika must "exert absolutely no pressure on her daughter…My situation is so difficult that God knows it is no pleasure to share it with me!" he exclaimed. Sophia, having no real option by this time but to broadcast joy at his choice, chuckled in her letter to the queen of Saxony at her son's naïveté. "But dear child, how can you believe that a woman would not be happy to ease your situation through grace and cheerfulness?" she reassured him.★

UP UNTIL THIS POINT, Sisi, the unconscious catalyst of this absorbing little drama, seems to have been doing her best just to keep up. The acute self-consciousness she had experienced during that first tea on the evening of August 16, where she had confessed herself so anxious that she couldn't swallow a bite, had carried over to the next day's dinner. "So far, Sissy has only eaten soup and lettuce, she must have imposed a fast day upon herself," the cousin seated next to her at the table had commented humorously to Archduchess Sophia. Close on the heels of this second meal came the ordeal of her first ball, with its sudden, bewildering focus on herself rather than on the resplendent Nene. (Asked later whether she had understood the significance of Franz Joseph's bestowing his bouquet on her, she had replied, "No, it just embarrassed me.") And the next day brought yet another surprise invitation, this time to occupy the coveted seat of honor next to her handsome cousin the emperor at his birthday luncheon, and afterwards to go for a drive with him, her aunt, and her sister.

This was the sum total of Sisi's interaction with Franz Joseph when, soon after she and Nene had returned from the afternoon's outing, she was informed that her imperial cousin wished to marry her. "The dear little one did not suspect the deep impression she had made on Franzi," Archduchess Sophia disclosed indulgently. "Until the moment her

---

★ Please note that Franz Joseph, who had ostensibly been leading a vast empire of some 34 million subjects for the past five years, was here referred to by his mother as a "dear child," while Elisabeth was suddenly promoted to a "woman."

mother spoke to her about it, she was filled with nothing but the shyness and timidity inspired in her by the many people around her."

Faced with so surreal a development—within the space of twenty-four hours (eight of which had involved sleeping), she had somehow gone from tag-along little sister at a ball to future empress—Elisabeth evidently tried to make some sense of the situation. "But, how can he even think of me?" she asked her mother incredulously. "After all, I am so insignificant."

In truth, there was not much Duchess Ludovika could reply to this. Her daughter was correct. From the Austrian perspective, the match was clearly an inferior one. But from her family's point of view, it was vital that Sisi accept, and accept promptly. Anything less than ardent enthusiasm risked losing the offer or, worse, insulting the suitor. Duchess Ludovika was already aware that her eldest daughter's matrimonial prospects had been damaged, perhaps irretrievably, by Franz Joseph's having rejected Nene so conspicuously, and there were three other girls, all of whom were going to need husbands, coming after Elisabeth. Sisi had it in her power to help all of her sisters, and to raise the entire family's standing, just by saying yes. And this was without even considering what effect a "no" might have on the future state of Bavarian defense, or on the kingdom's political, strategic, and economic interests. Her mother was as wary of this proposal as Sisi was—the next day, she broke down and observed to a member of Franz Joseph's household, "With how much trepidation she looked on the hard task facing her daughter Elisabeth, since she was ascending the throne literally straight from the nursery"—but Ludovika also understood that there was no turning it down.

Luckily for the duchess, her second daughter's natural inclination toward dreamy romanticism, nurtured from childhood by Duke Max, helped to overcome any hesitancy Sisi might otherwise have felt. There was no denying that it was all very much like a fairy tale, or one of those Greek myths of which Elisabeth was so fond, where one of the gods comes down from Mount Olympus to woo a beautiful maiden. Franz Joseph was slender, and his features were still nonthreateningly boyish; his manner, too, was courteous and gentle. As he had looked the part of a soldier at the time of his ascension, so in the eyes of fifteen-year-old Sisi did he now appear to embody the role of handsome prince to her Cinderella. Asked by her mother whether she thought she could love her imperial suitor, Sisi exclaimed, "How could one not love that man!"

AND SO IT WAS DECIDED. That same evening—it was still the 18th of August—Ludovika dashed off a note of acceptance to Sophia. (How she broke the news to poor Helene is unknown.) The archduchess then passed along the glad tidings to her son, who by eight the next morning was already at his beloved's hotel. Duchess Ludovika opened the door to him; "he rushed towards Sissy and the two fell into each other's arms." As, by Elisabeth's own admission, her previous crush had not responded to her advances, it is highly likely that this was the first time she had ever been kissed.

The news spread quickly throughout Ischl. It was a Sunday, so many people were already off work, and by the time the imperial family went to mass at 11 a.m., the streets were packed with excited onlookers, all jostling to get a glimpse of the engaged couple. Those who were lucky enough to secure a spot near the entrance, or inside the packed church, were rewarded with a moment of high drama, when Archduchess Sophia paused and expressly stepped aside to allow Elisabeth, wearing a simple summer dress and straw hat, to enter ahead of her. This was the first public acknowledgment of the younger woman's superior future rank and the new order of precedence. Franz Joseph was so intoxicated with his fiancée—his mother described him as "radiant with joy"—that he could barely contain his elation. In front of the entire congregation, he took Sisi's hand and led her proudly to the officiating cleric. "Please give us your blessing, your Reverence," the emperor invited the priest. "This is my future wife."

From this point on, the official reaction to the match was one of unmitigated rapture. Duke Max, informed by telegram, gave his hearty approval to the engagement (Sisi's father was not a man to let his liberal democratic principles interfere with getting one of his daughters married off so prestigiously) and even showed up in Ischl a few days later to personally congratulate his future son-in-law and join in the general celebration. Sophia gushed to the queen of Saxony that "so much happiness was bestowed upon us within a few hours that one can no longer measure time." All the court officials expressed their delighted congratulations to the archduchess as well as to the emperor and his adolescent intended, and many of these long-serving retainers joined Sophia in tears of joy or were reported to be so overcome with emotion that they could not speak.

But behind this carefully orchestrated façade, cracks soon began to appear. Helene could no longer mask her wretchedness—it was one thing to put up a good front for a day or so, quite another to have to endure nearly two weeks of watching the man she had expected to marry lavish his affection on her younger sister. In tacit acknowledgment of her niece's sacrifice, Sophia presented Nene with the consolation prize of an ostentatiously elaborate diamond cross, after which she was allowed to return home early with her father. And Helene was not the only disappointed sibling. Archduke Karl was equally miserable upon being informed that he had been right to be suspicious after all; his eldest brother had indeed stolen the bewitching Sisi away from him.

The most worrisome fault lines, however, emanated from the future bride herself. As a series of ever more spectacular celebrations relentlessly succeeded each other in the days following the engagement—at one, the entire town was lit up, fireworks were set off, and Franz Joseph's and Elisabeth's initials, surrounded by a circlet of colored lights representing a bridal bouquet, were displayed brilliantly against the backdrop of the night sky—Sisi's emotions vacillated from starry-eyed enchantment to nervous insecurity. She was in tears so often from all the attention during the last week of August that Sophia felt compelled to address the issue. "You cannot imagine how adorable Sissy is when she cries!" the archduchess trilled cheerily, as though having a future empress who wept whenever there were too many people around was somehow an asset. Elisabeth also discovered to her dismay that she was expected to sit quietly for hours while having her portrait painted, although the tedium of modeling was somewhat alleviated by Franz Joseph's loyally attending these sessions, and by his thoughtfully ordering a tree swing be installed for her amusement. "I love the Emperor so much! If only he weren't an emperor!" Sisi was heard to exclaim.

AT LAST, ON AUGUST 31, the sojourn in Ischl came to an end. Pressing matters of state recalled Franz Joseph to Vienna, and Elisabeth, too, had work to do. Having by this time gotten used to the idea, Sophia recognized the engagement as a success. After all, the archduchess had gotten what she had come for—a marriage alliance with Bavaria and a daughter-in-law who, coming from her sister's family, could be relied upon to understand and uphold the values that Sophia herself held dear. That had been the crucial point: to procure a wife for her son who would not bring opposing ideas or the headache of foreign political considerations to the court. That it was not the niece of her choosing was immaterial. Sisi would do just as well—better, perhaps, as Franz Joseph was so obviously taken with her, and to see him so happy was a great joy and comfort to his mother.

But Sophia was under no illusions as to how ill-prepared her future daughter-in-law was for her new position. A wedding date was set for April of the following year, and, before everyone departed, Sophia discussed with Ludovika the requirements of an imperial trousseau and the extensive training Sisi would need prior to her appearance in Vienna for the ceremony. Also, the bride-to-be's deficiencies in personal hygiene were noted. "She has yellow teeth!" the archduchess scolded.

Although the wedding announcement made all the papers—"In this marriage...it is impossible to trace any political motive whatever," puzzled the *Times*—it was by no means the lead story coming out of Austria. That was reserved for the emperor's upcoming conference with the tsar, set for later that September at Olmütz. While Franz Joseph was busy falling in love, Nicholas had sent troops into the Turkish territories of Moldavia and Wallachia, with the intent of seizing

Crimea. It was clear that war was on the horizon; the question was, what position would the various European powers take on the invasion? It was understood that the emperor, because he had been forced to solicit Russian troops to help subdue Hungary, would be under great pressure to return the favor and send an army to aid the tsar in the dismemberment of Turkey. "FRANCIS JOSEPH owes his throne to NICHOLAS of Russia," an editorial in the *Daily News* pointed out bluntly.

But this was not the only consideration. There was a new wild card in the deck of European power players. France, Austria's traditional enemy, had recently come under the control of Louis Napoleon, nephew of the great Bonaparte himself.

Another Napoleon! Just the name brought dismay to the ruling autocrats (and hope to the oppressed masses). That the threat came so soon upon the heels of the violent revolutionary uprisings of 1848 only made it more penetrating—would the specter of *liberté* and *égalité* never go away? What if, under this new incarnation of the brilliant Corsican general, the French decided to take advantage of the distraction of the Russian invasion of Turkey to launch yet another campaign for European domination?

And so it was against this disturbing backdrop that the imperial party in Ischl reluctantly broke up and Franz Joseph took leave of his adored Sisi, kissing her passionately before setting off.

EUGÉNIE

Eugénie's father, Don Cipriano

4

The Reign in Spain

Toward France there journeyed two grenadiers
Who had been captured in Russia;
And they hung their heads and their eyes had tears
As they came to the border of Prussia.

They heard the terrible news again
That France had been lost and forsaken;
Her armies were beaten, her captains were slain,
And the Emperor, the Emperor was taken!

Together they wept, these two grenadiers,
To one thing their thoughts kept returning—
"Alas," cried one, half-choked with tears,
"Once more my old wound is burning...

What matters wife? What matters child?
With far greater cares I am shaken;
Let them go and beg with hunger wild—
My Emperor, my Emperor is taken!"

—Heinrich Heine

EUGÉNIE DE MONTIJO WAS BORN ON MAY 5, 1826, in the city of Granada, site of the wondrous Alhambra palace, in southern Spain. She was her parents' second child; her older sister, María Francisca, known as Paca, was just fifteen months her senior. There was an earthquake in Granada on the day of Eugénie's birth, and her mother, María Manuela, countess of Teba, would no doubt have liked to escape to more stable terrain to have this second daughter but, unfortunately, Eugénie's father, Don Cipriano, had been sentenced to house arrest for revolutionary activities and was confined with his family at their present abode, a modest residence far from the royal court in Madrid. So, María Manuela ended up giving birth to Eugénie in a tent in a garden rocked by tremors, rather than risk going inside and having the walls of her husband's domestic lockup collapse on her during labor.

Like Duke Max, Don Cipriano had an outsized influence on his daughter's development, but all similarity between the two men ended there. Duke Max was a professional dilettante, an amusing if provincial character; Don Cipriano was a bona fide international war hero, complete with an arresting black eye patch. Born into the house of Montijo, one of the oldest and most prestigious families in Spain, Eugénie's father could trace his lineage back to Saint Dominic, thirteenth-century founder of the Order of Friars Preachers. He counted celebrated ministers of state and distinguished cardinals among his ancestors. But Don Cipriano was only a second son, and the law of primogeniture applied in Spain. So, on his father's death, his older brother, Don Eugenio, had inherited the exalted title of count of Montijo, and with it, the considerable influence and wealth of the family, including a splendid palace in Madrid, while Don Cipriano was assigned the significantly less impressive insignia (and income) of count of Teba.

It is refreshing to report that none of this mattered to him. Don Cipriano was not interested in status or riches; in fact, as a lifelong soldier and man of action, he rather scorned them. He was instead passionately devoted to an ideal that transcended material concerns, a larger-than-life campaign to which he dedicated all his energies. The count of Teba was a devout follower and fearless champion of Napoleon Bonaparte.

Napoleon's effect on Spain was profound. The aging Spanish king, Carlos IV—or, rather, his wife and her favorite, Manuel Godoy, who were the people actually running the government—had eyed the French juggernaut looming on their northeastern border and, like Bavaria, prudently decided to ally early with their powerful neighbor. As a result, Don Cipriano had seen his first action at the age of twenty-one when, as a member of the Spanish military, he served beside French officers against the British navy at what turned out to be the famous Battle of Trafalgar of 1805. Eugénie's father lost the use of his left arm that day amid the hail of cannonballs and bullets. The French and Spanish lost a whopping nineteen warships. The English lost Admiral Horatio Nelson.

In the wake of this crushing defeat, the Spanish royal family began to squabble among themselves in a manner not destined to improve their prospects for a long and fruitful reign. The immediate problem was that Carlos IV's eldest son, Ferdinand, thought that he would make a better king than his father. Encouraged by a group of similarly minded aristocrats (including Don Eugenio), Ferdinand began intriguing against his parents. Carlos IV found out about it and, to shore up support for their respective positions, both father and son each appealed separately to their good friend and ally Napoleon to moderate.

This strategy was akin to two chickens asking a fox for help. Napoleon summoned the entire family to Bayonne and, when they arrived on May 5, 1808, bribed them to abdicate in favor of his brother Joseph, a deal that all took willingly. Carlos IV received lifetime ownership of the castle of Compiègne, plus a generous annuity; the queen and Godoy were also compensated. Ferdinand did even better: he was given the magnificent château of Valençay, one of the most beautiful estates in France, as well as the province of Navarre and a yearly allowance of 400,000 francs. So pleased was Ferdinand with this arrangement that he even wrote Joseph a heartfelt note congratulating him on his ascension to the throne of Spain.

The only people who weren't consulted about the details of this cozy transaction were the Spanish themselves. All they knew was that two months after the ruling family decamped for Bayonne, Joseph Bonaparte, accompanied by a large French army, suddenly showed up in Madrid, bearing documents indicating that he was now king. It was naturally assumed that both Carlos IV and Ferdinand were being held against their will in France.

Sometimes you don't know how much you want something until somebody tries to take it away from you. Nobody much cared about Carlos—he was obviously in decline, and there had already been violence against his government, with Godoy having barely escaped being torn to bits by a mob—but the vast majority of the citizenry took umbrage at Napoleon's high-handed assumption that they would welcome his brother Joseph as a substitute for Ferdinand, whom they considered the rightful heir to the Spanish throne.

But not Eugénie's father. Don Cipriano was thrilled at the chance to serve under King Joseph, because it meant a break from the repressive despotism of the past, which he blamed for the poverty and ignorance endemic among the population. As was his custom when taking over other countries, Napoleon had sent a constitution along with his brother. Among the terms of this treatise were articles abolishing the Inquisition and inherited aristocratic privilege. The count of Teba approved of all these reforms. "Many persons respectable for intelligence, rank, fortune, and even love of country, attached themselves to the fortunes of King Joseph from deep conviction of the necessity of a change in dynasty," explained a Spanish nobleman in a letter to a friend in England. "They looked to the genius and power of the Bonapartes... in the hope of bettering the condition of their country."

Don Cipriano, however, was one of only a very small minority who rallied to Joseph's side. Almost everyone else fought the invaders. An independent rebel government was set up in Cádiz, on the southwest coast of the kingdom. The rural population spontaneously organized itself into small groups and attacked the occupying French soldiers at every turn. Nobody paid their taxes. The new king found himself, his government, and his army under siege from all sides.★

Joseph's reign was consequently short-lived. In 1813, England, which had allied with Austria and Prussia against France, took advantage of Napoleon's disastrous Russian campaign to send 40,000 soldiers into Spain under the command of the soon-to-be-famous General Wellington. The native guerilla fighters did their part by pinning down large numbers of the hated French troops and retaking territory. Again, Don Cipriano, by this time one of Joseph's most experienced and trusted officers, remained loyal to his ideals and fought on the side of the Bonapartes, losing his right eye and taking a bullet in the leg during a battle with Wellington. "Isn't it fortunate that God has created us with two legs, two arms, and two eyes? Thus I still have one of each left," he would later jest mordantly to his daughters.

But it was clear that the French were overmatched. Napoleon, already reeling from his losses in Russia and facing a massive counter-offensive from the combined armies of Britain, Prussia, and Austria (newly reinforced by Bavaria), gave up on trying to hold Spain. He ordered his brother to return to France. So committed was the count of Teba to his hero that when Joseph and his much-reduced army withdrew to Paris, he went with them as the colonel in charge of artillery.

Ironically, while Eugénie's father was resolutely approaching France, Ferdinand was reluctantly leaving it.† Judging that his feckless houseguest was unlikely to be a threat to anyone except maybe his own countrymen, Napoleon abruptly cancelled Ferdinand's allowance, took back the fancy castle and the valuable province of Navarre, and

---

★ It was during this struggle that the term *guerilla war* made its first appearance. *Guerilla* is a diminutive of *guerra,* the Spanish word for war—thus, a "little war," meaning many small, ad hoc skirmishes rather than one big battle.

† The English had earlier sent a covert agent to Valençay to liberate Ferdinand so that he could come back to Spain and lead the revolt against Joseph himself, but, alas, the former heir to the throne, who was immensely enjoying his beautiful French estate, refused to budge and instead revealed the plot instantly to the local authorities. "The English ministry, deceived by the false idea that I am here against my will, under restraint, has proposed to me means of escaping!" Ferdinand had reported indignantly.

had him instead sign the Treaty of Valençay, which generously returned his kingdom to him on the condition that "all Spaniards who had adhered to King Joseph, and who had served him in civil, political, and military offices, were to preserve their property and rights." By March of 1814, Ferdinand had dutifully packed his bags and crossed the border into Catalonia, in the northeast corner of Spain.

The end came soon after this for Napoleon. Prussian soldiers invaded France and overran Paris. Don Cipriano was among those who made a last desperate effort to ward off the enemy attack on the French capital. It was he, a Spaniard, who heroically "fired the last shots...from the cannons of Montmartre," a resident noted.

In the wake of Napoleon's defeat, the victorious monarchies returned all the territory the Bonapartes had conquered to the dynasties who had ruled them two decades earlier. In France, this meant reinstating the family of Louis XVI. As there were no surviving sons of the executed king, the throne passed to his younger brother, Louis XVIII, who at sixty years old was in no condition to defend himself militarily and so had to be imposed on the populace by force, with his government protected by Prussian troops.★

Don Cipriano, who had managed to evade capture, had no desire to remain in Paris under these conditions. If he was going to have to live under a hated autocrat, it might as well be a Spanish one. So, he took advantage of the amnesty granted by the Treaty of Valençay and returned home. He had another, more pressing reason for going as well. The count of Teba was in love.

Her name was María Manuela Kirkpatrick. She was the niece of the count de Lesseps, a distinguished French diplomat. Her father, William, was a Scotsman who had fled the cold and poverty of his native land to settle in the balmy port town of Málaga, in southern Spain. Her mother, the elder sister of the countess de Lesseps, was the daughter of

---

★ Louis XVIII was the elder of Louis XVI's two surviving younger brothers. He is Louis XVIII because Louis XVII was the title the family gave to the dauphin (Marie Antoinette's second son), who perished in prison during the Revolution.

the wine merchant under whom the enterprising William had apprenticed on his arrival and then succeeded in the family business.

Don Cipriano had met María Manuela in Paris at her aunt's salon just prior to the Prussian invasion. She was nineteen, ten years younger than he, and had just graduated from one of the most fashionable girls' schools in the city. Beautiful and vivacious, she had impressed him as much with her passionate talk about art, music, literature, politics, and history as she had with her slender figure and raven hair. He had been about to declare himself when the war came and she was sent back to Spain for her own safety. Now he turned up at her father's wine shop in Málaga to propose.

Although her suitor might not have had the use of all of his appendages, his rank clearly dazzled her. Moreover, as his elder brother was currently without heirs, María Manuela understood that there was a chance that Don Cipriano (assuming he outlived Don Eugenio) would inherit the entire Montijo estate, including the fabulous palace in Madrid and the equally impressive title and income. But perhaps the most salient factor in her decision was that this one-eyed suitor was familiar with and appreciated the world outside of merchant-oriented Málaga. And it was in that world, the graceful world of Paris and Madrid, of society and ideas, and not just money and trade (although she by no means disdained money), in which María Manuela wished to live. She accepted the count of Teba's offer of marriage.

There was only one small problem. Don Cipriano was of such high birth that the king himself had to approve his bride, and it was unlikely that Ferdinand, now back on his throne, would allow an alliance between a member of one of the kingdom's most prestigious families and the daughter of a common Scottish tradesman. William Kirkpatrick, however, proved himself equal to the task of mustering ancestors every bit as venerable as any Spain could produce, by remembering from his school days that the name Kirkpatrick had appeared in historical records dating back to the thirteenth century. "You trace up to King Alfonso the Eleventh," William mused to his potential son-in-law. "If I trace up to King Robert Bruce, I suppose His Majesty will be satisfied?" A document to this effect was duly drawn up and subsequently presented at court, where it was apparently such a source of mirth that the king gave his consent. Without doubt, "Let the noble Montijo marry the daughter of Fingal [a fictional Scottish hero from a well-known poem]!" Ferdinand chortled.

And so Don Cipriano and María Manuela were married in Málaga on December 15, 1817. An American who knew her at the time of her wedding observed simply of the bride that she was "the most cultivated and the most interesting woman in Spain."

IF THE NEW COUNTESS OF TEBA was hoping that her husband would moderate his political views and focus on assuming his rightful place at the highest levels of Spanish society, with maybe a few trips to Paris sprinkled in between, she was sadly disappointed. They weren't married two years before a new insurrection erupted in Spain and he was in trouble with the crown all over again.

No one was more surprised than Ferdinand when, after being kicked out of his lovely château by Napoleon, he crossed over the border into Spain and discovered not only that his subjects wanted him back, but that they had been fighting for him all this time and were positively ecstatic at his return! They cheered his route and thronged his procession for miles, often pulling his carriage along themselves. They called him Ferdinand "the Well-Beloved" and "the Long-Wished-For" and shouted, "Long live the absolute king!" To the Spanish citizenry, particularly the rural peasantry, the monarch's return was a measure of their own success. They had pushed the hated French out and forced Napoleon to release their legitimate sovereign!

No sooner was Ferdinand safely ensconced in the family palace in Madrid, however, than all the old dissatisfactions began to creep out. The suffering during the years of occupation had been intense, and people expected conditions to improve quickly. But the military effort to oust the French had drained the kingdom's resources. To the crisis of a bankrupt treasury was added widespread unemployment. As the king's invariable response to these difficulties was simply to fire (or arrest) his ministers and replace them with new ones, who then helped themselves to whatever they could get their hands on before being themselves fired (or arrested), Spain teetered on the edge of economic collapse.

Still, the speed with which even a ruler as hapless as Ferdinand had gone from being wildly celebrated in the streets as "the Long-Wished-For" to having to hide in terror inside his palace while an infuriated mob gathered outside in those same streets, threatening to break down the doors, was impressive. Ironically, the gravest threat to Ferdinand's rule came from the military, the very people who had fought so long and hard, and suffered so much, to get him back. They had expected to be rewarded for their perseverance, but instead, due to the royal treasury's chronic lack of funds, their rations and salaries were hopelessly in arrears or had been cut entirely. On January 1, 1820, an enterprising Spanish colonel by the name of Rafael del Riego, fed up with the unfairness and corruption, took matters into his own hands and started a revolt.

And it was at this point that that pesky constitution resurfaced. Riego, being in Cádiz at the time, remembered that the rebel government established there during the reign of Joseph Bonaparte had actually written their own, homegrown declaration of liberties, called "the Constitution of 1812," to compete with the despised French treatise. The Cádiz version went even further than Napoleon's, calling not only for the abolishment of the Inquisition, but also for a national legislative assembly based on universal male suffrage. Riego, looking around for an issue that would help rally the kingdom to his side, decided to champion the Constitution of 1812 as being the most legitimate means of curbing the power of the monarchy. When at first the general population (most of whom still did not understand what a constitution was) failed to respond to his initiative, Riego had the happy thought to sweeten the deal by explaining that if the Constitution of 1812 was adopted, taxes would be drastically reduced. *That* got everyone's attention.

From Cádiz, Riego and his now numerous supporters marched

71

through southern Spain, attracting new volunteers along the way. Of course, when he got to Granada, where Don Cipriano now lived with his bride, the count of Teba could not resist joining the movement. Within months, Riego and his insurrectionists had mobbed Madrid, forcing Ferdinand to accept the Constitution of 1812 and, with it, a more liberal, representative government. In 1822, they went even further, deposing the king and taking him prisoner.

But a constitution is just a piece of paper with ideas written on it. It can't, on its own, fill the treasury with gold, put food on the table, find jobs for the unemployed, pay the salaries of soldiers, improve trade, or cure yellow fever. This seems not to have been clear to many of those who initially took violently to the streets in its favor.

When the improvements to the general living standard promised by Riego did not magically materialize, his supporters became disillusioned. At the same time, the overthrow of the king of Spain emerged as a source of considerable anxiety to his fellow monarchs, particularly Louis XVIII, who found Ferdinand's predicament entirely too reminiscent for comfort of his own experience of the early days of the French Revolution. To prevent Spanish radicalism from spilling over the border and threatening *his* life and rule, the French king raised an army of some 80,000 soldiers, which he then ordered to march into Spain to rescue Ferdinand and crush the constitutional government. As by this time the majority of the Spanish population was tired of the violence and chaos, the French regiments—*many of whom were the very same people whom these exact Spanish citizens had fought so bitterly to evict less than a decade before*—were cheered as deliverers throughout the countryside. Within months, Riego and his supporters were on the run, and a seriously aggrieved Ferdinand was released from captivity and returned to his throne.

Spoiling for revenge, and with the powerful French army behind him, Ferdinand felt confident enough to issue a series of decrees designed to ensure that no one ever tried anything like *that* again. Riego was captured, tried, and publicly hanged in Madrid on November 7, 1823, from the tallest gibbet the kingdom had ever constructed.

The Constitution of 1812 was abolished and thousands of people associated with it were executed, exiled, or arrested. The liberal universities were closed, the Inquisition was revived, and the Church was restored to its former position of power and privilege. "Vengeance and proscription are the order of the day," the editors of the London *Morning Chronicle* observed.

Don Cipriano was one of those who felt the fury of Ferdinand's wrath. The count of Teba was arrested, found guilty, and incarcerated in a penal facility over 600 miles north of Granada. There, he would later reveal darkly if somewhat obscurely to his young daughters, he was kept as "the prisoner of the Inquisition."

And there he would have stayed had it not been for his resourceful wife. María Manuela made a trip to Madrid to appeal personally to her husband's elder brother, Don Eugenio, the prestigious count of Montijo, for leniency. She must have impressed him, as Don Eugenio used his influence with the king to get his rebellious younger brother released into his wife's custody. In 1824, Don Cipriano was allowed to serve the remainder of his sentence in the small house in Granada that she shared with him.

The enforced intimacy resulted in the birth of Paca in January of 1825 and then a second daughter in May of the following year. Don Cipriano, wishing to honor his brother for putting family before politics, had clearly been reserving the count of Montijo's given name, hoping for a son the second time, but when another girl appeared he evidently felt he couldn't wait any longer, and so "Eugenio" was adroitly refashioned as "Eugénie."

Eugénie would spend the first four years of her childhood in the humble abode in Granada that served as her father's prison. For a toddler, this was not a deprivation. She had Paca to play with, and unlike Sisi's parent, Duke Max, who ignored his children for long stretches of time, Don Cipriano (being legally unable to leave the house) was always around. The count of Teba apparently held some strong opinions about child-rearing, and his influence was evident even at this very young age. Still nostalgic for the Napoleonic cause, Don Cipriano ensured that his daughters' first words were in his hero's native tongue. So, although a member of one of the most ancient and prestigious aristocracies in all of Spain, Eugénie would grow up with and use French to communicate with her family for the rest of her life.

Eugénie adored her father, and Don Cipriano, in turn, seeing so much of himself in her, gave her the attention she craved. Quiet Paca, black-haired, delicately pretty, sweet-tempered, and obedient, was a small replica of María Manuela, but Eugénie was her father through and through. It wasn't just that, with her honey-red hair and blue eyes, she looked so much like him. It was her personality — restless, spirited, outspoken, stubborn — that drew him to this strong-willed second daughter. With Eugénie he could relive the vibrancy of his youth, and the ideals he had cherished, in the hope that these would yet live on. He nurtured in her a love of the natural world, of independence, and, most importantly, of Napoleon.

5

Mademoiselle de Montijo

Only little girls understand great things.

—Stendhal

EUGÉNIE WAS FOUR YEARS OLD when her father was abruptly released from captivity and her family was finally allowed to move to a nicer house in Granada and travel freely.

Don Cipriano's sudden liberation was not the result of his having served his sentence but rather of yet another political crisis at the Spanish court. Fifty-five-year-old Ferdinand, already three times widowed and perennially heirless, had rewarded himself for surviving his brush with insurrection by marrying his beautiful twenty-three-year-old niece, Maria Christina (daughter of his sister, the queen of Naples), and this new young bride had done something that none of his previous wives had been able to accomplish: produced a child.

Alas, it was only a girl, and under Spanish law males alone could reign. But Maria Christina, who on her father's side was a great-granddaughter of the memorable Empress Maria Theresa, knew that there was a way to circumvent this obstacle. The king could unilaterally issue a decree, known as a pragmatic sanction, which, in the absence of a son, would allow a daughter to inherit the throne. There was even precedent for female rule in Spanish history: in the fifteenth century, Queen Isabella, one of Spain's most celebrated monarchs, had also held the crown in her own right. To make this connection even stronger, Maria Christina named her daughter Isabella and, in March of 1830, convinced Ferdinand to affirm the pragmatic sanction.

Legally designating an infant princess as the future sovereign of Spain at the last minute like this did not go over at all well with Ferdinand's younger brother Don Carlos, who (observing Ferdinand's failure at procreation for thirty years through three wives) had naturally expected to inherit the throne. Nor did the Spanish priesthood think much of this maneuver. When Don Carlos publicly protested the change in succession, the Church threw its support behind him. Maria Christina, understanding that she and Isabella were going to need domestic allies of their own to make this stick, prevailed upon Ferdinand, who was ill and starting to weaken, to restore the constitutional party to royal favor by freeing from exile or imprisonment the thousands of people he had just spent years persecuting (sadly, nothing could be done to bring back those he executed) and promoting them as a bulwark against Don Carlos's faction. This accounted for Eugénie and her family's improbably swift return to Spanish society as valued citizens.

The release from confinement was not the only change in Eugénie's life. While Don Cipriano was still under house arrest, news reached him from Madrid that his failing older brother, the formerly heirless widower Don Eugenio, had been manipulated into marrying a commoner of shady reputation, who had then suddenly announced that she was expecting. This was too much for María Manuela, who had no intention of letting her husband's inheritance slip away without a fight. She evaded the family detention and charged into Madrid to investigate the suspicious pregnancy. There she discovered Don Eugenio incapacitated from a stroke, and his new, very obviously *not* pregnant wife, who was arranging to pass off an orphaned baby as his son. The dissembler was no match for María Manuela, who overawed her upstart sister-in-law, got her to confess to the scam, and then adopted the boy herself to ensure that he could not be resurrected in the future as a threat to her husband's property.

Eugénie seems to have had a difficult time adapting to her family's reentry into society, much more so than Paca, though the age difference between the two sisters was only a little more than a year. Eugénie did not enjoy playing indoors with other children and caused scenes when forced to do so. She much preferred to spend her time outside riding, which she learned to do at an early age, and exploring. (A Gypsy camp on the outskirts of town apparently fascinated her.) In addition to the new house, Don Cipriano had a country estate at Teba, just outside Granada, and Eugénie spent her summers there, as Sisi had at Possi. To further improve his younger daughter's skill in the saddle, her father would take her out for long canters, after which they would frequently camp out in front of a fire under the stars, just the two of them. There, he told her tales of Napoleon's valor, as Sisi's father had told his daughter stories of Greek heroes.

Although María Manuela picked up her life where she had left off, expanding her social circle and throwing her home open to people of culture and importance, Don Cipriano nonetheless insisted that his daughters be treated as though they could all be reduced to abject poverty at any moment. "Let them be toughened by privation and suffering," he counseled. Eugénie would later praise her father for helping her to become more prepared for adversity. "But he carried things rather too far when he made us wear linen gowns in all weathers and in all seasons, and when he would not allow my mother to buy us umbrellas or even to take us with her in a carriage," she pointed out.

But there was one visitor whose company even little Eugénie enjoyed. He was a new friend of the family—a twenty-seven-year-old Frenchman journeying through Spain for the first time. Don Cipriano had happened upon the younger man, with whom he had fallen into an instant rapport, on one of his first journeys as a free citizen in 1830. Reflecting that the traveler, who had introduced himself as Prosper Mérimée, an author interested in Spanish culture and antiquity, was a stranger in Granada, Don Cipriano had graciously invited him home to dinner.

María Manuela must have recognized within minutes of his arrival that Mérimée was exactly the kind of erudite, amusing sophisticate she was hoping to cultivate. The son of Parisian artists—his father, an authority on Dutch Masters, was an official at the École des Beaux-Arts; his mother painted miniatures—Mérimée enjoyed sketching, but his real passion was literature. He came by this talent naturally; his great-grandmother, Jeanne-Marie Leprince de Beaumont, a governess and early champion of women's education, had published some seventy volumes of novels, short stories, articles, and fairy tales during her lifetime, including the classic *Beauty and the Beast*.

In fact, had María Manuela searched the world over, she could not have found a more direct route to the cosmopolitan set she so admired than through this obliging dinner guest. Not only was Mérimée already an up-and-coming author in his own right, but his circle of acquaintance was truly impressive. He counted the artist Eugène Delacroix and the writers Henri Beyle (who later adopted the pen name Stendhal) and Adolphe Thiers (a journalist and future newspaper publisher) among his close friends. In England, Mérimée kept company with the likes of the librarian of the British Museum. He went to parties with Ivan Turgenev and Balzac, and knew Victor Hugo well enough to avoid him.

As her new friend's stated purpose was to gather authentic material for stories about Spain, María Manuela flung her considerable energy and resources into this project. Through the family's Montijo contacts, Mérimée was granted access to private archives and was introduced to librarians and scholars in Madrid. Eugénie's mother herself acted as tour guide around Granada, gaily regaling Mérimée with snippets of local gossip, sensational regional crimes, and colorful legends of the Alhambra. One of the scandals with which she diverted him, about the murder of a neighborhood Gypsy woman by her lover, so captured Mérimée's imagination that he ended up turning it into a short story called "Carmen."

It all worked: Mérimée was utterly charmed. He raved to cronies in Paris that María Manuela "amazed and enchanted him by her grace, her mental activity, the variety of her conversation and the extent of her knowledge." To Stendhal, he observed that his hostess "is a complete and very beautiful type of the woman of Andalusia. She is an admirable friend." He was equally delighted with the rest of the family and especially with the younger daughter. "Fate willed it, that, through sheer lack of something else to do, I went to Spain where I met some very good and amiable people who gave me a hearty welcome. Among them was a little girl to whom I told tales, for whom I interceded when she did not know her lessons, to whom later I preached gentle sermons with a moral," he wrote. Mérimée had such a good time playing with the child he called "*la petite* Eugénie" that he even got down on his hands and knees and let her climb up on his back so he could take her for a ride around the living room floor. "I am interested by her chatter," he laughed.★

This serendipitous encounter could not have come at a more opportune time, for, within a few short years, Eugénie's life would be upended once more, and having a well-connected French friend turned out to be very convenient indeed.

The trouble again stemmed from the conflict between the newly revitalized liberal party, whose hopes were raised by the issuance of the pragmatic sanction and the possibility that Maria Christina, ruling as regent for her young daughter in the event of her husband's death, would be the kind of progressive sovereign they were hoping for, and the ultraconservatives, who swore undying allegiance to absolute monarchy and the Inquisition, as represented by Ferdinand's younger brother Don Carlos. In the summer of 1833, when Eugénie was seven years old, this conflict came to a head. Ferdinand, anticipating his imminent demise, demanded that the ruling elite — the grandees and other privileged members of the aristocracy, high church officials, and

---

★ Mérimée was not the only foreign author Don Cipriano brought home after he was first freed. Washington Irving, of "Rip Van Winkle" fame, was in Spain at this time, researching his book on the Alhambra. He, too, was a visitor to the home of the count of Teba. "Eugénie...whom, when a child, I have had on my knee at Granada!" he would later exclaim.

regional government executives, known in Spain as the Cortes—come to the capital to take a formal oath of allegiance to three-year-old Isabella as the legitimate heir to the throne. As Don Eugenio was by this time paralyzed and anticipating his own death, it fell to his younger brother to perform this service, and when Don Cipriano came to Madrid for the ceremony, he brought his family with him.

The move from Granada marked a big change for Eugénie. Granada was a sleepy little provincial city of some 60,000 inhabitants, where she could roam freely through the streets. Madrid, by contrast, was the bustling seat of government, boasting a population of nearly 200,000. The Spanish capital couldn't compare to the great metropolises of Europe, of course—Paris had 800,000 residents and London a teeming 1.5 million—but it was certainly vibrant enough to impress a seven-year-old. A contemporary author penned an affectionate description of what Eugénie and her family would have experienced on an average day in Madrid. "At dawn the motion of this numerous town begins slowly," he wrote. "The gates are opened to let in scores of villagers who bring their wares from the surrounding countryside...At nine o'clock, the tableau changes: the carriages of the magnates, and of the public functionaries, followed by hordes of jobseekers...roll to the government ministries and offices...At four o'clock the city is reanimated,...the shaded walks are peopled with individuals of all ranks; the bullfights, teas,...all remain happily in these activities until night approaches,... [while] others prolong their pleasures...in salons...or at gaming houses."

Eugénie's mother was among those who took full advantage of all the capital had to offer. María Manuela seems not to have bothered to wait until Don Eugenio was actually dead to begin the process of transitioning to her expected status as countess of Montijo. She, Don Cipriano, and the children all moved in with the invalid and his much-cowed wife at the magnificent family palace, located on the Plazuela del Àngel, one of the main squares in the very center of the city. Because of her husband's family connections and her own considerable intelligence, charm, and conversational talents, María Manuela made great inroads into fashionable society. She had the use of a box at the theater and the bullfights; she was invited to court; she went to masked balls during Carnival. She became acquainted with all the most notable people in the city and commandeered her ailing brother-in-law's salon to entertain them. She was seen so often in the company of the British ambassador, a smarmy bachelor who obviously appreciated female company, that she provoked rumors of infidelity. "There is no lack here of black eyes and pretty feet," the ambassador wrote home to his brother, enthusiastically describing his new position (and quite possibly Eugénie's mother). "Nothing can be more graceful than the dress of a Spanish woman—the manner in which she puts on and wears the mantilla—the variety of colors she manages to combine...her short petticoats, which show off the almost universally well-turned ankle and little foot...An ugly face may be overlooked—an ugly foot, never!"

Black eyes and pretty feet—the move to Madrid only highlighted blue-eyed Eugénie's growing awareness that, unlike her dark-haired mother and sister, her looks did not conform to the traditional notions of Spanish femininity so prized by the haughty and insular society around her. She later admitted that she "was not considered at all beautiful as compared to her more brilliant sister," and became "painfully self-conscious...and was especially ashamed of the color of her hair...which people called *red*." This was not a case of a child's oversensitivity but of a collective judgment that many in María Manuela's circle cruelly took no pains to hide. Relatives later confirmed "that they had heard it repeatedly asserted in Madrid that at that period Eugénie was plain almost to ugliness."

And her perceived homeliness was not her only source of confusion and anxiety. Eugénie was old enough by this time to know how to behave when she was taken to visit cousins or to meet the children of other members of the nobility, but the move to Madrid still took some getting used to. People noted with amusement the expressions of wonder on the faces of the count of Teba's daughters whenever Paca and Eugénie were first introduced to a new home and saw the opulence on display around them. Worried that they might become corrupted by their affluent surroundings, and not wishing to raise "timid, namby-pamby daughters" (as Eugénie later recounted to friends), Don Cipriano redoubled his efforts to toughen them up. One of his more innovative teaching methods was to have both Paca and Eugénie clamber up a rampart and onto the barrel of a cannon. He would then fire the cannon. If either "cried or winced," he would do it again and again until they learned not to flinch.

It was almost as though he was preparing them for battle. If so, this turned out to be prescient. For no sooner did they arrive in Madrid than Spain descended, for the third time in as many decades, into civil war.

THIS RENEWAL OF HOSTILITIES was again the crown's doing. The ritual that had drawn Don Cipriano to the capital in the first place — the formal swearing of fidelity to a three-year-old, with her young, foreign-born mother acting as regent during her minority — which Ferdinand had expected to settle the matter of succession, had somewhat predictably sparked the opposite effect. Ominously, the king's younger brother, Don Carlos, declined to attend altogether and instead fled to Portugal, where he was openly engaged in recruiting an army. "My rights to the crown are so clear, failing male issue to you, that I cannot ignore them," Don Carlos wrote pointedly to his elder sibling.

This was to be the brothers' last exchange; three months later, on September 29, 1833, Ferdinand died from a massive stroke. In a reign noted for its extreme incompetence, corruption, and general all-around selfishness, the crisis over the succession — ratcheted up by the oath ceremony — was to be the king's crowning act of mayhem. Within days, both Maria Christina (acting as regent for Isabella) and Don Carlos had claimed the throne; by Christmas, most of northern and rural Spain had declared in favor of the male contender; and by the summer of 1834, Maria Christina faced an army of some 35,000 Carlist troops intent on her overthrow. Upon being informed that the liberal party would not fight for her unless she adopted some form of constitutional government, Maria Christina bowed to political necessity and called for yet another gathering of the Cortes.

In the six weeks leading up to this proposed assembly, set for July 24, 1834, fantastic rumors swirled on both sides of the political spectrum. It was said that the meeting would either be prevented from taking place or, worse, if it did succeed in convoking, would be the scene of carnage. Conspiracy theories abounded, and were accepted as fact by a fearful public, who had been taught by their leaders to regard those of differing political views as inhumane disciples of Satan. Then, to the mounting anxiety that ghastly summer was suddenly added a new horror: disease. Fueled by fierce heat and the displacement of numerous villagers fleeing the economic devastation and violence of the civil war, a deadly wave of cholera hit Madrid.

Eugénie's parents would no doubt have liked to take the children and escape the capital for their country house, as many others were doing, but they could not. Don Eugenio, so long confined to his armchair, was finally on the brink of succumbing to his infirmities. The family was keeping a deathbed vigil around the invalid. For Don Cipriano, this was a matter of brotherly feeling. For María Manuela, it was a necessity. The inheritance was too valuable to leave to chance. To secure it, they had to be there. For eight-year-old Eugénie, this death, and the days that immediately followed, were terrifying.

It took until July 16, 1834, for Don Eugenio to breathe his last. As was customary, the corpse was placed in an open coffin and the children were brought to pay their final respects to the deceased. Eugénie was too young for this tradition. Forced to approach her uncle's lifeless body, she became so distraught that she ran to an open window and tried to climb out of it to get away.

The next day was no better. The family remained trapped in Madrid, waiting for the funeral and the legal transfer of the inheritance to take place. Meanwhile, the number of deaths due to cholera had exploded overnight and was causing a panic. Mobs of aggrieved citizens roamed the streets. "The last 24 hours we have been in a state of complete anarchy," the foreign correspondent for the *Times* reported grimly. "The angry passions of the two parties long arrayed against each other . . . [have] been found in the popular belief that the present mortality . . . has been produced by the diabolical machinations of those who wish to deter the Cortes from meeting . . . and who with this view are supposed to have been poisoning the waters of the public fountains."

Because of these fears, bands of self-appointed lookouts milled around the main squares, keeping a close watch on the water supply. As they were convinced that a heinous crime was sure to be committed, it was almost inevitable that they should identify a series of perpetrators—and so they did. "The first victim," the *Times* correspondent reported, "was a man in coloured clothes, supposed to be a Franciscan friar, who was seen yesterday forenoon with a paper in his hand, standing near the public fountain at the Puerta del Sol. The answer he gave to the charge of an intention to poison the fountain was not thought satisfactory by the bystanders . . . and in an instant he paid with his life for the thoughtlessness of making what proved to be only a paper cigar." This bloodletting in no way appeased the crowd; rather, it spurred the vigilantes on to new acts of slaughter. "This incident, in passing from mouth to mouth, became a strong . . . evidence against the friars as public poisoners, and within an hour afterwards three or four were killed in the streets," the journalist revealed.

By sheer coincidence, the Montijo mansion, where Don Cipriano and his family were staying, overlooked the fountain at the Puerta del Sol. Thus, Eugénie and Paca, drawn to the window by the angry shouts of the crowd in the street below, were unfortunately present to witness this butchery.

That was enough for their parents. The inheritance had come through; overnight Don Cipriano, formerly a gentleman of extremely modest income and assets, became the count of Montijo, one of the richest men in Spain. It was decided that he would remain behind in Madrid to lend his support to the liberal party, while María Manuela took the children and fled to Paris.

They left the very next day, traveling in a carriage drawn by mules.

It was a slow, harrowing journey. The streets were clogged with refugees trying to get away from the violence and disease, and there was always the threat that Carlist insurgents would attack. It took nearly ten days to reach France. María Manuela seems not to have stopped until the family made it across the northern border of Spain. She apparently wasn't using her new title yet, but, understanding that wealthy visitors were much more likely to be welcomed than penniless immigrants, made no secret of her improved position in life. Consequently, she was remembered. "Many Spaniards are passing through Perpignan; most of them come from Madrid," the governor of a French town noted in his diary. "The Countess of Teba, a woman of thirty-five—extremely intelligent—is going to Toulouse. She has a very considerable fortune," the obviously impressed official continued. "Madame de Teba...saw dreadful things done there [Madrid]. The City Guard maimed and assassinated the monks and the Jesuits, even in their churches."

As for Eugénie, the death of her uncle, followed by the shocking bloodshed at the fountain, the trauma of the flight, and the anxiety and longing for her father, who had elected to remain behind—these would stay with her for a very long time. A much less innocent girl arrived in Paris than the one who the year before had first come to Madrid. "None of us is dead, which is what really matters," this new Eugénie wrote home soberly to her father.

ACTUALLY, AT LEAST FOR MARÍA MANUELA, it was a little better than that. There is nothing like coming into a vast fortune to ease the pain of relocating—especially when you are relocating to one of the great cities of the world. And, in truth, this separation from Madrid seems to have come at a good time for María Manuela. Certainly, she and Don Cipriano did not make a great effort to live with one another once the inheritance came through. Perhaps there was something to those rumors about the British ambassador after all.

For Eugénie, of course, it was different. Soon after the family's arrival, she and Paca were bundled off to the Convent of the Sacré-Cœur, the most expensive and fashionable girls' school in Paris. The nuns there followed a classic, highly regimented, French Catholic curriculum, quite different from anything María Manuela's daughters had experienced previously. In addition to this, they were foreigners. The other students, all from elite French families, became especially disdainful once it became clear that the Montijo sisters (their mother began using the title once she got to Paris) did not have a great deal of money to spend on themselves. For although Don Cipriano was now a rich man, he continued to insist that his children practice frugality, and María Manuela bowed to his wishes (so long as they did not apply to herself). To the end of her life, Eugénie remembered how the other girls had ridiculed her and Paca for not having the same silk stockings everyone else wore at their First Communion. It was in April 1837, just before Eugénie's eleventh birthday. "Their small brains could not fathom it," she observed.

The girls' next educational experience was equally disheartening. María Manuela, wishing to visit London, parked her daughters at a boarding school in the small, provincial town of Clifton, just outside the port city of Bristol, in the southwest of England, to help them learn English. They only lasted there two months. Eugénie was teased so mercilessly about the color of her hair that she tried to run away with a girl from India, another outsider made wretched by taunting. The plan was to stow away on a ship to Bombay. When this ambitious scheme proved unsuccessful, María Manuela gave up, took Eugénie and Paca out of the school, hired a long-suffering British governess named Miss Flowers so her daughters could continue their English lessons, and brought everyone back with her to Paris.

This was an improvement. Eugénie and Paca, thrown together in their exile, were happy in each other's company and easily evaded the staid Miss Flowers's surveillance whenever the mood struck them. To supplement their convent school education, Don Cipriano insisted that his daughters attend an innovative girls' program run by an expatriate Spanish officer who had also fought for Joseph Bonaparte. The instructors stressed not the usual finishing school mishmash of feminine arts, but rather training in gymnastics. Here, at last, was an outlet for

Eugénie's restless energy, a place where her athletic talents were recognized and encouraged. Whereas she had struggled through her previous schooling, trailing always in Paca's shadow, at these classes, at least, she shone.

Eugénie was also buoyed by the presence of Monsieur Mérimée, as she called him, who, finding the charming family he had discovered in Spain conveniently transplanted to Paris, became such a regular visitor to their apartments that he might well have been considered an extension of the household. His interest in María Manuela was not romantic; rather, he enjoyed the countess of Montijo's hospitality and her amusing repartee, and brought his friends to her salon. But it was with her daughters that Mérimée was at his most generous. Perhaps, having grown up an only child himself, he was attracted to the warmth and playfulness he felt he had missed. He took the girls for walks and showed them the sights of Paris, bought them treats, romped with them, and helped them with their studies. When Don Cipriano, ever on guard against weakness and coddling, sent twelve-year-old Eugénie a set of pistols so that she could learn to defend herself, it was Mérimée who escorted her to the shooting range.

One red-letter day, he brought his friend Stendhal to visit. Stendhal—he was "Monsieur Beyle" to Eugénie—was fifty-four years old, short, overweight, and unattractive. The girls adored him. A perennial bachelor who loved women and Italy, Stendhal had caused something of a sensation a few years back by publishing a scathing social novel called *The Red and the Black* and was at work on a new one entitled *The Charterhouse of Parma*. This latest book was set during the Napoleonic wars, and Stendhal seems to have tried out some of the material, as novelists sometimes do, on the countess of Montijo's daughters. If he had had any doubts about the power of his storytelling, they were assuaged by his young audience's response. "Remember M. Beyle!" Eugénie burst out decades later when questioned about the author. "He was the first man who made my heart beat—and beat violently!... He came to my mother's every Thursday; that evening, in honor of our great friend, we went to bed at 9 instead of 8, we didn't have dinner, we were so impatient to hear him!" she laughed. "Whenever the bell rang we rushed to the door...at last we brought him back, in triumph, into the salon, each of us holding one of his hands, and we settled him in his armchair by the fire. He used to take one of us on each knee; we didn't give him any time to breathe before we reminded him of the victory where he had left our emperor, the emperor we had thought about all the week...We wept and laughed and shuddered, we went mad...He showed us the emperor radiant in the sun of Austerlitz, pale in the snows of Russia, dying at Saint Helen." Mérimée was perhaps a little jealous. "He felt that his words were listened to with admiration and fervor," the rival author could not help noting grudgingly of Stendhal's success with Paca and Eugénie. "To his satisfied vanity, nothing was more agreeable than the eager attention shown in those pretty eyes of the two little girls."

In fact, between Mérimée's shepherding and Stendhal's impromptu literary sessions, Eugénie ended up with one of the most sophisticated cultural educations it was possible for a young woman to obtain in Europe. It certainly dwarfed anything Sisi experienced in Munich, practicing circus tricks in her backyard. Eugénie visited the Egyptian museum in Paris and examined three mummies ("one large and two small," as she wrote home diligently to her father) and a statue of the Sphinx. She went regularly to Versailles to wander through the magnificent gardens and woods surrounding the palace, one of her favorite outings. She read French translations of *Robinson Crusoe* and *The Swiss Family Robinson* along with (at her father's suggestion, naturally) the memoirs Napoleon had dictated at Saint Helena. She attended sold-out performances at the Comédie-Française and was even introduced to one of Paris's most acclaimed young actresses. Eugénie became so comfortable in the worldly ambience of her mother's circle that she asked for a muff, "because I am grown up now and would like to be fashionable." She even began to sound a little jaded. "It is impossible to live in Paris; they are always trying to kill the king," she airily informed Don Cipriano.

But there was one aspect of her life in which she remained firmly a little girl, and this was in the depth of her desire to be with her father. The interlude in Paris represented the first time she had been away from Don Cipriano since birth, and she felt his loss keenly. In the five years following his family's escape from Madrid in the summer of 1834, Don Cipriano made only two short visits to Paris—one in 1835 and the other in the spring of 1837. Each time, he stayed for only a few months before the political situation in Spain drew him back. In letter after letter, Eugénie spilled her heart out to her father about how much she missed him and wished to be with him. "My dear Papa, when will I see you again, my heart longs for you," she wrote on August 6, 1836, when she was ten. The next year brought a series of entreaties: "Papa, you know how much I want to kiss you and that the day I am with you...my heart will burst with joy"; "I will be so happy on the day that I see you again, dear Papa, it will be the most beautiful day of my life"; "I love you with all my heart," and finally, plaintively, in September of 1838, when she was twelve, "My dear Papa, I hope you will come soon." At least some of her desperation seems to have sprung from her recognition that Don Cipriano understood and accepted her in a way María Manuela did not. "My mother wished to make everybody happy, but in her own way, not in theirs," she later observed pointedly.

But the count of Montijo was too heavily involved in the struggle for his country's future to spend much time in Paris. The war with the Carlists dragged on, and the longer it lasted, the more concessions the queen regent, Maria Christina, was forced to make to the liberal faction in order to stay in power. Chief among those bargaining points upon which she had yet to agree was the increasingly insistent demand for a constitution supported by a nationally elected assembly.

There was nothing new in these objectives—they were the same reforms the kingdom had already gone to war over twice in the past quarter century. But it was their very familiarity that made this time different. After some twenty-odd years of hearing the issues debated, far more of the Spanish citizenry understood what a constitution was, and why it was important, than had previously. They had had a chance to get used to the idea, and discovered they liked it.

Emboldened by the change in public opinion, Don Cipriano, too old and disabled for military service, had instead turned his focus to political leadership. In early 1836, he helped draft legislation that outlined voting rights. "With regard to the project of the Electoral Law...which established direct election," wrote the foreign correspondent for the *Morning Chronicle,* observing from Madrid on January 10, "the report recommending the adoption of the project, in all its parts, was read by the Count of Montijo."

Maria Christina, loath to share sovereignty with her subjects, did everything she could think of to wriggle out of it. But when, in the early hours of August 13, 1836, approximately 1,100 of her own soldiers decided to rally under the queen's windows, threatening to storm the palace, she surrendered to their demands. "They...gave the Queen the alternative of signing a decree adopting the Constitution, or submitting to the massacre of everyone in the palace," the *Morning Chronicle* reported helpfully. As these were apparently her only two options, Maria Christina chose to sign.

And this time, there was no going back. It was a turning point for the kingdom. Within a year, a new constitution had been written. This document, called "the Constitution of 1837," was a more moderate version of its earlier incarnation, but it still represented a decided step forward for liberalism and a break with absolute monarchy. It called for freedom of the press, abolished aristocratic privilege, and mandated equal protection under the law. It established an elected parliament that could initiate legislation, decide questions of succession, and hold the Crown's ministers to account. To prevent any future backsliding, the Crown's concurrence to these terms was written into the instrument itself.

For Don Cipriano, this represented a rare moment of triumph in a career otherwise steeped in adversity and frustration. Using the voting laws that he himself had helped draft, he was elected to the Spanish Senate.

But it was to be the soldier's last victory. In February of 1839, a message arrived in Paris informing María Manuela that her husband was critically ill and asking her to come to him. Leaving her daughters behind with Miss Flowers, she traveled alone to Madrid. She did not reveal the true nature of her trip to anyone in France. Paca and Eugénie were not even told their father was unwell.

Although she hurried as best she could to Don Cipriano's bedside, the winter snows made traveling difficult. By the time she arrived, the count of Montijo was past hope. The steadfast warrior who had devoted himself to Napoleon—"What matters wife? What matters child?...My Emperor, my Emperor is taken"—made his final journey to join his champion in death on March 15, 1839.

It was only when she understood that he would not last that María Manuela wrote to Paris instructing Miss Flowers to bring Paca and Eugénie to Madrid. She again gave no indication of the seriousness of her husband's illness. As a result, the girls did not even leave the city until March 17. ("You would not believe what grief I feel to see the children go," Mérimée confided to a friend.) They had the same problem with the winter snows that their mother had had, so it was over two weeks before their coach pulled up in front of the beautiful palace near the Puerta del Sol.

During the whole journey, twelve-year-old Eugénie had been feverishly awaiting the moment that she could throw herself once more into Don Cipriano's arms and know herself to be home. She and Paca ran out of the carriage and into the mansion. It was only then that they were told that they had missed their father's last days, that there would be no chance for a parting caress, or to say goodbye. He had been cold and buried even before they had departed France.

6

The Wild Countess of Teba

The uncertainty of the future is so frightening when it comes to the people we love.

—Eugénie

THE SUDDEN, GRIEVOUS LOSS OF HER FATHER, coinciding with the vulnerability and uncertainty of the onslaught of adolescence, affected Eugénie so profoundly that she barricaded herself alone in her room for two full days, refusing all attempts at comfort. When at last she did emerge, it was only to discover that the reassuring familiarity of her life in Paris was now also over. María Manuela, still in possession of all the trappings, privileges, and income (reported to be the equivalent of a thumping 500,000 francs a year) accorded to a countess of Montijo, but now freed from the inconvenience of having to conform her behavior and spending patterns to the dictates of her lately deceased spouse, had decided to uproot her children yet again and remain in Madrid.

This decision was made possible by the victory of the liberal party over the Carlists, which happened soon after the family's arrival. Having achieved their political objective of securing a constitution, the soldiers supporting Maria Christina and her daughter, Isabella, launched a new military offensive (this one, happily, against the enemy). The morale of their counterparts on the opposing side wavered, as they were already disillusioned with Don Carlos's leadership, particularly his habit of plundering his own partisans whenever he needed money, which was constantly. On August 24, 1839, Don Carlos's leading general was secretly bribed to defect to Maria Christina's side, together with all of his men. Don Carlos only discovered the intrigue when he boomed out in an address to his troops, "Do you acknowledge me for your King—are you ready to follow me wherever I please?" and instead of receiving the expected "Yes, yes! Everywhere! Long Live the King!" was met instead by an emphatic silence. "Gallop off, we are betrayed!" the disconcerted royal cried out to his entourage. "All the party mounted their horses without delay, leaving their baggage, etc.," and fled to France. As a result, "The cause of Carlism...is defunct," the correspondent for the *Observer* noted flatly.

With peace came not only the removal of the threat from the Carlists, but also the opportunity for preferment at the Spanish court.★ Buttressed by royal favor, María Manuela at once assumed a commanding position in the social hierarchy. An invitation to one of the countess of Montijo's magnificent balls—she hosted three a year, including a costume extravaganza, the first in Madrid—was as sure a sign of exclusive status as a centuries-old coat of arms.

But for Eugénie, conforming to her mother's societal expectations merely bred more unhappiness. She still had not grown into her looks, so again, everywhere she went, she was in pretty Paca's shadow. She missed the stimulating cultural and intellectual environment she had become used to during her time away. In December 1839, at the age of thirteen, she was already able to assess the political situation in Madrid with a lucidity far beyond her years. "Spain at present is much agitated," she wrote to Stendhal, with whom she kept up a brief correspondence before the author's death in 1842. "In Madrid great festivals have been held in honor of the proclamation of peace, but so often has

---

★ Just to be on the safe side, María Manuela, while abroad, had entertained and sympathized with many of the Carlists who were in exile in France. That way, if Don Carlos had won, the family would have some protection from the inevitable retaliation against the liberals. But she never crossed the line and openly supported him, so she managed also to maintain her standing with Maria Christina and her daughter, Isabella II. It was well played.

peace been proclaimed, that I am slow to believe it is yet an accomplished fact." Small wonder that after keeping company for so many years with the likes of Mérimée and Stendhal, Eugénie had trouble fitting in. "The young girls we meet can only speak of dress, or if they change their conversation it is to slander and backbite one another," she complained in a postscript to her letter. "I do not like such friends."

There was one exception to Eugénie's alienation, however, and that was her warm relationship with James, duke of Alba. In 1840, James was nineteen to Eugénie's fourteen (and Paca's sixteen). By all accounts a shy, somewhat diffident young man, the duke of Alba nonetheless more than made up for any dearth of personality or conviction with an overabundance of titles and wealth. A grandee who could trace his lineage back to the illegitimate son of King James II of England on one side, and the Scottish king Robert Bruce on the other, the duke of Alba was also the richest bachelor in all of Spain.

As such, he had been in María Manuela's sights for years. Eugénie had known him since she was seven and had first come to Madrid from Granada. She and Paca had been taught to call him "cousin" (anyone in Europe of Scottish descent who was worth knowing was evidently a cousin in María Manuela's opinion) and the three of them had more or less grown up together. James, too, had been sent to Paris to escape the violence and cholera in Madrid; his father, like Eugénie's, had also passed away while he was abroad. The three children had seen each other often in France; now that they were all back in Spain, they fell naturally into the old, easy pattern of friendship (much encouraged by the countess of Montijo). To forlorn Eugénie, James seems to have represented a lifeline of comforting stability. He was someone she could speak to of their old life in Paris, someone who understood her in a way that her more recent acquaintances did not.

It consequently did not take Eugénie long to fall in love with him. Like Sisi's first crush (the prematurely deceased young count for whose sake she had concealed herself for hours behind the bushes), Eugénie could not disguise her feelings. Unlike Elisabeth, however, she believed that her passion was reciprocated. It is possible, of course, that James led her on, but more likely than not, he simply did not know what to do with a sixteen-year-old's amorous declarations, and tried to be gently noncommittal.

Because it was always going to be Paca. She was the right age and temperament for the position of duchess of Alba (not to mention an ebony-eyed knockout of the traditional Spanish variety). There was gossip that María Manuela had steered James to her elder daughter, but that hardly seemed necessary. What she did do, however, was take the squirming suitor off the hook by breaking the news to her younger daughter for him in such a way that there would be no further discussion on the subject. Thus, Eugénie only found out that she was not going to be duchess of Alba when her mother announced, publicly and with great fanfare, that Paca and James were engaged to be married.

Eugénie's disappointment was very great, but it was nothing compared to her rage at being passed over in this way. Not being given to the composition of mournful poetry the way Sisi was, Eugénie instead fired off one of those imprudent letters, not uncommon to young women who have been slighted romantically, which in retrospect probably should not have been sent. "My very dear cousin," she began with dignity to James on May 16, 1843, "You will find it comic that I write you a letter like this, but as there is an end to all things in this world, and as my end is fast approaching [it was ten days before her seventeenth birthday], I want to explain to you everything that my heart contains…My character is strong, it is true…but when I am treated like a donkey, when I am beaten in front of the whole world, it is more than I can bear," she unloaded. "You will say that I am romantic and silly, but you who are good will forgive a poor girl who has lost everyone who loved her, and who is regarded with indifference by everyone, even by her mother, her sister, and, dare I say it, by the man she loves the most, for whom she would have begged for alms" (the duke of Alba had more money than the queen of Spain) "and even consented to her own dishonor." (Fortunately, it had not come to that.) Having thus poured out her emotions in satisfactorily melodramatic fashion, Eugénie went on to pronounce her intention "to end my life peacefully in the depths of some sad cloister, where no one will know I exist," adding stoically in a postscript, "Don't try to talk me out of it, that would be futile. My resolution is taken."

Her resolve might have been strong but it didn't last. When, the following year, James and Paca were married with great ostentation on February 14, seventeen-year-old Eugénie was in attendance. Washington Irving, who, based on his august literary reputation, had recently been appointed US ambassador in Madrid, was among the guests. Recognizing that the female members of his family would surely be interested in what was shaping up to be one of the highlights of the Spanish social season, he good-naturedly took the time to describe the festivities in a letter on March 15, 1844: "A grand wedding took place, shortly since, between...the present Duke of Alva [sic], about twenty-two years of age, and the daughter of the Countess of Montijo, another very rich grandee. The corbeille, or wedding presents of the bride, amounted to one hundred and twenty thousand dollars, all in finery. There were lace handkerchiefs worth a hundred or two dollars, only to look at; and dresses, the very sight of which made several young ladies quite ill. The young Duchess is thought to be one of the happiest and best-dressed young ladies in the whole world. She is already quite hated in the *beau monde*." In fact, María Manuela, in her eagerness to secure Paca's future as a member in good standing of the cream of *haute* society, had been so extravagant in her spending that she caught the attention of the foreign press. "The Duchess de Montijo, a Spanish lady...has just sent to Madrid a magnificent set of presents to her daughter and her future son-in-law...The most curious...is a Malay cane of great delicacy... [ornamented with] diamonds, emeralds, and amethysts," reported an Irish paper. "The duchess, on being reproached by one of her friends for this lavish waste of money, replied, 'You are quite right; the sum is considerable; but when one marries a daughter to the Duke of Alba one cannot hesitate about expense.'"

A social success as triumphant as this one was always going to be a tough act to follow. In the wake of the wedding, Eugénie, still hurting, and casting around for an outlet for her feelings, focused her resentment on her mother. In glorious teenage fashion, she understood instinctively that the best way to get back at María Manuela was not to bury herself in the dirge-like gloom of a convent, but rather to rebel against the manners and conventions that the countess of Montijo held so dear.

And so, at seventeen, Eugénie, who as a result of her sister's being made duchess of Alba had inherited Paca's former title of countess of Teba, determined to break free from many of the rules governing the behavior of unmarried young women. As this decision coincided with her finally shedding her adolescent awkwardness and blossoming into the full power of her beauty, which was considerable—Mérimée, who saw her when he came to visit, described her as "very tall, very fair, marvelously lovely, with the hair that Titian loved"—she caused something of a stir in Madrid. Always athletic (although not quite at Sisi's level), she raced bareback through the streets of the capital. She swam and fished at the extensive Montijo country estate on the out-skirts of the city, and was even known to take up a blade and fence. Her style was defiantly ostentatious. An anonymous admirer left a memo-rable description of Eugénie's appearance at one of Madrid's celebrated bullfights during this period. "Her slender figure is well defined by a costly bodice, which enhances her beauty and elegance," he recorded. "Her dainty hand is armed with a riding whip instead of a fan, and she generally arrives...on a wild Andalusian horse, and in her belt she car-ries a sharp-pointed dagger," he continued. "Her little feet are encased in red satin boots,...her broad golden plaits interwoven with pearls and real flowers...She is the recognized queen of beauty," he raved.

Consequently, at least in the beginning, suitors crowded around her. The duke of Osuna, much in favor at the royal court and, according to Washington Irving, "a tall elegant man about thirty years of age" (also the "richest grandee and greatest Dandy in Spain"), could have been brought to a proposal with the slightest encouragement; to her mother's chagrin, Eugénie gave him none. There were many others, but those who did propose were turned down. Eugénie danced and flirted but refused to commit herself. She had had her heart broken once and she would not give it away again so easily. She had long since forgiven Paca and James, however; if anything, she drew even closer to her sister. Eugénie was such a frequent visitor to the duke and duchess of Alba's home that it was almost as if she considered Paca as a refuge from María Manuela, with whom she lived on warily chilly terms.

But beneath this bold front there is evidence of extreme vulnerability. Still keenly interested in politics, she followed some of the more radical political theories then being tossed around in Europe and discovered the work of an obscure philosopher named Charles Fourier, who had a tiny but dedicated following in France. It is not difficult to surmise what caused Eugénie to embrace the reasoning of this particular visionary. Although many of Fourier's ideas were absurd to the point of comedy — he advocated setting up small agrarian settlements called "phalanxes" where everyone would eat nine times a day ("the key to wisdom and social policy is the art of keeping mankind's appetite up for his nine meals," Fourier, poor and perpetually hungry himself, noted) and workers would leap out of bed every morning at 3 a.m., so excited would they be to begin the day — his criticisms of current society, particularly the way women were treated, must have resonated deeply. "Is not a young woman a piece of merchandise put up for sale to the highest bidder?" he demanded. "Is she not tyrannized by prejudice from childhood and obliged to consent to any marriage that may be arranged for her? People try to persuade her that she is only bound by chains of flowers. But can she really doubt her degradation?" he asked. Fourier then went even further and presciently argued that "as a general rule: *Social progress . . . occurs in accordance with the progress women make towards freedom, and the social order becomes decadent in accordance with the reduction of women's freedom . . .* In short, *the extension of women's privileges is the general principle of all social progress.*"★

As the years passed and she turned first eighteen, then nineteen, then twenty without announcing the required wedding engagement, no one felt the pressure to conform to expectations more than Eugénie.

★ Many scholars now credit Fourier with introducing the concept of feminism.

She still held out idealistically for love, but occasionally cracked under the strain. At her mother's salons, it was noted that the countess of Montijo's younger daughter argued vehemently in favor of Fourier's ideas, incurring María Manuela's sharp displeasure. Rumors circulated that when General Narváez, the powerful head of both the army and the government, overheard Eugénie speak in this way, he took offense. "You ladies ought not to meddle with politics, for if things come to the worst you would not have the nerve to face cold steel," he interrupted severely. "Would I not?" retorted Eugénie, snatching up a knife from a nearby table and proceeding to stab herself in the arm.*

Behavior like this tends to give the average wooer pause. The pace of proposals dropped off. And an unmarried young woman of Eugénie's class could not even distract herself with a meaningful occupation. For a short period in 1847, there was some hope of a career at court, when María Manuela was appointed first lady-in-waiting to Isabella II and managed to get her younger daughter attached to the royal household as well. But even this opportunity was snatched away when both were forced to resign after only two months. Although tongues wagged that their dismissal was a result of Eugénie's having exceeded the bounds of propriety by taking an unchaperoned, late-night walk with a male member of the royal administration, the truth was that it was the revelation of María Manuela's support of the Carlists during her years in France that caused the rupture.

So, by the beginning of 1848, it was back to the endless round of parties and social calls, quadrilles, and bullfights, with no outlet in sight for Eugénie's restless spirit and intelligence. And then suddenly, out of nowhere, soon after the fiasco at court, Eugénie finally found the love for which she had been searching.

His name was José, but everyone called him Pepe. He was the

---

* The Spanish court had turned much more autocratic by this time. In 1844, General Narváez, using the army, had declared thirteen-year-old Isabella II queen in her own right and then taken over her government. He was notorious for using repression to establish order. It was said later that on his deathbed, when he was advised by his priest to forgive his enemies, Narváez replied that, fortunately, there were none to forgive because he "had shot them all."

marquis d'Alcañicès and duke of Sexton, twenty-three, handsome, charming, and ambitious: he would be appointed mayor of Madrid at the age of twenty-eight. Pepe had been born in Spain, but as a child he and his family had fled to Italy to escape the violence of the Carlist war. His father had died and Pepe had now returned to claim his titles and inheritance. It wasn't a vast fortune, like James's, but it was substantial enough to make the marquis d'Alcañicès a grandee and, as such, a highly desirable catch.

It is likely that none of this mattered to Eugénie. This was no fleeting schoolgirl crush. She was twenty-one and knew what she wanted; this was the overwhelming, electric feeling for which she had been hoping and waiting. Pepe, sophisticated and clever, understood and pursued her. The defenses she had built up so assiduously after the duke of Alba affair vanished and she fell hopelessly, helplessly in love. They saw each other often, sometimes daily, and were invited everywhere together. When, for one reason or another, Pepe could not be with her, he wrote her ardent notes. She had every reason to believe that he would propose.

And then it came out that the woman he really wanted was her sister, and that the only reason he had been playing up to Eugénie was to secure invitations to the duchess of Alba's home in the hopes of getting close enough to Paca to seduce her.

Eugénie's despair was profound. This time, she could not even blame her mother. She took poison.

She came very close to dying. At first, she refused all treatment. To get her to take the remedy, they summoned Pepe to the sickroom. He knelt beside her and, true to form, his first words betrayed his callousness. "Where are my letters?" he whispered, hoping to retrieve them and avoid culpability. In a moment her anger and disdain flared up and she agreed to take a purgative. "Like Achilles's spear he healed the wounds he made," she later recalled bitterly.

This was one scandal too much, even for freewheeling Madrid. As soon as Eugénie was well enough to travel, the countess of Montijo took her younger daughter on an extended trip abroad.

★   ★   ★

LIKE A CHARACTER TRAPPED in some nightmarish, real-life Jane Austen novel, Eugénie spent much of the next four years being dragged along in her mother's wake from one international capital or fashionable aristocratic resort to another, as María Manuela sought, with increasing desperation, to broker a suitably brilliant match (or indeed, after a while, *any* match) for her frustratingly recalcitrant progeny. They were in Paris for the spring of 1849, followed by a stint in Brussels and a month imbibing the healthful waters at chic Spa in Germany; 1851 saw them in London and then the high-society hot springs of Wiesbaden, outside Frankfurt; May 1852 found mother and daughter at the genteel mountain resort of Eaux-Bonnes, in the French Pyrenees, before flitting on to Paris again. Snatched in between this restless hurrying to and fro were brief visits back home to Spain. (The countess of Montijo, who had no intention of sacrificing her own hard-won place among the Madrid elite to her maternal responsibilities, always made sure to be back in time to host her expected costume ball during the winter season.) For Eugénie, the need to be constantly on display with strangers, no matter how accomplished or important, only served to deepen her misery. "I am very sad today and had to go with mother to Princess Mathilde's, where I knew absolutely no one," she wrote to Paca from Paris in 1849. "No one, absolutely no one spoke to me...My body was there, but my imagination was far away...I believe I will do without going out into the world whenever I can," she added, although it is likely, even as she wrote these words, that she understood that the number of invitations she could refuse was limited.

María Manuela's doggedness was compelled by her recognition that although her daughter's spirit might be subdued, her beauty was anything but. Eugénie grew lovelier as she aged. This, with her income and title—she was countess of Teba in her own right—ensured that despite her recent humiliation, Eugénie continued to be a marketable commodity. While they were away in France, María Manuela even managed to coax one of her daughter's old beaux back into the ring. "A marriage is said to be negotiating between the Duke of Osuna, the richest nobleman in Spain, and the Countess de Teba, daughter of the Countess de Montijo," one of the London papers announced on June 19, 1849.

But this engagement, too, failed to materialize. At twenty-three, Eugénie remained lonely, rebellious, and stubbornly single. Her outlook was one of defiance tinged with despair. "I like danger," she confided in a letter to Paca. "I don't know why I am so attracted to it, perhaps it is due to the little attachment I have to life."

And it was in this happy frame of mind that she first met Louis Napoleon Bonaparte, nephew of the great Napoleon Bonaparte himself.

THE CHALLENGE IN WRITING the history of Napoleon's extended family is not just that there were so many of them, but that they all played a role in his affairs. (Not to mention that they all christened their sons "Napoleon" to take advantage of the celebrity attached to the name.) The emperor had been the second eldest of eight children, and as a solicitous brother he naturally wanted to help his siblings along in life. Luckily, he had a large empire to run, so the easy solution was simply to make them all kings and queens of the various European realms he had conquered. Consequently, his older brother, Joseph (for whom Don Cipriano had fought), was allotted Spain; a younger brother, Louis, was named king of Holland; and Napoleon's sister Caroline ascended to the throne of Naples. Somewhere along the line, the emperor ran out of monarchies, so for his youngest brother, Jérôme, he ingeniously carved a whole new realm out of some French-controlled territory in northwest Germany, christened it "the kingdom of Westphalia," and plopped Jérôme down in it.

Louis Napoleon (the one Eugénie was introduced to) was the son and namesake of the brother who had been gifted Holland. His mother, Hortense, was the daughter of Napoleon's first wife, Josephine, by her husband from a previous marriage. Hortense and King Louis loathed each other but it was Napoleon who had proposed the match, and no one said no to the emperor. So, the couple had dutifully wed, and just as dutifully had children. Louis Napoleon, their second surviving son, was born on April 20, 1808, which made him eighteen years older than Eugénie.

As a baby, Louis Napoleon was dandled on his illustrious ancestor's knee, and had naturally picked up the family reverence for the great conqueror. But until Louis Napoleon was in his early twenties, he gave hardly any thought to politics. His tastes skewed much more towards beautiful women and fast horses. No one thought much about it, however, since it seemed unlikely, what with an older brother, and Napoleon's own son by his second marriage, ahead of him in order of seniority (Joseph had no sons), that Louis Napoleon would ever seriously have to consider taking over leadership of the dynasty.*

And then, in short succession, his older brother died in 1831 of measles and Napoleon's son succumbed in 1832 to tuberculosis, and suddenly Louis Napoleon, at the age of twenty-four, found himself the standard-bearer for global domination. It was a calling for which he was almost laughably unsuited, but luckily French politics during this period were so spectacularly chaotic that it gave him lots of time to practice. The speed with which one government after another in France improbably rose, and then just as impulsively fell during the first half of the nineteenth century was impressive. Teenagers are less volatile.

The political tug of war was over what type of government was best suited to France. Louis XVIII had been restored to the French throne by the victorious Prussians but, cognizant that his authority relied on the presence of foreign troops, he had trod carefully. One of the conditions of his restoration had been that he grant his subjects a constitution, so he had a weak one written up. Still, fearful that the kingdom would explode into revolution again if he pushed too hard to return to

---

* When Josephine failed to give Napoleon a male heir, he divorced her and instead married Marie Louise, daughter of the Austrian emperor Francis II (Archduchess Sophia's father-in-law). Marie Louise successfully gave birth to a son but took him with her when she escaped to Vienna after Paris fell to the Prussians in 1814. This child was given the title of Napoleon II in France, although he never ruled and was in fact raised in Austria.

absolute monarchy, Louis XVIII favored moderate councilors and reconciliation during his reign.

Alas, his younger brother, Charles X, who inherited the throne on
Louis's death in 1824, had no such compunctions. He appointed arch-
conservative royalists to his government, and when the representative
Chamber of Deputies tried to thwart him in 1830, Charles dissolved
the assembly and annulled the constitution. His brother had been right:
this did not go over at all well with liberal Parisians. In July, a mob rose
up and chased Charles and his family out of France.

The abrupt exodus of Charles X left the realm once more without
a king. The mob clamored for the marquis de Lafayette to take the
job, but the seventy-three-year-old hero of the American Revolution, still active in French politics, declined the honor. With the
withdrawal of the marquis, the choice had instead fallen on Louis
Philippe, duke of Orléans. This was because, by a strange twist of
fate, Louis Philippe literally embodied both sides of the political
spectrum. He believed in a constitution but was acceptable to the
monarchists because by birth he was a close relation of the ousted
Charles X. For their part, the Parisians identified him with the glorious achievements of 1789. It had been Louis Philippe's father who,
during the Revolution, had cast the deciding vote condemning his
cousin Louis XVI to execution.*

Having a foot in both camps in this way was a tricky act to pull off.
Louis Philippe's solution was to rule as a "citizen king"—to govern as
a monarch but not look like one. The new king of France eschewed
pomp and opulence and instead ambled around Paris dressed like an
affluent shopkeeper. In lieu of grand balls and glittering state dinners,
he took his family out for drives in an ordinary carriage, like any other
upstanding member of the bourgeoisie. "You ask me for news; and the

---

* Not everyone in France understood the distinction between an absolute and a constitutional monarchy. "The old women and children who were frightened [by the mob
who chased Charles X out], are now beginning to wonder what it has been all about, and
to ask why, if there has been a revolution, there are no gibbets or heads on spikes," commented the Paris correspondent for the London *Standard*.

only news I have to give you is, that I have seen a King of France walking yesterday with an umbrella under his arm in the rue St. Honoré," observed the *Standard* correspondent.

It was the citizen king who was in charge of France when Louis Napoleon suddenly found himself the most senior of the next generation of Bonapartes. To prepare himself for the great task ahead of him (his mother, Hortense, was already calling him "emperor"), the fledgling conqueror published a book on politics (Napoleon had published a similar treatise when he was younger) and another on artillery (Napoleon had started his career in an artillery regiment). Then, having established his credentials, Louis Napoleon attempted to take over France.

This first effort, launched on October 30, 1836, sadly did not go as well as might be hoped. Louis Napoleon showed up at 6 a.m. at a French garrison in Strasbourg where one of his friends was a colonel, announced who he was, and invited the soldiers there to join him in overturning Louis Philippe's government by marching through the streets shouting *"Vive Napoleon!"* The regiment declined this honor, and both Louis Napoleon and his friend the colonel were arrested. The whole affair was over in less than an hour.

In fact, so trifling was this "absurd insurrection," as one of the London papers called it, that the target of the sedition, Louis Philippe, took pity on the prisoner and agreed to banish him to the United States rather than have him languish in the Strasbourg city jail. The citizen king even provided the young agitator with some pocket money so he could have a good time in New York.★

This state-funded exile across the Atlantic didn't last long. The next year found Louis Napoleon back in Europe at his dying mother's

---

★ This leniency was arranged by Louis Napoleon's mother, who succeeded in obtaining a personal audience with the king, where she eloquently pleaded her son's case. Hortense was also responsible for having earlier saved her son's life when he got mixed up in a rebellion in Italy and couldn't get away because he had caught the measles. That time, Hortense swooped in and rescued him by disguising him as one of her servants and then hiding him in a daring carriage escape. She's the one who should have been emperor, if you ask me.

bedside, where, as a parting gift, Hortense left him an estate worth 3 million francs. This munificence was enough to allow Louis Napoleon to set himself up in London in grand style and still have money left over to take another whack at reclaiming France.

This second time, he went bigger. On August 5, 1840, Louis Napoleon, together with an entourage of some fifty-seven followers—including an aged general who had fought under Napoleon I, three colonels, and a handful of other officers—set off in a rented city of Edinburgh steamboat for Boulogne, on the northwest coast of France, in what had been billed to the captain and crew as a pleasure cruise. Upon arriving in the early hours of August 6, however, the entire party suddenly showed up on deck dressed in French military uniforms. Louis Napoleon then ordered the captain to hang around on the outskirts of the harbor while he commandeered the steamer's small rowboat to ferry his men in stages to the shore. Once arrived, they began running through the streets shouting *"Vive l'Empereur!"* and distributing money and copies of proclamations Louis Napoleon had had the foresight to draw up. One of these decreed that Louis Philippe and his family "has ceased to reign," and dissolved the current French government pending "the arrival of Prince Napoleon in Paris." The other, addressed to the army, read: "Soldiers! The great shade of the Emperor Napoleon speaks to you by my voice…Show it upon its arrival that you are worthy sons of the great Army!"

Strangely, this second attempt fared no better than the first. Louis Napoleon and his band of faux French soldiers appeared at the regular army barracks at 5 a.m., when the enlisted men were just getting up. The regiment was a little disconcerted when the visitors tried to convince them that everyone else in France had already rebelled in favor of the emperor, but a captain, hearing the commotion, hurriedly appeared and shouted *"Vive le Roi!,"* at which point everyone in the room understood that this was another attempt at a coup. Louis Napoleon, threatened with arrest, then pulled a pistol out of his pocket and leveled it at the captain; being out of practice, he missed his aim and ended up wounding one of the common soldiers, an unfortunate bungle that did little to recommend him to the men he was trying to recruit.

It went downhill pretty quickly from there. The National Guard was informed, and the mayor called for the citizenry to arm themselves against the intruders. Louis Napoleon's militia scattered. Most were quickly rounded up; one was shot dead and two were seriously injured. The officers in command of this abortive little insurrection made a beeline for the rowboat they had left on the beach, to try to get back to the steamer, but so many of them crammed themselves aboard that it overturned in the waves. Several drowned but four were plucked alive from the harbor, including Louis Napoleon himself, who was discovered clinging to a convenient buoy.★

This time, there was no fond mother available to make a pitch for leniency. Louis Napoleon was convicted of treason and sentenced to life in prison at the Château de Ham, a forbidding fortress in northeastern France. Fortunately for its new inmate, this stockade turned out to be not *quite* as secure as its massive stone walls and remote location might otherwise suggest. Over time, the warden of the Château de Ham, with only Louis Napoleon and a few of his most loyal officers to guard and nobody else nearly as interesting to talk to, became chummy with his charges. He visited Louis Napoleon's rooms every evening after dinner to play cards with this group. When, after six years of this, his congenial prisoner asked that repairs be made to the castle to make it more comfortable, the warden ordered a crew of carpenters from the local village to come in to help with the renovation. On May 25, 1846, Louis Napoleon, disguised as one of these workmen, and carrying a

---

★ An editorial in one of the London papers had some fun with this. "The Prince [Louis Napoleon], in one of his proclamations, ... says, with a fine mixture of the familiar and the sublime — 'When one has the honour to be at the head of a people like the French people, there is an infallible means of doing great things — it is to will them.' But how is 'one to have the honour to be at the head of a people like the French people' if there is to be a Mayor in the way, who mounts on horseback, and calls out the constable? How ... if there is to be a Captain to tell a handful of soldiers not to be humbugged? ... if a boat upsets when one is doing one's best to make one's escape from the Mayors and police officers?"

board to hide his face, walked out of the Château de Ham in broad daylight.

He made it all the way to the safety and freedom of London, where he was celebrated for his brazen escape. He had burned through his mother's fortune, but happily his newfound fame secured him the love and admiration of a young, beautiful, extremely wealthy mistress who was willing to bankroll him. He was thus positioned to attempt a third ineffectual takeover of France when, lo and behold, the year 1848 rolled around. Without warning, the Bavarians revolted against Lola Montez, the Austrians and Hungarians against Archduchess Sophia, and the French against Louis Philippe, all without Louis Napoleon's having to rent a single steamboat from the city of Edinburgh.

This latest revolution in France had been prompted, like the one in 1789, by economic hardship. A series of poor harvests had pushed the price of grain and other crops sky high; at the same time, the industrial revolution had closed down small businesses in favor of factories at which working conditions were horrendous. Paris was filled with angry, unemployed, starving people, many of whom had come from outside the capital in a desperate search for work. Radical leaders on the left, hoping to install a socialist republic, organized and inflamed these passions. Barricades were erected and there were riots in the streets. On February 23, a group of royal soldiers charged with keeping order made the fatal mistake of shooting into a crowd, killing over fifty and wounding dozens of others. The famous author Alexis de Tocqueville, a member of the Chamber of Deputies at the time, recorded, "On leaving my bed-room, I met the cook, who had been out; the good woman was quite beside herself, poured out a sorrowing rigmarole, of which I failed to understand a word, except that the Government was massacring the poor people."

That did it. The next day, February 24, 1848, a mob attacked the Palace of the Tuileries. Louis Philippe, taking the example of his predecessor, hastily abdicated, and fled to England with his family. In his place, a provisional government, whose ministers were dictated by the mob, was installed on the promise of a new constitution and the creation of a nationally elected republic in the fall.

This was exactly the sort of political upheaval that Louis Napoleon had sought to capitalize on in the past. But there's nothing like six years in jail to give an aspiring emperor perspective. Louis Napoleon thought about going to Paris—he even got on board a ship headed to France—but he turned around when the new provisional government made it clear that he wasn't welcome. This time, he knew he could afford to be patient. No need to go up against a capital in the grip of republican fever. Much better to wait around until the country had a taste of what it was like to be governed by the mob.

He knew what he was about. Over the next few months, the provisional government was so frequently threatened with violence, and the capital with riots, that they had to give in over and over to the more radical elements of the party. According to the British ambassador stationed in Paris, by the time elections for a new National Assembly were held in June, "the mass of the people had become so weary" of this sort of chaos that Louis Napoleon, although he had neither campaigned nor set foot in France as a free man for over three decades (except for those two ill-fated days when he had attempted coups), was voted in to represent no fewer than five different districts, based solely on nostalgia and name recognition.

And that foothold in Paris was all he needed. When, soon thereafter, it was announced that, rather than reinstating a king, the French republic would take on the model of the United States and elect a president for a term of four years, Louis Napoleon put his name on the ballot, and this time actively canvassed for the office. "The name which I bear is above all a symbol of order, of nationality, of glory," he hammered home repeatedly. Order and glory were code words for the days of the Napoleonic empire, when France ruled the world.

After nine months of ineffectual progressive rule, with the provisional government widely perceived as acquiescent to the demands of the violent Parisian underclass, this was clearly a message that resonated. On December 10, 1848, despite years of ignominy and international ridicule, Louis Napoleon was elected to the presidency of the new French republic with a landslide victory of 5,534,520 votes out of a total of 7,426,252 cast. Alexis de Tocqueville summed up the significance of this dark-horse upset for the benefit of the astounded British ambassador. "There only remains now one question, whether it is the Republicans or the Republic itself which the country cannot abide," he observed candidly.

A mere four months after this undeniable triumph, Eugénie met Louis Napoleon.

7

An Imperial Coup

*Is there any game of chance more frightful than an exclusive
and indissoluble tie [marriage], on which you stake a lifetime's
happiness or unhappiness?*

—Charles Fourier

EUGÉNIE'S INITIAL ENCOUNTER with the new president of France did
not bode at all well for an extended relationship. On April 12, 1849,
María Manuela managed to wrangle an invitation to a crowded public
reception at the Élysée Palace, Louis Napoleon's official residence, at
which the countess of Montijo made a point of introducing herself and
her daughter to their famous host. Although he barely spoke to her at
that time, Eugénie clearly made an impression on Louis Napoleon, as
the very next month, she and her mother were invited to another presi-
dential affair, this one a dinner at his summer residence, the sumptuous
Château de Saint-Cloud, just outside Paris.

Unbeknownst to his flattered guests, however, the entertainment
Louis Napoleon had in mind this time around was of a more intimate
nature. Despite having brought his beautiful, wealthy British mistress
with him to France and setting her up in a mansion right next door to
the Élysée Palace so he could slip over there whenever he wanted
(which was almost every night), the new president still frequently felt
the need to lighten the heavy burdens of his office by also generously

bestowing his charms upon whatever other radiant young female happened to wander into his orbit. As Louis Napoleon was aware that the unmarried Eugénie could not attend a fête without a chaperone, he thoughtfully included her mother in his invitation, to induce her to accept.

It worked: Eugénie and María Manuela, assuming that they had been asked to a grand society dinner, put on their most elaborate evening wear and arrived at the Château de Saint-Cloud, only to discover that the party was actually being held not in the great halls of the palace, but rather in the decidedly less impressive dining parlor of a little garden house on the estate, where they, along with a low-level official who was accustomed to facilitating this sort of tryst, were Louis Napoleon's only guests. Any lingering hopes they may have had that perhaps they had been chosen for this honor because the French president, knowing them to be former members of Isabella II's household, wished to consult them on Spanish politics, were dispelled when, at the close of this uncomfortable meal, Louis Napoleon abruptly rose and offered his arm to Eugénie, proposing that he and she take a stroll in the shadowy depths of the adjacent park. He might just as well have invited her to retire alone with him to the bedroom.

It must have been a blow to be treated like a hired courtesan, but by this time Eugénie had been humiliated by experts. She knew how to stand up for herself. "Monseigneur, my mother is here," she reminded her would-be seducer sweetly, sidestepping his arm. Caught, Louis Napoleon was forced to proffer his elbow instead to María Manuela, as she was of higher rank than her daughter, after which he sullenly escorted the countess of Montijo for a brief trudge through the gardens, while Eugénie tripped along behind them with his subordinate. That concluded the evening at Saint-Cloud.

Although Eugénie had handled this insult gracefully, the depth of her mortification may perhaps be measured by the speed with which she and her mother subsequently packed up and left Paris for Brussels. She would not see Louis Napoleon again for three years, after he had once more shocked Europe.

★ ★ ★

THE IMPETUS FOR HIS LATEST ESCAPADE had revolved around the restrictions on the chief executive's time in office. Louis Napoleon had understood when he was elected that the new French constitution limited the presidency to one four-year interval, but as the day drew nearer when he would have to voluntarily resign his administration to make way for somebody else, he discovered he didn't want to. He felt strongly that he deserved another term.

At first, he tried to achieve this desire through legal means. He pressured the National Assembly to alter the constitution to allow him to run for reelection. But the representatives, suspicious that what he really wanted was to make himself emperor (and they suspected with good reason, as it turned out), refused. "Because we once had Napoleon the Great must we now have Napoleon the Little?" demanded a scornful Victor Hugo on the evening of July 18, 1851, when the assembly took this matter up for debate. "What we ask of the President, and what we confidently expect from him, is not that he should retain power like a great man, but that he should quit it like an honest one," he declaimed forcefully to the accompaniment of "indescribable uproar and conflicting cheers."

The assembly's resistance did not, however, alter Louis Napoleon's determination to remain in office one bit. Stymied for the moment on the legal front, he began a backdoor campaign intended to arouse such sweeping public support for his candidacy that the representatives would have no choice but to accede to his reelection. His platform was based almost entirely on fear. He denounced the National Assembly as having been taken over by radicals who wanted to implement a socialist agenda based on mob violence. He warned that should he not be maintained in the presidency, France would be thrust into chaos, with law-abiding citizens subject to the mercy of anarchists and criminals. He painted those in opposition to him as effete Parisian intellectuals who had little in common with the rest of the country, and who considered themselves superior to those who lived outside the capital, particularly people in the conservative rural areas where Louis Napoleon's strongest support was based.

But these populist tactics, far from intimidating the members of the assembly, only stiffened their resolve. When he discovered that he could not secure a second term through the ordinary channels of political discourse, Louis Napoleon instead opted for a more direct approach to the problem and staged another coup.

It turned out to be much simpler taking over a country of which he was already the president. For starters, it saved having to round up a band of pretend warriors. This time around, all Louis Napoleon had to do was find a few like-minded officers of the French army who were eager for career advancement under a new regime. In the early morning hours of December 2, 1851, Parisians woke up to find the streets filled with soldiers from the regiments of these commanders. The National Assembly was dissolved by proclamation, and its leaders were ousted from their beds and arrested. In a nice ironic touch, the one general who might have prevented the army from obeying the president's orders was hustled into a carriage and exiled to a long prison confinement at the Château de Ham, now under new management.

Although there were pockets of violent resistance, these were easily subdued, and within a few days the capital had resumed its customary peaceful appearance. The general passivity of the citizenry to the sedition was in large part due to the president's having cleverly portrayed the action as his heroic, patriotic duty, necessary to prevent the machinations of the radical socialists. He also promised to hold a public referendum, whereby the country would by popular vote decide for themselves whether his initiative had been justified. "Frenchmen—the disturbances are pacified," trumpeted one of the many official proclamations distributed in the days following the coup. "Whatever be the decision of the people, society is saved!...If I no longer possess your confidence, if your ideas have changed, there is no need to cause precious blood to be shed; it suffices to depose in the urn a contrary vote," the president assured his constituents. "My sole ambition is to secure the repose and prosperity of France."

The referendum on Louis Napoleon's surprise attack on the republic took place two weeks later, on the 20th and 21st of December. Every

Frenchman over the age of twenty-one was eligible to vote. The wording on the ballot framed the issue as a straight yes-or-no question. Did the voter wish Louis Napoleon to continue as head of state, this time for a period of ten years, under a new constitution modeled on the one used during the glorious days of the empire, which would grant him basically unlimited powers?

On January 1, 1852, the votes were tallied and the numbers reported in the press. By a staggering margin of 7,439,216 to 640,737, the country that had once so famously stormed the Bastille and beheaded its long-standing monarch in the defense of liberty had voted roaring approval for Louis Napoleon's remaining in office as a virtual dictator, with an undeniable mandate to make France great again.

And it was at this point that Eugénie and María Manuela returned to Paris.

THREE YEARS OF WANDERING aimlessly around Europe with an unaffectionate, socially ambitious mother would dampen the spirits of even the most intrepid young woman. By the time she arrived back in the French capital, in September 1852, Eugénie was aware that she was fast approaching the age when she would reach the upper limit of her matrimonial desirability. If she did not somehow find a way to take control of her life, she would find herself condemned to reside as her parent's unhappy companion until María Manuela's death.

And perversely (considering the tawdry nature of their first encounter), Louis Napoleon had no more fervent admirer, at least in his public role, than the twenty-seven-year-old countess of Teba. In fact, Eugénie had been eagerly following his career from afar. Even before the coup d'état, when Louis Napoleon had first started agitating for a second term, Eugénie had written to him offering to help support his candidacy out of her own income. When he had struck, she had been thrilled by the daring of his strategy and the brilliance of his success. Here was a man of action committed to the glory of France, a modern hero who inspired emotions in her reminiscent of those that had been conjured in childhood, when she had sat breathlessly listening to first her father, and then Stendhal, narrate the stirring adventures of the original Napoleon.

And she was in town at just the right moment to catch him on the brink of yet another triumph. The representatives of the National Assembly had been right: Louis Napoleon's goal had always been to reinstate the empire. To rally support for this final step, he had set off on an extended goodwill tour of France, reaching as far south as Marseilles and as far west as Bordeaux to show himself to his subjects. Many of these smaller cities and towns had not received a visit from a French ruler since the days of the first Napoleon, and the excitement was tangible. The president was greeted everywhere with military parades and celebratory fêtes. The accounts of his progress were uniformly glowing, but even more importantly for his plans, his audience had spontaneously greeted him with exactly the sort of cheers he had hoped to elicit. "The enthusiasm of the Marseilles people burst out everywhere... The whole population of the town was assembled on the quays, and on the roofs of the houses. More than 60,000 voices, at the same time, raised the cry of '*Vive l'Empereur!*'" ran one of the newspaper reports. In Nîmes, "His Highness yesterday went through the whole town. On his passage an immense concourse of people uttered cries of '*Vive l'Empereur! Vive Napoléon III!*' The enthusiasm is extraordinary," proclaimed another.

Having thus pointedly demonstrated the opinions of those who lived outside the capital, Louis Napoleon returned to Paris, leading a triumphant procession through the city on October 16, 1852. A rapt Eugénie looked down on this spectacle from the windows of a spacious apartment occupied by yet another of the countess of Montijo's wide circle of acquaintance. The tenant of these well-placed rooms was a wealthy older English gentleman so "hopelessly in love with his fair guest," according to a diplomat who was also present on this occasion, that it was a source of mirth to the rest of the company. This English suitor had proposed years before and been flatly turned down, but he still hovered like a vulture circling a slowly weakening prey, awaiting the day when Eugénie's options would run out and she would be forced to reconsider his offer. Looking down now on the cheering crowds and the commanding figure (from a distance) of Louis Napoleon astride his magnificent stallion, Eugénie could not have helped but compare the unpalatable marital alternative represented by her host to the excitement inspired by the great leader passing before her on the street below.

And so, at the many gala events that marked the season in Paris that fall, Eugénie accepted more invitations, and shone in society as never before. Even her mother, who understood what she was doing, was impressed. "Paris talks of nothing but [Eugénie's] beauty," María Manuela wrote to Paca. "She has become the fashion of the day."

It worked. Louis Napoleon took notice and renewed his attentions to her, but this time in a far more respectful way. When, as he had intended, on November 7, 1852, the French Senate (made up entirely of loyalists appointed by the president) declared the republic abolished and recommended that another national vote be called to reestablish "the imperial dignity in the person of Louis Napoleon Bonaparte, with succession to his direct descendants, legitimate or adopted," the soon-to-be emperor celebrated by throwing himself a fabulous hunting party at Fontainebleau. It was the most sought-after invitation in Paris, and this time Eugénie and her mother were on the guest list.

The mighty Napoleon I himself could not have attained a greater victory in battle than Eugénie did at that hunt. Her fashion sense was only outdone by her riding. Her accessories were a marvel. According to an admiring spectator, along with her tight-fitting habit (consisting, provocatively, of a skirt "over grey trousers") she wore "patent leather boots with high heels and spurs." Her shining red-gold hair was set off to perfection by "a dainty felt hat, from which waved a magnificent long ostrich feather fastened by a diamond clasp," and she carried a pearl-handled crop. "She sat her horse like a knight, and despised the saddle ordinarily used by ladies," the admirer, clearly male, sighed in appreciation.

His host shared his sentiments. Louis Napoleon (who had conveniently left his devoted mistress back in Paris on this occasion) did everything he could think of to get Eugénie to sleep with him. She admired a clover in a field and he immediately sent to Paris to have his jewelers fashion a pin just like it out of diamonds. Having no mount of her own in France, Eugénie had been forced to borrow the thorough-bred Andalusian she had ridden at the hunt; the next day, Louis Napoleon gave it to her. His attentions were so pronounced that they caused comment. "You can't imagine what they are saying about me since I accepted that infernal horse," she fumed in a letter home to Madrid.

But no matter what inducement he proffered, she held out for wed-lock. The story went around that, when an increasingly frustrated Louis Napoleon demanded, "What is then the road to your heart?" Eugénie answered demurely, "That of the chapel, Sire." This cat-and-mouse sparring was observed with interest in diplomatic circles. "She has played her game so well that he can get her in no other way but marriage," the British ambassador to France informed London.

Her timing was perfect. Two weeks after the Fontainebleau house party, on December 1, 1852, the ballots from the public referendum were tallied, and Louis Napoleon was discovered to have won by his usual stupendous margin. When the results were read out in the Senate—7,824,189 votes in favor of establishing a second empire ver-sus 253,145 against—a cry of "*Vive l'Empereur!*" resounded. The fol-lowing day, December 2 (conveniently for the history books, the one-year anniversary of his coup d'état), Louis Napoleon was officially proclaimed Napoleon III, emperor of the French, and made his formal progress through Paris along the Champs-Élysées all the way to his new residence, the Palace of the Tuileries, accompanied by "a consid-erable body of officers in splendid uniforms," and heralded by trum-pets, drums, and a 101-cannon salute.

And it was coincidentally exactly this, the achievement of his decades-long dream, that gave Louis Napoleon's romantic skirmishes with Eugénie a sudden relevance. Because under the terms of his new employment, the forty-four-year-old emperor was going to need some heirs. But to have legitimate heirs (he had plenty of the other kind), he was going to have to marry, and the sooner the better. There was no wriggling around this uncomfortable fact.

Not that Eugénie was at first anywhere near the top of the list of potential candidates for the vaunted title of Empress of the French. Louis Napoleon knew that it was his job to make a prestigious marriage with a woman of royal birth, who brought with her a powerful international alliance that could be useful to France. Problem was, he couldn't find anyone who would have him. A match was proposed early in December with one of Queen Victoria's nieces, but this offer was quickly refused. The straitlaced Victoria, who had no intention of allowing her naïve, seventeen-year-old relative to wed a middle-aged man of Louis Napoleon's notorious reputation, observed pointedly to her foreign secretary "the sad fate of all the wives of the rulers of France since 1789," and that was that. As for the Austrian, Prussian, and Russian courts, they were so annoyed by the prospect of having to deal with a second upstart, potentially militant, Napoleonic empire that they refused even to recognize the French leader's status, much less discuss a possible marital alliance with him, until well into January of 1853.

But by that time, it was all over anyway. The more Eugénie held him off, the more Louis Napoleon wanted her and the less patience he had for the diplomatic squabbling necessary to secure the hand of what, given the snobbish attitude of the important powers, would clearly be an insignificant princess anyway. At the imperial Christmas court festivities, held at Compiègne, the emperor was observed to be "over head and ears in love with Mdlle. De Montijo," as one of the other guests recorded flatly in his diary. As for Eugénie, she was clearly attracted by the boldness of Louis Napoleon's success, and by his willingness to take the sort of dangerous risks that she found so exhilarating. "He is a man...who always stakes his future on a single card," she reported with admiration to Paca. "That's why he wins."

Matters came to a head on January 12, 1853, when a grand imperial reception was held at the Palace of the Tuileries. Dinner had been announced, and Eugénie was making her way into the banquet room, when the wife of the French foreign minister suddenly shoved her out of the way, at the same time scolding her for having had the presumption to enter ahead of her betters. It was akin to publicly calling Eugénie a tramp. Although visibly angry, the countess of Teba yet managed to control herself. "Pass, Madame," she spit out coldly, stepping aside.

She was still upset, however, and when she took her seat Napoleon III, who had not witnessed the incident, asked what was wrong. Aware that everyone was watching them, and not willing to give the rest of the amused company the satisfaction of believing her hurt, Eugénie refused to say anything at first. But after the meal, he persisted. "I will know the truth," demanded the emperor. "What has happened to you?"

"Sire, I have been insulted," Eugénie admitted. "But I shall not be insulted a second time," she added firmly.

It was an ultimatum, and he knew it. If he continued to refuse to legitimize their relationship with an offer of marriage, she would stop seeing him.

This turned out to be the pivotal jab. For, no matter what the contemptuous minister's wife had implied, despite two months of intensive lobbying, the emperor still had not gotten what he wanted from Eugénie. And this was approximately two months longer than Louis Napoleon was accustomed to waiting for what he wanted from a woman.

"Tomorrow no one shall dare to insult you," he told her.

ACTUALLY, IT TOOK A FEW DAYS longer than that. The emperor knew that there would be objections from his dismayed advisers, who sought a more useful diplomatic alliance, and from his family, who protested that Eugénie's inferior lineage degraded the imperial name. There was also the small matter of the beautiful British mistress who, having loyally financed Louis Napoleon's earlier political campaigns, had already on more than one occasion expressed the opinion that it was she who should be rewarded with marriage and the title of Empress.

But the smitten suitor had made up his mind. The all-important commitment appeared three days later, on January 15, in the form of a short note addressed to María Manuela. "Madame Countess," the emperor wrote, "I have loved your daughter and have wanted to make her my wife for a long time. Consequently, I come today to ask you for her hand, because no one is so capable of making me happy, nor is more worthy to wear a crown, than she." Although Louis Napoleon cautioned that, for the moment, it would be best if the bride-to-be and her mother kept quiet about the engagement to give him a chance to make "our arrangements"—i.e., to get rid of the mistress and figure out how to overcome the storm of resistance that would inevitably accompany the wedding announcement—Eugénie could not stop herself from writing immediately to Paca. "My dear and good sister," she rejoiced, "I want to be the first to announce to you my marriage with the Emperor. He was so noble, so generous with me, he has shown me so much affection, that I am still quite overwhelmed with emotion." Finally, someone who loved *her* to distraction, who was willing to risk everything for *her*, as she had loved and been willing to risk for others in the past—but had been turned down.

And he was as good as his word. A week later, on January 22, Louis Napoleon summoned his ministers, his state councilors, the members of the Senate, and his unhappy but clearly bested relatives to the Palace of the Tuileries. Standing before this august company against the imposing backdrop of the throne room, he formally addressed the nation and defended Eugénie as no one, save perhaps for her dead father, had ever defended her before. "I yield to the wish so often manifested by the country in coming to announce to you my marriage," the emperor began, getting straight to the point. "She who has been the object of my preference is of distinguished birth," he informed his audience. "French in heart, by education, by the recollection of the blood shed by her father in the cause of the empire,...endowed with all the qualities of the mind, she will be the ornament of the throne; in the day of danger she would be one of its courageous supporters...In fine, by her grace and her goodness she will...endeavor to revive in the same position the virtues of the Empress Josephine," he concluded, masterfully evoking the precedent established by his revered uncle, whose first wife (Louis Napoleon's maternal grandmother) had also lacked a royal pedigree.

"His speech produced a magical effect," a grateful Eugénie wrote, thrilled, a few hours later to her sister, "because it spoke to the people and to the heart." She and María Manuela had been whisked off to the Élysée Palace immediately following this public declaration, where they were to stay until the wedding ceremony the following week. "This whole moment is very sad," Eugénie suddenly confessed in the same letter to Paca. "I say goodbye to my family and to my country so that I may dedicate myself exclusively to the man who loved me to the point of raising me to his throne. I love him," she was quick to add loyally. "He is noble of heart and devoted to me, and that is the best guarantee of our happiness... Today for the first time came the cry of 'Long Live the Empress!' God grant it never changes, but adversity will find me firmer and braver than prosperity. Your sister who adores you, Eugénie."

"I love him," she had assured Paca in this letter, and perhaps she even believed it as she was writing it, but there is reason to doubt that hers was an all-consuming passion. Because it turned out that her sister was not the only person Eugénie had reached out to on the day Louis Napoleon's written proposal had arrived. That same evening, while there was yet time to change her mind, she had dashed off a telegram to Pepe, marquis d'Alcañicès, the man who had deceived her so cruelly that she had been reduced to swallowing poison. The emperor had asked her to marry him, Eugénie informed her former beloved. What did he think she should do?

It is difficult to believe that she did not pose this question hoping that competition from one of the most powerful men in Europe would induce Pepe finally to see her worth; that, realizing he could lose her forever, he would write back begging her not to do it, to come home to Madrid instead and marry him.

But Pepe remained true to form. "Accept my most cordial felicitations," he wrote back.

EUGÉNIE, COUNTESS OF TEBA, and Napoleon III, emperor of the French, were married in great state on Sunday, January 30, 1853. All of Paris turned out to watch the wedding procession. They lined the streets in vast crowds from the Palace of the Élysée to the Palace of the Tuileries, and from there to the venerable Cathedral of Notre-Dame, where the ceremony was to take place. They hung out of every window and balcony; even the roofs of the houses were packed with spectators who stood for hours to get a glimpse of the imperial couple. There were almost as many people taking part in the parade to the church as there were who craned their heads to observe it. Delegations from every trade marched, carrying huge flags and banners extolling the emperor. Bevies of young women, dressed in white and bedecked in blossoms, strewed flowers along the route. The inevitable bands of cavalry and soldiers with their splendidly clad officers were also heavily represented, for Louis Napoleon understood the source of his power and did not fail to give the military its due, even on this most romantic occasion.

The bride and groom were driven to the cathedral in a magnificently gilded carriage with large plate-glass windows, long a symbol of French royalty—in fact, the very coach that had once carried Marie Antoinette from Vienna on her wedding journey. It was pulled by eight superb horses, each outfitted in silk and cloth of gold and wearing a tall plume of white ostrich feathers on its head. Trotting alongside were footmen clad in matching livery. "The whole procession was gorgeous and splendid,... as if the dynasty of Louis Napolcon had been as old as the Bourbons," observed one of the many correspondents sent to cover this event (which was, of course, the point).

The same careful attention to detail and grandeur had been lavished on the decorations within the church. The nave was lit up with dozens of chandeliers and hundreds of candles intended to dazzle even the most jaded critic; the columns and altar were draped in yards of rich crimson velvet; gilded eagles, symbol of the empire, were much in evidence, as were flowers, gold stars, and the letter *N*. The ladies-in-waiting wore velvet gowns in an array of colors (María Manuela's was azure) and, like the horses, boasted high plumes of white ostrich feathers on their heads.

The bridal trousseau was extraordinary. There were so many matching sets of necklaces, bracelets, and crowns, some in white pearls and rubies, others in rare black pearls and diamonds, that they could not all be enumerated in the press accounts. Thirty-four morning frocks, in a profusion of colors and silks, many trimmed in Valenciennes lace, had been ordered, with another twenty evening gowns on the way, in embroidered silks and velvets, ornamented in silver and gold, and bedecked still further with a variety of flowers, flounces, and feathers. The extravagance was breathtaking. It made Paca's haul look like a shopgirl's.

Hand in hand, the emperor led his bride down the aisle to the transept, where two thrones had been placed on a raised platform covered with ermine. Eugénie wore a white velvet gown, its bodice glittering in diamonds, with a matching diamond crown from which fell a sweeping veil of delicate, handwoven English lace. She was observed to be "exceedingly pale, but perfectly composed." The ceremony was conducted by the archbishop of Paris. Eugénie took her place on the throne beside Louis Napoleon's for the first time while the rings were exchanged, and then the couple knelt at the altar for the archbishop's blessing. Afterwards, a Te Deum was performed.

She was in it now.

ELISABETH

Kaiser Franz Josef I. und Kaiserin Elisabeth.
Porträts aus dem Jahre 1854.

The engaged couple

8

The Rose of Bavaria

Thou seemest like a flower,
So pure and fair and bright;
A melancholy yearning
Steals o'er me at thy sight.
I fain would lay a blessing
My hands upon thy hair
Imploring God to keep thee
So bright, and pure, and fair.

—Heinrich Heine

ON AUGUST 31, 1853, exactly seven months after Eugénie's magnificent wedding, fifteen-year-old Elisabeth kissed Franz Joseph goodbye at Ischl and got into a carriage with her mother for the journey back to Possi. Still dazed by her whirlwind courtship, Sisi was happy to be going home, away from all the attention (although she clearly missed her handsome imperial fiancé and longed to be with him again). There are no records of Duchess Ludovika's state of mind during this extended coach ride back to Bavaria, but her degree of anxiety may perhaps be judged by the numerous immutable directives issued to her by Archduchess Sophia just prior to the family's departure. Sisi's marriage would take place in Vienna in the spring, Elisabeth's future mother-in-law had informed her sister firmly. In the interim, the bride would have to learn both French and Italian, and improve her dancing. Ludovika would also have to arrange for an appropriate trousseau. Lists of the exact items required would be forthcoming. Additionally, the bride-to-be must be educated in court protocol and master the various forms of address used by the imperial family to acknowledge the myriad archdukes, duchesses, barons, ambassadors, and other classes of underlings with whom Sisi, as Franz Joseph's wife, would be required to interact. Unspoken but nonetheless manifest in these instructions was the archduchess's expectation that by the time Elisabeth stepped off the imperial steamboat that would ferry her to Austria early the following year, she would look and behave like an empress. And Sophia meant an empress with clean white teeth.

Duchess Ludovika knew to take her lofty sister's injunctions seriously. Upon Sisi's return to Possi, she was met with a barrage of lessons conducted not by her governess, but rather by professors from the University of Munich. Any portion of her day not given over to education was swallowed up by dental hygiene and the endless fittings necessary to produce the mountain of apparel insisted upon by the Viennese court. The lists that arrived by imperial courier called for a minimum of fifty-four separate garments, including ball gowns, evening wear, formal silk dresses, and cotton day frocks, each embellished with flounces, flowers, and ribbons, and all accessorized with either hats or hair ornaments. Protocol also stipulated dozens of sets of silk undergarments, gloves, and over a hundred pairs of shoes.

For Elisabeth, who prior to her engagement had spent her life rolling out of bed, feeding her numerous pets, and then ducking away as much as possible to practice her riding or go swimming or fishing with Gackel, her younger brother, all of this enforced inactivity — the need to sit or stand still for long periods while repeating French phrases or being measured by one of the army of local seamstresses recruited by Duchess Ludovika — was difficult. Moreover, Sisi was unaccustomed to concentrating on subjects in which she was not particularly interested. "Unfortunately, my children have no facility in learning foreign languages," Duchess Ludovika fretted in a letter to her sister in Saxony.★

The one highlight of Elisabeth's new, accelerated educational program was the result of her father's intervention. Among Duke Max's broad Munich literary acquaintance was a rather down-on-his-luck Hungarian named Johann Mailáth. Formerly a resident of Vienna, Mailáth had decamped for Bavaria soon after the imposition of martial law and was currently attempting to scrape by while researching the origins of local folk tales for a new book. But Duke Max was aware that the émigré author was best known for his previous work, *History of the Austrian Empire,* a five-volume exploration of the Habsburg dynasty, and it was for his expertise in this area that Sisi's father solicited Mailáth's services, entreating the scholar to teach his daughter a little bit about the background of the court in which she was soon to find herself.

It was an inspired choice. Much like Stendhal with Eugénie, Mailáth was first and foremost a storyteller, and he saw history as a thrilling ride through the past. There is no record of the specific episodes he used to instruct his teenaged pupil, but it seems he was careful to avoid any mention of present-day conditions, as Sisi was unaware at the time of her marriage of the repressive military autocracy established by her husband and his mother. It is, however, highly likely that at least some of the material for these sessions came from the final volume of Mailáth's massive study, published only three years earlier, in which the author had covered the dramatic events of the previous century, when the venerated Maria Theresa had reigned. It would have been negligent of him *not* to teach a future empress the story of so revered a past one.

And so Sisi very likely listened as Mailáth described how, as a young mother, Maria Theresa was attacked without warning by the wily king of Prussia, Frederick the Great, who invaded Silesia almost as soon as she

---

★ Actually, this was not true. Both Sisi and Nene had mastered English, and often used it as a secret language when they didn't want other people to understand what they were saying.

had ascended her throne. As we know also that Elisabeth's admiration for Hungary was kindled by this professor, he surely stressed the large role his countrymen had played in rescuing the imperial court at this critical moment. In his book, Mailáth described the powerful scene in which Maria Theresa took her infant son, the future emperor Joseph II, into her arms and raised him up before the entire Hungarian Diet as a symbol of her commitment to the kingdom, until they roared their approval and voted her the army she needed to defend herself. Whatever content Mailáth chose to communicate, the material was so compelling that in no time at all, he had half the family listening in on his lectures.

It was thus only by the barest serendipity that Elisabeth was exposed to Hungarian history in a way that moved her. A little over a year later, cold, hunger, and poverty would force Johann Mailáth, together with his adult daughter, who served as his research assistant and secretary, to drown themselves in Lake Starnberg, on whose shores Sisi's beloved Possi also stood. The chronicler never knew the service he had done his country by capturing his imperial pupil's imagination, for by her own admission, Elisabeth never forgot those stories of the brave Hungarians who saved the empire.

WHILE SISI ABSORBED THE LESSONS of history and struggled to learn how to make basic conversation with a baroness in French and a duke in Italian, an elated Franz Joseph returned to Vienna with his mother. The infatuated bridegroom no sooner arrived than he wanted to turn around again. "I cannot stop thinking about her," he confessed to Archduchess Sophia.

But of course he couldn't go back, at least not right away; other issues demanded his attention. There was, for example, a great deal to do to prepare for the wedding. Mindful of the resentment still harbored by the population for the brutal military takeover of 1848, the imperial family deliberately promoted the marriage as a new beginning for the monarchy, a way of showcasing the emperor's softer, more human side. Along these lines, even before he left Ischl, Franz Joseph had signed a decree freeing Vienna and Prague from the military rule under which the two cities had suffered for the past five years. "The abolition of the state of siege," observed the *Times* correspondent in Vienna, "may be considered a sure indication that the highest authority in the empire will very soon order milder measures to be employed... The state of public feeling in Vienna was such that it would be good policy to bury the past in oblivion."

The anticipation of an opulent wedding celebration was also welcomed by the imperial court as a distraction from the hardships of daily life, of which there were many. The royal treasury was hopelessly overloaded with debt, commerce was depressed, and scarcity and destitution were rampant. It is a sad economic truth that having to maintain hundreds of thousands of soldiers to subdue a hostile citizenry over a vast territory stretching from Venice to Hungary can have a deleterious effect on cash flow. Franz Joseph really had no choice but to reduce his military presence, and his upcoming marriage to Sisi allowed the court to frame the retrenchment as a further benefit of the storybook imperial romance.

It was therefore extremely inconvenient of the Russian tsar to choose this exact moment to invade Crimea. Even more inopportune was Nicholas's natural expectation that Franz Joseph, who had become so cozy with Nicholas that he called him "Thee, dear friend," in his letters, would assist him in this unprovoked aggression against Turkey, as reciprocity for the tsar's previous intervention in Hungary.

Not that Nicholas hadn't made it perfectly clear in the months leading up to Franz Joseph's engagement what he intended to do, and what he expected from Austria. As early as July 1853, the tsar had been quite open about his desire to wrest territory from Turkey, and he had even offered to compensate Franz Joseph for his participation. "Perhaps Constantinople might be made a free city, without territorial rights; the Dardanelles being held by Thee, the Bosphorus by us," he had dangled as one possible outcome of a successful collaboration.*

---

* The Dardanelles and the Bosphorus were the two most strategic waterways in Turkey because it was only by navigating through both of these narrow straits that a ship from the Black Sea, where Crimea was located, could reach the Mediterranean. So this was quite a generous offer on Nicholas's part, and implied great trust in Franz Joseph's friendship.

Tempting as this proposition was, Franz Joseph had no desire to join Russia in a war against Turkey. It wasn't just that he didn't have the money to do it. He didn't *want* to acquire more territory to the east, where large numbers of foreign-speaking, non-Catholic Turks and Romanians lived. The emperor's focus was on maintaining his unruly Italian possessions, and securing imperial leadership of Germany, which was currently being contested by Prussia. He knew that if he transferred soldiers away from Venice to help the tsar in Crimea, his Italian subjects might take advantage of their absence to rebel. And if he took troops from Hungary and brought them down to Venice to put out the Italian rebellion, his Hungarian subjects might revolt. And while he was busy putting out all of these fires to the south and east, the Prussians might easily go behind his back and expand into Germany, and he would have to start all over again, this time redeploying an army to the west. So, as fond as he was of the tsar, he was going to have to decline this kind offer. To blunt the pain of his refusal, Franz Joseph resolved instead to offer his services to mediate a peaceful solution to Nicholas's disagreement with Turkey. Pleased with this clever compromise, he traveled to Olmütz on September 24, 1853, to meet personally with the tsar to inform him of his decision.

And it all worked out beautifully, just the way he had thought it would. Nicholas was disappointed at first but in the end he accepted that Franz Joseph would remain neutral and attempt to arbitrate. The tsar further pledged that under no circumstances would Russian troops ever cross the Danube, the navigation of which was vital to Austrian interests. Franz Joseph, having secured the assurances he had been looking for, was so confident that his side of the Crimean crisis had been defused that he continued with his planned cost-cutting and ordered a further reduction of the imperial forces immediately following this meeting. He also rewarded himself by making a flying visit to Possi to see Sisi, traveling straight through for nearly two days to arrive on October 11.

There he found his bride-to-be even more adorable than he remembered her. They went for long rides, just the two of them, where

Elisabeth, joyful in her own surroundings, showed off her expertise. Although it is clear from his letters back to Vienna that he had been instructed by Archduchess Sophia to try to curtail this aspect of his fiancée's routine, even someone of Franz Joseph's limited imagination could see, from how exceptional she was on horseback and how much she loved the sport, that this prohibition was likely to fail. "As you advised me, I begged my Mama-in-law not to let Sisi ride too much; but I believe that will be hard to enforce, since Sisi is unwilling to give it up," he noted in a letter dated October 17, 1853. To compensate for Elisabeth's stubbornness in this one area, Franz Joseph made haste to reassure his mother that Sisi was otherwise taking all of her suggestions to heart. Her teeth, for example, he reported enthusiastically, were now beautifully white.*

In his euphoria at being with her again, even her noisy, somewhat disorganized family appeared charming—at first. Helene had recovered her equilibrium and, along with everyone else, welcomed him warmly into the household.† After a few days at Possi, the entire clan went back to Munich for a series of court entertainments, which included a performance at the theater and a palace ball. Elisabeth, who was used to spending her winters roaming around the capital in complete anonymity, was so embarrassed by the ovation she inspired when she and the emperor arrived at the opera that she shrank back into the box and hid herself. But none of this mattered to Franz Joseph. "I love Sisi more every day," he insisted jubilantly in a letter home to his mother, "and feel surer than ever that no woman could suit me as well as she does."

This happy time was abruptly cut short, however, by urgent dispatches from Vienna. Turkey had declared war on Russia, and there were skirmishes between the two hostile armies. As a result, the

---

* The negative effects of all this harping on a perceived flaw in a sensitive teenaged girl was that, *for the rest of her life,* Elisabeth smiled with her lips closed, and mumbled and cupped her hand over her mouth when she spoke, so that no one could see her teeth.

† Observing the pressures loaded on Elisabeth, Helene might well have considered herself fortunate to be out of it. Whatever her reasoning, she never blamed Sisi for the rejection she suffered, and she remained staunchly loyal to her sister for the rest of her life.

conflict had now expanded to include Britain and France, who, determined to keep the tsar from challenging their naval superiority in the Mediterranean, had sent a joint fleet to defend those two critical waterways, the Dardanelles and the Bosphorus. Franz Joseph needed to get going on his peace negotiations.

Before he left, though, he sat Sisi down and spoke seriously to her. The natural mannerisms and easygoing habits displayed by her family would not do at the imperial court, he cautioned. Elisabeth had erred, for example, when, in a recent thank-you note to Archduchess Sophia, she addressed her future mother-in-law familiarly, as she did her parents and other close relatives. Even he, the emperor, used formal grammar when speaking or writing to his mother. And lateness or missing appointments was not tolerated in Vienna as it was at Possi. Already, the trousseau was behind schedule. "Nor do I think it is going to be very pretty," he sniffed in an aside to his mother (although he kept that part to himself with his fiancée).

Elisabeth agreed to everything, particularly after Franz Joseph tenderly emphasized how their love for each other would allow them to face these sometimes tiresome duties together. But at fifteen she could not really have understood the suffocating rigidity to which she was committing herself. It's one thing to be warned in general terms about the demands of protocol and etiquette, quite another to experience them daily with no possibility of reprieve. The time she had spent at Ischl, when everyone had been on holiday and the whole town had been swept up in the ebullient chaos of the emperor's love, was her only touchstone to his family's behavior. She could not have known that this emotional period was in no way reflective of the imperial court's ordinary demeanor.

After this little talk, Sisi redoubled her efforts to comply with Franz Joseph's wishes. She stood without complaint or too much fidgeting for the hours of fittings with the dressmakers and practiced protocol by making dreary formal visits with her mother to the royal palace in Munich, where she struggled to exchange meaningless pleasantries with the diplomatic corps. By the time Franz Joseph returned to

Bavaria two months later, just in time for her sixteenth birthday on Christmas Eve, he was able to affirm to his mother that Sisi had made progress and was now "learning many new and different things."

It was another affectionate meeting, greatly enhanced by the wonderful presents the ardent emperor showered on his beloved. Despite the many demands on his time, Franz Joseph had clearly given great care and thought to these gifts. Elisabeth received a sparkling bracelet studded with precious gems and inset with a miniature of her devoted fiancé; a large diamond brooch fashioned to resemble a spray of flowers; a gorgeous winter cloak of deep-blue velvet lined in sable with a matching sable muff; and, from Archduchess Sophia, a bouquet of fresh-cut roses, messengered all the way from the imperial greenhouses of Vienna, which miraculously arrived in full bloom. By this time, however, Franz Joseph knew enough to also bring along an addition to his bride-to-be's menagerie—in this case, an exotic parrot able to squawk a few phrases. Sisi's delight in this bird immediately eclipsed the reception she had given the jewelry, the flowers, and the cloak.

But this gladsome holiday, too, was cut short by the appearance of vexing dispatches. Perplexingly, the emperor's mediating strategy was not getting much traction. While the negotiations were proceeding, Russian troops had destroyed an entire squadron of the Turkish fleet, mercilessly slaughtering the thousands of sailors on board. This appalling massacre, which caused outrage across Europe, was an indication that Nicholas was perhaps not taking the peace initiative as seriously as he had previously implied he would. In fact, by the time the beleaguered bridegroom returned to Munich on March 15, 1854, for one last sojourn with Sisi's family before the wedding, the tsar's forces had crossed the Danube and invaded Turkey; Britain and France had broken off negotiations and were on the brink of declaring war; and Franz Joseph had been forced to recall all the soldiers he had formerly furloughed to save money.

But the emperor did not allow the threat of a cascading European conflict to mar his enjoyment of this final premarital visit with his betrothed. On this occasion, there was only time for a quick outing to

Possi. So buoyant were his spirits, so complete his happiness in his future wife's company, that Franz Joseph, not a man ordinarily given to eloquence, waxed almost poetic in his description of this romantic excursion. "It was a wonderful sunny day," he gushed in the inevitable letter home to his parent. "The snow-covered mountains reflected in the deep blue lake looked near enough for us to be on their slopes, and clouds of wild geese were flying over the water."

But for Elisabeth, this period leading up to her marriage was defined by far more mixed emotions. When her younger sister Marie noted with satisfaction that, once Sisi was gone, she had obtained permission to move into her old bedroom, the bride-to-be burst into tears. Marie was taken aback. "But aren't you happy you are going to be an Empress?" the twelve-year-old had asked incredulously. It wasn't that Elisabeth didn't love Franz Joseph—when she was with him, she felt she did—but she was bereft at the idea of leaving her family, pets, and Possi, and feared the foreignness of the imperial court. "If only he were a tailor," she sighed.

This was the situation as the day of her departure drew nearer and nearer, until at last it arrived. On April 20, 1854, the streets in front of the family's Munich residence were stuffed with pedestrians eager for a glimpse of the future empress as she left the city to begin the first stage of a three-day trip to Vienna. In a sign of her soon-to-be vastly superior rank, both kings of Bavaria, the reigning Maximilian II and the deposed Ludwig I (who had gotten over his infatuation with Lola Montez sufficiently to begin pestering another beautiful, if unwilling, young woman with his attentions and treacly lovesick poetry), came to Duke Max's house to see Elisabeth off, rather than having her stop off at the royal palace on her way out of town, as would have been the case if she had been marrying almost anyone else. The tearful bride, accompanied by her family, climbed into one of the carriages waiting to take them to the Danube town of Straubing, ninety miles north of Munich, where they would transfer to a steamboat for the rest of the journey. So resounding was the cry that greeted her appearance that Sisi spontaneously stood up in her coach to acknowledge the heartfelt felicitations, waving to the crowds of well-wishers as she passed, every inch the princess they wanted her to be.

UNLIKE EUGÉNIE'S WEDDING, which for all its splendor had occurred so quickly after the announcement of her engagement that there was a whiff of the dance hall, rather than the throne room, about it—"the Montijo marriage sets me agreeably at rest because no European princely house need unite itself with the parvenue," sneered Wilhelm, younger brother of the king of Prussia, when he was told of it—Elisabeth's nuptials unfolded with a stately dignity suitable to a celestial visitation. By spring, her sweetly youthful likeness was everywhere—hanging in the shop windows, painted on decorative plates and cups, and fashioned into delicate miniature porcelain figurines that were hawked throughout the capital. A drumroll of carefully choreographed acts of imperial benevolence sounded in the days preceding the bride's arrival. On April 9, 1854, Franz Joseph signed an order finally dispensing with martial law in the remaining territories of Hungary, Kraków, and Venetia, "a popular act, which...eloquently appeals to the lively sympathies and warm affections of a people...who, convinced of the error of their ways, have been happily brought back to the fold of their legitimate and liege shepherd," piously rejoiced the Vienna *Gazette,* the official publication of the imperial court. This decision was followed soon thereafter by a grant of amnesty to political prisoners, the cancellation throughout the empire of all outstanding criminal prosecutions for treason, and the distribution of 200,000 florins to the poor to help mitigate the effects of the economic downturn, which were unfortunately exacerbated by the increased expenses associated with the wedding and the rapidly deteriorating foreign situation.

This none-too-subtle campaign had an unintended effect. By associating these acts of compassion so closely with his upcoming marriage, Sophia and Franz Joseph immediately conditioned the population, particularly the lower classes, to attribute the improvements in their lives to Elisabeth's influence rather than crediting the emperor with their genesis. *She* was assumed to be their guardian angel, not him.

Consequently, the citizenry mobbed the banks of the Danube all along her route — tens of thousands of people, all straining to get a glimpse of their good-fairy future empress. From Munich, the family had traveled to Passau, on the border with Austria, and from there to Linz, only a day's journey away from Vienna on the powerful imperial steamship that the emperor had sent to ferry his bride to the capital. At every stop, there were formal receptions and public celebrations. Sisi had to show herself to the crowds, meet all the local officials, review parades, accept mountains of bouquets from little girls in white dresses (as part of the publicity associated with her marriage, Elisabeth had been described in popular verse as the "Rose of Bavaria"), and listen to regional military bands belt out the Austrian national anthem, which had been rewritten specifically to include a stanza about her.

Sisi, who hated being the center of attention — "on show like a freak in the circus," was the way she bitterly described these appearances to her mother — was thus already under significant strain before she even set foot in the capital. Franz Joseph, on the other hand, was so excited for his bride's arrival that he impetuously rushed to Linz the night before her official entry into Vienna to be near her. The emperor allowed himself this small indulgence because just the day before, on April 20, 1854, he'd received some very good news: at the prodding of his mother and her sister Elise, the queen of Prussia, his uncle King Frederick William IV had signed a defensive treaty with Austria whereby the Prussians had committed themselves to sending an army to help Franz Joseph if any of his property was attacked, and vice versa. It's true that the wording of this agreement was a little vague, but the pact allowed the imperial court to trumpet a comforting, much-needed diplomatic success to coincide with the wedding, which had clearly been his mother's and his aunt's fond intention.

This moment of spontaneity was fleeting, however. There was barely time for the emperor to accompany the bride and her family to the evening's planned festivities—a local theatrical performance, followed by fireworks—before he had to dash back to Vienna to be there in time to take part in the official welcoming ceremony. Still, this tender gesture could not have helped but buoy Sisi, as did her discovery the next morning that the deck of the palatial steamboat sent to fetch her for the final leg of her journey had, on her future husband's order, been so loaded with roses that the ship resembled a gigantic floating arbor.

No other vessel was allowed on the Danube between Linz and Vienna on that memorable day. Elisabeth stood for hours in the sun and a strong wind, gamely smiling and waving to the throngs gathered along the shores at each town along her route. At last, around 4 p.m., to the competing cacophony created by the sounding of a thunderous cannon salute, the clanging of every church bell in the capital, and the blaring of the inevitable military bands, the great ship docked at Nussdorf, about six miles from the center of the city.

Here, too, the port was jammed with spectators, the wealthier flocking in carriages, the poorer on foot. They had been streaming in for hours, filling the cobblestone streets and taking up posts all along the way to Schönbrunn Palace, where it was known that Sisi would stay the night. They crowded on flag-draped terraces and cheered through upper-story windows thrown open to reveal vases of roses in Elisabeth's honor and celebratory plaster busts of the imperial couple. The landing dock itself was reserved for the official welcoming party. "The preparations for her reception today at Nussdorf are made upon a truly magnificent scale," admitted the correspondent for the *Morning Chronicle*.

At least this time, she did not have to face the multitudes alone. The steamship no sooner slid into the pier than Franz Joseph was aboard. In a romantic gesture that won the full-throated approval of all who gazed on the charming scene, he swept Sisi (who wore an appropriately rose-colored, diaphanous silk gown, matched with a small bonnet and white lace mantilla) into his arms and kissed her as passionately as though he had not seen her in months.

There followed a rigid hierarchy of greetings, beginning with

Archduchess Sophia and the other members of the extended imperial family; Elisabeth's formal disembarkation down the gangplank, clutching the emperor's arm and smiling and waving as the legions roared and the bands played; and a long, triumphal six-mile procession to Schönbrunn Palace, where she rode, not with her future husband in the lead carriage, but rather in the second coach with his mother.

It was only when the procession finally drew up beside the sprawling, ornate château and she saw the crowds gathered in the gardens as well as the crush of high aristocrats and court officials waiting in the great hall and along the staircase to greet her, that an already exhausted Sisi likely realized that the day's ordeal was far from over. She had to stand between her future husband and mother-in-law and be introduced to all these people, one by one, a slowly snaking reception line that took hours; to publicly survey the wedding gifts, which included, from a beaming Franz Joseph, yet another dazzling emerald-and-diamond tiara, complete with a matching bejeweled waist-cinch, called a "corsage" (which, by the time it was presented, Elisabeth was far too tired to appreciate); to make a generous appearance on the terrace overlooking the packed public gardens and acknowledge the hundreds of Viennese who wished to see her but were not of sufficient rank to merit entry into the palace; and finally to keep up a brave face while trying, as the guest of honor and center of all eyes, to remember who everyone was at a formal state dinner.

Teenaged girls, as a rule, are not known for their forbearance, and Sisi was no exception. When she awoke the next morning in her unfamiliar bedroom at Schönbrunn and was handed a thick schedule by her new Mistress of the Household, Countess Esterházy, a grim-faced, fifty-six-year-old scold appointed by Archduchess Sophia to mold Elisabeth into a docile empress, and realized that she was expected to spend her entire day at formal receptions, with no exercise or fresh air, and without ever once being alone with her future husband, or being alone at all, for that matter, she began to sob. Her mother had to be called in to quiet her, but that afternoon, when she finally emerged, she wept all the way to the Hofburg Palace, as could be clearly seen through the windows of the glass coronation carriage in which she was conveyed.

But of course there was no getting out of it now. And Franz Joseph reassured her that the trying public ceremonies would be over shortly, and then it would be just the two of them. "We shall soon forget all about it at beautiful Laxenburg," he soothed her, referring to the imperial estate just outside Vienna where they would spend their honeymoon.

And so the next morning, April 24, 1854, Elisabeth woke up at the Hofburg Palace and prepared to become empress of Austria. At 10 a.m., the bells in every church in Vienna rang out, and special prayer services were offered for the bride and groom; at the same time, Sisi attended a private mass in company with Franz Joseph's family and her own in the ancient Hofburg chapel. She then retired to begin the long hours of dressing for the nuptial ceremony, which was to be held next door at the venerable Church of the Augustinians, traditional site of imperial marriages. Maria Theresa herself, among many other illustrious Habsburg ancestors, had been wed at this same altar.

The first guests began arriving at 6:30 p.m., and were immediately dazzled by the palace's high, vaulted interior, which had been transformed for the occasion by over 100 chandeliers of varying sizes, containing some 10,000 candles in all. "The brilliancy of the illumination surpasses all description," marveled a correspondent. At seven o'clock, the wedding procession left the Hofburg for the short journey to the sanctuary. First came the numerous officers of the court, the state councilors, and the great noblemen. They were quickly followed by the emperor's brothers, and then finally Franz Joseph, alone and on horseback, dressed in the formal white uniform of a military field commander. Behind the groom rolled the carriage bearing Archduchess Sophia, Duchess Ludovika, and the bride. Elisabeth's dress was of shimmering white silk, richly embroidered in gold and silver. The bodice was adorned with white roses, and on her head was perched her mother-in-law's diamond-and-opal wedding crown, draped in a veil of gold lace. Her sisters' carriages brought up the rear with those of the imperial ladies-in-waiting.

The archbishop of Vienna conducted the proceedings. It was remarked that the bride was composed but very pale and spoke so softly when it was time for her responses that she could not be heard. After the rings were exchanged, the nuptial couple knelt before a throne that had been mounted on one side of the altar and bowed their heads in prayer. A Te Deum was sung and a burst of cannon fire signaled the end of the service to the waiting city. It was done.

EUGÉNIE

Eugénie as a young bride

9

Making France Great Again

Policy consists in watching for an opportunity.

—Napoleon III

WHILE ELISABETH STOOD TREMULOUSLY AT THE ALTAR, linking her fate with that of one of the most ancient and exalted ruling dynasties in Europe, Eugénie and her husband, Louis Napoleon, were in the process of bursting onto the world stage like a pair of uninvited dinner guests who somehow manage to take over the whole party.

The new empress of the French had spent her wedding night with her husband at the Villeneuve-l'Étang, a charming garden residence on the grounds of the Château de Saint-Cloud. The emperor often used this romantic country villa as an escape from the cold formalities of palace life.* Although gossip would later taunt Eugénie with accusations of frigidity, it is interesting to note that this supposed defect was nowhere in evidence at the start of their union. On the contrary, Louis Napoleon remained every bit as infatuated with his bride after the marriage had been consummated as he was before. His dentist, Dr. Thomas Evans, an expatriate American who tended to the imperial court, visited the couple upon their return to Paris just a week after the

---

* This was *not* the same little house he had employed the first time he invited Eugénie and her mother to Saint-Cloud, when he had so crassly propositioned her. Luckily, Napoleon III had enough domiciles available to avoid just this sort of awkwardness.

wedding (Eugénie had a toothache) and reported "the strong and romantic attachment of the Emperor to his lovely wife." After "coming upstairs from his cabinet several times to inquire how she was feeling," Dr. Evans continued, Louis Napoleon impulsively presented Eugénie with "a magnificent string of pearls, which he placed around her neck." Although he had been intending to save the gift for a special occasion, "touched by a feeling of love and compassion, his Majesty had been unable to keep his secret from her any longer," the dentist observed.

The newlyweds returned to Paris after only a week, not because they were tired of each other's company but rather because they were excited to begin their reign together. Louis Napoleon had large schemes for France. He was committed to establishing a new, Second Empire based on the principles of the first Napoleon's vision, but with a distinctly modern twist.

Advancements in industry and science were proceeding at a breakneck pace; humanity had never experienced anything like this sort of progress all at once before. Railroads had the potential to move people and goods with a rapidity that was surpassed only by the dizzying speed at which information could suddenly be transmitted by telegraph. Because he had been forced into exile (or to run for his life) for so many years, Louis Napoleon was extremely well traveled. He had seen firsthand the commercial and technological improvements made by other countries, and he recognized that whoever took the lead in the race to modernize would have an advantage that could be used for political ends. He was determined that France win this competition, and he intended to use the power that came with the resulting prosperity not only to improve the lives of his subjects but also to return the empire to the heady days of world dominance that it had enjoyed during his uncle's tenure.

Louis Napoleon could not have chosen a life partner more thoroughly in accord with these laudable ambitions, or more eager to be of assistance in bringing them to fruition. "I have an immense desire to help those unhappy classes who are deprived of everything, even of work...to serve as a mediator between those who suffer, and the one man who can remedy that suffering," she declared passionately in a letter to Paca on the eve of her wedding. "I thank God for having placed in my path a heart as noble and devoted as that of the Emperor." She was in earnest: her first official act was to politely decline a wedding gift of jewelry worth 600,000 francs from local functionaries, tactfully requesting that the funds be used instead to help the poor. "Monsieur Le Préfet," she wrote. "I have been moved greatly by hearing of the generous decision which the Municipal Council of Paris has taken," she began. "Nevertheless, it would pain me to think that the first public document to which my name is attached...should record a considerable expense for the city of Paris...You will make me happier by using for charitable purposes the sum that you have appropriated for the purchasing of the diamond set," she demurred gently but firmly.

The disadvantaged and impoverished among her subjects were not the only people whose welfare Eugénie was determined to champion. Taking to heart the philosopher Charles Fourier's maxim that social progress could not be achieved in the absence of a corresponding improvement in feminine independence, she was also fervently devoted to broadening the career opportunities available to women, and to recognizing their achievements. "What woman wants, God wants," she told Paca. Accordingly, the Municipal Council of Paris took the 600,000 francs originally earmarked for jewels and instead established a vocational school for 300 underprivileged girls, so that upon graduation they would have the skills necessary to obtain employment and support themselves. The empress took this institution under her protection; it was one of many charities to which she lent her support.★

But these initiatives were only a small component of the grand scheme. To return France to its intrinsic position of dominance after so many

---

★ Eugénie would eventually augment her household to include a full-time staff whose job it was to "inquire into the condition of the poor and suffering, and to report the result of their investigations personally," as recorded by Dr. Evans. "Frequently, and especially in winter,...the Empress left her palace *incognito*, accompanied by one faithful attendant only, to visit the dwellings where she had been informed there was destitution and distress," the dentist noted.

years of stagnation would require bold action on many fronts. The other European heads of state, suspicious of the emperor's motives, were going to have to *want* French friendship, alliance, and commerce. This meant that their citizens were going to have to clamor for imperial goods, expertise, and culture. Both emperor and empress understood that people must be attracted irresistibly to France the way they were drawn naturally to the seaside in summer.

And Louis Napoleon had thought of just the way to do it: remake Paris. Like a master gardener pruning away withered blossoms and dead branches to allow the beauty below the rot to flourish, the emperor was determined to tear down the filthy, cramped, centuries-old buildings at the center of the city and widen the dank, narrow, cobblestone passageways, so habitually clogged with garbage and sewage. An irrigation system including state-of-the-art drainage and water pipes could then be installed to chase away any lingering effects of these evil-smelling slums. In their place would rise long, elegant avenues and clean, sunlit, public parks, an aesthetically pleasing prospect that had the additional advantage of making it much more difficult for revolutionary mobs and other bothersome troublemakers to blockade the streets and rain bullets and paving stones down on the heads of the imperial troops sent to vanquish them. ("Barricades will be impossible—and without barricades disturbances [i.e. riots and protests] will cease," explained Baron Heeckeren, a Dutch financier who had been a childhood friend of Napoleon III and frequently advised him on money matters.) Thus would the emperor "make of Paris the supreme city of the world, the capital of Europe, beautiful and magnificent beyond all reach of rivalry...'That,' said Napoleon to me, 'is my plan,'" the baron revealed.

Eugénie did not have to be told what her role in all of this would be. It wasn't enough to enhance the capital architecturally. The French empire under the first Napoleon had reveled in displays of wealth and grandeur, but subsequent rulers, particularly Louis Philippe, the citizen king, fearful of provoking the ire of the unruly lower classes, had cautiously hewn to revolutionary principles and deliberately projected a humble, middle-class image. Eugénie's task as empress was to obliterate this timid demeanor by returning the imperial court to its blazing former brilliance, enticing others to emulate her, and evoking the envy of Europe.

This responsibility must have been much on her mind, because on the very first day of her marriage, immediately following her wedding night, she asked Louis Napoleon to drive her to Versailles so she could visit the Petit Trianon, private home of the beautiful, tragic Marie Antoinette.

Although the doomed queen of France was so vilified during the Revolution that today her name is synonymous with outrageous profligacy and heartless self-absorption, throughout the centuries there has always been a stalwart cadre of partisans, predominantly women, who identified with and defended her. Eugénie was one of these. (She spoke often of Marie Antoinette, especially "of the Queen's sad fate," Dr. Evans reported.) The empress, who knew herself to be treading a similarly dangerous path, saw the executed sovereign not as an agent of her own destruction, but rather as one of the first victims of the Terror, a martyr to the sort of violent mob rule from which Eugénie's strong, noble husband, Louis Napoleon, had just rescued France.

But unlike the legions of Marie Antoinette fans who came after her, Eugénie was in a position to act on her fixation, and she did so by salvaging as much as she could of the ill-fated queen's luster. Every stick of furniture, every knickknack, portrait, article of clothing, or strand of jewelry that she could identify from the dead queen's possessions, was authenticated and purchased. She rounded up so many of Marie Antoinette's belongings that she had to set up a gallery, the Musée des Souvenirs, to house her collection. Much of what survives of the queen's effects today is due to Eugénie's efforts.

The empress also clearly took inspiration from her predecessor's daring aesthetic. Eugénie knew that before Marie Antoinette's arrival, the French court at Versailles had become so fusty that everyone still followed the same customs and styles that had been prevalent a half century earlier. Marie Antoinette's refusal to dress as her grandmother had, and her determination to create her own style, had broken the iron hold of the past on the court, and turned the queen into an icon whose glamour was replicated all over Europe. This lesson was not lost on Eugénie. "The Empress, ever since her marriage, has been, and is still, the leader of fashion," Baron Heeckeren observed flatly.

And so, between her fascination with the beautiful, beheaded queen and the long years she had spent being dragged across the continent by her mother to every swank dinner party and salon that would have them, Eugénie was as prepared to step into the role of empress as if she had been born to it. Although she would no longer have María Manuela's immediate guidance — Louis Napoleon, who had already had enough of the countess of Montijo's enforced company during the courtship, settled a handsome sum on the older woman on the condition that she return to Spain — Eugénie no longer really needed it. She was already perfectly proficient at charming ambassadors, be it in French, Spanish, or English, and at mingling graciously with the various representatives of high society at crowded receptions. "I have two incurable defects," María Manuela announced dramatically to Mérimée upon hearing of Napoleon III's well-compensated ultimatum. "I am a foreigner and a mother-in-law." Mérimée was consoling. "What a dreadful thing it must be to have daughters and to see them married!" he commiserated. However, "now that you have done your duty as a mother (and none can deny that you have effected brilliant matches for your daughters) you must begin to live for yourself, and try to cultivate a little selfishness," he counseled.★

But other than dismissing her mother, Louis Napoleon did not attempt to interfere with his wife's preferences. If anything, he went out of his way to please her, as when he appointed Mérimée a member

---

★ Notwithstanding the prickly nature of their relationship, Eugénie expressed sympathy for her parent's exile. "I believe that despite the miserable situation in which we lived, due to the incompatibility of our characters, she will now be very lonely and sad," she wrote to Paca on February 22, 1853. "Our house in Madrid is full of reminders of me and from afar the faults will disappear, leaving only the good memories." She didn't have to worry; María Manuela took Mérimée's advice and resumed her previous role as a society hostess in Madrid, where, as she was the matriarch of a family that now included both the French empress and the wealthy duchess of Alba, invitations to her balls and salons were even more sought after than before.

of the French Senate. "I am a little dazed, to tell the truth," the author confided in a letter to María Manuela. "The Empress kissed her husband most affectionately when it was announced." In the same manner, Eugénie sought to reward those who remained loyal to her husband and his family. The head of her household, an elegant older woman chosen to lend dignity to the court, was the daughter-in-law of one of Napoleon I's most decorated generals. Another of Eugénie's ladies-in-waiting was married to the emperor's chamberlain, who was himself descended from a member of the great Corsican's devoted inner circle. But the empress was also able to surround herself with trusted and diverting attendants, like a Spanish countess who had been a close friend of hers and Paca's since childhood; and even a new acquaintance, a young American heiress married to a French baron, who was much admired for her superb horsemanship, making her a welcome addition at Eugénie's side during the hunting season.

The establishment of the empress's household coincided with the launch of a sweeping imperial charm offensive, in which the Parisian upper classes were treated to the kind of social whirl that had not been experienced in France for over a generation. There were official court galas with guest lists in the thousands—formal balls at which Eugénie presided, her shoulders bared above a voluminous swirl of tulle or silk, a diamond tiara in her hair; elaborate costume parties; and amusing masked fêtes. Interspersed with these were the empress's regular Monday evening receptions, where dinner and music or dancing were provided for a select company of 500 or so close friends and officials, as well as bucolic weekend jaunts to the nearby Château de Saint-Cloud. In the spring, the court moved to Fontainebleau for stag hunting and fireworks followed by seaside excursions to Biarritz, Eugénie's favorite summer resort. Fall found the imperial couple back in Paris before heading out to Compiègne for the annual November hunting excursion with its weeks-long recreation, attended by a rotating roster of some sixty houseguests. Finally came the return to Paris for the winter holiday festivities. "Social entertainments have gone on literally without a pause," attested the Dutch banker with awe.

And right from the beginning, Eugénie was the driving force behind the spectacle. "That young Empress, let us speak of her, for already she is playing a great part," observed the celebrated author and playwright George Sand (the pen name of Aurore Dupin, a bisexual French-woman), whose novel *Mauprat* was being staged in Paris that year.★ "She arrived with a Spanish chic that she wears well, and the piquancy of strong emotions," the writer reflected. "She is adroit at the game of the fan, has a passion for clothes, sprinkles gold in her hair, and...is possessed of all the graces, even that of kindness, for she is good and charmingly generous. Here all the men are in love with her...and try to make their wives into faux empresses," she reported, amused. "These solid, conventional women strive to copy the beautiful Eugénie; they powder their hair, real or false, with gold and copper; they put on make-up, they become redheads." And it was not only her own sub-jects who responded strongly to the empress's appeal. Within months of the wedding, Madame Tussaud's in London had added a Eugénie exhibit "in her beautiful Bridal Dress of exquisite lace of great value," and the English papers ran regular advertisements for "RIMMEL'S GOLDEN HAIR POWDER (as worn by the Empress Eugénie and the élite of the French nobility)," which, for a mere 10 shillings and sixpence per box, "gives a most enchanting and unique brilliancy to female beauty, and is adopted at all the balls of the 'Haut ton.'"

There were those who jeered that the opulence was vulgar, a glitter-ing charade intended to disguise the uncouth origins of many of the imperial courtiers. This was to be expected. The ancient aristocratic families allied with the previous monarchies sneered at the Spanish Eugénie and the Napoleonic usurper, as did the intellectual and artistic cliques who had backed the republic. "It only takes one individual more distinguished than the others to create a noble lineage these days," sniffed George Sand. "The grandmother who wore clogs had a daughter who wore shoes; the granddaughter now wears high heeled slippers."

★ Also in the Parisian theaters that summer of 1853 was a production of *Uncle Tom's Cabin,* which, according to Baron Heeckeren, drew "floods of tears."

But there was no denying the energy of the new regime, or the aura of optimism radiating from it. Within the first months of 1853, Louis Napoleon had already begun laying out what would eventually become thousands of miles of railroad tracks linking Paris to regional cities throughout France, to make it easier to bring business and visitors to the capital. The emperor also announced his intention to organize a mammoth Exhibition Universelle (modeled openly on London's enormously successful Great Exhibition, held two years earlier, which Napoleon III intended to best) to showcase art, industry, and agriculture from France and around the world. And he brought in a new administrator, Baron Haussmann, an extremely competent Parisian who had languished for years managing the governments of provincial cities like Vienne and Bordeaux, to help turn the imperial vision of a modern, beautified Paris into reality. Demolition began almost immediately, and plans were drawn up to build canals and sewers, along with a sprawling central marketplace encased by an avant-garde design of iron latticework. "My God, Monsieur," cried one amazed architect to Haussmann. "What a coup of the pickaxe!"

In fact, the only setback to this otherwise impressive rollout came in April, when Eugénie, who had to her elation discovered herself to be pregnant at the end of March, sadly lost the baby in a painful miscarriage two weeks later. She was in bed for nearly a month afterward. "I was desperate that I had suffered so greatly in vain," she revealed to Paca in a letter of May 1, 1853, in which she informed her sister of her great disappointment. "I would have been so happy to have had a beautiful baby like yours," she added poignantly. In the ensuing weeks, she went through various stages of grief, looking for answers, trying to find solace. "You ask me the cause of my accident," she wrote again a few days later. "I confess to you that neither I nor anyone else can tell what happened. It's true that I took a lukewarm bath (not hot) but according to two doctors the damage was already done." Ill and depressed, the empress unburdened herself to her sibling. The months of smiling constantly for the spotlight, the endless rounds of parties and politicking, the criticism and often open disdain from the patrician elite (which included her husband's family) had taken their toll. "I won a crown," Eugénie confided bitterly, "but what does that mean if not that I am the first slave of my kingdom, isolated among people, without a friend, and never alone for a moment? It would be unbearable if I did not have in compensation a man near me who loves me madly but who is also a slave like me to the country...Right now, my sister, I give thanks to God for not having realized a hope that filled me with joy because I think with horror of the poor dauphin Louis XVII, of Charles I, of Mary Stuart, and of Marie Antoinette. Who knows what the sad fate of my child might have been!"

Fortunately, by June she had recovered her equilibrium sufficiently to return to her myriad social duties. "You can't imagine how exhausting summer was, with so many balls and ceremonies," she told Paca in September. But Eugénie was also clearly much buoyed by the evidence of domestic support for the throne, especially outside Paris. "I assure you that our journey this summer [through the French countryside] was a true triumph," she raved, adding that everywhere they went they were greeted with "the greatest enthusiasm."

But popularity at home and glamour abroad were not enough for the emperor. No man who bore the name Napoleon could neglect the military's desire for glory, nor the need to establish France as the preeminent world power and acknowledged leader of Europe. The question was how best to do this.

And then, as if on cue, Nicholas I invaded Crimea.

THE TSAR'S ACTION CAME as no surprise to Louis Napoleon. The emperor had long suspected that the Russians intended to expand into Turkey. One of the reasons his uncle the first Napoleon had launched his ultimately disastrous attack on Moscow was because he had anticipated just this sort of threat. "Once mistress of Constantinople," the great Corsican general had warned as early as 1817, from his prison cell at Saint Helena, "Russia gets all the commerce of the Mediterranean; becomes a great naval power; marches off to India an army of seventy thousand good soldiers; and God knows what may happen...I see into futurity farther than others," the captive conqueror had concluded modestly.

Louis Napoleon had taken his uncle's concerns to heart. Months before Nicholas's offensive, the emperor had cornered the English ambassador after a dinner at the Tuileries and expounded on the prodigious dangers to the future of mankind in the event of a Russian invasion of Crimea. "He [Napoleon III] said…that two great subjects were now paramount—namely the [defense] of the Turkish Empire and the new International Code broached by America called the 'Monroe Doctrine,' and that these two points comprehended the whole policy of the world, the maintenance of peace, and the advance of human civilization and improvement," the somewhat disconcerted English envoy noted of this little chat.★

Unlike his namesake, however, Louis Napoleon had no wish to confront the Russians on his own. The old approach of raising large armies and taking over the rest of Europe by force held little appeal for him. It was too expensive and risky, and got in the way of his ambitious railway-and-beautification agenda. Rather, the emperor envisioned the role of the French military as being at the head of a consortium of like-minded powers intent on policing, rather than subjugating, their neighbors. This was the route to glory! "The time for conquest is passed beyond return," he declared in a speech to the Senate. "It is no longer in extending territorial limits that a nation can hereafter be honored and powerful; it is in placing itself at the head of generous ideas, and in causing the principles of law and justice everywhere to prevail."

But to be head of a consortium meant that the other great powers had to be willing to go along with your program, and here Louis Napoleon had what may generously be described as a trust problem.

★ The Monroe Doctrine asserted that the US would not tolerate European colonization or interference in the Americas. Louis Napoleon, who did not like having his options limited in this way, took offense at the directive and cautioned that something might have to be done about it. "Russia was a barbarous Monarchy, and America a barbarous Republic, but both were young, vigorous, and full of beans," he groused to the British ambassador.

For obvious reasons dating back to the first Napoleon's alarming tendency to view other people's kingdoms as fair game for annexation, not to mention Louis Napoleon's own recent willingness to use military force to wrest sovereignty away from his domestic political opponents, France was not generally thought of internationally as a team player.

This had to change, and to effect this makeover, the emperor enlisted his wife. As Eugénie had not much experience of foreign policy (at least not the way Louis Napoleon practiced it), he took it upon himself to educate her. And so, at more or less the same time that the recently-engaged-but-not-yet-married Sisi was learning how to make diplomatic small talk in French, Eugénie was getting lessons from her husband in the finer points of power politics.

These were, like the man himself, a curious mixture of the wily pragmatic and the mildly delusional. Louis Napoleon evidently viewed the world as a vast tile puzzle whose pieces could be moved around at will. To push the Russians out of Crimea, he explained to Eugénie, it would be best if France could have the help of both the British and the Austrians, the two major powers in Europe. The English, jealously protective of their naval superiority, were as anxious as Louis Napoleon to keep the tsar from gaining access to the Mediterranean, and had already signaled their willingness to work together for this purpose. It was the Austrians who were the problem. Traditionally, they were allied with Nicholas, and so must somehow be coaxed away from the Russians. The emperor considered Franz Joseph's stated policy of mediation based on nonintervention to be hopelessly naïve. "Neutrality is impossible for Austria in a war between Russia and England and France in the east," Louis Napoleon declared flatly.

But how best to separate Franz Joseph from the tsar? Although willing to use intimidation, on the whole the emperor much preferred bribing his way to success by offering compensation in the form of other people's property. "It would be a great advantage if we could agree upon granting her [Austria] an equivalent somewhere else—but where? There seemed none but some Turkish province," he mused to the British ambassador.

Eugénie took instantly to this game of find-the-right-puzzle-piece. Loyally casting around for a way to help her husband, she came up with a novel plan that would tie the Austrian monarchy not only to French interests, but to those of her native land of Spain as well. In January 1854, with an amateur's enthusiasm (and Louis Napoleon's permission), she sought out the Austrian ambassador, Baron Hübner, who had been invited to one of her regular Monday evening entertainments, to sound him out discreetly on the virtues of her inspired scheme.

Unfortunately, as she was new to the exciting world of political intrigue, her approach left something to be desired. In fact, she might have taught a class in how *not* to conduct a clandestine negotiation. To introduce her subject, Eugénie suddenly observed out of nowhere to her bewildered guest that the reign of Isabella had become so corrupt that it was obvious that the Spanish queen would soon be overthrown and exiled. While the startled Hübner was digesting this bit of misinformation and wondering why he had been singled out as the beneficiary of his hostess's confidence, Eugénie began speculating aloud as to who might take Isabella's place in the event of an uprising against her. "How," she exclaimed brightly, smiling as though she had just come up with the idea for the very first time, "about the Archduke Maximilian, brother of the Austrian emperor?"

Of course, the experienced envoy saw through her instantly. "Ah, Madame, you do diplomacy!" he flattered her, parrying expertly. Alas, not only did the ambassador decline to take the bait, but the empress gave away more than she had intended with this clumsy overture, which conveyed a strong whiff of desperation. "This is not the first time that she has spoken to me this way," the baron noted in his diary entry for January 23, 1854. "Only these insinuations are too sewn with white thread [not to be trusted]. They need the Austrians to help them win in the East," he concluded sagely.*

---

* Fortunately, Eugénie's misstep was not fatal, and in fact, when the ambassador went back to Vienna three months later to attend the wedding of Franz Joseph with Elisabeth—"a very young girl," Hübner recorded in his diary—he did try to convince his sovereign to ally with France and England against Russia.

The failure of her Spanish plan was not the only disappointment Eugénie experienced in the coming months. Her marriage was already beginning to show cracks. As had been expected by absolutely everyone who knew him (except his wife), Louis Napoleon had begun to cheat on her. The English mistress, in particular, had her revenge: she was reinstalled in the emperor's good graces before the year was out, and was only set aside a second time, with much reluctance, after Eugénie found out and caused a scene. "I was faithful...during the first six months of our union, but I need little distractions," Louis Napoleon explained airily. However, "I always return to her [Eugénie] with pleasure," he added virtuously.

But the biggest blow lay in her inability to perpetuate her husband's dynasty. Eugénie became pregnant again in 1854, and again miscarried. This was extremely worrying. The empress was already twenty-eight years old and the fear that she might never bear an heir was demoralizing. It could not have helped but color her relationship with her spouse, who had wed specifically to produce a legitimate son.

And the second year of her reign was going no better than the marriage. After an encouraging beginning, the emperor's much-heralded domestic program was provoking some sharp criticism. Parisians whose houses were torn down, or whose streets were dug up, complained that they now had nowhere to live. There were aggrieved accusations of favoritism as to compensation, with the emperor's friends receiving far more for their destroyed property than others who did not have access to the court. The complaints of dust, inconvenience, and general unsightliness rose in direct proportion to the mounds of rubble. Commerce fell and the economy contracted; even the weather refused to cooperate, resulting in a poor harvest. The price of bread, a leading indicator of consumer dissatisfaction that no French ruler since the Revolution could afford to ignore, climbed ominously.

But it was the necessity of readying for war that was the real culprit. In truth, Louis Napoleon, fearing just this sort of financial downturn, had done all he could to prevent the outbreak of open hostilities with Russia. At the last minute, he even wrote a personal letter to the tsar offering him a dignified way out. "If your Majesty desires as much as I do a pacific conclusion, what can be more simple than to declare that an armistice will be signed immediately...and that all the belligerent forces will retire from the places which they have occupied?...There is truly nothing in this plan which is not worthy of your Majesty, nothing which can wound your honor," he urged. But Nicholas, confident that Franz Joseph would never ally against him, was having none of it, and threw down the gauntlet. "Russia, as I can guarantee, will prove herself in 1854 what she was in 1812," the tsar retorted, referring to the catastrophic defeat suffered by the first Napoleon at the hands of the Russian army.

There was no backing down in the face of so insulting a taunt, particularly as it was followed, on February 6, 1854, by Nicholas's officially breaking off diplomatic relations with Britain and France. Preparations for combat began in earnest. Both kingdoms levied soldiers, ships, and supplies for an attack. "Three battalions of the Guards and other troops to the number of 10,000 go immediately to the East," reported the British ambassador on February 13. "The regiments depart in a few days," Eugénie informed Paca on February 22. "To think that many of these robust men, who leave so full of life and hope, will never see their homeland nor families again! I assure you that when I consider the war from this point of view, I am horrified...Pardon your little sister for burdening you with all of this but my spirit is so afflicted that I can't talk about anything else," she agonized.

But nothing hindered the dogged tread to the battlefield. On March 27, Britain and France officially declared war on Russia. On April 10, 1854, exactly two weeks before Sisi stood at the altar, Louis Napoleon signed a military alliance with England to defend Turkey from Russian encroachment. He and Queen Victoria invited all the other nations to join them in this pact, hoping to convince the tsar to withdraw his forces by isolating Russia from the rest of Europe. Of course, to have any hope of succeeding, they needed to bring Austria on board. But Franz Joseph was able to reject their overtures because on April 20, as a wedding present, his mother and aunt had protected him from diplomatic isolation by arranging for Prussia to sign a defensive treaty with Austria. And as long as Franz Joseph refused to join with France and England, the tsar had no need to worry about his western borders and was left free to concentrate all his forces against Turkey.

And so began one of the most savage and deadly conflicts of its age: the Crimean War. In a period rife with wretchedness, this struggle stood out for its sheer, senseless suffering. But it was also novel for another reason. Because of the invention of the telegraph, this was the first theater of operations to be reported on persistently, in depth, and in real time by international newspapers. It brought the battle-field home to the public at large, marshaled popular opinion, and launched the careers of foreign journalists. It introduced the world to the courageous competence of Florence Nightingale and the mad, tragic heroism of Alfred, Lord Tennyson's "The Charge of the Light Brigade." With the Crimean War, combat entered the modern era.

ELISABETH

Elisabeth as a young bride

10

Love in the Time of Cholera

Into the valley of Death
Rode the six hundred.
                    —Tennyson, "The Charge of the Light Brigade"

UNLIKE EUGÉNIE, ELISABETH WAS NOT CONSUMED by the marshaling of soldiers and the ominous jostling for alliances that signaled the approach of war. She was still just trying to get through the rest of her wedding.

The religious ceremony at the Church of the Augustinians had not marked the end of her ordeal. As, by her murmured acceptance of the vows at the altar, she was now officially empress of Austria, it was necessary that she be acknowledged as such by the members of the imperial court. This involved having everyone of any importance to her new husband and his family approach her one by one to kiss her hand and present their felicitations. When, immediately after the church service, Sisi returned to the Hofburg Palace and saw the crush of people lined up waiting to perform this ritual, she ran into a small side chamber and sobbed.

They calmed her down and got her out, but it was clear that she was unhappy, and was only submitting to the required protocol under protest. She particularly objected to having women her mother's or grandmother's age kiss her hand. Baron Hübner, back in Vienna for the wedding, witnessed her resistance. "How," Elisabeth demanded, "can I have my hand kissed by women so much older than me? Never!" she exclaimed. "The Emperor had to intervene to persuade her to submit to the formalities of etiquette," the ambassador noted with amusement. Similarly, when Sisi finally saw some young women she knew—two cousins she had grown up with who had been invited to the wedding—and tried to hug them as she always had, she was quickly rebuked by her mother-in-law. Hugging was not permitted to empresses, Archduchess Sophia scolded her.

It took over two hours for the hand-kissing exercise to be over, after which the wedding banquet, mercifully limited to members of the imperial family, began. Elisabeth, ordinarily so full of energy when she was at home at Possi, was visibly subdued and barely ate. The conclusion of this meal, which everyone but the bride seemed to enjoy, marked the end of the day's festivities. There was no grand ball that evening (although boisterous celebrations among the common people of Vienna went on long into the night). There was only the final indignity of being led by her mother and a dozen imperial footmen wielding candelabras from the banquet hall to the bedroom. Upon her arrival, Sisi discovered her new Mistress of the Household, the formidable Countess Esterházy, on hand to supervise her undressing by her new ladies-in-waiting, all still strangers to her; at least Duchess Ludovika lingered to help put her daughter, who was still painfully modest about displaying her naked body, as many teenaged girls are, to bed. The departure of her mother and ladies was the cue for the bridegroom, escorted by his parent, to enter the chamber. So completely was Sophia in control of the imperial court that, although Franz Joseph's father attended the ceremony, it was she who conducted her son to his wedding night.

The archduchess had no doubt been intending to say a few soothing words of blessing and joy to the young bride, but she was prevented in this, as, upon her entrance, Elisabeth dove under the covers, hid her face, and pretended to be asleep. All that Sophia could see of her daughter-in-law, as she tenderly bade her son good night and closed the door, was Sisi's wild, beautiful hair cascading out from among the pillows.

★   ★   ★

FRANZ JOSEPH WAS A GENTLEMAN about it. He did not force her that first night—as both mothers discovered to their disappointment when they burst in before breakfast the next morning. (The servants talked, so everyone else at the court also knew from the unsullied state of the sheets.) Nor were husband and wife to be given any privacy that day, or indeed for the next several days. Elisabeth's waking hours were swallowed up by diplomatic audiences, where she stood sandwiched between the emperor and his mother, dressed in whatever regional costume was appropriate, greeting deputations from various provinces of the Austrian empire. Evenings were given over to official court functions, like a grand celebratory ball, but even here she was expected to waltz, not with Franz Joseph, but with his most senior officials. Sophia noted disapprovingly in her diary that her daughter-in-law still had to be coached on the correct dance steps.

The one highlight of her first experience of married life came a full four days after the wedding, when the court left the palace grounds to view a special public performance of the famous Renz circus, staged in honor of the newlyweds. A rapt Sisi came to life as the expert riders, gorgeously costumed in medieval dress, put sixty horses through choreographed routines and acrobatic tricks. The ringmaster, Ernst Renz himself, contributed to the spectacle with a virtuoso solo demonstration of equestrian artistry. "It really was too lovely!" Elisabeth breathed to Franz Joseph after watching this presentation. "I must get to know that man."

But this, too, she was informed by her scandalized mother-in-law, would not be allowed. Sisi was not even permitted to wander around the rooms of the Hofburg alone with her husband; they had done it once and Sophia had found out and immediately put a stop to it. There was to be no softening of propriety, no easing of the rules to accommodate individual taste or inclinations, no changes at all to the rigid imperial routine established by the archduchess, simply because her son was now married. This fact was brought home to Sisi on the morning of her third day of wedlock. Franz Joseph had finally, gently prevailed upon her to consummate the marriage the night before, and she had awakened understanding that his mother would query him about this as soon as she saw him. Elisabeth was mortified that something so private would be discussed openly, and begged to be allowed to miss the regular morning meal with Archduchess Sophia and the rest of the imperial family. But Franz Joseph refused to allow her to remain behind. He always had breakfast with his mother, and he expected her to do the same. Sisi would remember this humiliation for the rest of her life. "The Emperor was so used to obeying her that he gave in to this demand as well," she recounted bitterly. "But it was horrible for me. I went only for his sake."

However, even Franz Joseph could tell that Sisi was miserable after her family made their farewells on the morning of April 29, 1854. (Her father, who found the stultifying, self-satisfied atmosphere of the court intolerable, instructed her to look him up the next time she was in Bavaria, as he was *never* coming back to Vienna.) To cheer her up, the emperor cancelled his afternoon obligations and made good on his promise to take his bride to Laxenburg, the imperial family's peaceful country estate situated about fifteen miles outside of Vienna. After a week of unrelenting public appearances, they were finally to begin their honeymoon, just the two of them.

THE IMPERIAL ABODE OF LAXENBURG, which sat on over 600 acres of parkland, gardens, and woods, boasted not one but three residences: the old castle, a fortress dating from the Middle Ages where nobody stayed; the new castle (called the Blauer Hof or Blue Court), a stately palace furnished in the rococo fashion favored by Maria Theresa, among whose immense crystal chandeliers and ornately painted ceilings Elisabeth would spend her honeymoon; and the Franzenburg, a smaller, heavily idealized faux-medieval castle, complete with armory and working dungeon, that had been built by Franz Joseph's grandfather as a sort of updated gazebo. By Habsburg standards, Laxenburg was considered rustic country living.

Of course, the surroundings couldn't compare to those around Sisi's beloved Possi, with its white-capped mountains and windswept lake (Laxenburg had more of a pond) but at least she could go riding, which she hadn't been able to do in over a week. Franz Joseph had thoughtfully brought along not only her horses but her parrots as well, so that she would be surrounded by her pets. The improvement in her mood was immediate, and the two of them set off at once on a long gallop through the woods, just as they had during the carefree days of their courtship. That evening they had their first meal alone, and Elisabeth was her old, lively self, in love with her husband and delighted to be in his company.

This happy state of affairs lasted until the next morning, when Franz Joseph had to get up early to go back to work in Vienna, and his mother showed up to keep her daughter-in-law company.

Sisi hadn't realized it, but her husband had never intended to be away from his desk for any length of time during their honeymoon. It wasn't just the impending war. There were all sorts of decisions to be made, no matter how mundane, that only the emperor could authorize, like who should be appointed as the new junior member of the secret police in Hungary, or the punishment to be meted out to "two disorderly women" in Milan (as the official report read) who had dared, as a small act of rebellion against the Austrian military occupation of their city, to sing patriotic Italian songs. (Thirty lashes with the whip, with the wounds subsequently doused in vinegar.) That's one of the sad drawbacks of totalitarian rule—no time off for a holiday.* And of course, there were also larger issues to be resolved, although these Franz Joseph tended to deal with expeditiously. "Is what you have written exactly in line with what we did before?" he would query his minister, and if the answer was yes (which it always was), then he would add his signature to the proffered document. The Russian ambassador to Vienna, who knew the emperor well, reported in frustration during this period that

---

* The Austrian general in charge of the imperial forces in Italy, besieged by pleas for mercy from the local population, consistently replied, "I cannot do it. It is not in my power to grant pardon. Irrevocable decisions have been made above me." There was only one person in the government of higher rank than this commander: the emperor.

Franz Joseph "is blinded by his self-will and the foolish assumption that he can *judge and decide everything entirely by himself.*"

Actually, this was not completely true. There was one person with whom the emperor discussed matters of policy, often for hours at a time: his mother. This situation did not change simply because he had married. Unlike Napoleon III, who took Eugénie into his confidence at once, Franz Joseph shut his wife out of his government, and consequently out of her subjects' lives, from the very beginning. Sisi's job was merely to *project* the image of an empress, not to *be* one. That position—the position of power—remained firmly in Sophia's hands.

And so Franz Joseph would go off to his office at the Hofburg Palace every day of his honeymoon to sit at his desk for hours signing paperwork while Elisabeth remained at Laxenburg with her ladies-in-waiting, supplemented by frequent visits from his mother. All of the women surrounding Sisi understood that it was their job to mold the teenager into Archduchess Sophia's ideal of what her son's wife should be.

It takes a very strong spirit to survive the sort of hectoring to which Elisabeth was consequently subjected. Her every movement was scrutinized and found lacking. She was criticized for not wearing gloves often enough, and for wearing her shoes too often. (An empress was supposed to slip her feet into a new pair every morning, and give yesterday's slippers to one of her women, an extravagance that Sisi considered shamefully wasteful.) Elisabeth was to be found at all times dressed beautifully and formally, sitting quietly with her ladies, her mother-in-law informed her.★ Nothing from her old life, or the person she had been, was to carry over into her new role as figurehead. Sisi was to limit her riding, and in any event, never to venture out on horseback unless chaperoned by guards. What she should be doing, Sophia lectured, was spending the long, captive hours of each day indoors

---

★ The gowns Sisi wore during this period were influenced by Eugénie. Baron Hübner noted that French style was widely imitated in the salons of Vienna. The great ladies of imperial society, which of course included the women of the court, were "fond of garish toilets all made in Paris, but not always chosen with taste," he deplored.

learning French and the details of imperial protocol, and perhaps perfecting her needlepoint. Even the simplest request, like asking for beer when she was thirsty, was scornfully denied her. Empresses did not drink beer. She was not to visit a museum, shop, or street in Vienna unless surrounded by court officials and police, all of whom had been notified in advance of her plans. She could not choose a single servant or lady-in-waiting, as Eugénie had; or take a drive or attend a theater performance, unless the outing was approved in advance by her mother-in-law, and the archduchess almost never approved of anything Sisi wanted. "Your Majesty evidently thinks you are still in the Bavarian mountains," was Sophia's common refrain, dripping with sarcasm. On those few occasions when she was not available to supervise her pupil personally, the severe Countess Esterházy, who was one of Sophia's oldest and closest friends, was authorized to act as imperial surrogate, treating Elisabeth as one would a wayward child, and reporting back any infraction, no matter how small.

Sisi resisted as best she could. She ducked away and went riding alone with just her groom for hours every day despite Sophia's withering opposition. When it rained, which it did frequently those first weeks, she shut herself up alone in her room and played with her parrots or sat at her desk crying and writing letters home to her family, telling them how much she missed them. "The mere thought of that time constricts my heart," a much older Elisabeth would later confess of this honeymoon interval at Laxenburg. "I was alone all day long and was afraid of the moment when Archduchess Sophie came. For she came every day, to spy on what I was doing at any hour...Everything I did was bad. She passed disparaging judgments on anyone I loved...The whole house feared her so much that everyone trembled. Of course they told her everything. The smallest thing was an affair of state."

There was only one person in all of Europe who had the authority to stop Archduchess Sophia from interfering with the empress, and that was the emperor, so it is important to understand Franz Joseph's role in all this. He would come back to Laxenburg every night at six, see Elisabeth's tearstained face, and hear her complaints about the way she was treated. He could not have helped but be aware of his wife's unhappiness.

But the emperor sided with his mother. Franz Joseph was so used to obeying Sophia, to relying on her judgment, that he did not think to question her methods, not even so much as to ask her to moderate her approach. This was just the way things were done. Sisi would have to get used to it. And so he consoled his wife by taking her out riding in the evenings, and holding her in his arms at night. "He was so frankly in love that it was a pleasure to see," Baron Hübner, who met with the emperor soon after the wedding, observed. "I am as much in love as a lieutenant and as happy as a God," Franz Joseph crowed in a letter to a friend.

Unfortunately, the same could not be said of his wife. On May 8, 1854, a mere two weeks into her marriage and at almost the same moment that her husband was boasting of his wedded bliss, Sisi was sitting at her little desk at Laxenburg, hiding from her mother-in-law and tearfully scribbling:

> *O that I had not left the way*
> *That would to freedom me have led!*
> *O that I had not gone astray*
> *On vanity's broad path instead! . . .*
>
> *I waken from a vision rich*
> *Wherein my spirit captive lay,*
> *And vainly curse the hour in which*
> *Freedom! I gambled thee away!*

THIS SITUATION DID NOT IMPROVE after the honeymoon ended and Elisabeth and Franz Joseph returned to Vienna and settled into their rooms at the Hofburg Palace.

The Hofburg was Sophia's domain. She ran the household according to a schedule and deportment that had been put in place while Franz Joseph and his brothers were growing up, and it was to this standard that Sisi was now expected to conform. The archduchess treated her daughter-in-law the same way she treated her youngest son, twelve-year-old Ludwig, who, with his older brother, twenty-one-year-old Karl, still lived at home. (Within months the spurned Karl would decamp for a position in Innsbruck.) Even Ludwig understood that all the rules that applied to him also applied to Elisabeth, and tattled on her conduct at breakfast one morning when he felt she had misbehaved.

Sisi's only reprieve from Sophia's sharp-eyed supervision came at the beginning of June, when Franz Joseph took her with him to Prague to introduce his Bohemian subjects to their new empress. As neither his mother nor Countess Esterházy was able to accompany them, Elisabeth was suddenly, mercifully freed from their incessant disparagement. Immediately, she recovered her old spirits and achieved a smashing success. She visited hospitals, charity schools, and asylums and charmed all with whom she came in contact. She stood for hours meeting delegations and hearing petitions from those in need. There were no tears, no scenes, no reluctance to perform her duties, no sign whatever of immaturity. On the contrary, it was clear that her popularity and the goodwill she engendered were of enormous benefit to the monarchy. The common people flocked to her whenever she and Franz Joseph appeared in public.

And this was not Elisabeth's only triumph. Upon her return home it was confirmed that the trip to Prague had been advantageous in another way. By the end of June, two months into her marriage, sixteen-year-old Sisi discovered herself to be pregnant. But rather than cementing her position at court and giving Elisabeth the respect due to the future mother of an imperial scion, Archduchess Sophia instead used it as an excuse to further constrain and control her daughter-in-law. Riding was now absolutely prohibited; the empress's only sanctioned form of exercise was to take a short walk in the palace garden, an activity that Sophia insisted occur regularly, as it served to exhibit Sisi's increasingly swollen figure to the public. Modest Elisabeth, embarrassed by the changes to her body, found this civic display humiliating, but Sophia, once again backed up by Franz Joseph, was adamant. The archduchess's dominion was so complete that even Sisi's pet birds were taken from her, on the grounds that if the expectant mother interacted with them too often the imperial child might end up look-ing like a parrot.

And this time Elisabeth could not fight back. She was too weak and ill. It was a difficult pregnancy; she couldn't keep anything down. She did not even have her mother with her, as Duchess Ludovika, loath to antagonize Sophia by interfering, stayed away. The archduchess's admonitions were motivated not by dislike of her daughter-in-law but rather by fear. Sophia had also conceived early in her marriage but had twice been unable to carry the child to term. She was determined to do everything in her power to see to it that Sisi did not lose this baby.

But Sophia also understood the political value of the imperial preg-nancy, and that is why she made Elisabeth show herself publicly. This joyful promise of an heir to the throne could not have come at a more opportune time. It served as a useful distraction from the increasingly dire foreign situation, and the privations and other hardships Franz Joseph's subjects were beginning to suffer. Because Napoleon III had been right after all: neutrality was impossible. The war had come to Austria.

By the end of June 1854, just as Sisi was beginning to experience the first signs of morning sickness, the French and British, working together as allies, had already landed troops at the port city of Varna (in present-day Bulgaria), on the western coast of the Black Sea, in prepa-ration for a major fall offensive against the Russians. Nicholas's force was holed up almost directly opposite on the eastern side, in the city of Sebastopol, the largest and best-defended naval base in Crimea.

By this time, Nicholas had also already broken his promise to Franz Joseph and moved some of his forces across the Danube into the princi-palities of Moldavia and Wallachia (basically Romania), only a couple of hundred miles to the north of the allied landing. So the French and English were facing the threat of Russia sweeping down on them by land as well as by sea. This they were desperate to prevent.

And for once, Franz Joseph was in agreement with them. Having Russian troops cross the Danube endangered his territory, which abutted the occupied principalities. He was forced to recall all the troops he had just been compelled to disband for lack of funds, and, when these were determined not to be enough to meet the threat, to order a new, general conscription of soldiers throughout the empire. There was, of course, no money for any of this, so Franz Joseph had also to raise cash through compulsory loans (the financial term for stealing), the brunt of which was squeezed from his already disgruntled subjects in Italy and Hungary. Still there was not enough, and so the throne was also obliged to borrow at exorbitant rates of interest that it could not afford. Inflation rose, the financial markets fell, and the common people, as always, bore the brunt of the economic crisis.

But after so many years of alliance and friendship, Franz Joseph was reluctant to break totally with Nicholas, and he knew that the older leader, already facing the French and British, would want to keep Austria out of the fighting. So, simultaneous with the military mobilization, the emperor fired off an ultimatum to the tsar ordering him to withdraw his troops from Moldavia and Wallachia or risk a declaration of war from Vienna. Franz Joseph, newly married, confident in himself

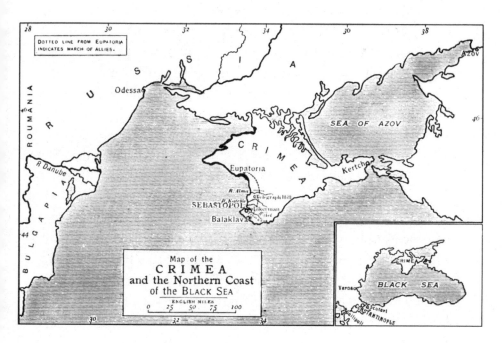

Map of the
CRIMEA
and the Northern Coast
of the BLACK SEA

and his army, and annoyed at having been deceived the first time, did not bother to couch this high-handed demand in diplomatic terms. Consequently, the tsar received it with fury—had he not helped Austria when they asked for Russian soldiers in Hungary?—and was on the verge of retaliating, when his response was tempered by timely family intervention. Hearing of Nicholas's rage, Franz Joseph's uncle the king of Prussia wrote soothingly to the tsarina (who happened to be his sister), "I know positively and believe that I can vouch with my word of honor that Franz Joseph is as far removed as heaven from earth in undertaking the occupation against Russia with any trace of enmity...God knows that, should Franz Joseph march, he comes as a friend and not as an enemy."

On the basis of this back-channel assurance that Austria would not declare war or ally against him, Nicholas reluctantly withdrew his men from the Danube provinces later that summer. On August 20, 1854, to ensure that the tsar kept his word this time, Franz Joseph sent 450,000 imperial soldiers into Moldavia and Wallachia, with instructions to hold the territory against any further Russian aggression.

The way was thus cleared for the French and British to invade Crimea. Within weeks of Austria's occupation of the principalities, the allied army gathered at Varna, which had grown to some 40,000 troops in all, was ferried across the Black Sea by their combined fleets. The regiments landed a little to the north of their principal target, the Russian-held port of Sebastopol, and commenced the attack.

At first, the war went well for the western powers. A great battle was held on September 20, 1854, on the banks of the Alma River in the hilly land surrounding Sebastopol. Despite the Russians holding the high ground, which allowed them to rain fire from heavy artillery—the London *Times* correspondent, who witnessed the scene, estimated the number of enemy cannon at 100 guns, and called the battle "one of the most bloody and determined struggles in the annals of war"—the French and English managed to cross the river and charge the hill where the main body of Russian infantry stood, breaking their lines and forcing the Russians back to the safety of Sebastopol. But the cost in human life was very great. The Russians lost nearly 5,000 men to capture or injury, with "nearly 3,000 killed or wounded on our side," the *Times* reporter noted grimly.

And it only got worse from there. The British and French decided to dig in and lay siege to Sebastopol, which meant a much longer war than either government had expected. Supplies ran short. Cholera and hunger decimated the allied forces. "Out of 35,600 men borne on the strength of the army there are not more now than 16,500 rank and file fit for service," the *Times* journalist estimated a month after the initial victory. The Russians took advantage of their opponents' weakness to stage a surprise counterattack outside the town of Balaklava, where many of the invalid troops had been sent to try to recover. Although the allies managed to repel this offensive, the effort was marred by mismanagement and, at least in one instance, by callous contempt for the lives of the soldiery.

Battles are always chaotic but there is no excuse for what happened to the British light cavalry. Six hundred men, armed only with sabers, with absolutely no covering support or nearby backup, were sent to charge across an open plain a mile and a half long, straight into the Russian artillery. In the hands of poet Alfred, Lord Tennyson, this episode was transmuted into a stirring, patriotic ode to the greatness of the British spirit. (It also conveniently served to distract from the contemptible behavior of those officers who failed to question an order that they knew would result in senseless slaughter.) The eyewitness accounts of those twenty minutes or so were considerably less romantic than art and nostalgia have made them out to be. "At ten minutes past eleven, our Light Cavalry brigade advanced," the *Times* journalist, stationed on a hill overlooking the battle, reported. "The whole brigade scarcely made one effective regiment...As they rushed towards the front, the Russians opened on them from the guns on the right, with volleys of musketry and rifles...We could scarcely believe the evidence of our senses!" the correspondent exclaimed. "Surely that handful of men are not going to charge an army in position? Alas, it was but too true...At the distance of 1200 yards, the whole line of the enemy belched forth, from thirty iron mouths, a flood of smoke and flame, through which hissed the deadly balls... Ere they [the riders] were lost from view the plain was strewn with their bodies and the carcasses of horses." The total number of British soldiers killed, wounded, and missing on that day was 387; of these, 305 came from the Light Brigade.

And then, as if the suffering was not already horrendous enough, almost immediately after this battle, winter blew in with a vengeance, and it was discovered that on the English side no preparations had been made for the cold weather. There were no tents, no wood to build huts or fires, no shelter from the days (and nights) of driving rain and freezing temperatures. Cholera, fever, and dysentery exploded. The British government was forced to appeal publicly to Florence Nightingale to organize a small group of volunteer nurses to go personally to the war zone to take charge of the situation.*

Although the forces Franz Joseph had sent to occupy Moldavia and Wallachia were not involved in the military action in Crimea, and so were spared this devastation, the pressure on him to use these men, already in position, to open up a second front against Russia, and so help to end the war quickly, increased in direct proportion to the allied troops' misery. Napoleon III, in particular, did everything he could think of to induce his Austrian counterpart to give up his cherished policy of neutrality. The French were better prepared for the harsh conditions in Crimea—their soldiers were provided with tents and wood, and so were able to build huts; and although their names are not famous today, nuns were already in place to provide nursing. "The wounded French are getting on very well, so are their sick... beds, coverlids, bandages, lint, &c., had all been prepared beforehand," the *Morning Chronicle,* which also had a foreign correspondent in Turkey, reported. "The French manage better," another London paper pointed out in frustration. "They have their newly baked bread, and from time to time they carry loaves to the

---

* She was so effective that it is clear that, had she been appointed to plan the supplies for the army, they would never have been in this position in the first place.

English soldiers, and exchange them for ration biscuit, which they employ chiefly when pounded up, for the purpose of thickening their soup." But despite this, France had also lost thousands of recruits, as well as experienced officers, to combat and cholera. To save what remained of his army, Louis Napoleon needed Franz Joseph to enter the war as soon as possible.

And the arguments against remaining neutral were compelling. Even Baron Hübner, back in Paris, warned Franz Joseph that, having already spurned Nicholas, he could not risk alienating both the Russians *and* the western powers. Cleverly, Franz Joseph's own foreign minister, who knew how the court at Vienna worked, went to Archduchess Sophia and persuaded her that her son risked the threat of French military intervention against Austrian interests in Italy if he did not take this chance to ally himself with Napoleon III. It was consequently Sophia who finally convinced Franz Joseph to abandon his signature neutrality and instead negotiate a defensive accord with the French and British.

This agreement, called the Treaty of Vienna, was signed on December 2, 1854. Although once again vaguely worded, it basically called upon Russia to agree to allied peace terms within thirty days or risk escalation and the entrance of Austria into the war. Having achieved his aim, Louis Napoleon rewarded his new ally by throwing in a bribe. A second, secret treaty was signed on December 22, two days before Elisabeth's seventeenth birthday, in which France guaranteed "the security of the Italian dominions of Austria" for the duration of the Crimean War.

The consequences of abruptly siding with France and Britain were clearly far more momentous than either Franz Joseph or his mother had anticipated. It severed the Austrian relationship with Russia so profoundly that it turned the formerly fatherly Nicholas into a betrayed, vengeful enemy. As soon as the treaty became public, the tsar ordered Franz Joseph's portrait dumped into the basement, and pointedly handed over a bust of his now despised protégé, which had been given to him as a gift, to a domestic. He then summoned the Austrian ambassador into his presence and asked him if he knew who the two stupidest kings in Europe were. "The first was King John Sobieski, who liber-ated Vienna [in 1683] from the siege laid by the Turks," Nicholas informed the envoy. "The second am I. For both of us...saved the House of Habsburgs."

But Russia's was not the only enmity Franz Joseph earned by his action. He lost the king of Prussia's goodwill as well. Signing a treaty like this one was exactly what his uncle had promised the tsarina his nephew would not do. Even worse, Franz Joseph had not even thought to inform his Prussian ally of the change in policy in advance of the signing. He just went ahead and did it. Consequently, his uncle also turned away from Vienna. This was a source of intense satisfaction to an obscure, low-level Prussian diplomat by the name of Otto von Bis-marck, who had for some time been arguing that it was not in the kingdom's interest to ally itself with Franz Joseph or to follow his lead. "In the long run we cannot coexist with each other," Bismarck declared bluntly of Austria. "We breathe the air out of each other's mouths; one must yield or must be 'yielded' to the other."

As before, Elisabeth was not taken into her husband's confidence. She knew that there was a war in Crimea that took up his time, but not much more. As she was unaware of the intolerance and repression with which Franz Joseph, with his mother's approval, ruled the empire of which she was now a symbol, so was she ignorant of the rancor to which he had exposed himself by signing the Treaty of Vienna and raising French and English expectations. *They* believed that this meant that Austria would open up a second front, or at least send an army to help them in Crimea. But in fact Franz Joseph had no intention of doing either.

EUGÉNIE

Eugénie and Napoleon III are received by Queen Victoria and
Prince Albert at Windsor Castle.

11

An Empress on the Rise

The Empress has great charm, and we are all very fond of her.
—Queen Victoria

THE NEWS THAT FRANZ JOSEPH had signed the Treaty of Vienna was greeted with a relief bordering on rapture by the French court. Word arrived at the Tuileries on Sunday, December 3, at the end of yet another formal state dinner. Louis Napoleon was so exhilarated by the tidings that he jumped up from his seat and in front of everyone ran over to Eugénie, kissed her passionately, and "held her tightly to his heart for a long time," Baron Hübner revealed. Up until that point, "a gloomy silence had reigned over the Imperial table," the envoy noted.

The British, too, considered the alliance to be a turning point in the war. The compact "is so far satisfactory that, although it contains no declaration against Russia, it shows such a decided adhesion to our policy...that it is pretty evident that, if a durable peace cannot be made soon, Austria will join us openly," observed Lord Malmesbury, the former ambassador to France and now an influential member of parliament. "The treaty now published must be so offensive to Russia that Austria must be aware she has forfeited all claim to her friendship."

It therefore came as a painful disappointment to discover thirty days later, when the January 1, 1855, deadline that had been set by the treaty for the tsar to withdraw from Crimea passed without the Russians conceding an inch, that Franz Joseph, despite having called up nearly a million soldiers, had no intention of using *any* of them to help his new allies. They were all to remain safely deployed on the Austrian-Hungarian side of the border with Russia, as a preventive against the war spreading to his territory.

While Britain and France were still grappling with this unhappy realization, heartbreaking intelligence reports from the front at Sebastopol continued to pour in. "The accounts from the Crimea are dreadful," Lord Malmesbury noted at the end of January. "Only 18,000 effective men; 14,000 are dead and 22,000 sick." "Cholera has made many a vacancy in our ranks," Baron Heeckeren grieved. "This frightful scourge has spared none...Officers and men have been alike attacked and have died by thousands."

Denied Austrian arms, the court scrambled for new allies. Eugénie tried to get her native land into the war by using her well-connected brother-in-law, the duke of Alba, as an intermediary. "My dear James," she wrote. "Lord Palmerston told me that the English government is obliged to send reinforcements to the Orient, and was going to ask Piedmont and perhaps the Swiss to levy men as well...The thought then came to me: Why not Spain? Spanish soldiers are sober and courageous, and I have no doubt that they would do their duty next to ours...If Spain enters into the treaty of alliance, there will be advantages," she coaxed. "It will not be only they who defend Cuba but France as well, as by signing we will be committed to protect it also." But even with this carrot, Isabella's government declined to intervene.

The one sovereign who understood instantly the bungle Franz Joseph had made of the alliance, and the profit to be had from it, was Victor Emmanuel, the king of Sardinia.

The realm of Sardinia encompassed not simply the Mediterranean island, but also a large chunk of northern Italy west of the Ticino River, which included Piedmont and Genoa, as well as the provinces of Savoy and Nice. Victor Emmanuel was an outspoken critic of what he viewed as the Austrian occupation of next-door Lombardy and Venetia, and as such had emerged as Franz Joseph's principal military competitor in the region. It was the Sardinian monarch's fond hope to free Italy from Austrian control and unite the country under one ruler—himself.

Victor Emmanuel's prime minister, Count Camillo di Cavour, who was even more ambitious than his sovereign, knew that they were going to need powerful allies willing to help them if Italy was serious about ousting a behemoth like Austria from its territories. He consequently graciously offered to send approximately 18,000 soldiers to Crimea to help fight the Russians, knowing that this would put France under obligation to his king. This proposal was gratefully accepted, and Sardinia officially signed the treaty of alliance on January 26, 1855.

And with this, preparations for yet another military campaign were set in motion. Even the death a few weeks later of fifty-eight-year-old Nicholas, who caught a cold reviewing his troops and succumbed soon thereafter to disappointment, depression, and pneumonia, in that order, failed to halt the conflict, as his son and heir, Alexander II, indicated immediately that he would remain faithful to his father's memory and continue to pursue Russian ambitions in Crimea to the utmost of his ability.*

Frustrated at the lack of progress in dislodging the enemy from its seemingly impregnable berth at Sebastopol, Louis Napoleon came up with a daring scheme to go himself to Crimea to take personal charge of the military operation there. He had originally appointed his cousin, Prince Napoleon (son of Jérôme Bonaparte, the former king of Westphalia), who was next in line to the throne should Eugénie fail to

---

* Franz Joseph, *still* not understanding the repercussions of his own foreign policy, sent Alexander a heartfelt condolence note, in which he fondly declared that "the memory of the bonds which unite me to the one whom we mourn [Nicholas] is only equal in my heart with the desire to cultivate the same relations with the heir to his throne," to which Alexander retorted, "I'm sure you can easily understand the effect the political events of the last year produced on his heart—he was afflicted—because instead of finding in you the faithful friend and ally on whom he relied, and whom he loved as his own son, he saw you following a political agenda that brought you closer and closer to our enemies and which will infallibly lead us...to a fratricidal war for which you will account for your actions to God!"

provide a male heir, to represent him as commander-in-chief, but the preening prince, who bore the ridiculous (but extremely helpful) nickname of Plon-Plon, had decamped at the first sign of cholera. Louis Napoleon, convinced that his presence would spur on the French troops, announced that he and the empress intended to sail for Turkey.

The project was singularly unpopular. Since Eugénie had so far failed to provide a son, Plon-Plon stood to inherit the throne if the emperor were to go off to Crimea and catch cholera, or be shot down by a Russian bullet. Nobody wanted *that*. Gossip asserted that, since the empress was going with him, it must have been her idea. Mérimée wrote worriedly to Eugénie's mother that "people are saying that he [Louis Napoleon] listens only to *one* person and that that *person* whose courage you know well enough is advising him to go, and wants to go with him." But, as the author-turned-senator soon discovered, Eugénie had in fact argued against the journey, and had only insisted on sharing the danger after it was clear that her husband was not to be shaken from his decision. "I had no need of her denials to realize that she had nothing to do with the idea," Mérimée made haste to inform María Manuela two weeks later, after he had seen Eugénie at one of her regular evenings at the Tuileries and questioned her about it. "We begin to know the stubbornness of your son-in-law," he added unhappily.

It was only the timely intervention of Buckingham Palace that persuaded Louis Napoleon to give up this adventure. Queen Victoria, hearing of the emperor's intention, was appalled. What if, by his going, French soldiers seized the initiative to win the war and cover themselves with glory at the expense of their British allies? "This we *never* could bear," she agonized. Accordingly, knowing that for some time Napoleon III had sought the international legitimacy that came with an official state reception by the British monarchy, she gritted her teeth and, to compensate him for abandoning the journey east, issued an invitation for the emperor and empress to be her guests at Windsor instead. On April 16, 1855, Eugénie and Louis Napoleon crossed the Channel and landed at Dover for a five-day visit to England.

★   ★   ★

IT IS NOT AN EXAGGERATION to say that this tour was an unmitigated triumph. Everywhere they went, Louis Napoleon and Eugénie were greeted by ecstatic crowds. Spectators lined the tracks all the way from Dover to the capital, straining just to get a look at their express locomotive as it chugged past. As they disembarked in London, "the Emperor and Empress were received by the people with the most deafening cheers," reported the *Guardian*; similarly, when they changed trains to continue on to Windsor, "the thunder of applause that rolled through the multitude...was something marvelous." In a truly stunning reversal, the British nation, which forty years earlier had fought a pitched battle at Waterloo with the first Napoleon, erected banners welcoming his descendant that read VIVE L'EMPEREUR, VIVE L'IMPÉRATICE, NAPOLEON, and EUGÉNIE, and had military bands belt out Napoleon III's signature anthem (a patriotic war tune written by his mother, Hortense) whenever he and Eugénie appeared.

There is no question that some of this popularity had to do with resentment of Franz Joseph. "If it be true that after all our patience and persevering hopes we shall not have the aid of Austria, there is all the more reason for cherishing the friendship of a power which is capable of a more generous and bolder resolution," the *Guardian* observed. But this sentiment represented only a fragment of the outpouring of affection with which the emperor and empress of the French were received. The English citizenry remembered that Louis Napoleon had chosen to live in London after his daring escape from his prison cell in Ham, and they showed their appreciation. "We never witnessed a more hearty and spontaneous greeting given by people to a sovereign," the correspondent for the *Morning Chronicle* remarked. Eugénie, too, was swept up in the general acclaim. "St. James's-street had the windows and balconies of all its houses filled with a large assemblage of ladies, whose curiosity and interest were no doubt strongly excited by the Empress, and who waved their handkerchiefs as she passed," noted the *Observer*.

But beneath "the beaming and inexpressively graceful smile of the Empress" were signs of faintness and fatigue; throughout the whole of this visit, Eugénie was again struggling with her health. The newspapers, upon being told that she needed rest one afternoon, put it down to seasickness from the journey, but this seems unlikely, as Eugénie was a practiced sailor who had endured far worse than a choppy crossing. It got so bad that on the last day of the trip, when she, Louis Napoleon, Victoria, and the queen's husband, Prince Albert, were on a tour of the Crystal Palace, which had been built to house the highly successful 1851 British international fair that Napoleon III was modeling his own upcoming world exhibition on, she suddenly had to sink into one of the newfangled rolling seats that made up part of the display. Prince Albert kindly rescued her by immediately purchasing the prize-winning wheelchair and "making a present of it." She finished the rest of the outing while being pushed around in this contraption by a servant.

Still, she soldiered on with charm and good humor through the grand receptions, state banquets, after-dinner concerts, and myriad other ceremonies that were crammed into the visit. On the evening of her arrival, when she was meeting the queen for the first time, she had to do without her hairdresser, who in the confusion had arrived too late to make the empress's train to Windsor. "I am in despair at being left behind!" he wailed. "What Her Majesty will do without me I cannot tell, but I feel like cutting my throat!" Upon being informed of his anguish, Eugénie laughed. Tell him "he must on no account commit suicide," she ordered with mock gravity. "We want no *affaire* Vatel here. My maids have done their best for me in his absence."★

Her sweet-natured resolve did not go unnoticed. Victoria, who had gone into the visit determined to appeal to the imperial couple's vanity through a show of pomp and courtesy, was pleasantly surprised to find herself the one beguiled instead. "How strange to think that I, the granddaughter of George III, should dance with the Emperor Napoleon, nephew of England's great enemy, and now my nearest and most

---

★ Vatel was a master chef during the reign of Louis XIV who famously ran himself through with a sword because he was afraid the fish would not arrive in time for the king's dinner.

intimate ally, in the Waterloo room, and that this ally, only six years ago, was living in this country an exile, poor and unthought of!" the queen confided to her diary after the magnificent ball held at Windsor on the first night of their sojourn. "That he *is* a very *extraordinary* man, with great qualities there can be *no* doubt... He is evidently possessed of *indomitable courage, unflinching firmness of purpose, self-reliance, persever-ance,* and *great secrecy,*" the queen continued later in a memorandum. "My impression is that... he has invariably been guided by the belief that he is *fulfilling a destiny* which God has *imposed* upon him... It is impossible to know him and not to see that there is much that is truly amiable, kind, and honest in his character." As for Eugénie, "She is full of courage and spirit," Victoria wrote, "and yet so gentle, with such innocence and *enjouement* that the *ensemble* is most charming. With all her great liveliness, she has the prettiest and most modest manners." It did not hurt that the empress, having no offspring of her own, instinc-tively reached out to the royal children (Victoria, only seven years older than Eugénie, already had eight). She made such an impression that the queen's eldest daughter, Vicky, wept when it came time to say goodbye at the end of the trip. The fourteen-year-old was only consoled when she discovered that she and her parents were invited to visit Paris that summer, when Victoria and Albert had agreed to be the guests of honor at Napoleon III's upcoming industrial trade fair, the grandiose Exposi-tion Universelle.

The boost in prestige that Louis Napoleon acquired by his reception in England was emphatic. It erased all suspicion of him as a charlatan who less than three years earlier had taken over France by force, and instead anointed him as the respected head of one of the greatest pow-ers in Europe. Eugénie's transformation was perhaps even more pro-found. Overnight she went from a scheming seductress who had married above her station with the aid of a pushy, social-climbing mother to a valued, upright, and endearing consort who had secured the famously straitlaced British queen's friendship. "Your Majesty has won all hearts," Victoria wrote affectionately to Eugénie.

And it was not just the empress's reputation that benefited by her newfound intimacy with the queen. Eugénie evidently also confided in Victoria about her problems conceiving and carrying a baby to term. It's even possible that she had recently had another disappointment in this regard, and that this was the source of her unexplained frailness during the visit. Having a chance to talk to a woman for whom motherhood had been a regular occurrence for eight years out of the last ten must have been irresistible.

Perhaps it was only a coincidence, but whatever advice Victoria gave turned out to be helpful. For within a month of returning to France, Eugénie found herself pregnant.

FLUSH WITH THE TRIUMPH of his London tour, and having been convinced by his British hosts to abandon his proposed expedition to Crimea, Napoleon III threw himself instead into the final preparations for his much-anticipated international trade fair, the Exposition Universelle, set to open on May 15, 1855, in Paris. This spectacle, intended to showcase French progress in technology, manufacturing, and agriculture and give a big boost to both the economy and the national spirit, was an immense gamble that cost over 10 million francs and required the construction, in less than two years, of three large buildings—the Palais de l'Industrie, the Galerie des Machines, and the Palais des Beaux-Arts. The area allocated to the initiative was equally impressive, encompassing a large portion of central Paris, all the way from the Champs-Élysées, down the Avenue Montaigne, and finally to the banks of the Seine. The fair was entirely reflective of Louis Napoleon's faith in ingenuity and consumerism as the route to future prosperity. As such, the Exposition Universelle represented a key test of his leadership. If it failed to spark the sort of electric enthusiasm that would attract the crowds necessary to justify the investment, particularly with the siege of Sebastopol dragging on so discouragingly, he would invite public humiliation.

They were still hammering on opening day, and many of the exhibits were not fully unpacked for weeks, but by June most of the glitches had been ironed out and the breadth of the accomplishment became clear. Exotic wares from as far away as America, Australia, Egypt, and Japan competed for attention with products from nearer-by Britain, Belgium, Austria, Prussia, Bavaria, Denmark, Sweden, and Switzerland. (Among the devices sent from the United States were Colt revolvers and Singer sewing machines.) The very latest in steam engines, locomotives, industrial drills, and pumps bellowed thunderously for purchase and order in the long Galerie des Machines down by the river. From France came exquisite silks and brocades, many from Lyon; delicate Sèvres porcelain; and fine wines from Bordeaux. The French physicist Léon Foucault exhibited his revolutionary pendulum, which demonstrated the earth's rotation, and in a somewhat less cerebral but equally popular display of recent French innovation, Monsieur Darbo presented for sale the *biberon,* a beautiful glass bottle equipped with a cork nipple, to be used for the feeding of infants, an invention that was soon to put wet nurses out of business.

With the opening of the doors came press accounts of the wonders within, and just like that, the exhibition caught on. Dignitaries and tourists alike streamed into Paris; the energy in the city was palpable. On any given day, upwards of 30,000 people visited the Palais de l'Industrie, where the chief attractions were a rotunda display of the world-famous Gobelins tapestries and the magnificent and mysterious Regent Diamond, presumed to be the largest and most valuable gem of its kind in Europe. "From morning to evening a train of people, like the *queue* at the doors of a theatre when a new piece from some popular author is to be represented, winds round and round, in a spiral fold, the base of the platform, each waiting his or her turn to behold the jewel which some believed to be a myth, and which many supposed to have unaccountably disappeared long since," reported the *Times*.* "Exhibition fever is now settling in," agreed the *Daily News*.

---

* The Regent Diamond was also a source of fascination because it was believed to be cursed. Discovered in a mine in India, the stone was secreted out of the country at the beginning of the eighteenth century. But before the smuggler, rumored to have been a runaway slave, could profit from it, he was killed for his prize. The gem eventually came into the possession of a London dealer, who set an enormous price tag on it and tried to sell it to George I. But the British king refused the offer and, after much haggling, the

But what really separated the Exposition Universelle from its predecessor and chief rival (Britain's Great Exhibition of 1851, the reason for the reconnaissance visit to the Crystal Palace) was the inclusion for the first time at a trade fair of a display of the fine arts. This was Eugénie's idea. Painting and sculpture were as critical to France's national identity as its vineyards and deserved to be showcased and promoted as well, she had urged. Her husband wholeheartedly agreed, going so far as to commission the building of a separate Palais des Beaux-Arts, where the collection would be presented, and appointing her the patron of the exhibit.

Although the empress did not herself choose the pieces to be shown—that task was performed by a select imperial commission headed by the omnipresent Plon-Plon (as a consolation prize for losing his war command) and the distinguished French artists Eugène Delacroix and Jean-Auguste-Dominique Ingres (who hated each other)—her presence was nonetheless much in evidence. In the main salon, where all the principal canvases were hung, were at least five by her favorite court painter, Franz Xaver Winterhalter, including a portrait of Eugénie sitting outside in a park surrounded by her ladies-in-waiting, their luxurious, richly colored silk dresses tumbling over the grass like garlands of peonies in full bloom. With Ingres's *Apotheosis of Napoleon I* (which depicted a naked, very buff Napoleon being carted up to the heavens in a golden chariot) and Delacroix's unfortunately chosen *La Chasse aux lions* (*The Lion Hunt*), in which picturesque Moroccan hunters enthusiastically slaughtered magnificent wild animals, the empress's group portrait was one of the most popular of the exhibit. It greatly

---

jewel ended up going instead at a deep discount in 1717 to the duke of Orléans, who at the time was acting as regent of France for the underaged Louis XV. (That is why it is called the Regent Diamond.) The stone subsequently acquired a well-earned reputation for bringing bad luck to the French monarchy. Marie Antoinette had it sewn into a hat and she was executed. Napoleon I used it to ornament the handle of his sword and he was defeated. His second wife, Marie Louise of Austria, pried the diamond out of the sword and escaped with it and her young son, Napoleon II, to Vienna; the boy contracted tuberculosis and died at twenty-one. Marie Louise's father, Emperor Francis II, graciously (and wisely) returned the stone to France, where Charles X put it in his crown and soon thereafter was forced to flee the kingdom. You'd think they would have known to get rid of it by this time but no—here it was.

enhanced Winterhalter's reputation, particularly in royal circles. Commissions poured in from courts all over Europe; every princess wanted to be painted like Eugénie.*

Disappointingly, the empress herself was absent from Paris that summer. She had clearly been looking forward to the Exposition. Her mother and sister were among those who had been invited to add international luster to the event, and to make it easier for them to attend, Napoleon III had so far relented about his in-laws as to purchase a house in town for them, which Eugénie had taken pains to furnish and decorate herself. The empress had even sent Winterhalter to paint Paca in Madrid so that her sister's likeness could hang near her own in the Palais des Beaux-Arts. On May 8, 1855, Eugénie wrote buoyantly to Paca, "We are waiting with great impatience for your portrait at the exhibition."

But then had come pregnancy, and with it the by now familiar faintness and fear of miscarriage. Eugénie's morning sickness was apparently acute, and she was ordered by her physician to ride out the first three months of her condition in the quiet of the remote spa town of Eaux-Bonnes, near the border with Spain. "Imagine, the doctors told the Emperor that, fortunately, they were still in time, but if I had waited [to begin bed rest], I would never have been able to bear children!" she exclaimed to Paca in a letter at the beginning of July. "Decidedly, I spend my life being sick. Who would have thought that when I was 16?" Even after she was feeling better, the enforced idleness took its toll on her spirit. "I know you go often to the Exposition and are having fun while I vegetate here," Eugénie fumed gloomily. "Please write to tell me if there are many people attending, I am very interested in the fate of the exhibition."

But she was back in Paris by the end of August, in time for the crowning event of the season: the promised return visit by Queen

---

* Plon-Plon was responsible for approving submissions and he did a singularly poor job of it. For example, he turned down *The Painter's Studio* by Courbet, which Delacroix, in his journal, called "one of the most remarkable works of our time." An artist found out that his canvas had been rejected when the crate was returned with the word "*Refusé*" stamped on it; thus we can all thank Plon-Plon for the later genesis of the Salon des Refusés.

Victoria, accompanied by Prince Albert and their two eldest children, Vicky, Princess Royal, and Edward, Prince of Wales, to the Exposition Universelle. This royal reunion prompted great excitement and a renewed flow of tourism. ("Half of England is here," grumbled Méri-mée.) Just prior to the British queen's setting foot on French soil, as if on schedule, Louis Napoleon's soldiers delivered a stinging blow to the enemy in Crimea by defeating a renewed Russian offensive intended to reinforce their beleaguered colleagues at Sebastopol. Eugénie, who had insisted on remaining up to date on the military intelligence coming out of Turkey despite her dreary confinement at Eaux-Bonnes, had hinted at this coming engagement in one of her letters to Paca. "At last, we are at a very decisive moment," she had written. The empress was correct: preventing the Russian reinforcement of Sebastopol would represent a turning point in the war.

The royal family's visit began on August 18 and ended ten days later. To say that this trip made a good impression on Victoria is a gross understatement. On August 23, the queen took time out of her busy schedule to dash off a letter to her uncle Leopold I, the king of the Belgians, from the summer palace at Saint-Cloud, where the emperor and empress had brought the British entourage to give them a respite from the heat of Paris. "I am *delighted, enchanted, amused,* and *interested,* and I think I never saw anything more *beautiful* and gay than Paris—or more splendid than all the Palaces," Victoria gushed. "Our entrance into Paris...was quite *overpowering*—splendidly decorated—illuminated—immensely crowded—and 60,000 troops out...who had come great distances to see me."

No more solicitous a host ever existed than Louis Napoleon. He squired his British houseguests through the myriad sights and charms of Paris and its surroundings with the zeal of an overpaid tour guide escorting a busload of wide-eyed foreigners. In his gallant presence, the queen and her family visited the Exposition (where Foucault personally explained the underlying laws of physics to Victoria, who then went with relief to look at the replica of Eugénie's boudoir and make a substantial purchase of silks from the Lyon exhibit). They attended a special performance of the opera, ogled fireworks, and were the guests of honor at a formal ball at Versailles. "Of the splendour of the *Fête* at Versailles I can really give *no* faint impression, for it exceeded all imagination!" the queen marveled in a later letter to her uncle. "The Emperor has done wonders for Paris," she added approvingly. The London papers agreed. "The Queen has passed through the principal streets of Paris—the most superb capital of Europe...and sees with her own eyes the prosperity of France," reported the on-the-scenes correspondent for the *Morning Post*. "The ordinary results of a century have been completed in the way of public improvements during the reign of Napolcon III. A railway connecting London and Paris with the Mediterranean is another historical event lately completed." In perhaps the most symbolic—and certainly the most bizarre—moment of the entire outing, the emperor escorted the British queen to the majestic tomb of Napoleon I, where they paid their solemn respects to the fallen conqueror—he to his ancestor, she to her kingdom's worst enemy—while a French organist sounded the stirring chords of "God Save the Queen" in the background.

Sadly, although she had returned to Paris expressly to welcome and honor Victoria and her family, Eugénie was still too weak to participate in many of the festivities surrounding the visit. "For the Emperor *personally* I have conceived a *real* affection and friendship," wrote the queen. "We have now seen him for full *ten days*, from twelve to fourteen hours every day—often alone; and I cannot say *how* pleasant and easy it is to live with him, or *how* attached one becomes to him...the dear Empress, who was all kindness and goodness, whom we are all very fond of, we saw comparatively little of," Victoria revealed, "as for *really* and *certainly very* good reasons she must take great care of herself."

But although Eugénie was unable to accompany her guests as much as she would have liked, her influence over their itinerary was nonetheless pervasive. (The empress did manage to attend the grand fête at Versailles, which she had clearly put a great deal of thought and work into. Victoria wrote that Eugénie looked like "a fairy queen or nymph, in a white dress, trimmed with branches of grass and diamonds—a beautiful *tour de corsage* [collar] of diamonds round the top of her dress and...the same round her waist, and a corresponding coiffure," prompting Louis Napoleon to exclaim on seeing her, "How beautiful you are!") It was the empress and her ladies who organized the wondrous balls that so excited the queen's admiration; she who had suggested the glamorous venues for her visitors' entertainment, and had so carefully arranged their schedule to both amuse and instruct. When Victoria, who despite her fondness for the previously displaced French king, admitted that "the Court and whole house [are] infinitely more *regal* and better managed than in poor Louis Philippe's time, when all was in great noise and confusion, and there was *no* Court," it was Eugénie's aura and elegance that the queen was commending.

Victoria's visit sealed the success of the Exposition. The millions of francs it had cost to build might not have been fully recovered, it is true, but the lift the fair gave to the national economy (so many orders flooded into Lyon that summer that the textile manufacturers had to raise wages to attract enough workers), and especially to French prestige abroad, was invaluable. And then, as though this vindication of Louis Napoleon's vision was not enough, a mere week after the British royal family had returned to Windsor, there came word of a second glorious victory for the French army in Crimea.

AFTER NAPOLEON III'S FORCES, assisted only by an advance regiment of Sardinian soldiers, thoroughly routed a Russian offensive intended to reinforce their beleaguered countrymen trapped in Sebastopol, the allies had seized the momentum. On August 17, 1855, they began a ferocious bombing campaign aimed at forcing the tsar to withdraw his men from the peninsula. For three weeks, the city of Sebastopol shook with the deafening explosions and brutal damage caused by 800 French and English cannons; it is estimated that 1,000 Russians died daily in the barrage. And yet, the enemy showed no sign of retreating. It became clear to the French and British commanders that a more decisive blow would be necessary to bring the war to a successful conclusion.

And so, a daring plan was devised. The allied armies were ranged in trenches outside Sebastopol; between this position and the city stood two fortresses, the Malakoff and the Great Redan, held by the Russians as their first line of defense. These barricades the French and British determined to seize in a surprise attack. The French, moving first, were to take the Malakoff; only after they signaled that they had secured it, by raising the distinctive tricolored French flag from the top of the tower, would the British begin their assault on the Great Redan. The day of the strike was set for September 8, 1855.

To catch the enemy off guard, the allies cleverly did not begin their offensive at dawn, as was common practice. Rather, they spent the morning pelting the city with cannonballs and explosive shells, as they had done every day for the past three weeks. But beneath the smoke and noise, 25,000 French soldiers led by General Pélissier, and supplemented by 5,000 Sardinians, crept into the trench closest to the Malakoff. At five minutes to noon, just when the Russians had been lulled into believing that all was as usual, Pélissier suddenly leapt to his feet and, waving his sword in the air, roared "Soldiers, forward! *Vive l'Empereur!*" and the French, "like a swarm of bees, issued forth from their trenches,... scrambled up its [the fortress's] face, and were through the embrasures [openings in the wall] in the twinkling of an eye," the London *Times* correspondent, who witnessed the scene, reported. "They crossed the seven meters of ground which separated them from the enemy at a few bounds—they drifted as lightly and quickly as autumn leaves before the wind, battalion after battalion, into the embrasures, and in a minute or two... the tricolor was floating over the bastion." So quickly did it happen that the British commander did not believe it and sent an officer to investigate. "My General wishes to know if you can hold your position," the officer said. "Tell your General that I am here and that here I stay," replied Pélissier firmly.

He was as good as his word. It did not take the Russians long to recover from their surprise and regroup. Desperately, they tried over and over again to retake the fort, knowing that it was central to the city's defense. "From twelve o'clock to half past seven in the evening, the French had to meet and repulse the repeated attempts of the enemy to regain the work," the *Times* correspondent noted.

Their British allies were of little help. Although it is true that, when they saw the tricolor go up, the first wave of English regiments threw themselves bravely at the Great Redan and managed to scale the walls, there were not enough troops to hold it, and the divisions meant to reinforce the initial assault refused to leave the confines of the trenches. It became clear pretty quickly that the problem was that the infantry did not trust its commanders. "In vain the officers, by voice and act, by example and daring valour, tried to urge our soldiers on," despaired the *Times* reporter. "The men...had an impression... that, if they advanced they would all be blown up."* It did not help when they saw the bodies of their captains, who in trying to get the troops to charge made themselves an easy target for Russian guns, fall in piles around them. Chaos spread; those regiments who had managed to make it into the Great Redan at the outset suddenly abandoned their posts and fled in a panic, scrambling over the fort's walls and out of the gun-openings, and running pell-mell down the incline back to their own lines. "It would be untrue to say that the result of our assault was not the source of deep grief and mortification to us," admitted the *Times* correspondent.

And so the enemy was able to concentrate all of its strength against Malakoff, and yet Pélissier held, as he had promised. This action by the French army was decisive. Around seven o'clock that evening, the Russian general, "weary of the fearful slaughter of his men, who lay in thousands over the exterior of the works, and, despairing of success...withdrew his exhausted legions," the *Times* report continued. To save what was left of his forces, that very evening, in a brilliant strategic retreat, the Russian commander ordered the evacuation of Sebastopol. Under cover of darkness, while his adversaries slept (an unforgiveable lapse of military judgment), he managed to get out not

---

* Difficult to believe that the earlier experience of the Light Brigade, for all of its deliberate glorification, didn't have something to do with this.

only his remaining troops, but all of his artillery and ammunition as well. That which he could not carry with him, he destroyed. He burned his own ships right under the noses of the allied fleet moored in the harbor. "When the first grey rays of morning came, the truth was plain," wrote the shocked *Times* correspondent. "The Russians were abandoning the city...And what were we doing? Just looking on," the reporter fumed in frustration, understanding that had the allied armies been alert, they could have so crippled the escape that the Russian general would likely have been compelled to surrender.

But this missed opportunity in no way overshadowed the magnitude of the previous day's achievement. News of the victory at Malakoff, and the subsequent withdrawal of the Russian army, dropped like an answered prayer on the court of France. "Sebastopol is in the possession of the Allies," the telegram from Crimea read.

AT THE TUILERIES, a much-relieved Louis Napoleon heralded the courageous action of the French soldiers with a cannon salute, a military parade, and a special noon mass on September 13 at Notre-Dame, at which a Te Deum was sung. Hordes of Parisians turned out to cheer the emperor as he and his entourage drove from the palace to the cathedral. "I come here to give thanks to Heaven for the success it has accorded our arms," Louis Napoleon proclaimed solemnly to the crowd. Pélessier was promoted to field marshal for his heroism.

Eugénie, still taking great care with her health, did not accompany her husband to Notre-Dame that day, but a week later was well enough to travel with him to the regimental headquarters at Rueil, near the palace of Saint-Cloud, where a number of those who had been injured in action had been sent to recuperate. She must have passed through the worst of the morning sickness because, in addition to staying a significant length of time conversing with the invalids and honoring their service, the empress used this opportunity to make public her pregnancy by assuming for the first time the right-hand seat next to her husband in the imperial coach, the centuries-old signal among the French that the wife of the sovereign was officially *enceinte*. From this point on, she was seen more frequently at court. On November 23, 1855, Lord Malmesbury went to a dinner at the Tuileries and found Eugénie "looking very handsome, and all appearances concealed by the large dresses now worn."★

Although the failure to disrupt the enemy retreat from Sebastopol meant that the Russian army was able to regroup and remain a threat in Crimea, Napoleon III was determined to use the victory at Malakoff to end the war while he yet had the upper hand. The emperor worked assiduously all through the fall and winter of 1855 to pressure the various combatants to agree to a diplomatic solution, and by January 1, 1856, had so far prevailed that he was able to announce that a new peace conference would be held in Paris. "The year has dawned in splendor; the fortunes of the Empire have attained their apogee," Baron Heeckeren wrote in wonder on January 10. "This war in the Crimea, which has ended so successfully for our arms, has added to the Imperial Crown the glittering jewel of glory. Paris is now the pharos [beacon] of the world. All hopes converge on her."

The peace conference opened in February, but even before the delegates could come to an accord, the French throne had achieved another triumph. On March 16, 1856, after a grueling, two-day labor, during which her screams could be heard throughout the palace, prompting her doctors to despair that either she or her baby must die, Eugénie gave birth to a healthy infant—*and it was a boy.*

Louis Napoleon, who had been by her side the entire time, and who had been forced to make the decision that, should it come to a choice, the empress's life should be saved over that of her child, could hardly believe it. "I got a letter from M. de Persigny, announcing that the

---

★ The fashion in oversized gowns to which Lord Malmesbury referred was achieved by a contraption called a caged crinoline, which the empress had adopted as her signature, over-the-top look. An update on the eighteenth-century pannier worn by her muse, Marie Antoinette, the caged crinoline created a skirt so broad that it often made it difficult for a woman wearing one to get through a doorway. Because they were all the rage at the French court, crinolines were immensely popular for years—Sisi owned one, as did Scarlett O'Hara in *Gone with the Wind*—but for Eugénie, the dome-shaped skirts had the added advantage, as Malmesbury pointed out, of hiding her condition, in case she miscarried again.

Empress of the French was safely confined of a son," wrote Lord Malmesbury. "The Emperor, who never left the room, was worked up into such a nervous state that for fifteen hours he cried and sobbed without ceasing; and when the child was born he was so overpowered with joy that he rushed into the next room and embraced the first five persons he met." The glad tidings were announced immediately. "It is four o'clock in the morning," Heeckeren recorded in his diary entry for March 16. "I am suddenly awakened by the firing of a cannon from Les Invalides. I count the guns. A son! The emperor has an heir!... Everybody is in great spirits; every face is beaming."

As for Eugénie, the birth was so exhausting and painful that, like a wounded soldier, it took her months to recover. In a gesture of respect, the representatives attending the Paris talks, aware of how important their work had been to her—"it is my overwhelming desire for peace that makes me believe in its possibility," she had written to Paca in February when the diplomatic conference first began—bestowed upon her the bejeweled eagle's quill with which they signed the treaty ending the Crimean War on March 30. She was still unable to walk without assistance when she celebrated her thirtieth birthday seven weeks later in May.

But she was well enough to attend her son's christening, held at Notre-Dame on June 14, 1856. It was estimated that some 300,000 people crammed the streets of Paris to watch the imperial procession as it made its way to the cathedral. Mérimée, by virtue of his position as senator and close friend of the family, was among the 4,000 notables fortunate enough to be invited to sit inside the church, and so was able to describe the elaborate ceremony to Eugénie's mother, and reassure her of the much-improved health of her daughter. "The Empress," he advised María Manuela, "was in great beauty and wore a diadem of diamonds worth no doubt two or three kingdoms." At the very center of this tiara, which had been a special gift by a grateful Napoleon III for the birth of his heir, gleamed the Regent Diamond.

ELISABETH

Sisi and Franz Joseph, with little Sophie and Gisela (in the cradle)

12

An Imperial Education

This is the olden fairy wood!
The linden blossoms smell sweetly,
The strange mysterious light of the moon
Enchants my senses completely.

I onward went, and as I went,
A voice above me was ringing;—
'Tis surely the nightingale's notes that I hear,
Of love and love's sorrows she's singing...

The nightingale sang: "O beauteous sphinx!
O loved one, explain the reason
Why all thy raptures with pains of death
Are mingled, in cruel treason?

O beauteous sphinx! Explain to me
The riddle so full of wonder!
I over it many a thousand years
Have never ceased to ponder."

—Heinrich Heine

ON THE MORNING OF MARCH 5, 1855, almost exactly a year before Eugénie experienced the harrowing birth of her son, Sisi awoke with labor pains. Being only seventeen, the Austrian empress had a much easier time of it than her French counterpart. That very afternoon, with both Franz Joseph and his mother there to hold her hand and encourage her, Elisabeth was safely delivered of a healthy child.

Disappointingly, the cannonade announcing this news to the expectant Viennese citizenry fired just twenty times, rather than the hoped-for 100: it was only a girl. Still, the birth was a welcome relief from the privations and worry associated with the ongoing war in Crimea. When, only a month after her confinement, Elisabeth made her first appearance at the opera, "the public, taken by surprise, rose to greet their adored young Empress amid hearty and long-continued demonstrations of joy," the press reported.

Sadly, becoming a mother did nothing to improve Sisi's subordinate position at court. As before, Archduchess Sophia usurped many of the prerogatives that rightly belonged to her daughter-in-law. It was Sophia who chose the baby's caregivers; she who organized the infant's schedule and authorized who would be admitted into the nursery and who would not. Elisabeth was not even allowed to choose her daughter's name; before the empress had a chance to say a word, her husband and his mother had already agreed that the girl should be called Sophie, after the archduchess.

If anything, the severity of Sophia's oppression increased with the birth of the child. The archduchess, intent on raising the girl herself, actually physically removed her granddaughter from Sisi's care by arranging for the nursery to be attached to her own apartments, which were a considerable distance from the empress's rooms at the Hofburg Palace. This action was without precedent at the Austrian court. No one had taken Sophia's offspring away from *her* when they were growing up, and certainly no one would have ever dared remove a child from the custody of the revered eighteenth-century empress Maria Theresa, still the dominant role model for the imperial dynasty.* But once again, Franz Joseph, used to relying without question upon his mother's judgment and experience, sided with her against his wife, and

---

* I'd like to have seen somebody try.

without his active support, Elisabeth was powerless to overrule the archduchess's orders.

As before, these decisions were imposed on Sisi while she was in a weakened state. Although physically healthy, spiritually Elisabeth experienced the gloom endured by many women after giving birth. When she discovered that her husband intended to leave her that summer in order to tour the imperial troops protecting the border against Russia, she begged to be allowed to go visit her family at Possi, rather than stay in Vienna without him. To cheer her up, Franz Joseph gave in and granted her request despite his mother's disapproval.

He could not have bestowed upon his wife a more welcome—or beneficial—gift. It was like Scarlett O'Hara coming home to Tara. Sisi swam and fished in the lake, rode like the wind for hours in the woods, and scrambled for miles along the mountain paths. She poured out her heart to her mother and sisters and ignored the sneers and complaints of her Viennese ladies-in-waiting, who considered the family's manners vulgar.

Consequently, it was the old Elisabeth—the blooming, spirited Elisabeth, full of energy and fire—who left Possi in August to reunite with her husband and baby for Franz Joseph's regular weeklong birthday celebration at Ischl. This year, Sophia had arranged, as a special gift for her son, the culmination of a foreign policy objective very close to the archduchess's heart: the signing of a concordat with Rome that granted sweeping new powers to the Catholic Church, including the reestablishment of the Inquisition throughout the Austrian empire.

NOTHING BESPOKE THE FANATICALLY ultraconservative nature of the imperial court more than this concordat (the official Church term for an agreement with the pope), which Franz Joseph signed into law on his twenty-fifth birthday. By this contract, the emperor voluntarily gave over responsibility for education, both public and private, to the priesthood; recognized as legal only those marriages sanctioned by the Catholic Church, which effectively abolished civil unions and prevented Protestants from wedding Catholics (nuptials involving Jews were already out of the question); awarded the bishopric the power to stifle any publication deemed dangerous to public morals; and established courts of inquisition whose job it was "to impose censures on all the faithful who shall dare to violate and transgress the ecclesiastical laws."

The reaction abroad, particularly in France, was of disbelief. Louis Napoleon, who had tried everything he could think of to persuade Vienna to send soldiers to help fight the Russians in Crimea, including inviting Franz Joseph and Elisabeth to be his honored guests at the Exposition Universelle, cornered Baron Hübner at a dinner party at Saint-Cloud, told him outright that the concordat was an exercise in "stupidity," and asked him how he was supposed to negotiate "with a government that finds the Jesuits too liberal?" Even Eugénie (who had made Sisi a present of a lace gown worth 200,000 francs in an attempt to coax her and her husband to Paris), used to the heavy piety of the Spanish court, was shocked, and called the agreement "medieval."

But for Elisabeth, the signing of this pact offered the first glimmer of insight into her husband and mother-in-law's rule. On the subject of troop movements, foreign allies, and war she had no opinion; but religion was a different matter. She was personally acquainted with Archbishop Rauscher, who was her mother-in-law's confessor and the architect of the papal agreement, and she disliked him. With the signing of the concordat, she became aware for the first time that unlike in Munich, Protestants in the Austrian empire could not worship openly, nor marry Catholics. Sisi found this disturbing and said so publicly, much to the displeasure of the archduchess. "Where I come from," Elisabeth was quoted in a Viennese newspaper as telling a Protestant minister who had appealed to her, and to whom she gave a contribution from her allowance, "your coreligionists have enjoyed these rights, as I know, for fifty years already. My late grandfather used state funds to let the Protestants build the handsome church on the Karlsplatz in Munich." Intermarriage between religions had been allowed in Bavaria since the time of the first Napoleon; her cousin, the current queen, was a Protestant, Elisabeth noted.

These statements were not the naïve protests of a child transplanted to a foreign court, but rather the views of a vivacious young woman who was starting to understand her surroundings, and her own place within them. There was no question that, as she neared her eighteenth birthday, Sisi was growing up.

SEPTEMBER OF 1855 BROUGHT NEWS of the French victory at Malakoff, and the subsequent retreat of the Russians from Sebastopol. Franz Joseph, who had roundly snubbed all of Louis Napoleon's overtures, including the invitation to Paris, was taken by surprise. He had expected the war to grind on until the various participants became so fatigued that, from his vaunted position of qualified neutrality, he could swoop in diplomatically and impose peace terms favorable to Vienna. But now, suddenly, the French seemed to have the upper hand. The Austrian emperor's discomfiture was reflected in the length of time it took him to congratulate his imperial counterpart on his success. Not until October 15, after yet another dinner at Saint-Cloud, did Baron Hübner extend his sovereign's warm felicitations to Napoleon III on the glorious victory at Malakoff, prompting his host to wonder aloud, in a tone dripping with sarcasm, why Franz Joseph, "*his ally*," had not found it convenient to congratulate him sooner.★

This situation did not improve with the arrival of winter. Although Franz Joseph had tried to recover his authority by threatening finally to declare war on Russia if the tsar did not immediately sue for peace and withdraw his forces from Crimea, the western powers considered this too little too late. In December, the Austrian emperor discovered that the diplomatic conference responsible for ending the conflict would be held in Paris, not Vienna as he had expected. More than this—the perfidious (in Franz Joseph's opinion) king of Sardinia, by virtue of having

---

★ Poor Hübner. He also had to listen to Eugénie chastise him about Austria's lack of commitment to the allied war effort. "Let's see," she said. "What have you gained by your policy? You did not conciliate Russia, you have not regained your ascendancy in Germany, and you will not be able to count on the good offices of France and England!"

contributed troops to active combat, had been granted a seat at the negotiating table!

And the worst of it was that, by first appearing to have joined the allied war effort and then backing away from it, he had so isolated Austria from the rest of Europe—not even his uncle, the king of Prussia, was willing to listen to him—that Franz Joseph had no choice but to acquiesce. What had seemed to him at the time to be an honorable neutrality had instead struck everyone else around him merely as false friendship, with the upshot being a significant loss of Austrian influence and prestige. By the time the peace negotiations opened in Paris early the next year, even Franz Joseph could not have helped but recognize that if there was one clear winner to emerge from the struggle in Crimea, it was France.

ABOUT THE ONLY CHEERING INTELLIGENCE the Viennese court received that season was the news that the empress was pregnant again. This was not as happy a prospect for Sisi as it was for everyone else. Pregnancy meant no more riding or traveling; dreary hours spent in the company of her ladies, with whom she had nothing in common and whom she could neither remove nor replace; and the required humiliating public promenades in the garden to showcase her expanding waistline. As she grew heavier, it became more and more difficult to climb the stairs to her daughter's nursery in the archduchess's apartments, and even when she made the effort, either Sophia or her women were always there, so Elisabeth never had any time alone with her child. She complained often to Franz Joseph about this but he declined to confront his mother.

Sophia's authority remained supreme. The archduchess kept a tight hold on her daughter-in-law's communication with her subjects, especially after Sisi's more liberal views on religion got out. To every letter and petition that poured in begging the empress to use her good offices with her husband to soften some blow, Elisabeth's household was instructed to write back, "Her Majesty does not exert any influence." Sisi could not even get Sophia to let her put in a separate bathroom. As had been the custom during the time of Maria Theresa, Elisabeth was forced to sit in a tub behind a screen in a drafty passageway. Her mother-in-law lectured her that what was good enough for the greatest of the Habsburg empresses was certainly good enough for a little princess from Bavaria. To which Sisi retorted that "at Possenhofen there was always the lake to bathe in and in Munich there was the *Hammam* [bath house] her father had installed on his return from his travels in the East."

In March of 1856 came word from France of Eugénie's successful delivery of a son and heir, another triumph for Napoleon III that only put more pressure on Elisabeth. Franz Joseph, wary of the growing affinity between the kingdom of Sardinia and the French court, decided to use the birth as a pretext for sending a high-ranking emissary with his personal congratulations to Paris, to nose around and surreptitiously report back on Louis Napoleon's views and ambitions. For this subtle task, he chose his brother Max.

Max—Archduke Maximilian when he was being formal—was the sibling closest in age to Franz Joseph, which made him next in line to the throne (unless Sisi gave birth to a son). The archduke was to his brother the emperor what champagne is to beer. Max was *fun.* He was drawn to poetry and the arts, and had a passion for Italy, adventure, and the sea. He was more humane and liberal in his political views than the rest of his family but knew to couch these opinions in loyally Austrian sentiments. An officer of the imperial navy from an early age, Max had traveled far more extensively than his elder brother and had acquired a breezy sophistication the latter lacked. He was proud of his lineage to the point of arrogance and longed for glory. The archduke concealed what was essentially a deeply romantic, aspiring character beneath an amusingly cynical exterior. To expose someone of twenty-three-year-old Max's temperament to Louis Napoleon was like sending Don Quixote to sound out a seasoned snake oil salesman.

Although the archduke arrived in Paris in May with his usual hubris intact, it took just twelve days for his host to win him over. In his first report home, Max assailed Napoleon III as a vulgarian, "which hardly produced a favourable impression on me," the archduke sniffed. "His short, unimposing stature, his exterior, which is utterly lacking in nobility, his shuffling gait, his ugly hands, the sly inquiring glance of his lustreless eyes...At the table the Emperor was so ill at ease that the conversation was never entertaining, and it was all I could do to infuse a little life into it," he complained. A few days later, however, Max admitted that he might have been somewhat hasty in his initial assessment of Louis Napoleon. "The Emperor can be very attractive in his frankness and amiability," Max was forced to acknowledge. "He speaks well and with animation...and gives utterance to some very shrewd ideas." By the close of the visit, the archduke had so far revised his opinion that he now characterized Louis Napoleon as "one of those men who do not produce a favourable impression at first sight, but know how to attract on closer acquaintance by their calm, easygoing and open nature. In the frequent conversations which he sought with me, I had occasion to appreciate the sound principles that seemed to inspire him."

Max didn't see much of Eugénie, who was still recovering from her ordeal. "I found the Empress...in a state of great weakness and lassitude; she took extraordinary pains to be nice...Her beauty, which is undeniably great...was dimmed by the imperial memories of Vienna," he made haste to reassure Franz Joseph, referring chivalrously to Sisi. But the archduke *did* have a chance to tour the capital. "It would hardly be believed what transformations Napoleon has effected in the outward aspect of Paris within a short time," he raved. "New streets, new boulevards, countless new buildings, all of gigantic dimensions...in all of his building enterprises, he seems to have...borne in mind not only the beautification of the city, but also strategic advantage," Max noted astutely. "Witness the Palace of Industry, which he himself pointed out to me as a splendid rallying-place for troops...witness the macadamized [tarred] roads, which are very pleasant to drive along, and have also the advantage of doing away with what used to be material for barricades; witness the squares, which are intended to provide open spaces for the troops, . . . [and] the filling up of the trenches, which makes attacks by cavalry possible," he emphasized.*

Nor did the imperial emissary neglect his true mission, which was to clarify his host's position on Sardinia. Were the French intending to reward King Victor Emmanuel for his help in Crimea by supporting his territorial ambitions against Franz Joseph in Italy? Napoleon III was only too happy to relieve his guest's mind on this point. "The Emperor gave me his assurance that his desire was always to act in agreement with Austria," Max was pleased to inform Vienna.

Having reached an understanding on this critical issue, the archduke departed Paris for Brussels, where he was scheduled to visit the Belgian king, who had a pretty daughter the sovereign was hoping to marry off quickly. "Our leave-taking was markedly friendly on the Emperor's side," Max reported with satisfaction in his final letter. "Indeed, I was far better pleased with his manner . . . than I could at first have expected. The Empress's amiability remained unaltered up to the last moment," he added gallantly.

A MONTH LATER, ON JULY 15, 1856, while Max was still traveling around Europe inspecting potential brides, Elisabeth gave birth to her second child. Again, the cannons alerting the populace fired only twenty rounds. Another girl.

The court made no attempt to hide its disappointment. The infant was christened Gisela, after which she, too, was whisked away to the nursery in the archduchess's quarters, to be brought up with her elder sister Sophie by their grandmother.

But this time around, the empress was ready for her mother-in-law. Elisabeth worked on Franz Joseph, pleading with him to return her children to her. It took over a month, but she finally got him to agree to order the imperial princesses transferred to rooms adjacent to her

---

* Franz Joseph took the hint and the very next year ordered Vienna's ditches to be filled in and the streets widened, following the French model.

own. Still, so difficult was it for the twenty-six-year-old emperor to confront his mother, that he shied away from telling Sophia in person. Instead (prudently, as it turned out), Franz Joseph informed the archduchess of his decision while he and Sisi were away on a two-week tour of southern Austria.

Recent scholarship has suggested that the empress's portrayal of her mother-in-law as unsympathetic and controlling was unfairly biased. As evidence, these biographers point to the numerous entries in Sophia's diary where she wrote approvingly of her daughter-in-law's appearance and demeanor (particularly when Elisabeth was being devout and respectful), and of the younger woman's "magical charm." But it is easy to be magnanimous when you are winning all the time. Sophia's reaction to having her authority overturned by her son was far more telling. The enraged archduchess fired off two furious letters to Franz Joseph objecting strenuously to the transfer, claiming that the new rooms would deprive the children of sunlight, and threatening to move out of the palace altogether if she could not have her way.

But her son was out having a glorious holiday in the mountains with his enchanting wife, away from his mother's intimidating presence, and the archduchess's reprimands fell like harmless arrows launched too far from their target. He even wrote bluntly that it was not just Elisabeth who objected to "seeing our children enclosed in your apartments," but he as well. As for Sophia's bitter accusations that the empress was trying to keep her grandchildren away from her, Franz Joseph returned mildly that, on the contrary, Sisi had "specifically asked me to write to you and tell you that they will always be entirely at your disposal."*

When the imperial couple returned to Vienna later in September from their excursion, the nursery was relocated. The empress had her daughters back.

THAT FALL, WITH THE WAR in Crimea over, Franz Joseph finally had time to turn his attention to some of the other problem spots in his

---

* As I said, it is much easier to be generous when you are winning.

realm. An inspection tour of his Italian provinces, for example, was long overdue. The commander in charge of his forces there (still Radetzky, who was among those who had helped Sophia take over in her coup) would be celebrating his ninetieth birthday in November, and it was thought that the general's advanced age and possible senility might have something to do with the puzzlingly persistent unrest among the civilian population. A visit by the emperor would naturally stabilize the situation and smooth the way for a change in military leadership. As a further expression of imperial goodwill, it was agreed that the empress would accompany her husband on the journey. Everyone at court knew that Italians responded favorably to beautiful women, and when it came to imperial allure, no one beat Sisi.

For Elisabeth, who would be nineteen on Christmas Eve, had at last grown into her looks. Her face had lost its adolescent roundness. Allowed once again to ride for hours and clamber up the sides of mountains with Franz Joseph on their recent travels through southern Austria, she had recovered easily from her second pregnancy and was as tall and slender as any nymph out of Greek mythology. Her sublime auburn tresses, which when loose flowed in cascades to below her waist, were a marvel.*

The empress, who loved to get away from the dull routine of her existence in Vienna, was eager to go, but only if she could take her elder daughter with her. Gisela, not yet six months old, was too young for such a trip, but Sophie was by this time a toddler. The Italian tour was expected to take months, and this, Sisi felt, was too long to be away from a child who had only recently been returned to her care. If she left Sophie now, Elisabeth would have to start regaining the child's trust all over again when she returned.

Sophia was appalled. Sophie, pretty and prattling, was her grandmother's favorite. The archduchess, who had raised only boys—the one daughter she had borne had died tragically at the age of five—adored the

---

* You begin to get a sense of why Franz Joseph was starting to listen to her, and not his mother.

toddler. But Sophie was also often ill. The child was too delicate to go on such an arduous journey, Sophia remonstrated. She must be left at home.

But Sisi insisted. In effect, her mother-in-law, still unreconciled to losing control of her granddaughters, left her no choice. (One of Sophia's more withering observations was that she was not about to have the imperial children brought up by someone who "did not know how to bring up herself.") Elisabeth recognized that she was in a competition that she could not afford to lose. Again, Sisi was forced to appeal to her husband, arguing that the milder climate in Italy might actually improve Sophie's health. And gratifyingly, Franz Joseph once more ruled in her favor. In fact, so far had the emperor come that he did not even feel the need to leave town first before informing his mother of his decision.

And so, against the backdrop of the archduchess's icy disapproval, Sisi, Sophie, and Franz Joseph left the Hofburg Palace on November 17, 1856, to begin the long trek southward to their first stop, Venice.

It took almost two weeks to get there. Although plans for a railway linking Vienna to the port of Trieste on the Adriatic Sea had been approved, construction had been held up by lack of funds, and the project was nowhere near completion. Most of the trip was conducted by carriage (it took thirty-seven horse-drawn coaches to transport the accompanying imperial entourage and all the luggage), followed by a journey westward across the sea. Elisabeth loved being on the water and was clearly excited to be visiting a city as storied and romantic as Venice.

And yet, she could not have helped but notice that their arrival was greeted by suspicious, not to say threatening, behavior. Just before they were to board the vessel that would ferry them across the Adriatic to their destination, the ship's distinctive crystal crown, signifying its imperial status, mysteriously shattered. There was no getting away from the impression that this seemingly random act of destruction might have been the result of deliberate sabotage.

And it only got worse when they landed in Venice. It's true that the principal square of Saint Mark's was crammed with spectators who had gathered specifically to view the emperor's procession into the city. But in an obviously coordinated and extremely persuasive exercise of passive resistance, rather than the usual cheers, the assembled multitude remained *completely silent* as Franz Joseph and Elisabeth rode past. "The crowd's only feeling was one of curiosity to see the Empress, whose reputation for marvelous beauty has naturally penetrated even to this place," reported the British consul stationed in Venice.

In fact, during the whole of the emperor and empress's six-week stay, the Venetian citizenry treated their Austrian visitors as though they were war criminals (which, in their opinion, they were). Theater boxes usually occupied by the high nobility remained empty when Franz Joseph and Sisi attended a performance. Fewer than a quarter of the guests invited to imperial entertainments showed up, and those who did had to dodge the abuse hurled at them by swarms of bystanders. It was difficult for Elisabeth even to venture out into the streets, for she was mobbed by those petitioning her husband for clemency. The only time the native population showed any cordiality at all to the couple was on December 3, when they applauded Franz Joseph at the opera for having just declared a general amnesty for political prisoners.

And it was the same everywhere they went throughout the rest of the tour. They left Venice on January 5, 1857, stopping in the rural municipalities—Vicenza, Verona, Brecia, and Bergamo—on their way to Milan. Again, the eerie, contemptuous silence of the onlookers as the imperial procession entered each town; again, the abrupt departure of the privileged classes, and their humiliatingly low attendance at official fêtes; again, the risk of violence. (The threatening message, "The Emperor arrives at 1500. We will get him at 1600," had to be scrubbed off a wall in Bergamo just prior to their arrival.) In Milan, the Austrian military resorted to paying the peasantry to crowd the streets and warned the population that "if anybody by criminal political obstinacy persisted in not frequenting the theatre, such conduct would be regarded as the silent demonstration of a criminal disposition, which merited being sought out and punished." But though they took the money and filled the plaza, the spectators still maintained their fraught silence, and domestic servants were outfitted with gloves signifying bereavement and sent to take the places of the noble families in the boxes at the famous opera house.

Nothing like this had ever happened to Elisabeth (or to Franz Joseph, for that matter). Throughout her previous travels in Austria and Bohemia, the empress had only to set foot outdoors to be mobbed by enthusiastic well-wishers. Her appearance at a concert or the theater was considered a great favor, and provoked heartfelt, spontaneous applause.

Now, for the first time, both she and her husband saw how much the Austrian regime was hated. Sisi could not speak Italian but she did not need the language to understand that the common people were suffering under military rule, and she did her best to intercede on their behalf. Countess Esterházy, whom Elisabeth had been forced to bring along on the trip (and who functioned as a spy for Sophia), reported to the archduchess that "the Empress is now committed to the *sans culottes* [the rabble] and ruins Imperial prestige by sympathizing with every rascal."

Sophia may have fumed at this breach of protocol, but in fact Sisi was a considerable asset to Franz Joseph on this trip. She did not shirk her duty once, but remained loyally by his side at every function, which helped to both humanize him and add an appealing glamour to his efforts. (Her spectacular crinoline evening gowns, modeled on Eugénie's, were so bouffant that on one occasion the archbishop of Milan became entangled with her dress merely by passing her on a staircase, and to her barely repressed giggles, could only be liberated by tearing off some of the outer folds.) It was Elisabeth who, in a flood of tears, convinced Franz Joseph to defy his military advisers and declare a general amnesty for those exiled on political grounds (an intervention strongly opposed by Count Grünne, another of Archduchess Sophia's close friends and spies, who was attached to the emperor's household). Taxes were reduced and expropriated property returned to its rightful owners. The ninety-year-old Radetzky was gracefully retired, and the military regime replaced by a civilian authority.

For the new position of governor-general of Lombardy-Venetia, the emperor thought to appoint his brother Max. Max had decided to marry the Belgian king's daughter after all—her name was Charlotte—and, since this meant that he would be starting a family, the archduke would need a more prestigious and lucrative employment anyway. Also, in contrast to his previous administrators (and Franz Joseph himself), the emperor remembered that Max actually *liked* Italy and the Italians.

And so, by the time the imperial entourage departed Milan on March 2, 1857, to begin the long ride back to Vienna, the first real steps to soften the harsh Austrian rule, in place for nearly a decade, had been taken. It would never have happened if it had been Archduchess Sophia, rather than Elisabeth, who had embarked on the journey with the emperor. "Italy has been allowed to go on too long feeling the conditions of 1848 [martial law]," Franz Joseph admitted on the way home.

There was one additional benefit to this otherwise disconcerting northern Italian tour: to the relief of her parents, little Sophie's health stabilized. She did seem to respond to the milder climate, and the joy Sisi took in having her daughter with her was palpable. In that respect, at least, the visit could be deemed a success.

THE EMPEROR AND EMPRESS had no sooner returned to Vienna in mid-March than plans were put in place for yet another official state tour, this time to rambunctious Hungary. Having personally witnessed the adverse effects of prolonged military rule on his Italian provinces, Franz Joseph now thought to investigate some of the other volatile regions under his dominion, to see if perhaps adjustments were due in these places as well. And chief among those citizens still agitating for relief from repression were the Hungarians.

Hungary was the emperor's largest and most important realm. Thirteen million people lived in Hungary. (By contrast, Bohemia had 7 million, and the Austrian population numbered only 4 million.) More than this, the kingdom had a wealth of natural resources and provided a useful geographical barrier to potential enemies. For centuries, Hungary had been all that stood between Vienna and the

Turks to the south, and the Russians to the east. Without the Hungarians, Franz Joseph's domain looked more like a vulnerable, oversized duchy than an empire.

Although they had only just returned from nearly five months of travel, the visit was scheduled for early May, less than six weeks away, and the empress was again expected to accompany her husband. Elisabeth's beauty had by this time been so acclaimed in the press that her Hungarian subjects would have been disappointed not to see her, and might possibly even have taken her absence as a snub. The imperial court could not take the chance that Sisi's failure to appear would reflect poorly on the emperor and work against the success of the mission. She had to go.

But after seeing Elisabeth's effect on Franz Joseph and his Italian possessions, the faction at court headed by her mother-in-law now identified the empress as a possibly potent threat to their authority. Sophia and her allies believed Slavic and Magyar Hungarians to be racially inferior to Austrians of German lineage like themselves. They despised and feared the neighboring kingdom as a hotbed of revolutionary activity that could only be controlled through coercion and intimidation. They were aware that the empress must accompany her husband on the visit, but were resolved to do all they could to prevent her from interceding on behalf of the common people, as she had in Italy.

And so, soon after her return, Sisi walked into her rooms after riding one morning to find that someone had mysteriously placed an old pamphlet, printed in Paris in 1774, on her desk. It was a scurrilous treatise written about Marie Antoinette, which had been brought to Vienna the century before in an attempt to extort money from the French queen's mother, Maria Theresa, to suppress it. (No luck there. The empress had simply threatened to have the blackmailer thrown into prison.) The tract had been deliberately left open to these lines: "The natural destiny of a Queen is to give an heir to the throne; and the King who says to his wife, 'Madame, We look to you to give Us sons and not advice,' and thus puts the ambitious creature in her place, has taught a lesson to all Queens in the world...If the Queen is so fortunate as to provide the State with a Crown-Prince, this should be the end of her ambition—she should by no means meddle with government of an Empire."

Impossible to determine who had placed this insulting text in her room. Elisabeth, although wounded, kept this petty harassment to herself and never investigated. It is difficult to believe that this document could have found its way to the empress without at least the tacit approval of the archduchess, as there was not much that went on in her daughter-in-law's apartments of which she was not informed. What can be said with certainty, however, is that there is no greater sign of how far Sisi had come, and how close she was to taking her rightful position at court, than that her worried adversaries felt the need to resort to this level of spite.

THE IMPERIAL FAMILY LEFT VIENNA for Pesth, Hungary, on May 4, 1857. Their entourage, which included 100 horses and several ornate state carriages, was sent on ahead of them the week before.

This time, Elisabeth insisted on taking nine-month-old Gisela along, as well as two-year-old Sophie. The empress had been unhappy to return home from Italy to find that her youngest daughter did not know her, and had cried for her grandmother when Sisi tried to hold her. She did not want to leave her baby again so quickly. Sophia had as usual protested that it was unhealthy for the children to travel and that they should be left at home in her care, but she again lost the argument. Franz Joseph agreed with his wife, especially as a voyage to Hungary wasn't nearly as long or fatiguing as going to Italy. After all, the warmer weather had arrived, and Pesth was only a little more than a day's steamboat ride from Vienna.

Hungary was a kingdom Elisabeth had been looking forward to visiting ever since her history tutor, Johann Mailáth, had regaled her with stories of his countrymen's gallantry and valor. She was not disappointed. She and Franz Joseph arrived on May 5 to an immense throng, estimated to be some 60,000 people. Their progression into the city was preceded by troops of Hungarian Lancers in splendidly colorful dress uniforms, dozens of court trumpeters, and regional magnates in elaborate equipages, with packs of uniformed footmen running beside them. Sisi rode in a "state glass coach drawn by magnificent grays," detailed the London *Times* correspondent, who was there. "Her Majesty, who looked remarkably well, wore an Hungarian headdress... That their Majesties were received with loud cheers and flourishes of trumpets need hardly be said."

The next day, she rode on horseback to survey the troops with her husband. Again, the crowds came out to see her. "The grace and beauty of the young Empress fascinates all hearts," another of the London papers reported. "All who see her remark on her beauty." For her part, Elisabeth felt a strong affinity with the populace and the landscape. She was charmed by the wild, rustic allure of Hungary.

Of course, by this time, accounts of the empress's sympathetic attitude towards the repressed had reached the Hungarians. Part of the enthusiasm they displayed for her was because they were hoping that she would use her influence to convince Franz Joseph to reinstate their long-standing constitution and allow them an autonomous, representative government. These ambitions, however, the emperor had no intention of granting, and Sisi, whose education in Hungarian history did not extend to the brutality of 1849, would not have thought to interfere.

What Franz Joseph did do was to issue a general amnesty on May 10 for all political prisoners, including those who had been in exile, complete with the return of their property. Although Elisabeth was given credit by the general population for his action, this time around there had been no need for tears or pleading. The emperor was simply granting the Hungarians the same concessions he had just approved for his Italian subjects.

It wasn't enough for the majority of the citizenry, but it was a start, and the visit was clearly going well. The splendid balls were well attended, and bouquets of fresh flowers were transported daily from the imperial gardens in Vienna by steamer to enhance the décor of the emperor and empress's dinner parties. Sisi visited a number of philanthropic institutions, including a children's hospital.

And then, on May 13, just as Elisabeth and Franz Joseph were about to begin a two-week tour of eastern Hungary, Gisela fell ill. Sisi insisted on postponing the excursion to sit with her baby. Within a week, the crisis had passed, and she and Franz Joseph were just beginning to think about starting off again when, on May 19, as so often happens with children, the high fever and intestinal distress that had attacked Gisela spread to Sophie. In Sophie's case, however, it was much more severe. She was up all night with intense stomach pain. "The little thing cries and screams incessantly in the most heart-rending way," an obviously shaken Franz Joseph wrote home to his mother in Vienna. Again, Elisabeth refused to leave her daughter's side.

But then, mercifully, the fever passed, just as it had with Gisela. By May 23, Sophie was so much better that her relieved parents, assured by the Viennese court doctor (appointed by Archduchess Sophia) that the worst was over, were able to resume their tour of Hungary. Of course, both children were left in Pesth with the physician and a full staff to rest and recover.

Only it wasn't over. The imperial party had just reached the town of Debreczen, nearly 150 miles to the east, when a telegram arrived from the doctor, warning the emperor that Sophie had relapsed. Elisabeth and Franz Joseph rode all day and night to be back with their child. They reached Pesth on the morning of May 29 to find their cherished two-year-old in a stupor, struggling to survive.

The end came at nine thirty that evening. For eleven hours, Sisi sat by the bed of her small daughter, watching her die.

ELISABETH'S GRIEF WAS PROFOUND. Franz Joseph, too, was affected, but her suffering was the more devastating because she was so sensitive and vulnerable. There was guilt there, too—guilt for having listened to the doctor, for having left her child to go on some obligatory ceremonial procession for protocol's sake. The blackness surrounding her was all encompassing; she could not stop weeping.

The rest of the trip to Hungary was called off; the imperial entourage packed its bags, and the emperor and empress left Pesth on May 30 to return to Laxenburg. They would not arrive until the following day. But, significantly, the papers had the story almost immediately. By June 1, 1857, the London *Times* correspondent stationed in Vienna had already wired his editor. "Although firmness is one of the most prominent features in the character of the Emperor Francis Joseph," the journalist wrote, "he is greatly afflicted at the loss of his little daughter, and reproaches himself for not having followed the advice of the Archduchess Sophia, his mother, which was that the two little girls should be placed under her care during the Hungarian journey. The grief of the bereaved mother is also very great," the correspondent added. "The Hungarians aver that the spring water at Buda is excellent, but it disagreed with the Imperial children... during the week preceding the decease... water was sent twice a day from Schönbrunn."★

There was only one possible source for this information: the Hofburg Palace. Freedom of the press was prohibited throughout the empire. The papers were only allowed to print the government-approved version of a news item. What is so striking about the *Times* account, which was repeated in the Viennese papers, is its obvious slant and level of detail. The imperial court was not known for its transparency, and yet in this instance the public was treated to a rare, behind-the-scenes look that could only have come from one place — Archduchess Sophia's faction.

★ There is no way to know with certainty what Sophie died of, as no autopsy was performed, but it was suspected at the time to be typhoid fever, which comes from contaminated water. That is why the palace was so intent on demonstrating that it had done everything it could, even to the point of shipping the children's drinking water to Hungary, but it had been too late for little Sophie. The irony is, of course, that if it was typhoid fever, it might well have been the Schönbrunn water that was responsible, in which case the two-year-old would have been equally likely to contract it had she stayed home. Notably, Archduke Max had come down with typhoid fever while visiting Vienna in the early spring of 1851.

In fact, this was nothing less than a blatant attempt to lay the blame for the death of a beloved two-year-old on her devastated nineteen-year-old mother, in order to keep the empress in line. In doing so, it anticipated by 150 years future attacks on other beautiful, spirited women who refused to conform to the pattern dictated by a royal family. And like today, it could not have been printed without the approval of the reigning sovereign—in this case, Archduchess Sophia.

Upon the imperial couple's return from Hungary, Franz Joseph returned the care of their surviving daughter, Gisela, to his mother.

EUGÉNIE

The countess of Castiglione

13

The Disciples of the Dagger

Usually, it is man who attacks; as for me, I defend myself, and
I often capitulate.

—Napoleon III

THE BIRTH OF HER SON, known as the prince imperial (and familiarly by
his parents as Louis), cemented Eugénie's position at court.* By bringing forth a male heir, she both ensured the future of the dynasty and
displaced her husband's inept cousin Plon-Plon from his formerly
prime spot in the line of succession. She could not have done the
emperor and his subjects a greater service.

But this triumph had come at a great cost. So difficult had been the
birth that the empress's doctors warned her that she would not survive
another pregnancy. Eugénie could have no more children. This grim
disclosure, exacerbated by her weakened state and long, fitful recovery,
weighed heavily on her. "My little man does well, thank God," she
wrote to Paca on June 6, 1856, just before her son's christening. "It's
the only rosy aspect my eyes can discern."

And so, that August, while Elisabeth was recuperating from the

---

* He was of course christened Napoleon for maximum brand identification, just like
every other male in the family. Worse, in homage to his father (and no doubt to the
despair of countless historians and biographers), his full name was Louis Napoleon. Thus,
my reliance on the title prince imperial.

birth of Gisela (and trying to convince her husband to stand up to his mother and return her daughters to her), Eugénie, hoping to restore both her health and her spirits, gathered up her husband and infant son and escaped to her palace in Biarritz for an extended family holiday.

Biarritz was to Eugénie what Possi was to Sisi. Located on the southwestern coast of France, close to the border with Spain, Biarritz boasted access to both the Atlantic Ocean and the foothills of the Pyrenees. It was a sleepy little fishing village when Eugénie first discovered and fell in love with it. To please her, Louis Napoleon had a palace built right on the beach, which became known as the Villa Eugénie.* Here she could swim, or board the dispatch boat that the emperor kept harbored nearby for a day-trip across the Bay of Biscay, or saddle a horse for a ride through the countryside, or drive out in a carriage to scale the mountains on a burro led by guides from the local Basque community. "At Biarritz, everything reminded her of her native land," remembered a visitor. "Climate, customs, even language, for at the Villa Eugénie, as well as on the sea front, one heard Spanish frequently spoken."

Political discussions were banned at Biarritz; Louis Napoleon, too, had been worn down by overwork and needed rest. All formality was cast aside. ("Come without knee-breeches," the empress instructed Mérimée in the telegram she sent inviting him to visit.) Evenings were given over to dancing, dinners with friends, and parlor games. "Biarritz was the only seaside residence of the Empress, who loved the sea and everything and everybody connected with it," the same friend observed. "I think that Biarritz was the place where she was most truly herself, simply because there she could, as far as was possible to a French Sovereign, do as she pleased, say what she thought, and see whom she liked."

The six weeks Eugénie spent with her husband and child in the relaxed atmosphere of her beach house revived her. She took some form of exercise every day and laughed and danced in the evenings. The prince imperial's doctor, who accompanied his small charge on

---

* It's a hotel today. You can stay there!

this journey, recorded the change in her appearance in a series of letters to his family. On July 8, 1856, just prior to the trip to Biarritz, he was shocked by how ill the empress looked. "The first time I saw her in 1854, I should have said she was twenty-four to twenty-five years old," he wrote. "Today she looked a good thirty-five." But happily by September 22, near the end of the holiday, he was able to report, "In the evening she is blooming with youth and beauty...Since we have been at Biarritz there has almost always been a ball twice a week. I do not think I have ever seen such a number of such pretty women together," he confessed. "But I cannot compare them with the Empress. She shines in the midst of these ladies like the fairest flower in the garden."

Significantly, as had Franz Joseph and Elisabeth, Eugénie and Louis Napoleon consulted their son's doctor as to whether it would be dangerous to bring the infant along on a trip to southern France. But even though Biarritz was three times as far from Paris as Pesth was from Vienna, the physician saw no reason the five-month-old should not accompany his parents. "We spoke of the health of the Prince,...the objections to a stay in the South, the dangers of travel, and the sanitary condition of Paris and Biarritz," he noted. "I sought to reassure their Majesties...that with a few precautions there will be no ill results." The doctor was proved correct: the prince imperial thrived. And having her baby, whom she adored, with her no doubt also contributed to the empress's strong recovery.

With the return of health came a more optimistic outlook and the renewal of Eugénie's natural vivacity. There was, after all, much to celebrate. Yes, she could not have more children, but she did have a precious, robust son, and with this, and the successful conclusion of the war, the emperor and empress were more popular than ever.

For the first time in three years, France was at peace. The courageous soldiers had returned; the economy, fueled by advancements in transportation and industry, and especially the investment in railroads, was strong. "Truly this year...is happy after the fashion of Nations which have no annals," Baron Heeckeren, the banker, crowed with satisfaction. "I can prove it by the receipts of the theatres." For once, the imperial couple did not have to worry about battles or troop movements. Eugénie could look forward to a brilliant social season.

It was well that she returned from her holiday rested. Because in the nineteenth century, no sooner did one problem spot die down than another flared up. That Italy would be next on the list was signaled in rather unorthodox fashion by the arrival of a drop-dead knockout from Turin by the name of the countess of Castiglione.

ITALY IN 1856 WAS DIVIDED into eight pieces, like the uneven shards of a broken urn. In the north, Austria occupied Lombardy and Venetia, while the king of Sardinia, Victor Emmanuel, held Piedmont, Savoy, and Nice. In the south, the king of Naples, Ferdinand II, ruled over everything below Rome, plus the island of Sicily. In the middle were five small fiefdoms held by the pope, the grand duke of Tuscany, and the more minor (but no less puffed-up) dukes of Modena, Parma, and Lucca.

It was consequently a nightmare to try to travel through, or sell goods and services in, Italy. Each piece of the pottery, no matter how small, had its own identity papers, customs duties, and tax rules (as was reflected by the maddeningly long lines at the borders). Each despot had his own military and secret police force, which did not cooperate well with the others'.

For decades—actually, for centuries—there had been a call from within to unify Italy, but by the fall of 1856, this clamor had become a shriek. Because nothing was ever easy, there were two warring schools of thought on how this could best be accomplished. On one side was the king of Sardinia, who believed it was necessary above all to oust Austria first, and *then* unify under a strong leader—himself. Having fought Franz Joseph's troops in the past and lost, however, he was reluctant to confront them again without the aid of an experienced foreign army. Hence Victor Emmanuel's alliance with France against Russia, and the pressure his prime minister, Count Cavour, put on Napoleon III to reciprocate for the soldiers Sardinia had sent to fight beside the French in Crimea.

On the other side of the argument was a messianic Genoese philosopher, freelance editor, and media influencer by the name of Giuseppe Mazzini. Mazzini had been given a classical education as a child (big mistake) and had become enamored with the Greek ideal of a republic. He was as committed to *not* having a king as he was to unifying Italy. Mazzini despised and distrusted Napoleon III, because at the pope's request, France had sent soldiers to Rome to help the papacy ward off

Italy before unification

revolution. Mazzini's plan—and he was forceful about it—was for the Italians to conduct guerilla warfare until such time as they could all come together as one nation, cast off the foreign troops, revolt against all the despots, and proclaim a republic.

By the fall of 1856, the feud between these two sides had devolved into a ferocious, real-world game of capture-the-flag. It was understood that whoever succeeded first in his objectives would determine the future of Italy. As it was obviously much easier for Victor Emmanuel to coax one man—Louis Napoleon—into providing military support than for Mazzini to get millions of people from all classes of society across the peninsula to put aside their provincial prejudices and come together for the good of the country, the faction favoring a republic was at a distinct disadvantage. To even the odds, members of the Mazzini party embraced an age-old ideology which in the nineteenth century went by the romantic designation "the theory of the dagger," and which today is identified as political assassination.

The emperor had already felt the hot wrath of one of these volunteer executioners. The year before, he had been out riding peacefully along the Champs-Élysées when suddenly a nearby pedestrian pulled out a gun and took two shots at him. Luckily for Napoleon III, both bullets missed. (This perhaps gives a sense of why it was not called "the theory of the pistol.") The would-be killer was tried and guillotined as a warning to others, but the threat lingered.

With the opposing Mazzini faction launching covert assassins at the French emperor as though they were long-range artillery shells, it wasn't too difficult for Count Cavour to persuade Louis Napoleon that his true interests lay in an alliance with Victor Emmanuel. And just to demonstrate to the French emperor who his *real* friends in Italy were, the prime minister thoughtfully sent him a little gift.

The countess of Castiglione—"whose Christian name, Virginia, was in marked contrast with her real nature," as a wit observed—was nineteen when she first appeared in Paris. "I must frankly confess that when I saw her for the first time her beauty really took my breath away," remembered the wife of an embassy official. "She was wearing a white tulle dress, strewn with long-stemmed roses; she wore no ornament in her magnificent hair, which in front was dressed to resemble a tiara. She had the figure of a nymph; her neck, shoulders, arms, hands... all seemed to be hewn out of rose-coloured marble of the most delicate shade," the woman marveled. "Though the bodice of the dress was cut extremely low, it hardly looked indecent, to such a degree did this splendid creature resemble an antique statue. And her face was the equal to her body; its shape a delicious oval; the complexion fresh and exquisite; dark green velvety eyes... Never have I seen anyone so beautiful; never again shall I see anyone so beautiful."

The countess of Castiglione happened to be Count Cavour's cousin. She was married at a young age and already had a son; having done her duty by her husband, she subsequently took as small account of him as he did of her. She had been idling around Turin, marking time by engaging in an obligatory, desultory affair with Victor Emmanuel, when the prime minister decided that Virginia could make better use of her considerable talents in France. Appealing to the countess's patriotism, which in fairness was deep and genuine, he recruited her to travel to Paris as (literally) an undercover agent, instructing her to do everything in her power to get Napoleon III to send an army to Piedmont to help fight the Austrians. He even gave her a code book, so she could report back secretly on her progress. "I advise you that I have enrolled in the ranks of diplomacy the very beautiful countess, enjoining her to be coquettish and, if need be, to seduce," Cavour wrote to a contact in France.

Mata Hari she wasn't, but with her looks and style she didn't have to be. Virginia, disdaining both the caged crinoline and the ordinary corset as distracting unnecessarily from her natural assets, opted for a slinkier silhouette. When she entered a ballroom or strolled insouciantly through a crowded assembly, clad only in sheer muslin, the fabric clinging suggestively below her plunging décolletage, many of the male guests were prompted to clamber up on chairs to get a better view.

Impossible for the empress to compete with this degree of ravishing sensuality. Louis Napoleon was aware of the countess's flaws—she was described by another courtier as being "utterly devoid of charm...Indeed, in watching her move and converse, one would almost have declared that she was an animated bit of sculpture"—but chose to overlook them. Nor was the emperor taken in by the countess of Castiglione's obvious attempts to sway him in favor of military action against Austria. Her conversation bored him, but then, he wasn't there to chat.

Eugénie could not help but be aware of her rival—everyone was. Her husband was infatuated and his mistress flaunted it. The countess of Castiglione was invited everywhere—to hunt at Compiègne that November, to the Tuileries and Saint-Cloud for the holidays, to Fontainebleau in the spring of 1857, to Plombières in the summer. The emperor and empress would attend a grand fête, only to have Louis Napoleon sneak out into the garden and depart with his Italian paramour, leaving his wife to bear the knowing glances of the other guests. He and Eugénie would be sitting in the imperial box at the theater, when the countess, seated with friends below, would suddenly make a great show of feigning illness and withdraw, whereupon the emperor, too, would suddenly find himself indisposed and exit, requiring Eugénie to sit abandoned through the rest of the performance. Eventually, Louis Napoleon just went ahead and bought Virginia a house in Paris, No. 53, Rue Montaigne, which he visited every evening at 11 p.m. sharp whenever he was in the capital.

It was utterly humiliating for the empress. "Last night there was a fancy-dress ball at the Ministry of Foreign Affairs," a gossipy courtier reported on February 18, 1857. "The Countess de Castiglione, who, they say, is on the most intimate terms with the Emperor, had the most fantastic and daring costume imaginable. Half Louis XIV, half modern, it won her the title of *Dame des cœurs* [Queen of Hearts]...More than one woman let loose her jealousy; impartial men thought, but did not say, 'I would like to be the Emperor,'" he noted gleefully. Publicly, Eugénie kept her head high, but privately she stood up for herself, and there were bitter fights and tears, which were overheard and circulated in the press despite the court's best attempts to suppress them. "The

Count and beautiful Countess Castiglione have left Paris, at the suggestion of those who think that the lady's absence might be conducive to the domestic happiness of the tenants of the Tuileries," snickered one such news item after a particularly contentious marital altercation that resulted in Virginia's (temporarily) hightailing it out of town.

The affair was *so* widely reported in fact that (despite the countess's diligent use of her code book) the Mazzini faction took notice and tried to ambush Napoleon III on one of his regular nocturnal visits to the Rue Montaigne. Fortunately, the Italian liberators once again proved inept, and the conspiracy failed. "An attempt was to have been made on Tuesday evening upon the Emperor as he left the abode of the Marquise de Castiglione, the beautiful Sardinian lady, whom the Emperor greatly admires," one of the London papers noted on April 12, 1857. "The plot was discovered, and its originators are already ruminating over their disappointment in their [prison] cells."

Poor Eugénie! It was a terrible year for her. Not only was she being taunted by a well-endowed teenager, she was also roundly snubbed by the tsarina of Russia, who initially declined to accompany her husband, Alexander II, when he arranged to meet Napoleon III and Eugénie in Stuttgart that October, an action that forced her French counterpart to withdraw as well. "No sooner, however, was the absence of that illustrious Lady [Eugénie] certain, than . . . the Empress of Russia . . . hastened to Stuttgardt and partook of its pleasures, without involving herself in a personal recognition of Empress Eugénie. The insult is plain and unmistakable," the correspondent for the *Daily News* noted. Another London paper pointed out that "the Czarina is also said to have expressed her determination not to make the acquaintance of the Empress Eugénie, whom some of her Court ladies irreverently call 'the lady of the crinoline.' "

The Russian indignity was the last straw. Upon his return from Stuttgart, Louis Napoleon sent the countess of Castiglione (whom, his ardor satiated, he discovered he did find tiresome) back to her homeland. But this was a hollow victory for his wife, whose pain is manifest in a letter written to Paca two months later, on December 31, 1857, in which Eugénie, without mentioning any names, railed against the newspapers and the gossips, and poured out her distress. "Perhaps tired of fighting against a hostile fate, I closed my eyes and let myself go adrift...I often wonder if it is worth fighting for, and I lack courage," she despaired. Then, quickly, so as not to cause her sister undue anxiety, she added, "But please erase that little frown and believe as I do that '*it was written.*' If the maxim is not new, at least it is consoling," she finished soothingly.

Eugénie may have been unsure she had the fortitude to go on, but this proved to be erroneous. The empress was every bit the valiant two weeks later when the disciples of the dagger struck again.

THIS NEW AND FAR MORE DESTRUCTIVE ATTEMPT by Italian nationalists to assassinate Louis Napoleon occurred on the evening of January 14, 1858, as the emperor and empress, accompanied by a procession of friends and attendants, were on their way to the opera. It was about eight thirty, and darkness had already fallen, but the streets were crowded with revelers jockeying to see the members of the imperial party as they alighted from their carriages. All at once, the boulevard in front of the theater was shaken by a volley of blasts that filled the air with broken glass and shards of wood and metal. Baron Heeckeren, who happened to be nearby, was on the scene within minutes. "As I was passing through the Rue Lepelletier...I suddenly heard from the direction of the Opera three explosions one after the other. I saw the people rush in that direction...and I hastened after them," the banker recorded in his diary that evening. "I saw a horrible sight. The street was strewn with wounded...the Imperial carriage was riddled by the splinters of a bomb," he continued, aghast.

It was the largest civilian attack of the period. A small group of conspirators, led by a thirty-eight-year-old Italian revolutionary named Felice Orsini, had smuggled in fulminate of mercury (an explosive similar to dynamite, which itself had only been invented the year before), and packed this substance, along with a quantity of homemade caps that acted as shrapnel, into a cast-iron shell small enough to be carried around and hidden in the recesses of a jacket. The effect when thrown against a hard surface like pavement was to produce a detonation capable not only of blowing up windows and buildings, but also of discharging a cluster of deadly projectiles.* Orsini's group hurled three of these handy new pocket grenades, one after another, into the crowded street as the imperial procession passed. One hundred fifty-six people were gashed, including eleven children; twenty-six horses were maimed as well, seven fatally. At least eight of the wounded spectators would die of their injuries.

But Napoleon III was not among them. Miraculously (for the imperial carriage was pierced in seventy-six different places), he and Eugénie both survived with minimal injuries. Orsini and his men got the emperor's hat but not the monarch himself; Eugénie just missed losing her eye to a shard of glass. Both had contusions to their faces, but nothing more. The general sitting across from them in the coach was not so lucky. He sustained a serious head wound.

Both Eugénie and Louis Napoleon maintained their composure throughout the tragedy. As soon as it became clear that the explosions had stopped, they clambered out of their carriage and immediately set about trying to aid the victims. "I could see the Emperor and Empress," Baron Heeckeren continued. "Their gestures expressed their distress...the Empress's dress was stained with blood."

"Do not bother yourselves about us, it is our trade," Eugénie reassured those who crowded frantically around her. "Take care of the wounded." Nor did she or her husband allow the bombing to alter their plans for the evening. Once they were confident that the injured were obtaining the help they needed, the imperial couple resolutely made their expected entrance into the theater, "where they were received with indescribable enthusiasm," the banker concluded.

In the wake of the attack, expressions of support flowed in from across Europe. Eugénie's demeanor under fire was especially admired.

---

* Today, law enforcement and other surveillance agencies call a weapon of this type an IED, or "improvised explosive device." You might say that Orsini, by cobbling together these do-it-yourself bombs, launched the world into the modern terrorist age.

Queen Victoria's brother-in-law happened to be in Paris and was already in his seat at the opera when he heard the explosions. "He rushed down, the noise and cries were dreadful, as well as the rush of the crowd, many bleeding," Victoria wrote in her journal after hearing his description. "The Empress wonderfully composed and courageous, even more so than the Emperor." Franz Joseph and Elisabeth sent a telegram expressing their sympathies, which Sisi followed up the next day with a personal letter to Eugénie, in which she applauded her counterpart's "courageous firmness." Baron Hübner added a postscript in his diary that a person he knew, "whose veracity I have no reason to doubt, and who followed Louis-Napoleon and his wife to their box at the opera that evening, told me that the Emperor appeared completely demoralized, while the Empress was admirable in her fearlessness and self-possession."

Eugénie herself described her feelings a week later in a letter to her mother. "Certainly, I am not going to pretend that the moment between the second and third bomb wasn't full of emotion, but honestly, I would have thought I would have been more frightened," she told her. (Clearly, those early lessons sitting on the barrel of the cannon with Paca while her father fired the gun beneath them had come in handy.) "This evening I am giving a grand ball," she continued. "I think we will have a lot of people because everyone is rushing to see us ... I compare it to the fourth bomb," she concluded drily. But she also admitted that "the enthusiasm there was for us afterward, ... the consoling expressions of sympathy, ... went straight to my heart."

The conspirators were easily rounded up. Orsini had himself been injured in the second blast, and was discovered and arrested in bed, where he was recovering from his wounds. Interest in the trial, set to begin on February 25, 1858, was so extensive that Napoleon III decided to allow the transcripts of the proceedings to be published in full; consequently, they were carried by every major newspaper. It was one of those criminal cases that come along once in a generation, like the later Dreyfus trial, and capture the imagination of a worldwide audience, and in so doing, secure for the accused a platform and celebrity that would have been unattainable otherwise. This was an advantage that the educated, charismatic Orsini was quick to exploit.

Unerringly, from the commencement of his interrogation by the prosecution, to the final line of his testimony, he was masterful. "From my youth I have only had one object, and one fixed idea — the deliverance of my country, and vengeance against the Austrians," Orsini began passionately. "We have always regarded the French as brothers and friends, and...we only wanted to get rid of the Austrians...I witnessed ridiculous attempts made by Mazzini, who sent 15 or 20 men to Italy, where they lost their lives. I tried legal means. I went over to England, and...advocated the principle of nonintervention." But after years of fruitless pleading, he had become horribly discouraged. Gradually, the notion that only by assassinating the emperor of the French could he effect change possessed him. "I said to myself, 'Let us put down the system; Napoleon is all powerful in Europe; if he falls, Italy will rise of herself.'" The devastation the homemade bombs had caused seems to have taken him by surprise, for he appeared genuinely contrite. "As to the victims, I am very sorry that so many people were wounded," he said soberly. "If my blood could repair the misfortune, I am quite ready to give it for the people; here it is."

But Orsini's real victory came after his testimony, towards the close of the trial, when his advocate obtained permission to read aloud a letter that the defendant had written to his intended target from his prison cell. "To Napoleon III, Emperor of the French," Orsini's letter began. "The depositions which I have made against myself...are sufficient to send me to the scaffold, and I shall submit to my fate without asking for pardon...I wish, however, to make a last effort to assist Italy, whose independence has hitherto made me pass through so many perils, and submit to so many sacrifices," he explained. "I beseech your Majesty, restore to Italy the independence which her children lost in 1849 [when Archduchess Sophia and her generals ordered the military occupation of the imperial territories]...Let your Majesty call to mind that the Italians, among whom was my father, joyfully shed their blood for Napoleon the Great...that they were faithful to him until his fall; and that, so long as Italy shall not be independent, the tranquility of Europe and that of your Majesty will only be vain illusions...May you deliver my country, and the blessings of 25 millions of citizens will follow you to posterity!" he finished fervently.

The effect on public opinion of Orsini's testimony, and especially this letter, was acute. It shifted the focus of the trial completely away from the crime itself and instead directed a white-hot spotlight on the cruel sufferings endured by an innocent population struggling for independence against the Austrians. Orsini himself was transformed into a hero and a martyr. His bold words, gallant demeanor, and unwavering commitment to his cause were the source of much admiration. Many people were converted by his words.

Among them, incredibly, were Eugénie and Louis Napoleon. Since childhood, the empress had revered daring, romantic warriors like her father, and she recognized these qualities in Orsini. She could not bear the thought of executing a man who appeared to her so honorable. Her husband, too, was moved. "Fancy the Emperor telling me yesterday that he could not help feeling the greatest sympathy for Orsini," an astonished Lord Cowley, the British ambassador to Paris, reported to London in a letter of March 3, 1858. "I should not be in the least surprised if he pardoned him, or at least mitigated his punishment. The Empress is upon her knees to him to do so."

But Louis Napoleon's reaction to these events was far more complex than his wife's. His narrow escape from the assassins' bombs had shaken him to his core. Weeks after the attempt, he was still visibly disturbed. "I thought the Emperor very low," Lord Cowley advised his superiors towards the end of January. "The other day a fair lady who is supposed to stand at the moment high in his good graces asked him if he was ill as he looked so miserable. 'No,' was the reply, 'I am just profoundly sad and discouraged.'"

Much of this had to do with Napoleon III's anxiety over the peaceful succession of his adored son. In the wake of the attack, the emperor had hurriedly named Eugénie as regent in the prince's name, to be aided by a council of high-ranking officials, should the desperadoes' next bullets take out more than his hat. But even this might not be enough. The prince imperial was only nearing his second birthday and already there were threats against him. "The poor Empress is tormented to death by anonymous letters telling her that the little Prince is to be carried off," Lord Cowley confided to London. "The poor child is now never let out of sight of the house."

And so, the harsh truth voiced by Orsini in his letter — that so long as the struggle against Austria remained unresolved, Napoleon III and his family would be considered fair game by the terrorists associated with the Mazzini faction — hit home. Shrewdly, however, the patriotic Orsini (who, despite Eugénie's pleas, *did* mount the gallows on March 13) had in the same letter provided the emperor with the solution to his problem: turn intimidation into blazing glory by walking in the footsteps of his exalted uncle and liberating the Italians from their tormentors. "His Majesty [Napoleon III] has evidently been tickled (I can use no other expression) by Orsini's letter read at the trial, in which it is said that the fate of Italy is in His Majesty's hands," an exasperated Lord Cowley reported home. "There was never a man more easily caught by flattery of this kind," he lamented.

But intervening militarily in Italy, Louis Napoleon recognized, was a very tricky business. All the other powers were likely to be suspicious of his motives and might ally against him. An ambitious state like Prussia might even take advantage of the situation to try to filch off bits of French territory while his army was otherwise engaged. Nor was the emperor confident that his own subjects were ready to support another war so soon after the last one. For all of these reasons, then, he could go to war in Italy only if it looked like he was not the aggressor but had instead been forced to take action by unforeseen circumstances beyond his control.

Luckily, to manufacture such an excuse was not difficult for a man of Louis Napoleon's resourceful imagination and undeniable talent for duplicity. He began by reaching out surreptitiously to his Sardinian ally, Count Cavour, to arrange for a secret meeting. (He sent his doctor as his emissary.) The emperor told no one of his plans — not his ministers, nor his ambassadors, not even Eugénie. As far as everyone else knew, Napoleon III was spending his summer as he always did—relaxing, fooling around with other women (he had a new favorite, the wife of his foreign minister, who also happened to be a good friend of the empress's), and traveling around to his regular vacation spots. One of these was Plombières, a spa town about 250 miles east of Paris, near the border with Germany and Switzerland. Plombières boasted a hot springs, which the emperor visited every July for his health, usually alone (or in the company of female society other than his wife); it was his favorite summer palace, as Biarritz was Eugénie's.

And it was here, on July 21, 1858, that Cavour, sporting an assumed name and disguised as an ordinary tourist, met with Louis Napoleon to plot out a joint campaign against Austria. As he was only a minister, he had to report the whole scheme in detail back to Victor Emmanuel to obtain the king's approval, and his letters make for enlightening reading. Napoleon III "began by saying that he had decided to support Sardinia with all his might in a war against Austria, provided that the war was fought for a...cause...which would be justified in the eyes of diplomacy and more especially by public opinion in France and Europe. The search for this cause presented the most difficult problem," Cavour noted. "My position was becoming embarrassing, for I had no...tangible proposal to make." Fortunately, "the emperor came to my assistance," he reassured his sovereign with relief.

In fact, Napoleon III, like an artist creating a whimsical new painting out of an old masterpiece, already had the whole deal sketched out. In exchange for providing the king of Sardinia with 200,000 troops to fight the Austrians, as well as state-of-the art artillery and ammunition, including a fleet of French warships, the emperor imposed the following conditions: (1) Upon the liberation of Lombardy and Venetia, Victor Emmanuel was to cede Savoy and Nice to France as compensation for imperial assistance. (2) All of Italy was then be divided into three kingdoms. Sardinia would rule the upper realm, comprising all the territory conquered from Austria *and* the province of Romagna (currently controlled by the pope). A new, middle kingdom, cobbled together out of Tuscany (at present, property of the grand duke) and the rest of the papal states (also to be stripped from the pope), was to be created. The southern Italian dominion of Naples was to be left intact, although, like Tuscany, it was to be governed by a player to be named later. ("In the probable event that Your Majesty's uncle and cousin [the grand duke and king, respectively] will prudently retire to Austria, the choice of Sovereigns for Florence and Naples has been left in abeyance," Cavour explained helpfully.) To compensate the pontiff for the loss of all of his property except Rome, the other Italian kingdoms would form a confederation of which he would be president. "I consider this arrangement entirely satisfactory. As sovereign by right of the richest and strongest part of Italy, Your Majesty will practically rule the whole peninsula," Cavour joyfully pointed out.

The only potential snag was the emperor's third condition: that the king of Sardinia marry his eldest daughter to Plon-Plon. Victor Emmanuel protested that the girl had only just turned fifteen, whereas the proffered bridegroom was thirty-six. But Louis Napoleon insisted. He needed to compensate his cousin —who was, after all, a Bonaparte and next in line for the French throne, after the prince imperial—for having been passed over for the imperial regency in favor of Eugénie. The best way to do this was to secure another throne for Plon-Plon, and here were two new ones—Tuscany and Naples—that were sure to be available soon in Italy! Recognizing how touchy the Italians were about being ruled by outsiders, however, the emperor understood that his cousin was going to need stronger ties to the country to appease them—hence the emphasis on the Sardinian marriage. Besides, Napoleon III assured the anxious father, there was no need to worry about Plon-Plon's suitability as a husband; the emperor could vouch for the fact that his cousin had always "shown very good feelings in his relations with his mistresses."

Victor Emmanuel weighed his daughter's happiness against the tantalizing prospect of increasing his power and territory by orders of magnitude and came down unsurprisingly on the side of property. The bargain was struck, although for the moment the deal remained secret, as the conspirators needed a few months to lay the groundwork for the coming campaign. They also needed time to set up the agreed-upon rationale for the war. And so, slowly and deliberately over the course of the next year, Napoleon III and Count Cavour set a trap for Austria.

And Franz Joseph walked right into it.

ELISABETH

A despondent Sisi with Franz Joseph, Gisela, and Crown Prince Rudolf
(in his soldier's uniform, on a toy horse)

14

Three Weddings and a War

Ghastly shadows rise unbidden,
Black night round mine eyes is thrown;
In my trembling breast is hidden
A sad whisp'ring voice unknown.

Unknown sorrows, unknown anguish
Toss me wildly to and fro,
And I pine away and languish
Tortured by an unknown glow.

But the cause why I am lying
Rack'd by fiery torments now,—
Why from very grief I'm dying,—
Love, behold!—The cause art thou!

—Heinrich Heine

THE GUILT—THE GUILT!

The death of two-year-old Sophie on May 29, 1857, propelled Elisabeth into an abyss of despair. Like a wraith, she would climb into a carriage draped in black and take the short drive to the Capuchin Church, there to submerge herself in the dank gloom of the imperial crypt, sitting for hours by the side of her child's tomb, weeping and praying, as she had by her sickbed. She stopped eating. She saw no one.

All the progress she had worked so hard to attain at court—getting her husband to confront his mother, wresting away control of the nursery, convincing Franz Joseph to take her political views seriously and moderate his approach to his subjects—all of this was instantly nullified. The emperor, too, grieved and felt culpable—but his remorse centered on having been too fond of his beautiful wife, and having given in to her childish whims, rather than holding steadfastly to the sensible course recommended by his excellent mother.

No word of reproof ever dropped from the archduchess's lips. It wasn't necessary. That Sisi was to blame for her darling granddaughter's death was communicated much more effectively by Sophia's icy avoidance of the subject. Nor could Elisabeth fail to feel her debasement. When she demanded the dismissal of the doctor who had misdiagnosed and underestimated the seriousness of her child's condition, Franz Joseph, acting in accordance with his mother's wishes, refused to grant her request. Not only this, but Elisabeth was forced to continue to accept the medic as her physician as well, despite the doctor's having despicably tried to absolve himself after the fact by claiming that she was "quite unfit to be a mother, and throughout the journey had persistently ignored his advice."

No parent comes out of a tragedy like this unscarred, but to have to bear the loss of a child while shackled within the confines of such a perniciously hostile environment would defeat even the most stable psyche. It broke Sisi, who was, after all, only nineteen.

All that summer, while Eugénie was waging a losing battle for her husband against the easily accessed charms of the countess of Castiglione, Elisabeth remained prostrate with misery. She barely left her rooms, withdrawing emotionally even from Franz Joseph and Gisela.

LIFE AT THE IMPERIAL COURT moved on without her. Archduke Max had finally made up his mind and on July 27, 1857, married the king of Belgium's pretty daughter, Charlotte, with great fanfare in Brussels.

Only his younger brother Karl was sent to represent the family at the ceremony, so as soon as the customary three days of festivities following the nuptials ended, twenty-five-year-old Max hastened to Vienna to introduce his seventeen-year-old bride to his family.

She was a huge hit. Although only a year older than Sisi had been at her wedding, Charlotte had been born into a royal court and thoroughly trained for her position. Her pedigree was impeccable—between her father, who was Queen Victoria's uncle, and her grandmother, a former queen of France (wife of Louis Philippe, the deposed Citizen King), Charlotte was related to half the crowned heads of Europe. She was consequently fluent in French, German, English, and Italian. Growing up, she had been instructed in history, government, literature, and philosophy. At the age of eleven she was reading Plutarch. "She is very clever, which is a bit worrying," Max had written of Charlotte to his brother Karl. "But no doubt I will get over that," he added airily.

The contrast with Elisabeth was unmistakable. When, on August 6, barely two weeks into her marriage, Charlotte was formally introduced to the imperial court, including all the government ministers and the diplomatic corps, she "was so easy in her manners and so graceful in her movements," the London *Times* correspondent observed, "that His Majesty the Emperor declared his new sister-in-law to be one of the most charming persons he had ever seen." Archduchess Sophia was in raptures. "Charlotte is charming, beautiful, attractive, loving, and gentle to me," she wrote triumphantly in her diary. "I feel as if I had always loved her," she fawned after she had known her new, better daughter-in-law for two days.

But by this time, Elisabeth didn't care. She greeted Charlotte affectionately but made only one wan appearance during the couple's abbreviated stay—at the private family dinner held at Schönbrunn Palace to celebrate the marriage. Max, in his new position as governor-general of Lombardy-Venetia, was in a hurry to get back to Italy, and left on August 7, after only two days. Franz Joseph had signaled by his brother's appointment that he was open to a more tolerant approach to imperial administration, and Max was anxious to begin the process of putting his own ideas of governance to work.

Nor would Sisi agree to accompany Franz Joseph when, the day after Max and Charlotte's departure, he resumed the couple's interrupted tour of Hungary. As she was clearly in no condition to appear in public, he did not press her. He might even have been somewhat relieved to escape her tears, as he seems to have participated happily enough in a shooting match held in Pressburg (present-day Bratislava) for his bene-fit, and only cancelled a performance at the theater (which bored him anyway) on the grounds of mourning. But although she wasn't physi-cally there, Elisabeth's presence nonetheless dominated his visit. The Hungarians, touched by her anguish, had taken Sisi into their hearts. Her portrait was displayed in private homes and shop windows, and Franz Joseph was laden with gifts and good wishes for her. "The Empress Elizabeth...is never forgotten in the homage which all pay to her husband," a London correspondent noted.

The emperor's tour of Hungary was followed by a meeting on October 1 in Weimar, Germany, with his Russian counterpart. This was the first time Franz Joseph had met personally with Alexander II since the death of the tsar's embittered father, Nicholas. Significantly, Alexander had just come from his rendezvous with Napoleon III in Stuttgart.

It was reported in all the papers that the two sovereigns met amica-bly enough and spent some time conversing in private. Although Franz Joseph later "expressed himself highly satisfied" with this interview, it is worth noting that the tsar did not invite the emperor to come along with him when he went out shooting immediately after their tête-à-tête, even though this was a sport Franz Joseph loved and at which he excelled.

Elisabeth did not attend the Weimar meeting either, although pro-tocol dictated that she should have, as (unlike with Eugénie) the tsarina had not feigned illness but instead had openly accompanied her hus-band on his journey. Rather, Sisi, still in pain, had chosen to remain behind in Ischl, where she and the rest of the imperial court were waiting to celebrate the emperor's twenty-seventh birthday.* Elisabeth had begged her mother to join her so that she would not have to be alone with Archduchess Sophia while they waited for Franz Joseph to finish up in Weimar, so Duchess Ludovika was also there. She brought along Sisi's younger sister, sixteen-year-old Marie, who, with her magnificent hair and slim, athletic figure, resembled a miniature of Elisabeth herself. Even Duke Max put in an appearance that October, for this was to be a double celebration: the gamble Ludovika had made on Elisabeth had paid off. Because of Marie's relationship to the empress of Austria, the heir to the throne of Naples had asked for her hand in marriage. There was to be another queen in the family.

This happy news, which Elisabeth was able to celebrate with her loved ones around her, made it easier for her to function and take the first steps towards returning to a semblance of normal life. She even managed, once Franz Joseph arrived, to put on a brave face and renew intimate relations with her relieved husband. And so it was that in December, just before her twentieth birthday, the empress found herself expecting again. Still so guilt-ridden was Sisi, so listless and unhappy, that this time she meekly followed all of her mother-in-law's strictures.

GETTING HIS WIFE PREGNANT AGAIN was one of the few positive achievements the emperor could claim going into the new year. Despite his conciliatory efforts with Tsar Alexander, Austria remained isolated internationally, and this just at a time when political unrest in Lombardy and Venetia, where Max was governor-general, exploded, fueled by the publication in March 1858 of Felice Orsini's stirring letter to Napoleon III in newspapers all across Europe. This missive spread through northern Italy, in particular, like a fever. There were angry demonstrations in the streets of Milan and Venice, and in the weeks following Orsini's execution, aristocratic audiences attending theatrical performances wore

---

* His real birthday was August 18 but the usual festivities, as well as the court's annual holiday, were delayed that year due to the extended period of mourning.

mourning in the patriot's honor. In response, Franz Joseph appointed a new, significantly more aggressive army officer, Field Marshal Gyulai, as commander of the Austrian forces in Italy (replacing the finally deceased Radetzky) and sent him down to Lombardy with instructions to quell the unrest.

Max, who had been diligently governing the region since his marriage the summer before, protested this decision. The archduke had initiated a number of reforms that were helping him win the trust of his subjects. He'd brought in respected Italian scholars to improve the educational system, and had already begun restoring the many public squares, churches, and theaters that were crumbling from decades of neglect. He made a point of addressing the public in their native language, the first Austrian administrator to think to do so, and had even proposed establishing a more autonomous government, complete with a representative assembly, to make imperial rule more responsive to the needs of the citizenry. Now here came Field Marshal Gyulai, seemingly intent on destroying all the goodwill he had just spent eight months building up. The disagreements between the archduke, who advised letting tensions die down on their own, and the field marshal, who only knew one way to handle resistance — crush it — became so pronounced that in May of 1858, Max made a special trip to Vienna to personally plead his case for leniency to his elder brother.

He might have saved himself the trouble of traveling. With Elisabeth's influence diminished, her competency demeaned, and her opinions belittled, Max's was the only voice for tolerance at the court. All the improvements he had initiated were treated with derision by Sophia's faction, firmly in control of the government and led by her cohort, Count Grünne, Franz Joseph's military attaché. This group, exploiting the natural tendency towards sibling rivalry that often exists between brothers, persuaded the emperor that what the archduke really wanted was to be king of northern Italy in his own right, and perhaps (it was darkly intimated) even to one day overthrow and replace Franz Joseph himself. The emperor, jealous of his dignity, and inclined by his early military training and experience to favor harsh treatment towards those who did not instantly follow his orders, was unfortunately only too easily convinced of Max's supposed malevolence. He chastised his younger brother firmly, revoking Max's reforms, and transferring his powers and authority instead to the reliably bureaucratic Gyulai. "Neither now nor ever can there be any question of the Italian provinces being governed independently of Vienna," Franz Joseph curtly informed his younger sibling.

Furious at his demotion, an offended Max, reduced to a figurehead, announced that he was going on holiday and took Charlotte for an extended cruise around the Adriatic. Consequently, he was not in residence in Milan in July, when Count Cavour slipped away from Turin to plot secretly with Louis Napoleon at Plombières.

IT WAS AGAINST THIS BACKGROUND of deliberate misdirection, back-stabbing, and a relentlessly developing crisis, that a month later, on August 21, 1858, to the utter astonishment of the imperial court, Sisi was delivered of a son. She could hardly believe it herself. "Of course! It must be another girl!" Elisabeth kept repeating nervously even after she was informed of the newborn's gender, until finally the baby was held up for her inspection, and she heard the extended roar of the hundred cannons fired to herald the joyous news.

Franz Joseph, like Louis Napoleon before him, was in ecstasies. At last, the long-hoped-for heir! The infant archduke was not alive twenty-four hours before he was made a colonel in his father's forces and awarded his own regiment. "I resolve that the son whom the grace of God has bestowed on me shall belong to the army from the moment of his entrance into the world," declared Franz Joseph solemnly in the first public statement issued by the imperial court in the aftermath of the birth. There was a special church service the next morning, at which a Te Deum was sung, and fireworks that evening. The emperor donated 20,000 florins to the poor (of whom there were many in Vienna that summer), and an additional 400 florins to the parents of every legitimate child born on the same day as the little crown prince.

Even Archduchess Sophia gave out 6,500 florins to her favorite religious institutions and charities in her grandson's honor.

Together, the emperor and his mother decided to name the child Rudolf, after the much-revered thirteenth-century founder of the Habsburg dynasty. Naturally, there was no thought of handing over the care of so precious a charge to a proven child murderer like Elisabeth, so Rudolf joined Gisela in the nursery under Sophia's supervision.

But by this time, Sisi was resigned to her inferior position at court. She had not expected to be allowed to raise Rudolf and had not the strength to fight a battle that she knew she would lose anyway. Although ordinarily the birth of an heir cemented an empress's status in imperial circles as second only to her husband's, that didn't happen here. Franz Joseph rewarded his wife for her accomplishment with an extravagant pearl necklace—but not his confidence. Archduchess Sophia remained firmly in control. Elisabeth still could not even choose her own ladies-in-waiting.

And yet, her son's birth was not without its effect. With the delivery of Rudolf, Sisi fulfilled her primary obligation to her husband and his subjects. This realization brought with it a slow-gathering renewal of spirit and sense of personal freedom. The days of conforming to the archduchess's dictates, and the stuffiness of the old rules of etiquette, were nearing their end. The empress no longer cared what her mother-in-law said or thought.

THE NEWS OF THE ARRIVAL of a healthy heir forced Max to cut short his idyll in the Greek islands and return to Italy so that (in his now much more limited role as governor-general) he could arrange the appropriately grandiose festivities ordered by Vienna to celebrate the great event. Accordingly, he and Charlotte dutifully hurried back to Venice.

They disembarked at the end of August to find the population of that city, as well as those of all the other municipalities throughout their northern Italian territories, seething. In the few months that Max and Charlotte had been away, Field Marshal Gyulai, acting on Franz

Joseph's orders, had enforced a number of sweeping new directives. An expanded military draft had been put in place, forcibly compelling thousands of reluctant young Italian men to serve in the Austrian army. To ensure that these new recruits did not try to wriggle out of their compulsory conscription by claiming family obligations, it was further decreed that no male under the age of twenty-three would be allowed to marry. Nor had Vienna neglected to make changes affecting the older citizenry. To help pay off the huge debt accumulated by the imperial army during the Crimean War, Franz Joseph's ministers had had the happy thought to require its subjects in Lombardy and Venetia to trade in their old regional coinage for a new Austrian silver florin at a penalizing exchange rate so that, without warning, the Italians living in these provinces woke up one morning to discover themselves significantly poorer than they had been when they had gone to bed the night before.

If its ambition had been to *try* to get the inhabitants of the region to rise up in disgust and overthrow the hated Austrians, the imperial government could not have done a better job of it. An appalled Max attempted to quit his position altogether, but the emperor refused to accept his resignation. The governor-general had to stay, otherwise it might look like he disapproved of his older brother's policies (which of course he did). "I cannot expect you always to agree with my decisions," Franz Joseph wrote icily in his response, "but I have got to be sure that what I have decided upon will be promptly carried out and that the opposition will not be encouraged in the idea that you are on their side." "If I did not feel it was my sacred duty to remain here, I would have left this unhappy country where every day I feel more and more humiliated at having to represent a...government totally devoid of common sense," Max complained bitterly in a letter to his mother.

It consequently did not take much for Count Cavour to exploit this situation to his sovereign's benefit. Bit by bit, word of his secret meeting with Napoleon III began to leak out. Lacking details, speculation was rife about what the two leaders might have discussed, when suddenly in November 1858 came word that Plon-Plon was to marry the king of Sardinia's fifteen-year-old daughter, Princess Clotilde.

This announcement was greeted with great excitement in Italy. As it was clearly not a love match, it was naturally assumed (as the French emperor had no doubt intended) that the alliance signaled a commitment on the part of Louis Napoleon to aid his cousin's future father-in-law, King Victor Emmanuel, by joining forces militarily.

The king of Naples certainly thought so. The aging monarch had been conducting negotiations for his son's wedding to Sisi's sister Marie at a leisurely pace for months, demanding first that the bride learn Italian, and later trying to ensure she was sufficiently pious for the Neapolitan court. In the wake of the news of the Sardinian match, however, he speeded things up and arranged for Marie to be married by proxy just after New Year's. "He thinks Austria strong enough to defend him from foreign states [like France]," a London correspondent stationed in Naples observed flatly. At nine o'clock on the evening of January 8, 1859, Marie was officially wed to the Neapolitan crown prince, with another member of the extended Bavarian royal family standing in for the absent groom at the ceremony in Munich.

Five days later, the bride bade a tearful farewell to her family and left Bavaria for her new home in Italy. As she had a week or so before she was scheduled to arrive in Trieste, where a ship would be waiting to take her to her royal husband, she went first to Vienna to spend a few days with her older sister.

Elisabeth was thrilled to have Marie with her. The months following Rudolf's delivery had been all too familiarly bleak for the empress. Her recovery from the birth had been impeded by Sophia's insistence on employing a wet nurse, rather than allowing the new mother to feed her baby herself, despite Sisi's entreaties that she be permitted to do so. The result had been a breast infection that manifested itself as an intermittent fever and persistent fatigue, ailments that had dogged Elisabeth through her twenty-first birthday and into the new year.

Now, basking in her sister's lively company, the gloom that had settled around Sisi lifted. Heedless of her mother-in-law's interminable harpings about maintaining decorum, the empress took her younger sibling everywhere — to the theater, to the shops, for sightseeing drives around the public park, even to the circus. The Viennese, who hadn't seen this much of their empress since her marriage, cheered the two charming young women wherever they went. Marie, unused to the splendor and adulation, was dazzled, and Sisi, experiencing the city through her sister's eyes, was suddenly reminded of her own popularity and exalted position in the world.

When, soon into the sojourn, the imperial court was informed that the old king of Naples had caught cold, Marie's departure was put off until the beginning of February. She and Elisabeth consequently had more than two weeks together. By the time this holiday had drawn to an end, Sisi had remembered what it was like to be young and have fun again.

The empress insisted on accompanying her sibling to the port of Trieste, where she saw Marie safely aboard the yacht that would deliver the royal bride to her new realm. The kingdom of Naples was all the way at the southern tip of Italy, over 500 miles from Milan and Venice, so Elisabeth had the comfort of knowing that Marie would be safe from the violence threatening to break out in the northern imperial provinces.

For, even as Sisi waved goodbye to her sister, and watched her ship pull away from the shore on February 3, 1859, word was spreading rapidly through Europe that Plon-Plon had married his adolescent Sardinian princess in Paris on January 31, and that both the bride's father, Victor Emmanuel, and the groom's cousin, Napoleon III, were calling up soldiers in preparation for war.

SINCE THE BEGINNING OF JANUARY, Franz Joseph had found himself perplexingly on the receiving end of a series of escalating crises orchestrated by Count Cavour and Louis Napoleon. First, on New Year's Day, Napoleon III had, by all accounts out of the blue, tried to pick a fight with the Austrian ambassador, Baron Hübner. Then, on the evening that Plon-Plon was married, the opera house in Milan had to be closed in the middle of a performance when the chorus on stage sang a refrain that included the words "*Guerra! Guerra!* [War! War!]," and all the Italians attending the production suddenly demonstrated their loyalty to their homeland by standing up and chanting "*Guerra! Guerra!*" as well. (Not to be outdone, the many Austrian soldiers present, led by Field Marshal Gyulai, who also happened to be in the audience, reciprocated by taking out their sabers, banging the handles of the swords on the floor, and chanting back ominously in turn, "*Si, Signori, Guerra! Guerra!*")★ For Franz Joseph, this parade of provocations was like being in a tennis match where, no matter what he did, the other side kept serving and he had no choice but to keep hitting the ball back.

As public challenges of this sort obviously could not be tolerated, the emperor felt he had no choice but to send in more soldiers. But the more troops he transferred to Lombardy, the more men and arms Victor Emmanuel also conscripted, and the more reservists and cannons Napoleon III called up and shipped to his ally. Mérimée wrote to a friend in England, "Great preparations [for war] are being made here quietly. The old soldiers are being recalled, . . . all the *matériel* of the artillery has been changed; and there are three hundred new field-guns, which will, so they say, decapitate a fly at three hundred kilometres." Baron Hübner, surveying the obvious mobilization of these forces from his apartments in Paris, agreed with him. "The shipment of troops and armaments continue on a large scale here," the ambassador warned Vienna bluntly on March 9.

And it was at this point that Austria took the bait. Convinced that, in the face of overwhelming imperial power, Victor Emmanuel would back down, Franz Joseph employed a shortcut. On April 19, 1859, Vienna issued an ultimatum, ordering the Sardinians to disarm unilaterally or face the consequences. It was exactly what Franz Joseph had done to the tsar at the beginning of the Crimean War. There was only

---

★ This scene could have come right out of the film *Casablanca,* where the opposing patrons of Rick's bar vie with each other in singing patriotic songs, and the Nazis end up shutting down the place.

one small miscalculation with this strategy. Nicholas hadn't wanted to go to war with his protégé. Victor Emmanuel and Napoleon III did.

With joy, Count Cavour realized that this ultimatum gave Louis Napoleon the pretext he had been looking for to intervene. Accordingly, the court at Turin made haste to scornfully reject the imperial demands, leaving a surprised Franz Joseph no choice but to make good on his threat. Max was publicly sacked, and Field Marshal Gyulai was told to prepare for open hostilities. "At last we breathe again!" Cavour exulted. "Thank God, the dear Viennese government intervenes, and in its usual way manages to . . . ruin its chances by recalling the Emperor's brother, because his wise reforms had displeased the old die-hards in Vienna."

Two days later, on April 21, 1859, Austria officially declared war on Sardinia. Since in doing so, Franz Joseph clearly made himself the aggressor in the eyes of the world, Napoleon III at last had his excuse to invade Italy.

EUGÉNIE

The Empress chairs a council meeting.

15

Regent of the Empire

We have been made regular dupes.

—Queen Victoria

EUGÉNIE FOUND OUT THAT HER HUSBAND was conspiring to support Sardinia in a war against Austria the same way everyone else in France did—on January 1, 1859, when, out of the blue, Napoleon III went up to Baron Hübner, who along with the rest of the diplomatic community had been enjoying the traditional New Year's Day reception at the Tuileries, and, in an obviously premeditated provocation, greeted the startled Austrian ambassador with the cold phrase, "I regret that our relations with your government are not as cordial as I would like them to be."

He might just as well have slapped the discomfited envoy in the face with his glove and demanded a duel, so aghast was the assembled company at this sudden change in attitude. By noon, even ordinary passersby on the street had heard of the affront. "An extraordinary thing happened to-day at a quarter past twelve," Baron Heeckeren recorded in his diary. "I had this conversation with a financier-friend: 'Have you heard the great news?' he asked. 'Prices are down a franc...Frazer has it from M. de Hubner himself, that there was a scene between him and the Emperor!' *'Diable!'* Heeckeren swore. 'A scene? Really?' 'Well, at all events there were some painful words exchanged,' conceded the friend. 'That is serious indeed,'" the baron fretted.

And he was not the only speculator who found this worrying. The money markets fell, not simply in Paris, but also in London. Even a soothing article in the *Moniteur,* the official mouthpiece of the Tuileries, reassuring the citizenry that there had been no change in policy (which "the Emperor, at my instigation, has caused…to be published in order to avert financial catastrophes," Heeckeren boasted), failed to arrest the panic. That was because "the truth is otherwise," the banker admitted. "I know for certain that clouds are gathering."*

Nor did the publication soon thereafter of a pamphlet entitled "Napoleon III and Italy," which outlined the emperor's plan for a federation of kingdoms under the presidency of the pope (leaked by Louis Napoleon himself, of course), help to calm the situation. To Napoleon III's chagrin, the other major powers, including Britain, Prussia, and even the papacy itself, somehow failed to appreciate the brilliance of his geopolitical reordering and vehemently rejected the scheme. "The Emperor is extremely irritated at our not concurring in his views on Italy," the English foreign minister notified Queen Victoria towards the end of January. Only the tsar, thrilled at the chance for payback for Crimea, came to the conspirators' aid. Gleefully giving Franz Joseph a taste of his own medicine, Alexander, while outwardly professing his neutrality, publicly condemned the Austrian occupation of Italy, offered to mediate on the side of Sardinia, and secretly pledged to muster enough troops along his western border that Franz Joseph would be forced to leave behind at least 150,000 soldiers to protect against a possible Russian invasion.

Eugénie, too, was caught by surprise; Hübner reported that the empress's first reaction to the threat of a war with Austria was dismay. But Louis Napoleon knew how to win his wife's sympathies. Within a

---

* Baron Rothschild, Eugénie's close friend and the most important financier in France, met personally with Count Cavour during this period to try to ascertain whether the Sardinians were serious about going to war. "There are many chances for peace," responded Cavour opaquely. "And—there are many chances for war." "Always droll, Count," observed Rothschild. "Well, Baron," Cavour volunteered, "I'll make a proposition to you. Let's buy shares in the funds together, and play for a rise,—I will resign, and there will be a rise of three francs." "You are too modest, Count," Rothschild corrected him glumly. "You are worth at least six francs."

month, he had convinced her that combat in northern Italy was inevitable (although it is unlikely that he volunteered just how much he was doing to help push it along). Without French aid, the plucky Sardinians, who were after all only asking for independence from a brutal occupation, would be massacred by the vast Austrian army. The grand Napoleonic legacy that they both venerated demanded that he fight on the side of the oppressed against a corrupt monarchy. It was thus a matter of honor. On February 8, 1859, Eugénie demonstrated just how persuasive his arguments had been, by penning a long letter to Paca in which she deplored the antipathy of the senators, ministers, and other court officials in Paris to her husband's program. "If you could see...the deputies who have decided in advance to be discontented,...everyone piling on, who repeat in all tones that *they are afraid,*...those who adopt the attitude of oracles, predicting the end of the world, and, finally, those who believe that the Emperor has lost his mind and that nothing can be done to calm him," she fumed. "Some people here would have liked him to say that *he would never make war,* in short, *the peace at any price* of King Louis-Philippe... For my part, I am not a warrior, far from it, but I cannot approve of this shameful rout," she decried, referring to the uneven match between the Austrians and the Sardinians. "By the way," she confided, repeating the position that Louis Napoleon had clearly represented to her, "the Emperor does not want to do it."

And ironically, by the time Eugénie wrote this line, it was probably the truth. The intrigue hadn't gone at all the way Napoleon III had expected. He had hoped for a coalition in support of intervention against Austria, as he had had against Russia in Crimea; instead, he was being roundly condemned and was in danger of isolation. And he couldn't even get out of it. Every time he tried to back away from the conflict, Count Cavour and Victor Emmanuel would threaten to publish the many incriminating letters he'd unfortunately been so indiscreet as to have written arranging the plot. It was a very effective form of blackmail. If those letters ever got out, no other European leader would ever trust him again.

And then mercifully, on April 19, 1859, Franz Joseph had come to

Louis Napoleon's rescue and issued his ultimatum to Sardinia, followed two days later by a declaration of war. Victoria, who was rapidly revising her initial impression of Napoleon III as an extraordinary man honest to the core, was exasperated. "Though it is *originally* the wicked folly of Russia and France that have brought about this fearful crisis," the queen wrote indignantly to her uncle, Leopold (Charlotte's father, the king of Belgium), a week later, "it is the madness and blindness of Austria which has brought on the war *now!* It has put *them* in the wrong, and entirely changed the feeling here... into the most *vehement* sympathy for Sardinia," she concluded in frustration.

In France, too, public opinion swung precipitously in favor of military intervention, just as Louis Napoleon had predicted. To capitalize swiftly on this helpful turn of events, the emperor declared war on Austria and immediately began a full-scale deployment of French troops to Alessandria, about sixty miles south of Milan, in preparation for an assault on Lombardy. "We are a funny nation!" Mérimée exclaimed in a letter to a friend on April 29. "I wrote to you a fortnight ago that there was only one man in France who was anxious for war [Napoleon III]... and the contrary holds good today!" he marveled. "The soldiers might be going to a ball. The day before yesterday they wrote in chalk on the carriages: 'Excursion trains for Italy and Vienna.'"

Although she was naturally worried about the well-being of those who would be risking their lives in the conflict, Eugénie fully supported the military initiative. "Our poor Empress has her eyes swollen as large as eggs, but she appears full of resolution and devotion," Mérimée attested. "She bids a tearful adieu to each regiment as it leaves, and the men cheer her to the echo."

But this time, Eugénie had a much larger role to play than simply providing comfort and encouragement to the troops, as she had during the previous conflict with Russia. This time, to reduce mismanagement and ensure that hostilities did not drag on as they had in Crimea, Louis Napoleon insisted on joining his army in Italy and leading his men himself. Consequently, it had become necessary to name a temporary regent to run the French government during his absence.

This was an important job. Not only would whoever the emperor appointed be responsible for the day-to-day administration of the regime, but the regent would also be required to manage diplomatic relations during the crisis, as well as keep abreast of any changes in domestic public opinion. It is a measure of just how far Eugénie had progressed in her understanding of politics and foreign affairs, and how much he trusted her abilities, that Napoleon III felt comfortable naming his wife to this position.*

And so, on May 10, at five thirty in the afternoon, Eugénie drove in an open carriage beside Louis Napoleon from the Tuileries to the train station in Paris to see her husband off to war. Baron Heeckeren, who had the honor of accompanying Napoleon III as part of his administrative suite, witnessed the imperial couple's arrival. The emperor, he reported, "was greeted by the people in the streets with the greatest enthusiasm." A tearful Eugénie embraced her spouse and then watched as he climbed onto the train. Beside her stood Plon-Plon's teenaged bride, there to see her own husband as he set off to help defeat the Austrians and in this way earn his expected kingdom.

The engine chugged out of the station to prayers and cheers. The carriages returned to the Tuileries. The empress was now in charge.

By ALL ACCOUNTS, Eugénie did an excellent job as regent. She certainly took her responsibilities very seriously. She read every report that crossed her desk. She chaired the imperial council and met with the government ministers three times a week. She lived quietly with her son at the palace of Saint-Cloud, where she spent her evenings cutting and rolling cloth into bandages for the soldiers. There was no unrest in France during her tenure—far from it. "The public spirit here is excellent," Mérimée assured his friend. "Even the *salons* are in a more fitting frame of mind."

---

* Eugénie's appointment came as an unpleasant surprise to the rest of her husband's family. Louis Napoleon's elderly uncle, Jérôme Bonaparte (Plon-Plon's father), was particularly incensed at having been bypassed for the position in favor of the empress. "What stupidity...to entrust the government to a fashion plate," he sneered. He made such a fuss that, for appearances' sake, Napoleon III was obliged to create a special office of adviser to the regent just for him.

The empress was helped enormously in her task by the favorable reports emanating from the front. Field Marshal Gyulai, who had been perfectly comfortable threatening a theater full of unarmed citizens, turned out to be decidedly less sanguine when faced with the prospect of going up against people who might actually shoot back. He advanced so cautiously into Piedmont that it took him a week to go twenty miles. By the time he got to the outskirts of Turin, he'd already had second thoughts about attacking the city, and decided that it would be better to return to Lombardy and wait until Franz Joseph and the rest of the Austrian forces arrived before making the attempt. He retreated without firing a shot, saving the Sardinian capital from occupation. "What *are* the Austrians about?" Victoria demanded in a letter to her uncle on May 9. "They would *not* wait when they ought to have done so, and *now* that they should have long ago made a rush and an attack with their overwhelming force, they do *nothing!*...Leaving the French to become stronger and more *fit* every day!!" she lamented. "Up to the present time the Austrians could not have played our game better if they had tried," Mérimée agreed.

And in Cavour, Louis Napoleon possessed an extremely energetic and wily ally. The count had had months to organize for this campaign and he had used his time wisely. By May, he'd managed to recruit an army of some 64,000 soldiers, mostly infantry. Ironically, thousands of these were young men fleeing the expanded Austrian draft in nearby Lombardy. Figuring that they were going to be forced into military service anyway, and wishing to fight *against* their imperial oppressors rather than for them, these youthful patriots "quit their families clandestinely [to] escape on foot, penniless, [and] cross the rivers by swimming or fording," the wife of a Sardinian official reported. To encourage them, Cavour issued orders that any potential volunteers be allowed to pass into Piedmont without the required papers. "The customs officers shut their eyes," the official's wife noted.

Nor had Cavour limited himself to military preparedness. Recognizing (like Napoleon III himself) that public opinion and internal political will mattered almost as much as the number of men under arms, he had secretly reached out to like-minded citizens all over central Italy and established what were essentially undercover governments-in-waiting in all the major cities north of Rome. These partisans he instructed to stall until the outbreak of hostilities and then do everything they could think of to incite the native population of each province to flood the streets, expel their respective heads of state, and vote to adopt Victor Emmanuel as their king.

But Count Cavour's undoubted masterstroke was to convince Giuseppe Garibaldi to fight on the side of Sardinia. Garibaldi was the most famous commander in Italy. Born into a seafaring family in Nice in 1807, Garibaldi left home at an early age and sailed all over the world, from Constantinople to Uruguay. As most of these exotic locales tended to be engaged in prolonged conflicts, Garibaldi would arrive at port only to find himself in the middle of combat. Lacking formal military training (which turned out to be a good thing), he consequently learned to fight on the fly in all terrains, picking up various winning strategies and techniques as he went along. Returning to Italy in 1848, Garibaldi had early fallen under Mazzini's hypnotic influence, trying valiantly to free Rome from the foreign troops the pope used to protect his property. Although he was unsuccessful, his bluff, honest manner, combined with his bravery and audacity under fire, won him the hearts of all Italians. Now, at the age of fifty-two, his reputation had so grown over the years that his very name was magic. When Cavour reached out and persuaded Garibaldi that Italy's best shot at independence and unification was not to wait to establish a republic, as Mazzini had led him to believe, but instead to join Victor Emmanuel and battle the Austrians, it was like recruiting Hercules.

To this excellent regional preparation was now added a French army composed of 132,000 infantry, 9,000 cavalry, and 10,000 heavy cannons and field guns. In addition, the French navy was speeding to the Adriatic to set up a blockade around Venice.

But even so, a confrontation with the Austrian empire presented a daunting prospect. By the middle of May, Vienna had already mustered an extra 100,000 men to augment Gyulai's divisions, bringing the total number of their forces in Italy to 200,000, with more on the way, and they had enough big guns to match those of the French. The Austrians held the superior strategic position as well: they were strongly established in Milan and possessed a line of seemingly impregnable forts that protected Venetia. Worse, after hearing that Napoleon III was himself going to Italy to assume command of the French divisions, Franz Joseph had decided to orchestrate his own campaign, both to inspire his men and to ensure rapid, decisive responses to changing battlefield conditions. He arrived in Verona on May 30.

Franz Joseph was twenty-eight and in excellent physical condition. Louis Napoleon, on the other hand, was fifty-one and inclined to paunchiness. Franz Joseph had trained as a soldier since childhood; Louis Napoleon's knowledge of military strategy was gleaned by poring over his uncle's half-century-old battle plans. About the only thing the two opposing commanders had in common was that neither of them had ever led an army before.

And back in Paris, Eugénie, who was in daily telegraph communication with her husband, waited anxiously with the rest of Europe for news of the approaching cataclysm.

IT DID NOT TAKE LONG. Garibaldi, straining at the bit, started it. Before Franz Joseph even had a chance to get to Verona, the storied commander led 3,000 volunteers (colorfully nicknamed "the Hunters of the Alps") across the Sardinian border into Varese, only about thirty-five miles north of Milan. Within three days, he had chased the much larger Austrian force stationed nearby even farther into Lombardy, all the way to the town of Como. Field Marshal Gyulai took fright and pulled his forces back even farther, at which point Napoleon III, acting on his ancestor's famous maxim to employ speed as a weapon, pursued Gyulai and his men before they could be reinforced, and provoked a battle on June 4, 1859, at the town of Magenta, just fifteen miles west of Milan.

The encounter began at noon, when the French crossed the Ticino River and began an assault. Both sides fought bravely, but the

Austrians, who had not seen action in Crimea, could not match the tenacious ferocity of their more experienced French opponents. By nightfall, unnerved by the multitude of corpses piling up on the battle-field, Gyulai called once more for a retreat. "At half-past eleven o'clock, a great victory was won at the bridge of Magenta," an exhausted Louis Napoleon managed to telegraph Eugénie that same evening. "5,000 prisoners are taken and 15,000 of the enemy are killed or wounded." Four days later, a triumphant Napoleon III officially entered Milan to wild rejoicings by the local population. "An immense crowd awaited us," the comte de Fleury, Louis Napoleon's aide-de-camp, wrote home excitedly to his wife. The emperor "had really the air of a prophet," he continued. "Women waved their handkerchiefs; men applauded, crying, 'Long live the Liberator of Italy!' Flowers were showered, the bouquets even fell upon us; the people came to touch his hands, to embrace his knees; it was a delirium!"

But the conflict was by no means over. Franz Joseph, who by this time had managed to get to Villafranca, some twenty miles outside of Verona, was appalled by Gyulai's incompetence. The emperor officially assumed control of the imperial army, fired his former field marshal, and prepared to continue the war. "I was driven to Villafranca, where I had summoned Gyulai, and gave him the formal order of dismissal," Sisi's husband wrote to her on June 16. "He was very grateful for it," he noted.

Alas, Franz Joseph's idea of wartime command was exactly like his notions of peacetime government. After a brief survey of the area, he set up a field headquarters at Valeggio, on the border between Venetia and Lombardy, and remained there with his chief of staff, receiving reports and messages from the various Austrian battalions spread out along the front lines, and diligently attending to correspondence and other paperwork. He kept to a rigid schedule: early to bed and up at dawn.

He was consequently asleep at two o'clock in the morning of June 24, when Napoleon III and Victor Emmanuel, having stealthily advanced their armies closer to the border with Venetia the night before, ordered their divisions into position in preparation for a surprise attack. By dawn, the French calvary had already taken the town of Medole, only thirteen miles from Valeggio. By 8 a.m., intense fighting had commenced in a wide-ranging, full-scale assault on the Austrian defenses.

Not that Franz Joseph had any idea that a pitched battle was underway. Eight a.m. was when he took his breakfast. He'd been up earlier, of course, but that time he spent in his rooms, answering his correspondence. At nine o'clock he dressed; a report of gunfire had reached him, and he thought he might just wander out and have a look. It wasn't until 11 a.m., at which point his army had already been fighting for six hours, that he understood the enemy had launched an offensive.

Even then, he had no idea of the strength or placement of the forces against him. Not everything went smoothly on the French side, but at least Napoleon III knew to clamber up to a high vantage point so that he could take in the whole front and see which of his battalions were gaining and which were falling behind on their objectives. Franz Joseph, by contrast, stayed put at headquarters and relied on messengers and communiqués. Shells were already exploding around his office at Valeggio at three thirty in the afternoon when the young emperor received the alarming dispatch, "I can hold out no longer, and I find myself forced to beat a retreat...I regret not to be able to announce to Your Majesty a better result," from one of his front line commanders. In fact, the situation was not as dire as this message indicated; the emperor still had a quantity of fresh troops waiting to enter the field. But Franz Joseph did not wait to investigate this unsettling first assessment. Rather, he at once ordered what remained of his army to fall back, and fled Valeggio on horseback.

"Great battle — great victory," a much-relieved Louis Napoleon telegraphed home to Eugénie very late that same evening. "This night I sleep...in the room previously occupied by the Emperor of Austria," he gloated.

IT IS NOT DIFFICULT to imagine Eugénie's elation when she was awakened early the next morning and handed this telegram. The empress didn't even wait for her ministers to appear but instead hopped out of bed, dressed quickly, and ran into the garden to share the triumph with the palace guard. Within hours, the news was all over Paris. Two great victories—and both in the very first month of battle! Why, the revered Napoleon I himself could hardly have done better!

To celebrate, a special thanksgiving service was scheduled to take place at Notre-Dame at noon on Sunday, July 3. In Paris, people started lining up as early as 9 a.m. to get a glimpse of the empress as she made her way to the cathedral. At 11:30 a.m., Eugénie, dressed in white, accompanied by the three-year-old prince imperial, came out of the Tuileries. Mother and son climbed into one of the grand ceremonial open-air carriages used on these occasions, the cannons of the Invalides were fired, and the pair set off at the head of a retinue for Notre-Dame. As the imperial coach came into view, trumpets blared and the crowd burst into spontaneous cheers. "The carriage conveying the Empress and the Prince was literally filled with flowers thrown in by the people as it passed slowly along," reported one of the many foreign correspondents who witnessed the procession. "One could but contrast all this joy and animation...with the present feelings of the inhabitants of Austria's capital. How dull must Vienna have been this day!"

Eugénie had been through celebrations like this before with Crimea, but this one was different. Napoleon III had been in Paris for that war and so of course the adulation had naturally been directed mostly at him. This time, it was *she* who was the principal beneficiary of the multitude's rapture. It must have been a heady experience for a woman who had been dismissed as a no-account Spanish social climber by so many at the beginning of her reign. It also completely justified her husband's gamble to intervene militarily. *This* was the reward for acting with vision and honor.

But there is such a thing as winning too big. The other European heads of state were none too pleased at the astonishing speed and success of the French army. Prussia, in particular, found the military progress made against Austria entirely too reminiscent of the first Napoleon's victories a half century earlier—victories that had resulted in the crushing defeat and occupation of Germany. There were calls in Berlin for an attack on France, either through Italy or across the Rhine, to discourage Napoleon III from following too closely in his uncle's footsteps.

The intelligence Eugénie received on the growing belligerence in Germany was sufficiently worrying that she immediately sent her husband a long letter apprising him of the development. "Here," she wrote, "some danger... is felt to be pending... A diplomat... tells me that... Prussia demanded... that all the federal troops be mobilized and announced her intention of an armed mediation in Italy... The old feeling of 1813 is rekindled, and no pacific assurances on your part will satisfy Prussia," she warned.

This letter reached Louis Napoleon just as the novice commander-in-chief was awakening to the staggering cost to human life engendered by his brilliant victory. The morning after the battle, he toured the field and found it littered with the gruesome remains of the dead and dying. Over 10,000 Frenchmen had been killed or wounded, among them several of his closest and most distinguished generals. His officer corps had been decimated as well. The suffering was palpable and intense. A shaken Napoleon III realized that he had not prepared for such carnage. There were not nearly enough doctors or medical supplies to see to the vast number of casualties. It was horribly hot and the victims were without clean water; their untended gashes festered in the heat; infection and typhus set in. The voices of men piteously begging for aid—for Austria had left over 13,000 of their own dead or wounded, and the Sardinians 4,000—could be heard from every direction.

And the slaughter was by no means over, he knew. The Austrians had retreated to the security of their line of fortresses. Franz Joseph still had many men under arms throughout his empire; he could likely deploy another 100,000 soldiers to Italy within weeks. Besieging an entrenched enemy holed up inside a citadel was a far riskier operation than surprising an army in the field. And now here was Eugénie's letter alerting him of the Prussian intention to open a second front against him.

Yet to free Venetia, as he had promised the Sardinians, he would have to go on. How many Frenchmen would he lead into death *then*? And for what? In addition to everything else, the political situation wasn't going at all the way Louis Napoleon had envisioned. Before the battle, he had sent Plon-Plon with a force into Tuscany as a first step towards securing the monarchy of the emperor's planned middle kingdom. But before his cousin had even had a chance to get there, the citizens of Florence had risen up all on their own, chased away their lawful duke, and voted to unite themselves instead with Victor Emmanuel. Nor was this a unique situation. Parma had also sent its duchess into exile; similarly, Romagna (which belonged to the pope) as well as Modena had rebelled and declared loyalty to Sardinia. With shock, Louis Napoleon realized that he had just sacrificed over 10,000 of his countrymen, not to bring his plan for an Italian federation under the presidency of the pope to fruition, but rather to expand Victor Emmanuel's domain and power.

It was at this point that Louis Napoleon understood that he had better find some way to get out of it—and fast. Without bothering to consult his Sardinian allies (who he was beginning to suspect had not been completely transparent with him about their aspirations to rule a united Italy), Napoleon III sent his aide-de-camp, the comte de Fleury, secretly to Franz Joseph in Verona with the offer of an immediate ceasefire followed by a personal meeting. "Here is a letter you are to take to the Emperor of Austria," Napoleon III instructed as he handed Fleury the note. "I am making an appeal to his humanitarian feelings, and proposing a suspension of hostilities in order to give time for diplomatic negotiations looking to a peace."

Fleury took off at once and reached Verona a little after ten on the evening of July 7. He located the villa in which Franz Joseph was staying without much difficulty and demanded an immediate audience. There was a momentary hesitation on the part of the imperial staff, as the Austrian emperor, as was his practice, had already gone to sleep, but it was decided, based on the urgency of the matter, to take the risk of awakening him. Informed of his visitor, Franz Joseph got out of bed, was hurriedly helped back into his uniform, and went to meet Fleury, who handed him Napoleon III's message.

Franz Joseph read the letter, thanked the emissary for his trouble, and told him that he would get back to him. Louis Napoleon, for whom speed was a priority, had clearly prepared for this response, as Fleury rejoined politely that he was afraid that his imperial highness only had until first thing in the morning to make a decision, otherwise the fleet of forty powerful French battleships currently aiming their large and very destructive guns at Venice would open fire and level the city. This proved an effective negotiating tactic.

A clandestine interview between the two emperors was quickly arranged for three days later at the fortress of Villafranca, about halfway between Verona and Valeggio. Franz Joseph was not enthusiastic at the prospect of being sequestered alone with his counterpart. "A meeting is in store for me which I dread, namely one with that archscoundrel Napoleon," he moaned in a letter to Sisi.

He needn't have worried. His rival had many faces and Louis Napoleon put on his best one to help him wriggle out of his by now muchregretted conspiracy with Sardinia. The Napoleon III that Franz Joseph met at Villafranca was the same man who had initially so charmed both Archduke Max and Queen Victoria. He could not have been more solicitous or sincere. Arriving first, the French emperor took immediate control of the situation and, like a greeter luring in a hesitant customer, made a point of riding out to meet Franz Joseph as he approached from the opposite direction, graciously helping to escort the younger man to their destination.

This good-natured, fatherly treatment continued for the duration of the negotiations, which took several hours. Franz Joseph was pleasantly surprised to discover that his former nemesis intended to be magnanimous. The Austrians would have to give up Lombardy to Victor Emmanuel, as too many French and Sardinian lives had been lost fighting for it, but France was willing to allow Vienna to keep Venetia if Franz Joseph would just agree to support Napoleon III's plan for a confederation of independent Italian kingdoms under the presidency of the pope. The archdukes of Tuscany and Modena, who were members of the extended Austrian imperial family, could also return to their dominions, provided they were not imposed on the citizenry by force of arms. Only the duchess of Parma would lose her small state, as Louis Napoleon would need to give this city to Victor Emmanuel as compensation for welching on his promise to liberate Venice.

These were far less onerous terms than the defeated sovereign had had any hope to expect, and, in spite of himself, the younger man was cajoled by his host's sympathetic manner. ("He was much affected by the gentle tones of Napoleon's voice...[and] by the kindness and affability visible in his features," a member of Franz Joseph's suite later confided to Fleury.) The Austrian emperor seems also to have found that he had more in common with his French opponent's political views than he had anticipated, as the following day, when Louis Napoleon sent Plon-Plon with the written version of this agreement for his formal authorization, Franz Joseph told him, "I am making a great sacrifice in thus ceding one of my finest provinces. But if we can agree, the Emperor and myself, as to Italian affairs in general, there will no longer be ground for differences between France and Austria." Despite the paternal atmosphere in which it was dressed, however, there was no getting away from the harsh reality of the punishment for losing. "Prince, I hope that it may never be your doom to sign a similar treaty," Franz Joseph sighed as he scribbled his name to the peace accord.

THE REACTION IN ITALY to this speedy armistice, which left Venetia still under Austrian control, was one of anger and disbelief. Count Cavour, informed of the details of the agreement, resigned on the spot. "I say to you...this peace will never be made! This treaty will never be executed!...No, a thousand times no! Never, never!" he raged. "The Emperor of the French departs. Let him go!...By God! *We* will not stop halfway!"

Victor Emmanuel, more politic than his minister, tried to limit the damage and keep his options open by swallowing his disappointment and thanking his ally for all that he had done for Sardinia already, but he, too, was indignant. Even the French army was against it. "What news is this—sudden, appalling—which paralyses the soldiers who were waiting to continue the struggle?" Baron Heeckeren exclaimed in his diary entry for July 12. "Napoleon has proposed an armistice to Francis Joseph! He has signed the preliminaries of a Peace at Villafranca! People are astounded."

In France, too, there was dissatisfaction, especially when the terms of the accord were published. "The people here have not received the news of peace very favorably," Mérimée confided from Paris, also on July 12. "They like war and want to make an end of the enemy. The *bourgeoisie* [businessmen], on the contrary, are delighted," he observed wryly. Objections were made especially to the pope's being stripped of Romagna and being accorded the dubious honor of president of an Italian confederation instead. "Another enigma—What is an honorary president?" Mérimée wondered. "Generally speaking, an old fool who is fit for nothing and who has something given him to play with.... And what is to be done with all the princes who have been turned out of doors by their subjects, or are fleeing from them?" he asked sensibly.

The senator was not the only one to question the details of the treaty. The regent was none too pleased either when her husband wired her about his handiwork. Although Eugénie had written to Paca on June 28, when the shocking extent of the casualties became known, "I hope that Peace will not be delayed, because with the weapons of destruction that we possess today, a battle resembles a slaughterhouse," she, too, worried that the agreed-to document compromised French honor and interests. "But will you be able to check the unity movement which seems destined to prevail?" she demanded of Napoleon III. Reports of unrest in France, particularly in the rural areas where the Church still had a strong hold, began to pile up on her desk, and she forwarded this intelligence to her husband, urging him to take action to return the pope's lands to him. Even Mérimée, who did not have access to the data that Eugénie did, could see that this issue threatened the tranquility of the home front. "Our bigots are riding the high horse, and are beginning to cause some anxiety," he observed. "They are making as much fuss as the devil would in holy water, and are telling the peasants that war is being made against the Church."

But Eugénie's concern over the treatment of the papacy paled in comparison to her fury when she discovered that Parma was to be annexed by Sardinia. What! The cowardly archdukes of Tuscany and Modena, who had abandoned their subjects at the first hint of trouble, were to be reinstated, but the duchess, who had bravely stayed until the war had come to her very doorstep, forcing her to flee only at the last minute, was not? Where was the justice in *that*? Not to mention that the duchess was ruling Parma as regent for her underaged son. Was this the precedent Louis Napoleon—who was after all at that very moment exposing himself to the dangers of a foreign battlefield, and who could thus easily leave his own wife and child in a similar position—really wanted to set? "It is impossible for Parma to be joined to Piedmont; everybody will see in it an act of spoliation and will believe you are persecuting a woman of a race enemy to yours. I implore you in the name of your honor to not do such a thing," Eugénie fired back by telegram. So outraged was she that an abuse of this magnitude could be directed at another female sovereign while she and Louis Napoleon were in charge, that she made plans to travel immediately to Italy to argue the duchess's cause personally, and was only dissuaded at the last minute, when it was impressed upon her by the French foreign minister that as regent "she ought not to leave the territory except for very exceptional reasons."

As it turned out, remaining in France was the right decision, although not necessarily for the minister's rationale—rather, had she left to join her husband, Eugénie might very well have missed him. So reviled had Napoleon III become in the immediate aftermath of the peace accord, Baron Heeckeren reported, that the emperor "had to leave in haste on July 12th and flee from the field of victory," and that "at Turin the enraged populace would have done him some injury if Victor Emmanuel had not got him out of the town in his carriage during the night." The man idolized only weeks before in Milan as the savior of Italy was forced to slink back to the palace of Saint-Cloud "incognito, like a criminal," the baron observed dolefully. The war was over.

THE WAR, YES. THE CONSEQUENCES, NO.

In the months following his return to France, Napoleon III did everything he could think of to impose his concept of a federation of regional kingdoms overseen by the pope on the people of northern and central Italy. He called for a peace conference to be held in Paris, attended by representatives of all the major powers, to iron out the details and legitimize the scheme. He conjured up tweaks to his initial vision, hoping to find the one recipe that would overcome enough objections to navigate the narrow path to success. Many of these demonstrated his wife's influence. For example, "I think that if Tuscany recalled the Grand Duke... the Duchess of Parma might be transferred to Modena," Louis Napoleon suggested brightly in September. But these gambits were uniformly rejected for what they were—the inventions of a man desperate to curtail the political turmoil that he himself had unleashed.

Because by then it was clearly too late. A popular assembly was elected in Florence, which voted that "Tuscany should form part of a strong Italian kingdom under the constitutional scepter of King Victor Emmanuel." Modena, Parma, and Romagna were petitioning for annexation as well. By January 1860, Victor Emmanuel felt confident enough of his position to recall Count Cavour to office, an appointment that signaled his intention to pursue a policy of national unity, raising the specter that Louis Napoleon might have to intervene all over again, this time against Sardinia, in order to protect the terms he had negotiated with Austria.

To forestall this possibility, the ever-resourceful Count Cavour, ten steps ahead of his former ally at every turn, had the perfect solution: bribery. The original deal between France and Sardinia had called for Nice and Savoy to be traded for the liberation of Lombardy and Venetia. Sadly, as Venetia remained in Austrian hands, these terms had not been met. But there was no reason the agreement could not be amended to reflect changing conditions. What if they simply substituted central Italy for Venetia, and ceded Savoy and Nice to Napoleon III in exchange for Victor Emmanuel's keeping Tuscany, Modena, and Parma?

And that is exactly what happened. Although Louis Napoleon tried to dress up this transaction as an act of national security ("Confronted by this transformation of Northern Italy...it was my duty, for the safety of our frontiers, to reclaim the French slope of the mountains," he intoned solemnly when news of the payoff became public), the veneer fooled no one. To continue the charade that this was not extortion, but rather a voluntary transfer of authority, referendums were held in Nice and Savoy in April on whether the citizens in these provinces favored joining France. Napoleon III, taking no chances, dispatched agents and troops to each locality in advance of the vote, to ensure the requisite enthusiasm among the populace. Consequently, even though a majority of the citizens of Nice (birthplace of the revered Garibaldi) identified as Italian, the French papers were able to gush after the election that "6,810 persons voted for annexation to France and only 11 against it."

It was all over by the end of April, when Savoy, too, voted by a wide margin to become French. As Louis Napoleon had calculated, although the other great powers expressed their displeasure with this naked land grab, the acreage involved was sufficiently limited that they declined to go to war over it. "Really, it is too bad!" Victoria seethed in a letter to her uncle. "*No* country, no human being would ever dream of *disturbing* or *attacking* France; every one would be glad to see her prosperous; but *she* must needs disturb every quarter of the globe and try to make mischief and set every one by the ears...It is really monstrous!"

But there was no denying that it was a win for Napoleon III. Nothing bespeaks success like imperial expansion. The domestic propaganda campaign worked; even Eugénie believed the acquired provinces had agreed voluntarily to the transfer, and would be much better off under imperial rule. Savoy "had been so abandoned by the Piedmontese government, especially during the last few years, and so pressured by taxes, that it is impoverished," she confided to Paca. "Thus, I hope that, after a little time, the French administration will bring this beautiful country, which in any event asks only to unite itself to France, back to life."

Paris was consequently in a festive mood that spring. The highlight of the social season was a masked costume ball arranged by Eugénie for April 24, 1860, the same day news of the Savoy vote was published. "The most extravagant expectations had been excited," the newspapers observed, and by ten o'clock in the evening, the jam of carriages waiting to reach the venue testified to the veracity of this report. Inside the main salon, delicate Louis XV–styled shepherdesses clad in extravagant silks mingled with diamond-bedecked countesses dressed to represent fairy-tale characters or primal elements such as water, earth, and night. The banquet hall boasted a huge fountain, upon which shone the new invention of electric light, "so adjusted as to give the watery spray as it rose and fell the appearance of frosted silver," one correspondent reported in awe. "The scene was most beautiful, and called vividly to mind those abodes only read of in the *Arabian Nights*." At six the next morning, the last of the guests found their happy way to the coaches still waiting on the street outside. "Too much praise cannot be attributed to her Majesty, . . . who planned so magnificent an entertainment," was the general consensus. "It was worthy of an Empress."

Two weeks later, General Garibaldi led 1,000 men into Sicily and the whole thing started over again.

ELISABETH

Franz Joseph meets Napoleon III at Villafranca.

16

His Cheatin' Imperial Heart

My bread they have utterly poison'd,
And poison'd my cup too of late;
While some with their love have annoy'd me,
The others pursue me with hate.

My songs with poison are tainted,
But how could it otherwise be?
My blossoming life thou hast poison'd,
And made it hateful to me.

My songs with poison are tainted,
But how could it otherwise be?
In my heart many serpents I carry,
And thee too, my dearest love, thee.

—Heinrich Heine

ELISABETH HAD NO SOONER RETURNED to Vienna from seeing her sister Marie off to become the future queen of Naples than the buildup to the war in northern Italy began in earnest. In the months preceding the actual outbreak of hostilities, Franz Joseph had tried to summon military aid by appealing to his long-standing ally the king of Prussia, but alas his uncle, who had always been so generous and accommodating in the past, had been incapacitated by a stroke the year before and was no longer in power. Ruling as regent in his place was his younger brother, sixty-two-year-old Prince Wilhelm, a decidedly less deferential in-law. Wilhelm let it be known that he would only send troops to Italy if the emperor agreed to place the imperial army under Prussian command, an insulting concession tantamount to reducing Austria to the position of an inferior power in Germany. Confident of the professionalism of his forces, Franz Joseph had demonstrated his contempt for this impertinence by issuing his April 19 ultimatum to Sardinia without even bothering to inform Wilhelm in advance.

The speed with which the conflict escalated in the wake of this unilateral attempt at intimidation, however, shocked the court. Having no idea, of course, that an overt act of coercion was precisely what Cavour had been seeking, Franz Joseph was somewhat disconcerted to discover his demands immediately and roundly rejected. Believing himself honor bound to make good on his threat, he had issued an official declaration of war on April 21, even though the Austrian military was by no means prepared for an extended fight. His subjects barely had time to digest this development when, two weeks later, he received the dismaying intelligence that Napoleon III, too, would be sending an army against him. The following week revealed that a large number of French regiments, complete with artillery, had already gathered at Alessandria; this news was followed swiftly by a report that a fleet of enemy warships had been spotted steaming their way towards Venice. Lastly came word that Louis Napoleon, who had announced his decision to lead his own troops, had acted with such energy and alacrity that by May 14, 1859, he was already ensconced in Italy, directing his men. As a personal challenge like this naturally could not be ignored, Franz Joseph, too, belatedly announced his intention to travel to Lombardy and take command of his soldiers himself.

Sisi was compelled to watch these events unfold from her helpless position on the political sidelines, for the emperor was fully under the sway of his mother's warmongering conservative faction, as represented by Count Grünne, the emperor's chief military adviser. Franz Joseph's decision to risk his life at the front terrified Sisi, but nothing she said could dissuade him. As if to drive home the precariousness of her situation, just before he left, Franz Joseph made plans for a regency to be put in place should he fall victim to enemy fire. Although the details of this arrangement were never published, it defies reason to believe that he had suddenly decided to entrust his wife with such an important office. Rather, all signs point to the inevitable conclusion that he had once again chosen his mother to rule in his stead, until his son and heir, nine-month-old Rudolf, should grow to his majority.

Elisabeth was thus faced not only with her anguish over her husband's safety, but also with the prospect of what her life would be like in Vienna with Franz Joseph gone forever and her mother-in-law firmly in charge for the next seventeen years. Her love for her husband, and his for her, was the only sliver of light that made the dark emptiness of her life at the palace bearable. She wept and begged him to change his mind, and when he would not, she wept and begged to be allowed to go with him to help keep him safe. "For my sake and the children's, think of yourself, too, and not only of your work and the war," she pleaded.

His departure from Vienna on May 29, 1859, was painful. Like Eugénie, Elisabeth, crying all the way, drove with him and the rest of the family to the station, but unlike her counterpart, she then sent the children home and rode the train with him as far as the first stop, frantically demanding last-minute promises from his suite that they would protect him and send him home to her quickly. She then returned alone to a court where she had not a single friend in which to confide, and where she was surrounded by a circle of back-biting adversaries who wore their malice for her openly. The doctor who had presided over the deathbed of little Sophie, still attached against the empress's will to her household, made a point of disparaging her whenever he could. "She is unfit for her position both as Empress and as wife, though she really has nothing to do," he opined severely to the minister of police. "Her relations with the children are most perfunctory, . . . an icy gulf separates her from the Archduchess Sophie, and the Mistress of the Household, the Countess Esterházy, has absolutely no influence over her," he lamented.

The accusation that consequently circulated that Sisi was indifferent to her children was the most hurtful—and the most unfair. Subsequent events would demonstrate that Elisabeth loved Gisela and Rudolf very much and wished to spend time with them. But the archduchess had the imperial prince and princess on a rigid schedule that made no accommodation for their mother, and even when the empress did manage to catch them at a free moment, her visits were always conducted under the watchful eyes of Sophia's women, which oppressed her.

Small wonder, then, that in this hostile environment Sisi slipped once more into despondency. She kept to herself as much as possible. She lost her appetite, shunning the heavy meals relished by the rest of the imperial court. To distract herself from her unhappiness, she went riding for hours with only her groomsman for company. She stayed up long into the night, writing to her husband and family, weeping as she poured out her heart in page after page. "Her letters are soaked in tears!" her mother exclaimed.

Significantly, the absent Franz Joseph (who presumably had plenty to do while he was away running a war in Italy) *also* took the time to write long, tender missives to his wife almost daily, an indication that he relied on her for emotional support every bit as much as she did on him. He called her "my dearest angel Sisi," and begged her to take care of herself. Her letters, not the state of the war, nor his generals' plans for defense or attack, were the first thing he read when he awoke each morning—he "simply devoured them while still in bed," he told her. And yet, even here, Sophia's grievances against her daughter-in-law reached him. "I have thought over the question of your riding and I cannot allow you to ride alone with Holmes, for it is not proper," he instructed.

The emperor's focus on trivial family dissensions like these may perhaps be excused, or are at least rendered more understandable, when placed within the larger context of the war. It must certainly have been easier to grapple with the difficulties presented by his wife's riding etiquette than to contemplate the enormity of his trouncing in Italy.

For, coincident with Franz Joseph's arrival in Verona, his subjects in Vienna were treated to news of a litany of Austrian setbacks, each more devastating than the last. What! The vaunted imperial army, on which so much treasure and sacrifice had been lavished over the past decade, had allowed itself to be bested by the French on June 4, leaving 10,000 casualties, 5,000 taken prisoner, and Milan in the hands of Napoleon III? And then, less than two weeks later, they had taken *a second* thrashing, even more horrific, from which 22,000 brave imperial soldiers were now reported wounded, missing, or dead?

Overnight, the mood of the citizenry turned ugly. Resentment against the heavy hand of autocracy, which the impoverished populace had endured stoically for so many years, burst forth. While the ebullient crowds in the boulevards of Paris strewed flowers before Eugénie in celebration, Austrians and Hungarians gathered in menacing mobs on the street corners of their respective capitals to protest and vandalize. There were calls for revolution and the adoption of a constitution and representative government. "Such is the general dissatisfaction that even in public places in Vienna shameless criticisms are directed at the course of military operations, and even the majority of the army do not conceal their sympathy with such views," read the official proceedings of the imperial council meeting of June 9, 1859. So worried was the court about the unrest that the foreign minister traveled specifically to Verona to bluntly warn Franz Joseph that if he did not find a way to placate his subjects soon, "the very existence of the monarchy . . . [could] be imperiled."

Sisi knew it. The wounded were beginning to stream into Vienna, so she could see for herself the price of these defeats. On her own initiative, she set up a military hospital at Laxenburg, where she did what she could to console the soldiers and their families. With the archduchess's hard-line approach temporarily in disrepute, Elisabeth saw her chance and wrote to her husband, imploring him to consider offering his Italian provinces a degree of liberalization and autonomy and by so doing "put an end to this horrible war." "Your political plan contains some very good ideas," Franz Joseph condescended to her in his reply.

"But for the present... there must be no thought of negotiating with the enemy," he concluded sternly.

And then, within days of this exchange, the comte de Fleury showed up in Verona with Napoleon III's offer of face-to-face peace talks, and an outmaneuvered Franz Joseph, presented with the prospect of a swift exit, adjusted his principles accordingly, signed the treaty of Villafranca on July 11, and like his French counterpart, hightailed it home.

MASSIVE PUBLIC FAILURE AFFECTS PEOPLE in different ways. Archduke Max, for example, who had been by his older brother's side throughout the war, was so humiliated by the defeat and the subsequent ceding of Lombardy that he could not even face his own wife. As soon as the peace was signed, Max fled, not to his spouse in the city of Trieste, but rather to the seclusion of Miramare, about five miles up the coast, where he was in the process of building an elaborate vacation home. "What is happening to Austria, and what will happen to her now?" he wrote to Charlotte in despair from this isolated location.

But of course Franz Joseph knew that, as emperor, he did not have the luxury of running away and hiding like his brother. His job was to carry on as he always had, making the difficult decisions that he thought best for his people. It helped enormously that he did not view the present situation as permanent. "We shall get Lombardy back in a year or two," he observed complacently soon after signing the agreement of Villafranca. In fact, by the time he returned to Vienna on July 16, 1859, the emperor had so far recovered his equilibrium that the very first thing he did was to issue an official manifesto, published in the papers, explaining exactly what had happened and why it wasn't his fault. "The valiant army of Austria has in this instance again given proofs of its tried heroism and its incomparable perseverance, so brilliant that... I experience a legitimate pride in being the chief of such an army," he boasted. "Our enemies, in spite of the greatest efforts, in spite of the superior forces which they had for a long time been preparing for the conflict... obtain only advantages, not a decisive victory,"

Franz Joseph declared, adroitly sidestepping the inconvenient reality that it had actually been the Austrian army, and not the French and Sardinians, that had possessed superiority in both troop numbers and field position. No, according to the emperor, blame for the performance on the battlefield must be shouldered by the true architect of the tragic defeat: Prussia. "In spite of the ardent sympathy…which the justice of our cause has inspired…in the journals and peoples of Germany, our natural allies [the Prussians], our most ancient allies [again the Prussians, for emphasis], have obstinately refused to recognize the great importance of the grand question of the day,…[leaving the imperial army] all alone to face the events which were being prepared for," Franz Joseph accused. Fortunately, he consoled his subjects, "the honor of Austria coming intact out of this war, I have resolved…to see the blessings of peace assured afresh to my beloved people."

Having thus absolved himself of all culpability in the disaster that had befallen his countrymen, the emperor, relieved to be home again with his lovely wife, immediately set off with Elisabeth on a well-earned holiday to Reichenau, sixty miles south of Vienna, so he could go hunting and she riding. Even his mother was a little shocked by this, although she attributed her son's carefree attitude to youthful naïveté. He "is…so innocent, for he is cheerful," Sophia recorded in her diary. "Actually that surprised me," she acknowledged.

ALAS, WHILE FRANZ JOSEPH did not blame himself for the losses in Italy, it turned out that just about everyone else did. This fact was made clear to him on his return from his hunting trip, when an assassination plot against both the emperor and his mother (but not the empress) was uncovered and foiled at the last minute.

And that was by no means the end of his woes. Hungarian revolutionaries, led by the charismatic statesman Lajos Kossuth, still in exile from the last rebellion ten years earlier, had had their hopes raised by the French intervention in Lombardy and were in active talks with Count Cavour to put additional pressure on Austria by staging an uprising of their own.* Foreign bankers were threatening to push the empire into bankruptcy unless the government curtailed its spending drastically and launched an investigation into possible fraud and theft in the military. Count Grünne and other members of the archduchess's faction deemed responsible for hurrying an isolated, unprepared Austria into war were vilified in the press, forcing the emperor to sack them.

Worse, the deal Franz Joseph had struck with Napoleon III to return the dukes of Tuscany and Modena to their respective principalities was already falling apart. These two kinsmen, together with their families, being unable to return safely to their castles in Italy, were now staying with the emperor at the Hofburg Palace, where they complained loudly at mealtimes that Victor Emmanuel was stealing their property. Not to mention that the Prussians were none too pleased with Franz Joseph for publicly attempting to make them the scapegoat for the whole fiasco, especially since it had been Prince Wilhelm who had cut the war short and saved Venice for Austria by threatening Louis Napoleon with invasion.

It was in the midst of these trying circumstances that the imperial family met glumly in August to talk things over and celebrate the emperor's twenty-ninth birthday. Max and Charlotte came in from Miramare for the occasion. This did not improve the general mood. There had been much speculation in the press that the more liberal archduke would take over the government of Venetia, and even some dark murmurings that Max should replace Franz Joseph as emperor. Stung, the emperor icily informed his brother that he no longer required his services in Italy—or, indeed, in any official position within the imperial government. A resentful Max realized that he had been demoted from commander of the Austrian navy and possible ruler of wealthy, glamorous Venice, to unemployed, exiled outsider.

The quarrel between the brothers was amplified by their wives'

---

* Ironically, it was only because Franz Joseph lost so quickly in Italy that he managed to keep Hungary—the peace of Villafranca was signed before Kossuth had time to organize an insurgency.

dislike of each other. Charlotte, still childless after two years of marriage, was dismayed by Franz Joseph's treatment of her husband, and his refusal to help his younger sibling rise to a level of success worthy of his talents. Max was "too striking not to leave his mark on the destiny of the world," she wrote to her family in Belgium in frustration. Elisabeth, whose lineage was inferior to her sister-in-law's, and yet who had everything Charlotte wanted, made for an easy target. Every court in Europe knew that earlier that summer Sisi's eldest brother, Ludwig, had publicly humiliated the family by giving up his rights of inheritance in order to marry his commoner mistress, a Protestant actress (whom the newspapers snidely accused of actually being "a Jewess, the daughter of a jeweller") with whom he had already fathered a daughter. Elisabeth, rather than ostracizing her sibling, had instead fully supported her brother in this decision and gone out of her way to be kind to his new wife. From Archduchess Sophia and her ladies-in-waiting, Charlotte heard how spoiled and selfish the empress was; how she shirked her obligations to the court and made her husband's life difficult by her constant demands for attention. All this from a woman who at nearly twenty-two years of age still practiced circus tricks and mangled her French pronunciation! It was a disgrace.

Nothing annoyed Sisi more than snobbery, particularly when it was directed at her Bavarian upbringing and family. She had made an effort with Charlotte; the previous year, aware of her sister-in-law's fondness for expensive jewelry, the empress had presented her with a glittering bracelet for her birthday, a gesture much appreciated at the time. Now Max's wife was siding with Sophia and treating Elisabeth with barely concealed disdain. The empress retaliated by referring to Charlotte as "that pretentious little . . . Belgian goose."

Elisabeth might have been more generous to her sister-in-law if she hadn't been so miserable herself. Although she was grateful to have her husband back safely from the battlefield, his return had brought her neither renewal of health nor peace of mind. After nearly six years of marriage, Sisi was no longer the adoring adolescent whom Franz Joseph had wooed so assiduously to the altar. She was not as easily intimidated and controlled as had formerly been the case, and there was almost nothing about the court that she respected. She held strong opinions and became impassioned when, instead of taking her seriously, her spouse tried to put her off as he had in the past. Although it was true that Elisabeth had not kept up with her French, this did not mean she was ignorant. Far from it. The empress was an avid reader, and not only of poetry. Sisi had developed an interest in politics, and read books by liberal authors like Rousseau and Lamartine, as well as numerous regional periodicals. The experience of her tour of Italy combined with the debacle of the recent war had hardened her view that her mother-in-law's brand of conservatism was cruel and outmoded, and would lead to ruin. She was vocal in her denunciation of these policies, urging Franz Joseph to grant both Venetia and Hungary more representation and autonomy, and to honor the calls for a constitution. After all, Bavaria had a constitution, she reminded him, and nobody seemed the worse for it.

But by far the imperial couple's most intense arguments were over Gisela and Rudolf. Elisabeth wanted control of her children back. Her brush with a potential regency under her mother-in-law was enough for her to take up the issue again with urgency. She opposed the rigidity of the schedule enforced by Sophia and disliked the governesses, nurses, priests, and doctors chosen by her mother-in-law. Increasingly, Sisi tried to countermand the archduchess's authority in the nursery. But she was always overruled by her mother-in-law, and all that came of these attempts was a torrent of bitter words and tears.*

Her husband, however, remained unmoved. Just as he had no intention of granting his subjects a constitution, so he declined to remove his mother from her position as superintendent of the imperial prince and princess's care and education.

Again, Sisi's emotional torment took a physical toll. The loss of

---

* Some historians point to Sophia's diary entries during this period, which sweetly praise Elisabeth's dress or manner, as an indication that Sisi was unreasonably antagonistic or unfair to her mother-in-law. Again, it is behavior that counts. The archduchess's diary entries are often in conflict with her actions.

appetite persisted through the fall, and was this time accompanied by a worrying cough. Despite these ailments, she continued to spend long hours exercising; physical activity was her only refuge from the oppressive atmosphere that surrounded her. She set up a gymnasium in her rooms, complete with hanging rings and a high bar from which to swing, and began each day with a strenuous routine (another source of eye-rolling ridicule by the rest of the court). She went riding for hours at a time, pushing herself and her horse as though trying to outrun her thoughts. She became painfully thin and nervous, crying easily, which only added to Franz Joseph's conviction that she was not competent to take over care of the children.

His wife's ill health and dark moods were not the only irritants rankling the emperor that fall and winter. Under pressure from his new ministers and foreign creditors, he was compelled to make all sorts of compromises he found distasteful. Protestants were suddenly to be granted greater freedom of religion and citizenship rights, and even Jews, who could neither marry nor move from place to place without prior governmental approval, were to have increased privileges. To calm the unrest in Hungary, Franz Joseph was forced to agree to consider the formation of a representative assembly, although its influence would be extremely limited. ("We are certainly going to have a little parliamentary life, but the power remains in my hands," the emperor assured his mother, who emphatically disapproved of these concessions.) The investigation into the imperial finances yielded evidence of massive theft, obliging the emperor to sell an imperial railroad to raise cash, and causing suspicion to fall on one of his most loyal administrators, who slit his throat in despair after Franz Joseph, bowing to public opinion, demanded his resignation. Only later was it determined that the official had been wholly innocent of the charges.

Such persistent adversity was undoubtedly wearing, particularly to a ruler used to having the way smoothed for him by his mother and her advisers. To relieve the strain under which he labored during this challenging period, Franz Joseph had recourse to a time-honored remedy embraced by many of his esteemed and noble predecessors: to make himself feel better, he cheated on his wife.

The object of his affections was reputed to be a charming Polish countess whom he had known before his marriage, and who happened to be visiting Vienna that winter. Maliciously, the imperial court made sure that Elisabeth was informed of her husband's transgression.

What was almost certainly a passing fancy for Franz Joseph was an act of the deepest betrayal to Sisi. The intensity of his love for her was the lifeline to which she had clung from the beginning. It was what had given her the strength to try to endure a life diametrically opposed to what she would have chosen for herself. It was his passion that had brought her to this grim prison where, like a blossom deprived of sunlight, her soul struggled to survive. Now she discovered that the adoration he had so often and eloquently pleaded to have for her was an illusion.

As he had hurt her, so Elisabeth set out to wound him. And she had been in Vienna long enough to know just how to do it. She went right after his most precious possession: his dignity.

Like a hussar wielding a razor-sharp saber, Sisi sliced through the court's vaunted rules of etiquette. For the first time since her marriage, she cultivated her own social circle. She threw exuberant late-night parties in her rooms, to which (scandalously defying custom) neither her mother-in-law nor any of her adherents were invited. She appeared at all the most fashionable galas outside the court, where (again scandalously defying the traditional role of empress) she made a point of dancing with whomever she pleased until the early hours of the morning; one time, she stayed out all night. She smoked Turkish cigarettes, and sometimes even cigars, in public. She continued to avoid family meals, and the few times she was coerced to the table, swallowed two spoonfuls of sorbet and left.

Her health continued to decline. Determined to remain slender, she ate so sparingly that it is possible her nutrition was affected. She still exercised rigorously, but her cough had worsened. And yet her beauty remained undiminished. She had grown over the years and now, at five foot seven, was taller than her husband. Despite having given birth to three children, she maintained a weight of 110 pounds, with a waist as narrow as a girl's. Her face was a charming oval, her eyes large, her lips delicate. Her wealth of luxurious hair was a wonder.

But the adulation Sisi inspired cannot be explained simply by her outward appearance. Elisabeth exuded vivacity and personal magnetism the way a diamond sparkles in the light, but it was her innate sense of fairness, her obvious empathy for the downtrodden, that drew the populace to her. In distinct contrast to Franz Joseph, who was so disliked by his subjects that they watched in pointed silence whenever he ventured out in his carriage, Sisi could not show herself in Vienna without at once attracting a mob of well-wishers. On April 6, 1860, after word got out that that empress had been seen walking the short distance from the palace to the cathedral, so many bystanders swarmed to see her that she had to be rescued by the police.

The imperial family had never experienced anything like this before. Elisabeth's popularity, especially with the lower classes, existed on a different plane. It transcended the poverty, the anger, the despair. They *knew* that this ethereal creature was on their side.

Public fascination to this degree is a power unto itself. Although Sisi did not yet recognize this, others did. "She is...their idol," Sophia conceded.

SOON AFTER ELISABETH'S BESIEGEMENT at the cathedral, Max returned to Vienna for a visit. This time, perhaps hoping for a less contentious atmosphere, he came without Charlotte.

Sisi was glad to see him. She had always liked Max, but now they had a special bond. Both were outliers at the court, demeaned and stifled for their opinions, poets and dreamers chained by birth and marriage to smug, suffocating conformity. At least Max could get away. The archduke had just returned from a five-month voyage to Brazil, with a stop at Madeira, and Elisabeth drank in his stories of exotic travel. He spoke eloquently of the wild beauty of the seascape and the island's lush green foliage, heavy with tropical fruit. He had gone, he revealed melodramatically, "to seek on the waves of the Atlantic the peace that tottering Europe can no longer give my worried soul."

But he couldn't drift forever, and upon his return he had been stunned to discover that none of the conditions negotiated at the peace of Villa-franca had been met. Victor Emmanuel had somehow become the recognized ruler of just about everything north of Rome (except for Venetia), and Napoleon III, rather than adhering to the treaty, had played false and was now in the process of helping himself to the spoils by annexing Nice and Savoy. And the situation in Vienna was, if anything, even more ominous. "I found the condition of our poor country...tangled and gloomy," he wrote to Charlotte's father immediately following this visit. "Corruption on the one hand and unrest on the other are growing stronger and more disquieting every day...I am making all preparations for a crisis." So imminent did Max believe a revolt against his brother's rule to be that he asked the king of the Belgians if he thought he should sell his Hungarian bonds.

But Max's concerns, like Sisi's, were dismissed, and he was again sent away without being given any official position in the government. No sooner had he left than word arrived that Garibaldi had invaded Sicily. To Elisabeth's great alarm, the war in Italy had come for Marie.

HER YOUNGER SISTER'S MARRIAGE had not gotten off to a promising start. The eighteen-year-old had arrived in Bari in February the year before to find her father-in-law, Ferdinand II, the reigning king of Naples, so sick from the chill he had caught as the royal family slogged its way through the snow in carriages to meet her that he could not get out of bed. (The modern convenience of railroads had yet to make an appearance in southern Italy.) Her new husband, twenty-three-year-old Francis, Ferdinand's eldest son, whose sainted mother (literally—she was in the process of being beatified) had died two weeks after giving birth to him, had been raised in such exaggerated holiness that he viewed his approaching conjugal responsibilities with a trepidation bordering on terror. The strained relationship between bride and groom was not improved when, on the evening of her arrival, Francis ate something that disagreed with him at the wedding feast and was consequently "violently ill nearly the whole night," as Marie later recounted to Sisi. The servants having locked the doors of the nuptial bedchamber, there was no way to call for help or get out, and "the unpleasant state of things which confronted the officials the next morning...may be well imagined," family lore afterwards expressed with distaste.

The utter failure of her wedding night was not Marie's only problem. Ferdinand II's second wife, the current queen, disapproved of her new daughter-in-law's high spirits and, like Archduchess Sophia, had appointed a much older woman as mistress of her household. As had also happened to Elisabeth, Marie was prohibited from riding and was instead pressured to spend her days in prayer or sitting quietly with her retinue.

But then, on May 22, 1859, some three months after her arrival, just as Franz Joseph was in the process of leaving Vienna to join his troops in northern Italy, Ferdinand II unexpectedly succumbed to a bronchial infection induced by his chill, and Francis ascended to the throne. Although Marie's marriage had not yet been consummated, her bashful husband stood in such awe of his wife's beauty and vitality that she was soon able to ignore her mother-in-law's strictures with impunity and go riding whenever she pleased. Similarly, the lady-in-waiting, who had been installed, like Countess Esterházy, to scold and spy, was instead charmed by her lively charge, and turned into a fond second mother, while Francis's younger half brother, next in line to the throne, was so enamored of Marie that, hoping for a replica, he asked for her sixteen-year-old sister Mathilde's hand in marriage. Her subjects liked her, too: When, on July 24, 1859, Marie and Francis were crowned at the cathedral of San Gennaro in Naples, multitudes turned out despite the oppressive heat to cheer their new young sovereigns. "The whole affair was brilliant," the *Times* correspondent admitted. "The houses hung out their best tapestries; the ships were all...dressed out in gala fashion."*

---

* The coronation ceremony included an ancient relic containing a smear of the blood of San Gennaro, said to flow if the saint approved the ritual. According to the newspaper reports, the blood was indeed observed to liquefy, and this momentous omen "much

But of course Marie knew very little about her new realm. The kingdom of Naples encompassed the entire southern boot of Italy: everything south of Rome, plus the island of Sicily. In antique times the mainland had shared this name, so Francis's domain was also sometimes referred to as the kingdom of the Two Sicilies.

This nomenclature—alluding as it did to a territory split into distinct parts—was illustrative of the kingdom's true character. The mainland was dominated by the city of Naples, an exuberant capital of some half a million inhabitants, the largest municipality in Italy. The mainland was where the royal family lived—in the elegant palace of Caserta, with its high, vaulted ceilings, vast marble staircases, and opulent interiors, built to out-grandiose Versailles; or at the Palazzo Reale in the capital, where the court could attend performances at the famous Teatro di San Carlo, perhaps the most renowned opera house in Europe. Naples, known for its tremendous natural beauty, relaxed morals, and cheap prices, was an extremely popular tourist destination. Even the struggling author Herman Melville, morose over the commercial and critical failures of his latest string of novels, including a long one about a whale, was charmed by Naples. The capital was the "gayest city in the world," he recorded in his travel diary. "No equipages flash like these; no beauties so haughty. No cavaliers so proud, no palaces so sumptuous."

But it was a different story on the island of Sicily. Although the scenery was just as jaw-droppingly magnificent, few tourists ventured there, and even the king himself stayed away. Instead, a royal governor, aided by a Neapolitan general, several regiments of soldiers, and a cadre of secret police, ruled in the sovereign's name from the island's capital of Palermo. The local population openly resented these officials, and the authorities in turn were contemptuous of their subjects, many of whom were peasants who could neither read nor write, and who had not the weapons to fight back. There were many instances of repression and persecution.

---

gratified his Majesty, and so overcame the Cardinal that he fainted." Marie appears to have been somewhat less impressed. "The Queen...seemed to be struggling to conceal a very inopportune smile," a correspondent noted.

The Sicilians, treated by their government as second-class citizens, were consequently rife with discontent, which in turn made them particularly susceptible to Cavour's arguments in favor of Italian unification. For nearly a year after the defeat of the Austrians, Sardinian agents tried to get the local population to rise up on its own, as Florence's had done. But when on April 4, 1860, one such insurrection attempt failed miserably, it was decided that the Sicilians needed a little help, and the ever-intrepid Garibaldi volunteered to lead a covert expedition of 1,000 battle-hardened recruits to the island to give them a hand.

For an invasion that was supposed to be secret, Garibaldi and his band certainly garnered publicity. Their every movement, even before they shipped off the coast of Genoa in the early hours of May 6, 1860, was reported in the papers, so that just about everyone in Europe, including their intended target, knew they were coming. As a result, the waters surrounding Sicily were filled with foreign observers, almost all of them deeply admiring of Garibaldi. The British, jealous of their naval rights in the Mediterranean, professed neutrality but sent warships to try to help him; the famous French novelist Alexandre Dumas *père,* author of such swashbuckling classics as *The Count of Monte Cristo* and *The Three Musketeers,* sailed his yacht to Sicily specifically to meet Garibaldi and volunteer his services as an unofficial press agent; the foreign correspondent for the London *Times* did Dumas one better and passed the great general surveillance information detailing the exact number and location of the enemy forces. Even the United States, about to become embroiled in its own civil war, sent a gunboat to Sicily, where the captain, perceiving Garibaldi's musket to be old and rusted, lent him his own pistol for the campaign.

The Sicilians, too, had advance notice of the landing. Hundreds of peasants, some armed with obsolete blunderbusses, others with the scythes they used for cutting hay, set out to join their deliverer. From the cramped streets of Palermo to the most isolated mountain village, the island quivered with excitement. If the Virgin Mary herself had been scheduled to make an appearance, she could not have been assured a warmer welcome. "He is coming!" were the watchwords murmured from house to house.

And yet, even with all of this, Garibaldi should not have stood a chance. His musketry was so antiquated that the guns could only be used as bayonets. His men were outnumbered by a ratio of 25 to 1. The Neapolitan navy had four battleships cruising around the island ready to intercept him. The fact that he was able to land at all (and in broad daylight, at two in the afternoon, no less) was due entirely to the protective presence of a British frigate hovering off the western coast of the island, near the port of Marsala, the legendary general's intended point of entry. Although the commander of the Neapolitan cruiser on patrol spotted Garibaldi's two boats in plenty of time to intervene and prevent the invasion, he did not dare bombard the vessels, for fear that the powerful guns on the watchful British battleship floating nearby would then be turned on *him*. It was only after Garibaldi and his men, together with all of their arms and equipment, including their five corroded cannons (which took a considerable amount of time to hoist and unload), were off the boats, and the band had swarmed safely ashore, that the Neapolitan commander felt it was safe to move in and fire on the empty ships. In terms of military effectiveness, this was the equivalent of boldly attacking the cage from which a mountain lion had just escaped.

But the British drew the line at committing a land force, and there were still some eighty miles and 25,000 enemy soldiers between Garibaldi's troops and the capital city of Palermo, which had to be captured for the insurrection to be successful. The world waited anxiously for the outcome of this contest. It was like watching a performance of Italian opera play out on a global stage. The problem for Francis and Marie was that, while Garibaldi and his men were staging a thrilling drama in which they heroically risked their lives in pursuit of a just but seemingly impossible goal, the action on the crown's side, directed by a pair of aged Neapolitan generals, played out more like a comic farce.

Incompetence in battle is not a new concept; history is full of examples of inept commanders. But Francis's generals were such clownish bunglers that they made Field Marshal Gyulai look like George S. Patton. They hoarded their soldiers, dribbling out only small groups for reconnaissance, so Garibaldi never had to face more troops than his men could handle at any one time. They retreated in a panic at the first sign of combat and begged Naples for reinforcements, which they received but then didn't use. They fell for every piece of misinformation and refused to credit valid intelligence when it contradicted what they wanted to believe. The prisoners in the city jail knew more about Garibaldi's plans and whereabouts than did the Neapolitan army headquartered at the royal palace at Palermo, and when the great general and his men stole into the capital through a weakly defended back gate at four o'clock in the morning on May 27, 1860, the main squares were already full of celebrating Sicilians ready to join him.

Even then, when he knew exactly where Garibaldi was and had him completely surrounded, Francis's commander took fright, and to the astonishment of Europe, abruptly surrendered to the rebel force on the condition that he and his 25,000 soldiers, the vast majority of whom had not once been called upon to fight, be allowed to leave the island in safety. "Look, Your Excellency!" exclaimed one old warrior, as he watched the seemingly endless line of his comrades parade humiliatingly out of the city on June 7, bound for the ships that would ferry them back to the mainland. "Just see how many we are! Must we really leave like this?" "Be off, you drunken sot!" snarled the royal general.

Back in Naples, panic gripped the royal court. Sicily, ruled by powerful Neapolitan monarchs for over six centuries, had been lost to Garibaldi in less than a month! And now the victorious rebel leader and his men (augmented by ships laden with arms and volunteer warriors sent by a grateful Victor Emmanuel) threatened to cross over to the mainland and overthrow the crown completely. "Things wear daily a more menacing aspect," warned the London *Times* correspondent based in the capital. "I think the Court are fully persuaded of the dangers of the position, and everyone must feel the deepest sympathy for the young, attractive, and right-minded Princess whose misfortune it is to be Queen of Naples."

★　　★　　★

In Vienna, an already distraught Sisi, watching these events unfold, began to fear for Marie's life. The empress's state of mind was not improved when her mother, an equally frantic Duchess Ludovika, sent two of Elisabeth's brothers to the Hofburg Palace on behalf of the rest of the family to try to convince the emperor to come to the Neapolitan court's aid. All throughout the month of June, Sisi begged Franz Joseph to send ships and soldiers to Francis and Marie before it was too late, but her husband had no desire to risk further military intervention in Italy. His refusal led to yet another rift in their relationship, and this time the empress was defiant enough to act on her unhappiness. That July, without a word of advance notice to anyone, she suddenly scooped up four-year-old Gisela and bolted home to Possi.

Taking her daughter along was both an assertion of her rights and a calculated risk. It wasn't that she didn't love two-year-old Rudolf, but she knew that she could not abscond with the precious heir to the throne, even just temporarily to see his grandparents in Bavaria, without her husband or his mother insisting on retrieving him. Elisabeth gambled that, although Sophia undoubtedly disapproved, Gisela, being only a girl, would be allowed to stay with her—and she was correct. As small as was this test of wills, it represented Elisabeth's first victory over her mother-in-law since the death of little Sophie three years earlier.

As always, the time Sisi spent with her family at Possi revived her. By the end of the visit, she was strong enough to ride every day and the cough that had plagued her in Vienna had subsided. Her mother described her as blooming. The empress was only able to stay in Bavaria for six weeks, however, as she was expected to return to the imperial court with Gisela in time to celebrate Franz Joseph's thirtieth birthday on August 18, 1860. No sooner had she complied with this obligation than word arrived that Garibaldi, flush with recruits, had crossed over the straits between Sicily and Naples, and her anxiety for her sister skyrocketed again.

For her part, in preparation for this attack, Marie had begun to assert herself. She convinced her husband to institute a series of reforms, including issuing a constitution. "A constitution is not a misfortune," she informed Francis, echoing Sisi's argument with Franz Joseph. "In my country, in constitutional Bavaria, the royal family is respected and beloved." She helped to free her spouse from his stepmother's authoritarian influence by encouraging the queen mother's withdrawal from the court. "The immediate cause of the departure of the ex-Queen from Naples proceeds from nothing less than a violent dispute and personal altercation with the reigning Queen," asserted one of the London papers. "One day, after the family council had received unpleasant accounts of the state of affairs, the young Queen could not restrain her feelings, but proceeded to the apartment of the Queen-Dowager, and after making her acquainted with the bad news just received, she told her that the throne of Naples was lost forever, and that she, the ex-Queen, might consider herself the cause of the ruin of the family, owing to the bad advice and example which she had always offered to the late king," the news item continued. Whereupon "the ex-Queen, without uttering a single word, rose up from her chair, and, report says, they came to blows."

But Marie was limited as to what she could achieve by her husband's inexperience and weak appearance. What was needed was a forceful presence to galvanize the army and the mass of the citizenry (who in truth remained loyal to the crown, particularly the rural peasantry and the urban lower classes). Quiet, pious Francis, who telegraphed frequently to Rome to ask for advice and prayers, was patently not up to the task. Even the pope referred to him as "the little Job."

Lacking strong leadership, the Neapolitan commanders behaved exactly as they had in Sicily. Towns and garrisons were surrendered without a fight and whole regiments deserted their units. Within a week of Garibaldi's landing, the celebrated general and his army had reached Salerno, only thirty miles south of Naples. On September 6, to save the capital from destruction, Francis and Marie, hoping to draw those of their forces still loyal to them, fled the palace for the coastal fortress of Gaeta, some sixty miles north of the capital, the most secure stronghold in the kingdom—there to make one last, desperate stand.

For Sisi, the worry over her sister, combined with the black despair she felt at being back at the imperial court, provoked a physical crisis. The coughing fits increased alarmingly and were accompanied by a troubling new symptom—a swelling of the feet so pronounced that she could barely walk. A respiratory specialist was brought in who diagnosed advanced, and potentially fatal, lung disease. He urged swift relocation to a warmer climate. Obviously influenced by Max's romantic depiction of the sea and its charms, and clearly hoping to retire somewhere as far away from her life in Vienna as possible, Elisabeth at once chose the island of Madeira for her convalescence. As Franz Joseph declined to make one of the imperial vessels available for her journey, Queen Victoria graciously offered the empress the use of her personal yacht.

Sisi left Vienna on November 19, 1860, bound by train for Antwerp, and from there by ship to Madeira. She would not return to the imperial court for more than a fleeting visit for the next two years.

EUGÉNIE

Sisi's sister Marie at Gaeta

A Toxic Triangle

Elisabeth as a young bride

Her handsome young husband, Franz Joseph

…and his mother, Archduchess Sophia

Eugénie by Xavier Winterhalter

...and Napoleon III by Winterhalter

Eugénie and her ladies-in-waiting by Winterhalter

Eugénie at Biarritz

Dinner at the Tuileries

A Luminous Mystique:

Sisi on horseback

...in black, the only color
she wore after Mayerling

...visiting a soup kitchen

The Cult of Sisi

A daring portrait of the empress by Winterhalter

Delusions of

Max as emperor

Charlotte as empress

The Execution of the Emperor Maximilian by Edouard Manet

Empire

The surrender of Napoleon III on September 1, 1870

Dr. Thomas Evans (Courtesy of the University of Pennsylvania Art Collection, Philadelphia, Pennsylvania)

Eugénie fleeing Paris (Courtesy of the University of Pennsylvania Art Collection, Philadelphia, Pennsylvania)

Mothers and Sons

Eugénie with the prince imperial as a baby
by Winterhalter

Louis in 1874

Crown Prince Rudolf before
his death

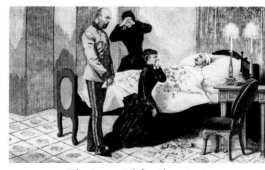

The imperial family grieving

17

Imperial Expeditions

There is nothing like a dream to create the future.

—Victor Hugo

IN THE SPRING OF 1860, six months before Sisi's abrupt decampment to Madeira, while the Austrian court struggled with bankruptcy and the wrath of its citizenry, the French, by contrast, were in a celebratory mood. By his victories in both Crimea and northern Italy, Napoleon III, like his uncle and namesake, had proven the armed forces of France to be superior to those of every other major European power, and he had reaped the rewards of his daring. The annexation of Nice and Savoy had recently been confirmed by a majority vote in each province, and although the balloting had been spurious in the case of Nice, this fact was not generally well known. Even if it had been, it wouldn't have made a difference, as it was naturally assumed in Paris that the Niçois would be much better off under French rule anyway.

More than this, the construction undertaken at the beginning of Louis Napoleon and Eugénie's reign seven years earlier had largely been completed, and the results were stunning. "The slums are vanishing and broad roads multiply," Baron Heeckeren noted in his diary. "Yesterday, you walked through a crooked, nefarious-looking alley. Today you find on the same spot a magnificent and sunlit boulevard." It was all going so well that the capital had been expanded to include the neighboring towns of Belleville, Montmartre, Batignolles, and Passy, among others. "By this extension, Paris has doubled its area," the baron crowed. "It now...contains 2,000,000 inhabitants. A city of faëry [enchantment]!" he marveled. "Paris has become Imperial; Paris has become great."

To underscore his achievements, Napoleon III announced his intention to visit Nice and Savoy later that summer to welcome his new subjects to France. As the point was to promote the empire, he asked Eugénie to accompany him. The acknowledged leader of fashion in Europe, she embodied the beauty and glamour of the capital. Louis Napoleon knew that the regional authorities, whose goodwill he needed to cultivate, would be disappointed, and possibly even insulted, if she did not appear.

But by this time, Eugénie had progressed politically far beyond her image as a style icon. She had proven herself during her regency, so much so that her husband now included her in his council meetings. As always, when she believed something, she held passionately to her point of view, and expressed these views forcefully. And in the early summer of 1860 there was no subject about which she was more passionate than the current state of chaos in Italy.

Like everyone else in France, the empress had watched in disbelief as Garibaldi landed in Sicily with his thousand volunteers in the early afternoon of May 11, 1860, and in less than a month intimidated the far superior Neapolitan force into surrendering to him at Palermo. "Garibaldi's expedition is one of the most comical pieces of history that has ever come under my notice," Mérimée laughed in a letter to a friend on June 15, 1860. "For twenty thousand men to capitulate to a handful of badly armed adventurers is somewhat astonishing."

But it wasn't funny to the empress. The Sardinians had Eugénie's sympathy when they were being oppressed by the Austrians, but now that they were proving themselves to be the aggressor against legitimate sovereigns like the pope and the young king and queen of Naples, her loyalties shifted. Rome itself might be threatened if Garibaldi was not stopped, she knew. Although Napoleon III already had troops stationed at the Vatican, she wanted him to do more. She wanted him to use the French military to defend the papal states, defeat Garibaldi, and restore the liberated territory to its rightful owners. Encouraging her in these views was the new Austrian ambassador to Paris, Prince Richard von Metternich.

Recalling Baron Hübner and replacing him with Prince Metternich was perhaps the most astute decision Franz Joseph made during his entire reign. The thirty-one-year-old prince hailed from the highest nobility and the most important political family in Austria. His father had been the greatest statesman of the first half of the nineteenth century. Handsome, cultured, and intelligent, "his manners were of the most polished description, and his attitude...most gallant and charming," remembered Amélie Carette, one of Eugénie's ladies-in-waiting. "He was enabled to fulfill the most delicate diplomatic tasks with unfailing honor and credit."

But it was his twenty-four-year-old wife, Princess Pauline, "that wondrously brilliant and popular woman," as Amélie raved, who was the new ambassador's greatest asset. "The Princesse de Metternich left in Parisian society a memory which never will be effaced, and which was for many years unequaled by that of any other woman," the lady-in-waiting testified solemnly.

Pauline combined the wit, grace, and charm of a *grande dame* with the high spirits and *joie de vivre* of youth. Although not classically pretty—Amélie called her "charmingly ugly"—she was nonetheless "possessed of wondrous powers of fascination." The princess would have succeeded at court in any event, but her career was jump-started in the spring of 1860 by her unerring eye for a bargain. By her own account, she was sitting at home one day reading when her maid interrupted her to tell her that a young woman, the wife of an unknown clothes designer, was begging to see her. Her visitor had brought along a little sketchbook of her husband's designs for Pauline to peruse, and if the princess would only consent to allow them to make her a dress, she could name her own price.

"What is the man's name?" Pauline interrupted.

"His name is Worth, and he is an Englishman," her maid replied.

"An Englishman! He must be bold indeed if he contemplates dressmaking here, in Paris. The idea is absurd," Pauline scoffed. "Nothing will induce me to have anything to do with him."

"Nevertheless your Highness would do well to glance at these sketches," her maid returned shrewdly, handing her the notebook. "To my mind, they are very charming."

Pauline opened to the first drawing and immediately changed her mind. "Bring this Englishwoman to see me," she instructed.

"She is pure French," corrected the exceptional domestic. "There is nothing English about her."

The upshot of this interview was that Pauline ordered two dresses, one for day, one for evening, for which she paid only 300 francs each. The Wednesday after the frocks were delivered, she wore the evening gown, a showstopper made of billows of white tulle, delicately embroidered with a halo of silver spangles, to a ball at the Tuileries. "Hardly had the Empress entered the Throne-room...than she immediately noticed my dress," the princess reported. Eugénie made straight for Pauline, complimented her on her ensemble, inquired as to the designer's name, and had the Englishman at the Tuileries by 10 a.m. the next morning. "Worth was launched, and I was done for; no dress costing three hundred francs ever again saw the light of day," Pauline concluded ruefully.★

The Metternichs very quickly became one of Eugénie's favorite couples. They were such good fun—the prince was also an accomplished pianist—that they were included in every official social event and were even invited to spend time with the imperial family during their private summer holidays at Biarritz. This gave the new Austrian

---

★ Charles Frederick Worth—for that was the English designer's full name—would go on to become Eugénie's principal dressmaker and consequently the most sought-after couturier in Europe. He was the first to display his clothes on live models rather than using the little dolls common to the time of Marie Antoinette, and is generally credited with originating modern-day haute couture.

ambassador time to present his country's case to the empress. As for Pauline, "Much has been said of the intimacy of the Princesse de Metternich at the Tuileries," reported Amélie. "Her Majesty had a great sympathy for this fascinating woman," she admitted, "but the Empress was intimate with no one."

This was not quite true. There was one person with whom Eugénie was very close: her sister Paca. It was Paca to whom she wrote regularly, spilling out her heart, her hopes and fears. With Paca she could be herself without the worry of having to maintain an appropriate imperial distance, or being misunderstood, or having her confidences leaked. From the very beginning, it had been the two of them against the world—not even her rejection in favor of her sister by her first love, the duke of Alba, had separated them.

Paca was ill that summer and had been for some time; she had pain and trouble breathing; she tired easily. Concerned, Eugénie insisted that she come to Paris for treatment, where, as with Sisi, the doctors diagnosed lung disease—a serious condition that required extensive rest but fortunately was not life-threatening. Eugénie herself had been rundown, and in preparation for her trip to Nice and Savoy—which had been extended by her husband, so long as they were already in the vicinity, to include a quick sea voyage to the French colony of Algiers—she had retreated to the healthful waters at the mountain spa of Eaux-Bonnes. But she returned to Paris in August to sit daily by her sister's bedside, sometimes driving out with her in the evenings so that Paca, reclining in the imperial carriage, could get a bit of air. María Manuela was also with her daughter, living in the beautiful mansion in Paris that Eugénie had had built for them, so the empress knew she was leaving her sister in good hands. And after all, it was only for a few weeks.

She and Napoleon III left the capital on August 23, 1860. Eugénie had never been to southeastern France before, and the scenery enchanted her. Like a tour guide, she did her best to convey what she saw to her sister, as though to bring her along on the journey. It was clear from the number of letters she wrote that Paca was always in her thoughts. "The country is magnificent," she raved to the invalid from

Lyon on the 25th. "We were received with an enthusiasm impossible to describe." Chamonix on September 4 boasted an astonishing glacier: "Imagine the sea being frozen suddenly during a heavy storm and you will have an exact idea of this immensity of ice," she exclaimed.

But her real excitement came two days later, when she was able to relate an experience that could only truly be shared with Paca. "I am in Grenoble, the homeland of M. Beyle [Stendhal]," she revealed joyfully to her sister. "This morning I went to the museum and the first thing I saw was his portrait, which I recognized on the spot. All our childhood memories came rushing back, and it was with the delight of seeing an old friend again that I looked at his image, which is a true likeness of him, just as we knew him when he told us the thrilling stories of the Emperor's battles that we listened to with such pleasure. How far from our thoughts then could it have been, that my son would be the descendant and representative of that dynasty!" she marveled.

But to this volley of letters, Paca did not respond. "I hope to hear from you in Marseilles," Eugénie wrote worriedly. From there she and her husband would be boarding a ship for Nice, and then on to North Africa on September 13. "I want to know what the doctors said at their last visit."

Up until this point, the trip had been a signal success: one brilliant reception after another, each event more crowded than the last; in Marseilles alone over 100,000 people crammed into a public ball to get a glimpse of the emperor and empress. But when they arrived in Algiers on September 17, Louis Napoleon told Eugénie that Paca's condition had worsened. In a panic, she wrote to both her mother and her brother-in-law, begging for an update. "The dispatch I just received is driving me mad," she agonized in her letter to María Manuela. "I don't know what I am doing or saying. The thought that Paca is sicker has put me in mortal anguish. I have prayed so much that it seems to me impossible that my sister does not recover... I am so unhappy being so far away and without details. I cannot live with this anguish, I am only waiting for answers by telegraph to leave."

But in fact the emperor, with a full schedule of celebratory events in front of him, to which all the most important officials from all over Algeria had been invited, had lied to her — Paca was already gone. It wasn't until September 21, when she had forced him to cut short their tour anyway, and they were onboard ship approaching Marseilles, that he advised Eugénie that it didn't matter how much they rushed, she would not be back in time to see her sister, as Paca had actually died before they had even reached Algiers, and so had been entombed the day before, on the 20th.

The similarities between Paca's passing and that of her father were unmistakable. Eugénie had initially been told both were ill, but not seriously, a falsehood meant to be soothing but which only made her grief that much more devastating when the truth came out later. She had been far away from each of these dear ones, blithely writing bright letters back to them, the only one not to know that they were languishing on their deathbeds. She had hurried back to both, believing she would see them again, only to be denied even the final farewell of burial. Although it is possible that he was unaware of her history, the emperor's decision to take political appearances into consideration and not tell his wife the truth at once was a betrayal for which Eugénie would never forgive him.

It was a terrible time for her. The first thing she did on her return to Paris was to have Paca's coffin transferred from La Madeleine, the church where her sister was initially interred, to the chapel at Rueil, which was closer to Saint-Cloud, and which held the tombs of the Empress Josephine, Napoleon I's first wife, and Queen Hortense, Louis Napoleon's mother. This was not simply so that she could be nearer to Paca's remains during the interim period while arrangements were being made for her final removal to Spain, but also to make a political statement. Eugénie had been incensed to learn that in her absence, M. Fould, the French foreign minister, had refused to give her sister a proper state burial. This had caused yet another rift with her husband. "On the death of the Duchess of Alba, M. Fould refused all official participation with the Court, and nothing in the funeral ceremony recalled the near relationship of the deceased to the Ruler of France," the *Guardian* reported.

315

"The Duc d'Alba complained to the Empress, who, in extreme anger, said she would never more receive M. Fould or anyone of his family. The Emperor replied, 'All very well; but as a minister you must receive him.' The answer was, 'Then I will henceforth receive no minister.'...The consequence of all this was scenes of the stormiest description," the journalist observed.

The guilt for having been absent, which had allowed this insult to her sister to take place, gnawed at her, and mixed in with her grieving. Paca was only thirty-five years old, and left three young children, a boy and two girls. "[The empress] seems to have been a good deal *choquée* [shocked] that she had been dancing in Africa when that poor sister of hers was dying," commented Leopold, king of the Belgians, to his niece Queen Victoria. Eugénie did her best to step in as a substitute parent for her ten-year-old nephew, Carlos, who remained in Paris after his father returned to Spain to make preparations for his wife's interment there. "My dear James," Eugénie wrote to her brother-in-law from Saint-Cloud. "Carlos's health is very good and he is very considerate, however, it is necessary to keep a close watch on him because he is also very dazed. I am searching diligently for a skilled tutor. I know how important this is to you, as it was also to my beloved sister, I only find it difficult because it is such a heavy responsibility. In my opinion, this child is capable of learning even without much work...He listens easily and is amused: we do our best to answer the hundred thousand questions he asks every day," she relayed in a valiant attempt at levity.

But she still seethed with sorrow and anger, and this was exacerbated by the deteriorating situation in southern Italy. At first, to appease her, Louis Napoleon agreed to send the French fleet to the port of Gaeta, where Sisi's sister Marie and her husband, Francis, were holed up with some 13,000 loyal Neapolitan troops who had refused to go over to Garibaldi's side. Eugénie had heard all about the young queen of Naples from her new friends the Metternichs, and through them had established a correspondence with her. Marie was exactly the sort of modern, courageous female the empress wished to encourage. Determined to remain by her husband's side as they fought for their kingdom, Marie rode out every day, dressed adorably in a military-style cape and cap, and always in the liveliest spirits, to boost the morale of those of the royal soldiers stationed on the front lines. She appeared so faithfully that these units were nicknamed the "Queen's battery." "It is very rude of the enemy never to leave me in peace anywhere!" the beautiful nineteen-year-old would joke in mock indignation as the cannonballs burst around these outposts. "They have driven me from one room to another, and now they will not even let me be here."

But although the queen of Naples's bravery won her European admiration, this unfortunately did not translate into active military support. Rather, Victor Emmanuel continued to rack up victories, both martial and political, including a referendum held in Naples on October 21, in which the population, as expected, cast their ballots in favor of annexation to Sardinia. It seems to have bothered no one that a majority of the participants in this novel exercise had no idea what they were voting for. "It was well worth seeing them yesterday, these barefoot ragamuffins who had become citizens, clutching their voting cards which they were unable to read," noted an observer. Five days later, Victor Emmanuel and his army crossed into the realm, and Garibaldi rode out to meet him. "I hail the first King of Italy!" the great general exclaimed graciously to the sovereign, ceding the kingdom to him.

Francis, alas, proved not so accommodating. He and Marie both stubbornly refused to recognize the results of the referendum and vowed instead to stay and fight to recover their domain or die in the attempt. As it was obviously inconvenient to have two monarchs claiming the kingdom at the same time, Victor Emmanuel took his predecessor at his word and in November 1860 marched his 30,000 soldiers to Gaeta to defeat his opponent's force, which was only one-third the size.

In vain, Louis Napoleon tried to get Francis, who clearly didn't stand a chance, to withdraw of his own accord. He wrote a letter reassuring the pious sovereign that he had done all he could to uphold the honor of his name, but that the time had come to retire with dignity for the sake of those who would otherwise perish for him in a futile cause. When this appeal fell on deaf ears—"His Majesty the King or ex-King of the Two Sicilies is a great booby," Mérimée noted, expressing the general opinion of Europe—the emperor took a more extreme approach. To get the besieged couple to accept the reality of their situation, Napoleon III announced that he was withdrawing the fleet from Gaeta, and if the king and queen of Naples did not take this opportunity to escape aboard one of the French ships, they would be on their own to face the far superior land forces under Victor Emmanuel as well as a full-scale sea bombardment by the fast-approaching Sardinian navy.

For Eugénie—whose grief and guilt over Paca's death were so acute that she, like Sisi, had started to cough—this ultimatum represented yet another betrayal by her husband. It didn't help that, confronted with his spouse's tears and recriminations, Louis Napoleon found refuge, like Franz Joseph, in infidelity (although the French emperor's indiscretions went far beyond his Austrian counterpart's). Napoleon III had now begun to cheat on Eugénie openly and with gusto, seemingly with whoever happened to be passing by—maids, actresses, wives of court officials, even women whom the empress had counted among her friends.

"The death of her sister...had thrown her into a very nervous and excitable state," remembered Anna Bicknell, governess to the children of one of the great families at court, who lived at the Tuileries and knew the empress. "At the same time she had serious domestic sorrows, into the cause of which the world was only too completely initiated." The arguments between the imperial couple escalated and made the rounds as gossip. "While the Empress grew angry and cried," ran one of these stories, Napoleon III "merely bent his head and let the storm pass, limiting himself to saying "Ugenie...'Ugenie...you go too far'...She cried out, still weeping: 'I am going away...I shall take Louis.' 'If you do that, I shall have you locked up.' 'I will do it.' 'No, you shall not.' 'I shall go mad...Lock me up if you wish. I shall be less unhappy in a convent or in prison than in this palace, where I am an object of derision.' "Ugenie!'

'No, I will never accept this degrading position of a slave who panders to your caprices.' 'You know my affection...' 'I do not believe in it any-more,'" she was reputed to have cried.

Gossip or not, Eugénie *did* go away. Abruptly and without her son, she fled suddenly on November 14, 1860, to the home of friends in Scotland. Scrounging around for an excuse for her absence, the court gave out that the empress, on the advice of her physicians, was journey-ing to the drizzly cold of the northern country for health reasons. ("Eugénie's expedition is most astonishing," the king of the Belgians commented drily when he first heard the news. "I have never heard Scotland recommended for winter excursions.") Her one preparation had been to write personally to Victoria, begging to be allowed to visit the realm incognito.★

The queen of England saw Eugénie twice on this trip. "She is very amiable, and one must like her," Victoria declared earnestly to her uncle on December 4, 1860. "There seems to be no doubt that there were many scenes...on account of her sister's funeral...She looked very pretty, but very sad—and in speaking of her health and of her return from Algiers began to cry. She seems to be much better, how-ever, for her journey; before she could neither eat nor sleep, nor would she take notice of anything. She never mentioned the Emperor but once when she offered his compliments...It is very strange," Victoria puzzled.

Eugénie's retreat into private citizenship lasted only a month, but it was enough. Under the quiet influence of unfamiliar surroundings, the blackness lifted. Strength returned, and with it, the empress's desire for, and belief in, her role as a public figure. Within two weeks she had come out of seclusion and was touring factories and museums. Victoria caught up with her again at the end of her visit, by which time Eugénie had clearly recovered her equilibrium. "The Empress is still here, and

---

★ She and Sisi each broke down and fled at almost exactly the same moment. They must have literally passed each other on the English Channel, Eugénie crossing over from France, Sisi sailing south from Antwerp to Madeira, both recipients of Victoria's generosity.

enjoys her liberty of all things," the queen informed her uncle on December 11. "We went to town for the Smithfield Cattle Show yesterday, and visited her at Claridge's hotel...She looked very pretty, and was in very good spirits, but again carefully avoided any allusion to her husband,...although she talked a great deal about all she was seeing!" complained Victoria, who, familiar with her own factories, likely found Eugénie's travelogue somewhat tedious.

This renewal of spirit persisted even after Eugénie's return to Paris, where she faced one last torment: the transfer of Paca's remains to Spain. "I had a terrible time seeing my sister's corpse being carried away," Eugénie confessed poignantly to her brother-in-law in a letter dated December 29, 1860. "It seemed to me that my soul was being torn away...But God having given me back my strength, I wanted to stay close to her until the very last moment, this being the only duty I could render her, and the only memory that can stay with me."

Thus ended those dreadful few months, the worst she had experienced since she had assumed the throne. But she had weathered the adversity, and it was with resolution, and a renewed sense of purpose, that the empress turned to face the future. Eugénie was a fighter.

HAPPILY, THE FESTIVITIES CELEBRATING the new year were particularly splendid that season, and so provided a welcome distraction. "All goes well," Baron Heeckeren boomed with satisfaction in his journal entry for January 1861. "The Bourse [the Parisian stock exchange] is excellent" (always important to the baron), "the Emperor in good health...the people contented...There is skating in the Bois, dancing in the Faubourg, receptions at the Tuileries. The Empress is entrancing," he noted appreciatively. "There is music everywhere, flowers, perfumes, songs, and love. Oh! The beautiful women one enjoys the sight of at these gatherings,...a whirlwind in which one grows intoxicated," he sighed with pleasure.

Under the influence of the general merriment, Eugénie seems to have yielded to Louis Napoleon's protestations of enduring affection—he did seem to love her—and so the couple was reconciled (although this in no way stopped him from further cheating). "I think that when a man breaks away and seeks other women, he is impelled by boredom and curiosity," Eugénie reflected later. "Boredom with that which is identified with his own personality and curiosity to know a fresh mind or fresh moods...It's the *sameness,* that fatal *sameness*—in fact what we call monotony," she continued in frustration. "One gets so used to acting and speaking and thinking together that at last neither interests the other. So...man roams!"

But just because she had resigned herself to her husband's straying didn't mean that Eugénie intended to back down on any of her other opinions. The new year had brought fresh danger to Francis and Marie, still huddled at Gaeta with a small force. On January 19, 1861, the armistice Napoleon III had proposed after the withdrawal of the French fleet from the harbor ended without a peaceful resolution, with the consequence that the fortress housing the beleaguered king and queen was shelled by the Sardinians for some eight hours on the 22nd. All the windows were blown out and Marie's dressing room was destroyed. "Well, Madam," one of the foreign ministers who had stayed with the couple observed, "you wanted to see the bullets at close range; you have been served to your heart's content." "All the same, I should have liked a little wound!" Marie countered.

Eugénie took the couple's cause to heart and made every attempt to rescue them. "The *salons* here have bestowed on the King of Naples a reputation for heroism, and one runs the risk of being set down as churlish if one suggests that he had not done anything very great, and that he has been somewhat late in beginning," Mérimée grumbled to a friend. "The ladies in society are subscribing to present the Queen with a silver buckler," he noted with amusement.

But by February, the situation was truly desperate. The destruction continued; food was scarce; typhoid broke out. Marie was beloved by the soldiers for working at the hospital and soothing them on their deathbeds by promising to transmit messages and wages to their loved ones, but it was clear that the Neapolitan force could not hold out much longer. At this point, Eugénie took matters into her own hands.

"The Attaché to the French Embassy at Rome has demanded permission [from the Sardinians] . . . to convey a letter from the Empress of the French to the young Queen at Gaëta," the *Times* reported from Naples on February 12, 1861. "This permission has been granted. The French steamer *Mouette* is said to have received orders to be in readiness to receive the family of Francis II." In her letter, Eugénie urged Marie to agree to an honorable surrender in order to forestall further bloodshed, and to use the ship Napoleon III was sending to escape to Rome in the hope that diplomacy could achieve what armed conflict had not. "You can be assured of all my admiration, of all my sympathy, and furthermore, you have right and justice on your side," the empress emphasized.

This appeal worked. Francis signed the terms of surrender, ceding his kingdom to Victor Emmanuel, on February 13, and the next day he and Marie withdrew from Gaeta. "It was a scene of august simplicity," revealed an onlooker. "Ragged and exhausted soldiers presented arms to their Sovereigns for the last time, tears rolling down their cheeks." The queen, too, broke down. "Gentlemen, do not forget me," Marie cried, just before boarding the *Mouette*. "I declare," Francis was reported to have said solemnly, "that the Emperor of the French is the only Sovereign who has held out a hand to me in my distress."

Thus was Sisi's beloved sister saved, not by Naples's long-standing ally Franz Joseph, but rather through the kind efforts and at the insistence of Eugénie.

BUT OF COURSE, HOWEVER much affairs in Italy might dominate conversation at the Parisian salons, they had no impact on the social season, which, with the empress at the helm, continued to dazzle the continent. "At that time there was a sort of intoxication in the very atmosphere of Paris, a fever of enjoyment—a passion for constant amusement, for constant excitement, and, amongst women, for extravagance of dress," reported Anna, the Tuileries governess. "This was encouraged by the court, with the intention of giving an impetus to trade and of gaining popularity by favoring constant festivities and consequently constant expense."

Actually, the lavish court balls and the rapidly increasing cost of Worth evening gowns (at a minimum of 1,500 francs each) were the least of it. There were also the still-unpaid bills for the thousands of miles of new railroad tracks, for the demolition and reconstruction of Paris, and for the massive military outlays in Crimea and Italy, all expenditures that Napoleon III had financed on credit. For the very first time, a note of apprehension crept into the Dutch banker's diary. "*Reflections on the Finances of the Empire,*" Baron Heeckeren wrote in his entry for February 1861. "Certain fears take hold of me," he confessed. "The public debt grows and grows in an alarming fashion. To-day it is 320 millions...and the deficit keeps growing. It is a bottomless pit...They will have in the end to add to it fresh wars and taxes not yet scheduled...Our feet are sinking ever deeper and deeper into the mire," he worried. "We want 200 millions, that's the truth. It is no use playing with figures."

Where was this money to come from? Louis Napoleon was confident that the improvements in transportation and technology he had made, so necessary to his vision of France as the future economic powerhouse of Europe, would result in a surge of commerce and trade more than sufficient to pay down the debt. This optimistic view was, however, dealt a heavy blow when, on April 12, 1861, an obscure military base on the far shore of the Atlantic called Fort Sumter was fired on by a Confederate brigadier general and the United States suddenly erupted in civil war.

Although both Eugénie and Napoleon III were personally appalled by slavery, and the practice was outlawed throughout their empire, this moral indignation did not, alas, extend to a ban on the French commercial class's enthusiastically (if indirectly) profiting from the heinous system through trading partners. Consequently, by the time the Civil War broke out, America, and particularly the Southern states, represented a substantial source of income to those dealing in imperial manufacturing and luxury goods. The textile industry, centered in Lyon, absolutely depended on this market. When the US demand abruptly disappeared, the deleterious effect on the French economy was immediate. "Commercial interests were deeply concerned, and became more and more so as the war went on," Eugénie's dentist, Dr. Thomas Evans, a native of Philadelphia, testified. "National industries were paralyzed and markets lost. Thousands of working men were idle."

And as if this were not bad enough, the summer brought yet *another* major financial setback. In July, the new president of Mexico, Benito Juarez, the first member of the Indigenous population to hold high office (all the previous heads of state for the past forty years had been of aristocratic Spanish ancestry), faced with an economic crisis brought about by decades of in-fighting and corruption, suddenly announced that he was reneging on some 75 million francs' worth of foreign bonds owed to France, Spain, and England. What was particularly provoking was that, while he was at it, Juarez also announced that he was unilaterally appropriating all the property owned by the Catholic Church in Mexico (conservatively estimated at some $150 million or about a quarter of all the land in the country), so it could be sold off to benefit the national treasury. The howls of protest from the papacy and the clerical class — Mexico was a state where there were more priests than cacti — only added to Napoleon III's domestic problems, as he was already under attack at home for allowing the pope to be stripped by Victor Emmanuel of his Italian states.

To her husband's rescue came Eugénie. Having grown up in Madrid, she had met many Mexicans (of the aristocratic Spanish variety, of course). Like other well-born travelers and courtly dignitaries to the capital, they were welcomed into María Manuela's social circle and attended her famous salons and costume balls. For some time, a handful of these men, exiled from their homeland by Juarez's policies, had been proposing that a European monarch, accompanied by a few experienced regiments, take control of the situation and impose a degree of order over the chaos in Mexico. Eugénie now began to listen to this scheme. "It has...been said that the Empress was the person who conceived the Mexican expedition... There is some truth in this assertion," the comte de Fleury admitted.

After eight years of marriage, Eugénie had been by Louis Napoleon's side long enough to have fully absorbed his somewhat quixotic teachings. Her view of the role of the French empire in world affairs, Prince Metternich warned in a letter home to Vienna, was a "mash of good intentions and impracticable notions, of sound reasoning and utopian phantasies." Consequently, she never for a moment considered carrying on a war of conquest. On the contrary, Mexico was to remain an independent country with a constitutional monarchy; the citizenry was simply to be relieved of the chaos they were enduring under Juarez's (to her mind) corrupt rule.

And the beauty of the plan was that it was so simple, and so easily accomplished. A right-minded Catholic prince with liberal views, who was yet capable of imposing order and bringing the fruits of European culture and civilization to the native population, was to be recruited to take over the Mexican monarchy. To aid this champion in claiming his throne, the French court would in the beginning provide a small military force until such time as the new ruler was sufficiently established to mobilize his own army from within his domain. There was no question that success would crown the efforts of whoever was bold enough to grab at the opportunity. After all, if Garibaldi, with his thousand poorly armed volunteer soldiers, could take over the kingdom of the Two Sicilies in a matter of months, think what a few regiments of the French army, the best-trained and most modern-equipped warriors in the world, could do against the undisciplined, impoverished, misguided Mexicans currently supporting that tyrant Juarez! Why, it would be a rout.

Providing Mexico with a stable, friendly government would solve the empire's financial problems as well. The country was rich in natural resources, particularly silver, and surely a sovereign who owed his crown to French intervention would be open to negotiating favorable trade agreements. Even the timing was optimal—with the United

States currently using its army to slaughter large numbers of its own population, there wouldn't be soldiers available to intercede on behalf of Juarez. In fact, the Confederacy, with its strong ties to France, could be counted on to welcome a sympathetic government on its southern border.

Really, the most difficult part was going to be finding a prince with the necessary principles and experience who was worthy of the honor. He could not come from France or the emperor's family—that would appear too much like annexation and might arouse the opposition of the other powers. Casting around, Eugénie mentally ran through and rejected various candidates from Spain and Portugal until finally it came to her.

Of course! That talented Archduke Max.

ELISABETH

Sisi and her ladies-in-waiting at Madeira

18

An Imperial Time Out

Hail to thee, O thou Ocean eterne!...
Methought whole winters long I sat
An invalid, in darksome sick-room,
And now I suddenly leave it,
And with dazzling rays am I greeted
By emerald Springtime, the sunny-awaken'd,
And the snowy blossoming trees are all rustling,
And the youthful flowers upon me gaze
With eyes all chequer'd and fragrant;
There's a perfume and humming and breathing and laughing,
And the birds in the azure heavens are singing—
Thalatta! Thalatta! [The Sea! The Sea!]

—Heinrich Heine

SHE WAS BETTER THE MOMENT she set sail from Antwerp on Queen Victoria's yacht.

This improvement did not mean that Elisabeth wasn't seriously ill when she left, or was somehow feigning infirmity (a supposition many at the imperial court in Vienna took malicious pleasure in circulating). The king of the Belgians, who took an instant liking to Sisi, clearly believed her to be in mortal danger, much like Paca, who had just died of a similarly chronic respiratory ailment. "I think there is something very peculiar about her, which is very pleasing," Leopold wrote to Victoria on November 21, 1860, after escorting "the young and very nice Empress of Austria...already dressed for her departure" to the harbor and seeing her safely aboard the borrowed ship. "Poor soul, to see her go away under, I fear, not very safe circumstances, as she coughs a great deal, quite grieves one," he lamented.

But the journey to Madeira, despite being rough, was immediately beneficial. Sisi loved the adventure of the voyage and the vast wildness of the ocean. Alone among her entourage, the empress was free of seasickness, and she who could not be coaxed to take more than a few mouthfuls at an imperial family dinner, ate with appetite in the mess of the tossing boat while everyone else aboard moaned and heaved over the railings.

Elisabeth was equally delighted, during the first weeks of her stay, with Madeira. It was all just as Max had described: exotic flowers, an enchanting shoreline, the peace and quiet of solitude. Her cough subsided and her strength began to return.

There are several schools of thought as to what had caused Sisi's symptoms. A story made the rounds that just before she left, the empress had taken advantage of Franz Joseph's absence at a diplomatic meeting in Poland to sheath herself from head to foot in a heavy black veil and in this disguise visit a Viennese specialist outside the court, who diagnosed her as having been infected with a sexually transmitted disease. However, as there has never been any firsthand evidence that this interview took place, and there was no indication at all in later life that either Elisabeth or Franz Joseph showed symptoms of the malady, this version of events seems unlikely. More feasible is the hypothesis that her health problems were due to anemia, brought about by loss of appetite or excessive dieting. Insufficient nutrition might have explained the swelling in her feet and face, as well as her fatigue, and could also have depressed her immune system, thus accounting for the fevers and cough.

Today, a wealth of research has been conducted indicating that emotional problems can adversely affect health and that young women in particular are susceptible to eating disorders. Neither Sisi nor her physicians, of course, could know this. All Elisabeth understood was that she was ill and desperately unhappy with her life in Vienna. Ironically, by removing herself from the pernicious atmosphere of the imperial court and settling somewhere so isolated that she could not be disturbed, she had instinctively chosen the best possible treatment for her condition.

To her ladies-in-waiting, the empress's daily activities, which included hours of card games, reading, and playing with dogs, were so trivial and monotonous that, as first weeks and then months went by, they complained openly of tedium. Even Elisabeth acknowledged that she was bored. "I want always to be on the move," she yearned. "Every ship I see sailing away fills me with the greatest desire to be on it." But she lingered in Madeira, for there was safety in seclusion. Her state of mind, and the degree to which she was struggling with the constraints of her position and the hostility surrounding her at court, are evidenced by her letters. "If I didn't have the children, the thought of having to resume the life I have led until now would be quite unendurable," she wrote simply.

As if to prove her point, Sisi was subjected, even on a sparsely inhabited island over 2,000 miles away from Austria, to spies and gossip. It was reported back to Vienna that she spent an inordinate amount of time with one of her groomsmen, a handsome young Hungarian count, the brother of one of her ladies-in-waiting. In fact, he was giving her lessons in his native dialect, which Elisabeth, drawn to the kingdom's romantic history and landscape, wished to learn. Although there was never a hint of impropriety, the count could not help but show his appreciation for his pupil's beauty. Rumors flew around the imperial court that the empress had abandoned her husband and children in order to have an affair, and he was immediately transferred.

And so it was to exactly the same carping environment that Sisi returned when she finally left Madeira on April 28, 1861. Franz Joseph met her in Trieste to bring her home. The emperor embraced her lovingly; he had clearly missed his wife. Elisabeth, for her part, was reported as being cheerful and healthy. By May 20 she was back in Vienna, having stopped along the way with Franz Joseph to pay a courtesy call on Max and Charlotte at their palace at Miramare.

Of course, the very first thing she did was to fly to Gisela and Rudolf, whom she had not seen for six months. But just as before, her visits to the nursery were overseen by Sophia's women, and Sisi was again prohibited from interrupting or altering the children's schedules in any way. Nor did official protocol make any concessions to the illness from which the empress had only recently recovered. Rather, almost as a punishment, Elisabeth was immediately thrust into a full routine of dreary formal receptions and state dinners at which she was expected to stand for hours among crowds of condescending Viennese aristocrats who made it clear that they believed her to be a self-centered whiner who had deliberately shirked her imperial and familial responsibilities.

The court did its work well. It took only a few days before Sisi stopped eating and was coughing again. The fevers and nausea returned, and with them, the tears and despondency. She cancelled all her appointments and retreated once more into her rooms at Laxenberg. Within weeks she was even worse than she had been before leaving for Madeira. She had frequent, prolonged fits of coughing at night that kept her from sleeping; her exhaustion was apparent. Elisabeth was too debilitated even to attend her sister Mathilde's marriage to the Neapolitan count of Trani, younger brother of the deposed Francis, held in Munich on June 5, although she had already accepted the invitation and had been looking forward to seeing her family.

Alarmed, her physicians again insisted on a warmer climate. Sisi thought at once of the enchanting island of Corfu, on the western coast of Greece, which she had toured briefly on her return voyage from Madeira and thought idyllic. As it was somewhat humiliating (and smacked ever so slightly of heartlessness) for a powerful ruler like Franz Joseph to have to rely on Queen Victoria's generosity to transport his critically ill wife a second time, the emperor had his brother Max run Elisabeth down to Corfu on his yacht instead.

Elisabeth left Vienna on June 22, 1861. She wept and clung to her children; it is clear she was so weak and sick that she did not feel she would recover. Worse, she did not seem to wish to. She wrote to her mother just before her departure that she had become such a burden that her husband would be better off without her—"if she were no longer alive, the Emperor could marry again." This was not histrionics. Sisi's health had declined so dramatically during the month she had been back that the general impression, even among the court and her family, was that she was dying. Certainly, the thousands of ordinary citizens who stood vigil at the train station to see her off believed they were taking leave of their empress for the last time. "There was a profound silence, broken only by women's sobs," an eyewitness reported solemnly.

AGAIN, SHE NO SOONER set sail than her condition improved. Max was astounded to see her appetite begin to revive even on such a short journey—they were only aboard ship two days before landing in Corfu. It was "nothing short of miraculous," the archduke confided to Vienna. By July, the imperial doctor who had accompanied her was so confident that the danger had passed that he left his patient, who wasn't following his advice anyway (he complained that Elisabeth went swimming too often), and returned to Vienna to resume his official duties.

Frustrated at his wife's erratic moods and symptoms, Franz Joseph sent Count Grünne, Archduchess Sophia's old confidante, to Corfu to act as his intermediary and try to arrange an understanding that would encourage the empress to return to court. This was a poor choice. An older man, Grünne held a rather jaundiced view of marriage. Although there is no record of their conversation, from Sisi's horrified reaction to his suggestions, and her later comments about this encounter, it seems he gave her the impression that it was assumed at court that she was unfaithful to the emperor, and he to her, and that this was all perfectly fine so long as she was discreet about it and didn't leave written proof, such as diary entries or love notes. As there is no evidence that Elisabeth had ever cheated on Franz Joseph, she was dismayed that her husband's emissary—and by extension the emperor himself and the rest of the court—believed the slander against her to be true. Sisi also seemed to be finding out for the first time that the emperor had strayed more than once, and that everyone but she knew about it. By the end of Grünne's visit, she was no longer speaking to the envoy, and had once more stopped eating and relapsed into tears and despair.

It was at this point that her family stepped in. Nene was enlisted to travel to Corfu to investigate the situation. She arrived in August to find Elisabeth in so wretched a state that Nene was shocked by her appearance. The empress was very thin. Her cough had returned, and her feet were swollen to the point that she could barely walk. Sisi's face, too, was disfigured by bloating.

Nene had not wished for this assignment. Three years earlier, in a feat of inspired matchmaking, Duchess Ludovika had found her eldest daughter a husband. The prince of Thurn and Taxis, although not a member of a ruling dynasty like Elisabeth's, Marie's, and Mathilde's spouses, had other attributes close to a mother's heart: he was the richest man in Germany. (His family owned the exclusive rights to the postal service.) Nene now lived in a palace that boasted more rooms than Versailles. Corfu was far from her home in Regensburg, and she was worried about leaving her two small daughters—she had by this time a one-year-old and a two-year-old—for so long an absence.*

But her stay was a boon to her younger sister. As Paca had been Eugénie's only real confidante, so was Sisi able to unburden herself to Nene in a way that she could not with her ladies-in-waiting or other members of her entourage. It must have been a great relief to the empress to be able to pour out her marital troubles to someone she knew she could trust. Within a month, Sisi was so much better, eating meat and drinking beer daily under Nene's guidance, that she was able to resume physical activity, and the visit ended with the two sisters

---

* The Thurn and Taxis postal system was so lucrative, and so famous, that the family (whose descendants *still* live in the same opulent palace) remains prominent in Germany today, and there even exists a board game commemorating their vocation.

enjoying their time together, sailing and swimming along the shore in the fine weather.

And now it was Sisi's turn to send her spouse an emissary. On her way back from Corfu in September 1861, Nene stopped at Vienna to pick up her husband (the prince of Thurn and Taxis had kept the emperor company by going hunting with him while their wives were away) and to speak with Franz Joseph. In her quiet way, she seems to have given her brother-in-law and former suitor an earful. The upshot of this conversation was that the emperor decided to visit Elisabeth for a few days in October himself. "I feel the greatest longing to be there after such a long separation," he explained to his disapproving mother (by letter, of course).

If Franz Joseph had been secretly hoping for a complete reconciliation, and to bring his recovered spouse back with him to Austria, as he had after Madeira, he was quickly disabused of this conceit. Elisabeth's entourage reported that the empress was kind to her husband, at least in public, but not intimate with him. This was the first indication that their roles had begun to reverse: his emotional need for her was greater than hers for him. She was not yet ready, physically or spiritually, to return to Vienna, but she was amenable to spending the next few months in Venice, which was still part of imperial territory (albeit against the local population's will). This compromise also worked well for Franz Joseph, who badly needed his charming wife to help him win over his disaffected Italian subjects. But Elisabeth made it clear that she would agree to winter in Venice only if she could have Gisela and Rudolf with her. She knew that for this to occur, her husband would have to confront his mother, and that nothing would change for her unless he was willing to do so. On this condition she was adamant: no children, no Sisi.

Sophia fought back with everything she had. Gisela and Rudolf were still too young for such an arduous journey, and to revolutionary Italy, of all places! The archduchess reminded her son what had happened the last time he had given in to his wife and traveled with the children. And what of the water in Venice, which was known to be unhealthy? Was he really intending to risk sickening and perhaps even losing Rudolf, the precious imperial heir, as he had little Sophie?

Caught between his wife and his mother, Franz Joseph temporized. Gisela and Rudolf were sent to Venice, but they were put in the charge of Countess Esterházy, whose duty it was to ensure that they followed the strict routines established by their grandmother. As another concession to the archduchess, water for the children's needs was transported regularly from Schönbrunn Palace to Italy at great expense. "One more sacrifice for our poor martyr, their excellent father!" Sophia lamented.

Sadly, the imperial family's residence in Venice, which began at the beginning of November 1861, was not a success. Sisi's joy at seeing her children was marred by the presence of the severe countess, who countermanded any changes Elisabeth attempted to make to the archduchess's directives, causing further friction between them. It took over two months, until well into January 1862, but Sisi was finally able to convince Franz Joseph that as empress she should be allowed to choose her own household. Countess Esterházy was sacked and sent home, replaced by a much younger lady-in-waiting more to Elisabeth's taste.

But this success did not bring solace. Sisi had been away so often over the past two years that Gisela and Rudolf, now five and three, did not really know their mother, and a long stay in unfamiliar surroundings was not calculated to comfort them. They were homesick; they missed their grandmother. That hurt. The empress herself was unhappy in Venice. The local people, heavily taxed to support the losses sustained by Austria in the war with Sardinia, and aware that they were the only province on the whole peninsula that had been denied the right to join the unified kingdom of Italy, openly resented and shunned their imperial visitors. The atmosphere was even more forbidding than it had been the last time Elisabeth visited, some five years before. Depressed, she stopped eating and the cycle of symptoms started up again: her feet swelled, preventing exercise; her face puffed up; she cried often.

To distract herself, she began what appeared a curious hobby—she collected photographs of striking women, which she solicited from ambassadors all over the world. But of course for Sisi, who had grown up in Munich during King Ludwig's reign (he of the famous portrait gallery of beauties and the Lola Montez scandal), there was nothing unusual about the idea. She, like her deposed uncle, was attracted to glamour, although not for the same reasons. His interest had been sexual. The empress was seeking affirmation and inspiration.

At last Duchess Ludovika, worried by accounts of the return of her daughter's symptoms and the despairing tone of Elisabeth's letters home, took matters into her own hands and dragged the family doctor, who had known Sisi since childhood, with her to Venice. The physician diagnosed dropsy caused by malnutrition and recommended a rest cure at the spa town of Bad Kissingen, about 200 miles north of Munich. By the time the empress's coach rolled into this pastoral German venue, towards the end of June 1862, she was so exhausted, and the swelling in her feet was so pronounced, that "her appearance is that of a delicate invalid — pale, with much suffering [and] she cannot walk without support, from the feebleness of her limbs," the newspapers observed.

And then Elisabeth saw her father standing on the street waiting for her. He had taken rooms in Kissingen for the length of her cure. He was there to watch over her, lift her out of despondency, and bring her back to herself. And Duke Max was not the only family member to put in an appearance. Her eldest brother, Ludwig, was also there to help take care of her and her younger brother Gackel was on the way.

The salubrious effect of this unexpected male support group was immediate and profound. For the first time in years, Sisi felt herself surrounded by people who loved, understood, and valued her for the fearless, fiercely competitive athlete and free spirit she had been before her marriage. Within a week she was back on her feet. "Her Majesty, who on arrival here was obliged to be lifted from the carriage and conveyed to her chamber, now appears daily in the public gardens, drinks 'ragoczy' [mineral water from one of the local springs], and walks up and down the alleys leaning on the arm of her father, the Duke Max in

Bavaria, replying to the salutations of the visitors by a friendly smile," a correspondent for the *Morning Post* reported. By July 10, the empress had evidenced so remarkable a recovery that there was no longer any need for her to remain at the spa. Still, she did not even consider going back to Vienna. Rather, Elisabeth and her unshakable retinue of ladies-in-waiting and servants left Kissingen and traveled instead with her father and brothers to Possi.

There, to her delight, she found two unexpected guests: her younger sisters Marie and Mathilde. But joy turned to concern when she discovered the reason for their visit. The ex-queen of Naples was in big trouble.

AFTER THE SURRENDER of the fortress of Gaeta the year before, Marie and Francis had been deposited in Rome by the warship sent at Eugénie's insistence by Napoleon III. Upon their arrival, the pope had put them up in one of his own residences, the magnificent Quirinal Palace. This mark of respect was taken as quite a good sign. The sumptuousness of their surroundings seemed to indicate that they had lost none of their prestige and that it was only a matter of time before the Neapolitans, unused to a king like Victor Emmanuel, who understood none of their customs—he had not even bothered to consult the blood of San Gennaro on his accession—and who moreover did not even live in the south, would revolt against the Sardinians and recall their legitimate monarch to his throne.

But as the months passed and this did not happen, Marie became restless. There was nothing for her to do in Rome. Francis was content to pray and plot to retake his kingdom with that portion of the Neapolitan nobility who had followed him into exile, but his wife found these sessions tedious, particularly after the excitement of dodging cannonballs at Gaeta. Similarly, her compatibility with her husband, not strong to begin with, suffered a further deterioration once the thrill of facing danger together in a noble cause faded. Francis continued to be gentle and considerate to Marie but they had by this time been wed for over two years and he had still not shown the slightest inclination to consummate the marriage.★

The queen's mood improved somewhat when her sister Mathilde married Francis's stepbrother the count of Trani (at the ceremony in Munich that Sisi had been too ill to attend) and moved with her new husband to Rome. Mathilde was eighteen to Marie's twenty. The countess of Trani was perhaps not as pretty as her older sister but she was just as lively. "The Queen's married life is unhappy, as is that of her sister the Countess of Trani," a resident of Rome observed in his diary on December 1, 1861. "Various stories are told about them. The ex-Queen drives with her sister in the Corso every afternoon...she rides, smokes, practices pistol-shooting in the Quirinal, and drives four horses, seated on the box," he noted. Marie and Mathilde also kept each other company by going daily for long gallops into the country-side for amusement.

These would prove to be the queen of Naples's undoing. Mathilde, it turned out, was not Marie's only riding companion on these scenic rural excursions. A handsome young man was apparently also in attendance. It is an open question as to whether he was a Belgian captain whose regiment was charged with keeping the royal family safe, or a German prince known to be residing in Rome during this period. Whoever this dashing mystery man was, Marie fell hopelessly in love and conse-quently strayed ever so slightly from what would ordinarily be consid-ered a strict interpretation of her marriage vows. By the spring of 1862 she was pregnant. As even Francis would probably have been able to figure out that this was likely not immaculate conception, both Marie and Mathilde fled to Possi in July to escape detection and scandal.†

★ Previous historians have sought to explain the king's disinterest by relying on the old chestnut that there was something wrong with his penis, which required a small operation (of which there is no record). Although no one can know with certainty what the problem was, an alternate explanation is perhaps suggested by the testimony of Fran-cis's confessor, who once peeked through the keyhole of the royal bedroom and found the king twirling around the room dressed in his wife's crinoline.

† Ironically, the highly public nature of Sisi's illness, which was reported in all the European papers, helped her sister disguise her plight. "I regret deeply, though I am

Elisabeth was intensely loyal to her family. Her distress at her failure to convince Franz Joseph to send soldiers to Naples had accelerated her symptoms, and led ultimately to her flight to Madeira. Once there, she had been too far away to follow the press reports of the bombardment of Gaeta, and so had been forced to beg for letters and news of her younger sister from the official couriers who appeared intermittently on the island. When at first she did not receive any correspondence from or about Marie, she assumed the worst and shut herself up in her rooms to cry for a day and a half. It was only after she heard that her sister was safely in Rome that Sisi's health really began to improve.

Now she listened to Marie with sympathy. Although Sisi was likely shocked that the queen had been unfaithful to her husband, it was clear that her sister was suffering deeply. Marie was wretched at being separated from her lover. She couldn't bear the thought of giving him up, and yet to run off with him would bring deep disgrace on the Neapolitan throne, just when the monarchy needed all the legitimacy it could get. Her only honorable option as queen was to remain in hiding until the child was born, give the baby away, and go back to her passionless existence with Francis. But, after experiencing romantic love, this alternative was so depressing that she could not reconcile her heart to it. "If only a bullet had struck me at Gaeta!" she moaned.

The three sisters, twenty-four-year-old Elisabeth, twenty-one-year-old Marie, and nineteen-year-old Mathilde, each faced with disappointment, adversity, and uncertainty, remained at Possi all that July. Ensconced safely in their childhood home, they behaved much as young women at this stage of life have been known to do. They huddled together discussing and rediscussing their situations long into the night. They left their crinolines and accessories lying around and crowded the house with their overflow of luggage and servants. Sisi's ladies-in-waiting had to be accommodated at meals, and

---

scarcely astonished to hear, that bad health is the reason of the young Queen leaving here," lamented the Roman correspondent for the *Daily Telegraph*. "She has all the delicate and dangerous brilliancy that betrays a frail constitution, and her sister the Empress of Austria is a confirmed invalid."

otherwise sat or stood disapprovingly, sniping among themselves at the general lack of decorum.

It is usually difficult to pinpoint with accuracy a specific catalyst that alters the course of events. There are always myriad factors to consider—so many possible pressure points, political actors, or technological and military developments to sift through and weigh. But in this instance, there is no question that the sweep of Austrian history was forever changed by one fed-up father.

Duke Max had taken it as long as he could. He had originally been philosophical about Marie's predicament. (Well, well, "these things happen," shrugged the man who had impregnated half the villages around Possi.) But within a month he'd had enough. It was one thing when Elisabeth had been seriously ill, but by this time she was back riding and hiking again. He'd already done his duty by stoically (for him) enduring two decades of a home front overstuffed with daughters. Duke Max felt strongly that it was now their husbands' turns to deal with them, and one evening in early August he expressed this belief forcefully by abruptly throwing all three—the empress, the queen, and the countess—out of the house.

It is not clear that Sisi would have gone back to the imperial court without this impetus. She was still so vulnerable that she brought Gackel along with her for moral support. But she had to for Marie's sake. Nene had agreed to house the queen of Naples temporarily, but to reduce the risk of scandal, Marie was going to need a more powerful protector. She required an empress.

And so, on August 14, 1862, at eight in the evening, after an absence of nearly two years, Elisabeth returned to Vienna by train. The reaction of the citizenry to her reappearance can only be described as euphoric. "No sooner had the town...heard of the impending arrival of the popular Empress than an extraordinary excitement was visible in all classes of society," the Austrian reporter for the *Standard* confirmed. Although given almost no advance warning, thousands turned out spontaneously to meet her at the station and welcome her home with shouts of joy. The following evening, an even more ecstatic reception awaited her when a special torch procession organized for her benefit drew an astounding 200,000 spectators. So many people crowded into the avenue leading to Schönbrunn Palace that it was difficult for the parade to pass, and many of her admirers climbed up onto the street-lights or hung out of the windows of buildings to get a better view. The procession itself was thrillingly theatrical. "There were between 14,000 and 15,000 lamp-bearers, and the effect produced by the lamps—which were extremely elegant in form and brilliant in colour—was almost magical," the *Times* correspondent marveled. When Sisi stepped out onto the balcony with Franz Joseph to acknowledge her subjects and thank them for their support, the accolades from the dense throng below were long and thunderous.

Sisi was back. And this time, she intended to win.

EUGÉNIE

Marguerite Bellanger

19

The Empress Rolls the Dice

Life resembles a novel more often than a novel resembles life.
—George Sand

As VIENNA REJOICED at the unexpected return of their lovely sovereign, Eugénie, feeling herself at thirty-six to be at the height of her political abilities, prepared to step out of her husband's shadow and launch the most ambitious project of her career: the conquest of Mexico.

Coincidentally, the empress's self-assertiveness had begun to climb just as her husband, beset by difficulties on all sides, began to question himself. By January of 1863, Louis Napoleon, fast approaching his fifty-fifth birthday, was beginning noticeably to wilt under the burdens of high office. He had put on weight and his trademark goatee was streaked with gray. He had not his old, youthful energy—at one of the court's famous skating parties early that year, a pretty young American named Lillie Moulton, who had married a banker living in Paris, observed merrily that when the emperor met her on the ice, he "stopped like an engine nearing a station, puffing and out of breath." Nonetheless, he rarely followed his doctors' advice to eat and drink less and avoid late-night carousing. Like many men his age, he was plagued by urine retention problems but in his case, his symptoms were exacerbated by a lamentable dose of gonorrhea.*

---

* I can't think how he could have picked this up.

But Napoleon III's real problem was the truly daunting set of challenges he had set in motion by conniving to intervene on the side of Sardinia in the Italian independence movement. All sorts of unintended complications had spiraled out of *that* decision. Now it wasn't just the citizens of Venice and Rome who clamored to be relieved of the evils of autocratic occupation. The unexpected triumph of Garibaldi and Victor Emmanuel had raised the hopes of oppressed peoples all over Europe. Suddenly, the Poles were threatening to rise against the Russians, the Hungarians were demanding their autonomy from Vienna, and the Prussians wanted to liberate two provinces from Denmark. Any one of these regional conflicts, Louis Napoleon knew, could draw in the other powers and escalate into a full-blown European war that might spill over into France.

The last thing the fatigued, middle-aged emperor wanted was to have to raise and lead another army, which he would have to do to protect his borders. Soldiers and battles were bad for business and threatened the growth and prosperity he had worked so hard to promote. Already, the Civil War in America was dragging on with no end in sight, and it was dragging the French economy right down with it.

Rather than armed conflict (which in addition to wasting precious lives and destroying property was unpredictable and might turn out against him), Louis Napoleon much preferred a diplomatic solution to these myriad disputes. His idea was to invite all the major powers to a conference in Paris at which international borders would be tweaked and provinces exchanged by mutual agreement, just as one would rearrange the furniture in the various rooms of a palace. To bring this about, however, required that the path towards compromise be smoothed in advance by clandestine understandings and alliances. And there was no ruler in Europe whom the French emperor needed secretly to convince of the advantages of switching the sofas more than Franz Joseph. It was clear to Louis Napoleon that there would be no peace in Italy, and consequently no way to quell the unrest and intrigues surging out of it, until Austria could be voluntarily induced to give up Venice.

Eugénie, too, was committed to securing an alliance with Vienna, although for different reasons. She was still incensed at what she considered the perfidy of Garibaldi and the Sardinians in taking property that didn't belong to them, ousting legitimate monarchs like Franz Joseph's relatives, the pope, and Francis and Marie in the process. She wished to do something to recompense the Austrians for France's failure to rein in Victor Emmanuel and adhere to the peace of Villafranca.

And so she had come up with the idea of offering Mexico to Archduke Maximilian. This unselfish bestowal of so rich a prize on a member of Franz Joseph's immediate family would surely convince Vienna that she and Napoleon III had only their best interests at heart. "It seemed to the Empress a sort of compensation to the House of Austria, which France had humiliated in the Italian campaign," the comte de Fleury explained. "It appeared to her chivalrous...to unite in an effort to give good government to a land...with such a magnificent future before it, but then cursed with envious leaders and threatened with anarchy."

Her husband thought offering the crown of Mexico to the archduke was an excellent idea as well. It served his purpose of securing repayment for the French loans in default under the current president, Benito Juarez, while providing future access to the country's considerable silver reserves—and all without upsetting the other great powers (who would definitely have objected had he tried to appropriate Mexico outright). Both Max and Franz Joseph would owe him for helping to establish their dynasty in America, and this political indebtedness could be parlayed to French advantage in Europe. Napoleon III was thus happy to let Eugénie broach the subject through diplomatic channels with the court of Austria, which dutifully passed the proposition on to Max.

Max and Charlotte were by this time living in their renovated, out-of-the-way castle in Miramare, on the northeastern shore of the Adriatic Sea near Trieste. Although they had been married for over five

years, the couple still had no children, so it was just the two of them.★
As Franz Joseph, suspicious of his brother's popularity and liberal
views, still refused to give him a position in his government, Max had
nothing to do but putter around, landscaping the garden; Charlotte
read and painted. The atmosphere surrounding the household was
evidently thick with the humiliation of political insignificance. Visitors were infrequent and generally limited to relatives. "I feel so sorry
for my poor sister, falling from the grandeur of Milan and Venice into
that little house, a collection of past glories, and really just a storage
place for furniture," deplored Charlotte's brother, who came to investigate her situation for himself. "My brother-in-law [Max] has put on
some weight...his teeth are worse, and to put it simply, the poor boy,
who by the way is now quite bald, has not improved with age," he
carped.

Max was very bitter about his treatment at the hands of his older sibling. The archduke knew he had done a good job as governor-general
in northern Italy. If only Franz Joseph had listened to him, Austria
might not have lost Lombardy. It was consequently extremely satisfy-
ing to discover that Napoleon III, arguably the most successful ruler in
Europe, thought so highly of Max's talents that he was offering him his
very own empire. The archduke could not help taking a swipe at his
brother in the memorandum he composed in the wake of this overture.
"Owing to the pressure of contemporary conditions, the pristine glory
of our house has become dimmed," he observed severely. "None sees
more clearly than I that it is the duty of our house to wipe out this
stain; and so I cannot fail to see what an impression would be made
upon the world, and above all upon an enfeebled Austria, if the proposition in question were carried into effect." And he indicated his willingness to consider accepting the honor, pending further discussion.

Both Eugénie and Louis Napoleon were delighted with this response
and set about putting their plan in motion. Max, who knew very little

---

★ There is no way to tell what the problem was. Meaningful research into the causes of
infertility would not be conducted until the next century.

about Mexico—he had never visited the country, didn't speak Spanish, and had only a vague idea of its history and general geography—naturally had questions about the project, which Napoleon III made haste to answer. It was intended to be a turnkey operation, with French troops smoothing the way for the new monarch's arrival. The archduke would not have to set foot in his empire until the entire country was pacified and a referendum was held confirming Max's government by majority vote as the will of the people. Only then would he and Charlotte cross the Atlantic and settle in their new land. Once established in the capital, Max would naturally raise his own force from among his subjects, and the French divisions would be withdrawn. "I do not believe there will be any serious resistance there," Napoleon III assured his protégé.

While the emperor communicated with the archduke, Eugénie began a separate correspondence with Charlotte. It was ever the empress's desire to promote the role of women and so she included the archduchess in the ongoing dialogue over the operation. "I know in advance what a providence Your Imperial Highness will be for all these peoples at present abandoned to demoralization [the Mexicans], but who are nonetheless ready to rally round those who will henceforth throw in their lot with that of the people," Eugénie declared fervently to her sister sovereign, whom she had never met.

For Charlotte, the empress's overtures, brimming with confidence (for Eugénie had never been to Mexico either and knew only what those whom Juarez had removed from power and wealth, and who were consequently seriously keen to get it back, told her), were as opportune as they were flattering. Finally, a position and purpose commensurate with the life for which she, as the daughter of a king, had been trained! No more languishing in embarrassing exile at Miramare, pretending to enjoy the solitude of the peaceful countryside. "To found a dynasty and work for the good of a people...isn't [this] the path that dear Father marked out with his example?" Charlotte wrote earnestly to her brother. To succeed would be "quite a beautiful thing....This year will decide whether or not you will become the brother-in-law of an emperor," she teased.

★   ★   ★

IT IS ASTONISHING HOW PROBLEMATIC a straightforward operation like taking over Mexico, a country of 9 million inhabitants spread out over an area more than three times the size of France, possessed of significant mountain ranges and a nearly 2,000-mile border with a potentially hostile neighbor to the north, separated from Europe by 5,000 miles of ocean, and already in the hands of an entrenched leader with a loyal army at his disposal, can be. The first combat unit the French sent over—a company of some 7,000 soldiers—lost 1,000 men to malaria and dehydration before they ever encountered the enemy. When this weakened battalion finally advanced inland far enough to reach the fortress town of Puebla, which had to be subdued before any assault on the capital, Mexico City, could be considered, they were repulsed in a single day by Juarez's forces, and compelled to fall back all the way to the coast.

This unexpected failure was enough to considerably dampen Louis Napoleon's enthusiasm. With Mérimée's help, he was busy researching and writing a life of Julius Caesar, a far more pleasurable activity than his usual cares of office. The empress's pet project was not merely an annoyance that took time away from this important scholarly endeavor, it was also beginning to cost him precious public support that he could ill afford to lose. "There is great anxiety about Mexico, and the general regret on the score of the expedition increases day by day," Mérimée observed on February 3, 1863. The emperor would just as soon have let the whole idea fade away.

But Eugénie wouldn't let him. She was absolutely committed to the venture. More than this, she argued, the honor of France was at stake. They could not let this first defeat stand. Her husband reluctantly agreed and sent two infantry divisions as reinforcements under a new general, who was under orders to resume the campaign. From the first, the emperor had tried to get England and Spain to send troops as well, but both countries, fearing the wrath of the United States should the North win the Civil War, declined to participate.

Again, Eugénie refused to take this as a warning sign that she was seriously underestimating the degree of difficulty involved and was risking the lives and reputation of the French military on a caprice. Rather, she assured Charlotte that their isolation should be considered an advantage, as now the new general would not have to waste time coordinating with the other powers. *"Here we are, thanks be to God, without allies!"* the empress exclaimed without irony in a letter to the archduchess. "Since our action has been freed from all constraint, the country feels safe enough to express its wishes," she explained. "Unfortunately many mistakes were made at first; but I have never had any doubt of the success of the enterprise."

This was bravado. The reinforced French army, now numbering some 28,000 men, was taking its time progressing towards the interior. In fact, both Eugénie and Louis Napoleon were anxious about the outcome of the invasion. The empress was aware that she had staked the dignity of her office, her husband's popularity, and perhaps even his rule and that of her son, on this gamble. Weeks passed without intelligence from the general beyond the fact that he had reached the heavily defended town of Puebla. And then finally, in June 1863, word arrived.

It was a victory. A big, smashing, unequivocal success. Juarez's defenses were routed. Thousands of prisoners were taken, including many in the Mexican president's high command. Juarez himself was forced to flee the capital, which the French army entered in triumph on June 7. "News has this moment been received of the capitulation of Puebla," Mérimée reported. "The Mexicans were completely defeated."

The invigorating effect of this victory cannot be overstated. It justified everything the emperor and empress believed about the glory of bold intervention in world affairs and allowed them to proceed with both Max's investiture and the prospective international conference to rearrange large parts of Europe for the benefit of mankind. Napoleon III, who had been in an agony of doubt over the possibility of another shameful loss at Puebla—"for the last week, he simply had not lived," Ambassador Metternich confided to Vienna just before the news came in—was so thrilled and relieved that he was reduced to tears. Eugénie beamed when she was informed that the French army had been applauded on their arrival in Mexico City, and that her portrait in particular had been prominently displayed by cheering crowds.

Events proceeded quickly from this point. An assembly of notable citizens from across Mexico (all of them previously dispossessed by Juarez) convened in the capital at the beginning of August and naturally voted overwhelmingly in favor of installing a balding, thirty-year-old, supercilious Austrian aristocrat, whom none of them had ever seen, as their new leader. Informed of this development, an exhilarated Max humbly accepted the honor (pending a fuller vote, which required an intimidation campaign throughout the surrounding countryside by the French troops). "The Archduke Maximilian has written the Emperor a letter of eight pages to thank him," Mérimée noted drily on August 21, 1863.

A proud and confident Eugénie chose this moment for a holiday to Spain. It was the first time she had visited her homeland since her marriage. Of course, she wanted to see her mother, who was aging, and pay her respects at her sister's tomb. But there is no getting away from the fact that the voyage was also in the nature of a victory lap.

The empress set off in the beginning of October from Biarritz, sailing first to Lisbon, then Cádiz, Seville, and Valencia, where she graciously accepted an invitation from Queen Isabella to attend a formal state dinner at the royal palace in Madrid. Upon her arrival at the capital, Eugénie, who had been ostracized as a child for not being as pretty as her older sister, and was further rejected as a teenager for her rebellious spirit, was fêted with bullfights and a magnificent procession, public celebrations reserved only for guests of the highest order. But her true revenge came when she appeared in full court attire at the banquet. "Her dress!" gasped the American ambassador. "The ladies contemplated it in silent awe, and even grave diplomatists were in raptures."

Pressing her advantage, the empress used this occasion to urge Isabella to provide military support for Max. Although she could not convince the queen to send ships or troops to help the archduke—Isabella wondered why her eleven-year-old daughter had not been chosen as ruler of Mexico instead—Eugénie did get her hostess to agree to recognize Max's regime once he had established himself in Mexico.★ Eugénie also cleverly flattered Isabella by promising that for the first time, Spain would be among those invited to attend the great power conference that Napoleon III was planning for early the following year in Paris.

It was thus with high hopes and at the pinnacle of success that the empress returned to France. The hunting season at Compiègne was particularly brilliant that year. "Many guests…notabilities of all countries, all nobilities, of every fortune and every social position, of every school in Art and Literature [are here]," Baron Heeckeren gushed. "The dinners…are magnificent functions…and include as many as one hundred guests. The general aspect of the table is superb…The dishes pass round; all choice and exquisite wines in abundance. Metternich, the sly dog, supplies an excellent Johannesberg which fills his pockets and wins golden opinions," the banker pointed out jealously.

The baron was not the only visitor to Compiègne to betray that emotion. Evidence of just how far the empress had climbed in influence and standing is indicated by Plon-Plon's treatment of her that November. The prince was so resentful of Eugénie that he could not bring himself to toast his hostess in front of a tableful of dinner guests, an unthinkable breach of etiquette that left his fellow diners aghast. "You do not wish to propose the health of the Empress?" Napoleon III demanded of his cousin in disbelief. "If Your Majesty will excuse me, I would rather not," replied his unruly relative.

Eugénie saved the situation—"I am not particularly anxious for a speech," she smiled at Plon-Plon. "You are very eloquent, but your speeches occasionally alarm me." But Mérimée, who was there that evening, observed that no one spoke to the offender for the rest of the night. "I never saw a man so wanting in courtesy," he wrote. "The

---

★ To Isabella's complaint that the Mexican empire had not been offered to her child, Eugénie countered soothingly that there was plenty of unclaimed territory in Central America that would become available once Max's empire was secured, and that it was best to wait until the Spanish princess had grown up a little before ceding it to her.

Prince who, I suppose, dreams sometimes of playing a part in politics, renders himself obnoxious."

The empress was able to laugh off this rudeness because the reports emanating from Mexico were just as promising as she had predicted. The French general, striking out into areas outside the capital previously held by Juarez, was able to relay the happy news that no sooner did his soldiers appear in a town or village than the opposition melted away without a fight, and that all those left in each of these rural municipalities had, under the benevolent eye of the occupying troops, *also* voted overwhelmingly for a new government headed by the archduke.

In fact, the success of the intervention in Mexico was the only real foreign policy achievement the French could claim that year. Humiliatingly, by December 1863 Louis Napoleon's plans for a sweeping international conference had to be scrapped. It seems that his fellow heads of state were not interested in being pressured to trade territories as though they were playing cards. "The Emperor Napoleon has written a circular to all the sovereigns of Europe inviting them to a congress at Paris to settle the affairs of Europe," Lord Malmesbury noted in his diary. "As... he talks of sacrifices to be made for the public good, I suspect there will be a great disinclination to respond... Probably England would be required to give up Gibraltar." The diplomat was correct; the British government was so antagonistic to the very idea of the conference that it published its refusal to attend in the newspapers even before the foreign minister had received his invitation. As no initiative that did not include the most formidable naval power in the world could hope to prevail, Napoleon III had been forced to give up the whole idea.

That left Max as France's last best chance to coax Austria into an alliance that would solve Louis Napoleon's Italian problems by peacefully persuading Franz Joseph to cede Venice to Victor Emmanuel. Getting Archduke Max to stop quibbling over details and set sail for his new empire as quickly as possible was also Napoleon III's only hope of getting both his money and his soldiers out of Mexico. As for Eugénie, she was so convinced of the glory and rectitude of the enterprise that when the American ambassador warned her bluntly in January 1864 that "the North is going to win [the Civil War], France will have to abandon her project, and things will end badly for the Austrian," she retorted passionately, "For my part, I assure you that if Mexico were not so far off, and my son were not still a child, I should want him to place himself at the head of the French army, in order to write with his sword one of the fairest pages in the history of this century." "Madame, you may thank God that Mexico *is* so far away, and that your son is still a child," the ambassador replied.

It took until the spring, but the emperor and empress, working together, finally achieved their purpose. The deal was clinched in March, when Max and Charlotte stopped for a week in Paris as part of a general farewell tour to members of the archduchess's family in Belgium and England. Although the couple traveled as private citizens, under an alias, attention was lavished upon them and they were treated and addressed as visiting royalty. Concerts and receptions were given in their honor, and they attended the first performance of a new comedy by Alexandre Dumas *fils*. "They could not but be flattered by the kindness of the Emperor and Empress of the French," observed the correspondent for the *Morning Post*. "The Court painter, Winterhalter, has contrived to execute the Empress Eugénie's orders for portraits of the future Emperor and Empress of Mexico, although he was allowed only two sittings by each."*

This was heady treatment for a husband and wife who had spent the bulk of their marriage being disdained by the Austrian court as inconsequential nobodies. In addition, Napoleon III had already thoughtfully arranged for Max to receive the proceeds of a large loan to get him started. (Well, not *all* the proceeds. About 60 percent was going to the French treasury to help Louis Napoleon recoup some of his losses.) But

---

* The artist was unfortunately unable to complete the work under such hurried conditions, so the commission was passed on to Albert Gräfle, a German painter who had apprenticed under Winterhalter for six years in Paris before striking out on his own. That's why Gräfle's famous painting of Charlotte, completed the following year, looks so much like a Winterhalter portrait.

certainly there would be enough left over to bankroll the fledgling government until the new emperor could begin collecting taxes and arranging profitable commercial ventures with interested parties on his own. And there was no need to worry about security; Napoleon III pledged on his honor that the French troops would stay until Maximilian—who was now to be addressed as His Imperial Highness, Emperor Maximilian I of Mexico—felt completely comfortable dismissing them.

That did it. On April 14, 1864, in front of a packed crowd of well-wishers at the port of Trieste, their Imperial Highnesses of Mexico climbed aboard an older Austrian gunboat (escorted by a large French warship) and began the long journey to their new home. The former archduke, surveying the dazzling coastline, was suddenly struck by the finality of his departure. He seems to have realized for the first time how much he was going to miss his quiet, gracious home at Miramare. "Look at poor Max!" Empress Charlotte exclaimed in surprise to her lady-in-waiting. "How he is weeping!"

But for Eugénie, who saw only the nobility and excitement of the enterprise, this voyage marked the jubilant culmination of nearly three years of effort. "We congratulate Your Majesty with all our hearts," she enthused to Charlotte in a celebratory telegram sent just before their departure. "We wish all happiness to Your Majesties, and prosperity to the lovely country over which you are called to reign. May Heaven bless the new empire," she concluded fervently.

ALAS, NO SOONER WAS the Mexican crisis resolved than a new and alarming peril, one that threatened not only Eugénie's throne and that of her son but also the balance of power in Europe, and the French empire's dominant place within it, made its appearance.

Louis Napoleon had fallen in love—again.

Her name was Marguerite Bellanger. She was twenty-six in 1864, a farmer's daughter turned second-rate actress. (Marguerite was her stage name; she was really plain old Julie Leboeuf from a hick village near Saumur.) The emperor was so besotted with her that he did not even try to keep up appearances. Unlike the countess of Castiglione, whose conversation had bored him, Louis Napoleon wanted Marguerite as much for her vivacious, irreverent personality as her slender, supple body. Nicknamed "the Laughing Margot," Marguerite, coarse and convivial, enjoyed life and made the most of her time in Paris, often staying up until the small hours of the morning drinking and reveling. Napoleon III swooned for this new passion with the puppy-dog devotion common to graying, middle-aged men desperate to recover their lost youth.

Eugénie could not help but be aware of her rival. The emperor's attentions had made Marguerite the most famous courtesan in Paris.* He had bought her *two* houses, one in Paris—"I several times met the Emperor driving up to the Champs-Élysées of an evening in his brougham to the Rue des Vignes, where Margot held a veritable court," reported an English journalist living in France at the time—and the other at Saint-Cloud, right on the edge of the palace grounds, so that Eugénie had to drive by it every time she took the air. The empress, by this time more than used to her husband's dalliances, ignored the liaison for over a year. But this became impossible when, in the summer of 1864, she was gleefully informed by a spiteful gossip that Marguerite had given birth to a son.

This was too much; the dam burst and Napoleon III had the worst of it. "It may easily be imagined that her Majesty was highly incensed at this," the English journalist noted. "She had tolerated mistresses, but she would not tolerate a bastard; this was an insult to herself and to her son...the terms in which the Empress expressed herself were said to have been violent, picturesque, and Spanish." And then, as though the revelation of a male love child were not bad enough, soon after being found out, Louis Napoleon, tottering home a little the worse for one of his late-night soirées with his sprightly playmate, briefly lost consciousness and

---

* Marguerite was such a celebrity that she was almost certainly the inspiration for Édouard Manet's *Olympia*, exhibited the following year in 1865. Although Victorine Meurent, Manet's favorite model, sat for the painting, *Olympia*'s unashamed posture, frank stare, and silken surroundings immediately label her as an elite Parisian paramour, and this would have brought Marguerite instantly to mind.

collapsed, prompting his already exasperated wife to fly to Margot's doorstep and confront her adversary directly. "Mademoiselle, you are killing the emperor!" Eugénie exploded.

The empress's concern was not misplaced. The prince imperial was only eight years old; Napoleon III's continued longevity was thus a matter of the utmost importance not only to his wife but to the welfare of France. Eugénie had lived through the devastation of the decades-long civil war in Spain, when King Ferdinand's younger brother Don Carlos had contested the regency of Maria Christina and the succession of her then three-year-old daughter (the present Queen Isabella). It was clear from his truculence at Compiègne that Plon-Plon was similarly spoiling for a fight. The premature demise of the emperor might give this jealous cousin his opportunity and thrust France into a similar conflict. The existence of an illegitimate son also threatened the prince imperial's succession, as this child, or others working in his name, might try to use his parentage to try to usurp the throne.

The most demeaning part was how public it all was. They could not even fight about it without the entire court overhearing. "The Emperor's private conduct was a constant subject of conversation," Anna the governess relayed matter-of-factly. "In general society, both in Paris and the provinces, everything was known and freely talked about... The Empress was violently jealous... multiplying vehement scenes and threatening extreme measures of public scandal." Eventually, as before, Eugénie fled. This time, she chose Schwalbach, a spa town in Germany outside Frankfurt. "The Empress travels in the most private way possible... The present trip to the Duchy of Nassau appears to have been a sudden resolution," the Paris correspondent for the *Morning Post* reported on September 8, 1864. "The Emperor remains at St. Cloud," he added pointedly.

At Schwalbach, at least, her sense of dignity was renewed. Other heads of state went out of their way to visit her. The queen of Holland came to tea and King Wilhelm of Prussia arrived, solicitous behind an impressive armload of roses. She was calmer when she returned to France a month later, but still anguished. With Paca gone, she had lost her confidante, and in her despair she turned to someone whom she had trusted since childhood, who seems by this time to have assumed almost the role of a surrogate father—Prosper Méri-mée. "I had a chat of four hours with her, the subject of which you can divine," the author wrote guardedly to María Manuela on October 11, a few days after this interview. "She needed *sfogarsi* [emotional release]. Everything is very sad, more so even than you can imagine, but do not say a word to anybody. I have given good advice, I believe," he continued, "though...whether my advice will be followed is quite another question."

Eugénie evidently took it, as she stayed with her husband. Domestic peace was eventually restored by a contrivance. Following her encounter with the empress, it was felt best by all concerned that Marguerite be bundled out of Paris to her childhood home near Saumur until a solution to the marital dilemma could be negotiated. In the end, a trusted intermediary was sent to "persuade Margot to confess that she had deceived the Emperor with regard to the child, which was not his, but the son of another lover," recounted the English journalist. The imperial emissary found the glamorous courtesan "dressed as a peasant, short petticoat and wooden shoes, ... sitting at a table with her parents round some cabbage soup flanked by pitchers of cider." Under these rustic conditions, which no doubt reminded her strongly of how far she had come (and how quickly it could all go away), Marguerite was only too happy to be of service to the emperor. The envoy helped her to write two letters—one to him, one to Napoleon III—in which she swore on her honor that the baby had actually been fathered by one of her other admirers. "These letters, shown to the Empress and accompanied by expressions of contrition on the part of the chief culprit, brought about a reconciliation between their Imperial Majesties," the Englishman explained.* "Harmony reigns in the household of our friends; after the clouds which might have brought on a storm, fine

---

* I know, I know, this all sounds too implausible to be true but here's the thing—the letters existed and were found afterwards at the Tuileries, and were even the subject of a caricature in the British press.

weather has reappeared," Mérimée confirmed with relief in a letter of November 27, 1864.

Napoleon III could congratulate himself that he had skirted more than just conjugal disaster that year. Denied the advantage of a coordinated international conference, he had yet wangled a means of disengaging from the perilous conflict over Venice and Rome by bribing Victor Emmanuel (Cavour had died) with the promise of official French recognition of the united Kingdom of Italy in exchange for the Sardinian's taking over the role of papal protector, a position Louis Napoleon sorely wished to vacate. It was a slick way for the emperor to withdraw the regiment of French soldiers stationed in Rome (something he was desperate to do, as they were expensive to maintain and deeply resented as an occupying force by Garibaldi and his followers, who were threatening to send new disciples of the dagger to Paris), while still technically upholding the vow he had made to the French clergy and their many rural supporters that he would never abandon the pope.

This agreement with Victor Emmanuel, tactfully announced while Eugénie was out of the country visiting the Schwalbach spa, was discouraging for the empress but not unexpected. It had been two years since Francis and Marie were chased out of Naples, and even Eugénie, who had once scornfully informed the Sardinian ambassador, "I would drown myself sooner than lend a hand to your highway robberies," could see that the dispossessed king of the Two Sicilies had not the temperament for the sort of bold military action necessary to reclaim his former realm. As for the removal of the French regiments from Rome, her husband had wired her soothingly that the deadline for the withdrawal was still two years away, and that he would not hesitate to break the accord if Victor Emmanuel did not adhere strictly to its terms.

The setback in Italy was not Eugénie's only disappointment that year. Despite the many incentives that she and Napoleon III had dangled in the hopes of securing an alliance (including arranging for his brother to acquire his very own empire), Franz Joseph had turned them down. Instead, the Austrian emperor had concluded a military pact with Prussia. Prussia, of all places! A second-rate power whose conniving chief minister, Otto von Bismarck, had politely but firmly declined their gracious invitation to attend an international conference in Paris. ("I would rather die than permit our position...to be discussed at a European Congress," Bismarck had snorted privately to his counterpart in Vienna.) "You ally with this one and that one, and you will end up at the tail end of the world," Eugénie had scolded her friend Prince Metternich when news of the Austrian-Prussian collaboration was made public.

Thank goodness, she could still pride herself on the success of the Mexican initiative. Although strangely, here, too, Charlotte's letters had gone, in a mere six months, from "The Emperor has everywhere been received with great enthusiasm, greater, he tells me, than any he had ever witnessed before," to "I am sorry to have to tell Your Majesty that...the pacification of the country is again much hampered." But of course, a few impediments were to be anticipated, especially in the beginning. Eugénie knew from experience that nothing worth achieving came easily.

ELISABETH

Sisi stuns in fur.

20

The Metamorphosis

Because my lightnings are so striking,
You think that I can't thunder too!
You're wrong, for I've a special liking
For thunder, as I'll prove to you.

This will be seen with awful clearness
When the right moment is at hand;
You'll hear my voice in startling nearness—
The word of thunder and command.

—Heinrich Heine

To the consternation of the imperial court, the Elisabeth who returned to Vienna in the autumn of 1862 bore little resemblance to the easily intimidated invalid, enfeebled by sickness and despair, who had withdrawn in tears two years earlier. This Elisabeth, healthy and glowing from a summer in Bavaria, was far more assertive. It wasn't so much that she flouted protocol as that she appeared entirely indifferent to it. She moved in an orbit all her own, where she, and not historical precedent, set the rules. No rush of objections or criticism made the least impression on her; disapproving looks and hurtful comments that would have sent the old Sisi coughing and crying to her rooms now bounced off her harmlessly. It was as though the empress had somehow developed a suit of armor.

And, in a way, she had. While she had been abroad collecting photographs of notable sirens, Sisi had come to recognize the power of glamour. Beauty she always had, but there is an art to employing it, and this art she had set herself to master, as she had once mastered riding. Glamour can be both sword and shield, and upon her return, this new Elisabeth wielded her growing allure to hack through the stultifying thicket of court etiquette to get what she wanted.

Her first priority was to establish an atmosphere supportive of her mental and physical health. With this in mind, she took a red pen to the list of household staff who had been appointed to her suite at the time of her marriage. Out went anyone loyal to Archduchess Sophia, and in came charming young women closer to the empress's own age. One of them, a Hungarian countess who was also a knockout, became her best friend. Sisi was confident enough of her own good looks to revel in those of her companions, and thus the intimate circle surrounding the empress only added to her luster. These younger women, proud of their exalted positions and staunchly devoted to their mistress, also formed a barrier of privacy that helped protect her sister Marie from scandal. The ex-queen of Naples spent September with Elisabeth before retiring to a nunnery to give birth, and no hint of her condition reached the public. Rather, it was implied that Marie was considering joining the sisterhood. "It is said that the Queen of Naples has entered a convent and demands the annulling of her marriage which, she says, has never been consummated," Mérimée reported from Paris on October 15, 1862. "All these old dynasties end in impotence," he added, obviously accepting the court's cover story.*

The following year saw the appointment to the empress's household of yet another strategic ally, the value of whose support cannot be overstated: She finally found the right hairdresser. As Eugénie had the

---

* The baby, a little girl, was born on November 24, 1862, and immediately given up for adoption, after which Marie very reluctantly went back to her husband.

overweight, pretentious, middle-aged Monsieur Leroy, given to pronouncements to the effect that, had Marie Antoinette been fortunate enough to engage him as a stylist, "she would never have been guillotined. Oh, no! He would have found a means to prevent that," Sisi recruited Fräulein Fanny Angerer, a clever commoner as slender as Elisabeth herself, culled from the ranks of the theatrical community. Though she was still a teenager, Fanny's skills, honed on some of the city's reigning actresses, gave Leroy's a run for their money. It took until April 1863 for Elisabeth to overcome the objections of the court—Archduchess Sophia was particularly aghast at this latest eccentricity of her daughter-in-law's, which she felt lowered the prestige of the throne—but Sisi just went ahead and hired the talented Fanny anyway, adding fuel to Sophia's ire by not only granting the *coiffeuse* a position and title formerly reserved exclusively for members of the aristocracy, but also paying her at an annual rate commensurate with that of a doctor of theology at the University of Vienna.

Of course, none of this would have been possible if Franz Joseph had elected to side with his mother, as he had in the past. But the emperor had changed. During Elisabeth's extended absence, Franz Joseph had discovered that he missed his wife. He loved her and ardently desired to return to their former intimacy. But for Sisi, who had found that she could do quite well without her husband, the question of whether she would continue to reside at court was entirely conditional on being able to carve out an environment suitable to her temperament. That the fulfillment of her demands amounted to an ultimatum was brought home to the emperor when, early upon her return, Elisabeth informed him that her doctors had warned that her health was not yet strong enough to support a fourth pregnancy, and so, sadly, she would be unable to renew marital relations until such time as she felt herself to be completely recovered. Thus was Franz Joseph induced to brave his mother's recriminations and approve the appointment of the lowly overpaid hairdresser.

Because even he could see that these alterations to the empress's habitat, which seemed so preposterous to the rest of the court, were having a beneficial effect on her health and outlook. Elisabeth approached each day with the discipline of an athlete in training for a professional sporting match. She began her mornings with a gymnastics routine, after which came hours of riding. In the summer, this activity was supplemented by long hikes into the woods or mountains. Vigorous exercise was followed by a three-hour session with Fanny, whose elaborate creations—which involved plaiting her mistress's sumptuous locks and then wrapping the braids atop her head in an intricate, interlocking pattern—were the envy of the entire female population of Vienna. Sisi monitored her diet rigorously but, significantly, she no longer strayed into unwholesome fasting. The empress had found a weight—110 pounds—that allowed her to keep her famously willowy figure while still providing her with the energy she needed to maintain her active lifestyle. Although the court, used to the heavy, multicourse meals that were the expected rewards of wealth and privilege, sniffed that the empress starved herself when she passed on dinner in favor of fruit and a glass of milk, this was clearly not the case. Starving people do not bloom and glow as Elisabeth did. "The Empress," the American ambassador stationed in Vienna wrote home to his mother in awe on March 16, 1863, "is a wonder of beauty."*

If anyone at the Austrian court required further confirmation of this diplomatic assessment, the arrival of the world-famous Xaver Winterhalter, court painter to the acknowledged doyenne of European fashion, Empress Eugénie, settled the matter. The official portrait he produced, of Sisi sheathed in an extravagantly diaphanous, off-the-shoulder Worth gown imported from Paris and glittering with sequins, her magnificent tresses held in place by a cascade of oversized diamond

---

* This envoy was not generally given to superlatives, nor, as a representative of democratic America, was he in any way cowed by his imperial hosts. "English society is very interesting, because anybody who has done anything noteworthy may be seen in it," he noted. "But if an Austrian should be Shakespeare, Galileo, Nelson, and Raphael all in one, he couldn't be admitted into good society in Vienna unless he had the sixteen quarterings of nobility which birth alone could give him." Yet Sisi turned even this cynical Yankee into a romantic schoolboy. "She is in great beauty this year—more radiant, lambent, exquisite than ever...How I do wish that I was a 'sentimental sort of fellow,'" he sighed after one diplomatic dinner with her. "What pretty and poetic things I would say. How many sonnets I would have composed to those majestic eyebrows."

stars arranged by the brilliant Fanny, announced her presence on the world stage as nothing else could. Copies of this painting were displayed and sold in every major European capital. Insular, aristocratic Viennese society, once disdainful of Sisi's gaucheness, was utterly vanquished by this broadside.

But the real blow was delivered by the unveiling of two additional portraits Winterhalter painted of the empress during his stay in the capital. These were likenesses of Elisabeth dressed for the boudoir. In them, the artificial trappings of majesty—the fairy-tale gowns, the dazzling jewels—were stripped away. The more provocative of the two depicted Sisi in profile from behind, her extraordinary hair, fully unloosed, tumbling voluptuously almost to the floor. Her peignoir, too, was slackened, casually revealing her bare shoulders and back, as though she had just arisen from bed. And yet, though intimate, the effect was not overtly titillating. Sisi's bearing was too pensive for that. Rather, the portrait conveyed the dual message of dignity and vulnerability. It was a window into the soul of a public figure, and an acknowledgment that here was a beauty that required no crown to embellish it.

No empress in the history of the Habsburgs had ever allowed herself to be portrayed on canvas as anything other than exalted. Indeed, no female sovereign in Europe had ever tested the boundaries of her office quite so blatantly. Not even Marie Antoinette, who had once scandalously (for the period) posed in a rustic muslin day dress for Elisabeth Vigée Le Brun, would have ever permitted herself to be painted slipping out of her wrapper with her hair down. In its emphasis on Elisabeth in her private life, the painting radically challenged long-held, conservative assumptions about the necessity of upholding the rigid social barriers of the past. It functioned as both a declaration of modernity and an announcement of emancipation. And it was aimed right at Archduchess Sophia.

Since her return, the feud between Sisi and her mother-in-law had entered a new, cold-war phase. The angry scenes that had formerly characterized their relationship had given way to detachment and distance. The empress and the archduchess stayed away from each other as much as possible.

But for Elisabeth, nothing had really changed. Sophia remained in full control of the imperial prince and princess's households and schedules, and by her orders the empress was treated as an outsider. At the beginning of August 1863, a year after Sisi's return to court, five-year-old Rudolf fell while shimmying up a ladder to a tree house at Schönbrunn Palace and cracked his head on a stone. None of the adult members of the immediate family were at home—Sophia was already at Ischl enjoying her customary summer outing; Franz Joseph was in Salzburg, conferring with the king of Prussia; and Elisabeth, on the advice of her doctors, was again taking the waters at Kissingen (this time as a preventive rather than a cure). The crown prince's household at once reported the accident to the archduchess by telegram. Sophia notified the emperor and then rushed home to nurse the boy herself. Franz Joseph, too, hurried back to Vienna to check on his son. Finding Rudolf weak but stable, and his capable grandmother in charge, Franz Joseph returned with relief to his German guests. Neither believed it necessary to notify the empress that her son had had a dangerous fall until Sophia had determined that he was well enough to receive visitors, thereby denying Sisi the chance to comfort her child. By the time she *was* told, and had hastened back, Rudolf was so far himself again that she was reduced simply to showering him with presents, as any member of the court or extended family might have done. Small wonder that both the crown prince and his older sister, seven-year-old Gisela, although of course aware that Elisabeth was their parent, nonetheless regarded Sophia as their real mother.

The political divide between the archduchess and the empress persisted as well. Sophia remained committed to absolute monarchy supported by a strong military. When, on November 15, 1863, the king of Denmark unexpectedly died, and Bismarck, now minister-president, leapt at this doleful accident to try to usurp two Danish duchies, Franz Joseph did not have to consult his mother as to what she thought Austria should do. He knew Sophia would approve the alliance he concluded on January 10, 1864, which called for Vienna and Berlin to jointly send troops to invade and occupy the helpless provinces. Similarly, although forced by public dissatisfaction to introduce a legislative assembly, the emperor shared his mother's disdain for representative government and stripped the chamber of all real power, a ruse not lost on its delegates. "We have got a little parliament here, which we call the *Reichsrath,* and we are as proud as Punch of it," observed the American ambassador, writing from Vienna to a friend. "It has worked two years admirably well, only the Opposition members, who make up two thirds of it, never come, which makes it easier for the administration," he chuckled. Imperial Vienna boasted "a parliamentary government without a Parliament," cracked a French wit.

But Elisabeth did not subscribe to these views. Her sympathies were with the outcasts and the downtrodden. She did not believe, as Sophia did, that Germans and Catholics were superior to all other ethnicities and religions, and that those of her husband's subjects possessed of dissenting opinions should be brought ruthlessly into line by the authorities. And nowhere was this clash between the empress's and the archduchess's political perspectives more openly, insistently rancorous than in their attitudes toward the Hungarians.

To date, Hungary had refused all of Franz Joseph's empty blandishments to participate in Austria's limited representative government. Determined to settle for nothing less than their right to exist as an independent kingdom with its own historical constitution, not a single Hungarian attended the meetings of the *Reichsrath.* As punishment for their resistance, the native Diet had been disbanded and the government taken over and administered by a herd of imported imperial officials who spoke only German. Taxes were imposed and collected by force; military service was also compulsory. Those who attempted to protest this system, whether through articles in the press or by demonstrations in the streets, were subdued harshly.

Consequently, when Elisabeth decided in 1864 to devote herself to becoming fluent in Hungarian, it was taken for the political statement it was, and made the papers. "The Empress of Austria takes lessons in the Hungarian language daily from Professor Homoky," observed a Viennese paper. "Her Majesty is so fond of this language that she has recently taken into her service a *femme de chambre*...who speaks nothing but Hungarian." Sophia, understanding that Sisi's public embrace of the dialect would give hope to those in Pesth pressing for a softening of imperial policy, made her disapproval known. But she was again overruled by her son, who, remembering how bewitched the Hungarians had been by his charming wife on her formal state visit seven years earlier, reflected upon what an asset she might be in helping to win over these recalcitrant subjects.

No, there was almost nothing that Elisabeth and her mother-in-law agreed on. The great exception to this rule was Max. Neither Sisi nor Sophia wanted Max to accept the tantalizing plum dangled in front of him by Eugénie and Napoleon III. In this they were hardly alone. "The step is exceedingly unpopular in Austria," observed the American ambassador. "That a prince of the house of Hapsburg should become the satrap of the Bonaparte dynasty, and should sit on an American throne which could not exist a moment but for French bayonets and French ships, is most galling to all classes of Austrians. The intrigue is a most embarrassing one to the government," the envoy continued. "If the fatal gift is refused, Louis Napoleon of course takes it highly in dudgeon. If it is accepted, Austria takes a kind of millstone around her neck in the shape of gratitude for something she didn't want, and some day she will be expected to pay for it in something she had rather not give," he finished astutely.

The imperial family did its best to dissuade the archduke and duchess from taking this irreversible step. At first, they used subtle means. Max was so touchy, Franz Joseph dared not forbid the adventure outright—he knew that nothing would launch his resentful brother more surely into the enterprise than if he thought it was being deliberately withheld from him. The Viennese government played along, showing Max and Charlotte the respect they craved by employing high-ranking, official ministers and envoys to pass messages and information about the project along to out-of-the-way Miramare. Franz

Joseph even held a personal audience with his brother in Venice to discuss possible terms on which to base his acceptance, hoping these would not be met.

When these methods failed, and Max, blinded by French assurances, gave insufficient credence to the many hidden dangers of the scheme and continued to pursue the opportunity, the family tactics became more obvious. Sophia shared firsthand reports of violence and disorder among the Mexicans, imploring her second son to reconsider. Since Max had the same difficulty confronting his mother as did Franz Joseph, Charlotte took it upon herself to answer these concerns. "It is far from being the case that matters are worse now than before," Sophia's favorite daughter-in-law reassured her. "On the contrary, they are moving towards a favorable and dignified solution," she concluded brightly. During this period, a revolution in Greece left the throne vacant, and there was hope that the archduke would consider substituting this much-closer-to-home honor for that of faraway Mexico. Max, however, rejected the offer. He'd been to Greece. "I am too well acquainted from personal observation with modern Hellas and its present corrupt state not to have been convinced for a long time past that that crafty and morally degenerate people is incapable of offering a firm foundation for an independent State," airily returned the man who had never set foot in either North or Central America.

It wasn't until March 19, 1864, when Max and Charlotte, having recently been gloriously fêted by Louis Napoleon and Eugénie in Paris, arrived in Vienna to say goodbye before embarking on their big adventure, that Franz Joseph made one final effort to change his sibling's mind. Aware that his brother and sister-in-law responded to flattery, the court held a magnificent reception for the couple, where Max and Charlotte were treated as visiting royalty, complete with the titles of his-and-her imperial majesty. The next morning, however, the archduke was informed that he would be taking part in another, less welcome ceremony—the renunciation of his rights of inheritance. Max could not be emperor of Mexico *and* heir apparent to the Austrian throne after Crown Prince Rudolf. He must choose.

It almost worked. Max was furious. He categorically declined to sign the renunciation. But Napoleon III and Eugénie protested vigorously (he to the archduke, she to Charlotte) that the undertaking had gone too far to turn back now, that they had already secured a large loan, which the emperor of Mexico was responsible for repaying. At their combined umbrage, Max swallowed his own, and bitterly signed away his inheritance. "I was never a great admirer of the much-admired sagacity of Louis Napoleon," the American ambassador admitted. "But I have been forced to give in at last. The way in which he has bamboozled that poor young man is one of the neatest pieces of escamotage [knavery] ever performed. If he does succeed in getting the Archduke in, and his own troops out, and the costs of the expedition paid, certainly it will be a *Kunststück* [sleight of hand]," the envoy exclaimed. "Meantime, he [Max] has smart new liveries made at Brussels, to amaze the Mexican heart. Likewise he has been seen trying on an imperial crown of gilt pasteboard, to see in the glass if it is becoming…But I am told he hasn't got a penny. Louis Napoleon is squeezing everything out of him that he may have in prospect," the American snorted.

For Elisabeth, the departure of the entertaining Max, whom she considered her closest friend among her husband's family, and the only other voice for poetry and liberalization at court, was a great loss.* She who had to steel herself every day to bear the restrictions of imperial office, who yearned for the freedom to wander, scribble, ride, and dream, could not comprehend why anyone of sense would actively lobby to don the straitjacket of sovereign rule. But she could see how much they wanted it, and so she put aside her own feelings and generously reached out to Charlotte to make her feel valued and supported. Her sister-in-law remembered this magnanimity in a letter sent later from her new empire. "I do not forget how much heart you showed toward us this time a year ago," she wrote gratefully to Sisi.

---

* It has been hypothesized that they were lovers, but there is absolutely no evidence of this. Sisi desired male admiration but, perhaps because she had been compelled to experience physical love before she was ready for it, did not seek it out, either with her husband or anyone else.

And so Max and Charlotte sailed away to Mexico. The very first thing the new emperor did while at sea was to write up a legal document officially reneging on the renunciation of his Austrian inheritance.

BY THE TIME OF MAX AND CHARLOTTE's departure in the summer of 1864, Elisabeth had regained her footing sufficiently to begin to undertake once more her many public duties as empress. She helped to nurse those wounded in the successful Austrian-Prussian campaign against the vastly overpowered Danish duchies, and that December attended the celebratory opening of a new hospital, "the first edifice built by the State for pacific purposes during the reign of the Emperor Francis Joseph," as the London *Times* correspondent made a point of noting. She attended the opera and took part in the expected processions commemorating religious holidays. No matter where she was, the moment she appeared in public, people flocked to her. On February 18, 1865, she traveled to Dresden for Gackel's wedding to the youngest daughter of her aunt Amalie, the queen of Saxony, and caused a sensation. "You simply cannot imagine what enthusiasm was aroused here by the Empress's beauty and amiability," exclaimed the queen. "I never saw our quiet Saxons so moved before...they were all simply off their heads about her," she added in astonishment.

In her private life, too, Sisi had made progress. By 1865, she and Franz Joseph had resumed conjugal relations, and some of their old affectionate rapport had returned. The American ambassador sat next to her at a state dinner that year at which she accidentally knocked over her glass. "I am so clumsy," she apologized, blushing "in the most adorable manner, like a school-girl," the envoy reported. Her husband, noting her embarrassment, playfully stepped in. "The Emperor coming to the rescue, very heroically upset another, so there was a great mess," the envoy laughed.

But there was one issue that remained an open wound: the children. And the gash only deepened as time passed and Elisabeth saw how her offspring were being raised, particularly Rudolf, who was approaching his seventh birthday. Unlike his nine-year-old sister, Gisela, who had inherited her father's grounded, stolid temperament, the crown prince was clearly his mother's child. Spirited, intelligent, impulsive, and fanciful, Rudolf was also sensitive and skittish. He cried easily and was prone to nightmares.

These latter traits were considered a worrisome liability, even in so young an heir. Rudolf's future was marked out for him. He would command both the military and the empire. To his father and grandmother, these two institutions were inseparable. Consequently, the year before, when Rudolf had turned six, Franz Joseph, with Sophia's approval, had removed him from the nursery, where he had lived since birth with his adored older sister, and replaced his fond, gentle, also adored nanny with an overzealous male governor, Count Gondrecourt, who was instructed to make a soldier of his small charge.

Gondrecourt, who despised weakness, even in six-year-olds, took to the task with the brisk dedication of a future psychopath torturing a puppy. He barked orders at his pupil, made him practice military drills until he vomited, threw him into cold baths, and berated him for the slightest misstep or hesitancy. "The little boy was...taught five languages...at the same time by five different nationalities," the correspondent for the London *Times* reported. "Every now and then he was awakened in the night in order that he might learn to have his wits about him." Unsurprisingly, coincident with the count's appointment, Rudolf began to complain of headaches and nausea. These rapidly escalated into coughs and fevers. He was ill so often that his old nanny feared for his life. But the archduchess and the emperor believed in Gondrecourt's methods, and so he was untouchable at court.

And then, in the summer of 1865, the count, frustrated that none of the usual torments seemed to be having the desired effect, bethought himself of a clever maneuver. He took Rudolf into the woods outside the palace and left him there, darting back inside the large gate separating the forest from the safety of the manor grounds. Closing the door behind him, he turned and shouted to the boy that a wild boar was coming right at him.

Rudolf behaved exactly as would any six-year-old. He screamed, cried, and begged to be let inside the gate. Since this exercise was formulated as a lesson in bravery, Gondrecourt prolonged his small charge's terror by refusing to open the door, all the while shouting that the boar was getting nearer. Rudolf was beside himself for days afterward.

Sisi was of course aware of the count's aggressive tactics to mold her son's character. She had already protested the punishingly cold baths and voiced the scathing opinion that subjecting a child of six to such treatment was lunacy. Determined to end it, she confronted Franz Joseph. Despite her insistence, however, the emperor declined to intervene, just as he had previously refused his wife's appeals in regard to the children on so many occasions.

But Elisabeth was no longer the empress of the past. She left her husband's office, went to her rooms, and picked up a pen. After living with him for over a decade, she knew how to get his attention. Without hesitation, she composed an official memorandum, to be filed among the legal papers of the court. This manifesto was brief and unambiguous. Addressed to the emperor, it demanded "that full and unlimited powers should be reserved to me in all things concerning the children, the choice of those by whom they are surrounded and of their place of residence... I alone must decide everything up to their majority." Additionally, the empress required that all "my own personal affairs, ... the choice of those about my person, my place of residence, all changes in domestic arrangements, etc., etc., should be left for me alone to decide." The document was signed and dated August 27, 1865, six days after Rudolf's seventh birthday.

Franz Joseph understood the implications of this paper when it was handed to him. Unless he acceded to his wife's demands, she would leave him.

The emperor was above all else conventional in his viewpoint. He wanted a traditional home and family. He believed in societal norms and avoided scandal where possible. It wasn't just that he loved Sisi and wanted her, although he did. It was a matter of appearances. He knew she meant it. How would it look to Vienna—to the rest of Europe—if this ethereal creature walked out on him? Such a thing had never happened to a reigning Habsburg before.

Count Gondrecourt was summarily relieved of his duties, and a discomfited Sophia was informed that the households of the imperial prince and princess would henceforth be under the direction of the empress, with new, more enlightened scholars and physicians assigned to educate them. The archduchess fought as usual, but this time her scoldings were of no avail and she was reduced to bemoaning her grievances to her ladies and sisters. It had taken eleven long years and a wrenching ultimatum, but finally, at the age of twenty-seven, Sisi had won back her children.

EUGÉNIE

Eugénie and Napoleon III with Louis, prince imperial,
in military uniform

21

Government by the Heroine

There is no more Eugénie. There is nothing but the Empress.

—Prosper Mérimée

BY 1865, JUST AS ELISABETH was rekindling intimate relations with Franz Joseph, Eugénie's marriage had disintegrated to the point where the imperial couple was no longer sleeping together. This decision seems to have helped the empress salvage a modicum of self-respect. The result was an improvement in domestic harmony. Mérimée, in whom the empress confided her resolve, reported "a renewal of confidence and friendship on both sides."

This did not mean that husband and wife did not still have their personal differences, of course. One area of recurrent disagreement focused on the manner in which Louis, the prince imperial, was to be raised. Although both adored their son, their parenting styles often clashed. Napoleon III simply could not bear to say no to the boy. Consequently, whenever his father was around, the prince could make as much noise as he liked, jump all over the furniture, interrupt important ministerial conversations, stay up late, and generally wheedle whatever he wanted out of his fond papa. "The Emperor could not be induced to resist the child's wishes in anything he fancied," Anna, the Tuileries governess, recalled. "I *could* not," Napoleon III would explain piteously. "He would not love me."

This left Eugénie as the disciplinarian. "It is impossible to bring up that child properly!" she would fume. The empress, like her father before her, worried that excessive coddling would result in her son's growing up to be "a milk-sop." Although there is no record that she made him sit astride a cannon while it was being fired, she did, when Louis was having a riding lesson at the age of three (according to Anna), send his pony cantering, causing the groom, who managed to catch the colt before his small charge was thrown, to "express his feelings with an amount of vigor very unusual in courts," while Miss Shaw, the boy's English nurse, "indulged in more respectful lamentations: 'Oh! Your Majesty! You shouldn't, your Majesty! You've only *one,* you know!'" Similarly, Louis was introduced to swimming at Biarritz by being thrown headfirst into the sea. Mérimée, who was present at this lesson, was aghast. "He [Louis] was reproached for his timidity, and asked the reason why he, who would not flinch before a loaded cannon, was afraid of the sea," the author reported. "He replied, ... 'Because I command the cannon and I don't command the sea.' Philosophical enough for a Prince not yet six years old," Mérimée noted, impressed.★

But there is also no question that she loved her son deeply and was an attentive, affectionate mother. In 1864, when the prince was eight years old, he caught scarlet fever from one of the guests at a costume ball hosted by his parents. It was a very serious case; the poor young woman from whom he caught it, only twenty years old herself, had been so determined to attend the imperial fête that she had hidden her symptoms from her mother. She was clearly highly contagious and infected others that evening, and the girl herself died the next day. "The same flowers that had adorned her ball costume decorated her casket," reported a lady-in-waiting sorrowfully. Eugénie, "with very natural anxiety and the greatest maternal devotion," sat by Louis's bedside day and night, nursing her son herself, until he was out of danger.

The empress also surrounded her child with a progressive, caring household. Miss Shaw, "whom he dearly loved," was devoted to him.

★ Who knows, maybe she did make him sit on a cannon while it was being fired.

His tutor was Augustin Filon, a charming and accomplished young professor of rhetoric at the University of Paris, and later the author of numerous novels and essays. Like Sisi's son, Rudolf, the imperial prince was expected to be a soldier, and so at the age of seven was assigned a general as a military governor. But Louis's governor, while strict, was in no way abusive and seemed to have a sense of humor. "The Emperor was wise enough to feel the necessity for this firmness, and was not sorry to hand over to another the control which might make his son 'love him' less," noted Anna. "His [Napoleon III's] over-tender feelings were, however, often tried severely. The young Prince was heard to say on some festive occasion: 'I should *so* like to stay! *He* [the general] won't let me.' The Emperor, with his usual indulgence, answered: 'Give me your cap; I will put it in my pocket—you can't go without it, and that will cause some delay.' The little Prince then said ruefully: 'It is of no use. I have tried that before! He has got another one ready!'"

It seems that Eugénie's methods worked; her son grew up rivaling his mother in courage and daring. Augustin Filon was there the day in Biarritz when the empress and the nine-year-old prince imperial went out for an afternoon's sail. Night had already fallen by the time their ship was making its return. The captain lost his way in the dark and missed the harbor; he steered instead into some boulders jutting out from the shore and wrecked the boat. His body would be fished out of the sea the next day. The empress and her son huddled together on the rocks in the blackness before eventually being rescued. "Louis, don't be afraid!" Eugénie had cried out in the first moments of confusion and danger. "A Napoleon is never afraid," had come back the staunch reply.

ALTHOUGH BY THE SPRING of 1865 Eugénie's domestic situation had stabilized, the same could not be said of the foreign challenges facing France. Prussia and Austria, having taken the Danish duchies together by force, were now squabbling over what was to be done with them, an argument that once more threatened to spill over into a wider European conflict; the Italians still seethed at the Austrian occupation of

Venetia, for which they continued to blame Napoleon III, once again prompting worries of disciple-of-the-dagger assassination attempts; and the promised riches from the expensive Mexican adventure had so far puzzlingly failed to materialize, further depressing the economy. And then, as though all of this was not frustrating enough, came the news of the North's triumph in the American Civil War, an unforeseen development (at least by Eugénie) that seriously compromised the welfare of Maximilian's empire, and with it French prestige, and, more importantly, the repayment of the large loan taken out to fund the project. SURRENDER OF GENERAL LEE AND HIS ARMY screamed the London headline of the *Guardian* on April 24, 1865.

This latest setback appears to have been one too many for Napoleon III. Having recently turned fifty-seven, the emperor was worn out with having energetically governed, planned, intrigued, bullied, negotiated, fought, and horse-traded, sometimes all at the same time, for the past thirteen years since taking over France in a coup. Abruptly, he decided he needed a break. As Eugénie had spontaneously escaped to the spa at Schwalbach the year before, so the emperor suddenly announced that he would leave for Algeria at the end of the month for what promised to be an extended tour.

A long trip to Algeria might not seem like the optimal getaway to many people, but Louis Napoleon's options were limited. He could not, as his wife had done, go as a private citizen to a foreign country and expect not to be bothered with royal visitors and ambassadors. As he consequently had to stay within French territory, Algeria, situated on the outskirts of the empire, presented the best alternative. It was far enough away that he wouldn't have to be troubled with the day-to-day business of imperial government, but not so remote that he could not be reached and hustle back quickly if a true crisis were to break out. To underscore that he did not wish to be disturbed except in an emergency, he again appointed his wife as regent during his absence. He seems also to have been feeling his mortality, as he further named Plon-Plon as consultant to the empress, thus setting up a dry run for what an idealized future government of France would look like in the event of his death.★

Based on Eugénie's past performance, his subjects had nothing to worry about. She was eager to rise to the occasion. One of the first challenges she faced was the assassination of President Lincoln, news of which reached Europe on the eve of Louis Napoleon's departure. In her horror at the violent act, Eugénie immediately set aside politics to communicate directly with her feminine counterpart. "Madame: The Emperor sends to Washington his official expressions of the indignation and sadness which have gripped the nation of France, for the fatal blow that struck President Lincoln," Eugénie gently addressed the grieving first lady. "However, aside from this national misfortune, your personal tragedy arouses profound feelings in my heart," she continued earnestly. "I would like...to offer my own condolences, as well as the assurance of my prayers that Heaven will grant you the strength to bear this cruel ordeal. Please believe, Madame, in my deep sympathy and my most sincere sentiments." The delivery of this letter, one of the first to arrive with personal condolences from a foreign head of state to the widow, made the US papers. LETTER FROM THE EMPRESS EUGENIE TO MRS. LINCOLN, blared the front page of the *New York Times*.†

Louis Napoleon was only away for about six weeks, but his wife managed to cram a surprising number of initiatives into the short interval. She worked with the minister of education on a plan to expand enrollment in advanced academic subjects, particularly the sciences, to young women; two years later, Paca's daughters would be among the

---

★ Plon-Plon managed to fail this test in predictably spectacular fashion. Napoleon III was not gone two weeks before his cousin gave a hectoring speech that was openly critical of the emperor's policies in Italy and Mexico. "The only thing talked of here is Prince Napoleon's latest freak," an exasperated Mérimée complained to his friend on May 23, 1865. Eugénie wisely ignored him. Upon Louis Napoleon's return, Plon-Plon found it expedient to decamp hurriedly abroad for a protracted stay.

† Victoria also sent a letter of sympathy to Mary Todd Lincoln, which was dated the day after Eugénie's. At the time, Eugénie was as much of a celebrity in the US as the English queen. In fact, when Mrs. Lincoln first arrived in Washington, she made a point of patterning her gowns after the empress's wardrobe.

first to take advantage of this program at the Sorbonne. Eugénie also insisted that a painting by Rosa Bonheur, known for her landscapes, be included in the Salon exhibition that year, and that the artist herself receive the Legion of Honor, France's most prestigious merit award, "the first time that distinction has been conferred on a lady," as one thunderstruck newspaper reported.

But for all that she held the promotion of women's equality dear, Eugénie's efforts during her regency went far beyond this one issue. The previous year, Napoleon III had acceded to demands for an elected representative legislature, so during her tenure there was a small but vocal opposition to the imperial government in Paris. The regent, in addition to chairing the ministerial council, now determined to engage personally with the leader of the opposing delegates. "The Empress Eugénie has had M. Emile Ollivier to dinner at the Tuileries, where, much to his astonishment, he found he had to sit down to table with M. Havin, the editor of the *Siècle,* who has often reproached him in his paper for his concessions to the Government. M. Havin was of course as much disconcerted at this *rencontre* [encounter] as M. Ollivier," snickered one London paper.

It turned out, however, that the empress's intention was not to embarrass her guests but rather to listen to them. One of Ollivier's principal grievances was the sorry state of the French penal system, particularly as it applied to juvenile offenders. Eugénie, alerted to the problem, took it upon herself to investigate and made a surprise visit to one of the largest of these institutions, the prison of La Roquette, which housed some 500 young criminals.

This was clearly the first time a sovereign had ever set foot inside this institution and what Eugénie saw appalled her. Children as young as seven were incarcerated, although most fell between the ages of fifteen and seventeen. Except for an hour's exercise a day, all were kept locked up individually, in what amounted to solitary confinement. "The names of the boys are not even known to the overseers, who call them by the number of the cell they occupy," wrote an English correspondent who reported on Eugénie's visit. "The Empress insisted on . . . interrogating many of the prisoners separately, drawing from them the history of their past lives and the details of the crimes for which they were incarcerated with such touching kindness that when she arose to quit the *salle,* where the young prisoners had been allowed to assemble at her request, several of them burst into tears, and literally sobbed with emotion as she took leave of them," he continued. "Those who were present say that the Empress herself was so much affected that she could not address them as she intended." At the next council meeting, Eugénie made an impassioned speech in favor of a more humane approach to rehabilitation. La Roquette was shut down and its youthful inmates spread out among smaller, rural institutions, where they worked outside on farms and became part of the community.

Towards the end of her regency, Eugénie was herself surprised by a visit. An emissary from Mexico suddenly turned up at court with a long letter for Napoleon III from Max, and the urgent request that (in the wake of the North's victory in the American Civil War) the great European realms publicly pledge to defend the Mexican empire in the event of future US aggression. Eugénie, understanding that obtaining such blanket guarantees would be highly unlikely, did her best to calm her protégé's fears. In fact, she had already met the new American ambassador to Paris, John Bigelow, who was a good friend of her much-esteemed Philadelphia dentist, Dr. Evans, and had ascertained that, far from threatening violence against Mexico, the envoy was keen to avoid conflict and to develop a strong working relationship with France. "Mr. Bigelow...is most pacific, and promises not only not to support [US] intervention [in Mexico], but even to prevent it," Mérimée observed with relief in a letter of June 2, 1865.

Armed with this knowledge, Eugénie saw no immediate cause for concern and simply forwarded Max's letter to Napoleon III in Algeria. She then sent a note of her own to her "very dear sister" Charlotte. "I can understand what an impression the events taking place in the North must produce on Your Majesty," she sympathized. "Here too they have created quite a strong sensation among the public, and yet, at the risk of appearing too optimistic, I confess that it has not surprised me that the Dissidents in Mexico have recovered their courage on the close of the war in the United States." She then reassured Charlotte that there was no pressing need to increase the number of French forces; nothing had really changed and so the soldiers they already had in place were sufficient to protect them. After all, "it is impossible to occupy the whole of Mexico," Eugénie observed.

Louis Napoleon returned to Paris much improved for his holiday. "The master of the house is as strong as a horse; he is ten years younger and in capital spirits," Mérimée reported happily on June 23. Even better, the foreign situation seemed to have stabilized. Prussia and Austria, to the great relief of most of the rest of Europe, had come to an agreement that divided the conquered duchies between them, thus averting a potential war. Max, while still pressing strongly for more money and troops, nonetheless wrote to Napoleon III on July 27, 1865, "Internal affairs are making good progress; I was much pleased with my last tour and especially with the touching and enthusiastic reception spontaneously accorded to me on my return to the capital."

It was all going so well. And then that fall, both cholera and Bismarck suddenly turned up in France at almost exactly the same moment. It is a matter of opinion which of these two scourges was the more dangerous.

OTTO VON BISMARCK WAS fifty years old and firmly ensconced as minister-president of Prussia, second only to King Wilhelm I in influence and authority, when he interrupted the imperial family's regular holiday stay at Biarritz in September 1865 to hold a private conclave with the emperor. Although the specifics of their conversation remained secret, it did not take much effort to surmise the topic under discussion, nor the general nature of the negotiations. That was because there was no statesman in Europe more enthusiastically vocal about his desire to foment hostilities than Bismarck. He didn't even *try* to hide it. "Make me an Under Secretary of Foreign Affairs, and I will produce for you in three weeks a civil war of the first quality," he had chirped happily on his way up the political ladder.

Bismarck's affinity for robust military intervention had sprung from the insights and frustrations connected to his long tenure as a career diplomat. He'd spent seven years in Frankfurt as the Prussian representative to the German Diet, another two in Russia, and two more in Paris. He was personally acquainted with the ministries of London and Austria as well. Familiarity with the heads of these various states had only convinced Bismarck of his own superiority. "I wasted several years of my life by the supposition that England was a great nation," he snorted. "Put Germany in the saddle and she will soon ride."

Thankfully for the rest of Europe, even his own sovereign had at first found Bismarck's pronouncements too belligerent to be taken seriously. After his inaugural speech, in which the minister-president stunned his countrymen by announcing that Prussia would "be unable to avoid a serious contest, a contest which could only be settled by blood and iron," Wilhelm had called Bismarck in for a private audience. "I can perfectly well see where all this will end," the king had lectured his chief official. "Over there, in front of the Opera House, under my windows, they will cut off your head, and mine a little while afterward." But Bismarck, who was unfortunately both smarter and more cunning than almost anyone else with whom he came into contact, had already taken the measure of his superior and understood that the key to handling Wilhelm was to play to his vanity. "Your Majesty must not think of Louis XVI," the minister-president had returned soothingly. "He lived and died in a condition of mental weakness, and does not present a heroic figure in history."

And after that, bit by bit over the course of the next three years, Bismarck had led Wilhelm, who had previously been happy to hobnob peaceably in the company of his fellow German sovereigns—the king of Saxony was his best friend—into tempting thoughts of greatness. "I reminded the King that every one of his immediate ancestors, not even excepting his brother, had won an increment of territory for the state," Bismarck noted. "His frame of mind, so far as I could observe, underwent a psychological change; he developed a taste for conquest," the minister-president concluded with satisfaction. Bismarck was not the only person to notice the alteration to Wilhelm's personality. A close friend of Victoria's wrote confidentially to London from Germany on August 27, 1865, warning the English queen that "he [Wilhelm] is under the influence of a clever, unprincipled man who has completely changed him, and for which there is no help, alas!"★

By September of 1865, Bismarck—now Count Bismarck, having been promoted as a sign of royal favor—had so far moved his sovereign along the glorious path towards unleashing unbridled slaughter against both Austria and his fellow Germans that he could commence making the sort of under-the-table arrangements necessary to the pursuit of his high political ideals. And who better to begin his intrigues with than the man who had so effectively lured Franz Joseph into a war with Italy?

The Prussian minister found a ready accomplice in Louis Napoleon. The emperor, who had been rebuffed again and again in his attempts to iron out an alliance that solved his Venetian problem, had lost patience with Vienna. He was happy to agree not to intervene on Austria's behalf should the Prussians decide to force a war with Franz Joseph, particularly as Bismarck hinted that France would gain by its magnanimity. There was nothing in writing; Louis Napoleon had learned from his experience with Cavour not to leave evidence that might be publicized against him in the future. He was content to leave the details of French compensation unspecified—after all, the emperor noted understandingly, "One cannot sell the bear-skin till one has killed the bear." "I believe that I may designate the present attitude of this Court as one that is in the highest degree favorable to us," a complacent Bismarck was able to report back to Berlin.

★ Queen Victoria had lost her husband, Prince Albert, suddenly in December of 1861, and had spent the years following this tragedy in a state of almost paralyzed mourning. Just before Albert's death, however, the couple had married their eldest daughter, Vicky (who had admired Eugénie so much as a child), to Wilhelm's eldest son, Crown Prince Frederick, known as Fritz. Prussia's increasing militarism, which put Vicky and her family at risk, greatly worried Victoria, and helped bring her out of her self-imposed seclusion. She sounds almost her old self in a letter to her uncle Leopold on August 3, 1865. "Prussia seems inclined to behave as atrociously as possible, as *she always has done!*" the queen wailed to the king of the Belgians. "Odious people the Prussians are, *that* I *must* say."

Eugénie was not included in these meetings, but she did not have to be. The empress had already discussed the deteriorating situation in Germany with her husband, and he had made clear to her his intention not to intervene or ally militarily with either side should war break out between Austria and Prussia. She had even communicated this position, which she agreed with, to her good friend Prince Metternich, assuring him "that in case Prussian proposals were made that might seem acceptable to the Emperor, she would openly and quickly warn me," as the Austrian ambassador made haste to report home to Vienna just prior to Bismarck's visit. As all that had happened during the count's stay was that Napoleon III had allowed himself to be bribed to maintain the neutrality he had intended to assume anyway, there was no need to alert Prince Metternich of a change in policy.

Besides, the empress had other, more pressing concerns that autumn. The imperial holiday at Biarritz was cut short by news of a severe outbreak of cholera in the capital. Eugénie, with the experience of her second regency behind her, was determined to ensure that the victims were getting the care they needed. On October 23, 1865, the English correspondent, who happened to be taking a morning stroll in Paris near the main hospital, was astounded to see an unpretentious dark carriage suddenly pull up, out of which popped the empress, dressed in black and accompanied by a single lady-in-waiting. Investigating further, the reporter learned that upon entering the hospital, Eugénie had "requested to be taken to the cholera wards, where she approached the bed of each patient, and in the case of the dying...knelt by their side and endeavoured to hear their last earthly wish...The enthusiasm excited by this visit...can hardly be imagined," the journalist continued warmly. "Her Majesty has won the heart of the country...Very different is the example set by some of the aristocrats...who have fled *en masse* to Versailles, or returned to their châteaux," he noted critically.

By New Year's, the threat from cholera had receded but the same could not be said of Count Bismarck. Armed with the assurance of Napoleon III's indulgent neutrality, which guaranteed that in the event of open hostilities, Vienna would be deprived of French arms, loans, and good offices, he set about laying a snare to entrap his prey. In February 1866, he sent an envoy to make discreet inquiries as to whether Victor Emmanuel would be willing to join with Prussia in a war of conquest against Austria, the reward for which would be Italy's longed-for annexation of Venetia. Victor Emmanuel, as it turned out, was very interested, and sent an emissary to Berlin to negotiate a secret treaty confirming this offer. The terms of this agreement, signed on April 8, 1866, stipulated that if "His Majesty the King of Prussia...be forced to take up arms,...then his Majesty the King of Italy...shall...[also] immediately declare war against Austria." Thus Bismarck significantly improved his odds for success by ensuring that Franz Joseph, should he be induced to take the bait, would have to split his forces in order to ward off combat on two fronts hundreds of miles apart.

That left only the problem of making Austria look like the aggressor, as the king of Prussia, willing but still hesitant, insisted that he not be the one to make the first move. To do this, Bismarck swiped a contrivance directly out of Louis Napoleon's playbook. Of course, it seemed too much to expect that Franz Joseph would fall twice for the same ploy, but it was worth a try.

ELISABETH

Count Gyula Andrássy

22

The Empress Takes a Stand

Princes wrangle, nations quarrel,
Each would bear away the laurel;
Conquest is the highest prize,
Highest worth in courage lies.

No proud helmet gives protection,
Death brings all things in subjection;
And the hero's blood is shed,
And the wicked win instead.

Laurel wreaths, triumphal arches!
On the morrow in he marches,
Who the better one o'erthrew,
Winning land and people too.

—Heinrich Heine

BISMARCK'S MACHINATIONS WERE STILL MONTHS in the future when Elisabeth succeeded in legally wresting control of her children's lives away from her mother-in-law in the summer of 1865. In fact, far from anticipating Prussian antagonism, Franz Joseph believed he had adroitly defused the tension with Berlin by agreeing, after much haggling, to divide the spoils of the recent war against Denmark fairly between the two victors. According to the Convention of Galstein, signed that August, Prussia was to administer the conquered duchy of Schleswig, while Austria would govern Holstein, the other occupied province. Relieved to have the family squabble settled, the emperor was able to turn his attention to other, more pressing, matters.

Chief among these was the question of what to do about Hungary. The kingdom was still under martial law for refusing to participate in the limited parliamentary system Franz Joseph had been forced to put into place after losing so ignominiously to Napoleon III and Victor Emmanuel in northern Italy. The standoff had been festering for years when suddenly in the fall of 1865, the possibility of compromise wavered on the horizon.

The emperor seems to have had his wife to thank for this development. Since her return to Vienna, Sisi had made no secret of her affinity for the oppressed people of Hungary. It was well known that she was intent on learning the language and took lessons from a local professor. Her favorite lady-in-waiting was a Hungarian countess, the sister of the young man who had been hastily bundled off the island of Madeira for having (in the court's opinion) demonstrated too great an interest in Elisabeth.

But by far Sisi's most public act of solidarity had come in the fall of 1864, when she had caused something of a minor sensation by appearing at the Vienna opera house attired in the outsized, crescent-shaped tiara customarily worn by Hungarian women. Since the dawn of Franz Joseph's and Archduchess Sophia's reign, no senior member of the imperial court had ever made such a provocative fashion statement. It was almost as though the empress was trying to get the Hungarians' attention.*

The leading politician in Pesth, Ferenc Deák, "the most popular and influential man in Hungary," as the Viennese correspondent for the London *Times* noted, certainly thought so. Deák, a proponent of nonviolent

---

* The London *Times* would later observe that "in the times when Hungary could only assert her rights by silent protests, ... the Hungarian dress was taken up as one of the most effective external signs of the feelings which the nation harbored within."

resistance long before Gandhi, appears to have been looking for a way to bypass official channels, which were so mired in bureaucracy as to be useless, and instead establish a more informal line of communication with the imperial court. When Elisabeth subsequently decided to supplement her language lessons by appointing someone to her household with whom she could converse in Hungarian, Deák saw his opportunity. On the dossier of possible candidates for this position were the names of six countesses from prominent aristocratic families, and one young woman of more modest birth, the daughter of rural gentry, whose nomination had obviously been added on the fly, after the approved list had already been compiled. The Hungarian baroness who had taken this risk knew the empress well: of course, Sisi chose the unpretentious country girl over the sophisticated society ladies.

And so, twenty-three-year-old Ida von Ferenczy moved from her parents' relatively modest quarters in rustic southeastern Hungary, some fifty-five miles outside of Budapest, to the imperial court in Vienna. Grateful for the opportunity (which, owing to her inferior rank, no other Austrian empress save possibly Maria Theresa would have given her), highly intelligent, and dazzled by her employer, she would prove to be Sisi's most loyal confidante.★ She and Elisabeth took to each other immediately. The empress found a way to circumvent the tiresome rule prohibiting someone of lower birth from joining her household by appointing Ida to the lesser title of "reader," although in every other way the younger woman functioned as her closest companion. During the three hours it took Sisi to have her hair brushed and arranged each morning, she and Ida would work on her pronunciation by conversing exclusively in Hungarian. As no one else in the room understood the language, it was like two secret agents communicating in code.

It is startling how quickly relations between Austria and Hungary improved after Ida's appearance at court. The Hungarians made the

---

★ Ida wasn't there a week before a member of Archduchess Sophia's household took her aside. "Pray consult me in everything and confide all Her Majesty says to me," the lady-in-waiting commanded. Not only did Ida refuse to succumb to this pressure, but she immediately informed Elisabeth of the encounter, thereby cementing the empress's trust.

first move just six months later, in June of 1865, by inviting Franz Joseph to attend the exhibition of the Hungarian Agricultural Association, a nonpolitical event. At his wife's urging, the emperor acceded to this request. Franz Joseph was so pleased with this visit (which happily coincided with Pesth's annual yacht and horse races, entertainments he enjoyed immensely) that he lifted martial law and gave a speech approving new elections for the Diet, to be held at the end of the year.*

Voting commenced in November 1865, and even before all the results were in, the *Times* reported "It is already evident that the Deak (Moderate Liberal) party will have a large majority in the Diet." "Deak's popularity and influence have never been so great as they are now," the correspondent added. "Indeed, in some parts of Hungary only the men of his recommendation have been elected." Elisabeth, delighted with Deák's success, asked her reader to obtain a signed painting of the statesman to hang in her bedroom, although Ida cautioned her contact in Pesth that the gift had to remain secret.

Ferenc Deák, portly and in his sixties, cleverly did his operative one better. In January of 1866, rather than simply forwarding an inanimate portrait to Vienna, he instead sent the darkly handsome Count Gyula Andrássy to the empress.

IF EVER A MAN was born to play the role of romantic knight to Sisi's good-fairy princess, that man was Andrássy. The count's political career had started early. He had been one of the youngest members of the rebel government brutally suppressed by Vienna with the help of the Russians at the very beginning of Franz Joseph's reign. The twenty-five-year-old had managed to slip out of the country before they could arrest him, so he ended up being one of those venerated patriots whom the frustrated Austrian military was reduced to hanging in effigy. Exiled from his homeland, the dashing Andrássy spent the next decade abroad, traveling first to London and then Paris, where he picked up a

---

* At this time, present-day Budapest was still divided into two cities, one on each side of the Danube. The royal palace, where the emperor stayed when visiting, was in Buda, while the Diet was in Pesth.

charming cosmopolitan manner, some sophisticated diplomatic ideas, and a wife and four children. Taking advantage of the imperial amnesty issued as part of Franz Joseph's limited liberalization policy, he returned to Hungary, where, as a loyal Deák partisan, he was voted into the Diet during the recent elections and was subsequently named vice president of the assembly. "This is not the first time that it has been the will of Providence Hungary should take part in the decisions of European questions," the now forty-two-year-old Andrássy reminded the Diet, referring to the reign of Maria Theresa, when his countrymen had come to the empress's rescue in the war against the Prussian king Frederick the Great. "Hungary, which had overcome so many dangers, and always issued from them stronger than before, will not belie her reputation upon this occasion as well," he vowed in a stirring speech delivered to his fellow representatives on December 20, 1865.

Impressed with his eloquence and gallantry, Deák included the count as one of a sixteen-member delegation, headed by the cardinal primate of Hungary (appointed to lend the spiritual authority of the Church), and sent this picturesque group to Vienna to convince Franz Joseph to return to Pesth to begin in-person negotiations with the new Diet as soon as possible. Aware that the empress was an ardent supporter of the kingdom, the representatives were instructed to petition her to make the journey as well. Andrássy was thus one of those ushered into Elisabeth's presence on January 8, 1866, when she granted the deputation an audience at the Hofburg Palace.

Sisi had done everything she could think of to demonstrate her affection and respect for these hopeful emissaries. She received the entire troupe in the magnificent hall of mirrors as though they were a massed conclave of the most powerful sovereigns in Europe and not merely a motley gaggle of provincial representatives from a vassal assembly. She wore a gown of sumptuous white silk, "trimmed with a braiding of diamonds," to which she had added a black velvet jacket embroidered "with precious stones"; her lace cap and apron were *à la hongroise* (in the style of Hungary), as the *Times* correspondent reported. She'd even raided the crown jewels for the occasion. "On the forepart of her head the Empress wore that splendid diadem of brilliants which is shown to visitors to the Imperial Schatz-Kammer [the vault]," the journalist noted. It was just past eleven o'clock in the morning.

But her effort went far beyond her regal appearance. When the cardinal primate, at the end of his "very loyal address to the Empress," added that "the Hungarian nation hopes and trusts Her Majesty will be pleased to accompany the Emperor when next he goes to Pesth," Sisi surprised her guests by responding to this overture in their native tongue. To cries of *"Eljen!* [Long life to you!]" she began, "Ever since it has pleased Providence — through His Majesty, my beloved Consort — to connect me by an indissoluble tie to Hungary, I have constantly taken great interest in the welfare of that country. (*Eljen! Eljen! Eljen!*) ... The feeling towards me, to which Your Eminence has now given expression, cannot but go to my heart. (*Eljen! Eljen!*) ... To those whose representatives you are I send my hearty greetings until such time as I, in accordance with the wish of the nation, can, in the company of my illustrious Consort, appear in the midst of them. (Prolonged cries of *Eljen!*)"

It is difficult to suppress the suspicion that Elisabeth, by arranging so theatrical a display, was not attempting to draw a deliberate parallel to the past. Her approach mirrored almost exactly the strategy employed a century earlier by Maria Theresa, who, finding herself under attack by Frederick the Great, had *also* donned Hungarian garb and reached out to the members of the Diet in their own language (in her era, Latin), to memorable effect. What is certain, however, is that it worked just as well for Sisi as it had for her predecessor. "The Empress produced a highly favourable impression on the Hungarians," the *Times* correspondent confirmed. The delegates, he marveled, even "gave me the assurance that she pronounces the Hungarian language more correctly than the Primate does."

Under these happy auspices, and at his wife's urging, Franz Joseph graciously accepted the Hungarians' invitation, and a month later he and Sisi journeyed to Pesth. Count Andrássy greeted them on their arrival and acted as Elisabeth's tour guide throughout the visit. Spirits were high on both sides; conditions for reconciliation had never seemed so promising. The imperial couple was welcomed excitedly into the city and fêted by a joyful populace. "No one expected that the Emperor would at once appoint responsible Hungarian ministers and restore the county authorities, [but] everybody believed that His Majesty would hint at the possibility of his being disposed to do [so]," testified the *Times* correspondent assigned to cover these historic negotiations.

But neither his wife nor his hosts had given sufficient credence to Franz Joseph's inflexibility. The emperor had never had any intention of giving in to the Hungarian demands. He felt he had already bent over backwards just by agreeing to let them air their arguments publicly without throwing them all in jail for treason. He had taken time out of his busy schedule to visit; he wanted them to know they were all his beloved subjects; but now, he told the kingdom's elected representatives in an address to the Diet on February 28, 1866, it was their turn to just do as they were told.

The delegates were stunned. There was one lone call of *Eljen* "but it was a very feeble one," the *Times* man observed. "The Emperor's reply... was listened to in silence, and... he appeared to be surprised and offended by the icy coldness with which his observations were received."

And so, having benevolently insulted the very subjects whose aid he would most need should hostilities break out against the empire, Franz Joseph, with Sisi in tow, returned to Vienna in March, just in time to get ambushed by Bismarck.

BY THE SPRING OF 1866, the Prussian count had almost all the elements of his many-sided intrigue in position. He had secretly secured French approval for a war against Austria by hintingly offering Napoleon III a bribe; he was in the final stages of formalizing a clandestine alliance with Victor Emmanuel to bring Italy into the coming hostilities; and he had taken the measure of the dilatory rulers of the other German kingdoms and knew that, faced with Prussian aggression, they would either be easily intimidated, or slow to arm, or both. He had been building up the army for years and had amassed a surplus of weapons, including a new state-of-the-art rifle called the needle gun, which was much faster to load and significantly more accurate in its aim. He even had a combat plan in place that drew heavily on the eighteenth-century military campaigns of his hero, Frederick the Great, whom Bismarck considered a "transcendent genius" and whose policies and tactics he unfailingly sought to emulate.

There was really only one impediment holding everything up, and that was the frustratingly pacific attitude of his own sovereign, Wilhelm I. No matter how many times the count patiently brought up the subject, Wilhelm persisted in shying away from the thought of war, and he most certainly did not want to be the monarch responsible for starting one. So, as in Shakespeare, Bismarck had to play Iago to Wilhelm's Othello, and convince the king that it wasn't Prussia that was being overly aggressive, but rather Franz Joseph who was betraying them by *pretending* that Austria wasn't arming in preparation for an attack when in fact it was, an accusation that absolutely everyone else in Europe, including Wilhelm's own son, Crown Prince Fritz (married to Vicky), knew to be false.

Bismarck's challenge was thus to goad Vienna into taking an action — any action — that could in some way be interpreted as menacing, so he could use it as evidence of Franz Joseph's hostile intent, and thereby get Wilhelm to order the military into the field. Problem was, Franz Joseph had been down this path before with Napoleon III and Count Cavour in Italy and had learned not to let himself get painted as the aggressor. So, no matter how hard he tried, the count could not get the emperor to make a threatening gesture, or even to put his soldiers on alert. Bismarck mobilized the entire Prussian army, calling it a training exercise; Vienna shrugged it off. He leaked plans to invade Saxony; the Austrian ambassador to Berlin merely asked if Prussia was intending to attack his neighbor, and was satisfied when Bismarck replied no, even though the count impudently pointed out afterwards that "if a power intended the next morning to march across its frontiers, it would also reply with a 'no' the evening before."

In fact, all the Prussian minister-president accomplished by engaging in these obvious ploys was create sympathy for Austria. Family and friends implored Wilhelm not to be taken in by Bismarck's belligerence. The Bavarian foreign minister offered his services as an independent, peaceful mediator. Even the Prussian citizenry protested the increased militarization of the kingdom. "The popular agitations against the war are assuming very unpleasant dimensions!" Wilhelm yelped to Bismarck on April 11, 1866.

And then, on April 20, the count's trump card came in when Franz Joseph received an alarming report from Venice that Victor Emmanuel had mustered some 40,000 soldiers and it looked like the Italians were going to attack Venetia in an attempt to liberate the province from imperial rule. As this was a threat the emperor could not afford to overlook, the next day Franz Joseph ordered the mobilization of both the army and the navy for deployment in northern Italy. (No getting caught unprepared by enemy warships in the Venetian harbor this time.)

And just like that, Bismarck had him. Reminding Wilhelm that, according to their recent secret treaty with Victor Emmanuel, an attack against Italy obliged Prussia to go to war in their ally's defense, the count characterized the Austrian call-up as a double-dealing act of belligerence, rather than defense. "Your Majesty will, I venture to trust, retain the conviction that it is contrary to my feelings, I may say my faith, to desire to influence...the highest sovereign determinations on war and peace; that is a domain in which I confidently leave to God alone the direction of your Majesty's heart," Bismarck demurred piously to Wilhelm in a masterpiece of literary passive-aggressiveness dated April 22, 1866. "At the same time I dare not disguise the conviction that if peace is maintained *now* we shall be threatened with the danger of war later, perhaps in a few months' time, under *more unfavorable conditions*," he warned ominously. "Anyone who, like your Majesty's most humble servant" — he was really laying it on — "has for sixteen years been most intimately concerned with Austrian policy, cannot doubt that hostility towards Prussia has become the chief, one might say, the only political aim in Vienna," he ended bluntly.

Wilhelm was convinced and the die was cast. The Prussian army began openly preparing for combat, and this time Franz Joseph had no choice but to respond. The emperor began calling up divisions to protect Bohemia in case of an attack by Berlin. He reached out to his German allies, especially Saxony and Bavaria, the two strongest, to muster troops to fight alongside those of Austria. He brought in his best general from Italy to command his soldiers in the north and sent an Austrian archduke to Venetia to meet the danger from Victor Emmanuel.

But the real worry was France. Franz Joseph was confident of victory, even with having to split his forces, if the threat came only from two lesser powers like Prussia and Italy. But he couldn't be sure that Napoleon III wouldn't take the opportunity to pile on as well. Franz Joseph had fought the French army before. If their might were added to the enemy battalions already allied against him, it would mean almost certain defeat.

And so he yielded to an expedient that he had resisted for years: bribery. In May, Prince Metternich was instructed to engage in covert negotiations with Louis Napoleon to determine what it would take for Austria to secure French neutrality in the coming conflict, although surely, after so many years of relentless pressure to vacate his remaining Italian territory, Franz Joseph already knew the answer to that question. "Could you promise...a cession of Venetia whether you whip the Italians or not?" a smug Napoleon III, aware that he had finally outmaneuvered his prey, inquired. "Your Majesty holds the knife at our throat!" the ambassador complained.

But there was no other way to ensure that he would not have to face French guns as well, so on June 12, Franz Joseph gritted his teeth and signed a "Secret Convention between France and Austria," in which he voluntarily ceded Venetia to Louis Napoleon, on the condition that, after Prussia was defeated, Austria would be compensated with Silesia. In return, Napoleon III, again after the war, would cede the province to Victor Emmanuel *even if Austria had prevailed in combat,* and so make good on his original promise to liberate Italy. By this document, then, Franz Joseph's soldiers in Venetia would be fighting and dying for territory which, unbeknownst to them, their sovereign had already given away.

The stage was set; the battle lines drawn. All of Europe knew that war was at hand. "There is much mischief brewing," the American ambassador stationed in Vienna mused in a letter to his daughter in the days just before combat commenced. "These people have been playing with edge tools ever since the beginning of January, and somebody may get hurt," he prophesied darkly.

AND NOW, FOR THE FIRST TIME, it was twenty-eight-year-old Sisi, and not sixty-one-year-old Sophia, who fully inhabited the office of empress during a period of crisis. In the months leading up to open conflict, it was to his wife that Franz Joseph turned for both emotional and political support, so much so that this time, when the issue of a possible regency was raised, it was understood by everyone at court that Elisabeth would be the one named to the position.

Fortunately, there was no immediate need of a surrogate, as the emperor prudently decided to remain in Vienna, rather than joining his forces in the field as he had before. All through that anxious spring and early summer, as relations between Prussia and Austria began to spiral out of control, the empress remained by her husband's side and did what she could to help him. Although she did not attend council meetings as Eugénie did, Sisi was nonetheless well informed on military developments. She knew that Franz Joseph was attempting to assemble a massive army of some 200,000 soldiers from across the empire, to which would be added an additional 23,000 or so men promised by the king of Saxony, to combat the threat from Wilhelm's divisions, which were expected to be of similar strength. A further 74,000 troops were also to be marshaled and sent to Italy to repel Victor Emmanuel's battalions.

But even these impressive numbers merely *matched* the forces arrayed against Vienna, and the Prussians had the advantage of a head start on mobilization, arms, training, and supplies. What Austria really needed was a second army in Germany to attack the enemy from the south, compelling Berlin to divert brigades meant for the main offensive. For this critical sortie, the emperor called upon his long-standing ally, Bavaria.

His timing could not have been worse. King Maximilian II had unexpectedly succumbed to illness just as the contest between Prussia and Austria was heating up. His death left his eldest son, Ludwig II, an extravagantly fanciful twenty-year-old with no prior preparation in government, and some rather odd notions as to how to go about his new job, on the throne of Bavaria.

Ludwig was not interested in troop movements, ballistics, combat plans, or joint command operations. Ludwig was interested in music, specifically the music of an out-of-work, on-the-run-from-his-creditors composer by the name of Richard Wagner, formerly the court conductor to the king of Saxony. The new sovereign had been introduced at an early age to the Wagnerian opera *Lohengrin,* about a mysterious medieval knight who appears in a gondola pulled by an enchanted swan to save a beautiful princess from her enemies. The two fall for each other, and Lohengrin (the knight) marries the princess on condition that she never ask his name. Of course she does, at which point he departs as dramatically as he arrived (this time with the help of a magic dove), while she perishes for having betrayed true love.* Ludwig's sole notion of kingship revolved around building a grand opera house that would bring the glories of Richard Wagner's music (and the composer himself) to Bavaria.

His ministers tried their best to get their monarch to see the danger emanating from Berlin, but the young ruler was impervious to their warnings. Instead of signing the papers necessary to muster an army, he went to his private island to watch fireworks. Even Sisi, who had known Ludwig since childhood, and who sympathized with his romantic nature (so very like her own), was nonplussed. "If only he would think a little more about government, now that times are so bad!" she fretted in a letter to her mother.

---

* Ironically, Ludwig was introduced to this composition at Sisi's home in Munich, when he found the score for *Lohengrin* propped up on Duke Max's piano.

Eventually, the more responsible members of Ludwig's administration induced him to approve a mobilization of the realm's forces, but by then it was too late to get an army together in time to play the vital role assigned to Bavaria in the hostilities. So, when Bismarck, employing Frederick the Great's tactics of speed and surprise, launched a lightning offensive against his neighbors in the very early hours of June 15, there were no opposing German divisions in place to slow the Prussians' progress. As a result, by the next day, Wilhelm's soldiers occupied both Saxony and Hanover, and his battalions were able to barrel forward at full strength into the imperial territory of Bohemia—exactly the scenario Franz Joseph had been most hoping to avoid.

AS SOON AS IT was confirmed that the Prussians had begun their invasion into Saxony, Elisabeth took the children to Bad Ischl for protection. But she left them there and returned to Vienna two weeks later to help care for the wounded, promising Rudolf, who was following the progress of the war with the natural keenness of a seven-year-old used to playing with toy soldiers, that she would keep him up-to-date on the latest intelligence. This pledge she faithfully executed. "Papa is looking well, thank God, and is filled with a calm and confidence in the future, which command admiration," she reassured her son in one of the lengthy, almost daily letters she wrote to the boy from the Hofburg Palace, "though the Prussian troops are terribly strong and their needle guns are having a prodigious success," honest Sisi was forced to add.

Franz Joseph, not being on the front line this time, repeatedly sent messengers into the field to urge his commander, who was holed up with his men in the secure fortress town of Königgrätz (modern-day Hradec Králové) about eighty-five miles east of Prague, to go on the offensive. The general, who had spent years in Venetia and knew absolutely nothing about the geography of the imperial lands bordering Prussia, was reluctant to make a move until he had a better sense of the terrain. For this very reason he had tried to turn down the assignment. "I told them at the War Office that on the theater of war in Bohemia I should be an ass, while in Italy I might perhaps be of some use," he had complained to his wife before his transfer. He was also concerned about the superior weaponry brandished by the enemy forces. During the last week of June, imperial troops had several skirmishes with the Prussians and had gotten the worst of the engagements each time. The general was getting a firsthand look at the destructive power of the needle gun, and it worried him.

Elisabeth, too, witnessed the trauma created by this new and improved firearm. Although the war had barely begun, the wounded were already pouring into Vienna, and these injured warriors caught at her heart. Her days were spent comforting those most in need. One young soldier resisted having his arm amputated until Sisi agreed to be there to soothe him. A member of Sophia's household noted that "the Empress is really admirable in never sparing herself, attending to everything and having thought for everybody in a most human and affectionate manner," and even the archduchess, although originally sniping, "At least she is here," felt compelled to write later to Rudolf, "Your dear mama remains at your father's side, like his guardian angel, and only leaves him to go from one hospital to another, bestowing consolation and help on every side."

Under pressure from Vienna, the Austrian general in Bohemia, who had originally asked to retreat and await reinforcements, realized that any new troops would have to be transferred from Italy and would likely arrive too late to make a difference. As this left confronting the enemy from a strong defensive position as his only real option, the commander scouted around for an advantageous location. He chose the forests and cliffs surrounding the village of Sadowa, on the bank of a nearby river, as his best shot. In order to press an assault, the Prussians would be forced to cross Sadowa's lone bridge, where they would be vulnerable to Austrian artillery, and once ashore they would be fighting in wooded areas and in hamlets where imperial troops could avail themselves of the cover of trees and huts, thus blunting the effects of the needle gun. The needle gun, the general knew, was at its most deadly when the target was out in the open.

But no position is invulnerable, and in this case, the general worried that his left flank, which occupied an exposed ridge, was at risk. There was no help for it, however, and he simply determined to watch for an attack and then protect this area as best he could.

He did not have long to wait. At one o'clock in the morning on July 3, 1866, the Prussians began their advance towards Sadowa. By dawn, the main army, some 150,000 strong, complete with artillery, had collected at the base of a hill above the village. A second Prussian force, of about 50,000 combatants, approached from the right. It had begun to rain, "and the wind blew bitterly cold," the *Times* correspondent, who had trekked with these divisions through the darkness of the predawn hours, attested. At 7 a.m., the cavalry, heralded by trumpets, led the charge to the river, with the intent of gaining the bridge. The battle was on.

The Austrian commander had planned his defenses well. Hour after hour, in the pouring rain, the Prussian troops tried to advance, only to be cut down by imperial artillery. "As soon as the Prussian fire actively commenced, Austrian guns seemed to appear, as if by magic, in every point of the position: from every road, from every village, from the orchard," the *Times* man reported. "On their left, came flashes of fire and whizzing rifle shells, which, bursting with a sharp crack, sent their splinters rattling among the guns, gunners, carriages, and horses, often killing man or horse...One shell came slap into a squadron...who were close beside the king...Bursting a moment after, [it] reduced the squadron by four files."

Into the afternoon the struggle raged, with terrible casualties on both sides. "The 27th Prussian regiment went in nearly 3,000 strong, with 90 officers, and came out on the further side with 2 officers and between 300 and 400 men standing," the correspondent recorded. "The fighting continued tree to tree, and the Austrians made many a rush,...but in this close fighting their boyish troops went down like ninepins...But when the defenders drew back a little, and their artillery played into the trees, the Prussians suffered fearfully," he revealed. Until finally, "the whole battle line of the Prussians could gain no more ground, and...it seemed as if it would be lost...The Generals became manifestly uneasy and they drew the infantry out of the battle."

And then, at three thirty in the afternoon, Crown Prince Fritz, with an additional 50,000 or so men, could be seen in the distance, moving in on the imperial left flank. In fact, Fritz was supposed to have rendezvoused with the other regiments hours earlier, but the Austrian commander had seen him coming and held him off on his first attempt, forcing this third Prussian force to march far out of its way before circling back and finding a path in. And now the overwhelming superiority of the needle gun in open terrain made itself manifest. The main Prussian corps had just spent the last eight hours throwing themselves at the imperial regiments and had gotten nowhere. Suddenly, *in fifteen minutes,* Fritz's divisions took out the entire left flank of the opposing army. They might as well have been wielding AK-47s. "In a quarter of an hour the Crown Prince's infantry was engaged...and their quick volleys of musketry, rapidly advancing, told that the Austrians were in full retreat," the *Times* correspondent, a stunned eyewitness to this turnaround, confirmed.

And in that moment, not only the tide of the battlefield but the entire power structure of Europe shifted—and cracked. For when the smoke cleared and the dust settled, it was revealed that some 80,000 of Franz Joseph's soldiers had been either killed, wounded, captured, or were missing presumed drowned; that 150 of his cannons had been seized; and that consequently there was no longer any effective deterrent to shield the imperial capital from the wrath of Bismarck and his victorious army.

"It looks awfully black for Austria at this moment, I fear," the American ambassador wrote worriedly to his daughter. "There is a general panic in Vienna. It is supposed the Prussians will occupy the city within a week."

EUGÉNIE

A determined Charlotte

23

An Unfortunate Fall-Off in Imperial Greatness

Do not deceive yourselves . . . our armies are mobilized; yours is not. You can imagine the consequences yourself.

—Bismarck to Napoleon III

DESPITE ITS STATED POLICY OF NEUTRALITY, the court of the Tuileries was not spared the anxiety that gripped Europe in the months leading up to the Prussian offensive. Eugénie, like her husband, was convinced that Austria would ultimately prevail in both Germany *and* Venetia, and that France would eventually be forced into the conflict, as the Italians would blame the emperor if he did not intervene militarily on their behalf. Sending French soldiers back to Lombardy was the last thing anyone in Paris wanted. In conversations with Prince Metternich, the empress had tried again and again to convince the ambassador to evacuate Venetia and take, say, Romania instead, or to at least allow the Italians to purchase the province through a loan arranged by Baron Rothschild, and so avert hostilities. But these proposals had all been rejected, and by spring it had become clear to everyone that war was imminent. "I never saw a more curious sight than the ball given by the Emperor on Monday evening," Mérimée remarked in a letter on May 9, 1866. "The faces of the foreign ministers were so long that they might easily have been taken for condemned criminals," he noted.

And so it had come as an enormous relief to Eugénie when, at the very last moment, Franz Joseph had come to his senses (as she saw it) and signed a secret treaty with Napoleon III ceding Venetia to France in exchange for Silesia. Now she could root wholeheartedly for the Austrians. "A power which can mobilize 700,000 men always negotiates better after or during a war than before it," she assured her good friends the Metternichs.

The brilliance of the French strategy was made immediately apparent when, on June 24, 1866, less than two weeks after the confidential agreement was signed, the Austrian army thoroughly trounced a much larger force sent by Victor Emmanuel at the small town of Custoza, near the border with Lombardy. This was exactly what Eugénie and Louis Napoleon, neither of whom thought much of the Italian military, had expected would happen. Now they did not have to worry about Austrian victories, however; they knew that after the war, Franz Joseph would take his compensation in Germany, and France would save the day by revealing the secret compact, and ceding Venetia to Victor Emmanuel despite the Italians having lost every battle.

It therefore came as a very rude shock when, just ten days later, on the morning of July 4, a telegram alerted the French court that the Prussian army, using a sneaky technological innovation called the needle gun, had pretty much annihilated the immense Austrian host massed against them at the tiny Bohemian village of Sadowa in the middle of nowhere. Napoleon III and Eugénie were still reeling from this bombshell—not one person in the imperial government had even considered the possibility of an outright Prussian victory—when suddenly a second wire came in with an urgent request from Franz Joseph, entreating his undercover ally Louis Napoleon to put pressure on Wilhelm I to agree to an immediate cease-fire.

An emergency meeting of the council was called to debate French options. Eugénie took the lead in enjoining that a show of force be made to intimidate the Prussians and prevent them from further encroachment. The ministers for war and foreign affairs concurred. "We can concentrate 80,000 men on the Rhine immediately and

250,000 within twenty days," the secretary of war declared. But the minister of the interior disagreed. The risk was too great, he cautioned. Some of their best troops were still in Mexico, he pointed out in a swipe at Eugénie. Because of the austerity measures enacted to try to reduce the ballooning national debt, the government had just spent the last few years *shrinking* the army, and as a result, none of the disbanded regiments now to be called up would be in peak form, let alone equipped with the terrifying needle guns. Worse, they would be joining the *losing* side, Austria, and throwing over their alliance with the successful Bismarck, who had promised compensation in exchange for French neutrality. His attitude infuriated the empress. "When the Prussian armies are no longer tied up in Bohemia and can turn back against ourselves, Bismarck will simply laugh at our claims!" Eugénie exploded, leaping to her feet in indignation.

Her vehemence, grounded in prudence, won over her husband. At the close of the session, which had lasted into the evening, Louis Napoleon agreed that the next morning he would announce a full mobilization of the imperial forces, and the immediate placement of 50,000 French troops on the border with Germany. But although she left the meeting confident that she had secured her point—"It was one of the great moments of my life," she would later recall—Eugénie neglected to take into consideration one important factor: the emperor's health.

By the summer of 1866, fifty-eight-year-old Napoleon III's high living had finally caught up with him. To the ravages of middle-aged debauchery was now added a bladder stone. The pain was apparently excruciating. Exhaustion ensued, and with it, apathy and indecision. "His sufferings and prostration bereft him for the moment of all independence of mind," Eugénie related. "In all the time I have known the imperial couple I have never seen the Emperor so completely *useless*," Prince Metternich railed in frustration in his report to Vienna.

The prospect of marshaling and leading an army into Germany—for Louis Napoleon knew well that history and honor compelled him, as a Bonaparte, to command his own forces against the Prussians—was too much for the emperor in his weakened condition. So, on the morning following the council meeting, he abruptly reneged on his decision to call up the French divisions, and instead fell back on an expedient that required significantly less energy. He sent two telegrams, one to Victor Emmanuel and the other to Bismarck, informing each belligerent that Austria had ceded Venetia to France, and that he had been empowered by Franz Joseph to mediate a peace. He then ordered both men to agree to an immediate cease-fire, pending further instructions.

To say that the recipients of these telegrams were not pleased to learn that the emperor had double-crossed them by first accepting a bribe to remain neutral, and then turning around and making a private side deal with Vienna, is something of an understatement. "Louis [Napoleon] shall pay for it," Bismarck vowed at this revelation. "He's a swine!" Victor Emmanuel spat out upon reading the wire.

Consequently, neither combatant felt the least need to acquiesce to the French demands. "To receive Venice as a gift from France would be humiliating," the general in charge of the Italian forces declared bluntly to Victor Emmanuel. "If you persist in this…we shall cross the Rhine…with 800,000 men and take away from you Alsace," Bismarck threatened Napoleon III.

Eugénie was beside herself at her husband's reversal, from which she foresaw only too clearly the dangers to France. "Really, you make me shiver," she told the special envoy sent by Bismarck to deliver the Prussian rejection of mediation. "The way your power is growing, we shall run the risk of seeing you one day in front of Paris. In the evening I shall go to sleep French and wake Prussian," she predicted sharply. But she couldn't rouse Louis Napoleon from his lassitude. "I found the Emperor deeply affected, I might say almost broken," the Prussian ambassador to Paris reported. "He had, he confessed,…committed a great blunder…If Prussia and Italy were now to persist in their opposition, he should be exposed to a deep humiliation…In some way or other, and most speedily, he must try to get out of this untenable position." Napoleon III's solution was to meekly acquiesce to Prussia's continuing its unimpeded conquest of Germany and Austria. He then further debased himself by whining for a piece of the spoils. "It would be a fine thing if the King

[Wilhelm] should do me a favor of this sort," he told the Prussian ambassador. "Everything taken into account, why should he not? We are such good friends now!" he wheedled.

It was thus left to Eugénie to inform Austria that France would not be sending an army into Germany to help save Vienna. It broke her heart to have to do it. "My Dear Prince," she wrote sorrowfully to Metternich on July 11, 1866. *"All that is humanely possible, I have done...My word has no more weight. I am almost alone in my opinion, to-day's danger is exaggerated the better to hide to-morrow's. As for me, I can tell you only one thing, and that is that I am miserable...If you could [only] give them a good drubbing!"* she agonized.

And it was precisely at this moment that Charlotte, in what can only be described as a monumental example of bad timing, popped up without warning to demand the requisition of fresh troops and funds for Mexico.

TRUTH BE TOLD, both Max and Charlotte had been shocked on their arrival by the somewhat primitive condition (by Western European standards) of their new empire. There was no telegraphic communication and the country's one railroad ran only a few miles inland from the Atlantic. Bandits operated with impunity, and the main road was so neglected that one of the imperial coaches carrying their retinue overturned on the long ride into Mexico City. The new emperor spent his first night in the capital sleeping on a billiard table because the palace sheets were infested with bedbugs.

Neither Max nor Charlotte ever let on that they were disappointed, however. To do so might have been taken as an admission that they had made a mistake. So they talked instead about the beauty of the scenery and the graceful culture they were encouraging. "I am sending you the program of a concert which we gave on Tuesday," Charlotte wrote to Eugénie after the couple had been in residence for six months. "It was not the Tuileries...but...one could not help considering it a very nice and presentable company...There were some very beautiful women, among them some of my ladies-in-waiting," she boasted.

But very quickly, numerous intransigent difficulties threatened to overwhelm them. Max, who wished to rule as an enlightened, benevolent sovereign, refused to buckle under to demands that the properties confiscated by Juarez be returned to their former aristocratic and priestly owners, and so he lost the backing of the influential conservative faction and the Church. The North's victory in the American Civil War emboldened Juarez and his supporters to escalate their attacks, and they began to make headway. The general in charge of pacifying the realm insisted that Max hang everyone caught conspiring with the enemy, or face the prospect of losing his empire; thus was liberal Max forced to employ even more brutal tactics than those for which he had so often criticized his brother Franz Joseph.

All of this was only exacerbated by a dearth of ready money. The proceeds of the original loan were long since spent; the silver mines were located in territory that Juarez still controlled; and swelling military expenses ate up what was left of customs and taxes. In December of 1865, Max was compelled to announce that he would be unable to reimburse France for some 25 million francs advanced to fund the Mexican army. In response, Napoleon III ordered the withdrawal of the French troops "as soon as possible."

An astonished Max protested this violation of their original agreement, but Louis Napoleon was quick to point out that it was the Mexican emperor himself who had first broken the contract by reneging on the payment. The general in charge of the French troops in Mexico strongly advised the imperial couple to decamp from the country under the protection of the departing force. Acceding to this counsel, Max prepared to abdicate.

And then Charlotte stepped in. She would under no circumstances hear of renouncing the throne. "Abdication amounts to pronouncing sentence on oneself, and writing oneself down as incompetent, and this is only admissible in old men and idiots," she scoffed. Instead, Charlotte insisted on making a personal appeal to Louis Napoleon to compel him to continue his support. "If one has neither credit nor money, one may win them so long as one has breath," she declared stoutly.

Shamed by her scorn, Max agreed to her plan, and Charlotte hurriedly left Mexico City on July 9, 1866, to sail to France. Neither she nor her husband had any idea that there was a war going on in Europe, much less that Prussia had just demolished the Austrian army and was in the process of marching on Vienna. Not that this seemed to make much of an impression on Charlotte once her ship docked in early August and she heard the news. Rather, she at once telegraphed to Napoleon III that she was coming to Paris to see him on an urgent matter.

As the emperor was still so debilitated that he spent much of his day in bed, it fell to Eugénie to handle the situation. She called on Charlotte at her hotel on August 10, the day after her arrival, and spent several hours listening as the empress of Mexico poured out a litany of grievances and explained the danger Max would be exposed to should the French withdraw their military and financial support now. Charlotte would afterwards report to her husband that, although Eugénie kept her countenance, she expressed such compassion for their predicament that Charlotte could feel that "tears were rising in her heart."

Eugénie knew better than to let sympathy cloud her judgment, however. Mexico had become an untenable burden, a drain on both the army and the treasury that, faced now with a direct threat from Prussia, France simply could not afford. Gently, Eugénie tried to make this clear to Charlotte.

But Charlotte would have none of it. She insisted on seeing the emperor. So, the next day, Eugénie had her former protégée driven out to Saint-Cloud, and both she and Louis Napoleon spent another long interview listening to Charlotte. Napoleon III was so weak and unhappy during this audience that he broke down and cried. Over the course of the next ten days, Charlotte also spoke to the minister for foreign affairs, the head of the treasury, and Prince Metternich. All turned down her requests. "I know more about China than these people here know about Mexico!" fumed the woman who had accepted the Mexican crown without knowing anything about Mexico, in a letter home to Max.

It was very warm in Paris, as August can be, and the visiting empress was often awake all night, running her arguments over and over in her head, and becoming more and more incensed at the injustice to which she and her husband were being subjected. These are the sorts of stressful conditions that can lead to a mental health crisis, and so it is not surprising that on August 22, after Napoleon III finally informed her bluntly that "it is henceforward *impossible* for me to give Mexico another *écu* or another man," Charlotte had one. "*He* [Napoleon III] *is the evil principle upon earth and wants to get rid of the good,*" she screeched in a long, incoherent letter to Max. "He is the Devil in person, and at our last interview yesterday he had an expression that would make one's hair stand on end, he was hideous... You must escape from his claws as soon as possible... It reminds me absolutely of the Apocalypse... It is enough to make any unbeliever believe in God to see the Devil so near," she ranted.

There is no question that both Louis Napoleon and Eugénie were distressed at having to say no to Charlotte, whose desperation was obvious. "I could plainly see how cruelly hurt she was," Napoleon III admitted. "We, too, were nearly crushed... by the sight of such anguish which nothing could appease." But neither he nor his wife expressed guilt, only disappointment. After all, they'd left the French regiments there for two whole years, more than enough time, they felt, for any halfway decent ruler to impose his will on a sprawling, turbulent, unfamiliar, fiercely contested new empire. "We have done our best by Maximilian," the emperor observed placidly, and Eugénie agreed.

Accordingly, as soon as Charlotte left Paris, Louis Napoleon wrote kindly to Maximilian, encouraging him to abdicate, and outlining how this could be done with honor, as he had once similarly advised the king of Naples. "The Empress of Mexico left Paris not very much pleased with her visit," Mérimée noted in a letter dated August 28, 1866. "She is going to Miramar... nobody doubts that she will speedily be rejoined by Maximilian."

The court was relieved to see her go. Max and Charlotte were but a sideshow; Bismarck was the main act. The Prussian army appeared unstoppable. They had rolled over the hapless Bavarian regiments, who had come into the field a month late. Wilhelm was collecting his forces for a final push through Bohemia.

"It is by no means improbable that there may be a battle with the Prussians over Vienna," Mérimée observed in a letter to England. "The great point is to find out what part the Hungarians wish to play. If they are not anxious to be shot in favour of the house of Hapsburg, the whole business will be finished in a fortnight by the collapse of Austria," he predicted coolly.

ELISABETH

Sisi in her Charles Worth coronation gown

24

The Empress to the Rescue

Thou hast pearls, thou hast diamonds also,
Hast all that mortals adore;
Thine eyes are among the fairest,—
My loved one, what wouldst thou have more? ...
And with thine eyes so beauteous
Hast thou tormented me sore,
And brought me to utter perdition,—
My loved one, what wouldst thou have more?

—Heinrich Heine

THE FEEBLENESS OF NAPOLEON III's response to Vienna's urgent request for aid in the week following the Prussian victory at Sadowa had caught the imperial court by surprise. Gaining the allegiance of a powerful nation like France, and thereby preventing Austria from becoming isolated like the last time, had after all been the whole point of ceding Venetia. Franz Joseph had certainly expected something more substantial for the province than two hectoring telegrams followed by a complete capitulation to Bismarck. "Ten days ago, Louis Napoleon was considered by his flatterers ... as master of the situation," the American ambassador stationed in Vienna apprised his daughter in a letter dated July 17, 1866. "He ... informs Prussia that she must at once make an armistice ... and orders Italy to stop short ... with an intimation that if she will sit up on her hind legs like a poodle and beg for it, he will one of these fine days toss her Venetia," the envoy snorted. "Prussia, . . . with one finger on her needle-gun trigger and another (let us suppose) upon her nose, laughed respectfully in the great Louis Napoleon's face . . . The moral of this . . . is . . . if you *will* be a great military power you must keep up with modern improvements. Especially if you will be dictator of Europe you must have something better than muzzle loaders," the ambassador noted drily.

In the light of the French betrayal, the failure to have come to terms with Hungary earlier in the year suddenly assumed alarming proportions. Franz Joseph could—and did—immediately recall his troops from Italy, so that they could be added to the 100,000 or so traumatized soldiers left of the northern army, but these would be insufficient to protect Vienna should the Hungarians decide to exploit the situation and revolt. And a rebellion of this nature was already in the planning stages. Bismarck, anticipating that he might need Hungary on his side, was in close communication with a disaffected Hungarian general who had men ready to fight against Franz Joseph. "I resolved to advise the king [Wilhelm] to make an appeal to the Hungarian nationality," the Prussian minister-president recorded later in his memoir of these events. "Our position might become so difficult that we should be obliged to seize every weapon offered us . . . in Hungary."

It thus became obvious, as soon as it was recognized that the approach to France had failed, that an imperial emissary must be sent to Pesth, charged with convincing the Hungarians to remain loyal to the emperor. There was never any question but that the individual best suited to this task was Sisi.

The choice of Elisabeth went far beyond her fluency in the language and her obvious sympathy for these recalcitrant subjects. Assigning this task to the empress was a deliberate reenactment of a celebrated episode in the entwined histories of the two realms. As Bismarck, in his arguments for the war, had evoked the brilliance (in his mind) of Frederick the Great, so the selection of Sisi for this risky mission was intended to conjure up the image of a young and beautiful Maria Theresa throwing herself on the mercy of the Hungarian Diet a century earlier in order to save Vienna from that same Prussian king. To make the parallel even more pronounced, Elisabeth resolved to take Rudolf and Gisela along, as Maria Theresa had taken her infant son, Joseph, the heir to her throne, and held him high before the Diet as a promise of her steadfast commitment to the gallant kingdom. Although Archduchess Sophia protested vociferously that the Hungarians were untrustworthy and it would be putting the imperial prince and princess in danger, Franz Joseph sided with his wife. "Take the children to Buda and be my advocate there," he told her.

And this was where the empress's long, lonely campaign in favor of Hungarian civil liberties, mocked for years by the court and Viennese society, paid off. Despite the best efforts of both the Prussians and an organized revolutionary movement bent on breaking away from Austria entirely—which took as its leader the fiery Hungarian statesman Lajos Kossuth, exiled in 1849 and now coordinating tactics from Italy—the reception given to Sisi and her children upon their arrival in Pesth on July 12 was flat-out heartwarming. It is doubtful that there was another person in Austria, including the emperor, who would have received anything close to a cordial welcome, let alone a mob of enthusiastic supporters. Elisabeth was used to it, but Rudolf, weeks from his eighth birthday, was so astounded at the hordes of people and the ringing cheers of *"Eljen!"* that he clung to his mother as they descended the station platform.

She entered immediately into conversations with Andrássy and Deák. The statesmen outlined the potentially explosive nature of the situation. At the moment, the majority of the population, whom they represented, still wished to remain united with Austria. But this could change at any moment. Both men assured Elisabeth that they would not attempt to exploit Vienna's current woes by increasing their demands. They asked only what they had asked before: an independent Diet and their traditional constitution, with a separate coronation for Franz Joseph and Sisi, for which there were also centuries of historical precedent, as an acknowledgment of Hungary's status as a kingdom within the empire. If these conditions were met, the Hungarians would remain loyal to Franz Joseph and his descendants, and would defend imperial territory as though it were their own.

Elisabeth had been around state councilors and other government officials in Vienna long enough to judge the superior vision and character of the men with whom she was now negotiating.* She knew they were telling her the truth. At once, Sisi notified her husband that she was sending Count Andrássy to Vienna, and that he must listen to him. Franz Joseph took her advice and met with the count, but when afterwards he informed Elisabeth that he remained unconvinced, she refused to back down. Rather, she renewed her pressure offensive, insisting that he speak to the venerable Deák himself. Again, while Franz Joseph conceded that the elder statesmen made a good impression, he remained obdurate. There would be no concessions to the Hungarians.

During this interval, the Prussians continued their relentless march southward, racking up victory after victory. "In a week or two of battles she [Prussia] has occupied Saxony, Bohemia, Moravia, and is looking grimly across the Danube into the very window of the Emperor's palace," the American ambassador informed his daughter. "On the right wing she has demolished Bavaria and the other south-western states, and she has occupied Frankfort. All Germany is in her grasp or at her feet." In response, Franz Joseph positioned his soldiers outside Vienna and prepared for an invasion. "The army, burning to wipe out the defeats of Bohemia,... is all for war," the American ambassador reported. "The emperor is for peace (I think). It is no joke to put an empire on one throw of the dice."

Elisabeth, still at the imperial palace in Buda with the children, was beside herself. "Whatever may happen, I shall be able to say honestly to Rudolf one day: 'I did everything in my power. Your misfortunes are not on my conscience,'" she presaged bitterly to her husband.

---

* Deák's loyalty may be measured by his observation, upon Sisi's arrival, "I should have considered it an act of cowardice to turn my back on the Empress in the day of her misfortune, after we had done homage to her when all was going well with the dynasty."

Battle was joined on the morning of July 22, 1866, when the Prussians attacked the Austrian forces arrayed outside of Pressburg, less than forty miles from Vienna. A ferocious firefight ensued. The artillery bombardment was intense; shells blanketed the area, spreading destruction and casualties. And then, suddenly, out of the blue, Franz Joseph's empire was saved—by Bismarck himself.

THE MINISTER-PRESIDENT'S RESTRAINT WAS born not of mercy, but rather of perspicacity and a thorough knowledge of previous military mistakes. To be too successful all at once invited an armed response from realms like Russia. Already, Tsar Alexander had put the Prussian ambassador on notice, warning, "The complete dethronement of entire dynasties troubles me."

Although Bismarck had as his ultimate goal the annexation of all of Germany, he was in no hurry to gulp down the whole region in one bite. Better to digest what they had already swallowed before going after the rest. To do this, a solid peace would be required, so that they would have time to build up the army again before renewing hostilities. "That a war with France would succeed that with Austria, lay in the logic of history," Bismarck reasoned coolly, "just as Frederick the Great had to defend the results of his first two . . . wars in the fiercer fire of the Seven Years' War." To prevent Austria from joining forces with Napoleon III at this inevitable future conflagration, it would be necessary "to avoid leaving behind in her any . . . desire for revenge," he concluded astutely.

And so, at the strategy meetings leading up to the attack, he had done his utmost to prevent the occupation of Vienna, which was a humiliation the Austrians would undoubtedly seethe to return. Rather, he urged the adoption of a cease-fire, followed by a generous peace. He even threatened to resign if his advice was ignored. "We get as easily intoxicated as discouraged," he wrote in frustration to his wife. "It is I that have the thankless task of pouring water into the foaming wine."

But his was the lone voice in the room for self-control. Not only the generals but also, comically, Wilhelm himself insisted on battle. The king had discovered (once he had begun winning) how much he liked war. He was particularly enraptured with the idea of giving Franz Joseph a good beating and then sweeping grandly into the Austrian capital as the acknowledged victor. There was nothing worse "than the existence of these small and powerless dynasties, who prolong their life at the expense of the national interests, [and] who perform their duties as sovereigns very unsatisfactorily," sniffed Wilhelm, the man who, less than two months earlier, had been exactly the type of monarch he now sought so gleefully to overthrow.

It had gone right down to the wire. The night before the battle began, a despairing Bismarck was standing in his room, wondering "whether it would not be better to fall out of the open window, which was four stories high," when the crown prince suddenly appeared. "You know that I was against this war," Fritz told the count. "If you are now persuaded that our end is attained and peace must now be concluded, I am ready to support you," and he went to see his father. He must have told him that he refused to fight, because thirty minutes later he was back with the news that the king, although irate, had agreed to call off the invasion. "Inasmuch as my Minister-President has left me in the lurch in the face of the enemy...I have discussed the question with my son; and...I find myself reluctantly compelled...to bite this sour apple and accept so disgraceful a peace," was the aggrieved note Wilhelm penned acknowledging this decision.

The cease-fire was called for noon the next day, July 22. At precisely that hour, the artillery bombardment already in process was halted, and the soldiers on both sides laid down their arms. Vienna was saved.

FRANZ JOSEPH WAS AGREEABLY surprised at the moderate terms offered by Bismarck. He had to give up all his influence in Germany, of course, and pay a hefty fine, but not only did he retain Vienna, Wilhelm also agreed to return all the territory the Prussians had conquered in Bohemia, including Prague. "We are severing our connection with Germany altogether," the emperor wrote to his wife. "After the experiences we have had with our dear German associates, I regard this as a piece of good fortune for Austria," he grunted. On the Italian side, Franz Joseph was forced to surrender Venetia and recognize the kingdom of Italy, but honor was saved when, improbably, just prior to the cease-fire, the tiny imperial navy won its first sea battle. "Poor Italy!" sighed the American ambassador to his daughter. "It was bad to be defeated...at Custozza. It was horrible to be insulted by the transfer of Venetia to France. But surely the deepest cut of all is to have her fleet signally conquered...by a small Austrian squadron, led by a colonel,...a most plucky affair on the part of the Austrians," the ambassador observed admiringly.

Elisabeth was naturally relieved to hear that Vienna had been saved from occupation (and that her brothers, who had fought with the over-matched Bavarian army against the Prussians, were not among the dead and wounded). But the speedy end of hostilities jeopardized the chances for a lasting political settlement with Hungary. Sisi knew her husband: once the pressure to compromise was removed, he would revert to his former, intractable stance that his Hungarian subjects follow the dictates handed down from Vienna. "There is no self-help, no ambition in Austria herself," the American ambassador asserted. "There is apoplexy [paralysis] at the top." Andrássy was more blunt. "The worst error of these [Austrian] Ministers is that they are asses," he told his wife.

The empress had seen firsthand the results of this rigid adherence to despotism and a centralized bureaucracy. Within a mere six years, Vienna had forfeited Lombardy, Tuscany, and Modena outright, as well as seeing imperial influence completely overthrown in Parma, Naples, and Rome. Now to this list of losses came Venetia and Germany. Sisi had visited Milan and lived in Venice, and so could contrast the difference in attitude between the citizenry in those locales and her Hungarian subjects. For heaven's sake, these people *wanted* to stay with Austria! To see them forced into the inevitable cycle of rebellion against Vienna's outdated policies, followed by brutal repression and military rule, when their leaders were advocating patient, peaceful arbitration, was more than she could bear.

Ministers like Bismarck, when they are unhappy with a decision, can threaten to resign; empresses cannot. There are, however, other ways for a wife to express her disappointment with her husband's choices, and her commitment to a cause. All that summer, Elisabeth kept up relentless emotional pressure on Franz Joseph. She positively tortured him. Except for a fleeting return to Vienna at the end of July, where they got into a big fight after he told her that it would be unfair to Bohemia to give Hungary special status, and another equally truncated visit in August, she remained in Buda.* To Sophia's wrath, Sisi did not even bring the children back to see their father on his birthday.† The harassed emperor, facing so much criticism that the Viennese papers were forbidden to report anything unfavorable about the war and its aftermath, was reduced to writing plaintive letters begging for her company, which he signed "Your poor little one," or "Your lonely little husband."

Even after she took Andrássy's advice and returned with the children in September, Elisabeth persevered in her efforts. As Bismarck, confident in his vision, had stood up first against public opinion, which had adamantly opposed the war, and later against Wilhelm's generals, who had lusted for conquest, so Sisi fought the Austrian court and aristocracy in her quest to convince her husband of the path she knew the crown had to take to survive. The empress's absence during the summer had provided the conservative faction in Vienna with ammunition against her—how could Elisabeth have left her husband and her Austrian and Bohemian subjects, made destitute by the war, at their time of need? In response, an unapologetic Sisi befriended a liberal, Jewish Hungarian journalist named Max Falk, with whom, to the horror of the court, she spent hours openly discussing the political situation, and from whom she obtained anti-authoritarian books banned by her husband's Jesuit educational minister.

It was a lonely battle. She was again ostracized as she had been at the

---

* The political situation in Bohemia was completely different from Hungary's. There was no equivalent to the moderate Deák-Andrássy majority in Prague. It was much more like Northern Ireland, with an entrenched Austrian-allied conservative minority in power. So Franz Joseph's rejecting Hungarian rights on this basis was comparing apples to oranges.

† I wonder where she learned that trick.

beginning of her marriage. But although the Viennese papers remained censored, the foreign newsmen were not, and they give perhaps a better sense of the stakes involved. "Though the Emperor's pride has received a series of rude shocks, and the mightiness of his dynastic and military power has been proved to be a mere spectral illusion, he is still full of prejudices, and utterly unlikely to adopt the principles of progress—popular rights, education, and press freedom—typical of the age we live in," observed the special Vienna correspondent for the *Daily Telegraph*. "How shall even as good a man as the Emperor is in many respects learn the truth...so long as he is surrounded by incompetent generals, who egg him on to foster his Frankenstein, the army, [and] by bigoted...Jesuits, amongst whose agents some of his most trusted Ministers are to be numbered?" the journalist queried hopelessly.

If Elisabeth needed any further evidence of how quickly the imperial family's position could deteriorate should Franz Joseph not hurry up and embrace a more enlightened approach, she had only to consider her sister Marie's situation. The queen of Naples had reluctantly returned to her husband, Francis, in Rome, only to have the war in Venetia break out. Although Victor Emmanuel lost in battle, he won the peace, and now the Eternal City was to be committed to the king of Italy's uncertain protection. By fall, the last of the French regiment that had been protecting the pope was in the process of withdrawing. Francis had been stripped of his estates and revenues, and the royal couple was so strapped for funds that Marie was obliged to unload a valuable pearl necklace at bargain basement prices to one of the wealthier Italian princesses. She and her husband, fearful of Victor Emmanuel's enmity, were actively considering emigrating to America.

At least they were until they saw Charlotte. *That* left a lasting impression. The empress of Mexico had originally departed Paris for Miramare but, conscious of her failure to help her husband, which preyed on her conscience, had decided to appeal personally to the pope and thereby obtain the additional funds and soldiers she had promised Max she would secure. She arrived in Rome towards the end of September.

The pope rewarded her with a private audience, but that was the extent of his generosity. Because Maximilian had not returned the church property seized by Juarez, the pontiff refused to sanction his government. A distraught Charlotte returned to her hotel, passed yet another sleepless night, and the next day exhibited the sort of behavior that could not help but attract the attention of the public.

The newspapers were full of the story: How the empress of Mexico had without warning burst into the Vatican at nine o'clock in the morning demanding to see the pope again, and raving "that there were designs on her life; that an attempt had been made to poison her at the Hotel de Rome; that she did not believe herself safe, and could not dine there." How the pontiff, concerned, broke off from his appointed schedule and had her brought to him, soothing her "with quite paternal kindness" and trying to get her to drink a cup of chocolate, which she at first refused, claiming it was poisoned, and then forgot was poisoned and drank. Towards the end of the day, the reports ran, the papal household tried to get her to go back to her hotel but she broke out in hysterics, wailing that she would sleep in the street rather than put herself in the hands of her treacherous entourage, so the pope had no choice but to indulge her again. A bed was accordingly set up for her in the library. It was the only time in recorded history that a woman was officially permitted to stay overnight in the Vatican.

The next day, they got her out by a ruse: the Mother Superior of a nearby convent came to collect her, ostensibly so that they could visit an orphanage. They made the mistake of touring the kitchen, where Charlotte abruptly plunged her hand into a pot of stew bubbling away nicely on the stove and burned herself so badly that she fainted. This gave the nuns the opportunity to return her to her hotel for medical care, but as soon as Charlotte came to and realized where she was, she began screaming. Convinced that she was going to die, she made out her will and wrote a few lines of farewell to her husband. Her Mexican retainers had to be dismissed as she accused them all, as well as Napoleon III, and sometimes even Max himself, of wanting her dead. Marie and Francis came to visit her during this period; she would only eat if a cat ate the food first. Eventually, her brother came to collect her and brought her back to Miramare, where a Viennese doctor was waiting to treat her. His prognosis was grim: "There is but a slender chance of recovery, because bodily health seems to be completely restored, while there is no trace of the mind perceiving the aberration that is clouding it, nor of any mental resistance." Almost as soon as Charlotte got there she tried to escape by jumping out of an upper-story window. They caught her in time and from then on she was kept on the ground floor under close supervision.

But neither Charlotte's predicament nor Marie's had any effect on Franz Joseph, who, caught as always between his mother's rigid conservatism and his wife's compassionate liberalism, had retreated once more behind the ponderous machinery of bureaucracy. And it was here, of all places, that Hungary found an unexpected ally.

As HAD HAPPENED THE LAST TIME Austria endured a devastating loss, popular anger was such that the emperor had been forced to sack his foreign minister, to whom (along with the commanding general, of course) was ascribed the official blame for the catastrophic defeat. Elisabeth immediately pushed her husband to assign Count Andrássy to the post, but Franz Joseph dismissed her choice, claiming that the appointment would show favoritism to the Hungarians. His rejection on this basis put him into a bit of a bind, however. He could not, in good conscience, approve a Bohemian candidate without falling prey to the same complaint from the Hungarians, and he'd already been through so many Austrian cabinet officials that there really wasn't anyone of sufficient rank and experience left to take the job.

This dilemma was ultimately resolved by the appointment of Baron Ferdinand Beust, formerly minister of Saxony. Although Franz Joseph had insisted as part of the peace settlement with Bismarck that the king of Saxony's realm be returned to him, it was clear that the monarch would have no need of an independent foreign minister, as it was understood that the Saxon government would follow Prussian policies or risk occupation again. It seemed a waste to let a competent official like Beust retire just when the empire was in such desperate need of a skilled diplomat, so despite the baron's idiosyncrasies—he was "a foreigner, a German, and a Protestant," as Franz Joseph's principal minister, a Jesuit, protested in alarm—the emperor nonetheless tapped the baron to fill the vacancy.

The demands of the Hungarians naturally fell within the new foreign minister's portfolio, and in December 1866, just before Elisabeth's twenty-ninth birthday, Beust made a quick trip to Pesth to meet with Deák and Andrássy. He wasn't there more than a few days before he came back to Vienna and told Franz Joseph in no uncertain terms to take the deal they were offering. The conservative faction again put up a fight, but Beust made it clear that it was him or them. In the end, Franz Joseph, "with tears in his eyes," fired his Jesuit councilor and accepted Beust's recommendation.

And so a man who could not speak the language, who had no real knowledge of Hungary, its institutions, leaders, peoples, or cultural or political history, and who had been in his post for less than six months, was credited with negotiating the groundbreaking power-sharing agreement known as the dual monarchy, whereby Franz Joseph and Elisabeth, in addition to their roles as emperor and empress, were to be crowned king and queen of Hungary, and the Hungarians, while still belonging to the empire, retained an independent, elected Diet and constitution. *It was the only time in the entire nineteenth century that seemingly intractable political differences between two states were resolved without recourse to bloodshed.*

And make no mistake, the path to this agreement was forged by Sisi. It was she who had devoted the past seven years of her life to mastering the difficult language necessary to convince the Hungarians of her sincerity; she who, employing glamour and celebrity, the two most potent weapons in her arsenal, had signaled her support of the kingdom's leaders, opening a direct channel of communication with them; she who had defied the disapproval and dogma of the court and the ruling aristocracy to promote their cause; she who had insisted on addressing this pressing political responsibility despite her husband's ardent desire to evade it. It is no exaggeration to say that Beust slipstreamed into the history books on the hem of Sisi's spectacular velvet-and-silk Charles Worth coronation gown.

The Hungarians knew it. Count Andrássy called her "the 'beautiful Providence' who watches over" the realm. The Diet, in grateful acknowledgment of her efforts, presented her with Gödöllő, a charming country estate that she had admired but been unable to buy due to the poverty of the imperial treasury. The coronation ceremony, which took place on June 8, 1867, was so jammed that the *Times* correspondent did not even try to estimate the size of the crowd. "It must be sufficient to say that the windows, the seats, the platforms, and the sides of the streets all along the route—at least three miles—were filled with people in their best...the centre of the world is just for the time this capital of Hungary on the lordly Danube," he admitted.

A magnificent procession, like something out of "a beautiful dream," preceded the ritual. Hussars in colorful uniforms and magnates in silks trimmed with pearls and fur sat astride horses draped in cloth-of-gold, sporting ostrich feathers and jeweled harnesses. Velvet-clad footmen ran beside the royal trumpeters and drummers. Elisabeth arrived at the church in a glass carriage that had been used by Maria Theresa herself.

She and her husband followed the age-old coronation rites. Franz Joseph was anointed with holy oil and then enveloped in the mantle of Saint Stephen (circa AD 1031 and looked it). The traditional Hungarian crown, also dating from the saint, had had to be returned to the capital for the ceremony (it had been kept in Vienna since the revolution of 1849 to prevent anyone else's being crowned with it). Andrássy had the honor of settling the heavy diadem on the new king's head.

Then it was Sisi's turn. "Words cannot describe this scene," reported the special correspondent for the *Morning Post*. "The Magnates advanced to meet her, and with that sweet, sad smile, that regal dignity, and that queenly step which are world-renowned, she moves towards the altar and kneels." Andrássy took the crown from Franz Joseph and held it over her head. The service concluded with Elisabeth taking her place on a throne beside her husband's, where "a lot more Latin was said," volunteered Rudolf, who was present at the ceremony and had to write a 400-word essay about it for his tutor.

There remained but one final ritual: the sword-waving ceremony. The entire company reassembled outside at the base of a small hill. Franz Joseph, seated on a white charger, grasped the heavy sword of Saint Stephen, lifted it high, and spurred his horse up the incline. Pausing at the crest, he pointed the blade north, south, east, and west as a symbol of his commitment to protect the kingdom from all directions, just as Maria Theresa had done a century earlier. "The enthusiasm became delirium," observed the London *Standard*.

Thus was the rift with Hungary, from which had snowballed so many disasters—the failure to reciprocate in Crimea after Russia had helped suppress the rebellion; the subsequent reneging on the military alliance with France, resulting in Austrian diplomatic isolation; the payback by Napoleon III in Italy, which in turn had led to the recent shellacking by Bismarck—healed. "I was not yet a member of the dynasty at that time, when a number of things were done in the name of my husband, then quite a young man, which he regrets more than anybody," Sisi told a Hungarian author who attended the coronation. "Were it in our power, we two should be the first to recall...the martyrs [of the brutal suppression of 1849] to life," the new queen of Hungary assured him.

"For three centuries we had tried faith, then again and again hope, till only one possibility remained: that the nation should be ready to love some member of the reigning house from the depths of its heart," a Hungarian poet observed. "Now that we have succeeded in this, I have no more fear for the future."

EUGÉNIE

Max leading his men

25

An Exhibition of Imperial Honor

The difference between treason and patriotism is only a matter of dates.

—Alexandre Dumas

IN THE FALL OF 1866, while Sisi was still forcefully expressing her displeasure at her husband's failure to compromise with his Hungarian subjects, Eugénie and Louis Napoleon were huddled at Biarritz trying to assess the damage done to their interests and influence by the unexpectedly brilliant showing of the Prussian army in its recent campaign against Austria and Germany. Although both were aware that French prestige had taken a blow, they were equally confident that the empire would soon recover from this setback. After enduring a prolonged period of crippling illness, Napoleon III was thankfully feeling well enough to resume the task of governing. Even better, he and Eugénie, faced for the first time in their reign with a serious threat from the Prussians, were brought together by the crisis. There were no more marital spats. From this time on, the emperor and empress supported each other and worked closely as a team.

The first order of business was obviously to rebuild and modernize the military, which had previously fallen victim to budget cuts. Louis Napoleon, who had been an artillery man like his famous uncle, recognized the need to equip his soldiers with a firearm that would rival the needle gun. "Here in France they are in earnest about getting this deadly weapon," the London *Daily Telegraph* testified. The imperial government surveyed 200 different types of rifles, including the American Remington, before coming down in favor of the French-made Chassepot as being superior even to the needle gun. "The Prussian weapon may be made to discharge eight shots in the minute, but the French no fewer than twelve," another paper observed. "As regards accuracy, it is well known that the needle gun is at long ranges very untrustworthy, while, with the Chassepot rifle it is a common thing for a soldier...firing from a distance of 540 yards at a target only six and a-half feet square, out of a hundred shots to hit [the target] a hundred times." Mérimée, invited to Biarritz that September, showed up with one of these state-of-the-art guns to give Eugénie a demonstration of its murderous efficiency. "A heavy expenditure will be required for the reorganization of the army, especially for renewing the armaments," the senator warned matter-of-factly.

But it wasn't just the imperial weaponry that required an upgrade. It had been made abundantly clear over the summer that the emperor had to be ready at a moment's notice to muster an immense army, should the Prussians and the Italians suddenly take it into their heads to combine against France as they had against Austria. This meant recruiting, training, and outfitting hundreds of thousands of men. To this chore were added France's numerous diplomatic worries. "The Emperor...is very much preoccupied with a number of things, each one producing its contingent embarrassments—Mexico, Venetia, Germany, the Pope,...the bad harvest, and needle guns. All these...have to be settled at one and the same time," Mérimée lamented.

There was one challenge that superseded all the others, however. The weakness Napoleon III had displayed over the summer had undermined his popularity, and this in turn threatened the longevity of his government. He and Eugénie needed to find a way to remind their subjects and the rest of Europe of the empire's greatness, and they needed to do it quickly.

Fortunately, they had just the vehicle. A second international exhibition, even more grandiose and ambitious than the one they had hosted during the Crimean War, was scheduled to open in Paris the following year. Louis Napoleon may have been unsuccessful at luring the other heads of state to the capital for a diplomatic conference, but who would say no to being entertained on a princely scale at what promised to be the party of the century? And what better way to reestablish the preeminence of France as the center of culture and technological progress, and bring pride and glory to its citizens (not to mention a much-needed increase in cash flow from millions of wealthy tourists), than to show off the newly modernized Paris in all its splendor? Invitations to attend the Exposition Universelle as a special guest of their imperial majesties went out to all the monarchs of Europe.

The emperor and empress's political instincts again proved unerring. The bait was irresistible. The acceptances poured in.

THE NEW YEAR'S FESTIVITIES of 1867 were celebrated at court with the same reckless gaiety as they had been in the past, and preparations for the international exposition, a vast undertaking involving industrial, agricultural, scientific, decorative, and cultural innovations and wares from nearly thirty countries—including, for the first time, Japan, Persia, and Egypt—proceeded apace. Both Eugénie and her husband projected an air of energy and optimism, and spent long hours planning and organizing the many brilliant entertainments necessary to amuse and impress their royal visitors. However, although Louis Napoleon had weathered what seems to have been a dangerous urinary tract infection over the summer, this didn't mean he was suddenly healthy. Sadly, bladder stones the size of robins' eggs don't go away on their own. "The poor Emperor was subjected to a terrible necessity of self-command at this time," attested Anna, the governess. "Sovereigns cannot have a headache with impunity; if they are reported to have the least indisposition, stocks fall, a financial commotion occurs, and fortunes are lost in a day. After the most intense suffering, the Emperor appeared at balls and theaters to pacify the public." By February, the strain was already beginning to show. Baron Heeckeren, who attended the opening session of the legislative assembly, was struck by the change in Napoleon III's manner. "Their Majesties' entrance seemed to me coldly received—a bad sign," the banker recorded in his diary. "The Emperor read his speech rather quickly, rather low...Never was I so much struck by this fact: *he is tired.* A tired Emperor, like a sick King...is a serious thing," he worried.

Diplomatic setbacks did not improve the situation. Bismarck scornfully refused to help Napoleon III save face and pretend that the war had somehow been a boon to France. He denied the emperor's many half-bullying, half-pathetic entreaties that the French be allotted some form of territorial compensation—the emperor thought Belgium would be nice—for having so graciously agreed to remain neutral during the conflict. And the Mexican venture had turned into an outright fiasco. Although a transatlantic cable had finally been laid linking the coast of Mexico to France, the line did not extend into the interior of the country, so communications were still delayed, which often resulted in conflicting reports from one day to the next. Just three months earlier, Max, having learned of Charlotte's collapse, had informed Louis Napoleon that he would be returning to Europe with the French forces. "At the moment of leaving a country where such hard trials awaited me, and which was to strike a blow at my tenderest affections, I write...begging you to assure Her Majesty the Empress of my respectful attachment...and the sincere friendship with which I am Your Majesty's good brother," was the gist of his fawning letter. And yet, despite this seemingly definitive resolution, there was no sign of Max when the last of the French regiments stationed in Mexico arrived in Paris in February 1867.

Puzzled, Eugénie made inquiries and discovered that the Austrian court had expressed the opinion that the hapless monarch should remain at his post. Franz Joseph was already unpopular enough for having lost the recent war against Prussia; the last thing the family needed was to have his humiliated younger brother crawl back to Vienna, another potent symbol of Habsburg failure. "I...*fully* approve the fact that, in spite of your natural desire to hasten to Charlotte, you have stayed in Mexico," Archduchess Sophia wrote to her son in January, the first of three times in one letter that she told him to stay put. "I can only rejoice in it, and hope profoundly that the rich people in the country will make your remaining there possible," she continued before reiterating forcefully in conclusion that, while she missed him, *"I am bound to want you to stay in Mexico now as long as this is possible, and can be done with honor."* To discourage Max even further, the court let it be known that he would not be welcomed home unless he renounced all claim to his Mexican title, a dignity for which he had already forfeited his Austrian succession rights. When Eugénie protested to Princess Metternich that the archduke should not be punished in this way, her friend replied that Vienna was within its prerogative to "refuse to have anything to do with an heir presumptive who had already accepted one throne and been unable to maintain himself upon it."

The ignominy associated with the withdrawal of the French army from Mexico was not confined to Max. Some 6,000 soldiers had died, and millions of francs had been squandered, in support of the failed enterprise. Public opinion, which had never been more than lukewarm to the undertaking, was now openly hostile. Many ordinary citizens, trusting in Napoleon III's government, had speculated in Mexican bonds; the returning regiments were thus ostracized as heralding the loss of these investments. The empress was roundly blamed for the disaster. The head of the secret police reluctantly reported to Louis Napoleon that the common people were angry about Mexico, and said of Eugénie, "it is the fault of the Spanish woman," as they had once said "it is the fault of the Austrian woman" about Marie Antoinette.

And so it was in the midst of this trying political environment that the emperor and empress of the French, in desperate need of a public relations triumph, opened the glorious Exposition Universelle of 1867.

SET ON THE CHAMP DE MARS, the main exhibition stadium, an enormous, two-story, steel-and-glass elliptical amphitheater, was designed to be the most technologically advanced building on the planet.

Equipped with hot and cold running water, piped-in gas, and electric lighting, it covered an area of 119 acres.* Something like 50,000 exhibits were on display. The building was divided into rings. The outer ring housed heavy machinery, with successive inner rings devoted to clothing, furniture, textiles, jewels, gadgets, science, and the fine arts. Encircling this immense structure were outdoor cafés at which visitors could sample various international specialties (the United States set up a bar), while a hot air balloon stood ready to offer an aerial tour of the surroundings. Those who found climbing the stairs to the upper floor tiring could take advantage of a new invention called "an elevator."

The exhibits themselves were a fascinating jumble of the exotic, the luxurious, and the ingenious. A Japanese tearoom vied for piquancy with a Buddhist temple and a replica of a villa owned by the Bey of Tunis. The Egyptian contingent brought an impressive model of the Suez Canal, which was in the process of being built by Eugénie's cousin, Ferdinand de Lesseps (at whose mother's salon a young María Manuela had first met her future husband, Don Cipriano). There was a "human aquarium," basically a large, glass-enclosed pool inside of which could be glimpsed "a fantastical being gamboling in the water," as one amazed visitor recounted. This mysterious creature, who turned out to be a man dressed in a bubble-helmeted diving suit, so captured the imagination of another spectator, a struggling French author by the name of Jules Verne, that he immediately went home and wrote a novel entitled *Twenty Thousand Leagues Under the Sea*.

The exhibition was a huge, unqualified triumph for the French throne. "The Exposition!" raved Baron Heeckeren. "The great event of the year! On April 1st, the opening day, a madding crowd. A hundred thousand people jostling and pushing for the barriers...and what wonders, to be sure—wonders upon wonders!" Lillie Moulton, the young American ice skater, agreed. "You can listen to the different national musics, and see the different national types and costumes, and

---

* The building utilized an early version of electricity called arc lighting. This technology was later supplanted by Thomas Edison's incandescent light bulb, which was not invented until 1879.

eat the different national foods," she prattled to her mother. "We go almost every day, and it is always a delight... The Exposition is a complete success. You pass from one lovely thing to the other."

In June, the illustrious imperial guests began arriving. "It rains kings, princes, and grandees in Paris," Baron Heeckeren observed. "The great ones of the earth appear one by one." Lillie helpfully listed some of them for her mother: "The Emperor of Russia, who is very handsome and stately; the King of Prussia, who is accompanied by the colossal Count Bismarck, very noticeable in his dazzling white uniform, and wearing a shining helmet with an enormous spread eagle on top of it, which made him tower still more above ordinary mortals... He clank-d his sword on the pavement, quite indifferent to the stare of wondering Frenchmen... The Prince of Italy looks rather small by the side of these German giants," she giggled. "The Khedive of Egypt, the Shah of Persia, the ex-Queen of Spain, and other sovereigns are flitting about." Franz Joseph and Elisabeth had also accepted but, due to the exhausting festivities surrounding their Hungarian coronation, were not expected until the end of the month.

Naturally, there were some small hiccups. A disgruntled Polish dissident took a shot at the tsar while he was being driven back from the Bois de Boulogne in an open carriage alongside his host. Luckily, the would-be assassin missed. Napoleon III did his best to make light of the incident. "Now we have been under fire together!" he exclaimed jovially to Alexander. And then suddenly, after having had no communication from Mexico for two months, the newspapers began reporting that Maximilian had somehow fallen into the hands of the opposition forces under President Benito Juarez and had been commanded to stand trial for treason. But this crisis, too, had been quickly and efficiently averted: the crowned heads of Europe had simply banded together to put pressure on the Americans to protect the unhappy monarch. "It is understood that the President of the United States,... having been addressed by several European sovereigns,... lost no time in communicating with Juarez," the Parisian correspondent for the *Morning Post* reported. "A telegram is said to have reached Vienna lately saying that the Austrian prince would be allowed to leave Mexico immediately after his trial." On June 17, William Seward, the American secretary of state, went out of his way to assure Franz Joseph's ambassador in Washington that Max's "life is quite as safe as yours and mine."

For Eugénie, the Exposition, and particularly the month of June, with its influx of lofty dignitaries, resembled nothing so much as an endurance test of her hospitality skills. One gorgeous, exquisitely rendered ball after another consumed her nights, while her days were spent organizing and attending a succession of receptions, teas, tours of the exhibition, speeches, and drives around the capital. "The sovereigns are working themselves to death, and almost killing their attendants," Lillie informed her mother flatly. Baron Heeckeren noticed as well. "How fatiguing for Napoleon and Eugénie!" the banker recorded in his diary. "Years like this use up a ruler, no doubt of that. His Majesty seems more and more weary."

But it was worth it. Both the empress and the emperor could feel the change in mood in Paris, the enthusiasm of the crowds, and the grudging respect of their royal guests. To underscore that whatever small frailty or indecision he might have displayed the previous year had passed, Napoleon III made sure to invite his fellow sovereigns to accompany him as he reviewed tens of thousands of French troops on parade. Even the cynical Mark Twain, in town with a tour group of Americans, was impressed with this patriotic demonstration of military capability. "With colors flying and a grand crash of military music, a gallant array of cavalry men emerged from the dust... After them came a long line of artillery; then more cavalry... The vast concourse of people swung their hats and shouted—the windows and house-tops in the wide vicinity burst into a snow-storm of waving handkerchiefs... It was a stirring spectacle," the humorist admitted.

But officers in dress uniform practicing drills are not the same as an experienced fighting force. Bismarck had a good look at Louis Napoleon's soldiers, as well as the Tuileries' offerings at the Exposition, and remained complacent. The French exhibits focused on luxury goods, textiles, and art. The Prussians by contrast, had brought with them a display "bristling with cannons," as one spectator noted. The huge guns were technically praiseworthy "if one did not feel tempted to place by the side of these figures the number of human beings these murderous engines are destined to kill," the visitor concluded thoughtfully.

Fortunately, the court had only to keep up this frenetic pace of revelry until July 1, when the emperor, the empress, and the eleven-year-old prince imperial were scheduled to hand out prizes for the most outstanding entries at the Exposition. This event, a star-studded, full-court dress affair, would mark the end of the bulk of the royal entertainments. The day at last arrived, and the auditorium was packed with foreign dignitaries and the cream of Parisian society awaiting the appearance of the exalted guests and their imperial hosts, when Napoleon III was suddenly handed an urgent telegram informing the French government that the emperor of Mexico had been shot.

MAX WAS ALREADY PACKED and ready to depart with the French troops when he received the intelligence that he would have to give up his title and pretensions to the thrones of both Mexico and Austria if he wished to be welcomed back to Vienna or Miramare. Even with this blow to his pride, he wavered. The news of Charlotte's insanity had come as a terrible shock to the Mexican emperor; as late as November 1866 Max had still been expecting his wife to return with some form of aid, either in terms of money or troops. When instead he learned that she was under the care of a doctor who ran a lunatic asylum, he broke down. Unable to make the decision himself, he queried everyone around him, even his personal physician, as to what he should do. The members of the conservative faction who had the most to fear from Juarez, as well as his servants and those officers of the national army who remained genuinely loyal to their sovereign, knew to appeal to his sense of duty. "If Your Majesty were to leave us, it would be a terrible misfortune for the people," the head of his household beseeched him.

In this way was Max induced to stay and put his faith in the approximately 4,000 soldiers who wished to fight for him. This group was not without initial success. Although Juarez's army far outnumbered Maximilian's, the enemy forces were not as well trained, and the imperial troops were able to surprise small groups of them at a time. In fact, at one of these early skirmishes, a cavalry captain almost succeeded in capturing Juarez himself, prompting Max to order that, should a similar opportunity occur in the future, the opposition leader was to be taken prisoner so he could stand trial for treason. These instructions were very inconveniently leaked and brought to Juarez's attention.

The capital being too easily penetrable to defend, in February 1867, Max and his men fell back on the fortress town of Querétaro, some 140 miles northwest of Mexico City.* Once arrived, the emperor tried to set up direct negotiations with the opposition to have the conflict resolved by a national congress. Juarez used the two months or so that Max spent promoting this idea to surround Querétaro with 40,000 troops. Although again, Max's men won some small sorties, they lacked money, and so rapidly ran out of ammunition and provisions. Eventually, it was decided that they should try to get away into the hills by breaking through the enemy lines. This plan was betrayed to Juarez's forces by one of the emperor's closest associates in exchange for 2,000 ounces of gold, on the condition that Max be allowed to escape unharmed.

And so, at four thirty in the morning of May 15, the traitor, one Colonel Lopez, let Juarez's men into Querétaro. The imperial forces, surprised in their sleep, laid down their arms; most joined with the enemy. Lopez tried to help the emperor evade capture, but Max considered it ignoble to flee. Rather, he insisted on ceremonially presenting his sword to Juarez's commanding general, after which he graciously volunteered to leave the country quietly, requesting only that he be escorted to a port on the Atlantic Ocean for this purpose. His opponent being unfamiliar with chivalric European customs, the whole

---

* Just as Sisi's sister Marie and her husband, Francis, had initially abandoned Naples for Gaeta.

sword gesture fell rather flat, and Max was taken prisoner and confined to a cell in a convent, in which were prominently displayed a crucifix and silver candlesticks. As Max was unfamiliar with the traditions of the Mexican penal system, he did not realize that the presence of these objects commonly signaled that the occupant of the cell had been condemned.

It is true that the United States, prompted by the outcry from Max's many sovereign relatives, sought to have the failed emperor released, and even guaranteed the independence and continuation of Juarez's rule against any subsequent European encroachment if the Mexican president would just agree to commute the prisoner's sentence. Other emissaries went even further: the Prussian ambassador tried to bribe Juarez, and the wife of one of Max's most loyal officers fell on her knees, wailing for a pardon. But the victorious Juarez remained obdurate. He had lost too many men in the war, and the country had suffered from the prolonged conflict. An example had to be made to prevent a repetition of this sort of escapade in the future.

On June 15, Emperor Maximilian of Mexico, along with two of his generals, was officially convicted of treason and condemned to the firing squad. He was given a grace period of three days in which to get his affairs in order. He wrote goodbye letters to his wife, his mother, his brothers, and many other friends and retainers.*

On June 19, 1867, Maximilian awoke and, together with his two generals, was taken to a small hill outside of Querétaro. It was a beautiful summer morning. Max did his best to keep up the courage of his companions. "What a glorious day!" he told them. "I have always wanted to die on just such a day." He had saved a gold piece for each member of the firing squad. "Muchachos, aim well, and aim right here," he told them, placing his hand on his heart.

They shot him five times, but he was still breathing when the officer in charge went to examine the body. Max had fallen forward on his

---

* He did not, however, write to Sisi, another indication that they were never romantically involved.

face but the captain ordered that the dying man be turned over. Pointing his sword at the emperor's chest, the officer indicated the need for another bullet. One of the musket men then stood directly over the body and shot Max through the heart at such close range that his shirt had powder burns. It was over.

EUGÉNIE AND LOUIS NAPOLEON, hoping against hope that the telegram they had received was just another example of the confusion they had experienced in the past when dealing with news from Mexico, went on with the prize ceremony as though nothing had happened. The winners were announced one by one, and made their way to the stage, where they took their awards from the hands of the shyly smiling prince imperial. The event went on for hours and no one was the wiser; Lillie gushed to her mother that "the gentlemen, splendid in their gala uniforms, were covered with decorations, and all the ladies present were *en grande toilette* and low-necked, and displayed every jewel they possessed."

But when it was over, and they were back at the Tuileries, they discovered that the report from Mexico was only too true. Eugénie retired to her rooms in tears, and the French court went into mourning for three weeks.

The news spread rapidly over Europe; the papers reveled in the details of Maximilian's trial and execution. "The feeling in Paris is very strong," reported the correspondent for the *Daily News*. "The Emperor Maximilian has been executed," observed one of the Parisian papers. "He has paid with his blood the cruel fault of an abortive enterprise, which will form the most lamentable page of contemporary history...Maximilian condemned to death, like a common criminal, by a council of war,...his wife bowed down by a woe which has extinguished her reason, slowly pining away at Miramar!" Lillie, who saw Prince Metternich soon afterward, wrote to her mother, "I never would have believed that he could be so affected as he seemed to be by this. He cried like a baby when he told us of the Emperor's last days, of his courage and fortitude." But not all the papers were respectful. "Prince Metternich was most indignant at…an article in *La Lanterne* [that] called the royal martyr 'the Arch-dupe,'" Lillie confided.

Eugénie agonized over what to do about the Austrian court. Franz Joseph cancelled his and Elisabeth's visit to the Exposition as soon as the news broke, and Prince Metternich urged that the emperor and empress of the French travel instead to Vienna to express their condolences personally to the family. "It will be the most painful thing in the world to find myself face to face with a brother and a mother to whose grief I have contributed by my insistence upon the expedition to Mexico," Eugénie protested. "If I had already known the Emperor, the Empress, and the Archduchess Sophie, I should long since have thrown myself into their arms to show them what I feel, though that they can hardly doubt. But since I do not know them, I am afraid I may seem too cold or too tragic," she quailed.

But she knew the ambassador was right, and so, after the required period of mourning, she plucked up her courage and accompanied her husband to Salzburg, where the Austrian court was then in attendance. For the first time in their reigns, Eugénie and Sisi, the two most fashionable empresses in Europe, were going to meet.

ELISABETH

Sisi's youngest daughter, Marie Valerie

26

The Empress Breaks Free

The rose and the lily, the dove and the sun,
I loved them all dearly once, every one;
I love them no longer, I love now alone
The small one, the neat one, the pure one, mine own.
Yes, she herself, the fount of all love,
Is the rose and the lily, the sun and the dove.

—Heinrich Heine

THE FESTIVITIES SURROUNDING FRANZ JOSEPH'S and Elisabeth's Hungarian coronations had barely ended, and the imperial couple, together with Gisela and Rudolf, had returned to Ischl, when a telegram suddenly arrived with the bewildering news that Nene's husband was dead. The prince of Thurn and Taxis was only thirty-five years old when he succumbed unexpectedly to illness on June 26, 1867. His health had perhaps been affected by his having stood loyally by his brother-in-law during the recent war. Courageously leading a cavalry brigade against the Prussians at Sadowa, Nene's husband was among those who, having survived this harrowing deployment, were then forced to endure the Austrians' grueling retreat. The family tragedy was compounded by the fact that Nene had only a month earlier given birth to her fourth child. The widow was in no condition to manage the distress, which included (now that Wilhelm ruled all of northern

Germany, another consequence of Franz Joseph's shellacking) Bismarck's insistence that the family cede their extremely lucrative ownership rights to the German postal service to Prussia. Although the count, as was his custom, tried to disguise the ruthlessness of the appropriation by offering the dynasty 3 million thalers in compensation, there was no hiding the reality that this was a forced sale.

The emperor and empress had at once hurried to Bavaria to provide what solace they could. The rest of Sisi's family was still gathering around the bereaved when, on July 1, Franz Joseph received the same shocking intelligence Napoleon III had just before the prize ceremony taking place that day in Paris, that Max, coincidentally also only thirty-five years old, had been shot. The emperor at once set off for Vienna to comfort his mother while a shaken Elisabeth elected instead to spend the night at Possi with her parents and siblings before heading back to Ischl to be with her children.

Upon his arrival, Franz Joseph found Archduchess Sophia in a state of collapse. She and the rest of the family had all believed Max to be safe; captured, yes, but facing exile, not execution. Now, confronted with the tragic results of its policies, the Austrian court belatedly attempted to justify its earlier behavior. The extent to which the family felt culpable may be demonstrated by the swiftness with which they, who so rarely commented publicly (Sisi's guilt in provoking the death of little Sophie being the big exception to this rule), released a statement. "The Vienna papers contain the following communication, which appears to be official," the foreign correspondent for the *Daily News* reported only two days after Max's death had been confirmed in Europe. " 'It may be interesting to learn the steps taken months ago by the Austrian government to avert this terrible catastrophe...Upon the withdrawal of the French troops, the Emperor of Austria, thinking that the Emperor Maximilian would leave Mexico...thought it advisable to take the question into consideration whether [his] return should not be facilitated by restoring to him all his rights...which he renounced before leaving...The reason for no further action being then taken in the matter...was that the Emperor Maximilian remained in Mexico.' "

The communiqué went on to disclose that, once Max had been imprisoned and charged with treason, it had been "at once resolved, at a council of the imperial family, to restore . . . all his rights," as a way of assuring his captors that the archduke, returned to his prestigious position as second in line to the Austrian throne, would have no further need to press his claims to the disputed territory, and could be safely exiled. But of course Juarez had not cared two sticks about the rights of the Austrian succession — it was *Max* to whom it would have made all the difference, had this concession been granted in time for him to withdraw with the French troops. Sophia's despair might possibly have been augmented by the remembrance that it was she who had strongly encouraged her second son to remain at his post, and that Max might yet be alive if they had all behaved a little more generously to him.

Sisi, surrounded by this atmosphere of death, sorrowing for both Nene and Max, was unwell again. "I am so utterly miserable that I could cry all day," she wrote to Franz Joseph, who was kept in Vienna laboring to get his brother's remains returned so they could be entombed in the family vault. She had been so happy in Hungary that she had even relented and begun sleeping with her husband again; now, depressed and ill, she protested at the thought of meeting the emperor and empress of the French, who had asked to personally express their condolences. But Franz Joseph told her how much he was dreading his interview with Napoleon III, and she knew it would be even worse for him if she were not there to entertain Eugénie, so towards the middle of August she steeled herself for the inevitable press frenzy associated with the visit, and traveled to Salzburg to receive her imperial guests.

The meeting seems to have gone better than either side expected, largely because Louis Napoleon, and especially his wife, worked so hard to be respectful and compassionate. "The Empress Eugénie astonished and delighted everyone by the graceful and yet dignified manner in which she held the receptions," the Austrian minister, Count Beust, reported. Although the newspapers made the event into a glamour contest, in fact this rendezvous, held in the shadow of Max's gruesome death, was the last place Eugénie wished to shine. "It was perhaps not without calculation that she arrived in an extremely simple traveling costume, and that throughout the visit she appeared in very unostentatious toilettes, being obviously desirous of yielding the palm of beauty to the Empress Elisabeth," Beust attested. Sophia had refused to meet Max's tempters and tried to get away with sending a polite note expressing her regrets, but Eugénie insisted on driving out with Sisi to nearby Ischl, where the archduchess was staying, to pay a personal condolence call. The empress of the French was so gentle and loving during this encounter, and was herself so obviously genuinely distraught over Max's death, that even his mother was won over. "The Empress was most gracious," Sophia conceded. As for Elisabeth, one of Napoleon III's servants, sent to Eugénie's rooms on an errand, discovered the two empresses with a tape measure, privately comparing ankle measurements and frock lengths as though they were sisters. But it was with Franz Joseph that Eugénie made a lasting connection. "For my part, I shall never forget the nobility and kindly tact with which he received the Emperor and myself at Salzburg, soon after Querétaro," she would later recall.

The imperial couples were together for only two days, so there wasn't much time to discuss European affairs. But Franz Joseph agreed that Bismarck remained a threat, and even seemed open to a possible defensive alliance with France, should the Prussians, who for the moment seemed content with their winnings, become aggressive again in the future. As further proof of the success of the audience, Franz Joseph and Sisi agreed to return the French courtesy call at Salzburg by attending the Exposition in Paris after all, and a date was set for October.

Elisabeth would end up not making this trip. For by the end of the month it was confirmed: she was pregnant again.

BOTH EMPEROR AND EMPRESS were joyful at the prospect of another child. It had been nearly a decade since Sisi's last pregnancy. After so much bitterness in the interim, here, at last, was a sign of genuine reconciliation. The empress was able to use her condition to politely excuse herself from visiting France, but it's likely she wouldn't have gone in any event. Sisi loved to travel, but only as a private citizen. She knew that a state trip to the Exposition meant that she would be on display as much as any of the exhibits. She had been willing to expose herself to the crowds for the Hungarians, but not the Parisians.

Franz Joseph, who, except for visits to relatives in Germany, rarely traveled outside of his own empire, was curious about the exhibition and kept the commitment. It was his first time in Paris and he was staggered by the city. "I had never thought it would be so overwhelmingly beautiful," he admitted, awestruck, in a letter to Elisabeth. Of the Exposition: "One cannot but be lost in astonishment at all the imposing, beautiful, and useful things one sees. It is like a dream." His hosts were thrilled to have him there, as it signaled that Vienna had decided not to hold Max's death against them. Eugénie was especially solicitous, and helped Franz Joseph pick out a beautiful fan and some other jewelry as gifts to take home to Sisi.

Elisabeth, absorbed with her condition, evinced no disappointment at staying behind, even after hearing her husband's glowing reports of Paris. For the first time, she did not have to follow her mother-in-law's dictates as to the manner in which an empress was expected to behave during pregnancy. There were no long days sitting quietly with her women, nor did Sisi make the expected daily promenades in the palace garden so that the public could scrutinize her expanding waistline. She did as she pleased.

The empress's rejection of these traditions was noted. Although in her sorrow Sophia had withdrawn from public affairs, many of the archduchess's loyal supporters, which included the majority of the court and the insular Viennese aristocracy, shared her conservative opinions and values. To them, Sisi was a dangerous liberal who would lead her husband to ruin. Since her return to Vienna five years earlier, Elisabeth had often scandalized this group by shunning her ceremonial societal duties in favor of less visible philanthropic activities. Like Eugénie, she made a practice of visiting hospitals, orphanages, and factories without warning, and in the company of a single lady-in-waiting. She held the hands of the dying, handed out sweets and compassion to poor children, and worked to improve industrial conditions for laborers. A passionate admirer of poetry and literature, Sisi was an avid reader who sought out writers regardless of their social status or religion. For this, she was deprecated by the ruling elite and adored by the lower classes and outcasts.

But what the high society Viennese matrons and their wealthy, entitled husbands really could not forgive was Hungary. The dual monarchy was not to them a way of preserving the empire (and with it, ironically, their own rights and property), but rather a deplorable degradation of Austrian superiority, for which they blamed the empress. They were already spoiling for a fight when it was announced that Elisabeth was pregnant, and in this disclosure they found the club with which they thought to bludgeon her. At once, the spiteful rumor went around that the baby was Andrássy's—and they made sure that Sisi heard it.

Now it was Elisabeth's turn to be unyielding. She was horrified by this insult, not simply because it was untrue, but because it besmirched the nature and achievements of a man—Andrássy—whom, with Deák, she respected more than anyone else of her acquaintance. Since she had come to Austria as a bride, the court and these society people had been nothing but hateful to her, but this! This time, they had gone too far.*

In February 1868, with the baby due in a little over two months, Sisi abruptly left Vienna for Hungary. Her intentions were clearly to remain away for an extended period; in fact, she was deliberately setting up a court in Buda to compete with the Habsburgs' traditional center of power. "Her Majesty is under the care of an Hungarian physician, has chosen an Hungarian wet-nurse,...an Hungarian governess, and last of all, an Hungarian *valet de chambre*," the London papers reported. The kingdom was thrilled at this mark of royal favor. In Hungary, Elisabeth was beloved by *all* strata of society, nobility and commoners alike. When the Hungarian chapter of the Jewish Benevolent Society asked

---

* For Elisabeth and the Hungarians, this slander was the equivalent of claiming she had slept with Abraham Lincoln.

to include her name as a member of their organization, so that they might pray for her as though she were one of their own, "the Empress wrote a gracious letter in reply, and sent a donation of 100 florins," the *Daily News* observed. "Her name now figures among those of the members of this body."*

On April 22, 1868, for the first time since the Habsburgs had taken proud possession of Austria centuries earlier, a princess of the imperial house was born in Hungary, not Vienna. Not only that, but with great pomp, she was *christened* in Budapest, thus forcing the very gossipmongers who had besmirched the empress to make the trip and mingle uncomfortably with Elisabeth's Hungarian courtiers in order to witness the ceremony, which protocol demanded they attend. "Numerous as the hotels are, they were overcrowded by visitors... Of course, Vienna furnished the largest contingent," the special correspondent for the *Times* noted. "With all that, there could be no mistake that it was the King and Queen of Hungary, not the Emperor and Empress of Austria, who were holding their Court," the journalist emphasized.

And it wasn't just her residence at the Hofburg that Elisabeth had determined to supplant. The imperial summer houses of Schönbrunn and Laxenburg, where the family was used to spending many of its holidays, were now also to be largely abandoned. In their place, Sisi substituted Gödöllő, the charming country estate twenty miles northeast of Budapest that had been presented to her by the Hungarians at the time of her coronation. If the emperor wanted to see the empress during the loveliest times of the year (which he did), from this time on he would have to come to Gödöllő.

Franz Joseph, who did not have his wife's strength of character, and who furthermore knew her to be innocent of the charges of infidelity,

---

* Sisi's decision to relocate to Hungary was the impetus behind the kingdom's expanding the capital to include the royal court. Within five years, the two cities on either side of the Danube, Pesth and Buda, would be officially linked. Accordingly, from now on, the capital will be designated by its present-day name of Budapest to reflect this transition.

acquiesced to these changes. Hungary was at least within imperial territory; if she was happy there, that was all that mattered.

In this way did Austria effectually lose its empress, the Hungarians gain a queen, and Sisi win her freedom. That October, the family spent its first holiday together at Gödöllő. "The Emperor Francis Joseph and the Empress are enjoying the fêtes and sports of the season," reported the Budapest correspondent for the *Daily News*. "While the Emperor is hunting in the environs, the Empress—a tenderly-loving mother—spends the time with her children, the greatest share of her maternal care being taken by the youngest,...Maria Valeria, who...is called 'the Hungarian Princess.'"

ELISABETH WAS ALREADY THIRTY YEARS OLD and the parent of a twelve-year-old daughter and ten-year-old son when she gave birth to her fourth child, Valerie. But her behavior suggests that, at least in her mind, this infant girl represented the empress's first real experience of motherhood. It demonstrates just how deeply she had been wounded by Sophia's usurpation of this role. Sisi would not let Valerie out of her sight. She trembled at every teething fever and cooed over every baby step. She took her with her everywhere (although not to Vienna). The imperial court, still smarting from the humiliation of the Hungarian christening, and deprived of a new addition to the imperial nursery, snidely referred to Valerie as "the one and only one."

For Gisela, and especially Rudolf, who up until this point, as the youngest child and only son and heir, had received the most attention, the favoritism displayed by their mother for this baby sister was perplexing and hurtful. They were often left at home in Vienna with their father and grandmother while Elisabeth took Valerie to Bavaria to see her family, or went riding at Gödöllő without them.

It was an inexcusable breach of parental bonds, for which Elisabeth was entirely responsible. The older children had done nothing to deserve this isolation; they were as much the victims of the long-standing feud between their mother and Sophia as Sisi was. But Elisabeth could not rise above her own pain enough to recognize others'.

Once she had Valerie, the daughter she could call her very own, she poured all of her love into her at the expense of everyone else.

Except perhaps for her own family in Munich. Even after all this time, Possi was still home to the empress. Elisabeth had trembled for her brothers, who had sided with Austria, and fought with the Bavarian army against Prussia in the recent war. But it had all worked out—although their regiment had been defeated, her siblings had all returned safely to Munich. Similarly, Bavaria itself had emerged more or less unscathed by the conflict. As he had with Franz Joseph, Bismarck had been surprisingly lenient in his peace terms with Sisi's cousin, the twenty-two-year-old King Ludwig II. The count had not asked to annex territory (well, except for the highly profitable post office), and had allowed the young monarch to retain his throne, demanding only that Bavaria pay Wilhelm a cash reparation of 30 million gulden for having fought against him.

Even better, in the aftermath of the war, Ludwig II actually seemed to take his state responsibilities a bit more seriously. True, he was still infatuated with Wagner, and continued to be absorbed in the details of the splendid new opera house he was building. And he had developed some other rather curious habits, like going for long nocturnal rides on the grounds of his country estate with only one of his groomsmen for company. But he *had* paid attention during the peace negotiations and signed the papers quickly. The most promising sign of maturity, however, was that Ludwig had agreed to marry, as was his duty as a sovereign, and had made a highly suitable match with his cousin, Sisi's youngest sister, twenty-year-old Sophie. All agreed that this heralded a new beginning and the start of a brighter future.

As was his nature, no sooner was his engagement announced than Ludwig threw himself into the nuptial preparations. A garish wedding chariot, so flamboyantly curlicued and doused in gold that it could have stood double duty as a Christmas tree ornament, was painstakingly constructed at a cost of 1 million gulden. To decorate the church, Ludwig ordered silks brocaded with scenes from his favorite opera, *Lohengrin;* he also referred to Sophie as Elsa, and himself as Heinrich, two of its main characters (although sometimes he was "the Eagle" and she "the Dove").

But even while Ludwig was writing heartfelt notes to "My dear Elsa!" he was also seen consistently in the company of his groomsman, Richard Hornig. It was Richard who accompanied the king to Paris for the Exposition; Richard who was by his sovereign's side when Ludwig wandered around Versailles for hours fantasizing that he was speaking to his favorite French monarchs, Louis XIV and Marie Antoinette; Richard whom Ludwig referred to as "Beloved of my Heart." When the pair returned from France, it was noticed that the king had cooled towards his prospective bride. He often avoided her company and kept putting off the wedding. One night he turned up very late and dragged Sophie out of bed to see if her crown would fit. He made her model it this way and that, openly expressing his dissatisfaction with her performance before leaving as abruptly as he had arrived. Poor Sophie was reduced to tears. "He is only playing with me!" she cried.★

Eventually, Duke Max got fed up again and went to the palace to ask the king if he was serious about marrying his daughter. With great relief, Ludwig took this interview as an excuse to wriggle out of it. "Your parents want to break off our engagement," he wrote solemnly to Sophie. "I accept the proposal." He was more candid in his diary entry that evening. "Sophie got rid of...Now I live again after this torturing nightmare," he rejoiced.

Elisabeth was incensed at the jilting. "How much both I and the Emperor are shocked about the King you can imagine. There is no expression for such behavior," she fumed to her mother. But it turned out to be a blessing for Sophie, who the very next year fell in love with the duc d'Alençon, grandson of Louis Philippe, the Citizen King, and married him on September 28, 1868.

Alas, the Bavarians, who could not switch sovereigns the way Sophie

---

★ Sophie's misery exasperated her mother, who considered her daughter's romantic expectations to be unrealistic. After all, Duchess Ludovika declared, "no one could be more tiresome and eccentric than her husband [Duke Max], and he did not even have the excuse of being a King."

exchanged fiancés, were not so lucky. For unbeknownst to his subjects and the rest of Europe, in order to keep his kingdom intact, Ludwig had signed a second, secret agreement with Bismarck at the time of the original peace treaty. This compact committed Bavaria to come to Prussia's defense should war be declared at any time in the future, and specifically put its military under the command of Wilhelm's generals, a snare that effectively brought the kingdom under Prussian control.

Bismarck, having set his trap, was content to wait. It was the count's desire that when its time came, Bavaria should accept its annexation willingly. The count felt strongly that a few years of the citizenry's exposure to Ludwig's extravagant fantasies could only push public opinion in the right direction. "We want to give the Bavarians time," Bismarck explained to his ambassador. "They will finger along the walls for a while and search for a way out, but they won't find any. Then they will at last resign themselves to their fate."

By 1870, the wily count could congratulate himself that he had everything in place. A north German government, incorporating all the conquered states, had been organized under Prussian leadership. The national army had been swelled by soldiers from those same defeated monarchies, like the kingdoms of Hanover and Saxony, which had formerly fought against it, and the royal treasury replenished by the millions in damages paid by Austria and Bavaria. The money had been used to provide the legions of troops under Wilhelm's command with the latest in weaponry, as developed by Prussian armaments experts and produced at Prussian factories. Bismarck saw to it that the regiments were drilled relentlessly, that battle plans were created based on speed and overwhelming strength, and that the ammunition and supplies for a prolonged conflict were stocked and ready.

All that was left was to pick a fight.

EUGÉNIE

Eugénie on camelback

27

The Reign in Spain—Again

My name... ought to be completely left out of everything...
They will cry "intrigue," they will be furious against me, but
without finding any point of attack.

—Bismarck's secret instructions to the
Prussian courier to Madrid

DESPITE THE UNDENIABLE SUCCESS of the Exposition Universelle, which lured millions of paying customers to Paris, the mood in France, particularly in the capital, had darkened considerably by the fall of 1867. Not even the well-publicized appearance of Franz Joseph during the closing days of the exhibition, a diplomatic triumph that signaled the possibility of future military cooperation, lifted the national spirits. Eugénie did not have to cast around for a reason for the discontent. She, like everyone else at court, saw plainly that Napoleon III had been weakened by chronic illness, and this, in combination with his advanced age—he was nearing his sixtieth birthday—was beginning to affect public confidence in the government. That's one of the unfortunate drawbacks of a glorious empire—they generally don't work without a fully functioning head of state. "Fall on the Bourse," Baron Heeckeren observed glumly in his diary entry for October 4, 1867. "The Emperor is unwell... Such panics are disastrous. They teach me to spread my investments widely, to be on my guard, to watch. The situation is growing tense. Can the Empire be coming to the dusk of its day?" he wondered.

Louis Napoleon was himself aware of the dangers to his rule, and particularly to that of his son. The prince imperial was not yet twelve, and the emperor, who was often in severe pain, was not at all sure he could last another six years until his heir reached his majority. He already did not have the energy to administer the government as he had in the past. So, the next year, he tried to improve his popularity by giving in to liberal demands to lift the censorship rules that had been imposed on the press since his coup d'état sixteen years earlier. Mérimée was appalled. "The Government is furnishing whips for its own castigation to people who lay hold of them eagerly," he exclaimed in the spring of 1868. The senator was correct: with freedom of the press came a slew of new publications dedicated to trumpeting grievances and stirring up unrest in the hopes of fomenting revolution. "And the most melancholy feature...is the utter absence of wit in them," Mérimée deplored to a friend. "Never have we been so stupid and vulgar. We are rapidly approaching the American style," he sniffed.

The French citizenry, particularly those in the capital, where most of these papers found an audience, bombarded for the first time with one scathing article after another about how corrupt and unjust the government was, and how terrible the present economic conditions (they weren't), began to believe it. In August, the prince imperial was openly insulted when he attended a student award ceremony in Paris. "He was received coldly whereas... [other] pupils...were cheered to the echo," Mérimée noted. "The Minister of Public Instruction, in the course of his speech, paid a compliment to the Prince. He was hissed," the senator reported, shocked.

And then, the very next month, as though to highlight just how tenuous the situation was, revolution broke out in Spain. Queen Isabella, whose ascension to the throne as a three-year-old some thirty-five years earlier had sparked the horrific violence of civil war (which the then eight-year-old Eugénie had witnessed from the window of her dead uncle's mansion before being swept off to Paris by her mother), was overthrown. Forced to flee Madrid, Isabella bolted for Biarritz, where the imperial family was spending its annual late-summer holiday, and threw herself and her eleven-year-old son and heir, Alfonso, who was only a year younger than the prince imperial, on the mercy of her countrywoman. Of course, Eugénie and Napoleon III took her in and gave her a beautiful château in the French countryside in which to live.

Distressingly, the revolt against Isabella only emboldened those in Paris who were hoping to replace the ailing Louis Napoleon's autocratic rule with a republic, or simply to wrest power away from him for themselves. (If the *Spanish* could do it...) By the beginning of 1869, there were anti-imperial demonstrations in the streets, and the army had to be called in several times to maintain the peace. In May, when new elections were held for the national assembly, the public appetite for change was made manifest. "Not a single official candidate has been approved in Paris," mourned Baron Heeckeren. "Ninety constituencies have nominated Opposition candidates."

Autocrats whose reigns are threatened in this way generally face two alternatives: either bring out the soldiers and impose martial law, or acquiesce to some form of power sharing. Franz Joseph had been confronted with the same choice in Hungary. To his credit, Napoleon III refused to employ oppression. In truth, neither the emperor nor the empress had any wish to rule by force.

And so, in place of an absolute monarchy, Louis Napoleon agreed to adopt a parliamentary system based on the British model. He would continue as emperor, but with vastly reduced powers. France would be run by a prime minister responsible to an elected assembly (called the Corps Législatif). "It is not easy to establish in France the regular and peaceful exercise of liberty," the emperor pointed out in his first address to this body. "But...we must...proclaim loudly the will of the country," he concluded, to loud cheers.

EUGÉNIE WAS NOT at her husband's side during this speech, although it wasn't because she disapproved of this course of action. He had sought her advice throughout this difficult period. "You must not be

473

discouraged, but continue in the course you have begun," she reassured him. "It is right to keep faith in the concessions that have been granted... I am persuaded that a *coup d'état* cannot be made twice in one reign," she added drily.

She was not in Paris for the commencement of the Corps Législatif because, ironically, at the very moment that her husband was handing over control of his government to a liberal French parliament, *she* was presiding over one of the empire's greatest and most lasting accomplishments: the grand opening of the Suez Canal in Egypt. Napoleon III had been too ill to travel to attend the ceremony, so Eugénie had undertaken the journey in his place. This was itself a novelty, as her voyage took her from Venice to Constantinople, and from there to Cairo and Alexandria, cities under the control of monarchs unused to fêting women. In Turkey, "a 'revolt of the harem' has broken out," reported the special correspondent for the *Daily News*. The women of Constantinople "have looked upon the lovely *Fransa Imperatrizassy* [French Empress]... They have seen the Lord of the Moslems himself give his arm to a woman, and not only conduct her to her palace, but accompany her in her carriage,... and they naturally ask why they should be obliged to veil their bright eyes and fair complexions in a cloud of gauze."

But Eugénie clearly reveled in her independence and enjoyed every minute of this exotic adventure. In Venice she toured by gondola; in Constantinople the sultan entertained her with fireworks and a magnificent feast; in Cairo she rode a camel surrounded by servants bearing torches for a night visit to the pyramids, which had been illuminated especially for her benefit. Franz Joseph was among the many heads of state, including the khedive of Egypt, to join her at Port Said for the ceremonial opening of the canal, a gargantuan undertaking imagined and constructed by her cousin, Ferdinand de Lesseps, whom she had supported from the beginning. "There have been few occasions in history... when the ships of war of all nationalities have been concentrated, and their... banners, their inspiriting music, their gallant crews, their cannon... made subservient to a common end," the special correspondent noted thoughtfully. "This is the case here."

But in Paris, even this monumental achievement failed to arouse the admiration of the populace; if anything, they resented the funds allocated for the empress's journey. "They wanted to overthrow the apparent dictatorship of the Emperor, and they have put in its place that of the Corps Législatif, which is worse still," Baron Heeckeren fretted. "The Emperor is sick. So is the Empire...Disturbances, hesitations, disputes, intrigues...What will happen in 1870? I am very sad at heart these last minutes of the year," read his diary entry for December 1869.

And it was just at this moment, with France torn by internal strife and Napoleon III "suffering, anxious, and humiliated," in the words of a Parisian journalist, that Bismarck made his move.

BY THE BEGINNING OF 1870, the Prussian count, who understood that timing was everything, was aware that the outlook for a triumphant assault against France (which would allow him to take over southern Germany, his real motive) was rapidly approaching its most advantageous point. He had consulted his commanding general, Field Marshal Helmut Moltke, who had informed Bismarck that "he regarded a rapid outbreak [of hostilities] as...more favorable to us than delay." Meanwhile, his minister of war, Albrecht von Roon, had assured him that, with France isolated and domestic conditions so chaotic, Napoleon III would be hard pressed to field an army of more than 300,000 men, whereas Prussia could deploy more than twice that number. But, as before with Austria, the count, now chancellor of Northern Germany, had to find a way to goad the French into making the first move, so that King Wilhelm did not appear to be the aggressor. "Success...depends upon the impression which the origination of the war makes upon us and others," Bismarck cautioned his fellow conspirators, Moltke and Roon. "It is important that we should be the party attacked."

He had just begun hunting around for a suitable pretext when the revolution in Spain unexpectedly provided one. After Isabella was chased out of the country, the administration of Madrid had been taken over by the Spanish minister of war, General Prim, who functioned as interim leader while the representative assembly, the Cortes, figured out what sort of government they wanted to put in the queen's place. Eventually, it was decided to try a constitutional monarchy—constitutional monarchies were clearly in vogue that year—and since this form of government unfortunately required the presence of a monarch, and nobody wanted Isabella back, it fell to General Prim to scrounge up a new one.

Problem was, nobody wanted the job. He offered the position to a number of candidates and every one of them turned him down. This lack of interest is perhaps best explained by the magnitude of the violence that enveloped the kingdom in the wake of the revolution. "The goings on in Spain afford food for reflection," Mérimée reported somberly to a friend. "Madame de Montijo sends me the most distressing accounts. Spain is at present divided into three zones... 1st. Cataláña and Galicia, Republican system; devoted to burning churches, archives, and castles. 2nd. Madrid and the center, Parliamentary system; stupid but not vicious... 3rd. Andalucia; Socialism and Communism. All landowners are ruined... accompanied by assassination, theft, and outrage."

Among those who had rejected the throne of Spain on the first go-round was Prince Leopold of Hohenzollern, one of Wilhelm's many cousins. Prince Leopold, who was in his early thirties, had originally been thought of because he was married to a princess of Portugal, and it seemed like a nice fit. Also, he wasn't doing much of anything else anyway, so he was available. But both Leopold's wife, who knew Spain, and who had no wish to exchange the safety of her comfortable German home for the dubious and potentially life-threatening rewards of an obviously unstable crown, and Leopold's mother, who still had Max's untimely demise fresh in her mind, were adamantly opposed to the move and had dissuaded him from accepting.

But in February 1870, Bismarck, who saw in the Spanish offer the opportunity he had been searching for, surreptitiously resurrected Leopold's candidacy. Although the information was kept carefully from the rest of Europe, and particularly from the French, the chancellor had Prim renew his appeal to the prince, and this time Bismarck energetically supported the proposal. "For dynastic and political reasons... [it would be] invaluable to have a friendly country in the rear of France," he urged Wilhelm, who, as head of the family, had to approve his cousin's acceptance. The count completely downplayed the danger to Leopold, assuring Wilhelm that General Prim had the rampaging under control. Finally, knowing how susceptible his sovereign was to flattery, the chancellor extolled the glory that would come to Prussia if they succeeded in placing the hapless Leopold on the Spanish throne — why, it "has only an analogy to the old Habsburg model!" Bismarck raved, aware of how jealous Wilhelm had formerly been of the reach of Franz Joseph's empire.

Pressure was accordingly brought to bear on the anointed candidate. He was told that all the ministers concurred that it was his "patriotic duty towards Prussia" to accept. On June 19, 1870, Leopold reluctantly agreed, and Wilhelm (who four months earlier had written firmly to Bismarck that he was "absolutely *against* the affair") now also consented, although the Prussian king, who clearly had no idea what his chancellor was actually up to, added that it was "with a heavy heart."

For once, however, Bismarck had underestimated his opponent. Although the exact nature of the conspiracy was not leaked to France until early July, Napoleon III, even sick as he was, knew to be on his guard against Prussia. It was clear that they were preparing for war. "A while ago I spent some time in Berlin," Baron Heeckeren noted. "The air there is highly electrified... You breathe a savor of powder... You should hear them discuss us — the defects of our armor-plating, our want of forethought, our guns, our arsenals, our military system, of which they know the weak points perfectly well. None of our Generals is unknown to them, while we know none of theirs."

The emperor had launched several initiatives in an attempt to protect against a Prussian attack. For over a year he had been in discussions with Austria and Italy to set up a defensive alliance so that France would not have to face Bismarck's legions alone. To ensure that the new Chassepot rifles lived up to their reputation, he sent them, along with a French brigade trained to use them, to Italy, where sixty-year-old Garibaldi and his band of volunteers were making one final run at occupying Rome. "It was a good opportunity to try the new weapon," the *Times* correspondent conceded, "although the poor, half-starved, half-armed Garibaldians were really hardly worthy of French lead and steel." Still, the guns worked as promised. "All was over so soon as the French came up," the journalist testified. As late as June 1870, Napoleon III proposed to boost the military budget to some 15 million francs to increase security on the eastern border, and ensure the prompt provision, transport, and arming of additional recruits. But in this, the emperor had been thwarted by the Corps Législatif. "They voted 4,000,000 [francs], and the papers laughed heartily at the alarmist prognostications," Baron Heeckeren reported.

And then, on July 2, 1870, Bismarck's intrigue leaked to the Tuileries, and by July 4 the French papers were reporting that a German prince had accepted the crown of Spain. The intent was obvious: to encircle France in the event of war.★

The timing could not have been worse for poor Napoleon III. On July 3, he was in such intense pain from his bladder stone that his doctors were recommending an operation. Of course, this remedy had to be put off in the face of the crisis. Instead, the Prussian ambassador to Paris was called in and told in the strongest possible terms that France "would not tolerate any Prussian prince on the Spanish throne." An alert went out to all the other major European powers, with the result that the governments of Britain, Austria, and Italy all promptly joined with the French in remonstrating strongly against this ploy. Under this pressure, the beleaguered Leopold, who hadn't been keen on the idea in the first place, was easily convinced to write a letter to Madrid formally declining the honor.

★ Having a Prussian prince on the throne of Spain meant that the French would have to divide their forces in the event of a German attack. Bismarck calculated that Napoleon III would have to divert at least "one or two army corps" from his eastern border to protect against a Spanish assault from the southwest.

But before this became generally known, Louis Napoleon, who had learned from his previous negotiations with Bismarck not to settle for vague promises, sought written confirmation not only that Leopold would withdraw his name from consideration, but that no Prussian prince would ever consider accepting the position in the future. Bismarck, anticipating this move, had made sure to retreat to his country estate as soon as the news became public.* Consequently, when the French ambassador in Berlin, Count Benedetti, tried to obtain official confirmation of Leopold's withdrawal, he was put off with the lofty explanation that Bismarck, while himself unfortunately unavailable for comment, had left word that "the Prussian government was absolutely ignorant of this affair, which did not exist for it"—an obvious piece of duplicity, which neither the ambassador nor the emperor believed for a moment.

Suspicious of the runaround, and harried by reports that the Prussians were already calling up soldiers in preparation for an offensive, Louis Napoleon knew he had no choice but to respond with a show of force. However, as war was the last thing the suffering emperor wanted, he cleverly decided to circumvent Bismarck and instead try to reason directly with the far more malleable Wilhelm. And so, at 10 p.m. on July 12, Napoleon III sent a telegram instructing Count Benedetti to track down the king, who was enjoying his summer holiday at a spa at Ems, some 370 miles southwest of Berlin, and get him to give his word in writing that he had withdrawn his support from Leopold. "So long as we have not an official communication from Ems,...we shall continue our armaments," Louis Napoleon declared flatly in his message to the envoy.

It was an inspired move. Benedetti hotfooted it down to Ems and cornered Wilhelm as he was making his regular late-morning stroll along the main promenade. The king was rather surprised to bump into the French ambassador like this, but, always the gentleman, he

---

* You can see what pros these guys are. Their cat-and-mouse over Leopold's candidacy is like watching two card sharps trying to outcheat each other during a high-stakes poker game.

stopped to speak with him. Wilhelm hadn't yet heard that Leopold had turned down the Spanish offer after all, but since the king had been against his cousin's accepting from the beginning, he did not have a problem assuring Benedetti that once Leopold's refusal was confirmed, the Prussian government would have "no more interest in the matter." Wilhelm was rather insulted when the ambassador insisted that official notification of this pledge be wired to Paris immediately—Wilhelm thought that his word as sovereign should be enough—but he nonetheless acceded to the request, telling Benedetti that he would have his aide-de-camp send the required telegram. Louis Napoleon's sleight of hand had worked; the emperor had sneaked a king from his sleeve while his opponent wasn't looking and averted the prospect of war.

THAT BISMARCK HAD INDEED been outmaneuvered by Napoleon III is evidenced by the chancellor's extreme displeasure at this new development. The count had come back to Berlin on July 12 to help oversee the mobilization of the Prussian army in preparation for what he confidently believed would be the start of imminent hostilities, when he was suddenly informed that Leopold had succumbed to international pressure and changed his mind. "I perceived in this extorted submission a humiliation of Germany...I was very much depressed," he admitted. And the next day came even worse news: to his fury, Bismarck discovered that Benedetti had gone behind his back and that Wilhelm had actually agreed to send a soothing telegram to Paris promising that this was the end of the affair. The count was at dinner with his co-conspirators, Moltke and Roon, when this communication was presented to him, and when he read aloud the contents of the message that the king had ordered be sent to the Tuileries, his guests' "dejection was so great that they turned away from the food and drink."

And it was while he sat morosely before his untouched dinner, reading and rereading the painful telegram he had been ordered to transmit (clearly searching for a loophole), that Bismarck had his epiphany. Wilhelm had, as usual, authorized his chancellor to make whatever changes to the wording that he saw fit, and the count now realized that, with a little deft editing, he could change the entire tone of the message. Quickly, "I reduced the telegram by striking out words, but without adding or altering," the count volunteered virtuously (pretending to have scruples). Moltke, impressed with this burst of creative chicanery, noted enthusiastically: "Now it has a different ring; before it sounded like a parley; now it is like a flourish in answer to a challenge!" In fact, out of what had been meant to be an accommodation, the chancellor had composed a sneering insult. With glee, Bismarck chortled, "[If] I at once communicate this text...not only to the newspapers, but also by telegraph to all of our embassies, it will be known in Paris before midnight, and not only on account of its contents, but also...its manner of distribution, it will have the effect of a red flag upon the Gallic bull." At this, his guests perked right up and "recovered their pleasure in eating and drinking."*

And so the revised message, known as "the Ems telegram," landed in Paris on the evening of July 13 with the insolence of a Prussian field marshal kicking his servant for not having polished his boots properly. "The French Ambassador...demanded...that his Majesty, the King, bound himself for all time never again to give his consent, should the Hohenzollerns renew their candidature," it read. "His Majesty, the King, thereupon decided not to receive the French Ambassador again, and sent the aide-de-camp on duty to tell him that his Majesty had nothing further to communicate to the ambassador." By the next day the papers had the story, and just as Bismarck had predicted, public opinion raged against the insult. The Corps Législatif took up the issue on July 15 and voted overwhelmingly for war. The assistant secretary to the American ambassador in Paris attended this fateful session, at which one lone representative, Adolphe Thiers, tried to stem the outrage. "Mr. Thiers rose, and attempted to address the House in a speech

---

* Napoleon III is sometimes criticized by historians for pressing for a written retraction and thus provoking the war, but in fairness there is no way he could have anticipated that Bismarck would so blatantly commit fraud in this manner. If any of the chancellor's subordinates had ever changed the tone of one of *his* telegrams like this, Bismarck would have had the offending official executed for treason. As for Wilhelm, he was too gullible to realize what had happened.

deprecating hostilities," the assistant secretary reported. "The great mass of the members sprung to their feet, pointed their fingers at the orator, yelled, and shouted '*Traître, traître! Allez à Berlin!* [Traitor, traitor! Onward to Berlin!]'"

Throughout this crisis, Eugénie, precluded by the transfer to a constitutional monarchy from having any say in the government, stayed conscientiously on the sidelines. Since her return from Egypt, the empress no longer attended council meetings. She did not try to impose her views publicly. She was in her husband's confidence, and sometimes took notes for him during diplomatic meetings, but she had no influence whatsoever over policymaking.

This did not mean she did not have an opinion, however. On the one hand, she understood the threat posed by the rise of Prussia and burned, like the rest of France, to teach Bismarck a lesson for his insults. "Everyone here, the empress foremost, is so desirous of war that it seems to me impossible that we shall not have it," observed one of Eugénie's ladies-in-waiting. But Eugénie was also well aware that the military was not as prepared as it should be for the conflict. Although the minister of war had assured the government that France had an army of 250,000 men ready to deploy immediately, with another 50,000 in reserve who could be called up within ten days, both she and Napoleon III understood that this might not be enough. They desperately needed Austrian help, and had been working with Franz Joseph's commanding general on a combined plan of attack. "The Empress had in her possession the minutes of these negotiations," the comte de Fleury testified. The campaign called for Franz Joseph to put an army in the field in Bavaria. "But all think the weak side of the plan the condition laid down by Austria that she must have six weeks to prepare from the moment the war breaks out," Eugénie noted of this arrangement. "The Emperor and the generals do not hide their anxiety as to whether the French armies could hold out alone for so long a time."

And it was more than just the lack of preparation. Although Louis Napoleon had not shared the results of his July 3 medical examination with her, or his need for an operation, she did not require a physician's report to worry about his health. Eugénie could see for herself how ill he was. He was clearly in no condition to lead an army and yet, as a Bonaparte, if war came, he would have to. And not only her husband but her son would have to go as well! The prince imperial was now fourteen, just old enough to accompany his father should open combat break out. For all of these reasons, then, the empress fully supported Napoleon III's efforts to find a peaceful solution to the Leopold controversy. "I am quite ready to assume the responsibility of all my acts," she would later reveal. "I admit that I exerted my influence in favor of the unfortunate Mexican expedition, but I stoutly deny that I ever approved of the struggle between Germany and France. Quite the contrary, I did what I could to prevent it."

But after the Ems telegram was made public, no one could do anything about it. The French people rose up and demanded war. They had been told so often over the past eighteen years that they were great that they believed it. It seems not to have occurred to anyone that they might lose. "I was present this morning at a scene never to be forgotten," Baron Heeckeren recorded in his diary. "I was on . . . an omnibus. Everybody was speaking at once. There was only one subject of conversation. A gentleman said: 'The war! Supposing it was to end in a defeat for France?' . . . They seized the man and threw him from the top of the moving omnibus onto the pavement. I can quite believe it killed him," the shaken financier reported.

Eugénie's misgivings, however, were nothing compared to the dread Louis Napoleon experienced as the inevitability of conflict became apparent. Just prior to the arrival of the Ems telegram, while the imperial court still thought that war could be averted, a dinner party had been scheduled for the evening of July 17. Although the event was hastily cancelled in the wake of the crisis, the American Lillie Moulton, who happened to be among those invited, did not get the message in time, and turned up at the appointed hour at Saint-Cloud. Out of an excess of politeness, the empress insisted she and her husband stay, and Lillie, for the same reason, felt she had no choice but to obey. "I never regretted anything so much in my life," she wailed to her mother before painting a vivid picture of her hosts' despair. "When we went into the drawing-room their Majesties were already there. The Emperor held out his hand, but did not say a word. He looked so ill and tired. Never had I seen him look like that!" she exclaimed. "There was no one beside ourselves and the Household, perhaps twenty in all. The Emperor never uttered a word; the Empress sat with her eyes fixed on the Emperor, and did not speak to a single person. No one spoke. The Emperor would receive telegram upon telegram; the gentleman sitting next to him opened the telegrams and put them before his Majesty. Every now and again the Emperor would look across the table to the Empress with such a distressed look it made me think that something terrible was happening."

Lillie was not kept in suspense for very long. Two days later, Louis Napoleon was forced to bow to public pressure and formally declare the commencement of an armed campaign against Prussia, making France the aggressor in the conflict. Bismarck had palmed an ace, and got his defensive war.

28

By the Skin of the Empress's Teeth

*I do not wear the uniform, but I am one of you in spirit. My
heart is that of a Musketeer.*

—Alexandre Dumas

ON JULY 28, 1870, just nine days after France officially declared war on
Prussia, Napoleon III and the prince imperial boarded a special train
from Saint-Cloud that would take them to Metz, some 200 miles due
east of Paris, on the border with Germany, where the French army was
gathering. It had been judged best not to leave from the center of Paris,
as the emperor had when he had gone off to command the army in
Italy with so much fanfare a decade earlier; this way, "the Empress and
her ladies could say their adieux without the crowd looking on," Lillie
informed her mother. Louis Napoleon was stoic throughout the brief
going-away ceremony, and Eugénie, too, put up a brave front. By contrast, the prince, dressed in his sublieutenant's uniform, was naturally
excited, as befitted his age, and beamed at his mother from behind the
large plate glass window of the imperial compartment until the engine
had chugged out of sight. "The Empress mastered her emotion," testified the prince's tutor, who was also present. But afterwards, the scholar
caught a glimpse of Eugénie in her carriage on her way back to the
palace. "The Empress was weeping, her face covered with her hands,"
he revealed soberly.

Eugénie had once again been named regent, as she had twice before, but this time her experience was very different. The prime minister and the Corps Législatif, not the throne, approved policies, administered the government, and passed the laws. So, although as regent the empress once again sat in on ministerial meetings, she was largely ignored. In fact, the ruling officials and the other elected representatives viewed her presence as a nuisance and political liability.

Despite this, Eugénie, devoted to aiding her country at this critical moment, strove to make herself useful. She gathered information assessing the mood of the citizenry and passed the data along to the ministry. She pored over reports from the front. These were not encouraging. Fewer than half of the promised 250,000 troops had so far materialized, and arms and supplies were similarly lagging. The rapid, overwhelming offensive that Napoleon III had planned to take the enemy by surprise had to be delayed. The first letter to arrive from her husband in Metz reduced the empress to tears. "He was *'navré'* [dismayed]," she confessed to one of her ladies-in-waiting. "Nothing was ready, nothing was in order."

Still, she, like almost everyone else in France, had an unshakable faith in the army. Had they not won in Crimea, in Italy, in Mexico? And, sure enough, the first news she received of an actual engagement—the battle of Saarbrücken—was of a victory. "Louis has received his baptism of fire," Napoleon III telegraphed on August 2, indicating, to Eugénie's immense pride, that her son had behaved bravely during combat.

Alas, this was to be the extent of the French military progress. There was no news at all from the front for the next few days and then suddenly, at midnight on August 6, she was abruptly awakened and handed a telegram from her husband that had been transmitted in cipher. "Our troops are in full retreat," the decoded message read. "Nothing must be thought of now beyond the defense of the capital."

Although her shock and disappointment must have been very great, Eugénie knew her duty and instantly steeled herself to handle the crisis. Within an hour she had traveled from Saint-Cloud to the Tuileries to call a middle-of-the-night emergency meeting of the ministers. In the absence of specific information as to the scale of the disaster, it was feared that the Prussian army could turn up at any moment outside the gates of Paris. It was above all necessary to keep the population calm in the face of this looming threat, while the government worked on ways to protect the city. By dawn, Eugénie had composed a proclamation, which was issued on the morning of August 7. "People of France, the war has begun unfavorably for us," it began. "Be firm in the presence of the reverse, and let us make haste to repair it... I am here in the midst of you... You will see me first in the place of danger to defend the flag of France." Mérimée saw her soon after this news broke. "I can conceive of nothing more truly admirable than the bearing of the Empress at this juncture," he wrote. "She does not deceive herself in the least, but yet she maintains a really heroic composure."

It must indeed have been difficult not to give in to despair. The military intelligence, as it trickled in over the next week, was as bad as it could be. In the four days since the victory at Saarbrücken, Napoleon III had lost not one battle but *three*. At each, the French troops had been outnumbered and outgeneraled, but also, and most significantly, outgunned. The Chassepot rifles had worked, it is true, but they were no match for the Prussian artillery. Those huge, prize-winning cannons that Bismarck had flaunted at the Exposition Universelle three years earlier had been replicated in quantity and lugged to the front, their murderous barrels pounding for hours at French soldiers. In the first battle, the Prussians boasted 66 heavy guns to the empire's 18. In the second, the imperial regiments faced bombardment from 108 cannons, at which point they lost over 20,000 men — and the war.

Realizing this, the emperor, defeated, exhausted, and ill, took the blame for the trouncings, relinquished his command to his most experienced senior officer in the hopes that this would restore the surviving soldiers' confidence in the military's leadership, and dispatched another practiced commander, General Trochu, to Paris to organize the defense of the city. He then proposed that, since he was no longer in a position of authority within the army, and was consequently simply in the way at the front, he should come back to Paris and help Eugénie prepare the capital for a possible Prussian invasion.

But by that time, the animosity in the city towards their long-standing ruler for having failed to provide the victory that everyone felt they deserved was so pronounced that the empress had to rush to dissuade her husband from undertaking the journey. "However sad it is for me to say it, the truth is that his popularity is lost, at least for the moment," she confided to General Trochu, when he made his appearance in Paris at midnight on August 19 and informed her of Napoleon III's plan. "I am told...that under existing circumstances, the Emperor would never reach the Tuileries alive if he were to attempt to return now," she revealed simply.

In fact, Paris was pulsing with anger, egged on by those on the far left, who wanted to take advantage of the turmoil over the war to overthrow the government and seize power for themselves. "I see nothing here but disorder and stupidity," Mérimée wrote on August 21. "I expect to hear the Republic proclaimed within a week, and to see the Prussians within a fortnight." To help calm the situation, the war minister assured the populace that the French army was in fact regrouping under its new command, with the intent of going to battle once more. "It is consoling to know that the situation is not as desperate as the alarmists would assert," Baron Heeckeren recorded with relief in his diary. "The army is effecting its retreat in good order, and the enemy only advances very cautiously and slowly. This will give us time to mass all our forces and make them ready to withstand a fresh shock—a decisive one this time, and one on which the issue of the whole war will turn," he reflected.

The minister, however, had erred on the side of optimism. While it was true that the remaining French troops were marshaling with the intent of engaging the Prussian forces in a last-ditch effort to halt their advance towards Paris, neither Eugénie nor her husband, nor even the soldiers who would be fighting the battle, were under any illusions as to the likely outcome of this campaign. "The army, occupying unfavorable positions and surrounded by the enemy, could only be beaten," one of the generals involved in the effort observed flatly. "The sole thing we could do, both for the honor of the army and the country, was to render our defeat as difficult as possible." Aware of this, the empress understood that it was now her job as regent to remain in the capital, doing her best to save it or die in the attempt. "The dynasty is lost. We must think only of France," she insisted.

She was shocked when the violence in Paris escalated during the last weeks of August and it was suggested that the army send a force to protect her from the wrath of those who fomented insurrection. "Once more, I beg of you, gentlemen, not to think of me...but only of France," she maintained firmly. "What terrible remorse would be ours, ... how ashamed we would be to stand before posterity, if it should be known one day that the presence of these... men at the front could have changed defeat into victory and yet we mobilized them here for our own defense! Do not lose an instant more discussing this painful subject."

And so the capital held its breath and waited in a state of armed restiveness as the last days of August slipped away and the noble remnants of the French army tried desperately to combine and rally before the Prussian behemoth fell upon them—until at last, on September 1, 1870, time ran out at a small fortress town inside the French border with Belgium called Sedan.

THE BATTLE BEGAN AT 6 A.M., and even the journalists covering the story could see how vastly outnumbered the French were. "The Prussian line extended for miles...as far as the great woods of Condé and Sedan, which run to the Belgian frontier," reported the war correspondent for the *Daily Telegraph*. "The number of the Prussian troops engaged was estimated by General Moltke at 240,000, and that of the French at 100,000." (In fact, the French commander had only been able to scrape together 80,000 men before the attack.) A 3:1 advantage, even without all the artillery, is generally considered insurmountable by the military, and this occasion proved no exception. "The Prussian...army corps formed a crescent round the town... About twelve o'clock this crescent became a circle...This circle grew ever smaller and smaller, until at length its circumference was inside...Sedan itself," the correspondent continued. Napoleon III, who, unable to return to Paris, had stayed to share the fate of his men, was among those caught in this vise. "Just imagine an army surrounding a strong town and itself being surrounded by far superior forces," he later explained to Eugénie.

When it was made clear to him that he had been repudiated by Paris, the emperor, like his wife, had understood that his reign was over. Again like Eugénie, Napoleon III recognized that the only honorable course left to him was to die on the battlefield. This he strove mightily to do during the approximately ten hours of combat outside of Sedan. Although in excruciating pain from his bladder stones, Louis Napoleon nonetheless managed to mount his horse and ride to the crest of the hill where the Prussians were directing the main force of their artillery. "He climbed, now on foot, now on his horse, the bombs in the meanwhile falling on all sides of him," reported a French general. "Reaching the top, there he stood...seemingly inviting death." "Silent and impassible he moved over the battlefield, as calmly as though he was crossing the grand drawing-room of the Tuileries," attested another. "Two bombs struck the ground quite near him...The horses...reared and fell, hurting their riders, while the Emperor was covered with fragments of earth and with smoke." But despite his deliberate exposure, Napoleon III remained unscathed. "I had no luck that day," he sighed.

By 4 p.m., those of the imperial troops who had managed to survive had been pushed back inside the walls of Sedan, where they jostled for space with frightened civilians. Wilhelm then ordered the bombardment of the city. "Houses were falling in and the panic-stricken inhabitants were fleeing and shrieking through the streets," an officer remembered. Fire was everywhere; terrified crowds snarled the traffic, making easy targets for Prussian shells; many died in their carriages. The town authorities found the emperor and begged him to do something to stop the destruction, and so to Napoleon III fell the bitter task of surrender. "I would have preferred death to such a disastrous capitulation," he told Eugénie later, "and yet...it was the only way of avoiding the butchery of 60,000 persons."

The emperor called for pen and paper, and Sedan hoisted the white flag. "Monsieur, my brother," Napoleon III wrote to Wilhelm. "Having been unable to die in the midst of my troops, I have nothing left but to hand my sword to your Majesty."

Forty-eight hours later in Paris, after days of dread marked by an absence of any communication from the front, Eugénie was handed another telegram from her husband. "The army is defeated and captured; I am a prisoner," it read.

SHE HAD BEEN EXPECTING WORD of his death, or of a defeat—since morning there had been a series of conflicting reports, impossible to confirm, delivered to the Tuileries from foreign sources; she knew that *something* had happened. But this...! The dishonor of surrender! Never had she imagined it possible. "A captive army and an imprisoned Emperor," a shaken Eugénie was heard to murmur over and over.

But there was one group in Paris who rejoiced at this news—the leaders of the far left. Ever since Napoleon III had first seized power from the representatives of the republic of 1852 (who had themselves seized power from Louis Philippe, the Citizen King, in 1848), these people had been waiting for their chance to turn the tables, and the debacle at Sedan gave them their opportunity. The army having just been crushed and therefore not available, the instigators fell back on their customary expedient and incited a mob. So premeditated was this coup that the organizers even helpfully put an announcement in the chief republican newspaper, the *Siècle,* notifying all those who wished to participate in the insurrection to meet the next day, Sunday, September 4, "at 2 p.m....in the square facing the palace of the Legislative Body."

The empress was of course aware like everyone else of the threat of revolt, and her first concern was that restraint be used in protecting the government. "If I can prevent it, I shall not permit the horrors of a civil war to be added to those of a foreign war," a grim-faced Eugénie insisted in yet another late-night emergency meeting on September 3. "I decline even to entertain the likelihood of Frenchmen killing Frenchmen, of Paris flowing with blood of her own citizens at a time when the whole country is in mourning." She was especially adamant that this proviso be applied to those responsible for her security. To General Trochu, who had previously announced that he was "ready to meet death on the steps of the Tuileries if the dynasty is in danger," she reiterated firmly: "For no price will I consent to the shedding of one drop of French blood for the preservation of my life."

She needn't have worried. In the aftermath of Napoleon III's surrender to the Prussians, General Trochu hastily reconsidered his political options and went over to the side of the insurrectionists. He and his troops were nowhere to be found on the afternoon of Sunday, September 4, when the mob stormed the Palais Bourbon, seat of the Corps Législatif. The aging Mérimée, in failing health—"I go from bad to worse, weaker and weaker every day...I cannot eat," he had complained earlier that year—was swept up in the tumult. "I am writing to you from the Senate," he scrawled urgently in a letter to his friend in London. "I am going to try to get as far as the Tuileries. As I write, the Corps Législatif is invaded and can deliberate no more." He never made it to Eugénie's side but was forced instead to flee Paris. The harrowing journey sapped his remaining strength and he succumbed three weeks later in Cannes, just shy of his sixty-seventh birthday. "These dreadful political events shortened his days," the distraught friend who announced his death observed in sorrow.

Having dispensed with the legislature, the leaders of the coup now leveled their sights at the regent. Their supporters, giddy with success, were incited to march on the Tuileries. A menacing crowd began to swell outside the gates. They pushed up against the barriers, trying to force their way in, and destroyed the statues of the imperial eagles. Cries of "Down with the Empire!" and "Deposition!" and "Hurrah for the Republic!" could be heard clearly from the windows of the imperial apartments.

Inside, all those who had taken refuge in the palace—including

Prince Metternich and his colleague Count Nigra, the Italian ambassador, both of whom had hastened to the Tuileries as soon as they realized what was happening—begged Eugénie to leave before the rioters broke through and began rampaging through the building. She refused. "Here I have been placed by the Emperor, and here I will stay," she stated firmly. "To abandon my post will weaken the power to resist the invasion...and leave France at the mercy of M. Bismarck." It wasn't until Metternich pointed out to her that she was risking not only her own life, but also those of her household, who refused to leave her so long as she remained, that she reluctantly consented to depart.

By that time, the mob was within minutes of pushing through the gates. Quickly, the two ambassadors led the empress, with only a single lady-in-waiting as a companion, by a roundabout back way through a connecting passage to the Louvre, and from there out a quiet side entrance removed from the path of the insurgents. And yet, even here, she was instantly recognized by a child who happened to be playing nearby. "*Voilà l'Impératrice!* [There's the Empress!]" he shouted, until Count Nigra, acting as decoy, distracted the boy while Prince Metternich desperately flagged down a closed carriage. Swiftly, he handed Eugénie and her lady-in-waiting, Madame Lebreton, inside the cab, and sent the driver trotting briskly on his way.

Where the empress and her companion were supposed to go once they had skirted the hordes of frenzied citizens who were jubilantly celebrating their prowess in overturning an unarmed, elected government while an army of some 250,000 Germans intent on exacting retribution moved relentlessly forward, however, was not at all clear. It had all happened so fast that there had been no chance to plan an escape route. Eugénie had left everything—money, jewels, dresses, top-secret documents, private letters—in her apartments at the Tuileries. She had not an umbrella nor a change of linen with her. Worse, there were toll-takers stationed at all the gates of the city whose job it was to inspect the papers of travelers and rummage through vehicles for smuggled goods; if a child had been able to recognize her at a glance, even in the plain black gown she was wearing, she would surely be discovered by these officials if she tried to slip out of Paris. She needed someone whose loyalty she could rely on without question to help disguise her identity.

She thought first of one of the imperial chamberlains, a man of long service to her husband, but when she and Madame Lebreton arrived at the official's private residence, there was no one home. It seemed too dangerous to wait on the step for his return; although the street outside his building was currently quiet, there was no knowing how long that would last. She and Madame Lebreton had to find someplace safe to hide. In her extremity, Eugénie appealed at last to a man who would turn out to be one of the great unsung gallants in history: Dr. Thomas W. Evans, her American dentist.

DR. EVANS HAD HAD a very busy Sunday. As president of the Paris chapter of the American Sanitation Committee, he had bestirred himself at an early hour to help organize a hospital to care for the flood of wounded soldiers the capital would undoubtedly be receiving in the wake of the horrific fighting at Sedan. He and his physician friend Dr. Crane (also a dedicated member of the committee) had spent most of the day at this activity, and although by the late afternoon both men were aware that there had been disturbances near the Tuileries, there had been no sign at all of unrest in the area where they were working. In fact, they were just about to take a drive to see what it was all about when Dr. Evans remembered that he needed to stop quickly at his house, so he could order food to be prepared for the small dinner he was hosting that evening for other members of the sanitation group. When the carriage brought him to his front door, he told Dr. Crane to give him a minute, popped out of the coach, entered the house, and discovered the empress and Madame Lebreton sitting in his study waiting for him. "I have come to you for protection and assistance, because I have full confidence in your devotion to my family," Eugénie said simply. "You see, I am no longer fortunate. The evil days have come, and I am left alone." And with that, the tears came.

Dr. Evans, bless him, sprang into action. It turned out that beneath the mild-mannered demeanor of a happily married, self-effacing member of the medical community, there lurked the valiant soul of a hero right out of an Alexandre Dumas novel. ("And if I felt a certain pride in having been chosen as the protector of this noble but unfortunate lady, I knew that I should have still better reason to feel proud and happy when I had justified the confidence she had placed in me," he later observed modestly.) Dr. Crane, still waiting patiently in the carriage, was immediately called in, briefed, and enlisted to play Watson to Evans's Holmes. Together, the two men huddled in conference and came up with a plan.

It was clear that the empress must be smuggled out of the country, but what was to be her ultimate destination? She could not go east through Germany, or south to Spain; this would put her in the hands of the enemy. Eugénie herself provided the answer: she wished to settle in England, which had remained neutral in the war. Victoria was a friend, and after all it had been to London that Louis Napoleon had turned for refuge after his escape from the prison of Ham those many years ago. Her protectors agreed that Britain was the empress's best and safest option.

By coincidence, Dr. Evans's wife was at that very moment enjoying a late-summer seaside holiday at Deauville, on the western coast of France, so it was decided to whisk Eugénie and Madame Lebreton off at once to Mrs. Evans's rooms at the fashionable resort, and from there try to book passage across the Channel. Although a train ride would have made their journey far swifter and easier, the empress would almost certainly be recognized by the other passengers, and so public transportation was rejected out of hand as being too risky.

This meant they would have to travel the approximately 125 miles to Deauville by carriage, also potentially dangerous to Eugénie, as it exposed her to local partisans who, eager to burnish their republican credentials, might seize the empress whenever the coach had to stop to change horses. An elaborate cover story was consequently hastily devised. Eugénie was cast as a languishing invalid, sickened by an unnamed-yet-serious disease in need of treatment; Dr. Crane was to impersonate the sick woman's physician (not much of a stretch there);

Madame Lebreton and Dr. Evans took the bit parts of the patient's loyal nurse and concerned brother respectively. Although the empress, who had not slept more than a few hours at a time in days, was already exhausted, Dr. Evans insisted on leaving just before dawn the next day, reasoning that the darkness and the earliness of the hour (the insurrectionists, having celebrated long into the night, were likely to be sleeping it off) provided their best chance of slipping out of Paris unnoticed. After a clandestine surveillance of the neighborhood streets to ensure that the coast was clear, he called for his carriage and within moments the four fugitives were on their way.

There was not one of them, on that long, fraught journey west, for whom the terrible consequences of Marie Antoinette and Louis XVI's doomed flight out of Paris during the Revolution was not uppermost in mind. In fact, it could be said that this was what saved Eugénie. They knew to move quickly and attract as little notice as possible. Dr. Evans's attention to detail was staggering. He might have been a trained operative for the secret services. When the carriage was stopped by the tolltakers and he had to draw the curtains and open the window to converse with the officials, he raised the newspaper he was pretending to read and held it at such an angle that he managed to hide Eugénie's face from the functionaries during the entire exchange. He kept the empress and Madame Lebreton secreted quietly in the back of the carriage the whole of the first day of the escape. When it became necessary to stop for sustenance, it was the two men alone who went into a local inn and sat down to a meal. Only afterwards, as though he had just thought of it, did Dr. Evans ask for a loaf of bread and a sausage, in case he and Dr. Crane got hungry again on the road; in this way he fed his charges. These precautions were clearly necessary, for they could hear cries of *"Vive la France!"* and *"Vive la République!"* as they passed through the various towns along the way, an indication that word of the fall of the empire had reached even the rural areas by telegraph.

After a day and a half, and despite pouring rain and a broken wheel that necessitated a change of carriage and left Eugénie standing exposed in a village street for more than an hour (luckily, by that time she was so bedraggled that no one who walked by would ever have conceived that the drenched woman shivering in a doorway was the glamorous empress of the French), the little company made it to the hotel in Deauville where Mrs. Evans was staying. As a further precaution, the dentist went up ahead of his companions to make sure that his wife's rooms were not being watched. Mrs. Evans was quite surprised to receive her husband and was able to assure him that there had been no word as to Eugénie's whereabouts since she had fled the Tuileries. "Oh, my God, I am saved!" the empress, worn out from her ordeal, breathed as she was ushered into Mrs. Evans's comfortable rooms and collapsed into an armchair.

Not quite. There was still the matter of the Channel crossing. Leaving Eugénie in his wife's care, Dr. Evans went out to investigate the possibilities. A stroll to the shoreline revealed a number of yachts moored in the harbor, one of which could perhaps be privately hired. He made inquiries about the vessel that seemed most suitable and discovered it to be owned by an English lord, Sir John Burgoyne, who was currently holidaying in Deauville with his wife.

Here was a piece of luck! Still exercising extreme caution, Dr. Evans, with Dr. Crane in tow for backup, arranged to meet Sir John on the pretext that he was in the market for a yacht himself and had taken such a fancy to Lord Burgoyne's that he wanted to get one just like it. Flattered, Sir John was only too happy to extoll the merits of his ship. The three fell into easy conversation and the dentist could find no reason to suspect that Lord Burgoyne was anything other than what he appeared: a prime specimen of British knighthood, bold as a lion, honest to a fault, and dedicated to the chivalric tradition. Even better, Sir John confided that he and Lady Burgoyne were intending to sail home the very next day. Still, Dr. Evans wanted to make sure of his archetype. "I drew him aside and told him...that I believed him to be a man in whose honour I could trust," the dentist revealed. "Sir John in answer...opened his card case, and giving me a card, remarked, 'I am an English gentleman, and have been in her Majesty's service in the army for some years.' These words quite assured me," a vastly relieved Dr. Evans added happily.

497

It therefore came as quite a shock to both him and Dr. Crane when, after taking the noble lord into their confidence and explaining how the empress had been forced to escape from a violent insurrection, the desperate plight she was in, and how necessary it was to whisk her away to England before she could be discovered by the usurpers, they were met by the cold reply, "I regret, gentlemen, that I am unable to assist you in this matter."

Stunned, Dr. Evans inquired as to his reasons. Sir John explained, among other excuses, that there was a storm brewing that might prevent his leaving as planned the next day, and if Eugénie was found on his yacht it might cause him some embarrassment. Neither medical man found this argument persuasive. They continued to press their case, but to no avail; Sir John remained obdurate. All entreaties for sympathy or stirring references to the worthiness of the enterprise fell flat.

Finally, Dr. Crane thought to switch tactics and, in an inspired bit of psychology, appealed instead to the recalcitrant lord's vanity and self-interest by reminding Sir John "that a man rarely had the chance to accede to such a request as we were making; that, were he to take the Empress over to England, he might someday be very glad he had once had the good fortune to be of service to her." Here, at last, was an argument that seemed to strike a chord. Unwilling to lose face and overturn himself, however, Sir John instead replied rather churlishly, "Well, gentlemen, you may submit the case to Lady Burgoyne. If she is willing to have the Empress come on board, she can come."

At once, Eugénie's two champions hastened to Lady Burgoyne's cabin and explained the situation to her. Without a moment's hesitation, as though it were the most obvious choice in the world, she put her husband's qualms to shame. "Well, why not?" Lady Burgoyne exclaimed. "I certainly shall be greatly pleased if we can be of any assistance to her...Let her come to us to-night, or as soon as she can safely do so."*

---

* Thus justifying Eugénie's long-standing campaign for the advancement of women. Clearly, Lady Burgoyne should have been the one carrying the card case.

And so, once again under cover of darkness, Eugénie and Madame Lebreton, along with Dr. Evans, who insisted on seeing his mission through to its safe conclusion on the shores of England (Dr. Crane remaining behind to assume charge of the Sanitary Committee), were taken aboard Sir John's commodious yacht, which set sail as promised the next morning. It was a terrible crossing. A fierce gale blew up, threatening to capsize the sails; in fact, the largest battleship in the British navy, with a crew of 500, was also caught in the Channel that day and sank with a staggering all hands perishing. Those on board the Burgoynes' smaller, nimbler vessel were buffeted for hours by ferocious wind and waves and assumed that they would share this fate. It gives a measure of the empress's despondency that she welcomed the thought of drowning. "I was sure we were lost," Eugénie conceded, "but, singular as it may seem, I did not feel alarmed in the least. I have always loved the sea, and it had for me no terrors then . . . death, perhaps, could not come more opportunely, nor provide me with a more desirable grave."

But she didn't die—none of them did. Sir John's pride in his ship was upheld, and by dawn of the next day, September 8, 1870, the yacht had weighed anchor on the shore of the British territory of the Isle of Wight. The empress could now safely take public transportation to the mainland, so the imperial party thanked their hosts profusely and disembarked. Dr. Evans, still in his role as stand-in for the Count of Monte Cristo, suggested that he escort Eugénie and Madame Lebreton on to Brighton, where they might find a suitable hotel and take their bearings, and the empress gratefully agreed.

The dentist had another compelling reason for choosing this spot. Since she had fled Paris on September 4, and even in the days prior to that, Eugénie had had no word of her son. Napoleon III's telegram had not mentioned the prince imperial. The empress did not know if her boy was dead or alive, imprisoned or free, wounded or whole, and she was wild with worry. The French papers had carried no mention of the prince either, but soon after disembarking from the yacht, Dr. Evans saw a British report that the imperial heir had been smuggled through

Belgium and, like his mother, had sought refuge in England, possibly in Hastings. Ever cautious, though, he did not wish to mention this and raise the empress's hopes until he had confirmed the intelligence. So he brought Eugénie to Brighton, the next large town over from Hastings, settled her into rooms, and went to get the latest edition of the London papers. Sure enough, these verified the initial notice, and even named the hotel at which the prince was staying. "This news had an electrical effect upon Her Majesty," Dr. Evans observed.

Eugénie at once demanded to go to Hastings. Nothing would stop her, not the lateness of the hour, nor the crush of press surrounding the prince; she must get to her son. Dr. Evans, determined that the family's first meeting be kept away from the papers, insisted on accompanying her and going up to the prince's rooms first to prepare the way. He saw at once that there was a back door into the imperial suite, so he came back and took the empress upstairs by this way, shielding her from the crowd in the front hall. Then he reversed his steps and entered the main room, nodding his head to the prince in the direction of the private inner chamber. The fourteen-year-old, recognizing the dentist, understood at once and ran out of public view to Eugénie, who pressed him to her heart as though to embed him inside of her. "The Prince, unable to control his emotion, sobbed as he rested in his mother's arms, and in broken sentences told how he had grieved for her, and how rejoiced he was to be with her once more," their benefactor revealed, just before he closed the door gently on the reunion.

ELISABETH

Ludwig II of Bavaria

29

The Search for Solace

And must I, then, myself constrain?
Would this, then, profit me?
But who would vanquished be, I pray,
Should I the conqueror be?

A foolish robber, sure, is he
Who thinks to gain more pelf
By lying ambushed in the woods
Only to rob — himself!

—Sisi

ALTHOUGH ELISABETH, LIKE EVERYONE ELSE in her family, naturally followed the course of the war between France and Prussia, the conflict had very little effect on her day-to-day life. For once, there were no wounded soldiers streaming into Vienna, no hospitals to organize, no having to be strong for her husband while he dealt with the aftermath of a crushing defeat. She could afford to take the role of cynical spectator. "We may possibly vegetate for a year or two more before our turn comes," she noted sardonically to Franz Joseph when news of the storming of the Tuileries circulated. "I hope you will tell me all the details of the Empress's flight. That interests me greatly," she added. Sisi was far more upset when, soon after the Prussian victory at Sedan,

Victor Emmanuel took advantage of the capture of Napoleon III to annex Rome, forcing her sister Marie and brother-in-law Francis out of their lovely papal villa and into permanent exile.

Franz Joseph, too, had very little to do with the war. The Austrian emperor could only sit by and watch helplessly as Bismarck raised Berlin to the dominant position on the continent, eclipsing Vienna. Within a month of the French surrender at Sedan, the Prussian army was outside the gates of Paris, and had set up headquarters at Versailles. When the capital stubbornly refused to capitulate, a blockade was installed to starve the city into submission. Not content with waiting for a formal surrender, on January 18, 1871, Bismarck had Wilhelm declared emperor of the Germans in a grand ceremony at the Hall of Mirrors, a stinging jab at the once all-powerful Louis XIV, the Sun King. Franz Joseph had been particularly disappointed to see how quickly the Bavarians, who had been Vienna's staunchest ally for over half a century, had abandoned him and fought on the side of the Prussians. Even his own in-laws were so ecstatic at the victory over snooty France that Sisi's youngest brother was among those who enthusiastically acclaimed Wilhelm emperor at Versailles, and it was noted pointedly in the *Times* that, in February 1871, when Paris finally capitulated and Wilhelm made his triumphant entry into the capital, Duke Max's palace was "the most brilliantly illuminated building in the whole town" at the Munich festivities celebrating the event.

But Elisabeth didn't care that Vienna no longer exerted influence over southern Germany, or that her husband had to swallow his pride and acknowledge Wilhelm, so recently his inferior in power and status, as master of an empire stronger than his own. After nearly two decades as empress, she had little respect for the system of government to which she was irrevocably tied. By now, Sisi openly favored a republican administration over a monarchy. "We do not need an Emperor," she wrote privately. Her sympathies were as ever with the lower classes. "Why should the people...love us, who live in excess, in the light, while the others, with all their hard work, barely have their daily bread and live in want?" the empress asked. "Our children in velvet and silks—theirs often in rags!"

But she was finished with politics. Her one foray into statecraft—her seven-year fight for Hungarian rights—had greatly embittered her. The calumnies leveled at her by the ruling conservative faction were so pervasive that they caused even those she had championed to doubt her. In July of 1871, fully four years after Elisabeth's coronation in Budapest, Count Andrássy was astounded to hear the Hungarian countess Marie Festetics, who would later become Sisi's closest friend and most ardent supporter, express reservations about joining the empress's entourage on moral grounds. "Does she deserve it?" the countess asked warily, implying that Elisabeth behaved in a wanton fashion. "What a question to ask!" Andrássy exploded. "The Queen is good, clever, and pure. They abuse her because she loves our country, and for that they will never forgive her."

Unwilling to subject herself to further persecution, but unable to extricate herself entirely from her position, Elisabeth attempted at first to walk a narrow line between her personal and public duties. In moments of family crisis, it was she to whom the others looked for strength and succor. In May 1872, when sixty-seven-year-old Arch-duchess Sophia came down with bronchitis, which worsened over the next weeks until it became clear she would not survive, it was Sisi who sent the others to eat and sleep while she sat steadfastly by her mother-in-law's bedside during the long final hours of her life, until the arch-duchess finally succumbed on May 28.

But even here, where her behavior was exemplary, she was vilified. The month before Sophia's death, fifteen-year-old Gisela had become engaged to her cousin, twenty-six-year-old Prince Luitpold of Bavaria, leader of the conservative Catholic party in southern Germany. Franz Joseph had arranged the marriage to curry favor with this faction but because the engagement was announced in Hungary, the match was attributed to Sisi, and tongues wagged that it was the empress's callous-ness that had really killed Sophia. "It is commonly said in Vienna that the Archduchess's first indisposition was brought about by the extreme pain and annoyance which she felt at not having been consulted with regard to her granddaughter's engagement," noted the foreign correspondent for one of the London papers.

In the wake of Sophia's death, Elisabeth, recognizing the void created by the archduchess's loss, went even further and made an attempt to conquer her revulsion for the court and step in to fulfill the traditional role of an Austrian empress. This resolution was put to an extreme test the following year, when Franz Joseph, taking advantage of the debilitation of Paris, decided to promote Vienna as the new capital of culture and commerce in Europe by imitating Napoleon III and hosting his own World Exhibition. The Austrian version naturally had to outshine the one he had attended in France, so Franz Joseph increased the scale of the project to cover an area approximately five times the size of the Exposition Universelle. He had to go into quite a bit of debt to do it but it was more than worth it, as it was confidently predicted that the exhibition would lure some 20 million visitors to Vienna.

For Sisi, however, a showcase like this was the stuff of nightmares. Taking yet another page from Louis Napoleon's playbook, Franz Joseph invited every sovereign of any importance in Europe and Asia to make an appearance, and many accepted. This meant that the empress was going to have to help officiate at long dreary ceremonies, dinners, and other court entertainments, where she would have to dress up and make insipid conversation for hours on end, as well as brave the crowds in the streets, who would jostle to view her as though she were one of the wares on display. It was everything she hated, and it was going to go on for *months*.

But she did it. The court saw more of Elisabeth that summer than they had in years. She entertained Crown Prince Fritz and his wife, Vicky; the Prince of Wales; Emperor Wilhelm and his wife, Augusta; the king of Belgium; the tsar. She toured the huge rotunda her husband had built, and endured the stares of those who dogged her steps and made it impossible for her to view the exhibits. In July, she escaped for a small holiday but came back early for a dinner with the Shah of Persia, who absolutely refused to leave until he had seen her.

But by that time it was clear that the fair was a disaster. Expectations had run very high, and many people had gone into debt, or speculated in the financial markets, in order to make an appropriately opulent appearance at court functions. When, due to unseasonably cold temperatures and excessive wind and rain during the first weeks of May, initial attendance fell below the numbers anticipated, there was a panic. The stock exchange crashed, causing many bankruptcies and even some suicides. The rain was followed by heat, which caused unsanitary conditions in the crowded areas, leading to an outbreak of cholera. Cholera is not a strong recommendation for visiting an exhibition. Elisabeth herself came down with a serious intestinal infection in September that kept her in bed for nearly two weeks. Foreigners stayed away, or left in droves. In the end, some 2,500 people died and the fair, which had cost 19 million gulden to produce, brought in only 4.2 million gulden in revenues.

Even after the exhibition closed, at the end of September, Elisabeth still had one last court appearance to make that year. December 2, 1873, marked the twenty-fifth anniversary of Franz Joseph's ascension to the imperial throne. There were fireworks, processions, and a banquet (albeit understated, due to the recent economic fiasco). Restless from attending audiences all day, Sisi decided to take a quick walk with Countess Festetics before dinner. She was dressed simply, and chose for her outing the newly completed Ringstrasse, the wide boulevard circling the city (inspired by Max's first visit to Paris in 1856, where he admired Napoleon III's expansive avenues and advised Franz Joseph to replicate them).

She had hoped to slip by unnoticed for a short stroll, but this was not to be. Those already out on the street, charmed by the appearance of the empress, cheered her loudly, and word spread rapidly that Elisabeth had been sighted. At this, people left their shops and homes and poured into the boulevard, making it impossible for either Sisi or her lady-in-waiting to move. Within minutes, there was a real danger that the crowd, in its enthusiasm to get near the empress, would trample her. "You are crushing the Empress! Help! Help! Make way! Make way!" shrieked Countess Festetics. Finally, they were rescued by a few men who forced a path through the crowd and helped the two shaken women into a carriage. Later, Sisi would confess: "An uncanny feeling overcomes me at the sight of the people. I want to help each and every one...but I fear the 'people' in the mass."

This seems to have marked a turning point. Sisi celebrated her thirty-sixth birthday that Christmas Eve. She had already spent more than half her life constrained by the rules of a position for which she was entirely unsuited and which she did not believe in. She could do it no longer.

FROM THIS POINT ON, Elisabeth pursued her own path. Despite everything that had happened to her, Sisi was still in many ways the same young woman she had been at fifteen, with a love of animals, nature, poetry, and athletics, and so her first inclination seems to have been to try to re-create the joyous, uncomplicated days of her youth.

She began by putting in a stable ring at Gödöllő at which to practice circus tricks, as her father had during her childhood in Munich; she also spent long hours riding through the surrounding countryside with friends as well as a hand-picked selection of exceptional Hungarian horsemen. An invitation from her sister Marie, who had landed on her feet with the fashionable equestrian set in England, brought her there in 1874 and introduced her to the rigors of an English hunt. Elisabeth would spend the next eight years of her life pushing herself to become the most accomplished and daring horsewoman on the field. To do this, she required the aid of an experienced sportsman (in hunting terms, a pilot) to guide her. Captain Bay Middleton, a Scotsman nine years her junior and considered the best at this vocation in England, was none too pleased when first asked as a favor to look after her. "What is an empress to me?" he scoffed. He soon changed his mind and became her most devoted hunting companion. This caused jealousy with her sister, as the captain had refused to pilot Marie when she had asked.

During this period, Sisi would dash off to Britain for six weeks at a time or longer to hunt and train with Middleton; in the offseason he came to Gödöllő. She loved the Scotsman's rough manners and contempt for titles as much as she appreciated his expertise; he admired her striking looks, fearlessness, and utter determination to excel. They were not lovers; there might have been an element of flirtation, but it was never acted upon—that would have ruined it for Elisabeth. They were something even closer, they were a team, in and out of the saddle.* Then, in 1881, he married and could no longer devote himself exclusively to his imperial client. Sisi tried again with a different pilot but the magic left with Middleton. In 1882, nearing her forty-fifth birthday, she retired from the sport.

Unable to live without intensive exercise but with her body beginning to show signs of pain and fatigue from the hours she had spent on horseback, the empress switched to walking and fencing. But again, she could do nothing in moderation. She marched at a brisk pace, almost a jog, for miles, until she was speeding along for five, then six, then seven hours at a time. No one could keep up with her; her entourage was forced to have chairs carried along on these outings so they could rest. By 1884, her feet were so swollen and she was subject to such intense sciatic pain that she was forced to consult a specialist in Amsterdam.

But she didn't just pursue athletics—Elisabeth also possessed a deeply romantic nature that sought expression in stories and verses. "Heine is my companion always and everywhere," she confided to Valerie. "Every word, every letter in Heine is a jewel." Now she began again to scribble her own poems, as she had as a teenager, which she kept secret from everyone but her youngest daughter. She also renewed her interest in classical literature, originally kindled by her father's thrilling rendition of the ancient world, with its warring gods and doomed heroes—tales which had held her rapt as a child. As she

---

* Interestingly, Victoria had a similarly close, also not sexual, relationship with her own Scotsman, John Brown, during this period.

approached her fiftieth birthday, she discovered Homer and set herself to learning Greek with the same intensity that she had previously devoted to mastering Hungarian.

But it didn't matter how determinedly she tried to distract herself; Sisi could not ride, hunt, walk, fence, or read her way out of her unhappiness. The anguish she had experienced, particularly in the years after the death of little Sophie, when the empress was so cruelly made to feel the blame for the tragedy, could not be easily vanquished. The pain lingered within her, festered, and grew, until, unable to expunge it, she began to withdraw more and more into herself. This in turn led to behavior that, particularly because of her high position, caused considerable comment.

It was during these years that the legend of Sisi was born. She fled from public observation and held a fan in front of her face, even when riding, to avoid being recognized. She shunned protocol wherever possible and, on those occasions when she was trapped into a particularly tedious court commitment, was not above feigning illness to escape. She indulged her love of travel and, to buy herself privacy while abroad, sometimes enlisted Fanny, her loyal hairdresser, who was of similar build, to impersonate her by dressing up as the empress and waving to the crowds from the deck of the imperial yacht, while Elisabeth, heavily veiled, would slip ashore unnoticed and tour the port.

Her relationship with Franz Joseph was another source of unrelenting criticism. His company clearly bored her, and the couple spent long periods apart; the intimacy between them had passed. Although in April 1879 she agreed to return to Vienna for a few days and stand by his side during the public parade held in honor of their twenty-fifth wedding anniversary, she made a point of signaling her indifference to the milestone by making only the most fleeting of appearances at the grand court ball celebrating the event. And yet, Elisabeth remained so concerned for her husband's safety that three years later, when Franz Joseph visited Italy for the first time since losing Venice, and there was a credible threat of assassination, she insisted on accompanying him, and even demanded the seat in the imperial carriage most vulnerable to attack, so that she might take the bullet, or absorb the effect of an explosion, before he did. Such was the emotional gulf between them, however, that when the emperor expressed loneliness at her frequent absences, rather than compromise her liberty, Sisi instead devised the very modern solution of introducing him to a placid, good-natured, Austrian actress named Katharina Schratt, twenty-three years his junior, to keep him company and take over the imperial marital duties.

It was noted also that the empress's attempts to hold on to her looks, upon which she based so much of her identity, became more extreme as time passed. She had a horror of aging, of wrinkles, of putting on weight. "The Empress took warm baths of olive oil, which she believed helped to preserve the suppleness of her figure," her niece, Countess Marie Larisch, daughter of Sisi's eldest brother (the one who had married an actress), volunteered in her memoirs. "She often slept with wet towels round her waist in order to keep its proportions slender...and drank a horrible decoction composed of the whites of five or six eggs mixed with salt." For a time, Elisabeth survived on broth, and then on milk, until the physician in Amsterdam informed her that she would age herself prematurely if she didn't start eating properly. Still, she successfully held herself to a punishing 110 pounds, the same weight she had maintained since her late teens. "'I want to be always young,' she repeated over and over again to me," Countess Larisch reported.

But even the most determined resistance cannot hold back the ravages of time forever. Although she preserved her gauntness, Elisabeth had spent a great deal of time outdoors exposed to the sun and wind. Her skin lost its dewy freshness; her face became wrinkled. By the time she was fifty, she refused to be photographed.★

Although she could still be fascinating and utterly delightful, especially in the company of those whom she was interested in or admired, as she grew older Sisi spent more and more of her time alone, daydreaming and writing verses. "Mamma talked to me about the poetry of her life of ideas, which nobody suspects, nobody understands,"

★ Poor Sisi, born too early! How she would have loved plastic surgery.

Valerie observed. "Oh, this shrinking from contact with people. How Mamma could be adored if she only wished it!"

Valerie was wrong. There *was* someone who not only appreciated Sisi's morbidly romantic tendencies but also shared her wistfulness and yearning for withdrawal: her cousin the king of Bavaria, Ludwig II. Ludwig revered Elisabeth and recognized her as a kindred spirit. A devout Catholic, the king was haunted by his homosexuality, which was in mortal conflict with his extreme piety. At war with himself, Ludwig, too, boasted a rich interior life, filled with heroic deeds, grace, and beauty. The difference between the king and the empress was a matter of degree: where Sisi was content to stare out the window and sigh for a fanciful country in which she ruled as queen of the fairies, Ludwig was determined to physically *live* in his imaginary world, by building it around him, piece by fantastical piece, as though it were an elaborate stage set.

He got away with it for nearly two decades. From 1868 to 1886, Ludwig conceived and erected two astoundingly extravagant castles: Neuschwanstein, at the top of a mountain ("It is just about the most beautiful spot one could find, holy and unapproachable," the king observed solemnly to his good friend Richard Wagner); and Linderhof, a Bavarian homage to Versailles, complete with a hall of mirrors. And he had no intention of stopping there—a third palace was under construction and three more were in the planning stages. Since it ruined the effect to have to drive up to the front gate of such imposing structures in the old, staid royal carriages, Ludwig replaced them with glittering golden coaches topped by royal crowns and driven by six white horses. In the winter he was ferried around in a sleigh shaped like a giant seashell. As the king slept during the day, and was awake only at night, he travelled from castle to castle in the dark, his procession lit by liveried servants in brilliant raiment, who wielded torches that flickered in the blackness like the fairy lights of an elfin prince.

While Sisi was fond of her cousin and shared his scorn for the tedium associated with royal etiquette (visiting monarchs were "people with whom one must babble," Ludwig sighed), she saw him only rarely, and even then sought to limit their interaction.* Being with the king was diverting, but he tended to go on too long, and it was difficult to get rid of him. Twice, he showed up late at night while she was visiting her family, and insisted on seeing her alone. "Save me, Marie, and think of some means of getting him away. I cannot stand it any longer," Elisabeth begged Countess Festetics on one of these occasions.

Ludwig's excesses tried the patience of all but his most loyal subjects. They didn't mind so much that he woke up at six o'clock every evening, consumed breakfast an hour later, stayed up all night, and then had an eight-course dinner served each morning around dawn for himself and a number of imaginary guests, one of whom was always Marie Antoinette, with whom he chatted and laughed while he ate. ("I love her better than any woman who ever lived," the king declared.) They could tolerate that he deigned to sign official documents only once a week, and that he shut himself away in his palaces, delegating the administration of the kingdom to his ministers.

But what they could not countenance was the expense. By 1885, Ludwig's magnificent castles, filled with marble halls and gilded ceilings, and stuffed with statues, paintings, and rich furniture, had had a ruinous effect on the royal treasury. Not content with draining his own resources, the king borrowed extensively to fulfill his vision, with the result that the kingdom was running a deficit of some 13 million marks, more than twice what it took in annually. His ministers sent him an official cease-and-desist letter, ordering him to halt all future building, and when he refused, they had the leading professor of psychiatry at the University of Munich, Dr. Bernhard von Gudden, declare the king insane. On June 8, 1886, Ludwig was consigned by the Munich government to Gudden's care (conveniently, the professor was also the director of the local asylum) and the most senior of the king's many cousins was appointed regent in his place.

Committing Ludwig in absentia was all very well, but actually

---

* Much has been made of their relationship, but between 1873 and 1886 she seems to have seen him only a handful of times.

taking him into custody proved challenging. A delegation was dispatched to the royal palace of Neuschwanstein, where the king was in residence, but when they arrived, at four in the morning on June 10, Ludwig, tipped off in the nick of time by a loyal retainer, resisted, calling out his guard and barricading himself inside the castle. The committee prudently retired, but two days later they returned, and this time they took the precaution of bribing one of the king's servants to betray him, and so caught their quarry. In the early morning hours of June 12, Ludwig was bundled out of Neuschwanstein in the company of Dr. Gudden and several burly male nurses, and taken to Berg Castle, a lakefront property less than twenty miles outside of Munich, where he was put under house arrest.

The king didn't stay there long, though. The very next day, June 13, 1886, Ludwig convinced Dr. Gudden that he was sane enough for the two of them to take a pleasant walk together without the necessity of guards. A little after six in the evening, the pair was seen heading off in the direction of the water. Two hours later, when they still had not returned, a search party was sent to look for them. Dr. Gudden was discovered facedown in the shallow part of Lake Starnberg with bruises around his neck. It was hypothesized that he had been strangled or held deliberately under the water. His patient was found a little distance away, in a slightly deeper part of the lake. Unlike the doctor's, the king's corpse showed no discernible signs of a struggle, although the water was just five feet deep, and it was well known that Ludwig was a strong swimmer. All the king would have had to do to live was to stand up.

EUGÉNIE

Eugénie and the prince imperial receive the
homage of the imperial party.

30

The Ex-Empress Steps In

The Empire is dead... It is the past, we are the future. It is hatred, we are sympathy. It is treason, we are loyalty.

—Victor Hugo

IN THE MONTHS FOLLOWING HER ESCAPE from Paris, Eugénie did everything she could think of to stop the war and save France from further destruction. She wrote urgent letters to Franz Joseph, to Tsar Alexander, to Wilhelm himself, begging for an end to hostilities and a negotiated peace. She made a personal visit to Victoria, who, despite being wholly on the side of the Prussians ("This dreadful war is vile and unforgivable!" the queen had fumed in the leadup to the battle of Sedan. "May God protect our dear, beloved Germany!"), could not help but be touched by Eugénie's plight. "The Empress bears her tragic fate with dignity," Victoria admitted in a letter to her good friend Augusta, Wilhelm's wife. "She looks very miserable and intensely sad, but still very beautiful, and so touching in her simple dignity... The Prince Imperial is a nice child, but terribly small," she added. Soon after this affecting meeting, the queen took it upon herself to intercede on France's behalf. "You have undoubtedly heard... with what keen interest I have heard of your great victory, how much I admired the courage of the German armies," Victoria flattered Wilhelm. "But now I should like to appeal to your generosity and

Christian charity... Would it not be possible for you to stop now and make peace?" she implored.

But it's difficult to come to terms with people who refuse to accept the reality of their situation. On the evening of Eugénie's flight from Paris, a republic had been declared and General Trochu, clearly by prearrangement, had suddenly resurfaced and taken over responsibility for the defense of the nation. In their euphoria at overthrowing the unprotected regent and Corps Législatif, and thereby finally attaining the political power denied them for nearly two decades, the members of the fledgling republic assumed that the difficult work was over and the war would end. The new minister for foreign affairs, Jules Favre, in a truly jaw-dropping display of naïveté, said as much in a proclamation circulated across Europe on September 6, 1870, in which he called on Germany to lay down its arms now that the French citizenry had liberated itself from the tyranny of its former government. "The King of Prussia declared that he made war not against France, but against the Imperial dynasty," Favre argued. "The dynasty has fallen to the ground. France rises, herself free. Does the King of Prussia wish to continue an impious struggle, which will be at least as fatal to him as to us?"

Well, actually, yes he did—or rather Bismarck did—unless the new German empire was awarded compensation commensurate with the scale of their crushing victory. The Prussian count (about to be raised to a prince for his efforts) felt that Wilhelm deserved not simply an immense monetary settlement, but also the conquered French territory near the eastern border. At this, Favre, on behalf of the new republic, took umbrage and thundered, *"We will not cede either an inch of our territory or a stone of our fortresses"*—and so the war dragged on.

Sadly, it did not take long before Favre's confident assertion that prolonging hostilities would be as fatal to the Prussians as it was to the French was proved spectacularly wrong. The suburbs surrounding Paris were decimated. The capital itself was besieged, starved, and eventually bombed. By November, the last remnants of the French army, who had been holding out against the enemy at the fortress of

Metz, had surrendered. They were taken captive and shipped off to join the rest of their defeated comrades in Germany, bringing the number of incarcerated French soldiers to over 100,000. As most of these men had neither food nor money, and possessed only the light summer clothing in which they had started off so buoyantly to the front in August, they suffered terribly from cold and privation in their German prison cells. Many died, and these, too, were casualties of the Parisians' refusal to accept defeat.

Eventually, however, even the capital was forced by hunger to surrender. An armistice was declared while elections were held for a new National Assembly, charged with negotiating peace terms. This latest attempt at government gathered in Bordeaux (safely away from Paris), where they voted nearly unanimously to have Adolphe Thiers, who had opposed the war from the beginning, as their chief executive, and sent him off to Versailles on February 20, 1871, to treat with Bismarck.

The terms to which Thiers was compelled to agree reflected, at long last, the inescapable truth of the French humiliation. It was a terrible, wrenching peace for the country, but by this time, the vast majority of the population wanted nothing more than to be done with the conflict and to bring their imprisoned sons, husbands, and fathers home. When it came time to read the negotiated settlement aloud to a hushed National Assembly on February 28, Thiers was so overcome with shame that he left in tears after a few sentences, and another delegate had to finish reading the despised treaty for him. By this contract, France forfeited "the fifth part of Lorraine, including Metz," as well as all of Alsace, less the town of Belfort. It had to pay 5 million francs to Prussia, the first million by the end of the year and the rest within three years; German troops would be withdrawn from French soil only proportionally to the amount paid. As a final indignity, the victors demanded the right to parade triumphantly into Paris over the course of three days. It was solely through his acceptance of this last debasing concession that Thiers had won the right to keep Belfort.

In England, Eugénie, stunned at the viciousness of the terms, was stricken that she had not been allowed to mitigate the months of unnecessary suffering by staying and fulfilling her duties as regent. "O God, if there had been no revolution we should have had a peace the very next day," she mourned to Victoria.

THE TREATY WAS RATIFIED and went quickly into effect. Successive waves of German divisions marched into Paris for their three days of glory beginning on March 1, 1871. They were met by "the most profound silence, as there were no spectators," one of the London papers observed. On the last day, in obvious imitation of Louis Napoleon's military parade four years earlier during the time of the Exposition, Wilhelm staged a gigantic review of 100,000 German soldiers in the Bois de Boulogne, but this, too, the citizenry ominously ignored. "The Prussian leaders appear disappointed at the cold and hostile attitude of the Parisians," a correspondent noted.

With the signing of the peace, the prisoners of war were released, and these included Napoleon III. Unlike the rest of the French army, the ex-emperor had spent his captivity in comfort, as a guest in one of Wilhelm's castles. He had had heat, food, affluent surroundings, and books, and had even been allowed visitors—Eugénie herself had made the trip some months earlier to assure herself of his well-being, and to discuss the family strategy going forward. On March 20, 1871, Louis Napoleon arrived at Dover. Baron Heeckeren was among those who had traveled to England to cheer his liberation. "The Empress and Prince Imperial ran forward to meet him," the banker reported. "A vast crowd had collected on the landing-stage. There were cries in French and English of 'Vive l'Empereur!' 'Vive l'Impératrice!' Old friends gathered round him...The Empress and Prince Imperial embraced him passionately. He pressed them to his heart, but was silent. An eloquent silence!" the baron exclaimed.

Eugénie had rented a private home in Chislehurst, about twelve miles southeast of London (discovered for her by the invaluable Dr. Evans), and it was here that the family settled after Louis Napoleon's release. Although the ex-emperor had written to his wife that, once he was freed, he just wanted to retire with her and their son to a quiet, ivy-covered little house, the news out of Paris in the aftermath of the peace was so infamous that he could not help being drawn back into politics.

The capital had not taken at all well to the terms of the treaty, or to the prideful parade of Prussians around the Arc de Triomphe, and, as was its wont, the citizenry now gave vent to its unhappiness and rebelled against their latest target, the Thiers government, which they held responsible for these misfortunes. Subduing this revolt was made significantly more complicated by the fact that the Parisians were well armed. During the siege, General Trochu (who, like his predecessors, was forced to resign for not having delivered the miraculous victory that everyone believed they deserved) had equipped the approximately 300,000 national guardsmen stationed in the city with cannons, paying them, as well as any other citizen who secured a rifle, thirty sous a day as defenders of France. For those segments of the capital impoverished by lack of work or resources, this stipend had often meant the difference between survival and an entire family's death by starvation. Desperate to improve their lives, this distressed underclass now challenged the new National Assembly by refusing to disarm.

Rather than confront the insurgency head-on, Thiers decided to be clever about it and deprive his opponents of their artillery by cunning. At four in the morning of March 18, just two days before Napoleon III's arrival at Dover, Thiers ordered some 15,000 troops into Paris to try to sneak the cannons out of the capital while the revolutionary element was still asleep. Alas, a successful subterfuge generally requires attention to small details like logistics, which Thiers had unfortunately neglected to consider. Specifically, he had failed to take into account that cannons are too heavy for human beings to transport without the aid of horses and wagons, and while his soldiers were standing around for hours waiting for these to appear, the Parisians woke up. Crowds lined the streets, the national guardsmen came out in force, and Thiers's troops, unwilling to open fire on their countrymen, left the artillery where it was and were welcomed as fellow patriots by the insurgents. The mob was substantially less forgiving of the regimental commanders, however, and by that afternoon two of the generals in charge had been violently taken into custody and summarily executed.

This was the genesis of the Paris Commune, a short-lived experiment at socialist self-government. It began altruistically, with the intention of nobly fulfilling the promise inherent in the revolutionary slogan "*Liberté, égalité, fraternité.*" Elections were held and committees established to divide wealth and opportunity more fairly among the populace and improve working and educational conditions. But implementing these objectives proved more elusive than anticipated, and when first disappointment and then chaos set in, the atmosphere in the city turned darker and more violent. Priests were attacked and the more affluent neighborhoods threatened and looted. After two months, Thiers's patience ran out and on May 21, 1871, he began bombing the capital and sent the army in to restore order. In response, the Commune burned down the city hall and the palace. The week that followed was among the deadliest in French history. Thousands of the Communards were executed, and many more imprisoned. By the time Thiers had reclaimed authority, Paris was in ruins. "Great was my astonishment when I drove through the streets of the capital and saw the extent to which the destruction had been carried," attested Dr. Evans, who returned to Paris the week after the Commune fell, to help with the wounded. "The devastation had not been the work of the Germans, but of the French themselves," he noted sadly.

For Eugénie and Louis Napoleon, the reports of this slaughter were just more proof of the incompetence of republican rule. Some of the newspapers went even further and suggested that the situation was deteriorating so quickly that it was only a matter of time before the emperor was reinstated. "Napoleon arrives in England to-day, and, in presence of the horrible events now happening in Paris, we may question whether Chislehurst may not prove to be the first stage on the road to the Tuileries," observed the correspondent for the *Morning Post.* Dr. Evans, returning to England to visit Eugénie later that winter, also remarked on the changing political environment, and the many courtiers who had begun soliciting Napoleon III's favor. "During the latter part of the year, the unsettled state of affairs in France ... was causing a manifest reaction in favor of the Empire," he disclosed. "The probability of its restoration at no distant day led the supporters of the Imperial dynasty to make frequent visits to Chislehurst and to speak of the future with hope and confidence."

But it was not to be. The next year, Napoleon III's old nemesis, his urinary tract blockage, reasserted itself. He became sicker and sicker. At last, in late December, the emperor submitted to an examination by the most respected urologist in London, who took one look at him and recommended an immediate operation. On January 2, 1873, he underwent surgery. The doctor who performed the procedure was shocked when he peered inside his patient and discovered the extent of the blockage. In fact, the stone had grown so large over the years that the surgeon couldn't crush it all at once, so a few days later, a second operation was performed. "The agony must have been constant. I cannot understand how he could have borne it," the specialist reflected soberly afterwards.

Even then, the physician could not get all of it and needed to schedule a third attempt. This last operation had to wait until Louis Napoleon recovered, which he did not do as quickly as he had after the first surgery. But he slept through the night of January 8 and seemed so well when he woke the next morning that his doctors thought they might perhaps try again that afternoon. Eugénie, who had been by her husband's side throughout, ordered a carriage made ready so she could fly to the prince imperial, who was attending a nearby school, to let him know his father was better.

She was on her way out the door when she was suddenly called back in. Louis Napoleon had sunk so quickly that they barely had time to summon a priest. The patient had contracted a blood infection that had passed from the bladder to the kidneys. Eugénie sent urgently for her son but he did not arrive in time to say goodbye. Her husband's last words demonstrated his preoccupation with his shameful defeat. "Conneau, were you at Sedan?" he whispered to one of the physicians huddled around his bed.

Napoleon III died just before noon on January 9, 1873. He was sixty-four years old. During the course of his long, improbable career he had been simultaneously idolized and reviled for being both wildly successful and spectacularly humbled. His achievement may be measured by the distance he had fallen. He built France into a modern economic power and Paris into the envy of Europe, only to see his dream of greatness fall victim to the very intrigues that he himself had put in motion.

Despite everything that had happened between them, Eugénie was shattered by her husband's death. When the prince, pulled out of his classes, appeared soon afterward, she gathered him in her arms. "I have only you, Louis!" she wept.

IN THE AFTERMATH of Napoleon III's demise, Eugénie devoted herself to ensuring that her son maintained his rightful position as heir to the imperial dynasty. The day after the funeral (which was held at Chislehurst in the midst of "a terrible crowd of onlookers and an enormous number of French people...Altogether 4,000 Frenchmen came over for the ceremony," as Victoria informed Augusta), fifteen-year-old Prince Louis appeared privately before a select group of military commanders, former imperial ministers, and aristocrats. A barely-under-control Eugénie, tears still streaming down her face, entered soon after, and together she and Louis went around the room. Every man present sank down on one knee and kissed the empress's hand as a gesture of loyalty to her and her son as they passed. "A week ago he was only the Prince Imperial—to-day he is Napoleon IV," observed one of the guests at this ceremony.*

Nor did Eugénie neglect to remind the world of the legitimacy of Louis's claim to the imperial throne whenever she could. On March 16, 1874, when the prince came into his majority at the age of eighteen, his

---

* Another reason for this formality was that (as expected) Plon-Plon was trying to take the regency of the prince imperial away from her. This was Eugénie's way of fighting back, and it succeeded. "Prince Napoleon is there with his wife and sister, which is very painful for the poor Empress!" Victoria gossiped to Augusta.

mother made sure the event made the papers. "Titled ladies by the score, ancient Deputies, Grand Crosses of the Legion of Honour, senators, members of the present Assembly, prefects and sous-prefects, officers of the Army and statesmen whose names are household words" packed the little church in Chislehurst, where the birthday mass was held, reported the *Daily Telegraph*. Thousands more stood outside shouting *"Vive l'Empereur!"*

Louis understood his role and welcomed it. "When I lost my father, my duty showed itself clear," he told his tutor. "From that day, I had only one end in life." As the Bonapartes were always soldiers first, the prince applied himself with energy to this vocation. He enrolled at an English military academy, where he developed a close cadre of friends and graduated towards the top of his class.

But unlike Spain, which, after a brief experiment with an imported sovereign, had returned Alfonso, Queen Isabella's heir, to the throne (Victor Emmanuel's second son had originally been coaxed to assume the crown, only to be run out of Madrid two years later), France remained stubbornly resistant to imperial rule. Ironically, because of the innumerable commercial, technological, and industrial improvements made during the empire—the railroads, the textile businesses, the financial system, the communications network, the prolonged growth in international market share—the economy had recovered quickly and Thiers had been able to pay off the Prussians ahead of schedule. There were still many supporters within the National Assembly who favored a return to some form of monarchy, but they were unable to coalesce behind a single candidate, and in the meantime, the years passed and the republic held.

Faced with this reality, Louis began to get impatient. By 1878, his friend Alfonso, humiliatingly some months younger than himself, had already been king of Spain *for three years* while he, Louis, heir to the magnificent Bonaparte legacy, was no closer to reestablishing the empire than he had been when his father died. "For if another august personality [Napoleon III] accustomed himself to exile, I do not wish to see mine prolonged indefinitely," Louis groused. The prince hated sitting around waiting for the political tide to turn his way. He felt he needed to do something to speed the process along, something courageous and useful that would remind the French of the brilliance of his family name, and the greatness that could once again be theirs if they would only put their trust in him. Luckily, the perfect vehicle for this was right at hand: the English war against the Zulus in South Africa.

Although the British government had been unwilling to intercede militarily in any of the recent conflicts in Europe, that did not mean they were against the use of force in principle. On the contrary, they simply preferred, under the pretext of spreading enlightened civilization, to pick fights with people who had lots of unprotected, useful natural resources. It was *so* much easier, and certainly more profitable, for example, to attack a South African kingdom like Zululand, which was rich in diamond mines but whose warriors lacked the sort of advanced weaponry necessary to shoot back.

When Eugénie first heard that her son wanted to run off and fight the Zulus, she was appalled. She tried every argument she could think of to dissuade him. "If anything happens to you, your adherents will not weep for you; they will have a grudge against you!" she warned him. She was greatly relieved when the British war office turned down his application to serve.

But Louis was distraught. He wept the day he received his official rejection, and fell into depression. His friends from school were all there; he wished to join them. He was aware that they made fun of him in France for his small stature and lack of achievement. She was unable to shake him out of it. "Do you want me to remain always the 'little Prince' to everyone?" he cried.

And so, against her better judgment, Eugénie intervened. She went to see the duke of Cambridge, who ran the war office. The duke, in turn, went behind Prime Minister Disraeli's back and interceded on the prince imperial's behalf with Victoria. Louis had written a letter outlining his reasons for wishing to participate in the conflict, and these touched the queen. "For eight years I have been the guest of England," Louis wrote. "I completed my education at one of her military schools... The war which England has been carrying on for more than a year at the Cape of Good Hope has assumed a gravity which it had not presented until now... I have not wished to remain a stranger to the fatigues and the danger of those troops amongst whom I have so many comrades," he finished plaintively.

A compromise was hammered out. Louis could go, but he would be attached in an unofficial capacity only, as an observer, to the commanding officer. Disraeli, forced to bow to the will of his sovereign, recognized Eugénie's hand in it and snorted that the scheme was the work of "two obstinate old women."

Louis shipped out on February 27, 1879, and reached Cape Town on March 26. He journeyed inland and joined the staff of the commanding general. There was no direct telegraph; it took weeks to receive news from Europe but the prince nonetheless managed to follow French politics. His reputation clearly remained uppermost in his mind. "Public feeling in France has then been, as I supposed, favorable to my decision," he wrote to his mother on April 20. "But it is not enough to go, I must come back with honor!" And he began to participate in reconnaissance missions, which frequently precipitated small skirmishes with bands of Zulu warriors. Still, he took the time to write to Eugénie, knowing how worried she was for him. "My Dear Mother, I am writing hurriedly on a leaf of my note-book; in a few minutes I am off to select a camping-ground for the second division... I did not want to let slip this opportunity of embracing you with all my heart," he scribbled reassuringly on June 1.

This was to be his last letter. That very afternoon, while he and the small scouting expedition he had joined were resting far from the main camp, a Zulu warrior was spotted in the distance. The horses were immediately called for. As the British officers were preparing to mount, some fifty Zulus suddenly charged out of the tall grass. There was chaos, one man was killed, and the rest of the unit galloped off—all except Louis. His horse, frightened by the noise, had shied and bolted as the prince, running beside it, tried desperately to mount. The saddle slipped and Louis fell off to the side as the horse raced on without him.

"The Prince is down!" cried one of the company, but his call went unheeded and the expedition continued its flight.

They came back later to look for the body. Realizing that he had been abandoned, Louis had evidently struggled to his feet and turned to face the enemy. Moving forward to meet his doom, he managed to get off three shots from his pistol before the Zulus fell on him. He was speared seventeen times in a matter of moments. Afterwards, the warriors tore off his uniform and distributed the clothing among themselves, leaving only Louis's medallions, which were hanging on a chain around his neck, on his mutilated, naked corpse.

It took two weeks for the news to reach London. "No, no, it can't be!" cried Victoria when she was handed the fatal telegram. "Poor dear Empress! Her only child, her *all*, gone!"

ELISABETH

Mary Vetsera

31

The Imperial Cabin in the Woods

Yonder, where the stars glow nightly,
We shall find those joys smile brightly
Which on earth seem far away.
Only in Death's cold embraces
Life grows warm and light replaces
Night's dark gloom at dawn of day.

—Heinrich Heine

LUDWIG II'S FORCED REMOVAL FROM RULE on the grounds of lunacy, followed almost immediately by his death by drowning, shocked Elisabeth. The empress happened to be in Bavaria just at this time, having
rented a house near Possi, just across the lake from Berg Castle where
the king had been taken after his capture. Despite her annoyance at his
tendency to overstay his welcome, Sisi had never found her cousin to
be anything but lucid. To her, Ludwig was simply a person who had
yearned to live a more poetic and romantic life than ordinary mortals,
just as she did. "The King was no madman," Elisabeth protested vehemently when she was told the morning after of Ludwig's apparent murder of his doctor, followed by his own despairing suicide. "Only an
eccentric who lived in a world of ideas." That the sort of make-believe
behavior in which the king had indulged qualified as insanity was
deeply unsettling to her. Her sister-in-law Charlotte, who after all

these years still had not recovered from the delusions that had beset her upon her return from Mexico — *she* was insane. But not Ludwig! "They might have treated him more gently, and so, perhaps, spared him such a fearful end," Elisabeth exclaimed angrily. She fell into a depression, weeping and even throwing herself on the floor in her grief, and worried that she, too, as a blood relation of the king's (albeit removed) carried the taint of lunacy. That year, she began to speak of taking her own life.

But for all her forebodings, the empress was not the person most at risk of despondency within the imperial family. Although he was not nearly as transparent about it, Rudolf, twenty-seven at the time of Ludwig's death, was actually far more fragile, both emotionally and psychologically, than was his mother.

Sisi's relationship with her son had been plagued over the years by a series of heartbreaking errors of omission and miscommunication. Rudolf had been seven when Elisabeth had finally managed to wrest control of his education away from Sophia in 1865 — old enough to understand and be grateful to her not only for freeing him from the sadistic methods of his former governor, but also for the new, liberal tutors who engaged him with art and literature, and more modern, inclusive ideas of government. He adored his mother, whose beauty and powers of fascination were then at their height, for speaking to him as to an adult of the situation in Hungary and bringing him with her to Budapest when the war broke out against Prussia. These were thrilling years for Rudolf. He idolized the gallant Count Andrássy, who rode so swiftly and fearlessly through the Hungarian countryside that he appeared to the boy like a medieval knight in a storybook, and when his parents were crowned in May of 1867, Rudolf felt himself to have been part of a great achievement for having been at his mother's side throughout, and not left behind in the protected banality of Ischl with his grandmother.

But then, the very next year, Elisabeth had given birth to his younger sister, Valerie, and everything had changed. Suddenly, his mother, consumed with the care of this latest child, had no time for him.

Rudolf was a very sensitive boy who needed love as much as did Sisi herself, and he was hurt by her long absences from Vienna, where he, as heir to the throne, was compelled to stay. "So in these difficult days poor Papa must be separated again from darling Mama," twelve-year-old Rudolf wrote bitterly in a complaint that was clearly as much about himself as his father.

Feeling himself abandoned, the crown prince naturally turned for consolation to his doting grandmother. But even this support was lost to him when Sophia succumbed to bronchitis in 1872. The archduchess's death brought Elisabeth back to court, but only for a brief interlude; mother and son both participated in the World Exhibition, but soon thereafter the empress resumed her wanderings, taking six-year-old Valerie with her. By that time, Gisela had married and was living in Bavaria with her husband and his family, and fifteen-year-old Rudolf was left alone with his tutors—and his father.

The pressures on him were enormous. The crown prince, highly intelligent, artistic, and imaginative, was as unsuited as his mother to the regimented court life and bureaucratic practices to which Franz Joseph insisted his son conform. Rudolf did his best. He entered the army, as his father had, and was promoted to commander of an infantry regiment in Prague. He accompanied Franz Joseph on state visits to Germany and made the acquaintance of ambassadors and government officials. In January of 1878, at the age of nineteen, he traveled to England and while his mother rode to hounds in the countryside, he toured factories and towns, charmed Victoria and her daughter Princess Beatrice, and made the acquaintance of Edward, Prince of Wales, the queen's rakish heir.

It was during this visit to Britain that his relationship with Elisabeth suffered a serious estrangement. The quarrel came as the result of the interference of Sisi's sister Marie. The ex-queen of Naples, who had won world renown as the courageous heroine of Gaeta, had not had a happy life afterwards. In 1870, after more than a decade of marriage, Marie had finally managed to conceive a child with Francis, only to have the baby die within months. Rome had fallen to Victor

Emmanuel soon thereafter, and the ex-queen now lived on the edge of fashionable society, having neither the income nor the prestige of genuine royalty. Although she claimed to enjoy her freedom, she clearly envied Elisabeth, who had everything Marie did not, and she took the opportunity of her nephew's visit to lash out at her sister by spitefully repeating to Rudolf the hurtful gossip that his mother was carrying on a scandalous affair with her pilot, Captain Middleton. When the prince expressed his outrage, Marie turned around and told Sisi that her son believed her to be an adulteress. Although Countess Festetics, worming the story out of Rudolf—"like a child he poured out his heart...with tears in his eyes he said...he had lost his most beautiful illusions"—rapidly disabused the prince of his suspicions, Elisabeth, wounded that her son could have believed such slander, did not trust him again for years.

But Rudolf never stopped loving or needing her. Two years later, in 1880, when Franz Joseph arranged for his son to marry Princess Stéphanie, daughter of Leopold II, king of the Belgians (Charlotte's brother), and Sisi broke off her travels to come to Brussels to meet her future daughter-in-law, it was noted how Rudolf's face lit up when she stepped off the train, and how gratefully he hugged her in greeting. The empress had had no part in arranging the match; it had been entirely her husband's doing and had come as an unpleasant surprise. It wasn't simply that Elisabeth found the Belgian royal family pretentious and tiresome. There was also the issue of Charlotte's madness—who knew if the bride-to-be harbored a similar malady? Countess Festetics reported that the empress turned pale when she read the telegram announcing the engagement.

The couple was married in May of the following year, Rudolf at twenty-three, Stéphanie at sixteen, exactly replicating the ages at which Franz Joseph and Sisi had been wed. Again in imitation of his parents, their honeymoon was spent at Laxenburg. (The Austrian court was nothing if not consistent.) By this time, the crown prince was beginning to show the first signs of frustration and unhappiness at his position. Rudolf had been educated by a small cadre of enlightened instructors who shared his mother's political sympathies, and his adoption of these values put him in direct conflict with his father. He resented Elisabeth's withdrawal from court, as it left him as the lone voice for liberalism in Vienna. "There was a time when the Empress... talked to the Emperor about serious matters, prompted by views diametrically opposed to those he held," Rudolf observed to one of his former tutors in December of 1881. "These times are past. The great lady no longer cares for anything but sport; and so this source of outside opinion... is now also closed... Three or four years ago the Emperor was, to some degree... reconciled to the nineteenth century. Now he is once again as he was in poor Grandmama's time," he concluded witheringly.

Over the course of the next five years, Rudolf flailed about, trying to find a way to force his father's government to adopt a more progressive attitude toward its subjects. He befriended the editor of Vienna's most liberal newspaper and surreptitiously sent him opinion pieces in which he emphasized the need for modern policies that would benefit formerly marginalized groups such as laborers and students, as well as oppressed minorities like Slavs and Jews. He met secretly with Hungarian politicians, who floated the idea of having him proclaimed king in his father's stead. He made similarly clandestine contacts with liberal politicians in Britain and France.

But everywhere he turned, he was met by the stone wall of his father's conservatism. By this time, Franz Joseph had appointed a new prime minister, Count Eduard Taaffe, whom he had known since childhood. Count Taaffe could be counted on to keep any troubling ideas of reform out of the government. The prime minister, to coerce the prince to remain in line, ordered the Austrian secret police to follow him; Rudolf was aware of the tail and its source. He despised Taaffe, who returned the favor. But it was all about who held influence with the emperor, and an immovable Franz Joseph, now in his fifties, naturally chose the static policies of his toadying minister over the more progressive notions of his volatile son.

Rudolf's marriage, too, was disappointing. His wife, fond of ceremony and privilege, had neither the gift of beauty nor the charm of fascination, and he soon grew tired of her. The birth in 1883 of a daughter, rather than the much-desired male heir for whom he had hoped, did not help. To fill the void inside him, Rudolf turned to sex. He was indiscriminate and voracious about it, and as he was the handsome heir to the Austrian empire, women flocked to him.

Inevitably, he contracted gonorrhea.★ The first sign was a very serious, painful urinary infection in February of 1886, just a few months before Ludwig II's suicide. To ease the torment, Rudolf began to drink heavily. A few weeks later, Stéphanie also fell ill from the disease; she became sterile. "After the birth of my daughter I was reproached with being unable to bear another child," she recorded grimly in her memoirs. "The court knew only too well whose fault that was."

The next year, the prince's infection flared up again, only this time, frighteningly, it attacked Rudolf's eyes. Although his doctors managed to ameliorate the worst of the symptoms, it was clear the sickness was progressing. The prince, approaching his thirtieth birthday, fell into such deep despair that he made out his will. To his drinking Rudolf now added opium for the pain. He prowled shady establishments that catered to debauchery and fell in with a fast crowd bent on hedonism. "He was spending his evenings in circles where I could not follow him," Stéphanie reported. "From that time onwards the Crown Prince would sometimes not return home until the early hours of the morning, and in an undesirable condition."

As he spiraled downward, his problems mounted until he could see only pain and infamy in his future. His body was polluted, he had fallen heavily into debt, his political career was under attack by his father's minister. His wife was threatening to go to the emperor if he did not reform his behavior. Elisabeth, coming home in May of 1888

★ For this diagnosis, see Fritz Judtmann's *Mayerling: The Facts behind the Legend,* pp. 17–21. Judtmann referred the evidence to medical experts, who concluded with "a very high degree of probability that the Crown Prince was suffering from a gonorrheal infection."

from one of her many trips abroad, was shocked when she saw him. "Are you ill?" she questioned him. But he brushed her off. "No, only tired and nervous," he said.

His mother, consumed with her own interests, utterly failed to perceive his distress. She could not know about Rudolf's condition—venereal disease was not a subject one discussed with one's imperial parents—but there were other signs that the prince needed help. That holiday season, Valerie's upcoming wedding was to be announced; Sisi had insisted that her beloved younger daughter be allowed to marry for love, and that this one child not be pressured to wed until she was old enough to know her own mind. Valerie had turned twenty that year, and had made her choice: the bridegroom was to be the grandson of the former grand duke of Tuscany (the one who had been run out of Florence after the Austrian defeat at Solferino in 1859 and had come complaining to Vienna about it). The entire family gathered to celebrate the joyous news on Christmas Eve, which coincided with Sisi's fifty-first birthday. Rudolf's gift to her on this occasion was a hugely expensive collection of rare Heine editions; he could not have expressed his love, nor begged for hers, more poignantly. But it was what happened after he'd presented her with the poems that was truly telling: the thirty-year-old prince suddenly threw himself into his mother's arms and gave himself over to uncontrollable sobs.

But still Elisabeth didn't see. It's true that, like Rudolf's illness, his drinking and adultery had been carefully kept from her. Franz Joseph knew some of it—not all, the worst had been withheld from him as well—but the emperor had not seen fit to share what worrying information he did possess with his wife. This does not absolve her, however. Sisi did not see because she had elected to be absent from her son's life, just as she had chosen to vacate her duties as wife and empress. There is no saying that Elisabeth could have done anything to alter the course of events, but of all the family, she held the most sway over Rudolf's heart.

It was decided that Christmas Eve to invite Valerie's future in-laws to a more formal celebratory dinner later in January, after the New Year. But first, the crown prince planned to do a little shooting at Mayerling.

MAYERLING WAS THE NAME of a small hunting lodge about twenty-five miles southwest of Vienna that Rudolf used as a convenient getaway for sporting holidays. It was only two hours from the capital by train and the surrounding woods were well-stocked with game. Rudolf liked to shoot birds there, and often invited similarly inclined friends to join him. One such gathering was arranged for three days beginning Monday, January 28, 1889.

But this was not to be an ordinary shooting party. The crown prince had lured his guests—there were two of them, one his steadfast friend and hunting partner, Count Josef Hoyos; the other his wife's brother-in-law, Prince Philipp of Coburg—to this spot under false pretenses. They were there to serve as blinds.

For months, Rudolf had searched for an honorable way out of his mounting despair. Like Sisi herself, he told several people he wished to kill himself. But suicide would not expiate him for his sins unless conducted as part of a larger dramatic narrative. He needed a cause greater than himself, greater than the sordidness of disease, debt, and political intrigue in which he was embroiled, to give him the appearance of a hero's death. A romantic like his mother, the idea of dying for love seemed to Rudolf the only solution. But when he asked his longtime paramour, Marie Caspar, a professional courtesan known as "Mitzi," to end her life with his in a passionate double suicide, she had only laughed and declined the honor.

And then he met Mary Vetsera.

Mary was the seventeen-year-old daughter of Baroness Helene Vetsera, a wealthy socialite who mingled in Viennese court circles through her intimacy with Elisabeth's niece, Countess Larisch, whom the baroness counted as one of her closest friends. In her youth, Helene had flirted so openly with Rudolf that even Franz Joseph, not generally known for his powers of observation, had taken notice and remarked on her brazenness. Now the baroness's daughter Mary—pretty, trusting, and naïve—came under the prince's spell and formed a crush on him. As Rudolf's unhappiness with his wife was common knowledge, Mary pestered her mother's good friend Countess Larisch to arrange a rendezvous with the object of her affections so she could confess her love.

Mary's timing was only too perfect. Countess Larisch happened to be experiencing some financial embarrassment of her own in November 1888. Her tastes were too extravagant for her unsympathetic husband's income and she had a debt of some 25,000 florins that needed to be repaid immediately if a scandal was to be avoided. The countess offered her imperial cousin her services as a discreet romantic intermediary if he could just see his way to advancing her the required sum. Rudolf, in desperate need of a little unconditional adoration, agreed to pay her to bring Mary to him.

The couple's first assignation occurred on November 15, when Mary made an excuse to stay home from a family evening at the opera, and Countess Larisch instead spirited her to Rudolf's rooms at the Hofburg Palace. They would meet several times over the course of the next two months, with the countess often employing the excuse to the baroness that she needed Mary's company on a shopping excursion. Everything about these trysts was designed to appeal to a schoolgirl's vision of romance. Mary did not find the fact that she had to be let in surreptitiously by Rudolf's valet at a side entrance, fly up the back stairs, cross a rooftop garden, and then climb in through an open window to meet her love demeaning; she thought it thrilling.

Two weeks into January, the inevitable happened. Mary wrote a letter to a friend in England swooning that "she belonged entirely" to the crown prince, and the couple even exchanged cigarette-cases to commemorate the occasion. (Mary's to Rudolf read: "In gratitude to a kindly fate! January 13th, 1889.") Five days later, chillingly, the seventeen-year-old made out her will. She also left a note for her sister that was meant to be found after her death. "We are both going blissfully into the uncertain beyond," she avowed. To her mother, she wrote, "Forgive me for what I have done; I could not resist love."

Even after he had clearly obtained Mary's assent to his plan, Rudolf seems to have wavered. But on the morning of January 26, he had a terrible fight with his father, where the emperor was heard to exclaim, "You are not worthy to be my successor!" The prince was observed to have left this interview shaking with rage, and it was then that Rudolf invited his friends Count Hoyos and Prince Philipp to go hunting. Unbeknownst to them, he also arranged with Countess Larisch for Mary to escape from home and drive out to Mayerling with him in two days' time.

And that is what happened. On the morning of Monday, January 28, the countess again appealed for Mary's aid in shopping, and the unsuspecting baroness gave her permission; her daughter never returned. Rather, in an elaborate bit of playacting, while the countess was loudly occupied in a shop, Mary slipped away and into a carriage that took her across town to Rudolf's coachman, who was waiting in another vehicle. The prince soon joined her and the two rode merrily off to the hunting lodge by back roads where they would be less noticeable. As planned, they arrived much later than Count Hoyos or Prince Philipp, who had both taken the train. While the men were inside the lodge's main room, waiting for dinner, Mary slipped easily into Rudolf's quarters without anyone but the valet seeing her. The next morning, Tuesday, January 29, Rudolf appeared at breakfast with his friends and told them he had a cold and was going to stay in that day. He had timed this holiday deliberately to coincide with Valerie's engagement party, at which he and his brother-in-law were both expected; Rudolf then told Prince Philipp to go back to Vienna that evening without him and make his apologies to his father for being too ill to attend the gathering.

His brother-in-law did as he was told and stayed in Vienna that night, after which he took the early morning train back to Mayerling. Count Hoyos had dinner alone with Rudolf that evening, then retired to his rooms, which were in a guesthouse outside the main lodge. He spent a peaceful night and awoke around eight. He was on his way to the main dining room to have breakfast when Prince Philipp, whose train had arrived at about the same time, showed up. At this point Rudolf's valet came urgently towards both men and told them he had been trying to awaken his master for some time and had received no response to his repeated knocking. He wanted to break down Rudolf's bedroom door, which was locked from the inside. The count gave permission to do this, and he and Prince Philipp both went along to investigate. However, they stopped short of actually going into the room, out of delicacy, after the valet admitted that the crown prince had a woman in the apartment with him.

The servant broke down the door. Inside, he found Mary's corpse stretched out on the bed, her eyes staring blankly, her long, beautiful hair flowing loosely down her shoulders, a rose clasped in her folded hands. She had been shot in the left temple and the bullet had exited just above her right ear; her face was untouched and peaceful. Rudolf, by contrast, presented a far more grisly sight. The prince was found sitting slumped over the side of the bed, surrounded by a pool of blood, the top of his head blown away, his brains spilling out from the gash in his skull.

THE COVER-UP BEGAN IMMEDIATELY. Count Hoyos, without getting a look at the bodies, left at once to inform the court. The valet, anxious to avoid being blamed for having missed or ignored the sound of gunshots, initially implied that the lovers had died from poisoning, and so this is what Hoyos told Rudolf's chamberlain when he got to the Hofburg Palace. Rudolf's chamberlain then went to Elisabeth's chamberlain and told him what had happened, and then the two of them approached Franz Joseph's aide-de-camp. Everyone was afraid to tell the emperor, so to lay the responsibility off, they got Sisi's chamberlain to convey the news to her instead.

And so Elisabeth had to absorb the shock first. She broke down in wild tears, but had only minutes before having to begin comforting the rest of the family. "Not yet! Do not come in!" she cried out as she struggled to control herself when her husband, understanding that something had happened, came to her door.

She told Franz Joseph, then Valerie, then Stéphanie. Valerie knew instantly. "Has he killed himself?" she asked. "No, no," Sisi insisted, aghast. "The girl poisoned him."

But try though they might to stifle it, the scandal began to leak out to the press. Franz Joseph took over and kept as many of the details from his wife as he could. Elisabeth likely never knew that Mary's corpse, her eyes still wide open and staring, had been hastily removed from Rudolf's room and flung unceremoniously into one of the outer cabins at Mayerling, with the bloodstained sheets piled on top of her; or that her body was later smuggled out in the dead of night in a carriage, where, to avoid suspicion, it was propped up as though she were still alive. As a final indignity, the seventeen-year-old was then secretly buried at four o'clock in the morning in the pouring rain in a small rural cemetery, before her distraught mother, who had been informed that her daughter was a murderer, could say a last farewell.

Nor was Sisi likely told the true nature of Rudolf's illness. Rather, suicide being a mortal sin, the court physicians instead diagnosed derangement, which allowed his remains to be interred in the imperial crypt. It was probably also kept from her that at the time of his death, her son was in debt to a French banker for some 300,000 florins, and that there were rumors he had been involved in treasonous activities in association with the more radical members of the Hungarian parliament.

But her husband's efforts to protect her from the more sordid aspects of her son's life in no way assuaged the empress's grief. Rudolf had left a number of farewell notes in Vienna, but only one had been written from Mayerling, and it was to Elisabeth. The letter had been composed in the darkness of the early morning, in the hours after the crown prince had shot Mary, where, in the presence of her carefully staged, lifeless body he sat alone, working up the courage to take his own life. The way Rudolf had laid out his "touchingly pure angel," as he called his victim, with her hair tumbling over her shoulders, was eerily reminiscent of the portrait of Sisi painted by Winterhalter, which hung in his father's study, and so it is perhaps not surprising that his last thoughts were of her. "I have no right to go on living; I have killed!" Rudolf confessed to his mother.

Later, Elisabeth acknowledged that she had suspected that her son was deeply unhappy in his marriage, but that she had deliberately refrained from meddling, "for I myself suffered so unspeakably under my mother-in-law," she wept.

ELISABETH
&
EUGÉNIE

Sisi and Eugénie, with Franz Joseph in the background, at Cap Martin

32

The New Disciples of the Dagger

But on, still on, no peace, no rest,
Thou never still mayst be;
What thou of yore didst love the best,
Thou ne'er again shalt see.

—Heinrich Heine

VICTORIA HAD OF COURSE BEEN CORRECT; Eugénie was devastated by the death of her son. The queen kindly sent a personal emissary to convey the intelligence as gently as possible, and the household at Chislehurst was duly instructed to withhold the news from the ex-empress until this delegation arrived. But this proved impossible when Eugénie, rising at an early hour, mistakenly read a letter intended for one of her staff that referred, obliquely, to some mysteriously dreadful event. Even then, she was told only that the prince imperial had been seriously wounded in action and that the war office was sending someone along with the latest update. After two hours of frantic worrying, the envoy finally made his appearance, and the terrified mother learned the truth.

For days, she could neither sleep nor eat. Victoria herself came to check on her. It was only after this visit that the ex-empress found the strength to send the briefest of notes to her mother, eighty-five-year-old María Manuela, herself in decline in Madrid. "I am still alive, but only because grief does not kill," Eugénie wrote hopelessly.

The prince's remains were returned to England and the funeral conducted at Chislehurst on July 12, 1879. The details of his gruesome end made all the papers, and expressions of condolence poured in. In Vienna, the entire court went into mourning for two weeks. In France, although it was reported that "all the Republican journals...[expressed] the opinion that with the death of Prince Louis Napoleon, Bonapartism is ended," a memorial service at the Saint Augustin church, built by Napoleon III during the glory years of the restoration of Paris, and as such a symbol of the empire, told a different story. "Countless hundreds...filled every nook and corner...It was a touching scene to witness that great gathering of all sorts of people, Princes and shopkeepers, the aristocracy of an Empire and workmen in blouses, ladies of high degree and children of the people, all...bent together in common grief at the death of one who was almost unknown to them," observed one correspondent. "It shows how the Napoleonic legend still lingers in the minds of Frenchmen," he added.

After the funeral, Eugénie's one thought was to see the place where her son had spent his last moments. The next year, at the age of fifty-four, she sailed to Cape Town and spent the next two months trekking inland with a small entourage and a military guide to the lonely site of the prince's massacre. She had timed this excursion to coincide with the first anniversary of his death. On the evening of June 1, 1880, she lit candles by the small stone cross that had been erected to mark the place where he had fallen, and held a solitary vigil. It was a windless night but towards dawn the flames suddenly flickered. "Is it you beside me?" the bereft mother cried out.

When she returned to England, she could not bear to live at Chislehurst, which held so many memories, and moved to a new house, Farnborough Hill, thirty-five miles west of London. There, she occupied her time with founding a small church adjoining the estate, in which she erected a family tomb, as her brother-in-law had built one for Paca. On January 9, 1888, fifteen years after Napoleon III's death, Eugénie had both her husband's and son's remains removed from Chislehurst and interred on either side of the altar she had built into the abbey at Farnborough Hill.

The termination of this project, almost a decade in the making, seems to have acted as something of a release. Later that year, she purchased a yacht and began traveling again. The republic having by this time held for twenty years, she was no longer considered a threat, so to escape the cold gloom of England, Eugénie took to spending her winters in the south of France. Mérimée had always loved it there, and now that he was gone, she followed his memory. In 1894, at the age of sixty-eight, the ex-empress found a beautiful spot along the shore in Cap Martin, near Monte Carlo, where she built a villa.

ELISABETH, LIKE EUGÉNIE, HAD been wild with grief over the loss of her son. She reeled as if from a series of actual physical blows at the cascade of revelations that ensued in the days following the initial news of his death. The official diagnosis of derangement, in particular, haunted her, as it had after Ludwig II's suicide. It reinforced the possibility that *she* had been responsible for passing along the fateful taint of insanity to her child. "Why did Francis Joseph ever enter my father's house?" she moaned. "Why did I have to see him and why did he have to know me?" Neither she nor Stéphanie nor Valerie had the strength to attend Rudolf's funeral on February 5, 1889, which, due to the cloud surrounding the bereavement, was restricted to the immediate family. But the empress, in her anguish, could not stay away from his final resting place, and four days later made a secret midnight pilgrimage to the imperial crypt. "I wish to be alone with my son," Sisi told the bewildered priest who let her into the Capuchin Church and down the steps to the prince's grave. "Rudolf!" he heard her cry out twice during the course of her solitary vigil, as Eugénie had cried out for her son in Africa.

But even at this moment of intense sorrow, the empress was again surrounded by hostility. Austria took sides in the tragedy. "Among all classes the sympathy felt for the Emperor is deep and sincere," the *Times* correspondent stationed in Vienna observed. Rudolf's often-absent mother, on the other hand, made for a convenient villain. Elisabeth was well aware of the campaign against her. "Now all these people who have spoken so much evil of me from the very moment of my arrival will have the consolation that I shall pass away without leaving a trace behind me in Austria," she told Valerie. It got so bad that on February 7, a mere forty-eight hours after Rudolf's funeral, Franz Joseph had to issue a strong public statement defending her. "How much I owe in these days of bitterness to my dearly beloved wife the Empress, and what a great support she has proved to me, I cannot describe," he emphasized. "How can I be sufficiently grateful that such a helpmeet has been given me. Tell this to everyone," he begged.

The pain of Mayerling robbed Elisabeth of what little peace of mind she had left. From this point on until the end of her life she dressed very simply, and only in dark clothing, as though she were in perpetual mourning. Her days stretched out before her bleakly, marked only by more grief: the next year she lost both Andrássy and Nene. Just before Rudolf's death, she had planned to build a villa on the Greek island of Corfu; now she went ahead with this project. She named the house after Achilles, hero of the Trojan War, and filled it with statues, including one of Heine. Here, too, she placed a memorial to her son, crowned by a winged figure holding aloft a scepter.

But even the beauty of Corfu could not hold her for long, and she would begin again her ceaseless wanderings, often on the imperial yacht once owned by Max. And then, one day in February of 1894, at the age of fifty-six, her journeys took her to Cap Martin.

ALTHOUGH AS A GENERAL RULE Sisi shied away from protocol, she made an exception in this instance, and paid a courtesy visit to Eugénie, who had just moved into her villa. It is not difficult to surmise what drew the notoriously private Elisabeth to the ex-empress's side. There was perhaps not another woman in Europe who could so fully share the experiences and sorrows of her life. There they were, two empresses, each once the pinnacle of fashion and beauty, now both in aging exile:

one forcibly cast out, the other's withdrawal self-imposed, but both had lost all, even to their only sons. They had a long conversation, and after that, Elisabeth would come to Cap Martin to visit Eugénie every season. They took walks together, or went on excursions in a yacht or carriage; sometimes Franz Joseph would join them. "It was like driving with a ghost, for her spirit seemed to be living in another world," Eugénie reflected later.

It took a few years, but it was to Eugénie, finally, that Sisi at last unburdened herself about Rudolf's final days. "Yes, I know the truth about the drama of Mayerling," the ex-empress recorded later. "I can even say that no one knows better than I do, for I had it directly from the Empress Elizabeth, who confided it to me during her last stay at Cap Martin." Sisi's rendition was understandably tainted by her desperation to cast Mary Vetsera as the villain of the piece. But she was probably accurate, at least, about her husband's role in the affair, and the contents of the letter the crown prince addressed to her in those dark hours before he took his own life. "Francis Joseph had a very heated interview with his son on the score of Mlle. Vetsera," Eugénie revealed. "He even threatened to disinherit him if he did not instantly put an end to the scandalous liaison. So violent was the tone of the Emperor's expression, that the Archduke took fright, and promised to break with his mistress... 'Don't forget that I have your word of honor, your word as a gentleman,'" Elisabeth had reported her husband's warning to Rudolf.

Sisi was convinced that her son had taken Mary to Mayerling two days later intending to keep his vow. But when Rudolf told his lover that he was ending the affair, Mary had flung "coldly" back at him that she was pregnant. "Whereupon there was a terrible scene of affectionate despair between the two adoring lovers," Eugénie explained. "They kept saying: 'We can't go on living! Let us die in each other's arms!'...In the paroxysm of their exalted state, Rudolph seized a revolver." Over the course of the next few hours, after he killed Mary, he poured out his agony to his mother in a long letter, then shot himself. "It was this letter which told...the exact course of the drama," Eugénie finished sadly.

This was to be the final confidence shared between the two empresses. For the following year, Elisabeth's odyssey took her first to Geneva, where, despite her well-known championship of those on the fringes of society, the seething fury of endemic poverty and despair, which are the inevitable by-products of years of destructive upheaval and the unrealistic promises of ambitious politicians, was by sheer coincidence waiting for her.

ALTHOUGH IN THE DECADES FOLLOWING the Franco-Prussian War, Western Europe managed to avoid another full-scale armed mobilization, this did not mean that political unrest had died down. On the contrary, there were calls for new and increasingly radical social experiments, many aimed, like the Paris Commune, at addressing the disparity in living conditions between the rich and the poor. Books like Karl Marx's *Das Kapital,* which inveighed against the industrial capitalist system, sold out within days of publication. The anger of the laboring classes also manifested itself in the rise of a new movement that advocated the violent overthrow of *all* authority: adherents of this philosophy were known as anarchists. Anarchists believed that every ruler, leader, government, or organized body, as well as any individual of wealth, property, or title, was responsible for the misery of the masses, and that it was thus an anarchist's heroic duty to assassinate as many of these people as possible, and so provoke a massive uprising that would lead to "the destruction of existing political, social and religious orders," as a journal promoting this philosophy helpfully explained.

Although there were anarchists all over the world, members of the indigent Italian underclasses were particularly susceptible to this enterprising reasoning. Every schoolchild knew that by taking fate into his own hands and attempting to murder Napoleon III, the revered martyr Felice Orsini had sparked the war against Austria, which had in turn led to the glorious unification of Italy. The anarchists seemed merely the modern equivalent of this legacy. And so, when in the aftermath of unity the marvels promised by the adoption of a single constitutional ruler had perplexingly failed to materialize and everybody remained just as poor as they had been before, it was natural that this ideology should find willing adherents. By definition, there were no rules to follow, no higher authority to consult; anarchists frowned on organization of any sort. All anyone needed was will and a weapon of choice, and he, too, could go down in history as "an avenger of wrong and a benefactor of humanity," as a contemporary professor observed.

In September of 1898, one of these would-be heroes, an unemployed former soldier from Parma named Luigi Luccesi, was drifting around Switzerland working odd jobs, when he happened to read in the paper that the duke of Orléans was going to be in Geneva. As a French duke certainly qualified as a member of the despised upper class who needed to be eliminated, Luigi hastened to the city, only to discover that his prey had already moved on to another fashionable watering spot. Disappointed but not dissuaded, he scanned the papers for another potential target and discovered that the empress of Austria was in town for the day. The society pages, thrilled with the visit of the celebrated, if reclusive, Sisi, even listed the hotel at which she was staying, and noted that she would leave the next day, September 10, and take the local steamboat to Montreux, on the other end of Lake Geneva.

After that, it was only a matter of hanging around near the dock waiting for her to show up. Luigi even knew what Sisi looked like, having spent a short time in Budapest, where she was a familiar sight. At one thirty in the afternoon, Elisabeth appeared, accompanied by a lady-in-waiting. Luigi had the murder weapon, a slender file that he had sharpened into a blade, concealed in his coat. Now he ran up to the two women, pushed the lady-in-waiting aside, stabbed the empress in the chest with the makeshift dagger, and ran off as she fell backwards on the pavement.

Her wound was so small that at first it seemed to Sisi that she was unharmed, and that the assailant had merely knocked her down at random. "Whatever did that man want?" Elisabeth asked, as she got up and dusted herself off. Since she felt no pain, she and the lady-in-waiting continued onto the boat. But Luigi, who was caught a short time later, knew better. "My blow went home," he told the police with satisfaction. "She must be dead."

He was right. The empress collapsed soon afterward, on the deck of the ship. Loosening her clothing in an attempt to revive her, her companion discovered a small trickle of blood seeping from a wound in her chest. The slender tip of Luigi's knife had pierced his victim's heart. The boat returned to the dock and Elisabeth was brought back to the hotel, but by that time she was unconscious, and the attending physician could do nothing to help her. A priest was brought quickly to perform the last rites, but she had already stopped breathing. Within minutes, the doctor confirmed that she was gone.

Sisi was sixty years old when she died. She had spent almost every moment since the day of her marriage struggling to maintain her individuality against a relentless, concerted effort to force her into conformity with a set of standards she did not believe in. The effort had cost her both health and happiness, and had heaped censure and slander on her head. But she had nonetheless refused to surrender. She was true to herself to the very end.

THE ASSASSINATION OF THE EMPRESS of Austria made headlines around the world. Franz Joseph, informed by telegram, held his head in his hands. "I see I am not to be spared any single misfortune in this world," he cried. Notes of condolence poured in from every head of state, and requiems were held in almost every capital in Europe. President William McKinley, who two years later almost to the day would himself be the victim of an anarchist's bullet, attended a memorial service for Elisabeth at a church in Washington, DC, along with members of his cabinet and other high government officials.

In Vienna, the citizenry suddenly woke up and remembered who their empress had been. "It is absolutely impossible to describe the feelings of despair, rage, and horror which swept yesterday over the Viennese when the intelligence of the murder...became known to the people," wrote the on-site reporter for the *Daily Telegraph*. "That such a crime could be perpetuated against this noble and unhappy woman,...who devoted her whole time to works of benevolence and to assuaging the woes of humanity...The murder of the Empress roused a tempest of wild rage such as has scarcely ever been seen in Vienna," he added. The grief was even more pronounced in Hungary, where the Chamber of Deputies unanimously adopted a resolution to have the "gratitude of the nation to their august protectress" permanently recorded in the official government statutes. "This is an honor which the Hungarians did not accord even to their great 'King' Maria Theresa," the *Times* correspondent noted.

Even the people of Cap Martin, who saw her only for a few weeks each year, were so appalled and bereft at the assassination that they erected a tall stone obelisk, surrounded by the olive and palm trees that Sisi had been known to admire, as a reminder of the time the wistful luminary had spent there.

It was observed that whenever the ex-empress of the French was in town, she would walk to this monument nearly every day to say a prayer for her lost sister in sorrow.

EUGÉNIE WOULD SURVIVE ANOTHER two decades. She outlived Victoria, who died on January 22, 1901, and Franz Joseph, who expired from pneumonia on November 21, 1916, at the age of eighty-six. During this time, she witnessed new marvels, like airplanes and the telephone, and even, towards the end, found herself being driven around in an automobile rather than a carriage. She watched Europe descend once more into the cataclysm of violence that marked the First World War and witnessed the return of Alsace-Lorraine, which was stripped from Germany as it had once been from France, after the triumph of the Allied armies.

Eugénie died on July 11, 1920, in Madrid, where she had been visiting her niece and nephew at Paca's former mansion, the Palacio de Liria. She was ninety-four years old. Her body was brought back to England and interred between the coffins of her husband and son in the crypt she had built at Farnborough Hill. The king and queen of England attended her funeral, as did the sovereigns of Spain and

Portugal. The French government made a point of objecting to the presence of foreign royalty and other honors planned during the service, as lending the deceased woman a legitimacy that they did not believe she merited.

But no matter how assiduously subsequent administrations in France have tried to eradicate the legacy of the empire over which Eugénie and her husband had presided, they have failed. It is there even today in the wide, tree-lined boulevards, spacious parks, and elegant architecture of the city; the enduring appeal of the fine arts and haute couture; the unrivaled devotion of the millions of visitors who year after year seek out Paris as the embodiment of all that is graceful, beautiful, and cultured. Echoes of the world Eugénie inhabited may still be found, with her portrait, in the magnificent Napoleon III rooms at the Louvre, and in the display case in which sparkles the Regent Diamond, whose curse she, fittingly, was the last to brave.

Acknowledgments

A sprawling work of European history like this one, which covers a full century of events—and what events!—demands the talents of more than just the author. In my case, I am again indebted to Barbara Ann Schmutzler, without whose German translations (particularly the one of Sophia's long letter to her sister, in which the archduchess hilariously glossed over her son's inexcusably callous public jilting of Helene, followed by his totally inappropriate engagement to fifteen-year-old Sisi) this book would not be possible. Similarly, I am deeply grateful to acclaimed Hollywood costume designer Madeline Weeks for taking the time to explain the philosophy behind fashion and glamour to me—"the lie"—thereby providing crucial insight into Sisi's and Eugénie's motivations and actions. I must also thank Lynn Smith Dolby, Director of the Penn Art Collection at the University of Pennsylvania, for sharing both the portrait of Dr. Evans and the haunting painting of Eugénie fleeing Paris. It is my hope that the stirring story of Dr. Evans's heroism as recounted here will promote interest in his life and the collection.

I am also fortunate to have the support of a team of exceptional publishing professionals to help bring the stories of these two amazing women to a general audience. My longtime editor Asya Muchnick at Little, Brown gave the manuscript her characteristic thoughtful read, sharpening the narrative. As always, I so appreciate her enthusiastic advocacy of my work! And thank heaven for Pat Jalbert-Levine, who patiently shepherded the book through production, as well as Lauren Roberts in publicity, who I know will do her absolute best to bring

Elisabeth and Eugénie the attention they deserve. Most important, though, is my gratitude to my agent, Michael Carlisle, who has stood by me, defended me, and steered my work through two of the most turbulent decades in publishing history.

But none of this, none of my books, nor the person I have become through writing them, would have been possible without my family. To my daughter, Lee, who is always there for me, and who bucks me up when I am down, thank you from the bottom of my heart. Your love and encouragement mean more than you can know. I am so lucky to have you, and so proud to be your mother.

And finally to my husband, Larry—Larry, who listened to and walked me through every line of this book; who generously put down his own important work on constitutional politics, so critical at this juncture in history, to rescue me from every technological difficulty; who over the course of the nearly four decades of our marriage (but most especially over the past three years while the nineteenth century welled up and took over our lives), has filled the role of loving cheerleader, sage, and therapist—thank you, thank you, thank you. For forty years I have lived my dreams and it is all because of you.

Notes

Epigraph

ix   Bowring, *Poems of Heine,* 6.

Introduction

4   "somewhat to the astonishment": *Leeds Mercury* (Leeds, UK), Thursday, August 22, 1867, 4.

5   "countenance of Elisabeth...covering concealed": Ibid.

5   "The Empress Eugénie": *Standard* (London), Wednesday, August 21, 1867, 5.

6   "In the whole demeanor": *Standard,* Tuesday, August 27, 1867, 6.

6   "The Empresses, who looked remarkably well": *Tennessean* (Nashville), Wednesday, September 25, 1867, 1.

Chapter 1. A Scandal in Bavaria

11   *The spirit of:* Heine, *Heine in Art and Letters,* 182.

11   "I was driven by": Maximilian, *Wanderung nach dem Orient im jahre 1838,* 1–2. Translated by Barbara Ann Schmutzler.

13   "The duchess LOUISA": *Times* (London), Thursday, January 4, 1838, 2.

14   "If you had not been": Corti, *Ludwig I of Bavaria,* 52.

14   1.2 million new Protestants: For this figure see Fisher, *Studies in Napoleonic Statesmanship,* 167.

14   "Religion is an affair": Ibid., 229.

14   on May 1, 1808: For more information on the religious rights of the Bavarian constitution, see Higby, "Religious Policy of the Bavarian Government during the Napoleonic Period," 127–28. Regarding the inclusion of Jews, see 168. To read this document in full, go to www.constituteproject.org /constitution/Bavaria_1808?lang=en.

15   "Have confidence in": Fisher, *Studies in Napoleonic Statesmanship,* 136.

15   "The extravagance of": Metternich, *Memoirs of Prince Metternich, 1773–1815,* vol. 1, 75.

15   "It produced an excellent": Corti, *Ludwig I of Bavaria,* 126.

16   "King Ludwig was": Ibid., 216.

17   pieces played at Buckingham Palace: See the *Standard,* Monday, June 16, 1845, 1.

18–19 "I don't want you to strut": Haslip, *Lonely Empress,* 16.

19   "I am never tired of walking": Tschudi, *Elizabeth, Empress of Austria and Queen of Hungary,* 14.

19   "there were times": Haslip, *Lonely Empress,* 15.

19   "If you and I": Ibid., 15–16.

19   "This is the only money": Tschudi, *Elizabeth, Empress of Austria and Queen of Hungary,* 16.

22   "a native of Seville": *Morning Post* (London), Monday, June 12, 1843, 5.

24   "Every conception": Corti, *Ludwig I of Bavaria,* 288.

25   "has insulted all classes": Seymour, *Lola Montez,* 130.

25   "Lolita": Ibid.

25   Duchess Ludovika had once cornered: See the *Morning Post,* Monday, April 9, 1838, 2.

26   "I feel constrained": Corti, *Ludwig I of Bavaria,* 320.

26   "an enormous fan": *Morning Post,* Monday, October 25, 1847, 6.

26   "grievances...Lola Montez": *Morning Post,* Saturday, October 23, 1847, 6.

27   ("I come after"): Seymour, *Lola Montez,* 178.

29   "The people have triumphed": Corti, *Ludwig I of Bavaria,* 338.

29   "It was public opinion": *Observer* (London), Sunday, March 26, 1848, 4.

30   "We have been graciously": *Morning Post,* Monday, March 27, 1848, 6.

30   "To Lola": Corti, *Ludwig I of Bavaria,* 348.

Chapter 2. The Empire Strikes Back

31   *In the world's history:* Heine, *Prose Writings,* 80.

31   "without delay...freedom and legality": *Examiner* (London), Saturday, April 1, 1848, 10.

31   "A very striking contrast": *Observer,* Sunday, April 16, 1848, 3.

32   "Their Majesties quitted Vienna": *Observer,* Sunday, May 28, 1848, 3.

34   "a cretin": *Observer,* Monday, May 29, 1848, 3.

34   "an idiot of the worst class": Ibid.

34   "mental nullity": *Morning Chronicle* (London), Tuesday, November 21, 1848, 5.

34   "a mess of students": Langer, *Political and Social Upheaval, 1832–1852,* 361.

35   "declared that they": *Morning Chronicle,* Friday, June 9, 1848, 6.

35   46 confirmed dead...130 wounded: For these numbers, as well as a more in-depth description of the conflict, see Pech, *Czech Revolution of 1848,* 148–62.

36   "even the slightest attempt": Ibid., 162.

36   "the Camarilla": Langer, *Political and Social Upheaval,* 361.

36   "setting things in order": Palmer, *Twilight of the Habsburgs,* 39.

37   2,000 people died: For these figures and a more detailed account of the shelling of Vienna, see Macartney, *House of Austria,* 114.

37   "an Emperor we can show": Hartley, *Man Who Saved Austria,* 267.

38   "God bless you": Macartney, *House of Austria,* 115.

38   "What a boy": *Daily News* (London), Monday, December 18, 1848, 3.

38   "Sophie says to her son": Hartley, *Man Who Saved Austria,* 278.

40   "From my childhood": Lincoln, *Nicholas I,* 313.

40   One hundred fourteen: For the numbers of Hungarians executed, imprisoned, or hanged in effigy, see Macartney, *House of Austria,* 124.

40   ("That's all right"): Hartley, *Man Who Saved Austria,* 338.

41   "The punishment...upon those": Lincoln, *Nicholas I,* 315.

41   "A Dynasty which is": Ibid., 298.

Chapter 3. An Imperial Bait and Switch

42   *One does not:* Hamann, *Reluctant Empress,* 16.

43   "as round-faced": Haslip, *Lonely Empress,* 15.

44   "hard truth": Corti, *Elizabeth, Empress of Austria,* 19.

44   "Soldiers administer": *Daily News,* Wednesday, October 1, 1851, 5.

46   "Long live Kossuth": Palmer, *Twilight of the Habsburgs,* 67.

49   "with profound delight": *Reichspost,* April 22, 1934. Translated by Barbara Ann Schmutzler. Sophia's letter was reprinted in this newspaper in celebration of what would have been Franz Joseph's eightieth anniversary.

50   "Nene is fortunate": Ibid.

50   "the moment the emperor": Ibid.

50   "As if he would look": Haslip, *Lonely Empress,* 43.

51   "Oh, but how sweet...yet so sweet": Hamann, *Reluctant Empress,* 13–14.

51   "not to rush...protract it": *Reichspost,* April 22, 1934. Translated by Barbara Ann Schmutzler.

52   "Many gentlemen": Ibid.

53   "Since she had never before": Ibid.

53   "talked a lot": Ibid.

54   "exert absolutely...grace and cheerfulness": Ibid.

54   "So far, Sissy": Ibid.

54   "No, it just": Ibid.

54   "The dear little one": Hamann, *Reluctant Empress,* 13.

55   "But, how can he": *Reichspost,* April 22, 1934. Translated by Barbara Ann Schmutzler.

55   "With how much trepidation": Hamann, *Reluctant Empress,* 18.

56   "How could one not love that man": *Reichspost,* April 22, 1934. Translated by Barbara Ann Schmutzler.

56   "he rushed towards": Ibid.

56   "radiant with joy": Ibid.

56   "Please give us": Corti, *Elizabeth, Empress of Austria,* 27.

57   "so much happiness": *Reichspost,* April 22, 1934. Translated by Barbara Ann Schmutzler.

57   "You cannot imagine": Ibid.

58 "I love the Emperor": Ibid.
58 "She has yellow teeth": Corti, *Elizabeth, Empress of Austria,* 28.
58 "In this marriage": *Times,* Thursday, August 25, 1853, 8.
59 "FRANCIS JOSEPH owes": *Daily News,* Friday, September 16, 1853, 4.

Chapter 4. The Reign in Spain

63 *Toward France there journeyed:* Heine, *Poems of Heinrich Heine,* 35–36. Translated by Louis Untermeyer.
66 "Many persons respectable": Latimer, *Spain in the Nineteenth Century,* 102.
67 "Isn't it fortunate": Kurtz, *Empress Eugénie,* 7–8.
67n "The English ministry": Quin, *Memoirs of Ferdinand VII, King of the Spains,* 103.
68 "all Spaniards who": Ibid., 108.
68 "fired the last shots": Filon, *Recollections of the Empress Eugénie,* 9.
69–70 "You trace up...daughter of Fingal": Sergeant, *Last Empress of the French,* 10.
70 "the most cultivated": Stoddart, *Life of the Empress Eugénie,* 13–14.
70 "the Well-Beloved...absolute king": Clarke, *Modern Spain,* 32.
71 "the Constitution of 1812": Payne, *A History of Spain and Portugal,* vol. 2, 425–27.
73 "Vengeance and proscription": *Morning Chronicle* (London), Saturday, November 29, 1823, 2.
73 "the prisoner of the Inquisition": Kurtz, *Empress Eugénie,* 9.

Chapter 5. Mademoiselle de Montijo

75 *Only little girls:* Richardson, *Stendhal,* 280.
75 pragmatic sanction: Clarke, *Modern Spain,* 83.
77 "Let them be toughened": Fleury, *Memoirs of the Empress Eugénie,* vol. 1, 4.
77 "But he carried": Filon, *Recollections of the Empress Eugénie,* 11.
78 "amazed and enchanted": Soissons, *True Story of the Empress Eugénie,* 1.
79 "is a complete and": Ibid., 10.
79 "Fate willed it": Fleury, *Memoirs of the Empress Eugénie,* vol. 1, 14–15.
79 "*la petite* Eugénie": Ibid., 8.
79 "I am interested": Ibid.
79n "Eugénie...whom, when a child": Williams, *Life of Washington Irving,* vol. 2, 381.
80 "At dawn the motion...gaming houses": Marichal, *Spain (1834–1844),* 58–59.
81 "There is no lack here": Maxwell, *Life and Letters of George William Frederick,* 73.
81 "Nothing can be more graceful": Ibid., 77.
81 "was not considered...almost to ugliness": Carey, *Empress Eugenie in Exile,* 328.
82 "timid, namby-pamby...cried or winced": Ibid., 332.
82 "My rights to the crown": Hume, *Modern Spain,* 296.
82 some 35,000 Carlist troops: For this figure and more on the beginning of the Carlist war, see Hume, *Modern Spain,* 307–9.

83–84 "The last 24 hours...killed in the streets": *Times,* Monday, July 28, 1834, 4.

85   "Many Spaniards are passing": Stoddart, *Life of the Empress Eugénie,* 19.

85   "None of us is dead": Seward, *Eugénie,* 5.

86   "Their small brains": Carey, *Empress Eugenie in Exile,* 333.

87   Monsieur Mérimée: Fleury, *Memoirs of the Empress Eugénie,* vol. 1, 8.

87   "Remember M. Beyle": Richardson, *Stendhal,* 280.

88   "felt that his words": Fleury, *Memoirs of the Empress Eugénie,* vol. 1, 7.

88   "one large...kill the king.": Eugénie, *Lettres familières,* vol. 1, 8–13. My translation.

89   "My dear Papa...come soon.": Ibid., 5–12. My translation.

89   "My mother wished": Filon, *Recollections of the Empress Eugénie,* 9.

90   "With regard to": *Morning Chronicle,* Thursday, January 21, 1836, 2.

90   "They...gave the Queen": *Morning Chronicle,* Friday, August 26, 1836, 2.

90   freedom of the press: See the *Morning Chronicle,* Monday, July 3, 1837, 2, for the entire text of the Constitution of 1837.

91   "What matters wife?": Heine, *Poems of Heinrich Heine,* 35–36. Translated by Louis Untermeyer.

91   ("You would not believe"): Fleury, *Memoirs of the Empress Eugénie,* vol. 1, 9.

Chapter 6. The Wild Countess of Teba

92   *The uncertainty of the future:* Eugénie, *Lettres familières,* vol. 1, 34.

92   500,000 francs: For this number see Sencourt, *Life of the Empress Eugénie,* 42, and Carlin, *William Kirkpatrick of Málaga,* 149.

93   "Do you acknowledge me...is defunct": *Observer,* Monday, September 16, 1839, 3.

93–94 "Spain at present...such friends": Loliée, *Life of an Empress,* 17–18.

95–96 "My very dear cousin...My resolution is taken": Eugénie, *Lettres familières,* vol. 1, 21–22. My translation.

96   "A grand wedding": Irving, *Life and Letters of Washington Irving,* vol. 3, 323.

96   "The Duchess de Montijo": *Freeman's Journal* (Dublin), Thursday, October 19, 1843, 4.

97   "very tall, very fair": Stoddart, *Life of the Empress Eugénie,* 27.

97   "Her slender figure": Tschudi, *Eugénie, Empress of the French,* 29–30.

97   "a tall elegant man": Irving, *Letters from Sunnyside and Spain,* 51.

98   "phalanxes": Spencer, *Charles Fourier,* 60.

98   ("the key to widsom"): Ibid., 69–70.

98   "Is not a young woman": Beecher and Bienvenu, *Utopian Vision of Charles Fourier,* 177–78.

98   "as a general rule": Spencer, *Charles Fourier,* 57. (Italics are Fourier's.)

99   "You ladies ought not": Stoddart, *Life of the Empress Eugénie,* 30.

99n   "had shot them all": Hume, *Modern Spain,* 374.

100   "Where are my letters": Seward, *Eugénie,* 21.

100   "Like Achilles's spear": Sencourt, *Life of the Empress Eugénie,* 45.

101 "I am very sad today": Eugénie, *Lettres familières,* vol. 1, 23–24. My translation.

101 "A marriage is said": *Morning Post,* Tuesday, June 19, 1849, 5.

102 "I like danger": Eugénie, *Lettres familières,* vol. 1, 25. My translation.

104 "citizen king": *Standard,* Tuesday, August 17, 1830, 2.

104 "You ask me for news": Ibid.

104n "The old women and children": Ibid.

105 *"Vive Napoleon": Standard,* Thursday, November 3, 1836, 2. The entire incident is reported in detail in this account.

105 "absurd insurrection": Ibid.

106 *"Vive l'Empereur"* . . . *"Vive le Roi": Morning Chronicle,* Saturday, August 8, 1840, 3.

107n "The Prince [Louis Napoleon]": *Examiner,* Sunday, August 16, 1840, 1.

108 "On leaving my bed-room": Tocqueville, *Recollections,* 44.

109 "the mass of the people": Normanby, *Year of Revolution,* 272.

109 "The name which I bear": *Caledonian Mercury* (Edinburgh), Monday, June 19, 1848, 2.

110 5,534,520 votes: See Normanby, *Year of Revolution,* 381, for these figures.

110 "There only remains now": Ibid., 375.

Chapter 7. An Imperial Coup

111 *Is there any:* Beecher and Bienvenu, *Utopian Vision of Charles Fourier,* 179.

112 "Monseigneur, my mother": Sencourt, *Life of the Empress Eugénie,* 62.

113 "Because we once had": *Daily News,* Saturday, July 19, 1851, 5.

113 "indescribable uproar": Ibid.

114 "Frenchmen—the disturbances": *Daily News,* Tuesday, December 9, 1851, 5.

115 7,439,216 to 640,737: For these results see *Morning Chronicle,* Saturday, January 3, 1852, 6. For the proclamation describing who could vote and when the voting would take place, see the *Observer,* Sunday, December 7, 1851, 5–6. For the exact language of the ballot, see the *Morning Chronicle,* Wednesday, December 3, 1851, 5.

116 "The enthusiasm of the Marseilles": *Morning Chronicle,* Thursday, September 30, 1852, 5.

116 "His Highness yesterday": *Morning Chronicle,* Monday, October 4, 1852, 5.

116 "hopelessly in love": Rumbold, *Recollections of a Diplomatist,* vol. 1, 163.

117 "Paris talks of nothing": Kurtz, *Empress Eugénie,* 33.

117 "the imperial dignity": *Guardian* (London), Saturday, December 4, 1852, 5.

117 "over grey trousers...used by ladies": Tschudi, *Eugénie, Empress of the French,* 51–52.

118 "You can't imagine": Eugénie, *Lettres familières,* vol. 1, 46. My translation.

118 "What is then": Soissons, *True Story of the Empress Eugénie,* 38–39.

118 "She has played": Sencourt, *Life of the Empress Eugénie,* 65.

118   7,824,189 votes in favor: For the official tally, see the *Guardian*, Saturday, December 4, 1852, 5.

118   *"Vive l'Empereur"*: Ibid.

118   "a considerable body": *Morning Chronicle*, Friday, December 3, 1852, 5–6.

119   "the sad fate": Kurtz, *Empress Eugénie*, 45.

119   "over head and ears": Viel-Castel, *Memoirs of Count Horace de Viel Castel*, vol. 1, 128–29.

119   "He is a man": Eugénie, *Lettres familières*, vol. 1, 53.

120   "Pass, Madame … insult you": Sencourt, *Life of the Empress Eugénie*, 67–68.

120   "Madame Countess": Eugénie, *Lettres familières*, vol. 1, 49. My translation.

121   "My dear and good sister": Ibid., 47.

121   "I yield to the wish": *Observer*, Sunday, January 30, 1853, 4.

122   "His speech produced": Eugénie, *Lettres familières*, vol. 1, 50.

122   "Accept my most cordial": Barker, *Distaff Diplomacy*, 7.

123   "The whole procession": *Examiner*, Saturday, February 5, 1853, 7.

124   "exceedingly pale": Ibid.

Chapter 8. The Rose of Bavaria

127   *Thou seemest like:* Heine, *Poems and Ballads*, 101.

128   "Unfortunately, my children": Hamann, *Reluctant Empress*, 24.

130   "I cannot stop": Ibid., 26.

131   "The abolition": *Times*, Saturday, September 3, 1853, 9.

131   "Thee, dear friend": Redlich, *Emperor Francis Joseph of Austria*, 138.

131   "Perhaps Constantinople": Ibid., 135.

133   "As you advised me": Hamann, *Reluctant Empress*, 27.

133   "I love Sisi more": Corti, *Elizabeth, Empress of Austria*, 33.

134   "Nor do I think": Haslip, *Lonely Empress*, 59.

135   "learning many new": Hamann, *Reluctant Empress*, 28.

136   "It was a wonderful": Palmer, *Twilight of the Habsburgs*, 74.

136   "But aren't you happy": Haslip, *Lonely Empress*, 53.

136   "If only he": Hamann, *Reluctant Empress*, 27.

137   "the Montijo marriage": William I, *Correspondence of William I and Bismarck*, vol. 1, 2.

137   "a popular act": *Morning Chronicle*, Thursday, April 20, 1854, 5 (quoting the Vienna *Gazette*).

138   "Rose of Bavaria": Corti, *Elizabeth, Empress of Austria*, 40.

138   "On show like": Haslip, *Lonely Empress*, 70.

139   "The preparations": *Morning Chronicle*, Wednesday, April 26, 1854, 5.

141   "We shall soon": Corti, *Elizabeth, Empress of Austria*, 46.

141   "The brilliancy": *Sheffield and Rotherham Independent* (UK), Saturday, May 6, 1854, 11. (Taken from the Vienna correspondent of the *Morning Chronicle*.)

Chapter 9. Making France Great Again

145 *Policy consists:* Senior, *Conversations with Distinguished Persons during the Second Empire,* 15.

146 "the strong and romantic...any longer": Evans, *Memoirs,* vol. 1, 100–101.

146 "I have an immense desire": Eugénie, *Lettres familières,* vol. 1, 52.

147 "Monsieur Le Préfet": Evans, *Memoirs,* vol. 1, 112.

147 "What woman wants": Eugénie, *Lettres familières,* vol. 1, 68.

147*n* "inquire into the condition": Evans, *Memoirs,* vol. 1, 113–14.

148 ("Barricades will be"): Ambès, *Intimate Memoirs,* 11–13. Ambès is the pseudonym Baron Heeckeren wrote under.

149 ("of the Queen's sad fate"): Evans, *Memoirs,* vol. 1, 100.

150 "The Empress, ever since": Ambès, *Intimate Memoirs,* 35.

150 "I have two incurable": Kurtz, *Empress Eugénie,* 67.

150 "What a dreadful thing": Loliée, *Life of an Empress,* 81.

150*n* "I believe that": Eugénie, *Lettres familières,* vol. 1, 64.

151 "I am a little dazed": Lyon, *Life and Times of Prosper Mérimée,* 244.

151 "Social entertainments": Ambès, *Intimate Memoirs,* 35.

152 "That young empress": Sand, *Impressions et souvenirs,* 23. My translation.

152 "in her beautiful": *Morning Post,* Tuesday, May 24, 1853, 1.

152 "RIMMEL'S GOLDEN": *Examiner,* Saturday, June 11, 1853, 14.

152 "It only takes one": Sand, *Impressions et souvenirs,* 24. My translation.

152*n* "floods of tears": Ambès, *Intimate Memoirs,* 36.

153 "My God, Monsieur": Sherard, *Twenty Years in Paris,* 107.

153 "I was desperate": Eugénie, *Lettres familières,* vol. 1, 76.

153 "You ask me": Ibid., 84.

154 "I won a crown": Ibid., 83.

154 "You can't imagine...greatest enthusiasm": Ibid., 89.

154 "Once mistress of Constantinople": Abbott, *History of Napoleon III,* 531.

155 "He [Napoleon III] said": Malmesbury, *Memoirs of an Ex-Minister,* vol. 2, 108–9.

155 "The time for conquest": Abbott, *History of Napoleon III,* 544.

155*n* "Russia was a": Malmesbury, *Memoirs of an Ex-Minister,* vol. 2, 108–9.

156 "Neutrality is impossible": Hallberg, *Franz Joseph and Napoleon III,* 51.

156 "It would be a great advantage": Malmesbury, *Memoirs of an Ex-Minister,* vol. 2, 109.

157 "How...about the Archduke": Hübner, *Neuf ans de souvenirs,* 204. My translation.

157 "This is not the first time": Ibid.

157*n* "a very young girl": Ibid., 229.

158 "I was faithful": Soissons, *True Story of the Empress Eugénie,* 82.

159 "If your Majesty": Abbott, *History of Napoleon III,* 543.

159 "Russia, as I can guarantee": Jerrold, *Life of Napoleon III,* vol. 4, 10.

159   "Three battalions of the Guards": Malmesbury, *Memoirs of an Ex-Minister,* vol. 2, 145.

159   "The regiments depart": Eugénie, *Lettres familières,* vol. 1, 104–5.

Chapter 10. *Love in the Time of Cholera*

163   *Into the valley of Death:* Tennyson, *Select Poems,* 152.

163–64 "How . . . can I have my hand": Hübner, *Neuf ans de souvenirs,* 231. My translation.

165   "It really was": Corti, *Elizabeth, Empress of Austria,* 49.

166   "The Emperor was": Hamann, *Reluctant Empress,* 47.

167   "two disorderly women": Tschuppik, *Reign of the Emperor Francis Joseph,* 46.

167   "Is what you have written": Redlich, *Emperor Francis Joseph of Austria,* 253.

167n "I cannot do it": Tschuppik, *Reign of the Emperor Francis Joseph,* 48.

168   "is blinded by": Ibid.

168n "fond of garish": Hübner, *Neuf ans de souvenirs,* 235. My translation.

169   "Your Majesty evidently": Tschuppik, *Reign of the Emperor Francis Joseph,* 124.

169   "The mere thought": Hamann, *Reluctant Empress,* 53.

170   "He was so frankly": Hübner, *Neuf ans de souvenirs,* 236. My translation.

170   "I am as much": Tschuppik, *Empress Elizabeth of Austria,* 33.

170   *O that I:* Corti, *Elizabeth, Empress of Austria,* 51.

174   "I know positively": Hallberg, *Franz Joseph and Napoleon III,* 68.

174   "one of the most bloody": Russel, *The War,* vol. 1, 181.

175   "nearly 3,000 killed": Ibid., 182.

175   "Out of 35,600": Ibid.

175   "At ten minutes past": Ibid., 231.

176   The total number: For the numbers on killed, wounded, and missing, see ibid., 234.

176   "The wounded French": *Morning Chronicle,* Saturday, October 21, 1854, 6.

176   "The French manage": *Observer,* Monday, December 11, 1854, 2.

177   "the security of the": Disraeli, *Debate in the House of Commons,* February 10, 1857, https://hansard.parliament.uk/Commons/1857-02-10/debates/c08aeea0-aaf3-462d-86e3-87dd3bcaf4ec/HouseOfCommons.

178   "The first was": Redlich, *Emperor Francis Joseph of Austria,* 156.

178   "In the long run": Steinberg, *Bismarck,* 122.

Chapter 11. *An Empress on the Rise*

181   *The Empress has great:* Sencourt, *Life of the Empress Eugénie,* 123.

181   "held her tightly": Hübner, *Neuf ans de souvenirs,* 204.

181   "is so far satisfactory": Malmesbury, *Memoirs of an Ex-Minister,* vol. 2, 169.

182   nearly a million soldiers: For these numbers and an account of their deployment, see Hallberg, *Franz Joseph and Napoleon III,* 82.

182   "The accounts from": Malmesbury, *Memoirs of an Ex-Minister,* vol. 2, 176.

182   "Cholera has made": Ambès, *Intimate Memoirs,* 59–61.

182   "My dear James": Eugénie, *Lettres familières,* vol. 1, 114–15.

183*n*   "the memory of the bonds": Hallberg, *Franz Joseph and Napoleon III,* 93.

183*n*   "I'm sure you can easily": Redlich, *Emperor Francis Joseph of Austria,* 159. My translation.

184   "people are saying": Kurtz, *Empress Eugénie,* 77.

184   "I had no need": Ibid.

184   "This we *never*": Aronson, *Queen Victoria and the Bonapartes,* 20.

185   "the Emperor and Empress": *Guardian,* Wednesday, April 18, 1855, 3.

185   "the thunder of applause": Ibid.

185   VIVE L'EMPEREUR: Ibid.

185   "If it be true": *Guardian,* Saturday, April 21, 1855, 7.

185   "We never witnessed": *Morning Chronicle,* Friday, April 20, 1855, 5.

185   "St. James's-street": *Observer,* Sunday, April 22, 1855, 5.

185   "the beaming and inexpressively": Ibid.

186   "making a present of it": *Morning Chronicle,* Saturday, April 21, 1855, 5.

186   "I am in despair": Vizetelly, *Court of the Tuileries,* 81.

186   "How strange to think": Lee, *Queen Victoria,* 256.

187   "That he *is*": Benson, *Letters of Queen Victoria,* vol. 3, 155–56.

187   "She is full of courage and spirit": Stoddart, *Life of the Empress Eugénie,* 75.

187   "Your Majesty": Sencourt, *Life of the Empress Eugénie,* 122. My translation.

188   10 million francs: See www.napoleon.org/en/history-of-the-two-empires /articles/1855-frances-first-international-exhibition/ and www .arthurchandler.com/paris-1855-exposition for precise details of the size and scope of the exposition.

189   America, Australia, Egypt…Singer sewing machines: For more on this see the *Morning Post,* Monday, August 27, 1855, 6.

189   the *biberon:* Forsythe, "History of Infant Feeding from Elizabethan Times," 133.

189   "From morning to evening": *Times,* Wednesday, August 1, 1855, 10.

189   "Exhibition fever": *Daily News,* Friday, June 1, 1855, 5.

190   Eugénie's idea: See Green, "France Exposed," 916.

191   "We are waiting": Eugénie, *Lettres familières,* vol. 1, 122.

191   "Imagine, the doctors": Ibid., 123.

191   "I know you go often": Ibid., 124–25.

191*n*   "one of the most remarkable": Trapp, "Universal Exhibition of 1855," 302.

192   ("Half of England"): Mérimée, *Letters of Prosper Mérimée,* vol. 1, 13.

192   "At last, we are at": Eugénie, *Lettres familières,* vol. 1, 123.

192   "I am *delighted*": Benson, *Letters of Queen Victoria,* vol. 3, 172.

193   "Of the splendour": Ibid., 175.

193   "The Emperor has": Ibid., 172.

193   "The Queen has passed": *Morning Post,* Wednesday, August 22, 1855, 5.

193   "For the Emperor": Benson, *Letters of Queen Victoria,* vol. 3, 177–78.

193 ("a fairy queen"): Jerrold, *Life of Napoleon III,* vol. 3, 85.

194 ("How beautiful you are"): Ibid. My translation.

194 "the Court and whole house": Benson, *Letters of Queen Victoria,* vol. 3, 177.

194 (so many orders): See *Daily News,* Tuesday, July 3, 1855, 4.

194 800 French...barrage: For these figures, and an account of the bombardment, see Palmer, *Crimean War,* 213.

195 "Soldiers, forward!": Abbott, *History of Napoleon III,* 562.

195 "like a swarm of bees": Russel, *The War,* vol. 2, 143.

195 "My General": Palmer, *Crimean War,* 217.

195 "From twelve o'clock": Russel, *The War,* vol. 2, 143.

196 "In vain the officers": Ibid., 150.

196 "It would be untrue": Ibid., 154–55.

196 "weary of the fearful slaughter": Ibid., 143.

197 "When the first grey": Ibid., 168–71.

197 "Sebastopol is in": Palmer, *Crimean War,* 219.

197 "I come here": Abbott, *History of Napoleon III,* 562.

197 *enceinte: Guardian,* Friday, September 21, 1855, 2.

198 "looking very handsome": Malmesbury, *Memoirs of an Ex-Minister,* vol. 2, 210.

198 "The year has dawned": Ambès, *Intimate Memoirs,* 83.

198 "I got a letter": Malmesbury, *Memoirs of an Ex-Minister,* vol. 2, 217.

199 "It is four o'clock": Ambès, *Intimate Memoirs,* 84.

199 "it is my overwhelming desire": Eugénie, *Lettres familières,* vol. 1, 126.

199 "The Empress": Kurtz, *Empress Eugénie,* 98.

199 the Regent Diamond: For a minute description of the christening, see Fleury, *Memoirs of the Empress Eugénie,* vol. 1, 90–94.

Chapter 12. An Imperial Education

203 *This is the olden fairy wood:* Heine, *Poems of Heinrich Heine,* 2–3.

204 fired just twenty times: For a description of the protocol and excitement surrounding the birth see *Lloyd's Weekly Newspaper,* Sunday, February 18, 1855, 8.

204 "the public": *Standard,* Tuesday, April 24, 1855, 3.

206 "to impose censures": *Morning Post,* Tuesday, November 27, 1855, 2. The entire document was translated into English here.

206 "stupidity": Hübner, *Neuf ans de souvenirs,* 352.

206 200,000 francs: See the *Observer,* Monday, April 23, 1855, 7.

206 "medieval": Hübner, *Neuf ans de souvenirs,* 372.

206 "Where I come from": Hamann, *Reluctant Empress,* 70.

207 "his ally": Hübner, *Neuf ans de souvenirs,* 342.

207n "Let's see": Ibid., 351.

208 "Her Majesty does not": Corti, *Elizabeth, Empress of Austria,* 56.

209 "at Possenhofen": Haslip, *Lonely Empress,* 96–97.

209–10 "which hardly...into it": Corti, *Maximilian and Charlotte of Mexico,* vol. 1, 48.

210 "The Emperor can be": Ibid., 55.

210 "one of those men": Ibid., 56–57.

210 "I found the Empress": Ibid., 48.

210–11 "It would hardly ... cavalry possible": Ibid., 51–55.

211 "The Emperor gave me": Ibid., 58.

211 "Our leave-taking": Ibid., 59.

212 "magical charm": Haslip, *Lonely Empress,* 88.

212 "seeing our children": Hamann, *Reluctant Empress,* 71.

212 "specifically asked": Ibid., 72.

214 ("did not know"): Tschuppik, *Reign of the Emperor Francis Joseph,* 104.

215 "The crowd's only": Corti, *Elizabeth, Empress of Austria,* 65.

215 "The Emperor arrives": Palmer, *Twilight of the Habsburgs,* 93.

215 "if anybody": Gribble, *Life of the Emperor Francis Joseph,* 126.

216 "the Empress is now": Haslip, *Lonely Empress,* 107.

216 (entangled with her dress): For the details of this incident see the *Morning Chronicle,* Tuesday, February 10, 1857, 5.

217 "Italy has been allowed": Redlich, *Emperor Francis Joseph of Austria,* 250.

218 "The natural destiny": Tschuppik, *Empress Elizabeth of Austria,* 57–58.

219 100 horses: For this information see the *Morning Chronicle,* Monday, April 27, 1857, 3.

220 some 60,000 people: For this number see the *Morning Post,* Monday, May 11, 1857, 5.

220 "state glass coach": *Times,* Friday, May 8, 1857, 7.

220 "The grace and beauty": *Morning Post,* Friday, May 15, 1857, 6.

221 "The little thing": Corti, *Elizabeth, Empress of Austria,* 73.

222 "Although firmness": *Times,* Thursday, June 4, 1857, 9. From an article obtained from Vienna on June 1.

222n Notably, Archduke Max: See Haslip, *Crown of Mexico,* 54.

Chapter 13. The Disciples of the Dagger

227 *Usually, it is man:* Soissons, *True Story of the Empress Eugénie,* 81.

227 "My little man": Eugénie, *Lettres familières,* vol. 1, 129.

228 "At Biarritz": Filon, *Recollections of the Empress Eugénie,* 44.

228 ("Come without"): Ibid.

228 "Biarritz was the only": Ibid., 45–46.

229 "The first time": Barthez, *Empress Eugénie and Her Circle,* 16.

229 "In the evening": Ibid., 105–6.

229 "We spoke of": Ibid., 40.

229 "Truly this year": Ambès, *Intimate Memoirs,* 91.

232 ("the theory of the pistol"): *Times,* Wednesday, June 25, 1856, 10.

232 "whose Christian name": Vizetelly, *Court of the Tuileries,* 110.

232 "I must frankly": Metternich, *My Years in Paris,* 130–31.

233 "I advise you": Soissons, *True Story of the Empress Eugénie,* 83.

234 "utterly devoid": Carette, *Recollections of the Court of the Tuileries,* 220–21.
234 No. 53, Rue Montaigne: See Vizetelly, *Court of the Tuileries,* 110.
234 "Last night": Soissons, *True Story of the Empress Eugénie,* 83–84.
234–35 "The Count and beautiful": *Reynold's Newspaper,* Sunday, May 3, 1857, 1.
235 "An attempt": *Reynold's Newspaper,* Sunday, April 12, 1857, 1.
235 "No sooner": *Daily News,* Friday, October 2, 1857, 4.
235 "the Czarina": *Reynold's Newspaper,* Sunday, October 4, 1857, 1.
236 "Perhaps tired": Eugénie, *Lettres familières,* vol. 1, 143.
236 "But please erase": Ibid., 144.
236 "As I was passing": Ambès, *Intimate Memoirs,* 108.
237 One hundred fifty-six: This attack, and the injuries that ensued, are described in detail in the *Times,* Thursday, February 25, 1838, 10.
237 "I could see": Ambès, *Intimate Memoirs,* 108.
237 "Do not bother": Soissons, *True Story of the Empress Eugénie,* 152.
237 "where they were": Ambès, *Intimate Memoirs,* 108.
237n "improvised explosive device": Crossland, "Radical Warfare's First 'Superweapon.'"
238 "He rushed down": Woodham-Smith, *Queen Victoria,* 392.
238 sent a telegram: See Hübner, *Neuf ans de souvenirs,* vol. 2, 91.
238 "courageous firmness": Barker, *Distaff Diplomacy,* 25.
238 "whose veracity": Hübner, *Neuf ans de souvenirs,* vol. 2, 92.
238 "Certainly, I am not...my heart": Eugénie, *Lettres familières,* vol. 1, 149–50.
239 "From my youth...here it is": *Morning Post,* Monday, March 1, 1858, 2.
239–40 "To Napoleon III...posterity!": Ibid., 3.
240 "Fancy the Emperor": Wellesley, *Conversations with Napoleon III,* 134.
240 "I thought the Emperor": Ibid., 133.
241 "The poor Empress": Ibid., 134.
241 "His Majesty": Ibid.
242 "began by saying...assistance": Ibid., 142.
243 ("In the probable"): Ibid., 145.
243 "I consider this arrangement": Ibid.
243 "shown very good": Ibid., 158.

Chapter 14. Three Weddings and a War

247 *Ghastly shadows:* Bowring, *Poems of Heine,* 2.
248 "quite unfit": Haslip, *Lonely Empress,* 119.
249 "She is very clever": Haslip, *Crown of Mexico,* 94.
249 "was so easy": *Times,* Tuesday, August 11, 1857, 8.
249 "Charlotte is charming": Hamann, *Reluctant Empress,* 78.
250 "The Empress Elizabeth": *Morning Post,* Wednesday, September 2, 1857, 5.
250 "expressed himself": *Morning Post,* Wednesday, October 7, 1857, 5.
250 shooting: Franz Joseph went instead for a drive with the grand duke of Weimar. See the *Times,* Monday, October 5, 1857, 7.

253 "Neither now nor ever": Haslip, *Crown of Mexico,* 122.

253 "Of course!": Corti, *Elizabeth, Empress of Austria,* 77.

253 "I resolve that": *Morning Chronicle,* Monday, August 30, 1858, 3.

255 "I cannot expect": Haslip, *Crown of Mexico,* 125–26.

255 "If I did not": Ibid., 125.

256 "He thinks Austria": *Morning Post,* Monday, November 29, 1858, 3.

258 "*Guerra! Guerra!... Si, Signori, Guerra! Guerra!*": *Times,* Tuesday, February 8, 1859, 10.

258 "Great preparations": Mérimée, *Letters of Prosper Mérimée,* vol. 1, 32.

258 "The shipment of": Hübner, *Neuf ans de souvenirs,* vol. 2, 313. My translation.

259 "At last": Haslip, *Crown of Mexico,* 127.

Chapter 15. Regent of the Empire

263 *We have been made:* Lee, *Queen Victoria,* 302.

263 "I regret": Hübner, *Neuf ans de souvenirs,* vol. 2, 244.

263 "An extraordinary thing...serious indeed'": Ambès, *Intimate Memoirs,* vol. 2, 117.

264 "the Emperor, at my": Ibid., 119.

264 "The Emperor is": Benson, *Letters of Queen Victoria,* 312–13.

264n "There are many...six francs": Thayer, *Life and Times of Cavour,* vol. 1, 577.

265 "If you could...want to do it": Eugénie, *Lettres familières,* vol. 1, 160–61.

266 "Though it is": Benson, *Letters of Queen Victoria,* 328.

266 "We are a funny nation": Mérimée, *Letters of Prosper Mérimée,* vol. 1, 39.

266 "Our poor Empress": Ibid., 41–42.

267 "was greeted by": Ambès, *Intimate Memoirs,* 135.

267 "The public spirit": Mérimée, *Letters of Prosper Mérimée,* vol. 1, 48.

267n "What stupidity": Barker, *Distaff Diplomacy,* 32.

268 "What *are* the Austrians": Benson, *Letters of Queen Victoria,* vol. 3, 425.

268 "Up to the present": Mérimée, *Letters of Prosper Mérimée,* vol. 1, 43–44.

268 64,000 soldiers: For the breakdown of these troops see Thayer, *Life and Times of Cavour,* vol. 2, 3.

268 "quit their families...shut their eyes": Ibid., vol. 1, 582.

269 132,000 infantry: For these and the Austrian numbers see Ibid., vol. 2, 2–3.

270 ("the Hunters of the Alps"): Ibid., vol. 1, 584.

271 "At half-past eleven": *Guardian,* Monday, June 6, 1859, 2.

271 "An immense crowd...a delirium!": Thayer, *Life and Times of Cavour,* vol. 2, 74.

271 "I was driven": Palmer, *Twilight of the Habsburgs,* 107.

272 "I can hold out": Thayer, *Life and Times of Cavour,* vol. 2, 45.

272 "Great battle": Ibid., 48.

272 "This night I sleep": *Times,* Thursday, July 21, 1859, 9. The *Times* correspondent at Verona disputed this statement, claiming that Franz Joseph

never actually stayed at that particular villa, but this is nitpicking. It was absolutely in close vicinity to where the defeated emperor *had* slept the night before.

273   "The carriage conveying": *Morning Chronicle,* Monday, July 4, 1859, 5.

274   "Here...satisfy Prussia": Fleury, *Memoirs of the Empress Eugénie,* vol. 2, 30–31.

275   "Here is a letter": Ibid., 36.

276   "A meeting is in store": Palmer, *Twilight of the Habsburgs,* 112.

277   ("He was much affected"): Fleury, *Memoirs of the Empress Eugénie,* vol. 2, 39.

277   "I am making": Ibid., 47.

277   "Prince, I hope": Abbott, *History of Napoleon III,* 588.

277   "I say to you": Thayer, *Life and Times of Cavour,* vol. 2, 113–14.

278   "What news is this": Ambès, *Intimate Memoirs,* vol. 2, 163.

278   "The people here...from them": Mérimée, *Letters of Prosper Mérimée,* vol. 1, 58–59.

278   "I hope that Peace": Eugénie, *Lettres familières,* vol. 1, 166.

278   "But will you be able": Fleury, *Memoirs of the Empress Eugénie,* vol. 2, 29.

278   "Our bigots are riding": Mérimée, *Letters of Prosper Mérimée,* vol. 1, 60.

279   "It is impossible": Barker, *Distaff Diplomacy,* 45.

279   "she ought not": Ibid., 46.

279–80   "had to leave...like a criminal": Ambès, *Intimate Memoirs,* vol. 2, 164.

280   "I think that": Fleury, *Memoirs of the Empress Eugénie,* vol. 2, 64.

280   "Tuscany should form": Thayer, *Life and Times of Cavour,* vol. 2, 133.

281   ("Confronted by"): Ibid., 210.

281   "6,810 persons": *Guardian,* Wednesday, April 18, 1860, 2.

281   "Really, it is too bad": Benson, *Letters of Queen Victoria,* vol. 3, 508.

281   "had been so abandoned": Eugénie, *Lettres familières,* vol. 1, 177.

282   "The most extravagant": *Daily Telegraph* (London), Monday, April 30, 1860, 6.

282   "so adjusted": *Daily Telegraph,* Monday, April 30, 1860, 6.

282   "Too much praise": *Morning Chronicle,* Thursday, April 26, 1860, 5.

Chapter 16. His Cheatin' Imperial Heart

285   *My bread:* Bowring, *Poems of Heine,* 81–83.

287   "For my sake": Corti, *Elizabeth, Empress of Austria,* 80.

287   "She is unfit": Ibid., 81.

288   "Her letters": Hamann, *Reluctant Empress,* 87.

288   "my dearest angel...it is not proper": Corti, *Elizabeth, Empress of Austria,* 81–83.

289   "Such is the": Tschuppik, *Reign of the Emperor Francis Joseph,* 70.

289   "the very existence": Ibid.

289   "put an end to": Haslip, *Lonely Empress,* 131.

289   "Your political plan": Corti, *Elizabeth, Empress of Austria,* 85.

290   "What is happening": Michel, *Empress of Farewells,* 80.

290 "We shall get": Redlich, *Emperor Francis Joseph of Austria,* 277.
290–91 "The valiant army...my beloved people": *Morning Chronicle,* Wednesday, July 20, 1859, 6. This edition contains the full text of Franz Joseph's manifesto.
291 "is...so innocent": Hamann, *Reluctant Empress,* 93.
293 "too striking": Michel, *Empress of Farewells,* 83.
293 ("a Jewess"): *Morning Chronicle,* Monday, August 8, 1859, 3.
293 "that pretentious": Michel, *Empress of Farewells,* 84.
294 like Rousseau: See Tschuppik, *Empress Elizabeth of Austria,* 79.
295 ("We are certainly"): Palmer, *Twilight of the Habsburgs,* 118.
297 "She is...their idol": Hamann, *Reluctant Empress,* 127.
298 "to seek": Michel, *Empress of Farewells,* 87.
298 "I found": Corti, *Maximilian and Charlotte of Mexico,* vol. 1, 91.
299 "violently ill...be well imagined": Wallersee-Larisch, *My Past,* 190.
299 "The whole affair": *Times,* Tuesday, August 2, 1859, 8.
299n–300n "much gratified...inopportune smile": *Morning Post,* Friday, August 5, 1859, 5.
300 "gayest city...so sumptuous": Melville, *Journal of a Visit to Europe and the Levant,* 187.
302 "He is coming": Trevelyan, *Garibaldi and the Thousand,* 161.
303 "Look, Your Excellency": Acton, *Last Bourbons of Naples,* 443.
303 "Things wear daily": *Times,* Tuesday, June 26, 1860, 6.
305 "A constitution": Tschudi, *Maria Sophia, Queen of Naples,* 100.
305 "The immediate cause": *Morning Post,* Monday, August 6, 1860, 5.
305 "the little Job": Acton, *Last Bourbons of Naples,* 477.

Chapter 17. Imperial Expeditions

309 *There is nothing:* Hugo, *Les Misérables,* 213.
309–10 "The slums...become great": Ambès, *Intimate Memoirs,* vol. 2, 201.
310 "Garibaldi's expedition": Mérimée, *Letters of Prosper Mérimée,* vol. 1, 118.
311 "his manners were": Carette, *Recollections of the Court of the Tuileries,* 43–44.
311 "that wondrously": Ibid., 34.
311 "charmingly ugly": Ibid., 36.
312 "What is...light of day": Metternich, *My Years in Paris,* 56–59.
313 "Much has been said": Carette, *Recollections of the Court of the Tuileries,* 38.
313 "The country is": Eugénie, *Lettres familières,* vol. 1, 175.
314 "We were received": Ibid., 176.
314 "Imagine the sea": Ibid., 179.
314 "I am in Grenoble": Ibid., 181.
314 "I hope to hear": Ibid., 180.
314 "The dispatch I just": Ibid., 185.
315 "On the death": *Guardian,* Tuesday, November 27, 1860, 4.
316 "[The empress] seems to": Benson, *Letters of Queen Victoria,* vol. 3, 415.

316 "My dear James": Eugénie, *Lettres familières,* vol. 1, 193.

316 some 13,000 loyal Neapolitan troops: For these numbers, see Acton, *Last Bourbons of Naples,* 509.

317 "Queen's battery": Tschudi, *Maria Sophia, Queen of Naples,* 147.

317 "It is very": Ibid., 149–50.

317 "It was well worth... King of Italy": Acton, *Last Bourbons of Naples,* 500.

318 "His Majesty the King": Mérimée, *Letters of Prosper Mérimée,* vol. 1, 147.

318 "The death of her sister": Bicknell, *Life in the Tuileries,* 134–35.

318–19 "While the Empress... anymore": Soissons, *True Story of the Empress Eugénie,* 99–100.

319 ("Eugénie's expedition"): Benson, *Letters of Queen Victoria,* 414.

319 "She is very amiable": Ibid., 418–19.

319 "The Empress is still": Ibid., 419.

320 "I had a terrible time": Eugénie, *Lettres familières,* vol. 1, 206.

320 "All goes well": Ambès, *Intimate Memoirs,* vol. 2, 227.

321 "I think that": Filon, *Recollections of the Empress Eugénie,* 34–35.

321 "Well, Madam": Acton, *Last Bourbons of Naples,* 514.

321 "The *salons* here": Mérimée, *Letters of Prosper Mérimée,* vol. 1, 187.

322 "The Attaché to": *Times,* Thursday, February 14, 1861, 9. [Quoting a February 12 telegram from Naples.]

322 "You can be assured": Barker, *Distaff Diplomacy,* 76.

322 "It was a scene": Acton, *Last Bourbons of Naples,* 521.

322 "Gentlemen, do not": *Weekly Dispatch,* Sunday, March 3, 1861, 2.

322 "I declare": Ibid.

322 "At that time": Bicknell, *Life in the Tuileries,* 117.

323 "*Reflections on the*": Ambès, *Intimate Memoirs,* vol. 2, 231–32.

324 "Commercial interests were": Evans, *Memoirs,* vol. 1, 143.

324 75 million: For these figures and a concise explanation of the events leading up to the repudiation of debt see Corti, *Maximilian and Charlotte of Mexico,* vol. 1, 26.

324 some $150 million: See Matson, "Church Wealth in Nineteenth-Century Mexico," 606–8.

324 "It has... been said": Fleury, *Memoirs of the Empress Eugénie,* vol. 2, 105.

325 "mash of good": Barker, *Distaff Diplomacy,* 54.

Chapter 18. An Imperial Time Out

329 *Hail to thee:* Bowring, *Poems of Heine,* 252.

329–30 "I think there... quite grieves one": Benson, *Letters of Queen Victoria,* 414.

330 There are several: Stephan, *Empress Elisabeth of Austria,* 48.

331 "I want always... unendurable": Hamann, *Reluctant Empress,* 104.

333 "if she were": Ibid., 107.

333 "There was a": Ibid.

333 "nothing short of": Haslip, *Lonely Empress,* 153.

335 "I feel the greatest": Corti, *Elizabeth, Empress of Austria,* 102.
336 "One more sacrifice": Haslip, *Lonely Empress,* 109.
337 "her appearance is": *Morning Post,* Monday, June 30, 1862, 6.
337 "Her Majesty, who": *Morning Post,* Saturday, July 5, 1862, 3.
339 "The Queen's married life": Gregorovius, *Roman Journals,* 148.
339n "I regret deeply": *Daily Telegraph,* Friday, July 25, 1862, 5.
340 "If only": Hamann, *Reluctant Empress,* 114.
341 ("these things"): Ibid., 113.
341 "No sooner had": *Standard,* Wednesday, August 20, 1862, 5.
342 "There were": *Times,* Saturday, August 30, 1862, 26.

Chapter 19. The Empress Rolls the Dice

345 *Life resembles:* George Sand, *Metella,* chapter 1; see www.gutenberg.org/cache/epub/12869/pg12869-images.html.
345 "stopped like an": Hegermann-Lindencrone, *In the Courts of Memory,* 22.
345 lamentable dose of gonorrhea: Napoleon III is cited in Berger and Edberg, "Infectious Diseases in Persons of Leadership," as having contracted gonorrhea. The authors, from Tel Aviv Medical Center, Ichilov Hospital, and the Department of Laboratory Medicine, Yale University, respectively, included only those individuals whose "infectious entity [was] described so well that its etiology met reasonable diagnostic criteria." Significantly, neither Franz Joseph nor Sisi met this requirement, and so neither was listed in this study as having contracted the disease.
347 "It seemed to": Fleury, *Memoirs of the Empress Eugénie,* vol. 2, 105.
348 "I feel so sorry": Michel, *Empress of Farewells,* 93.
348 "Owing to the pressure": Corti, *Maximilian and Charlotte of Mexico,* vol. 1, 115.
349 "I do not believe": Ibid., 144.
349 "I know in advance": Ibid., 369.
349 "To found a dynasty": Michel, *Empress of Farewells,* 107.
349 "quite a beautiful...an emperor": Ibid., 110.
350 "There is great": Mérimée, *Letters of Prosper Mérimée,* vol. 1, 315.
351 *"Here we are":* Corti, *Maximilian and Charlotte of Mexico,* vol. 1, 374.
351 "News has this": Mérimée, *Letters of Prosper Mérimée,* vol. 1, 325.
351 "for the last week": Corti, *Maximilian and Charlotte of Mexico,* vol. 1, 212.
351 Eugénie beamed: See ibid., 220.
352 "The Archduke Maximilian": Mérimée, *Letters of Prosper Mérimée,* vol. 1, 343.
352 "Her dress": Kurtz, *Empress Eugénie,* 179.
353 "Many guests": Ambès, *Intimate Memoirs,* vol. 2, 272–73.
353–54 "You do not...obnoxious": Mérimée, *Letters of Prosper Mérimée,* vol. 1, 359–60.
354 "The Emperor Napoleon": Malmesbury, *Memoirs of an Ex-Minister,* vol. 3, 178–79.

355 "the North...still a child": Corti, *Maximilian and Charlotte of Mexico,* vol. 1, 310–11.
355 "They could not": *Morning Post,* Monday, March 14, 1864, 2.
356 "Look at": Corti, *Maximilian and Charlotte of Mexico,* vol. 1, 359.
356 "We congratulate": Ibid., 403.
357 "I several times": Bingham, *Recollections of Paris,* vol. 1, 49.
357 "It may easily": Ibid., 46–47.
358 "Mademoiselle, you": Bresler, *Napoleon III,* 320.
358 "The Emperor's private": Bicknell, *Life in the Tuileries,* 189.
358 "The Empress travels": *Morning Post,* Thursday, September 8, 1864, 5.
359 "I had a chat": Mérimée, *Letters of Prosper Mérimée,* vol. 2, 19.
359 "persuade Margot...Imperial Majesties": Bingham, *Recollections of Paris,* vol. 1, 47–48.
359 "Harmony reigns": Mérimée, *Letters of Prosper Mérimée,* vol. 2, 25.
360 "I would drown": Barker, *Distaff Diplomacy,* 99.
361 ("I would rather"): Robertson, *Bismarck,* 138.
361 "You ally with": Barker, *Distaff Diplomacy,*118.
361 "The Emperor has": Corti, *Maximilian and Charlotte of Mexico,* vol. 2, 846.
361 "I am sorry": Ibid., 865.

Chapter 20. The Metamorphosis

365 *Because my lightnings:* Bowring, *Poems of Heine,* 179.
366 "It is said": Mérimée, *Letters of Prosper Mérimée,* vol. 1, 290–91.
367 "she would never": Bicknell, *Life in the Tuileries,* 141.
368 "The Empress": Motley, *Correspondence,* vol. 2, 153.
368n "English society": Ibid., 125.
368n "She is in": Ibid., 199.
371 "We have got": Ibid., 133.
371 "a parliamentary government": Clark, *Franz Joseph and Bismarck,* 15.
371 "The Empress of Austria": *Weekly Dispatch,* Sunday, May 10, 1865, 35. This article quotes the *Ost-Deutsche-Post* of Vienna.
372 "The step is": Motley, *Correspondence,* vol. 2, 138.
373 "It is far": Corti, *Maximilian and Charlotte of Mexico,* vol. 1, 241.
373 "I am too": Ibid., 203.
374 "I was never": Motley, *Correspondence,* vol. 2, 156–57.
374 "I do not forget": Corti, *Elizabeth, Empress of Austria,* 114.
375 "the first edifice": *Times,* Saturday, December 17, 1864, 26.
375 "You simply cannot": Corti, *Elizabeth, Empress of Austria,* 118.
375 "I am so clumsy": Motley, *Correspondence,* vol. 2, 199.
376 "The little boy": *Times,* Saturday, June 3, 1865, 21.
377 "that full and...to decide": Corti, *Elizabeth, Empress of Austria,* 123–24.

Chapter 21. Government by the Heroine

381   *There is no more:* Mérimée, *Letters of Prosper Mérimée*, vol. 2, 87.

381   "a renewal": Ibid.

381   "The Emperor": Bicknell, *Life in the Tuileries*, 148.

381   "I *could* not": Ibid., 146.

382   "It is impossible": Ibid., 147.

382   "milk-sop": Ibid., 145.

382   "express his feelings... you know": Ibid.

382   "He [Louis] was reproached": Mérimée, *Letters of Prosper Mérimée*, vol. 1, 238.

382   "The same flowers": Carette, *Recollections of the Court of the Tuileries*, 194–95.

382   "with very natural": Bicknell, *Life in the Tuileries*, 148.

382   "whom he dearly": Ibid., 144.

383   "The Emperor... one ready": Ibid., 149.

383   "Louis, don't be": Filon, *Memoirs of the Prince Imperial*, 27.

384   SURRENDER: *Guardian*, Monday, April 24, 1865, 3.

385   "Madame: The Emperor": Emerson, "A Medal for Mrs. Lincoln," 189–90.

385   LETTER FROM THE: *New York Times*, Monday, May 22, 1865, 1.

385*n*   "The only thing talked of": Mérimée, *Letters of Prosper Mérimée*, vol. 2, 62.

386   "the first time": *Daily Telegraph*, Wednesday, June 14, 1865, 5.

386   "The Empress Eugénie": *Pall Mall Gazette*, Friday, May 12, 1865, 9.

386   "The names of the boys": Peat, *Gossip from Paris*, 93–94.

387   "Mr. Bigelow": Mérimée, *Letters of Prosper Mérimée*, vol. 2, 65.

387–88   "very dear sister... whole of Mexico": Corti, *Maximilian and Charlotte of Mexico*, vol. 2, 908–9.

388   "The master of": Mérimée, *Letters of Prosper Mérimée*, vol. 2, 70.

388   "Internal affairs": Corti, *Maximilian and Charlotte of Mexico*, vol. 2, 914.

388   "Make me": Robertson, *Bismarck*, 112.

389   "I wasted": Ibid., 173.

389   "Put Germany": Ibid., 231.

389   "be unable": Bismarck, *Bismarck, the Man and the Statesman*, vol. 1, 313.

389   "I can perfectly... in history": Ibid., 314.

389   "I reminded the King": Ibid., vol. 2, 9.

389   "His frame of mind": Ibid., 19–20.

390   "he [Wilhelm] is": Victoria, *Letters of Queen Victoria: Second Series*, vol. 1, 273.

390   "One cannot sell": Sybel, *Founding of the German Empire by William I*, vol. 4, 235.

390   "I believe that I may": Ibid., 250.

390*n*   "Prussia seems": Victoria, *Letters of Queen Victoria: Second Series*, vol. 1, 271.

391   "that in case": Clark, *Franz Joseph and Bismarck*, 285.

391   "requested to be taken": Peat, *Gossip from Paris*, 125–26.

392   "His Majesty": Sybel, *Founding of the German Empire by William I*, vol. 4, 355.

Chapter 22. The Empress Takes a Stand

395 *Princes wrangle:* Bowring, *Poems of Heine,* 388.

396 "the most popular": *Times,* Friday, December 22, 1865, 21.

396n "in the times": *Times,* Saturday, May 2, 1868, 12.

397n "Pray consult me": Corti, *Elizabeth, Empress of Austria,* 117.

398 "It is already": *Times,* Saturday, December 2, 1865, 26.

399 "This is not": *Sunday Dispatch,* Sunday, December 31, 1865, 51.

399–400 "trimmed with...goes to Pesth": *Times,* Saturday, January 13, 1866, 6.

400 "*Eljen!* [Long life to you]": *Times,* Monday, June 12, 1865, 10.

400 "Ever since...cries of *Eljen!*)": *Times,* Saturday, January 13, 1866, 6.

400 "The Empress produced": Ibid.

401 "No one expected...were received": *Times,* Monday, March 5, 1866, 10.

402 "transcendent genius": Bismarck, *Bismarck, the Man and the Statesman,* vol. 1, 320.

402 "if a power intended": Clark, *Franz Joseph and Bismarck,* 368.

403 "The popular agitations": William I, *Correspondence of William I and Bismarck,* vol. 1, 63.

403 "Your Majesty will...in Vienna": Ibid., 64.

404 "Could you promise": Clark, *Franz Joseph and Bismarck,* 434.

404 "Your Majesty": Ibid., 435.

404 "Secret Convention": Ibid., 437.

405 "There is much": Motley, *Correspondence,* vol. 2, 217.

405 23,000...74,000: For these numbers see Rumbold, *Francis Joseph and His Times,* 261.

406 "If only he": Corti, *Elizabeth, Empress of Austria,* 135.

407 "Papa is looking": Ibid., 137.

407 "I told them": Rumbold, *Francis Joseph and His Times,* 255.

408 "the Empress is": Haslip, *Lonely Empress,* 192.

408 "At least she": Corti, *Elizabeth, Empress of Austria,* 136.

408 "Your dear mama": Haslip, *Lonely Empress,* 192.

409–10 "and the wind blew...in full retreat": *Times,* Tuesday, July 10, 1866, 9.

410 "It looks awfully": Motley, *Correspondence,* vol. 2, 230–32.

Chapter 23. An Unfortunate Fall-Off in Imperial Greatness

413 *Do not deceiv:* Sybel, *Founding of the German Empire by William I,* vol. 5, 421.

413 "I never saw": Mérimée, *Letters of Prosper Mérimée,* vol. 2, 149–50.

414 "A power which": Barker, *Distaff Diplomacy,* 141.

414 "We can concentrate": Paléologue, *Tragic Empress,* 111.

415 "When the Prussian": Ibid., 112.

415 "It was one": Ibid., 111.

415 "His sufferings": Ibid., 117.

415 "In all the time": Sencourt, *Life of the Empress Eugénie*, 196. My translation.

416 "Louis [Napoleon] shall pay": Robertson, *Bismarck*, 208.

416 "To receive Venice": Sybel, *Founding of the German Empire by William I*, vol. 5, 259.

416 "If you persist": Ibid., 421.

416 "Really, you make me": Sencourt, *Life of the Empress Eugénie*, 195.

416 "I found the Emperor": Sybel, *Founding of the German Empire by William I*, vol. 5, 273–74.

416 "It would be": Ibid., 415.

417 "My Dear Prince": Sencourt, *Life of the Empress Eugénie*, 193–94.

417 "I am sending": Corti, *Maximilian and Charlotte of Mexico*, vol. 2, 858.

418 "as soon as possible": Ibid., 931.

418 "Abdication amounts": Ibid., 639.

419 "tears were rising": Ibid., 670.

419 "I know more": Ibid., 671.

420 "it is henceforward": Ibid., 945.

420 "*He* [Napoleon III] *is*": Ibid., 685–86.

420 "I could plainly see": Fleury, *Memoirs of the Empress Eugénie*, vol. 2, 119.

420 "We have done": Ibid., 121.

420 "The Empress of Mexico": Mérimée, *Letters of Prosper Mérimée*, vol. 2, 186–87.

421 "It is by no means": Ibid., 179.

Chapter 24. The Empress to the Rescue

425 *Thou hast pearls:* Bowring, *Poems of Heine*, 219.

425–26 "Ten days ago...muzzle loaders": Motley, *Correspondence*, vol. 2, 231–32.

426 "I resolved to advise": Bismarck, *Bismarck, the Man and the Statesman*, vol. 2, 38.

427 "Take the children": Corti, *Elizabeth, Empress of Austria*, 141.

427 "*Eljen*": Rumbold, *Francis Joseph and His Times*, 296.

428 "In a week...of the dice": Motley, *Correspondence*, vol. 2, 237–38.

428 "Whatever may happen": Corti, *Elizabeth, Empress of Austria*, 144.

428n "I should have": Tschuppik, *Reign of the Emperor Francis Joseph*, 161.

429 "The complete": Sybel, *Founding of the German Empire by William I*, vol. 5, 431.

429 "That a war": Bismarck, *Bismarck, the Man and the Statesman*, vol. 2, 41.

429 "to avoid": Ibid., 48.

429 "We get as easily": Sybel, *Founding of the German Empire by William I*, vol. 5, 285.

430 "than the existence": Ibid., 450.

430 "whether it would...a peace": Hamerow, *Otto von Bismarck*, 149–50.

430 "We are severing": Corti, *Elizabeth, Empress of Austria*, 148.

431 "Poor Italy": Motley, *Correspondence*, vol. 2, 239.

431 "There is no": Ibid., 252.

431 "The worst error": Tschuppik, *Reign of the Emperor Francis Joseph*, 168.

432 "Your poor little one": Corti, *Elizabeth, Empress of Austria*, 148.

432 "Your lonely": Ibid., 151.

433 "Though the Emperor's pride": *Daily Telegraph*, Saturday, August 11, 1866, 5.

433 pearl necklace...America: See the *Pall Mall Gazette*, Thursday, August 23, 1866, 4.

434 "that there were designs...paternal kindness": *Morning Post*, Saturday, October 13, 1866, 4.

435 "There is but": *Daily Telegraph*, Friday, October 26, 1866, 3.

436 "a foreigner, a German": Tschuppik, *Reign of the Emperor Francis Joseph*, 168.

436 "with tears": Palmer, *Twilight of the Habsburgs*, 154.

437 "the 'beautiful Providence'": Corti, *Elizabeth, Empress of Austria*, 150.

437 "It must be...beautiful dream": *Times*, Wednesday, June 12, 1867, 9.

437 "Words cannot describe": *Morning Post*, Thursday, June 13, 1867, 6.

437 "a lot more Latin": Palmer, *Twilight of the Habsburgs*, 159.

438 "The enthusiasm": *Standard*, Tuesday, June 11, 1867, 5.

438 "I was not": Corti, *Elizabeth, Empress of Austria*, 162.

438 "For three centuries": Ibid., 161.

Chapter 25. An Exhibition of Imperial Honor

441 *The difference between:* Attributed to Alexandre Dumas, *The Count of Monte Cristo*. Although there is no specific passage in the original work that translates into this phrase in English, it is a theme of the novel.

442 "Here in France": *Daily Telegraph*, Thursday, November 8, 1866, 3.

442 "The Prussian weapon": *Pall Mall Gazette*, Friday, July 27, 1866, 5.

442 "A heavy expenditure": Mérimée, *Letters of Prosper Mérimée*, vol. 2, 197.

442 "The Emperor": Ibid., 194.

443 "The poor Emperor": Bicknell, *Life in the Tuileries*, 201.

444 "Their Majesties' entrance": Ambès, *Intimate Memoirs*, vol. 2, 335.

444 "At the moment": Corti, *Maximilian and Charlotte of Mexico*, vol. 2, 947.

444 "I...fully approve": Ibid., 770–71.

445 "refuse to have": Ibid., 778.

445 Some 6,000 soldiers: For this figure see Sergeant, *Last Empress of the French*, 313.

445 "it is the fault": Soissons, *True Story of the Empress Eugénie*, 164–65.

446 "a fantastical being": Rimmel, *Recollections of the Paris Exhibition of 1867*, 25.

446 "The Exposition": Ambès, *Intimate Memoirs*, vol. 2, 340.

446 "You can listen": Hegermann-Lindencrone, *In the Courts of Memory*, 154–55.

447 "It rains kings": Ambès, *Intimate Memoirs*, vol. 2, 340.

447 "The Emperor of Russia": Hegermann-Lindencrone, *In the Courts of Memory*, 156.

447 "Now we have been": Sergeant, *Last Empress of the French*, 316.

447 "It is understood": *Morning Post*, Tuesday, June 25, 1867, 5.

448 "life is quite as safe": Corti, *Maximilian and Charlotte of Mexico*, vol. 2, 825.

448   "The sovereigns are": Hegermann-Lindencrone, *In the Courts of Memory,* 165.

448   "How fatiguing": Ambès, *Intimate Memoirs,* vol. 2, 341.

448   "With colors flying": Twain, *Innocents Abroad,* 125.

449   "bristling with cannons": Rimmel, *Recollections of the Paris Exhibition of 1867,* 168.

449   "If Your Majesty": Corti, *Maximilian and Charlotte of Mexico,* vol. 2, 745.

450   40,000 troops: See ibid., 791.

450   2,000 ounces of gold: See ibid., 800.

451   "What a glorious": Ibid., 821.

451   "Muchachos, aim well": Martin, *Maximilian in Mexico,* 383.

452   "the gentlemen": Hegermann-Lindencrone, *In the Courts of Memory,* 174–75.

452   "The feeling in Paris…away at Miramar": *Daily News,* Friday, July 5, 1867, 5. Quoting the Parisian paper the *Temps.*

452–53 "I never would…'the Archdupe'": Hegermann-Lindencrone, *In the Courts of Memory,* 177.

453   "It will be": Sencourt, *Life of the Empress Eugénie,* 207–8.

Chapter 26. The Empress Breaks Free

457   *The rose and the lily:* Bowring, *Poems of Heine,* 66.

458–59 "The Vienna papers…all his rights": *Daily News,* Friday, July 5, 1867, 5.

459   "I am so utterly": Corti, *Elizabeth, Empress of Austria,* 170.

459–60 "The Empress Eugénie…Empress Elisabeth": Stoddart, *Life of the Empress Eugénie,* 171–72.

460   "The Empress was": Palmer, *Twilight of the Habsburgs,* 161.

460   "For my part": Paléologue, *Tragic Empress,* 152–53.

461   "I had never thought": Corti, *Elizabeth, Empress of Austria,* 175–76.

462   "Her Majesty is": *Sunday Dispatch,* Sunday, March 22, 1868, 51.

463   "the Empress wrote": *Daily News,* Monday, November 11, 1867, 5.

463   "Numerous as…their Court": *Times,* Saturday, May 2, 1868, 12.

464   "The Emperor Francis Joseph": *Daily News,* Saturday, October 10, 1868, 5.

464   "the one and only one": Corti, *Elizabeth, Empress of Austria,* 178.

465   1 million gulden: See Bertram, *A Royal Recluse,* 42.

465–66 "Elsa…'the Dove'": Chapman-Huston, *Ludwig II,* 117.

466   "My dear Elsa": Ibid., 119.

466   "Beloved of my": Ibid., 138.

466   "He is only playing": Bertram, *A Royal Recluse,* 44.

466   "Your parents": Chapman-Huston, *Ludwig II,* 135.

466   "Sophie got rid of": Ibid., 137.

466   "How much": Ibid.

466n "no one": Haslip, *Lonely Empress,* 216.

467   "We want to give": Richter, *Mad Monarch,* 136.

Chapter 27. The Reign in Spain—Again

471 *My name:* Lord, *Origins of the War of 1870*, 23–24.
471 "Fall on the Bourse": Ambès, *Intimate Memoirs*, vol. 2, 341.
472 "The Government is": Mérimée, *Letters of Prosper Mérimée*, vol. 2, 277.
472 "And the most": Ibid., 294–95.
472 "He was received": Ibid., 296–97.
473 "Not a single": Ambès, *Intimate Memoirs*, vol. 2, 366.
473 "It is not easy": Jerrold, *Life of Napoleon III*, vol. 4, 418.
473 "You must not": Stoddart, *Life of the Empress Eugénie*, 187.
474 "a 'revolt of the harem' ": *Daily News*, Saturday, November 6, 1869, 3.
474 "There have been few": *Daily News*, Monday, November 29, 1869, 5.
475 "They wanted to…the year": Ambès, *Intimate Memoirs*, vol. 2, 368–69.
475 "suffering, anxious": Stoddart, *Life of the Empress Eugénie*, 185.
475 "he regarded": Bismarck, *Bismarck, the Man and the Statesman*, vol. 2, 97.
475 300,000 men: For these figures see Moltke, *Extracts from Moltke's Correspondence*, 170.
475 "Success…depends upon": Bismarck, *Bismarck, the Man and the Statesman*, vol. 2, 99.
476 "The goings on": Mérimée, *Letters of Prosper Mérimée*, vol. 2, 335–36.
477 "For dynastic": Lord, *Origins of the War of 1870*, 20.
477 "has only": Eych, *Bismarck and the German Empire*, 167.
477 "patriotic duty": Lord, *Origins of the War of 1870*, 21.
477 "absolutely *against*": William I, *Correspondence of William I and Bismarck*, vol. 1, 123.
477 "with a heavy": Lord, *Origins of the War of 1870*, 22.
477 "A while ago": Ambès, *Intimate Memoirs*, vol. 2, 386.
478 "It was a good": *Times*, Monday, November 11, 1867, 8.
478 "They voted": Ambès, *Intimate Memoirs*, vol. 2, 396.
478 "would not tolerate": Jerrold, *Life of Napoleon III*, vol. 4, 459.
478n "one or two army corps": Robertson, *Bismarck*, 267.
479 "the Prussian government": Ibid., 268.
479 "So long as": Jerrold, *Life of Napoleon III*, vol. 4, 469.
480 "no more interest": Robertson, *Bismarck*, 513.
480–81 "I perceived…eating and drinking.": Bismarck, *Bismarck, the Man and the Statesman*, vol. 2, 93–99.
481 "The French Ambassador": Robertson, *Bismarck*, 513.
481 "Mr. Thiers rose": Hoffman, *Camp, Court and Siege*, 136.
482 "Everyone here": Barker, *Distaff Diplomacy*, 196.
482 "The Empress had…long a time": Fleury, *Memoirs of the Empress Eugénie*, vol. 2, 261.
483 "I am quite ready": Ibid., 257.

483 "I was present": Ambès, *Intimate Memoirs,* vol. 2, 398.

483 "I never regretted": Hegermann-Lindencrone, *In the Courts of Memory,* 250–51.

Chapter 28. By the Skin of the Empress's Teeth

485 *I do not wear:* Dumas, *Three Musketeers,* 55.

485 "the Empress and": Hegermann-Lindencrone, *In the Courts of Memory,* 252.

485 "The Empress mastered": Filon, *Memoirs of the Prince Imperial,* 68.

486 "He was '*navré*'": Jerrold, *Life of Napoleon III,* vol. 4, 477.

486 "Louis has received": Filon, *Memoirs of the Prince Imperial,* 69.

486 "Our troops are": Sencourt, *Life of the Empress Eugénie,* 251.

487 "People of France": Ibid., 252–53.

487 "I can conceive": Mérimée, *Letters of Prosper Mérimée,* vol. 2, 379.

487 66 heavy guns: For these statistics see Quintin, *The Franco-Prussian War,* vol. 1, 79–98.

488 "However sad it is": Fleury, *Memoirs of the Empress Eugénie,* vol. 2, 367.

488 "I see nothing here": Mérimée, *Letters of Prosper Mérimée,* vol. 2, 380.

488 "It is consoling": Ambès, *Intimate Memoirs,* vol. 2, 403.

488 "The army is effecting": Fleury, *Memoirs of the Empress Eugénie,* vol. 2, 279.

488 "The army, occupying unfavorable": Ibid., 279–280.

489 "The dynasty is lost": Sencourt, *Life of the Empress Eugénie,* 251.

489 "Once more I beg you": Fleury, *Memoirs of the Empress Eugénie,* vol. 2, 392–93.

489–90 "The Prussian line...Sedan itself": *Daily Telegraph,* Tuesday, September 6, 1870, 5.

490 "Just imagine": Fleury, *Memoirs of the Empress Eugénie,* vol. 2, 314.

490 "He climbed...inviting death": Ibid., 279–81.

490 "Silent and impassible...that day": Ibid., 285–86.

490 "Houses were falling": Ibid., 296.

490 "I would have preferred": Ibid., 313.

491 "Monsieur, my brother": Ibid., 297.

491 "The army is": Ibid., 403.

491 "A captive army": Ibid., 404.

491 "at 2 p.m.": Ibid., 415–16.

491 "If I can prevent it": Ibid., 405.

492 "ready to meet": Ibid., 393.

492 "For no price": Ibid., 407.

492 "I go from": Mérimée, *Letters of Prosper Mérimée,* vol. 2, 340–42.

492 "I am writing": Ibid., 388.

492 "These dreadful": Ibid., 390.

492 "Down with the Empire": Fleury, *Memoirs of the Empress Eugénie,* vol. 2, 457.

493 "Here I have": Evans, *Memoirs,* vol. 2, 326.

493 *"Voilà l'Impératrice"*: Ibid., 335.

494 "I have come": Ibid., 359–60.

495 ("And if I"): Ibid., 361.

496 *"Vive la France"*: Ibid., 413.

497 "Oh, my God": Ibid., 441.

497 "I drew him": Ibid., 444.

498 "I regret, gentlemen": Ibid., 445.

498 "that a man...safely do so": Ibid., 446–47.

499 "I was sure": Ibid., 463.

500 "This news had": Ibid., 467.

500 "The Prince": Ibid., 474.

Chapter 29. The Search for Solace

503 *And must I:* Corti, *Elizabeth, Empress of Austria,* 260.

503 "We may possibly": Ibid., 195.

503 "I hope you": Ibid., 196.

504 "the most brilliantly": *Times,* Monday, February 13, 1871, 4.

504–5 "We do not...in rags": Hamann, *Reluctant Empress,* 295.

505 "Does she deserve": Corti, *Elizabeth, Empress of Austria,* 200.

505 to curry: For the political rationale behind Gisela's engagement see the *Standard,* Monday, April 22, 1872, 5.

505 "It is commonly said": *Guardian,* Friday, June 7, 1872, 6.

507 2,500 people died: See Palmer, *Twilight of the Habsburgs,* 186.

507 19 million gulden: See https://artblart.com/2014/09/23 /exhibition-the-metropolis-experiment-vienna-and-the-1873-world -exhibition-at-wien-museum-vienna/.

508 "You are crushing": Corti, *Elizabeth, Empress of Austria,* 232.

508 "An uncanny": Hamann, *Reluctant Empress,* 295.

508 "What is an empress": Corti, *Elizabeth, Empress of Austria,* 272.

509 "Heine is": Ibid., 352.

511 "The Empress took": Wallersee-Larisch, *My Past,* 79.

511 " 'I want to be' ": Ibid., 90.

511 "Mamma talked to me": Corti, *Elizabeth, Empress of Austria,* 324–25.

512 ("It is just"): Richter, *Mad Monarch,* 198.

512 ("people with whom"): Ibid., 217.

513 "Save me, Marie": Corti, *Elizabeth, Empress of Austria,* 235.

513 ("I love her better"): Chapman-Huston, *Ludwig II,* 307.

513 13 million marks: For the financial situation and consequences, see Richter, *Mad Monarch,* 257–58.

Chapter 30. The Ex-Empress Steps In

517 *The Empire is dead: Pall Mall Gazette,* Saturday, September 10, 1870, 11.

517 ("This dreadful war"): Bolitho, *Further Letters of Queen Victoria,* 171.

517   "The Empress bears": Ibid., 180–81.

517   "You have undoubtedly": Ibid., 181–82.

518   "The King of Prussia": Landon, *Franco-Prussian War*, 279.

518   "*We will not cede*": Ibid.

519   "the fifth part of": *Morning Post*, Wednesday, March 1, 1871, 5.

520   "O God": Bolitho, *Further Letters of Queen Victoria*, 181.

520   "the most profound...of the Parisians": *Morning Post*, Saturday, March 4, 1871, 5.

520   "The Empress and": Ambès, *Intimate Memoirs*, vol. 2, 411.

521   300,000 national guardsmen: For these numbers see Mason, *Paris Commune*, 114.

522   "Great was my": Evans, *Memoirs*, vol. 2, 582.

522   "Napoleon arrives": *Morning Post*, Monday, March 20, 1871, 4.

522   "During the latter": Evans, *Memoirs*, vol. 2, 600.

523   "The agony": Ibid., 601.

523   "Conneau, were you": Sergeant, *Last Empress of the French*, 391.

524   "I have only you": Ibid., 392.

524   "a terrible crowd": Bolitho, *Further Letters of Queen Victoria*, 193–94.

524   "A week ago": Legge, *Empress Eugénie*, 101.

524n   "Prince Napoleon is": Bolitho, *Further Letters of Queen Victoria*, 193.

525   "Titled ladies": *Daily Telegraph*, Tuesday, March 17, 1874, 4.

525   "*Vive l'Empereur*": Ibid.

525   "When I lost": Filon, *Memoirs of the Prince Imperial*, 102.

525   "For if": Legge, *Empress Eugénie*, 221.

526   "If anything happens": Filon, *Memoirs of the Prince Imperial*, 185–86.

526   "Do you want": Filon, *Memoirs of the Empress Eugénie*, 290.

526   "For eight years": Legge, *Empress Eugénie*, 219–20.

527   "two obstinate": Kurtz, *Empress Eugénie*, 297.

527   "Public feeling": Filon, *Memoirs of the Prince Imperial*, 198.

528   "The Prince is down": Ibid., 211.

528   "No, no": Bolitho, *Further Letters of Queen Victoria*, 237.

Chapter 31. The Imperial Cabin in the Woods

531   *Yonder, where the stars*: Bowring, *Poems of Heine*, 4.

531–32 "The King was...fearful end": Corti, *Elizabeth, Empress of Austria*, 347.

533   "So in these difficult": Palmer, *Twilight of the Habsburgs*, 177–78.

534   "like a child": Hamann, *Reluctant Empress*, 229.

535   "There was a time": Palmer, *Twilight of the Habsburgs*, 224.

536   "After the birth": Judtmann, *Mayerling*, 18.

536   "He was spending": Ibid., 21.

536n   "a very high degree": Ibid., 20.

537   "Are you ill?": Corti, *Elizabeth, Empress of Austria*, 377.

538   "Mitzi": Judtmann, *Mayerling*, 47.

539   "she belonged": Ibid., 346.
539   ("In gratitude"): Ibid., 40.
540   "We are both": Ibid., 151.
540   "Forgive me": Ibid.
540   "You are not": Ibid., 50.
542   "Not yet": Corti, *Elizabeth, Empress of Austria,* 392.
542   "Has he...poisoned him": Ibid., 393.
542–43 "touchingly pure...killed": Judtmann, *Mayerling,* 147.
543   "for I myself": Hamann, *Reluctant Empress,* 331.

Chapter 32. The New Disciples of the Dagger

547   *But on, still on:* Bowring, *Poems of Heine,* 131.
547   "I am still": Eugénie, *Lettres familières,* vol. 2, 101.
548   "all the Republican": *Daily News,* Monday, June 23, 1879, 5.
548   "Countless hundreds": *Daily Telegraph,* Friday, June 27, 1879, 5.
548   "Is it you": Kurtz, *Empress Eugénie,* 317.
549   "Why did Francis": Corti, *Elizabeth, Empress of Austria,* 400.
549   "I wish...Rudolf": Ibid., 405–6.
549   "Among all classes": *Times,* Monday, February 4, 1889, 5.
550   "Now all these people": Corti, *Elizabeth, Empress of Austria,* 402.
550   "How much I owe": *Times,* Friday, February 8, 1889, 5.
551   "It was like": Kurtz, *Empress Eugénie,* 352.
551   "Yes, I know...of the drama": Paléologue, *Tragic Empress,* 162–64.
552   "the destruction of": Nitti, "Italian Anarchist," 602.
553   "an avenger of": Ibid., 599.
553   "Whatever did": Corti, *Elizabeth, Empress of Austria,* 477.
554   "My blow": *Daily Telegraph,* Monday, September 12, 1898, 7.
554   "I see I": *Times,* Monday, September 12, 1898, 3.
554   "It is absolutely": *Daily Telegraph,* Monday, September 12, 1898, 7.
555   "gratitude of the nation...Maria Theresa": *Times,* Monday, September 12, 1898, 3.

Bibliography

Abbott, John S. C. *The History of Napoleon III, Emperor of the French. Including a Brief Narrative of All the Most Important Events Which Have Occurred in Europe since the Fall of Napoleon I until the Overthrow of the Second Empire and the Death of Napoleon III.* Boston: B. B. Russell, 1873.

Acton, Harold. *The Last Bourbons of Naples.* London: Methuen, 1961.

Ambès, Baron d' [pseud. for Baron de Heeckeren]. *Intimate Memoirs of Napoleon III: Personal Reminiscences of the Man and the Emperor.* Edited and translated by A. R. Allinson, with illustrations from the collection of A. M. Broadly. Boston: Little, Brown, 1912.

Aronson, Theo. *Queen Victoria and the Bonapartes.* London: Cassell, 1972.

Artz, Frederick B. *France under the Bourbon Restoration: 1814–1830.* New York: Russell & Russell, 1963.

Barker, Nancy Nichols. *Distaff Diplomacy: The Empress Eugénie and the Foreign Policy of the Second Empire.* Austin: University of Texas Press, 1967.

Barthez, Ernest. *The Empress Eugénie and Her Circle.* New York: Brentano's, 1913.

Beecher, Jonathan, and Richard Bienvenu. *The Utopian Vision of Charles Fourier: Selected Texts on Work, Love, and Passionate Attraction.* Boston: Beacon Press, 1971.

Benson, Arthur Christopher, editor. *The Letters of Queen Victoria: A Selection from Her Majesty's Correspondence between the Years 1837 and 1861.* 3 vols. London: John Murray; New York: Longmans, Green, 1907.

Berger, Stephen A., and Stephen C. Edberg. "Infectious Diseases in Persons of Leadership." *Reviews of Infectious Diseases* 6, no. 6 (November/December 1984): 802–813.

Bertram, Werner. *A Royal Recluse: Memories of Ludwig II of Bavaria.* Munich: M. Herpich, 1900.

Bicknell, Anna L. *Life in the Tuileries under the Second Empire.* New York: The Century Co., 1895.

Bingham, D. *Recollections of Paris, by Captain the Hon. D. Bingham.* 2 vols. London: Chapman and Hall, 1896.

Bismarck, Otto von. *Bismarck, the Man and the Statesman; Being the Reflections and Reminiscences of Otto, Prince von Bismarck, Written and Dictated by Himself after*

His Retirement from Office; Tr. from the German under the Supervision of A. J. Butler... with Two Portraits and a Facsimile of Handwriting. New York: Harper & Brothers, 1899.

Blanc, Louis. *The History of Ten Years, 1830–1840; or, France under Louis Philippe.* Translated by Walter Keating Kelly. Philadelphia: Lea & Blanchard, 1848.

Bolitho, Hector, editor. *Further Letters of Queen Victoria.* London: Thornton Butterworth, 1938.

Bowman, Frank Paul. *Prosper Mérimée: Heroism, Pessimism, and Irony.* Berkeley: University of California Press, 1962.

Brereton, F. S. *A Gallant Grenadier: A Tale of the Crimean War.* New York: H. M. Caldwell, 1919.

Bresler, Fenton S. *Napoleon III: A Life.* New York: Carroll & Graf, 1999.

Cairns, William E., editor. *Napoleon's Military Maxims.* Mineola, NY: Dover Publications, 2004.

Carette, Madame. *Recollections of the Court of the Tuileries.* Translated from the French by Elizabeth Phipps Train. New York: D. Appleton, 1889.

Carey, Agnes. *Empress Eugenie in Exile.* With illustrations from photographs. New York: The Century Co., 1920.

Carlin, Colin. *William Kirkpatrick of Málaga: Consul, Négociant and Entrepreneur, and Grandfather of the Empress Eugénie.* Glasgow: The Grimsay Press, 2011.

Chapman-Huston, Desmond. *Ludwig II: The Mad King of Bavaria.* New York: Dorset Press, 1990.

Clark, Chester Wells. *Franz Joseph and Bismarck: The Diplomacy of Austria before the War of 1866.* Cambridge, MA: Harvard University Press, 1934.

Clarke, H. Butler. *Modern Spain, 1815–1898.* Cambridge: Cambridge University Press, 1906.

Corti, Count Egon Caesar. *Elizabeth, Empress of Austria.* Translated by Catherine Alison Phillips. New Haven, CT: Yale University Press, 1936.

———. *Ludwig I of Bavaria.* Translated by Evelyn B. Graham Stamper. London: Eyre & Spottiswoode, 1943.

——— . *Maximilian and Charlotte of Mexico.* 2 vols. New York: Alfred A. Knopf, 1929.

Cowley, Henry Wellesley. *The Diary and Correspondence of Henry Wellesley: First Lord Cowley, 1790–1846.* London: Hutchinson, 1930.

Crossland, James. "Radical Warfare's First 'Superweapon': The Fears, Perceptions, and Realities of the Orsini Bomb, 1858–1896." *Terrorism and Political Violence* 35, no. 2 (2023): 355–69. www.tandfonline.com/doi/epdf/10.1080/09546553.2021.1924692.

Cunliffe-Owen, Marguerite. *The Martyrdom of an Empress. With Portraits from Photographs.* New York: Harper & Brothers, 1900.

De Burgh, Edward. *Elizabeth Empress of Austria: A Memoir.* London: Hutchinson, 1899.

Dumas, Alexandre. *The Three Musketeers. Translated by William Robson with a Letter from Alexandre Dumas Fils, and Two Hundred and Fifty Illustrations by Maurice Leloir, Engraved on wood by J. Huyot.* New York: D. Appleton, 1922.

Emerson, Jason. "A Medal for Mrs. Lincoln." *The Register of the Kentucky Historical Society,* no. 2 (spring 2011): 187–205.

Eugénie [de Montijo], Empress. *Lettres familières de l'impératrice Eugénie. Publiées par les soins du duc d'Albe avec le concours de F. de Llanos y Torriglia et Pierre Josserand, préface de Gabriel Hanotaux, de l'Académie Française.* 2 vols. Paris: Le Divan, 1935.

Evans, Thomas W. *The Memoirs of Dr. Thomas W. Evans: Recollections of the Second French Empire.* Edited by Edward A. Crane. London: Unwin, 1905.

Eych, Erich. *Bismarck and the German Empire.* New York: Norton, 1968.

Fehrenbach, Charles Wentz. "Moderados and Exaltados: The Liberal Opposition to Ferdinand VII, 1814–1823." *Hispanic American Historical Review* 50, no. 1 (1970): 52–69.

Filon, Augustin. *Memoirs of the Prince Imperial, 1856–1879.* Boston: Little, Brown, 1913.

——— . *Recollections of the Empress Eugénie.* London: Cassell, 1920.

Fisher, Herbert A. L. *Studies in Napoleonic Statesmanship: Germany.* Oxford: Clarendon Press, 1903.

Flaubert, Gustave. *Madame Bovary: Provincial Manner.* Translated from the French. London: W. W. Gibbings, 1892.

Fleury, Maurice, comte. *Memoirs of the Empress Eugénie. Compiled from Statements, Private Documents, and Personal Letters of the Empress Eugenie; from Conversations of the Emperor Napoleon III and from Family Letters and Papers of General Fleury, M. Franceschini Pieui, Prince Victor Napoleon, and Other Members of the Court of the Second Empire.* 2 vols. New York: D. Appleton, 1920.

Forsythe, David. "The History of Infant Feeding from Elizabethan Times." *Journal of the Royal Society of Medicine* 4 (1911): 110–41. https://journals.sagepub.com /doi/abs/10.1177/003591571100401457.

Green, Anne. "France Exposed: *Madame Bovary* and the Exposition Universelle." *Modern Language Review* 99, no. 4 (October 2004): 915+.

Gregorovius, Ferdinand. *The Roman Journals of Ferdinand Gregorovius, 1852–1874. Edited by Friedrich Althaus and Translated from the Second German Edition by Mrs. Gustavus W. Hamilton.* London: George Bell & Sons, 1907.

Gribble, Francis Henry. *The Life of the Emperor Francis Joseph.* London: E. Nash, 1914.

Hallberg, Charles. *Franz Joseph and Napoleon III, 1852–1864.* New York: Bookman Associates, 1955.

Hamann, Brigitte. *The Reluctant Empress: Elisabeth of Austria.* Translated from the German by Ruth Hein. New York: Alfred A. Knopf, 1986.

Hamerow, Theodore S., editor. *Otto von Bismarck: Reflections and Reminiscences.* New York: Harper & Row, 1968.

Hartley, M. *The Man Who Saved Austria: The Life and Times of Baron Jellačić.* London: Mills & Boon, 1912.

Haslip, Joan. *The Crown of Mexico: Maximilian and His Empress Carlota.* New York: Holt, Rinehart and Winston, 1972.

———. *The Lonely Empress: A Biography of Elizabeth of Austria*. London: Weidenfeld & Nicolson, 1965.

Hayes, Carlton J. H. *A Political and Social History of Modern Europe*. New York: Macmillan, 1916.

Hegermann-Lindencrone, Lillie de. *In the Courts of Memory, 1858–1875, from Contemporary Letters*. New York: Harper & Brothers, 1912.

Heine, Heinrich. *Heine in Art and Letters*. Translated with a prefatory note by Elizabeth A. Sharp. London: W. Scott, 1905.

———. *Poems and Ballads of Heinrich Heine*. Translated by Emma Lazarus. New York: Hurst, 1881.

———. *Poems of Heinrich Heine*. Edited and translated by Louis Untermeyer. New York: Henry Holt, 1917.

———. *The Poems of Heine. Complete. Translated in the Original Metres. With a Sketch of Heine's Life*. Translated by Edgar Alfred Bowring. London: Henry G. Bohn, 1861.

———. *The Prose Writings of Heinrich Heine*. Edited with an introduction by Havelock Ellis. London: W. Scott, 1887.

Higby, Chester Penn. "The Religious Policy of the Bavarian Government during the Napoleonic Period." PhD diss., Columbia University, 1918. New York: Columbia University; London: Longmans, Green, 1919.

Hoffman, Wickham. *Camp, Court and Siege: A Narrative of Personal Adventure and Observation during Two Wars: 1861–1865; 1870–1871*. London: Sampson Low, Marston, Searle & Rivington, 1877.

Hübner, Joseph Alexander, count. *Neuf ans de souvenirs d'un ambassadeur d'Autriche à Paris sous le second empire, 1851–1859*. Paris: Plon-Nourrit, 1905.

Hugo, Victor. *Les Misérables*. Translated by Charles E. Wilbour. Abridged, edited, and with an introduction by Paul Bénichou. New York: Washington Square Press, 1964.

Hume, Martin A. S. *Modern Spain*. London: Unwin, 1923.

Irving, Pierre M. *The Life and Letters of Washington Irving*. 4 vols. New York: G. P. Putnam, 1863.

Irving, Washington. *Letters from Sunnyside and Spain*. New Haven, CT: Yale University Press, 1938.

Jerrold, Blanchard. *The Life of Napoleon III: Derived from State Records, from Unpublished Family Correspondence, and from Personal Testimony; with Family Portraits in the Possession of the Imperial Family, and Facsimiles of Letters of Napoleon I, Napoleon III, Queen Hortense &c*. 4 vols. London: Longmans, Green, 1874–1882.

Judtmann, Fritz. *Mayerling: The Facts behind the Legend*. London: George G. Harrap, 1971.

Kossuth, Louis. *Hungary and Its Revolutions: With a Memoir of Louis Kossuth*. London: Bohn, 1854.

Kurtz, Harold. *The Empress Eugénie, 1826–1920*. Boston: Houghton Mifflin, 1964.

Landon, Melville D. *The Franco-Prussian War.* New York: G. W. Carleton, 1871.

Langer, William L. *Political and Social Upheaval, 1832–1852.* New York: Harper & Row, 1969.

Latimer, Elizabeth Wormeley. *Spain in the Nineteenth Century.* Chicago: A. C. McClurg, 1898.

Lee, Sydney. *Queen Victoria: A Biography.* London: John Murray, 1904.

Legge, Edward. *The Empress Eugénie 1870–1910: Her Majesty's life since "the terrible year."* New York: C. Scribner's Sons, 1910.

Lincoln, W. Bruce. *Nicholas I, Emperor and Autocrat of All the Russias.* Bloomington: Indiana University Press, 1978.

Loliée, Frédéric. *The Life of an Empress (Eugénie de Montijo).* London: E. Nash, 1908.

Lord, Robert Howard. *The Origins of the War of 1870: New Documents from the German Archives.* Cambridge, MA: Harvard University Press, 1924.

Lyon, Sylvia. *The Life and Times of Prosper Mérimée.* New York: The Dial Press, 1948.

Macartney, C. A. *The House of Austria: The Later Phase, 1790–1918.* Edinburgh: Edinburgh University Press, 1978.

Malmesbury, James, 3rd earl of. *Memoirs of an Ex-Minister: An Autobiography.* 2 vols. Leipzig: Tauchnitz, 1885.

Marichal, Carlos. *Spain (1834–1844): A New Society.* London: Tamesis Books, 1977.

Martin, Percy F. *Maximilian in Mexico: The Story of the French Intervention (1861– 1867).* New York: C. Scribner's Sons, 1914.

Mason, Edward S. *The Paris Commune.* New York: Macmillan, 1930.

Matson, Robert W. "Church Wealth in Nineteenth-Century Mexico: A Review of Literature." *The Catholic Historical Review* 65, no. 4 (October 1979): 600–609.

Maximilian Joseph, Herzog in Bayern. *Wanderung nach dem Orient im jahre 1838.* Munich: G. Franz, 1839.

Maxwell, Sir Herbert. *The Life and Letters of George William Frederick, Fourth Earl of Clarendon, KG, GCB.* London: Edward Arnold, 1913.

Melville, Herman. *Journal of a Visit to Europe and the Levant, October 11, 1856–May 6, 1857.* Princeton, NJ: Princeton University Press; Oxford: Oxford University Press, 1955.

Mérimée, Prosper. *Letters of Prosper Mérimée to Panizzi.* Edited by Louis Fagan. 2 vols. London: Remington, 1881.

Metternich, Klemens von. *Memoirs of Prince Metternich, 1773–1815.* 2 vols. New York: C. Scribner's Sons, 1880.

Metternich, Pauline. *My Years in Paris.* London: E. Nash & Grayson, 1922.

Michel, Prince of Greece. *The Empress of Farewells: The Story of Charlotte, Empress of Mexico.* New York: Atlantic Monthly Press, 2002.

Moltke, Graf Helmuth von. *Extracts from Moltke's Correspondence Pertaining to the War of 1870–71.* Translated by Harry Bell. Fort Leavenworth, KS: Army Service School Press, 1911.

Moore, George Greville. *Society Recollections in Paris and Vienna, 1879–1904, by an English Officer. With thirty-two illustrations.* London: John Long, 1907.

Motley, John Lothrop. *The Correspondence of John Lothrop Motley.* 2 vols. New York: Harper & Brothers, 1889.

Nitti, Francesco S. "Italian Anarchist." *The North American Review* 167, no. 504 (November 1898): 598–608.

Normanby, Constantine Henry Phipps, Marquess of. *A Year of Revolution. From a Journal Kept in Paris in 1848.* 2 vols. London: Longman, Brown, Green, Longmans & Roberts, 1857.

Paléologue, Maurice. *The Tragic Empress: Intimate Conversations with the Empress Eugénie, 1901–1911.* London: Thornton Butterworth, 1920.

Palmer, Alan. *The Crimean War.* New York: Dorset Press, 1992.

——. *Twilight of the Habsburgs: The Life and Times of Emperor Francis Joseph.* New York: Atlantic Monthly Press, 1994.

Payne, Stanley G. *A History of Spain and Portugal.* 2 vols. Madison: University of Wisconsin Press, 1973.

Peat, Anthony B. North. *Gossip from Paris during the Second Empire: Correspondence (1864–1869).* Edited by A. R. Waller. New York: D. Appleton, 1903.

Pech, Stanley Z. *The Czech Revolution of 1858.* Chapel Hill: University of North Carolina Press, 1969.

Quin, Michael J. *Memoirs of Ferdinand VII, King of the Spains.* London: Hurst, Robinson, 1824.

Quintin, Barry. *The Franco-Prussian War, 1870–71.* Solihull, UK: Helion, 2007.

Rappoport, A. S. *Napoleon III and the Women He Loved, with 18 Illustrations and Facsimile Letters.* London: Holden & Hardingham, 1915.

Redlich, Joseph. *Emperor Francis Joseph of Austria.* London: Macmillan; Paris: Denton, 1868.

Richardson, Joanna. *Stendhal.* London: Gallancz, 1974.

Richter, Werner. *The Mad Monarch: The Life and Times of Ludwig II of Bavaria.* Chicago: H. Regnery, 1980.

Rimmel, Eugene. *Recollections of the Paris Exhibition of 1867.* London: Chapman and Hall, 1868.

Robertson, C. Grant. *Bismarck.* London: Constable, 1919.

Rumbold, Horace, Sir. *Francis Joseph and His Times.* New York: D. Appleton, 1909.

——. *Recollections of a Diplomatist.* 2 vols. London: Edward Arnold, 1902.

Russel, William Howard. *The War.* 2 vols. London: Routledge, 1855.

Sand, George. *Impressions et souvenirs.* Paris: C. Lévy, 1896.

Sencourt, Robert. *The Life of the Empress Eugénie.* London: Ernest Benn, 1931.

Senior, Nassau William. *Conversations with Distinguished Persons during the Second Empire, from 1860 to 1863, Edited by His Daughter, M. C. M. Simpson.* London: Hurst and Blackett, 1880.

Sergeant, Philip Walsingham. *The Last Empress of the French: Being the Life of the Empress Eugénie, Wife of Napoleon III.* Philadelphia: J. P. Lippincott, 1907.

Seward, Desmond. *Eugénie: The Empress and Her Empire.* Phoenix Mill, UK: Sutton Publishing, 2004.

Seymour, Bruce. *Lola Montez.* New Haven, CT: Yale University Press, 1996.

Sharp, William. *Life of Heinrich Heine.* London: W. Scott, 1888.

Sherard, Robert Harborough. *Twenty Years in Paris; Being Some Recollections of a Literary Life, with 8 Illustrations.* Philadelphia: George W. Jacobs, 1905.

Soissons, Guy, comte de. *The True Story of the Empress Eugénie.* With eight illustrations. London: John Lane, 1921.

Spencer, Michael. *Charles Fourier.* Boston: Twayne Publishers, 1981.

Steinberg, Jonathan. *Bismarck: A Life.* New York: Oxford University Press, 2011.

Stephan, Renate. *Empress Elisabeth of Austria, 1837–1898: The Fate of a Woman under the Yoke of the Imperial Court.* Austrian Imperial Edition. Vienna: Glattau & Schaar Verlag, 1998.

Stoddart, Jane T. *The Life of the Empress Eugénie.* With six illustrations in photogravure. New York: E. P. Dutton, 1906.

Sybel, Heinrich von. *The Founding of the German Empire by William I.* 7 vols. New York: T. Y. Crowell, 1890–1898.

Tennyson, Alfred. *Select Poems of Alfred Lord Tennyson.* Edited with notes by William J. Rolfe. Boston: Houghton Mifflin, 1895.

Thayer, William Roscoe. *The Life and Times of Cavour.* 2 vols. Boston: Houghton Mifflin, 1911.

Tocqueville, Alexis de. *The Recollections of Alexis de Tocqueville, Edited by the Comte de Tocqueville and Now Translated into English by Alexander Teixeira de Mattos.* New York: Macmillan, 1896.

Trapp, Frank Anderson. "The Universal Exhibition of 1855." *The Burlington Magazine* 107, no. 747 (June 1965): 300–305.

Trevelyan, George Macauley. *Garibaldi and the Thousand.* London and New York: Longmans, Green, 1909.

Tschudi, Clara. *Elizabeth, Empress of Austria and Queen of Hungary.* Translated from the Norwegian by E. M. Cope. New York: E. P. Dutton, 1901.

——. *Eugénie, Empress of the French: A Popular Sketch.* Translated from the Norwegian by E. M. Cope. London: Sonnenschein; New York: Macmillan, 1900.

——. *Maria Sophia, Queen of Naples: A Continuation of "The Empress Elizabeth."* Translated from the Norwegian by Ethel Harriet Hearn. New York: E. P. Dutton, 1905.

Tschuppik, Karl. *The Empress Elizabeth of Austria.* Translated by Eric Sutton. New York: Brentano's, 1930.

——. *The Reign of the Emperor Francis Joseph, 1848–1916.* Translated by C. J. S. Sprigge. London: George Bell & Sons, 1930.

Twain, Mark. *The Innocents Abroad* (1869). Reprint. New York: Hippocrene Books, 1989.

Victoria, Queen of Great Britain. *The Letters of Queen Victoria, Second Series: A Selection from Her Majesty's Correspondence and Journal Between the Years 1862 and 1878*. Edited by George Earle Buckle. 2 vols. London: John Murray, 1926.

Viel-Castel, Horace, comte de. *Memoirs of Count Horace de Viel Castel: A Chronicle of the Principal Events, Political and Social, during the Reign of Napoleon III from 1851 to 1864*. Translated by Charles Bousefield. 2 vols. London: Remington, 1888.

Vizetelly, Ernest Alfred [pseud. Le Petit Homme Rouge]. *The Court of the Tuileries, 1852–1870: Its Organization, Chief Personages, Splendour, Frivolity, and Downfall*. London: Chatto & Windus, 1912.

Wallace, William K. *Greater Italy*. New York: C. Scribner's Sons, 1917.

Wallersee-Larisch, Marie Louise von. *My Past: Reminiscences of the Courts of Austria and Bavaria; Together with the True Story of the Events Leading Up to the Tragic Death of Rudolph, Crown Prince of Austria*. New York: G. P. Putnam's Sons, 1913.

Wellesley, Sir Victor. *Conversations with Napoleon III*. London: E. Benn, 1934.

William I. *The Correspondence of William I and Bismarck, with Other Letters from and to Prince Bismarck*. Translated by J. A. Ford. 2 vols. With portrait and facsimile letters. New York: F. A. Stokes, 1903.

Williams, Stanley T. *The Life of Washington Irving*. 2 vols. New York: Oxford University Press, 1935.

Woodham-Smith, Cecil. *Queen Victoria: From her birth to the death of the Prince Consort*. New York: Alfred A. Knopf, 1972.

Illustration Credits

Page

x–xi Map of Europe in 1815. Hayes, *Political and Social History of Modern Europe*, 1.

9 Duke Max, with his zither. Rumbold, *Francis Joseph and His Times*, 316.

61 Eugénie's father, Don Cipriano. Public domain, Alamy.

125 The engaged couple (Franz Joseph and Elisabeth in 1854). Public domain, Alamy.

143 Eugénie as a young bride. Public domain, Library of Congress.

161 Elisabeth as a young bride. De Burgh, *Elizabeth Empress of Austria*, 31.

173 Map of Crimea. Brereton, *Gallant Grenadier*, 139.

179 Eugénie and Napoleon III are received by Queen Victoria and Prince Albert at Windsor Castle (1855). Public domain, Alamy.

201 Sisi and Franz Joseph, with little Sophie and Gisela. Public domain, Alamy.

225 The countess of Castiglione. Rappoport, *Napoleon III and the Women He Loved*, 158.

231 Map of Italy before unification. Wallace, *Greater Italy*, 6.

245 Sisi with Franz Joseph, Gisela, and Rudolf. Public domain, Alamy.

261 The Empress chairs a council meeting. Barthez, *Empress Eugénie and Her Circle*, 226.

283 Franz Joseph meets Napoleon III at Villafranca. Public domain, Alamy.

307 Sisi's sister Marie at Gaeta. Public domain, Alamy.

327 Sisi and her ladies-in-waiting at Madeira. Public domain, Alamy.

343 Marguerite Bellanger. Rappoport, *Napoleon III and the Women He Loved*, 218.

363 Sisi stuns in fur. Public domain, Alamy.

379 Eugénie and Napoleon III with Louis, prince imperial, in military uniform. Carey, *Empress Eugenie in Exile*, 88.

393 Count Gyula Andrássy. Public domain, Alamy.

411 A determined Charlotte (Empress of Mexico). Public domain, Library of Congress.

423 Sisi in her Charles Worth coronation gown. Cunliffe-Owen, *Martyrdom of an Empress*, 64.

439 Max leading his men. Public domain, Library of Congress.

455 Sisi's youngest daughter, Marie Valerie. Public domain, Alamy.

469 Eugénie on camelback. Public domain, Library of Congress.

501 Ludwig II of Bavaria. Moore, *Society Recollections in Paris and Vienna,* 102.

515 Eugénie and the prince imperial receive the homage of the imperial party. Public domain, Alamy.

529 Mary Vetsera. Public domain, Alamy.

545 Empresses Elisabeth and Eugénie at Cap Martin. Public domain, Alamy.

Insert p. 1 (top): Elisabeth as a young bride. Public domain, Alamy.

Insert p. 1 (middle): Her handsome young husband, Franz Joseph. Public domain, Alamy.

Insert p. 1 (bottom): . . . and his mother, Archduchess Sophia. Public domain, Alamy.

Insert p. 2: (top left): Eugénie by Xavier Winterhalter. Public domain, Alamy.

Insert p. 2 (top right): . . . and Napoleon III by Winterhalter. Public domain, Alamy.

Insert p. 2 (bottom): Eugénie and her ladies-in-waiting by Winterhalter. Public domain, Alamy.

Insert p. 3 (top): Eugénie at Biarritz. Public domain, Alamy.

Insert p. 3 (bottom): Dinner at the Tuileries. Public domain, Bridgeman Images.

Insert p. 4: (top): Sisi on horseback. Public domain, Bridgeman Images.

Insert p. 4 (middle): . . . in black, the only color she wore after Mayerling. Public domain, Alamy.

Insert p. 4 (bottom): . . . visiting a soup kitchen. Public domain, Alamy.

Insert p. 5: A daring portrait of the empress by Winterhalter. Public domain, Alamy.

Insert p. 6 (top): Max as emperor. Public domain, Alamy.

Insert p. 6 (middle): Charlotte as empress. Public domain, Alamy.

Insert p.6 (bottom): *The Execution of the Emperor Maximilian* by Edouard Manet. Public domain, Alamy.

Insert p. 7 (top): The surrender of Napoleon III on September 1, 1870. Public domain, Alamy.

Insert p. 7 (middle): Dr. Thomas Evans. Courtesy of the University of Pennsylvania Art Collection, Philadelphia, Pennsylvania.

Insert p. 7 (bottom): Eugénie fleeing Paris. Courtesy of the University of Pennsylvania Art Collection, Philadelphia, Pennsylvania.

Insert p. 8: (top left): Eugénie with the prince imperial as a baby by Winterhalter. Public domain, Alamy.

Insert p. 8 (top right): Louis in 1874. Public domain, Alamy.

Insert p. 8 (bottom left): Crown Prince Rudolf before his death. Public domain, Alamy.

Insert p. 8 (bottom right): The imperial family grieving. Public domain, Bridgeman Images.

Index

Note: Italic page numbers refer to illustrations.

Albert, prince of Saxe-Coburg and
    Gotha (1819–1861), *179*, 186–87,
    192–93, 390n
Alcañicès, marquis d', José, duke of
    Sexton, 99–100, 122
Alençon, duc d', Ferdinand, 466
Alexander II (1818–1881), tsar of Russia
    (1855–1881)
    Otto von Bismarck and, 429
    Eugénie and, 517
    Exposition Universelle of 1867 and, 447
    Franz Joseph I and, 183, 183n, 250,
        251, 264
    Napoleon III and, 235, 250
    World Exhibition in Austria and, 506
Alfonso XI, king of Spain, 69
Alfonso XII, king of Spain, 473, 525
Algeria, 384
Algiers, Algeria, 313, 314–15
Alma River, battle of, 174–75
Alsace-Lorraine, 416, 519, 555
Amalie Auguste of Bavaria (1801–1877),
    queen consort of Saxony, 46, 49–50,
    52, 53, 54, 57, 375
American Remington rifle, 442
American Revolution, 104
American Sanitation Committee, 494, 499
anarchists, 552–53
Andrássy, Gyula (1823–1890), count
    Ferdinand Beust and, 436
    coronation ceremony and, 437
    death of, 550
    Elisabeth and, 398–401, 427, 428, 432,
        435, 462, 505

    exile of, 398–99
    Hungary and, 431, 432n
    portrait of, *393*
    Rudolf and, 532
Angerer, Fanny, 367–69, 510
arc lighting, 446n
Augusta of Saxe-Weimar-Eisenach
    (1811–1890), queen of Prussia,
    German empress, 506, 517, 524, 524n
Austen, Jane, 101
Austria
    Bavaria and, 46–47, 55, 58, 67, 404,
        406–07
    Bohemia and, 432, 432n, 435
    Britain and, 178, 181, 185
    Catholic Church and, 205–06, 432,
        433, 436
    constitution of, 32, 34, 39
    Crimean War and, 131–34, 131n, 135,
        156–57, 159–60, 172–74, 176, 177–78,
        181–84, 204, 206, 207, 255, 258–59,
        271, 438
    Denmark and, 375, 383, 388, 395–96
    dissolution of Diet, 39
    economic conditions in, 131, 132,
        137, 172, 173, 507
    Exposition Universelle of 1855 and, 189
    France and, 59, 67, 156, 157, 157n,
        177–78, 181, 242, 256, 263, 266, 277,
        347, 354, 360–61, 372, 383, 390,
        391–92, 404, 413, 417, 425, 429, 438,
        477, 478, 482, 552
    Germany and, 46, 132, 274, 413,
        416, 430–31

Austria *(cont.)*
  Hungary and, 35, 36–37, 38, 39–41, 41n,
    42, 59, 131, 132, 137, 173, 174, 289,
    291–92, 292n, 294, 346, 371–72, 396,
    397–401, 421, 426, 432–33, 435, 438
  Inquisition reestablished in, 205
  Italy and, 35, 36, 38, 167, 167n, 173, 177,
    211, 213–15, 217, 230, 239–41, 242,
    243, 257–59, 264, 270–77, 287–89,
    291–92, 392, 401, 403, 404, 426, 442
  Mexican monarchy and, 372–73
  military rule of, 44, 129, 130–31, 137,
    167, 431
  Napoleon I and, 13–14, 15, 67, 273–74
  Napoleon III and, 119, 156, 172, 244,
    259, 263, 266, 388, 413
  Nicholas I as ally of, 156
  population of, 217
  Prussia and, 46, 132, 138, 160, 178, 208,
    273, 291, 361, 390, 391–92, 402, 403,
    404, 405–10, 416, 419, 428, 442, 444,
    467, 475
  religious tolerance in, 295
  Russia and, 172, 174, 181, 264, 429
  Sardinia and, 35, 36, 182–83, 209, 211,
    242, 258–59, 263, 264n, 265–70, 274,
    275, 276, 301, 310, 336
  Spain and, 157
  totalitarianism of, 41, 45, 167
  Venetia and, 35, 36, 137, 183, 217, 230,
    242, 251, 252–55, 270, 276, 277,
    280–81, 292, 294, 383–84, 403,
    404–05, 413, 416
  Venice and, 131, 132, 214–15, 276, 286,
    292, 335, 346
  World Exhibition of, 506–07, 533

Bad Ischl. *See* Ischl, Austria
Bad Kissengen, Germany, 337–38
Balaklava, Crimea, 175
Balzac, Honoré de, 78
Batignolles, Paris, 310
Battle of Trafalgar, 65
Bavaria
  Austria and, 46–47, 55, 58, 67, 404,
    406–07, 504
  constitution of, 14, 16, 25, 29–30, 294,
    305
  as electorate, 13
  Exposition Universelle of 1855 and, 189

Jews in, 14, 31
as monarchy, 14, 16
Napoleon I and, 67
Prussia and, 421, 428, 431, 465, 467, 504
reforms in, 31–32, 37
religious tolerance in, 14, 15–16, 25,
  31, 206
Bayonne, France, 65–66
Beatrice, princess of the United Kingdom
  (1857–1944), 533
Beauharnais, Hortense de (1783–1837),
  queen consort of Holland
  (1806–1810), 102–03, 105–07, 105n,
  108, 185, 315
Beauharnais, Josephine de (1763–1814),
  empress of the French, 102–03, 103n,
  121, 315
Beaumont, Jeanne-Marie Leprince de, 78
Belfort, Alsace, 519
Belgium, 189
Bellanger, Marguerite (stage name for
  Julie Leboeuf), *343*, 356–59, 357n
Belleville, Paris, 310
Berg Castle, 514, 531
Beust, Ferdinand, Count, 435–37, 459–60
Biarritz, France, 151, 228–29, 242, 312,
  382, 388, 391, 441
Bicknell, Anna (governess at Tuileries),
  318, 322–23, 358, 381, 382, 383, 443
Bigelow, John, 387
Bismarck, Otto von (1815–1898)
  cease-fire and, 429–30
  diplomatic career of, 4, 389, 395,
    431, 432
  Eugénie on, 482, 493
  Exposition Universelle of 1867 and,
    447, 448–49
  Franz Joseph I and, 178, 370–71, 392,
    401, 402, 407, 410, 429, 430–31, 435,
    438, 460, 465, 504
  on Frederick the Great, 402, 407, 426
  Germany and, 389, 390, 428, 429,
    475, 518
  Leopold, prince of Hohenzollern,
    476–77, 478
  Ludwig II, king of Bavaria and, 467
  Napoleon III and, 361, 388–89, 390,
    391–92, 401, 415, 416, 420–21, 425,
    444, 475, 477–79, 478n, 479n, 480–81,
    481n, 484

Adolphe Thiers and, 519
Victor Emmanuel and, 392, 401, 403
Wilhelm I and, 389–90, 392, 402, 403–04, 407, 426, 429–30, 477, 480–81
Black Sea, 172, *173*, 174
Blauer Hof (castle at Laxenburg), 166
Bohemia
Austria and, 432, 432n, 435
Habsburg empire and, 35
population of, 217
Prussia and, 404, 407, 408–09, 421, 428, 430
state visits to, 216
Bonheur, Rosa, 386
Bosphorus, 131, 131n, 134
Britain
Austria and, 178, 181, 185
Otto von Bismarck and, 389
Crimean War and, 134, 159, 160, 172–73, 174, 175–77, 181, 182, 184, 194, 195–96
defense of Dardanelles and Bosphorus, 134
Eugénie's escape to, 494–500
France and, 184, 478
Great Exhibition of 1851, 153, 186, 190
Italy and, 264
Napoleon I and, 67, 67n, 135
Napoleon III and, 155, 155n, 156, 354
naval superiority of, 134, 156
Russia and, 156, 157n, 159, 172, 173, 175–76, 177
Sicily and, 301, 302
war against Zulus in South Africa, 526
Brown, John, 509n
Buda, Hungary, 398n, 427, 428, 462, 463n
Budapest, Hungary, 463n
Burgoyne, John, 497–99
Burgoyne, Lady, 498–99, 498n
Burnett, Frances Hodgson, 20

Caesar, Julius, 350
Cambridge, duke of, 526–27
Cape Town, South Africa, 548
Carette, Amélie, 311, 313
Carlos, Don [Carlos María Isidro Benito de Borbón y Borbón-Parma] (1788–1855), 76, 79, 82, 92–93, 93n, 358

Carlos [Carlos María Fitz-James Stuart y Palafox] (1849–1901), 16th duke of Alba, 316
Carlos IV aka Charles IV (1748–1819), king of Spain (1788–1808), 65–66
Caroline Bonaparte (1782–1839), queen consort of Naples, 102
Caroline of Baden (1776–1841), 12
Casablanca (film), 258
Caserta, Royal Palace of, Naples, 300
Caspar, Marie (Mitzi), 538
Castiglione, Virginia Oldoini Rapallini, countess (1837–1899), *225*, 230, 232–35, 248, 356
Catholic Church
Austrian empire and, 205–06, 432, 433, 436
Charlotte, empress of Mexico's appeal to pope, 433–34
France and, 231–32, 310–11, 360, 442
Francis II, king of Naples and, 305
Hungary and, 399, 400
Italy and, 230, 231–32, 242–43, 243, 264, 269, 275, 276–77, 278, 279, 280
Mexico and, 324, 325, 418, 433–34
papal Rome properties and, 243, 269
papal states and, 243, 311
Romagna province of Italy and, 242–43
Sardinia as papal protector, 360
Vatican and, 311
Cavour, Camillo, count of (1810–1861)
Austria and, 183, 268–69
countess of Castiglione and, 232–33
death of, 360
Franz Joseph I and, 286
Giuseppe Garibaldi and, 269
Lajos Kossuth and, 291
Napoleon III and, 232, 241–44, 253, 255, 257, 259, 265, 268, 277, 280–81, 390, 402
Baron Rothschild and, 264n
Sicily and, 301
Charles I (1600–1649), king of England, 154
Charles X (1757–1836), king of France (1824–1830; legitimist pretender, 1830–1836), 104, 104n, 190n
Charlotte (1798–1860), empress/tsarina of Russia, 174, 178

Charlotte (1840–1927), archduchess of
    Belgium, empress consort of Mexico
    (1864–1867)
  on abdication, 418
  appeal to pope and, 433–34
  Elisabeth's relationship with, 249–50,
    292–93, 332, 374, 531–32, 534
  Eugénie's correspondence with, 349, 351,
    356, 361, 387–88, 417
  Eugénie's meeting with, 419
  Albert Gräfle's portrait of, 355n
  Maximilian I's marriage to, 217, 248–50,
    252, 292, 347–48, 348n, 349
  Maximilian I's relationship with, 253,
    254–55, 290, 356, 418–20, 434, 444,
    449, 451
  mental breakdown of, 434–35, 444–45,
    449, 452, 531–32, 534
  Mexico and, 355–56, 372, 373, 374,
    417–18, 444
  Napoleon III and, 419–20
  pedigree of, 249
  portrait of, *411*
Chassepot rifles, 442, 478, 487
Château de Saint-Cloud
  Eugénie and, 151, 192, 267, 315, 316,
    357
  Napoleon III and, 111–12, 145, 145n,
    192, 206, 207, 279–80, 357
cholera, 175–77, 182, 184, 388, 391, 507
Church of the Augustinians, Vienna,
    141, 163
Cipriano, Don (1784–1839), count of
    Teba, count of Montijo
  death of, 91, 92
  education of daughters and, 86–87
  Eugénie influenced by, 64–65, 73–74, 77,
    82, 86–87, 88, 89, 115–16
  Ferdinand VII and, 73
  friendships with authors and, 77–79, 79n
  on frugality, 77, 86
  house arrest of, 64
  inheritance of, 76, 83–84, 85
  María Manuela Kirkpatrick y
    Grivegnée's marriage to, 63–64, 68–70,
    73–74, 76, 85, 86, 91, 92, 446
  in Madrid, 80–82, 83, 89, 90–91
  Napoleon I and, 64, 68, 74, 77, 91, 121
  oath of allegiance to Isabella II, 80
  political leadership of, 90

  portrait of, *61*
  release from captivity, 75, 76, 77
  Rafael del Riego's movement and, 72
  in Spanish military, 64–65, 69
  in Spanish Senate, 90
Compiègne, France, 151, 353
Convention of Galstein, 396
Courbet, Gustave, 191n
Cowley, Lord, 240–41
Crane, Dr., 494–99
Crimea
  Alexander II and, 183
  map of, *173*
  Nicholas I's invasion of, 131, 131n,
    132, 154–56
  Nicholas I's plans for annexing of, 46, 59
Crimean War
  Austria and, 131–34, 131n, 135, 156–57,
    159–60, 172–74, 176, 177–78, 181–84,
    204, 206, 207, 255, 258–59, 271, 438
  Britain and, 134, 159, 160, 172–73, 174,
    175–77, 181, 182, 184, 194, 195–96
  France and, 134, 156–59, 160, 172–73,
    174, 175–77, 181–84, 194–98, 206,
    207, 208, 229, 231, 266, 273, 309, 323,
    443, 486
  Paris peace conference, 198, 199,
    207, 208
  Russia and, 131–34, 131n, 135, 154–56,
    158–59, 160, 172–78, 182, 183,
    194, 195–97, 198, 206, 207, 264, 265,
    266, 438
  Sardinia and, 182–83, 194, 195, 207–08,
    211, 231
  Sebastopol and, 172, 174–75, 182, 183,
    188, 192, 194–98, 207
Crystal Palace, London, 186, 190
Cuba, 182
Custoza, Italy, 414, 431

dagger, disciple of (political assassination),
    232, 236, 360, 384
Darbo, Monsieur, 189
Dardanelles, 131, 131n, 134
Deák, Ferenc, 396–99, 427, 428, 428n,
    432n, 436, 462
Delacroix, Eugène, 78, 190, 191n
Denmark, 189, 346, 370–71, 375, 388,
    395–96
Disraeli, Benjamin, 526–27

Dominic, Saint, 64
Dreyfus, Alfred, 238
Dumas, Alexandre *fils,* 355
Dumas, Alexandre *pere,* 301, 495
Dupin, Aurore, 152

Eaux-Bonnes, France, 101, 191, 192, 313
École des Beaux-Arts, 78
Edison, Thomas, 446n
Edward VII (1841–1910), prince of Wales (1841–1910), 192, 506, 533
Egypt, 474–75
electricity, 446, 446n
Elisabeth Amalie Eugenie, duchess in Bavaria (1837–1898), empress of Austria (1854–1898)
adolescence of, 43–44, 48, 50, 51, 94
Count Andrássy and, 398–401, 427, 428, 432, 435, 462, 505
Fanny Angerer as hairdresser of, 367–69, 510
appetite and eating habits of, 50, 164, 288, 294–97, 330–31, 332, 333, 334, 336, 368, 511
Archduchess Sophie's relationship with, 42, 49, 51, 54–57, 58, 128, 134, 140–41, 164, 165–66, 167, 168–72, 204–05, 206, 208–09, 211–14, 218, 219, 222, 228, 248, 251, 254, 256–57, 287, 288, 294, 294n, 296, 299, 304, 332, 366, 367, 369–70, 372, 378, 395, 397n, 408, 427, 432, 461, 464, 505–06, 543
athletic ability of, 19, 48, 97, 128, 337, 508
Bad Kissengen and, 337–38, 370
on bath accommodations, 208–09
beauty of, 213, 215, 218, 220, 296–97, 331, 366, 368, 368n, 369, 375, 509, 511, 550
breast infection of, 256
care for wounded in war with Prussia, 407–08
Charlotte, archduchess of Belgium's relationship with, 249–50, 292–93, 332, 374
childhood in Munich, 16, 17–18, 20, 22, 25, 42
clothing influenced by Eugénie, 168n, 216
Corfu convalescence and, 332–35

Corfu villa of, 550
cultural education of, 88, 134–35
dancing of, 165
death of, 554
demands of protocol and etiquette of Vienna court, 134, 163–66, 168–71, 254, 257, 296, 306, 331, 332, 365–66, 367, 368–69, 374, 432, 461–62, 464, 506–08, 510, 554
dental hygiene of, 58, 128, 133, 133n
diplomatic audiences and, 165
diplomatic small talk and, 134, 156
discipline of, 368
drawing of, 42
dual monarchy and, 436, 462, 463
education of, 128–30, 134–35, 293–94
as emissary to Hungary, 426, 427–28, 428n
engagement portrait of, *125*
English language fluency of, 129n
with Eugénie at Cap Martin with Franz Joseph I in background, *545*
on Eugénie's escape to Britain, 503
Eugénie's relationship with, 206, 238, 453, 459, 460, 550–52
exercise regime of, 295, 296, 368, 509
Exposition Universelle of 1867 and, 447, 453, 460
family background of, 11, 13, 16, 18
fashion of, 198n, 216, 396, 399, 453, 550
father's relationship with, 18–20, 55, 64, 73, 77, 166, 306, 341, 508, 509
first romantic crush of, 44, 56, 94
on Franco-Prussian War, 503–04
Franz Joseph I's birthday celebration and, 48, 49, 50–53, 54, 432
Franz Joseph I's choice as bride, 51, 52–58, 54n, 59, 127–28
Franz Joseph I's engagement to, 56–57, 127, 130–36
Franz Joseph I's infidelity and, 295–96
Franz Joseph I's marriage to, 137–42, 145, 157n, 163–67
Franz Joseph I's relationship with, 166–67, 168, 169–70, 178, 204–05, 211, 213, 213n, 214, 223, 248, 250, 251, 254, 271, 276, 286–87, 288, 289–90, 291, 293–96, 304, 305, 306, 331–32, 335, 340, 342, 367, 375, 377–78, 381, 405,

421, 427, 428, 430–32, 435, 460, 461,
463–64, 510–11, 550
Gisela's birth and, 211–12, 227–28
glamour of, 216, 337, 366, 436,
459–60
Gödöllő country estate of, 437, 463–64,
508, 509
gossip about, 165, 293, 330, 331, 333–34,
340–41, 463, 534
Greek language and, 510
health of, 294–97, 304, 306, 313, 319n,
329–30, 332–33, 336, 337, 339–40n,
365, 367–68, 459, 507
Helene's relationship with, 43–44, 48,
49, 50, 129n, 133n, 205, 334–35,
457–58, 459
horsemanship of, 18, 19, 42, 43, 44, 128,
132–33, 167, 168, 169, 170, 205, 208,
213, 220, 288, 291, 295, 304, 341, 366,
368, 464, 508–09
Hungarian coronation ceremony and,
437–38, 447, 457, 505, 532
Hungarian delegation and, 399–400
Hungarian language fluency of, 371–72,
396–97, 400, 426, 436, 510
Hungarian relocation of, 462–63, 463n
Hungarian-style clothing of, 399
Hungarian-style tiara of, 396, 396n
Hungary and, 371–72, 396, 436–38, 441,
462, 462n, 463–64, 505, 532, 553
Hungary tours and, 217–22, 250, 372,
400–401
infatuations of, 44
influence of, 5, 6, 7, 208–09, 215, 218,
220, 248, 252, 254, 436
Innsbruck visit and, 32–34, 42
Italian provinces trip and, 213,
214–16, 218
Italy tour and, 294
ladies-in-waiting of, 49, 164, 168, 169,
205, 254, 293, 327, 331, 334, 336, 338,
340–41, 372, 396, 397–98, 397n, 461,
505, 507–08, 534, 553
legend of, 510
Leopold I's impression of, 329–30
life-sized statue of, 4
Luigi Luccesi's assassination of, 553–54
Ludwig II and, 406, 466, 512–13, 513n,
531–32, 549
lung disease of, 306, 313, 329–30, 332

Madeira convalescence of, 306, 309,
319n, 330–32, 335, 340, 396
Maria Sophie Amalie's relationship with,
136, 251, 256–57, 285, 298–99, 304,
306, 322, 366
Marie Antoinette pamphlet and, 218–19
Maximilian I's execution and, 458, 459
Maximilian I's relationship with, 297–98,
330, 332, 333, 374, 374n, 451n, 453
military hospital at Laxenburg set up
by, 289
modernity and, 369
modesty of, 43, 164, 166, 171, 208
mother's relationship with, 11, 12, 13,
32, 43, 48, 54–56, 134, 138, 140–42,
164, 165–66, 172, 205, 251, 288, 304,
333, 337, 406
nursing wounded of Austrian-Prussian
campaign against Danish Duchies, 375
official memorandum on personal and
parental rights of, 377–78
as outdoorswoman, 43, 44, 88, 205
pets of, 18, 32, 42, 48, 128, 135, 136,
167, 169, 171–72
philanthropic activities of, 461–62, 555
photograph collection of striking
women, 336–37, 366
poetry and, 20, 42, 44, 95, 170, 294, 297,
374, 462, 508, 509, 511–12, 537
political views of, 371, 405, 427–28,
431–33, 435, 436–37, 504–05
popularity as empress, 137–39, 171, 213,
216, 220, 257, 297, 341–42, 372, 375,
400, 427, 507–08
portrait as young bride, *161*
portrait in Charles Worth coronation
gown, *423*
portrait in fur, *363*
portrait with Franz Joseph I, Gisela, and
Rudolf, *245*
portrait with Franz Joseph I, Sophie, and
Gisela, *201*
portrait with her ladies-in-waiting at
Madeira, *327*
at Possenhofen Castle (Possi)
summer estate, 18–20, 27, 30, 33, 42,
77, 127, 128, 130, 132–33, 134, 136,
167, 205, 209, 228, 304, 338, 340,
458, 465
Prague visit and, 171

pregnancies of, 171–72, 208, 251, 460, 461, 462
processions commemorating religious holidays and, 375
public duties as empress, 375
as queen of Hungary, 436
reading habits of, 294, 462, 509–10
on religious rights, 206–07, 208
Renz circus and, 165
romanticism of, 55
Rudolf's birth and, 253, 256
Rudolf's death and, 541–42, 549–50, 551
as Rudolf's regent, 405
Rudolf's relationship with, 287, 288, 294, 295, 304, 332–33, 335, 336, 370, 375–76, 377, 378, 395, 407, 427, 428, 432, 457, 464–65, 532–34, 536–37, 542–43, 550, 551
sense of personal freedom, 254
as Sisi, 11
social circle cultivated by, 296
Sophie's birth and, 203–04
Sophie's death and, 221–23, 227–28, 247–48, 250–51, 287, 304, 458, 509
state visit of Napoleon III and Empress Eugénie, 3–6
stories of, 509–10
subordinate position at court and, 204, 286–88, 293–94, 297, 331, 332, 333, 369, 370, 462, 463
sympathies towards oppressed populations, 215, 216, 220, 248, 297, 371, 435, 462, 504–05
Valerie's relationship with, 464–65, 509, 511–12, 532–33, 537–38, 550
in Venice, 335–37
Vienna journey and, 136–37
Vienna return of, 341–42, 345
wedding trousseau of, 58, 128, 134
Xaver Winterhalter's portraits of, 368–69
World Exhibition and, 506–07, 533
zither and, 18, 19
Elisabeth Ludovika of Bavaria (1801–1873), queen consort of Prussia (1840–1861), 32, 46, 50, 51, 138
Elizabeth I (queen of England), 6
Ems (spa town), 479–81, 483
Esterházy von Galántha, Countess Sophia, (Sophie of Liechtenstein) (1798–1869), 140, 169, 171, 216, 287, 299, 336

Eugénie (1826–1920), countess of Teba, marquise of Ardales, empress of the French
adolescence of, 92, 93–96, 97
Alcañicès, marquis d' José; duke of Sexton and, 99–100
assassination of Elisabeth and, 555
athleticism of, 87, 97
balls and court galas hosted by, 151–52, 154, 157, 184, 194, 282, 322–23
beauty of, 97, 101, 117, 152, 229, 310, 517, 550
at Biarritz, 228–29, 242, 441, 473
on Otto von Bismarck, 482
boarding school experience in Clifton, England, 86
bridal trousseau of, 124
in Cape Town, South Africa, 548
Cap Martin villa of, 549, 550
charities and, 146–47, 147n
Charlotte, empress of Mexico's meeting with, 419, 420
at Chislehurst, England, 520–21, 522, 523, 524–25, 547, 548
cholera outbreak in Paris and, 391
at Convent of the Sacré-Cœur, 85–86
correspondence with father, 85, 88, 89
countess of Castiglione and, 233–35
as countess of Teba, 97
country estate at Teba and, 77
country estate of Montijo and, 97
Crimean War and, 182, 192
cultural education of, 88
death of, 555
in Deauville, 495–97
diplomacy and, 156, 157, 157n
Benjamin Disraeli and, 527
early life of, 63–64, 73, 80–82, 83, 84–85
at Eaux-Bonnes spa, 101, 191, 192, 313
education initiative of, 385–86
education of, 85–87, 88
with Elisabeth at Cap Martin with Franz Joseph in background, *545*
Elisabeth's relationship with, 206, 238, 453, 459, 460, 550–52
English language instruction for, 86
escape from Paris, 494–500, 517, 518
Don Eugenio's death and, 83, 85
Thomas W. Evans and, 494–500, 520, 522

Eugénie (1826–1920) *(cont.)*
Exposition Universelle of 1855
and, 190–94
Exposition Universelle of 1867 and, 443,
445, 448, 449, 452
failure to produce heir, 183–84, 187–88
Farnborough Hill, England and,
548–49, 555
fashion sense of, 117, 150, 151, 152,
168n, 198n, 216, 235, 310, 312n,
322–23, 352, 368, 385n, 453, 550
father's death and, 91, 92, 315
father's influence on, 64–65, 73–74,
77, 82, 86–87, 88, 89, 115–16, 238,
240, 382
father's release from captivity and,
75, 76, 77
Miss Flowers as governess of, 86–87, 91
Charles Fourier and, 98, 147
Franco-Prussian War and, 485, 486–89,
517
Franz Joseph I's relationship with,
460, 461
French imperial court and, 148–49
French language and, 74
frigidity accusations and, 145
on Giuseppe Garibaldi, 310–11, 347
Germany and, 391
glamour of, 150, 310, 459–60, 497
gossip about, 145, 184, 234, 236, 318,
319, 357, 524n
health of, 186, 188, 191, 193, 197, 199,
210, 227, 228–29, 313, 318–19
horsemanship of, 77, 97, 117, 118, 151, 228
household established by, 151
Joseph Alexander Hübner and, 157,
157n, 207n, 238
on infidelity of men, 321
influence of, 5–6, 7
Washington Irving and, 79n
Italian nationalist assassination attempts
and, 237–38
on Italy, 310
ladies-in-waiting of, 151, 482, 486
Mary Todd Lincoln and, 385, 385n
Abraham Lincoln's assassination and, 385
Louis-Napoléon's birth and, 198–99, 203,
209, 227
Louis-Napoléon's death and, 528,
547, 549

in Madrid, 80–82, 83, 84, 91, 92,
93–94, 101
María Francisca's death and, 315–16,
318, 319, 320, 358
María Francisca's relationship with, 98,
101, 102, 119, 121, 122, 147, 150n,
151, 153–54, 159, 191, 192, 199, 227,
235–36, 238, 265, 278, 281–82,
313–16, 334, 352
Maria Sophia Amalie, queen of Naples
and, 316, 321–22, 338
on Marie Antoinette's aesthetic, 149–50
on Marie Antoinette's fate, 154
Maximilian I's execution and, 452, 453,
459–60, 461
Prosper Mérimée and, 79, 87–88, 91, 94,
97, 151, 184, 199, 228, 266, 359, 492
Pauline von Metternich and, 312, 316,
445
Richard von Metternich and, 311,
312–13, 316, 325, 361, 391, 413, 417
Mexico and, 324–26, 345, 347, 348–52,
354–55, 356, 361, 372, 373, 384,
387–88, 415, 417, 445, 453, 483
ministerial council and, 386–87, 405,
414–15, 482, 486–87
miscarriages of, 153–54, 158, 188, 191,
198n
mother's relationship with, 89, 93, 96–97,
98, 99, 100–102, 111–12, 115, 117,
150, 150n, 238, 313, 352, 359, 472, 547
as namesake of Don Eugenio, 73
Napoleon III's engagement to, 120–22
Napoleon III's imprisonment and,
491–92, 520
Napoleon III's marriage to, 122–24, 127,
137, 145–46, 147, 149, 158
Napoleon III's relationship with, 102–03,
110, 111–12, 115, 117–20, 145–47,
150–51, 154, 156, 157, 158, 168, 181,
183–84, 191, 194, 234–35, 237, 242,
248, 264–67, 270, 271, 272–74,
278–80, 309, 310, 314–16, 318–21,
356–60, 359n, 381, 415, 416, 441,
473–74, 482–84, 485, 490–91, 520,
524
Napoléon-Jérôme Bonaparte and,
353–54, 384–85, 385n
Ramón María Narváez on, 99
Nice visit of, 313–15

ostentatious style of, 97
parenting style of, 382–83
in Paris, 84–85, 86, 87–89, 92, 101,
   111–12, 115–17, 472
poison taken by, 100
political views of, 98–99, 157, 310, 319,
   321, 324–25, 345, 482
popularity as empress, 391, 442
portrait as young bride, *143*
portrait chairing a council meeting, *261*
portrait on camelback, *469*, 474
portrait with Napoleon III with Louis,
   prince imperial, in military
   uniform, *379*
portrait with prince imperial receiving
   homage of imperial party, *515*
position at court and, 227
pregnancy of, 191, 193, 197–98
Prison of La Roquette and, 386–87
on Prussia treaty terms, 519–20
Puerto del Sol slaughter and, 84, 85
red hair color of, 74, 81, 86, 117, 152
as regent for Louis-Napoléon, 240–41,
   243, 266–68, 267n, 273, 279, 310,
   384–87, 486
on republican rule, 522
reuniting with Louis-Napoléon in
   England, 500
romantic crush on James, duke of Alba,
   94–96, 98
Baron Rothschild and, 264n
rules governing unmarried women and,
   97, 98
in Schwalbach, Germany, 358–59,
   360, 384
in Scotland, 319–20, 319n
shooting range practice and, 87
on slavery, 323
Sophie, archduchess of Austria and, 460
in Spain, 352
Spanish language and, 228
state visit to Austria, 3–6
state visit to Britain and, *179*, 184,
   185–88
Stendahl and, 87–88, 93–94, 116,
   129, 314
strong-willed personality of, 74, 99
Suez Canal opening in Egypt and,
   474–75
threat of revolt and, 491–94

traditional Spanish femininity lacking in,
   81, 93
Venetia and, 414
Victoria, queen of United Kingdom and,
   179, 186, 187–88, 191–94, 238,
   319–20, 319n, 495, 517, 520, 524n,
   528, 547, 555
Franz Xaver Winterhalter's portrait of,
   190–91, 368
on women's achievements, 147, 349,
   385–86, 498n
Eugenio, Don (1773–1834), count of
   Montijo, count of Teba, 64–65, 69,
   73, 76, 80–81, 83, 85, 472
Europe, 1815 map of, *x–xi*
Evans, Thomas W., 145–46, 147n, 149,
   324, 387, 494–500, 520, 522–23
Exposition Universelle (Paris, 1855), 153,
   187, 188–94, 206, 443
Exposition Universelle (Paris, 1867), 443,
   445–47, 448, 471, 487

Falk, Max, 432
Favre, Jules, 518
feminism, 98n
Ferdinand I (1793–1875), emperor of
   Austria, 29–30, 34, 36, 37–39
Ferdinand II, king of the Two Sicilies,
   230, 231, 256, 257, 298–99, 305
Ferdinand VII (1784–1833), king of Spain,
   65–73, 67n, 75–76, 79–80, 82, 358
Ferenczy, Ida von, 397–98, 397n
Festetics, Marie, countess von Tolna, 505,
   507–08, 513, 534
Filon, Augustin, 383
Fleury, comte de, 271, 275–77, 290, 325,
   347, 482
Florence, Italy, 301
Flowers, Miss (governess to Eugénie and
   María Francesca), 86–87, 91
Fontainebleau, France, 117–18, 151
Foucault, Léon, 189, 192
Fould, Monsieur, 242, 279, 315–16
Fourier, Charles, 98–99, 98n, 147
France
   anti-imperial demonstrations of, 473
   Austria and, 59, 67, 156, 157, 157n, 177–78,
      181, 242, 256, 263, 266, 277, 347, 354,
      360–61, 372, 383, 390, 391–92, 404, 413,
      417, 425, 429, 438, 477, 482, 552

France *(cont.)*
Britain and, 184
Chassepot rifles of, 442, 478, 487
constitution of, 103, 104, 109, 113,
115, 482
Corps Législatif of, 473–74, 475, 478,
481–82, 486, 492, 518
Crimean War and, 134, 156–59, 160,
172–73, 174, 175–77, 181–84, 194–98,
206, 207, 208, 229, 231, 266, 273, 309,
323, 486
defense of Dardanelles and Bosphorus,
134
economic hardship in, 108, 158
economic prosperity of, 193–94,
229, 320, 524, 525
Eugénie's legacy and, 556
Exposition Universelle of 1855 and, 153,
187, 188–94, 206, 443
Exposition Universelle of 1867 and, 443,
445, 448, 449, 452, 466, 471
financial markets of, 264, 324
Germany and, 442
Italy and, 230–31, 233, 238–42, 259,
264–65, 270–75, 309, 323, 346, 347,
360, 413, 425, 431, 438, 442, 477, 486
Mexican monarchy and, 325–26, 347,
350–52, 354, 372–73, 384, 415,
417, 442
military rebuilding in, 441–42, 448,
478, 482
national assembly of, 14, 109, 113, 114,
116, 473
new National Assembly of, 519, 521, 525
Nicholas I and, 135, 159, 173
Paris Commune and, 522, 552
Paris defense from Prussia and, 487–89
parliamentary system and, 473
penal system of, 386
provisional government in, 109–10
Prussia and, 67, 68, 103, 241, 383,
414–15, 416, 420–21, 429, 442, 444,
475, 477–78, 483, 484, 485, 486–87,
519, 520
public debt of, 323
railroads of, 153, 155, 193, 229, 323, 525
representative legislature and, 386
republic of, 491, 518, 522
revolt against Louis Philippe, 108–09
revolt against Thiers government, 521

Russia and, 159, 172, 173, 176, 266
Sardinia and, 183, 209, 231, 265, 266, 269
U.S. Civil War and, 323–24, 326, 346
Venetia and, 275, 390, 404–05, 414,
416, 441
Francis II (1768–1835), emperor of
Austria, 15, 103n, 190n
Francis II (1836–1894), king of the
Two Sicilies, king of Naples
ascension to throne, 299
Charlotte, empress of Mexico and,
434–35
coronation ceremony of, 299, 299–300n
Eugénie and, 347, 360
at Gaeta fortress, 305–06, 316, 317–18,
321–22, 338, 450n
Giuseppe Garibaldi and, 302–03, 304,
305, 310, 347
Maria Sophie Amalie's engagement to,
251, 256, 285
Maria Sophie Amalie's marriage to,
298–99
Maria Sophie Amalie's relationship with,
305, 338–39, 339n, 433
Napoleon III and, 317–18, 322, 338
permanent exile of, 504
in Rome, 338–39
surrender to Victor Emmanuel, 322,
338, 433
Franco-Prussian War (1870–1871),
484, 485, 486–91, 503, 504, 517,
518–19, 552
Frankfort, Germany, 428
Franzenburg (castle at Laxenburg), 166
Franz Joseph I aka Francis Joseph I
(1830-1916); emperor of Austria
(1848–1916), king of Hungary
(1867–1916)
Alexander II and, 183, 183n, 250,
251, 264
Count Andrássy and, 428
ascension to throne, 37–41, 42, 507
on assassination of Elisabeth, 554
assassination plots against, 291, 510–11
in background with Elisabeth and
Eugénie at Cap Martin, *545*
birthday celebration in Ischl, 44, 47–50,
52, 53, 205, 251, 251n, 292,
304, 432
birthday mass of, 3–4

Otto van Bismarck and, 178, 370–71, 392, 401, 402, 407, 410, 429, 430–31, 435, 438, 460, 465, 504
Britain and, 185
on Charlotte, archduchess of Belgium, 249
concordat with Catholic Church, 205–06
Ferenc Deák and, 428
death of, 555
decree dispensing with martial law, 17
decree freeing Italian provinces from military rule, 216
decree freeing Vienna and Prague from military rule, 130–31
Denmark and, 370–71, 395–96
diplomatic audiences and, 165
discipline of, 33, 37–38, 52
dual monarchy and, 436, 462, 463
Elisabeth as choice for bride, 51, 52–58, 54n, 59, 130
Elisabeth's engagement to, 56–57, 127, 130–36
Elisabeth's marriage to, 137–42, 145, 157n, 163–67, 169–70
Elisabeth's relationship with, 166–67, 168, 169–70, 178, 204–05, 211, 213, 213n, 214, 223, 228, 248, 250, 251, 254, 271, 276, 286–87, 288, 289–90, 291, 293–96, 304, 305, 306, 331–32, 335, 340, 342, 367, 375, 377–78, 381, 405, 427, 428, 430–32, 435, 460, 461, 463–64, 510–11, 550, 551
engagement portrait of, *125*
Eugénie's relationship with, 460, 517, 551
Exposition Universelle of 1867 and, 447, 453, 460–61, 471
Frederick William IV and, 285–86
Germany and, 132, 431
Hungarian coronation ceremony of, 437–38, 447, 457, 532
Hungarian sword-waving ceremony and, 438
Hungary and, 372, 396, 397–98, 399, 400, 431–32, 432n, 463–64, 473
Hungary tours and, 217–22, 250, 372, 400–401
imperial finances and, 295
improvements to Vienna, 211n
infidelity of, 295–96, 333–34

Italian possessions and, 132, 167, 167n, 173, 182–83, 230, 251–55, 258–59, 264, 265–66, 270, 271–74, 286–92, 292n, 335, 390, 396, 403, 426
Italian provinces trip and, 213, 214–16
as king of Hungary, 436
manifesto on Italian conflict, 290–91
Maximilian I's execution and, 458, 459
Maximilian I's relationship with, 252–53, 255, 259, 292–93, 297, 298, 348, 372–73, 418, 444–45, 448, 451, 453
Richard von Metternich as ambassador to Paris, 311
mother's choice of bride for, 44–47, 49–50, 52, 53–54, 54n, 58
mother's relationship with, 169–70, 177, 178, 204–05, 211–12, 218, 222, 223, 228, 248, 286, 291, 294, 295, 335–36, 367, 370–71, 372, 435
Napoleon III and, 3–5, 207, 238, 244, 257, 275–77, 278, 280, *283*, 286, 289, 290, 292, 298, 346, 347, 360–61, 390, 402, 404, 414, 416, 425, 459, 506
Nicholas I and, 39–41, 41n, 46, 58–59, 131–32, 131n, 135, 156, 159, 160, 172, 173–74, 177–78, 183n, 207, 250, 258–59
portrait with Elisabeth, Gisela, and Rudolf, *245*
portrait with Elisabeth, Sophie, and Gisela, *201*
repressive autocracy of, 39–41, 178, 289, 431, 433
Rudolf's birth and, 253
Rudolf's death and, 541, 542
Rudolf's relationship with, 370, 533, 535, 538–39, 540, 551
Russia and, 167–68, 172–73, 176, 177, 182, 183, 205, 207
shooting matches and, 250
Sophie's death and, 221–23, 248
stabbing attempt on, 45–46
Suez Canal opening in Egypt and, 474
Treaty of Vienna and, 177–78, 181–82
Turkey and, 131, 131n, 132, 135
Weimar, Germany meeting with Alexander II, 250–51
Wilhelm I and, 286, 292, 402, 405, 414, 430, 458, 477
World Exhibition of, 506–07

Franz Karl (1802–1878), archduke of
Austria, 32, 34, 37, 164
Frederick II (1712–1786), king of Prussia
(1740–1786), Frederick the Great,
129–30, 399, 400, 402, 407, 426, 429
Frederick III (1831–1888), king of Prussia,
390n, 402, 409–10, 430, 506
Frederick William IV (1795–1861), king
of Prussia, 29, 32, 138, 174, 178, 208,
285–86, 358
French Revolution, 14, 29, 35, 59, 68n,
72, 104, 149

Gaeta, Italy, 305–06, 316, 317–18, 321,
338, 450n
Galerie des Machines, Paris, 188, 189
Gandhi, Mahatma, 397
Garibaldi, Giuseppe
Nice and, 281
Rome and, 310–11, 360, 478
Salerno and, 305
Sardinia and, 70, 269
Sicily and, 282, 298, 301–05, 310–11,
316–17, 325
Victor Emmanuel II and, 317, 346
George I (king of England), 189–90n
George III (king of England), 186
Germany
Austria and, 46, 132, 274, 413, 416,
430–31
Otto von Bismarck and, 389, 390, 428,
429, 467, 475
France and, 442
Napoléon III and, 391
Gilbert, Edward, 20
Gisela (1856–1932), archduchess of Austria
Archduchess Sophia's supervision of
raising of, 211, 212, 219, 223, 248, 254,
288, 294, 295, 332, 335–36, 370, 375,
395, 464
birth of, 211–12, 228
Elisabeth as emissary in Hungary
and, 427
Elisabeth's relationship with, 211–12,
213, 219, 223, 228, 248, 287, 288, 294,
295, 332–33, 335, 336, 370, 375–76,
378, 395, 427, 432, 457, 464–65,
505–06, 533
Elisabeth's trip to Possi with, 304
Hungary trip and, 219–21

illness of, 221
portrait with parents and
Rudolf, *245*
portrait with parents and Sophie, *201*
Gödöllő country estate, Hungary, 437,
463–64, 508, 509
Godoy, Manuel, 65–66
Gondrecourt, Count, 376–77, 378
Gräfle, Albert, 355n
Great Exhibition (London, 1851), 153,
186, 190
Great Redan, 195, 196
Greece, 373
Grünne, Karl Ludwig von (1808–1884),
count of Pinchard, 45, 216, 252, 286,
292, 333–34
Gudden, Bernhard von, 513–14
guerilla war, 67n
Gyulai, Field Marshal, 252–55, 258, 259,
268–71, 303

Habsburg empire, 35, 129, 178
Hanover, 407, 467
Haussmann, Georges-Eugène,
baron, 153
Havin, M., 386
Heeckeren, Baron
on assassination attempt on Napoleon
III, 236–37
on cholera, 182
on Corps Législatif, 475
on Crimean War, 198
on economy of France, 229, 323
on Eugénie's fashion sense, 150
on Exposition Universelle of 1867, 446,
447, 448
on France's military buildup, 478
on Franco-Prussian War, 488
on hunting season, 353
on Louis-Napoléon's birth, 199
as Napoléon III's adviser, 148, 263–64,
267, 278, 279, 444
on Napoléon III's health, 471–72
on Napoléon III's release from
Prussia, 520
on national assembly candidates, 473
on Prussia, 477, 483
on rejuvenation of Paris, 309–10
on *Uncle Tom's Cabin* production, 152n
Heine, Heinrich, 16, 19–20, 509, 537, 550

Helene in Bavaria (1834–1890), duchess
  in Bavaria
  Archduchess Sophia's relationship with,
    33, 34, 42–44, 46–47, 49, 51, 57
  death of, 550
  Elisabeth's relationship with, 43–44, 48,
    49, 50, 129n, 133n, 205, 334–35,
    457–58, 459
  English language fluency of, 129n
  Franz Joseph I's engagement to Elisabeth
    and, 133
  Franz Joseph I's marriage to Elisabeth
    and, 142
  husband's death and, 457–58
  Maria Sophie Amalie's pregnancy
    and, 341
  marriage of, 334, 334n
  mother's relationship with, 42–43,
    47–49, 56, 334
  potential marriage to Franz Joseph I and,
    46–52, 53, 54, 55, 56, 57, 133n
  as sister to Elisabeth, 11, 18
  Vienna visit and, 32–34
Hofburg Palace, Vienna, 141–42, 163,
  165, 170–71, 222, 292, 399, 407, 463
Holstein, duchy of, 396
Homer, 510
Homoky, Professor (Hungarian instructor
  to Elisabeth), 372
Hornig, Richard, 466
Hoyos, Josef, Count, 538, 540–41
Hübner, Joseph Alexander, count
  Elisabeth's and Franz Joseph I's
    relationship and, 170
  Elisabeth's clothing and, 168n
  Elisabeth's wedding protocol
    and, 163–64
  Eugénie's chastising Austria and, 207n
  Eugénie's diplomatic proposal and,
    157, 157n
  Eugénie's reaction to assassination
    attempt and, 238
  Eugénie's reaction to war with Austria
    and, 264
  Franz Joseph I and, 177, 311
  Napoleon III and, 206, 207, 238, 257,
    263
  Treaty of Vienna and, 181
Hugo, Victor, 78, 113
Hungarian Agricultural Association, 398

Hungary
  Austria and, 35, 36–37, 38, 39–41, 41n,
    42, 46, 59, 131, 132, 137, 173, 174,
    289, 291–92, 292n, 294, 346, 371–72,
    396, 397–401, 421, 426, 427–28, 431,
    432–33, 432n, 435, 438
  constitution of, 39, 427, 436
  Diet of, 130, 371, 398, 399, 401, 427,
    436, 437
  dual monarchy and, 436, 462, 463
  Elisabeth as emissary to, 426, 427–28
  Elisabeth's relocation to, 462–63
  Elisabeth's separate coronation in,
    427–28, 437–38
  Franz Joseph I's separate coronation in,
    427–28, 437–38
  Franz Joseph I's tour of, 217–21, 250
  liberalization policy and, 399, 473
  Prussia and, 426
  reaction to assassination of Elisabeth, 555
  Reichsrath and, 371
  representative assembly in, 295, 396
  sword-waving ceremony of, 438
  traditional costume of, 396, 396n

Ingres, Jean-Auguste-Dominique, 190
Innsbruck, Austria, 32–34, 35, 36,
  42, 48
Inquisition, 66, 71, 73, 79, 205–06
Irving, Washington, 79n, 96, 97
Isabella I (1451–1504), queen of Castile
  and León, 75–76
Isabella II (1830–1904), queen of Spain
  birth of, 75–76
  civil war and, 472–73, 476
  Crimean War and, 182
  Eugénie and, 157, 352, 353n, 473
  Exposition Universelle of 1867 and, 447
  María Manuela Kirkpatrick y Grivegnée
    and, 93n, 99, 112
  Maximilian I as emperor of Mexico and,
    352–53, 353n
  Ramón María Narváez and, 99n
  oath ceremony as legitimate heir to
    throne, 80, 82
  soldiers supporting, 92
  succession of, 525
Ischl, Austria, imperial villa in, 44, 47–49,
  52–54, 56–57, 59, 134, 205, 250–51,
  370, 407, 457, 458, 460

Italy
  Austria and, 35, 36, 38, 167, 167n, 173,
    182–83, 211, 213–15, 217, 230, 233,
    239–41, 242, 243, 251–53, 257–59,
    264, 270–77, 287–89, 383–84, 392,
    396, 401, 403, 404, 426, 431, 441
  division of, 230
  federation of independent kingdoms,
    276–77, 278, 279, 280
  France and, 230–31, 233, 238–42, 259,
    264–65, 270–75, 309, 323, 346, 347,
    360, 413, 425, 431, 438, 442, 477,
    478, 486
  independence movement of, 239, 240,
    269, 346
  Lajos Kossuth and, 427
  map before unification, *231*
  papal states of, 242–43, 311, 324, 433
  Prussia and, 264, 273, 274, 403, 442
  unification of, 230, 231–32, 238–39, 243,
    269, 278, 279, 301, 360, 552

James, Thomas, 21
James II, king of England, 94
James [Jacobo Fitz-James Stuart]
    (1821–1881), 15th duke of Alba,
    94–98, 100, 124, 182, 313–14, 316,
    320, 548
Jellačić, Josip, 36, 38–39
Jérôme Bonaparte (1784–1860); king of
    Westphalia, 102, 183, 267n
Jewish Benevolent Society, 462–63
Jews
  in Austria, 205–06, 295
  in Bavaria, 14, 31
  forced conversion of, 19
  Joseph Karl Stieler's Gallery of Beauties
    and, 23
John III Sobieski, king of Poland, 178
Joseph Bonaparte (1768–1844), king of
    Spain, 65–68, 67n, 71, 86, 102, 103
Joseph II (1741–1790), Holy Roman
    Emperor, 130, 427
Josephine, princess of Baden
    (1830–1900), 476
Juarez, Benito
  Battle of Puebla and, 350, 351
  Catholic Church's property seized
    by, 434
  French forces and, 354

  French loans defaulted under, 347
  Maximilian I and, 447, 449–51, 459
  policies of, 324, 325, 349, 352, 418, 449
Judtmann, Fritz, 536n

Karl Ludwig (1833–1896), archduke
    of Austria, 32–34, 47–50, 57, 171,
    249, 451
Karl Theodore (1839–1909), duke in
    Bavaria (Gackel)
  in Bavarian army, 431, 465
  birth of, 18
  Elisabeth's relationship with, 128, 337,
    338, 341, 375
  at Possenhofen Castle (Possi) summer
    estate, 32, 338
Kirkpatrick, William, 68–70
Kirkpatrick y Grivegnée, María Manuela,
    countess of Teba; countess of Montijo
  balls and salons hosted by, 93, 101,
    150n, 324
  Carlists in Spain and, 93n
  Don Cipriano's release from captivity
    and, 77–78
  education of daughters and, 85–86
  Eugénie's engagement to Napoleon III
    and, 120–21, 122
  Eugénie's health and, 199
  Eugénie's marriage to Napoleon III and,
    123, 150
  Eugénie's relationship with, 89, 93,
    96–97, 98, 99, 100–102, 111–12, 115,
    117, 150, 150n, 238, 313, 352, 359,
    472, 547
  Exposition Universelle of 1855 and, 191
  as first lady-in-waiting to Isabella II,
    99, 112
  inheritance of Don Cipriano and, 76,
    83–84, 85
  James, duke of Alba and, 94, 95
  in London, 86
  in Madrid, 80–81, 83, 91, 92, 93, 93n,
    101, 150n
  María Francisca's marriage to James,
    duke of Alba, 95, 96
  María Francisca's relationship with, 117,
    313, 314
  marriage to Don Cipriano, 63–64,
    68–70, 73–74, 76, 85, 86, 91,
    92, 446

Prosper Mérimée and, 77–79, 87, 150,
150n, 151, 184
Napoleon III and, 150
in Paris, 84–85, 88, 101, 111–12, 115–16
salons of, 150n
status as countess of Montijo, 80–81, 85,
86, 92, 96
Königgrätz, Bohemia, 407
Kossuth, Lajos, 40–41, 46, 291, 292n, 427

Lafayette, marquis de (1757–1834), 104
Lamartine, Alphonse de, 294
Larisch, Marie, countess von Moennich,
511, 538–40
La Roquette (prison in Paris), 386–87
Laxenburg (imperial estate outside
Vienna), 141, 166, 168–70, 289–90,
332, 463
Lebreton, Madame (lady-in-waiting to
Eugénie), 493–96, 499
Lee, Robert E., 384
Legion of Honor, 386
Lennox (lieutenant), 21–22
Leopold, prince of Hohenzollern, 476–77,
478, 478n, 479–80, 479n, 481, 483
Leopold I (1790–1865), king of Belgium
Charlotte as daughter of, 249
on Elisabeth, 329–30
Eugénie and, 316, 319
Maximilian I and, 211, 290
Victoria's correspondence with,
192–93, 266, 268, 281, 316, 319–20,
330, 390n
Leopold II (1835–1909), king of the
Belgians, 348, 349, 506, 534
Leroy, Monsieur (hairdresser to Eugénie),
186, 367
Lesseps, Ferdinand, count de (1805–1894),
68, 446, 474
Lincoln, Abraham, 385, 462n
Lincoln, Mary Todd, 385, 385n
Linderhof (Bavarian castle), 512
Liszt, Franz, 22
Lombardy
Austria and, 35, 36, 183, 217, 230, 242,
251, 252–55, 258, 266, 268, 270, 276,
280, 431
France and, 266, 268, 270, 413
Franz Joseph I and, 286, 290
López, Miguel, 450

Louis Bonaparte (1778–1846), king of
Holland, 102–03
Louise d'Artois, duchess of Parma,
275, 277, 279–80
Louis Maria of Bourbon-Two Sicilies,
count of Trani (1838–1886),
299, 332, 339
Louis-Napoléon (1856–1879), prince
imperial of France
attaining age of majority and, 524–25
at Biarritz, 228–29, 382, 383
birth of, 198–99, 203, 209, 227, 253
christening of, 199, 227, 227n
claim to throne as Napoleon IV, 524–25
death of, 528, 547
at English military academy, 525, 526–27
escape to Britain, 499–500, 517
Eugénie as regent for, 240–41, 243,
266–68, 267n, 273, 279, 310,
384–87, 486
with Eugénie in Scotland, 319
Eugénie's relationship with, 524, 527
Exposition Universelle of 1867 and,
449, 452
funeral of, 548
horsemanship of, 382
military combat and, 483, 485, 486, 499
military governor of, 383
Napoleon III's death and, 524
Napoleon III's release from Prussia
and, 520
parenting style differences and, 381–82
portrait with Eugénie and Napoleon in
military uniform, *379*
portrait with Eugénie receiving homage
of imperial party, *515*
public insults to, 472
revolt and, 492, 518
succession of, 240–41, 243, 351, 358, 472
Zulus and, 526–28
Louis Napoleon (nephew of Bonaparte).
See Napoleon III
Louis Philippe I (1773–1850), king of the
French (1830–1848), the Citizen
King, 29, 104–05, 108, 148, 194,
249, 265, 491
Louis Philippe II (1747–1793), duke of
Orléans, 104, 108, 148, 249
Louis XIV (1638–1715), king of France
(1643–1715), 186n, 466, 504

Louis XV (1710–1774), king of France
(1715–1774), 190n
Louis XVI (1754–1793), king of France
(1775–1792), 68, 68n, 104, 389, 496
Louis XVII (1785–1795), dauphin of
France, king of France (claimant,
1793–1795), 68n, 154
Louis XVIII (1755–1824), king of France
(8 June 1795–3 May 1814; 20 March
1815–8 July 1815), 68, 68n, 72,
103–04
Luccesi, Luigi, 553–54
Ludovika (1808–1892), princess of Bavaria
(later duchess in Bavaria)
children of, 17–18
Elisabeth's engagement and, 127
Elisabeth's marriage and, 127–29,
140–41, 164, 166
Elisabeth's relationship with, 11, 12, 13,
32, 43, 48, 54–56, 134, 138, 140–42,
164, 165–66, 172, 205, 251, 288, 304,
333, 337, 406
Elisabeth's wedding trousseau and,
58, 128
family background of, 12, 13–14, 15, 16
Franz Joseph I's birthday celebration and,
47–50, 51, 54
Helene's relationship with, 42–43,
47–48, 55
Innsbruck visit with sister Sophie and,
12, 32–34
Ludwig I and, 25
marriage of, 13, 16, 17, 18, 32, 43, 466n
political influence of, 159–60
Possenhofen Castle (Possi) summer estate
and, 27, 30, 32, 47, 127
Vienna visit with sister Sophie, 12
Ludwig I (1786–1868), king of Bavaria
abdication of, 30, 31, 37, 136, 293
as elder half-brother of Ludovika, 12,
16, 17, 25
Elisabeth's engagement to Franz Joseph
I and, 136
literary arts and, 16, 30
marriage and family of, 17, 22–24, 26
marriage to Protestant actress, 293
Lola Montez and, 22–27, 26n, 28, 29, 30,
136, 293, 337
Joseph Karl Stieler's Gallery of Beauties
portraits and, 23, 24, 337

University of Munich and, 28, 29
Ludwig II (1845–1886), king of Bavaria,
406–07, 406n, 465–67, *501*, 512–14,
531–32, 536, 549
Ludwig Viktor, 32, 171, 451
Ludwig Wilhelm (1831–1920), duke in
Bavaria, 11, 16, 17–18, 337–38, 431,
465, 511
Luitpold (1821–1912), prince of
Bavaria, 505
Lyon, France, textile industry of, 189, 192,
194, 323–24

McKinley, William, 554
Madame Tussaud's, London, 152
Mailáth, Johann, 129–30, 219
Malakoff (fortress at Sebastopol), 195,
196–97, 198, 207
Malmesbury, James Howard Harris, 3rd
earl of, 181–82, 198–99, 198n, 354
Manet, Édouard, 357n
Maria Alexandrovna (1824–1880)
empress/tsarina of Russia, 235, 250
Maria Christina (1806–1878), queen
consort (1829–1833) of Spain
Ferdinand VII's marriage to, 75, 358
Ferdinand VII's pragmatic sanction for
daughter Isabella II, 75–76, 79
as queen regent for Isabella II, 82–83, 89,
90, 92–93, 93n
Maria Clotilde, Princess of Savoy
(1843–1911), Napoléon-Jérôme
Bonaparte's marriage to, 243–44,
256, 257, 267
Maria Cristina of Savoy (1812–1836),
queen consort of the Two
Sicilies, 298
María Francisca (1825–1860), duchess of
Alba (Paca)
adolescence of, 94
Alcañices, marquis d', José and, 100
birth of, 73
boarding school experience in Clifton,
England, 86
burial of, 316
children of, 316, 385–86
at Convent of the Sacré-Cœur, 85–86
death of, 315–16, 318, 319–20, 358, 548
education of, 85–87
English language instruction for, 86

Eugénie's relationship with, 98, 101, 102, 119, 121, 122, 147, 150n, 151, 153–54, 159, 191, 192, 199, 227, 235–36, 238, 265, 278, 281–82, 313, 352, 555
Exposition Universelle of 1855 and, 191
father's death and, 91
father's influence on, 82, 86–87
father's release from captivity and, 77
Miss Flowers as governess of, 86–87, 91
illness of, 313–15, 329
James, duke of Alba's friendship with, 94, 95
in Madrid, 81–82, 84, 91, 92
marriage to James, duke of Alba, 96, 97, 98, 124
Prosper Mérimée and, 87–88, 91
mother's influence on, 74
mother's relationship with, 117, 150n
in Paris, 84–85, 86, 87
Puerto del Sol slaughter and, 84
as sister of Eugénie, 64, 73
Stendahl and, 87–88, 314
traditional Spanish beauty of, 74, 81, 93, 95
transfer of remains to Spain, 315, 320
Franz Xaver Winterhalter's portrait of, 191
Maria Luisa of Parma, queen of Spain, 65–66
María Manuela. *See* Kirkpatrick y Grivegnée, María Manuela
Maria Sophie Amalie (1841–1925), duchess in Bavaria, queen of Naples, queen of the Two Sicilies
beauty of, 299
characteristics of kingdom, 300
Charlotte, empress of Mexico and, 434–35
childhood in Munich, 18
coronation ceremony of, 299, 299–300n
death of infant and, 533
Elisabeth's relationship with, 136, 251, 256–57, 285, 298–99, 304, 306, 322, 366, 534
Eugénie's relationship with, 316, 321, 347, 360
Francis II's engagement to, 251, 256, 285
Francis II's marriage to, 298–99
Francis II's relationship with, 305, 338–39, 339n, 340, 433

Franz Joseph I's birthday celebration and, 51n, 251
Franz Joseph I's marriage to Elisabeth and, 142
at Gaeta fortress, 305–06, 316–18, 321–22, 338, 340, 450n
Giuseppe Garibaldi and, 302, 303, 304, 305, 310, 347
horsemanship of, 299, 339, 508
Mathilde's relationship with, 339–40
permanent exile of, 504
political influence of, 305
popularity as queen, 299
portrait at Gaeta, *307*
at Possenhofen Castle (Possi) summer estate, 339, 339–40n, 340
pregnancy of, 339–40, 339–40n, 341, 366, 366n
in Rome, 338–39
Rudolf's relationship with, 534
Maria Theresa I (1717–1780), ruler of Habsburg dominions
bathroom of, 209
Blauer Hof castle at Laxenburg and, 166
Elisabeth compared to, 141, 400, 426–27, 555
Elisabeth's use of glass carriage used by, 437
Frederick the Great and, 129–30, 399, 400
Hungarian sword-waving ceremony and, 438
Hungary and, 397, 399
pamphlet on Marie Antoinette and, 218
as role model for dynasty, 204
wedding of, 141
Maria Theresa of Austria (1816–1867), queen consort of the Two Sicilies, 299, 305
Maria Theresa of Spain (1638–1683); queen consort of France, 75
Marie Antoinette (1755–1793)
coach of marriage journey, 123
Eugénie compared to, 445
Eugénie on, 149–50, 154
fashion of, 198n, 312n
flight from Paris, 496
Monsieur Leroy on, 367
Louis XVII as second son, 68n
Ludwig II and, 513

Marie Antoinette (1755–1793) *(cont.)*
pamphlet written about, 218–19
Petit Trianon and, 149
portraits of, 369
Regent Diamond and, 190n
Marie Louise (1791–1847), duchess of
Parma; empress consort of the
French, queen consort of Italy,
103n, 190n
Marx, Karl, 552
Mary Stuart (Mary, Queen of Scots)
(1542–1587), 154
Mathilde Ludovika, duchess in Bavaria,
countess of Trani (Spatz, Sparrow),
18, 142, 299, 332, 334, 339–40
Maximilian Anton, hereditary prince of
Thurn and Taxis (1831–1867),
334–35, 457
Maximilian Emanuel (Mapperl), duke in
Bavaria (1849–1893), 42, 431,
465, 550
Maximilian I (1832–1867), archduke of
Austria; emperor of Mexico
Catholic Church and, 434
Charlotte's marriage to, 217, 248–50,
252, 292, 347–48, 348n, 349
Charlotte's relationship with, 253,
254–55, 290, 297, 356, 418–20, 434,
444, 449, 451
Elisabeth's relationship with, 297–98,
330, 332, 333, 374, 374n, 451n
as emperor of Mexico, 352, 354–56, 361,
387–88, 417–18
Eugénie's diplomatic proposal to Hübner
and, 157
on Eugénie's health, 210
Eugénie's proposal of Mexico for, 326,
347, 348–50, 354–55, 372, 373, 374
execution of, 451–53, 458, 459–60,
461, 476
Franz Joseph I's birthday celebration and,
49–50, 292
Franz Joseph I's relationship with,
252–53, 255, 259, 292–93, 297, 298,
348, 372–73, 418, 444–45, 448, 451
French forces supporting, 349, 352, 356,
388, 418, 444, 449–50, 458
as governor-general of Lombardy-
Venetia, 217, 249–50, 251, 252,
254–55, 259, 348

imprisonment in Mexico, 451, 459
on Italian defeat, 290
mother's relationship with, 252, 372, 373,
445, 451
Napoleon III and, 209–11, 276, 347,
348–49, 352, 355–56, 372, 373, 374,
387, 388, 418, 420, 444, 452
personality of, 209–10
portrait leading his men, *439*
at Querétaro, 450–51, 460
renunciation of rights of inheritance,
373–74, 375, 445, 449, 459
treason conviction, 451
trial for treason in Mexico, 447–48, 452,
459
typhoid fever of, 222n
unrest in Vienna and, 32
Maximilian II (1811–1864), king of
Bavaria, 30, 31–32, 46, 136, 406
Maximilian I Joseph (1756–1825), king of
Bavaria, 11, 13–14, 15, 16, 166
Maximilian Joseph (1808–1888), duke in
Bavaria (Duke Max)
Elisabeth's engagement to Franz Joseph I
and, 56–57, 129, 136
as Elisabeth's father, 11, 13, 17, 18–19, 55,
64, 73, 306, 337–38, 341
Elisabeth's marriage to Franz Joseph I
and, 166
faux-classical mansion of, 16, 17
Franz Joseph I's birthday celebration and,
47, 251
Heinrich Heine and, 19–20
horsemanship, 17, 19
illegitimate children of, 17, 43n, 341
Knights of the Round Table society
organized by, 17
liberal beliefs of, 25
literary arts and, 16
Ludwig I and, 16, 136
Ludwig II and, 406n
Maria Sophie Amalie's pregnancy
and, 341
marriage of, 13, 16, 17, 18, 32, 47–48, 466n
personality of, 11–12, 17
popularity with townspeople, 17
portrait with zither, *9*
Possenhofen Castle (Possi) summer estate
and, 18–20, 27, 30, 33, 42, 77
as professional dilettante, 64

relationship with children, 18–20, 42,
43n, 73
Wilhelm I and, 504
zither and, 9, 17, 18, 19
Mayerling (hunting lodge), 538, 540–41,
542, 550, 551
Mazzini, Giuseppe, 231–32, 235, 239, 241,
269
Melville, Herman, 300
Mérimée, Prosper
on Austria, 268, 421
at Biarritz, 442
on John Bigelow, 387
on Charlotte, empress of Mexico, 420
Don Cipriano and, 77, 79n
death of, 492, 549
Eugénie and, 79, 87–88, 91, 94, 97, 151,
184, 199, 228, 266, 267, 359–60, 381,
487, 492
on Francis II, king of Naples, 318, 321
on Franco-Prussian War, 488
French Senate appointment and, 150–51
on Giuseppe Garibaldi, 310
María Manuela Kirkpatrick y Grivegnée
and, 77–79, 87, 150, 150n, 151, 184
on Louis-Napoléon, 382, 472
on Maria Sophie Amalie, queen of
Naples, 366
on Maximilian I, 352
on Mexico, 351
Napoleon III and, 150–51, 266, 278–79,
350, 388, 413, 442, 472
on Napoléon-Jérôme Bonaparte,
353–54, 385n
on Prussia, 421
on Spain, 476
on state visit of Victoria and Albert, 192
on war in Lombardy, 258
Metternich, Pauline Clémentine Marie
Walburga von (1836–1921), princess
of Metternich, 311–13, 316, 414, 445
Metternich, Richard von (1829–1895),
prince of Metternich-Winneburg
zu Beilstein
as Austrian ambassador to Paris, 311
Charlotte, empress of Mexico and, 419
Eugénie and, 311, 312–13, 316, 325, 361,
391, 413, 414, 417, 493
on Maximilian I's execution, 452–53
Napoleon III and, 351, 404, 415

Metz, fortress of, 518–19
Meurent, Victorine, 357n
Mexico
Eugénie and, 324–26, 345, 347, 348–52,
354–55, 356, 361, 372, 373, 384,
387–88, 415, 417, 445, 453, 483
French support for monarchy in, 325–26,
347, 350–52, 354, 372–73, 384, 415,
417, 442, 444–45
Benito Juarez's default on French
loans, 347
Benito Juarez's policies and, 324, 325
Maximilian I as emperor of, 352, 354–56,
361, 387–88, 417–18
Maximilian I's execution in, 451–53, 458,
459–60, 461, 476
Maximilian I's imprisonment in, 451, 459
Maximilian I's trial for treason in,
447–48, 452, 459
silver reserves of, 325, 347, 418
Middleton, Bay, 508–09, 534
Milan, Italy, 46, 431
Miramare, Italy, 290, 292, 332, 347–48,
349, 356, 372, 420, 433, 452
Modena, Italy, 292, 431
Moldavia
Franz Joseph I and, 174, 176
Nicholas I and, 58, 172, 173
Moltke, Helmut, 475, 480–81, 489
Monroe Doctrine, 155, 155n
Montez, Lola (Eliza Gilbert) (Eliza James)
Bavarian citizenship of, 25–26, 30
as Bavarian countess of Landsfeld, 26,
26n, 27, 28, 30
Bavarian revolt against, 108
beauty of, 21
dog Turk of, 24, 24n, 27
education of, 20–21
expulsion from Bavaria, 29, 31
family background of, 20
Thomas James and, 21
Ludwig I, king of Bavaria and, 22–27,
26n, 28, 29, 30, 136, 293, 337
persona of, 21–22, 22n
University of Munich students and,
27–29
Montmartre, Paris, 310
Moravia, 428
Moulton, Lillie, 345, 446–48, 452–53,
483–84, 485

Mozart, Wolfgang Amadeus, 4
Munich
  Elisabeth's trip to Vienna and, 136–37
  royal palace in, 134

Naples, Italy, 243, 257, 300, 316–17, 321,
    338, 431
Napoleon I (Napoleon Bonaparte)
    (1769–1821)
  Austria and, 13–14, 15, 67, 273–74
  Bavaria and, 13, 14, 15–16, 20
  book on politics published by, 105
  Britain and, 185, 186–87
  Carlos IV, king of Spain and, 65, 66
  as champion of downtrodden, 15
  Don Cipriano's support for, 64, 68,
    74, 77, 115–16
  Élysée Palace of, 122
  extended family of, 102
  Ferdinand VII and, 65, 67–68, 70
  French empire under, 148
  generals fighting under, 106
  Germany and, 14, 15
  legacy of, 265, 273, 309
  memoirs of, 88
  Napoleon III and, 113, 116, 121, 146,
    193, 241, 265, 270, 274
  Regent Diamond and, 190n
  on religion, 14, 206
  Russian campaign of, 15, 67,
    154–55, 159
  Spain and, 15, 65–66, 68
  succession of, 103, 103n
  tomb of, 193
Napoleonic Wars, 15–16
Napoleon II (1811–1832), 103, 103n, 190n
Napoleon III (Charles-Louis Napoléon
    Bonaparte) (1808–1873), emperor of
    the French
  Algeria tour of, 384, 387
  anti-imperial demonstrations against, 473
  Marguerite Bellanger and, 356–59, 357n
  at Biarritz, 228–29, 441, 473
  Otto von Bismarck and, 361, 388–89,
    390, 391–92, 401, 415, 416, 425,
    444, 475, 477–79, 478n, 479n, 480–81,
    481n
  bladder stones of, 415, 443, 478, 490, 523
  books on politics and artillery published
    by, 105

British mistress of, 111, 117, 120, 121,
    158
Count Cavour and, 232, 241–44, 253,
    255, 257, 259, 265, 268, 277, 280–81,
    390, 402
Charlotte, empress of Mexico and,
    419–20
Château de Saint-Cloud of, 111–12, 145,
    145n, 192, 206, 207
at Chislehurst, England, 520–21, 522, 523
countess of Castiglione and, 233–35, 248,
    356–57
Crimean War and, 197, 198, 230, 309
death of, 523–24
early life of, 103
Élysée Palace of, 111, 122, 123
as emperor of the French, 59, 116–17, 118
Eugénie's engagement to, 120–22
Eugénie's marriage to, 122–24, 127, 137,
    145–46, 147, 149, 158
Eugénie's relationship with, 102–03, 110,
    111–12, 115, 117–20, 145–47, 150–51,
    154, 156, 157, 168, 181, 183–84, 191,
    194, 234–35, 237, 242, 248, 264–67,
    270, 271, 272–74, 278–80, 309, 310,
    314–16, 318–21, 356–60, 359n, 381,
    415, 416, 441, 473–74, 482–84, 485,
    490–91, 520, 524
Exposition Universelle of 1855 and, 153,
    187, 188, 191–94, 206
Exposition Universelle of 1867 and, 443,
    445, 448, 449, 452, 506, 520
failed insurrections of, 105–07, 105n,
    107n, 109
Fontainebleau hunting party of, 117–18
Francis II, king of Naples and, 317–18,
    322, 338
Franco-Prussian War and, 485, 487–92
Franz Joseph I and, 3–5, 207, 238, 244, 257,
    275–77, 278, 280, 283, 286, 289, 290,
    292, 298, 346, 347, 360–61, 390, 396,
    402, 404, 414, 416, 425, 429, 459, 506
freedom of the press and, 472
French military's role and, 155–56
funeral of, 524
gonorrhea of, 345
goodwill tour of France, 116
health of, 320, 345, 346, 415–16, 419,
    441, 443–44, 471–72, 474, 475, 477,
    478, 482–84, 487, 523

imprisonment at Château de Ham, 107–08, 185, 495
imprisonment in Franco-Prussia War, 491–92, 504, 520
infidelity of, 158, 233–35, 242, 248, 318, 321, 357–59
inheritance from mother, 106, 108
insurrection against, 491–92
international conference proposal, 346, 351, 354, 360, 361
Italian nationalist assassination attempts on, 232, 236–41, 237n, 552
Italy and, 231–34, 240–42, 259, 264, 270–74, 309, 324, 346, 384, 396, 438
legacy of, 556
Louis-Napoléon's birth and, 198–99, 253
on María Francisca's death, 315
Maximilian I and, 209–11, 276, 347, 348–49, 352, 355–56, 372, 373, 374, 387, 388, 418, 420, 444, 452
Maximilian I's execution and, 452, 459–60, 461
Prosper Mérimée and, 150–51, 266, 278–79, 413
Richard von Metternich and, 351, 404, 415
Mexico and, 350, 351–52, 372, 384, 444, 445
military rebuilding and, 441–42, 448, 478, 479
on modernization, 146
Nice visit of, 310, 313–15
optimism of regime of, 153
Felice Orsini and, 251, 552
Palace of the Tuileries of, 119–20, 121, 123, 181, 197, 198, 263–64
parenting style of, 381, 383
parliamentary system and, 473–74
political upheaval in France and, 109–10
popularity of, 442
portrait with Eugénie, Louis, prince imperial, in military uniform, *379*
power politics and, 156
as president of France, 59, 110, 111–14, 115
Prussia and, 119, 274, 388, 425–26, 477–78, 483–84
public reaction to, 154
referendum on coup of, 114–15

reinstatement of empire, 116–17, 118, 146, 148, 152, 156
rejuvenation of Paris and, 148–49, 153, 155, 158, 193, 210–11, 309–10, 323, 507, 525, 548, 556
release from Prussia, 520, 521
on republican rule, 522
Russia and, 119, 155, 155n, 158–59, 177, 192, 266
Sardinia and, 242–43, 256–59, 263, 264–68, 275, 276, 277, 279, 346, 360
Savoy visit of, 310
Sedan battle and, 489–91, 503–04, 517, 523
on slavery, 323
state visit to Austria, 3–5
state visit to Britain and, *179*, 184, 185, 186–88
Treaty of Vienna and, 181
troops at Vatican, 311
Turkey and, 155, 159, 183–84
urinary tract infection of, 443
Victor Emmanuel II and, 256, 257, 258, 259, 265, 271–72, 275–78, 279, 280–81, 346, 414, 416
Victoria and Albert's state visit and, 192–93
Wilhelm I and, 416–17, 475, 479–80, 481n
Napoléon-Jérôme Bonaparte (1822–1891) (Plon-Plon)
Crimean War and, 183–84
Eugénie and, 353–54, 384–85, 385n
Exposition Universelle of 1855 and, 190, 191n
Italy and, 275, 277
line of succession and, 184, 227, 243, 358, 524n
Maria-Clotilde's marriage to, 243–44, 256, 257, 267
Napoléon Louis Bonaparte (1804–1831), 103
Narváez, Ramón María (1799–1868), duke of Valencia, 99, 99n
needle guns, 402, 407–08, 410, 414, 415, 426, 442
Nelson, Horatio, 65
Neuschwanstein (Bavarian castle), 512, 514

Nice, France, 230, 242, 281, 298, 309, 310, 313–15
Nicholas I (1796–1855), tsar of Russia
  access to Mediterranean and, 131n, 134, 154, 156
  British diplomatic relations and, 159
  death of, 183
  Franz Joseph I and, 39–41, 41n, 46, 58–59, 131–32, 131n, 156, 159, 160, 172, 173–74, 177–78, 183n, 207, 250, 258–59
  Franz Joseph I's subduing of Hungary and, 39–41, 41n, 46, 59, 131, 174
  invasion of Crimea, 131, 131n, 132, 154–56
  Napoleon III and, 158–59
  Sebastopol and, 194
  Turkey and, 59, 131–32, 131n, 133, 135, 154, 160
Nightingale, Florence, 160, 176, 176n
Nigra, Count, 493
Notre-Dame Cathedral, Paris, 123–24, 199, 273

Ollivier, Emile, 386
Olmütz, Prussia, 36, 37, 38, 58
Order of Friars Preachers, 64
Orléans, duke of, 190n, 553
Orsini, Felice, 236–41, 237n, 251–52, 552
Osuna, duke of, 97, 101–02

Palais de l'Industrie, Paris, 188, 189, 191n, 210
Palais des Beaux-Arts, Paris, 188, 190, 191
Palermo, Sicily, 300, 301, 302, 303, 310
Palmerston, Lord, 182
Paris Commune, 522
Passy, Paris, 310
Patton, George S., 303
Pélissier, General, 195–97
Persia, Shah of, 507
Persigny, Madame de, 198
Pesth, Hungary
  Ferenc Deák and, 396–97
  democratic demands in, 35
  Elisabeth and, 400–401, 426, 427
  Franz Joseph I and, 38, 398, 399, 400–401
  imperial policy in, 372
  transition to Budapest, 398n, 463n

Philipp, Prince of Saxe-Coburg and Gotha (1881–1921), 538, 540–41
Piedmont, Sardinia, 35, 182, 230, 233, 268, 279, 281
Plombières-les-Bains, France, 234, 242, 253
Plutarch, 249
Poland, 346, 447
pragmatic sanction, for Isabella II, queen of Spain, 75–76, 79
Prague, Hungary, 35–36, 37, 430, 432n
Pressburg, Austria, 429
Prim, Juan General (1814–1870), 476–77
Prussia
  Austria and, 46, 132, 138, 160, 178, 208, 273, 291, 361, 390, 391–92, 402, 403, 404, 405–10, 413, 416, 419, 428–29, 442, 444, 467, 475
  Bavaria and, 421, 428, 431, 465, 467, 504
  Bohemia and, 404, 407, 408–09, 421
  citizen protests against militarization of, 403
  constitution of, 29–30, 32
  Denmark and, 346, 375, 383, 388, 395–96
  Exposition Universelle of 1855 and, 189
  Exposition Universelle of 1867 and, 448–49
  France and, 67, 68, 103, 241, 383, 414–15, 416, 420–21, 425–26, 429, 442, 444, 475, 477–78, 483, 484, 485, 486–87, 519, 525
  Franz Joseph I and, 291, 292, 395, 428, 460
  German kingdoms and, 401, 467
  Germany and, 132, 416
  Hungary and, 426
  Italy and, 264, 273, 274, 403, 442
  militarism of, 390n
  Napoleon I and, 14, 67
  Napoleon III and, 119, 274, 388, 425–26
  needle guns of, 402, 407–08, 410, 414, 415, 426, 442
  territorial expansion of, 4
  Victoria, queen of United Kingdom and, 390, 390n
  weaponry of, 467, 487, 489
Puebla, Mexico, battle of, 350, 351
Puerto del Sol, Madrid, 84–85

Quirinal Palace, Rome, 338

Radetzky, Joseph, 36, 38, 213, 216, 252
Rauscher, Archbishop, 206
Regent Diamond, 189, 189–90n, 199, 556
Reichenau, Germany, 291
Renz, Ernst, 165
Riego, Rafael del, 71–72
Robert the Bruce (1274–1329), king of
    Scots, 69, 94
Romagna, Romania, 242–43, 275,
    278, 280
Romania, 413
Rome, Italy
    Giuseppe Garibaldi and, 310–11,
        360, 478
    Marie, queen of Naples in, 338–39
    Maximilian Joseph (Duke Max) in, 11
    papal Rome properties, 243, 269
    Victor Emmanuel and, 433, 504, 533–34
Roon, Albrecht von (1803–1879), 475,
    480, 481
Rothschild, Baron, 264n, 413
Rousseau, Jean-Jacques, 294
Rudolf, crown prince of Austria
    (1858–1889)
    Archduchess Sophie's correspondence
        with, 408
    Archduchess Sophie's supervision of
        raising of, 254, 256, 288, 294, 295,
        332, 335–36, 370, 375–76, 395,
        464, 532, 533
    birth of, 253, 256
    debt of, 542
    demands of Vienna court and, 533
    Elisabeth as emissary in Hungary
        and, 427
    Elisabeth as regent for, 405
    Elisabeth's relationship with, 287, 288,
        294, 295, 304, 332–33, 335, 336, 370,
        375–76, 377, 378, 395, 407, 427, 428,
        432, 457, 464–65, 532–34, 536–37,
        542–43, 550, 551
    in England, 533
    Franz Joseph I's relationship with, 370,
        533, 535, 537, 538–39, 540, 551
    funeral of, 549
    Count Gondrecourt as governor of,
        376–77, 378
    gonorrhea of, 536, 536n, 537, 538, 542

    health of, 376
    Hungarian coronation ceremony and,
        437–38, 532
    Hungary and, 535, 542
    line of succession and, 373, 376
    Maria Sophie Amalie's relationship
        with, 534
    marriage to Stéphanie, princess of
        Belgium, 534–36
    military training of, 533
    murder/suicide of, 541, 542–43
    political views of, 535, 538, 542
    portrait with parents and Gisela, *245*
    psychological fragility of, 532
    regency of, 287
    sporting holidays of, 538
    Mary Vetsera and, 538–39
    World Exhibition and, 533
Rueil, France, chapel at, 315
Russia
    Austria and, 172, 174, 181, 264, 429
    battle of Alma River and, 174–75
    Otto von Bismarck and, 389, 429
    Britain and, 156, 157n, 159, 172,
        173, 175–76
    Crimean War and, 131–34, 131n, 135,
        154–56, 158–59, 160, 172–78, 182,
        183, 194, 195–97, 198, 206, 207, 264,
        265, 266, 438
    France and, 159, 172, 173, 176, 266
    Franz Joseph I and, 167–68, 172–73, 176,
        177, 182, 183
    Hungary and, 218
    Napoleon I and, 15, 67, 154–55, 159
    Napoleon III and, 119, 155, 155n,
        158–59, 177, 192, 266
    Poland and, 346
    Treaty of Vienna and, 177
    Turkey and, 133–34, 135, 154, 159,
        176–77

Saarbrücken, battle of, 486, 487
Sadowa, Bohemia, 408–10, 414, 425, 457
Saint Augustine church, Paris, 548
Salerno, Italy, 305
Salon des Refusés, Palais de l'Industrie,
    191n
Salzburg, Austria, 3, 49
Sand, George, 152
San Gennaro, blood of, 299n, 338

Sardinia
  Austria and, 35, 36, 182–83, 209, 211,
    242, 258–59, 263, 264n, 265–70, 274,
    275, 276, 301, 310, 336
  Crimean War and, 182–83, 194, 195,
    207–08, 211, 231
  Eugénie and, 310–11
  Franz Joseph I and, 286
  Italy and, 230, 346, 347, 360
  Naples and, 317, 321–22, 338
  Napoleon III and, 242–43, 256–59,
    263, 264–68, 269, 275, 276, 277,
    279, 346, 360
Savoy, Sardinia, 230, 242, 256,
  281–82, 298, 309, 313
Saxony
  Austria and, 404, 405
  Ferdinand Beust and, 435–36
  Otto von Bismarck and, 402
  Ludwig II and, 406
  Prussia and, 428, 467
  royal families of, 12
  Wilhelm I and, 389, 407
Schleswig, duchy of, 396
Schönbrunn Palace, Vienna, 139–41, 222,
  222n, 249, 336, 342, 370, 463
Schratt, Katharina, 511
Schwarzenberg, Felix, prince of, 36–37,
  38, 40, 45
Sebastopol, siege of, 172, 174–75, 182,
  183, 188, 192, 194–98, 207
Sedan, France, battle of, 489–91, 494, 503,
  504, 517, 523
Seven Years' War, 429
Seward, William, 448
Shakespeare, William, 402
Shaw, Miss (English nurse to Louis-
  Napoléon), 382
Sicily
  characteristics of, 300–301
  constitution of, 305
  Giuseppe Garibaldi and, 282, 298,
    301–04, 310–11, 316–17, 325
Silesia, 404, 414
Sobieski, John, 178
Sophie, archduchess of Austria
  (1855–1857)
  Archduchess Sophia's supervision of
    raising of, 204–05, 211, 212,
    213–14, 248

  birth of, 203–04
  death of, 221–23, 222n, 247–48, 250–51,
    304, 336, 458, 509
  Elisabeth's relationship with, 204, 205,
    210–11, 212, 213, 214, 217, 228,
    247–48, 250–51, 254, 256, 287
  health of, 214, 217, 221
  Hungary trip and, 219–21
  Italian provinces trip and, 213,
    214–15, 216
  portrait with parents and Gisela, *201*
Sophie Charlotte Augustine, duchess in
  Bavaria (1847–1897), 142, 465–66,
  466n
Sophie Friederike Dorothea Wilhelmine
  (1805–1872), archduchess of Austria
  assassination plot against, 291
  Bavarian revolt against, 108
  on Charlotte, archduchess of
    Belgium, 249
  daughter's death and, 213–14
  death of, 505–06, 533
  diplomatic audiences and, 165
  Elisabeth's birth of Sophie and, 204
  Elisabeth's horsemanship and, 133,
    171, 288
  on Elisabeth's popularity with public, 297
  Elisabeth's relationship with, 42, 49, 51,
    54–57, 58, 128, 134, 140–41, 164,
    165–66, 167, 168–72, 204–05, 206,
    208–09, 211–14, 218, 219, 222, 228,
    248, 251, 254, 256–57, 287, 288, 293,
    294, 294n, 296, 299, 304, 332, 366,
    367, 369–70, 372, 378, 395, 397n, 408,
    427, 432, 461, 464, 505–06, 543
  Eugénie and, 460
  Franz Joseph I's ascent to throne and,
    37–41, 42
  Franz Joseph I's marriage and, 44–47, 49,
    50–52, 53, 54–55, 54n, 56, 57, 58, 127,
    130, 133, 134–35, 136, 137–38, 140,
    141–42, 164, 165
  Franz Joseph I's policy and, 168
  Franz Joseph I's relationship with,
    169–70, 177, 178, 204–05, 211–12,
    218, 222, 223, 228, 248, 286, 291, 294,
    295, 335–36, 367, 372, 435
  Franz Joseph I's stabbing and, 45–46
  Helene in Bavaria and, 33
  Ludovika in Innsbruck and, 12, 32–34

Ludovika's relationship with,
    127–29, 172
marriage of, 32, 34
Maximilian I's execution and, 458,
    460, 461
Maximilian I's relationship with, 252,
    372, 373, 445, 451, 453, 459
miscarriages of, 172
political influence of, 34–41, 42, 159–60,
    177, 178, 213, 217, 218, 222–23, 239,
    248, 292, 294, 295, 370, 371
Rudolf's birth and, 254
supporters of, 461–62
Sophie Maria Friederike, duchess of
    Saxony, 375
Sorbonne, 386
Spain
    Austria and, 157
    autocracy of Spanish court, 99n
    Carlist insurgents and, 85, 89, 92–93,
        99, 100
    cholera epidemic in Madrid, 83–84
    civil war of, 82–85, 475–76
    as constitutional monarchy, 476
    constitution of, 66, 71, 82–83, 89–90, 92
    Constitution of 1812, 71, 72, 73
    Constitution of 1837, 90
    Cortes of, 80, 83, 84, 476
    economic problems of, 70–71, 72
    guerilla war in, 67, 67n
    inherited aristocratic privilege
        abolished in, 66
    insurrection in, 70, 71, 472
    Joseph Bonaparte as king of, 65–67, 71
    law of primogeniture in, 64
    liberal party in, 79, 82–83, 89, 92, 93n
    Louis XVIII and, 72
    Napoleon I and, 65–66, 70
    peace proclamation in, 93–94
    Puerto del Sol slaughter and, 84–85
    rebel government in Cádiz, 66–67
    restoration of constitutional party, 76
    revolution in, 475–76
    ultraconservatives of, 79
    universal male suffrage and, 71
Stendahl (Marie-Henri Beyle), 78–79,
    87–88, 93–94, 116, 129, 314
Stéphanie (1864–1945), princess of
    Belgium, 534, 535–36, 539, 542, 549
Stephen, Saint, 437, 438

Stieler, Joseph Karl, 23–24
Suez Canal, opening of, 446, 474–75
Sweden, 189
Switzerland, 189

Taaffe, Eduard, Count, 535
Tennyson, Alfred Tennyson, Baron, 160,
    175–76
Therese of Saxe-Hildburghausen
    (1792–1854), 17, 22, 23, 24, 26
Thiers, Adolphe, 78, 481–82, 519,
    521–22, 525
Tocqueville, Alexis de, 108, 110
Transylvania, 35
Treaty of Vienna, 177–78, 181–82
Trochu, Louis-Jules (1815–1896), 487–88,
    492, 518, 521
Turgenev, Ivan, 78
Turkey
    Eugénie in, 474
    Hungary and, 218
    military intelligence from, 192
    Napoleon III and, 155, 159, 183–84
    Nicholas I and, 59, 131–32, 131n, 133,
        135, 154, 160
    Russia and, 133–34, 135, 154, 159,
        176–77
Tuscany, Italy, 243, 275, 292, 431
Twain, Mark, 448

United States
    Civil War of, 323–26, 346, 350, 355, 384,
        387–88, 418
    Exposition Universelle of 1855 and, 189
    Maximilian I and, 447–48, 451
    Monroe Doctrine, 155, 155n
    Sicily and, 301
University of Munich, 27–28

Valençay, château of, 65, 67n, 70
Valençay, Treaty of, 68
Valerie (Marie Valerie), archduchess of
    Austria (1868–1924)
    birth in Budapest, Hungary, 463, 532
    christening in Budapest, Hungary,
        463, 464
    Elisabeth's relationship with, 464–65,
        509, 511–12, 532–33, 537–38, 550
    engagement party of, 537–38, 540
    as "the Hungarian Princess," 464

Valerie (Marie Valerie) *(cont.)*
    portrait of, *455*
    Rudolf's death and, 542, 549
Varna, Russia, 172, 174
Vatel (French chef), 186, 186n
Venetia
    Austria and, 35, 36, 137, 183, 217,
        230, 242, 251, 252–55, 270, 276,
        277, 280–81, 292, 294, 383–84, 403,
        404–05, 413, 425, 431
    France and, 275, 390, 404–05, 414, 416,
        425, 426, 431, 442
Venice
    Austria and, 131, 132, 214–15, 276, 286,
        292, 335, 346, 354, 431
    France and, 251, 269, 276
Verne, Jules, 446
Versailles, Napoleon III's *Fête* at, 193
Vetsera, Helene, Baroness, 538–39,
        540, 542
Vetsera, Mary, *529*, 538–40, 541,
        542–43, 551
Victor Emmanuel II (1820–1878), king of
        Sardinia, king of Italy
    Austria and, 35, 36, 182–83, 207–08, 211,
        258–59, 269, 292, 354, 392, 404,
        405, 414
    Otto von Bismarck and, 392, 401, 403
    Count Cavour and, 232, 242–44, 269
    countess of Castiglione and, 233
    Eugénie on, 347, 360
    Exposition Universelle of 1867 and, 447
    France and, 230, 232, 256
    Francis II's surrender to, 322
    Italy and, 230, 232, 271–72, 275, 276,
        277, 298, 324, 338, 396, 401, 403
    Naples and, 317, 322
    Napoleon III and, 256, 257, 258, 259,
        265, 271–72, 275–78, 279, 280–81,
        346, 360, 404, 414, 416
    Prussia and, 392
    Sicily and, 303
Victoria (1819–1901), queen of the United
        Kingdom of Great Britain and
        Ireland
    Albert's death and, 390n
    alliance with France against Russia, 159
    Austria and, 268
    John Brown and, 509n
    death of, 555

Elisabeth, empress of Austria's
        relationship with, 306, 319n,
        329, 332
    Eugénie and, *179*, 186, 187–88, 191–94,
        238, 319–20, 319n, 495, 517, 520,
        524n, 528, 547, 555
    Leopold I's correspondence with,
        192–93, 266, 268, 281, 316, 319–20,
        330, 390n
    Mary Todd Lincoln and, 385n
    Louis-Napoléon and, 526–27, 528
    Napoleon III and, 119, *179*, 184, 186–87,
        264, 266, 276, 281, 524n
    as nineteenth-century icon, 6
    Prussia and, 390, 390n, 517
    Rudolf and, 533
    state visit to France, 191–94
    Wilhelm I and, 390
Victoria Adelaide Mary Louisa
        (1840–1901) (Vicky), 187, 192,
        390n, 402, 506
Vienna, Austria
    Austrian imperial court, 128,
        134, 137, 163–66, 168 71, 208,
        254, 257
    martial law in, 37, 129
    military rule lifted in, 130–31, 137
    reaction to assassination of Elisabeth,
        554–55
    uprisings in, 32, 35–37, 38, 289–90
Vigée Le Brun, Élisabeth, 369
Villa Eugénie, Biarritz, 228
Villafranca, treaty of, 276–78, *283*, 290,
        292, 292n, 298, 347
Vincent, Count Benedetti (1817–1900),
        479–80

Wagner, Richard, 406, 465, 512
Wallachia
    Franz Joseph I and, 174, 176
    Nicholas I and, 58, 172, 173
Weber, Carl Maria von (composer), 17
Wellesley, Henry Richard Charles
        (1804–1884), 240–41
Wellington, Arthur Wellesley, duke of, 67
Wilhelm, prince of Prussia (1783–1851),
        137
Wilhelm I (William I) (1797–1888), king
        of Prussia; German emperor
    Bavaria and, 465, 467

Otto von Bismarck and, 389–90, 392, 402, 403–04, 407, 426, 429–30, 477, 480–81, 504
Bohemia and, 421
Ems telegram and, 480–81, 483
Eugénie and, 358, 517
Exposition Universelle of 1867 and, 447
Franco-Prussia War and, 490–91, 517–18
Franz Joseph I and, 286, 292, 402, 405, 414, 430, 458, 477
as German emperor, 457–58
military review in Bois de Boulogne, 520

Napoleon III and, 416–17, 475, 479–80, 481n, 490–91
World Exhibition in Austria and, 506
Windischgraetz, Alfred, prince, 35–40, 186
Winterhalter, Franz Xaver (court painter), 190–91, 355, 355n, 368–69, 543
Worth, Charles Frederick (designer), 312, 312n, 323, 368, 437

Zululand (South African kingdom), 526–27

About the Author

NANCY GOLDSTONE is the author of seven previous books: *In the Shadow of the Empress: The Defiant Lives of Maria Theresa, Mother of Marie Antoinette, and Her Daughters; Daughters of the Winter Queen: Four Remarkable Sisters, the Crown of Bohemia, and the Enduring Legacy of Mary, Queen of Scots; The Rival Queens: Catherine de' Medici, Her Daughter Marguerite de Valois, and the Betrayal That Ignited a Kingdom; The Maid and the Queen: The Secret History of Joan of Arc; The Lady Queen: The Notorious Reign of Joanna I, Queen of Naples, Jerusalem, and Sicily;* and *Four Queens: The Provençal Sisters Who Ruled Europe.* She has also coauthored six books with her husband, Lawrence Goldstone. She lives in Del Mar, California.